HINDI-ENGLISH ENGLISH-HINDI DICTIONARY

HIPPOCRENE BOOKS

New York

Copyright© 1993 Hippocrene Books, Inc.

For information address:
HIPPOCRENE BOOKS, INC.
171 Madison Ave.
New York, NY 10016

ISBN 0-7818-0084-6

Printed in the United States of America.

HINDI-ENGLISH
ENGLISH-HINDI
DICTIONARY

HINDI-ENGLISH DICTIONARY

Dr. R.C. Tiwari
Dr. R.S. Sharma
& Krishna Vikal

ABBREVIATIONS
USED IN THE DICTIONARY

a — adjective
adv— adverb
conj — conjugation
ind — indeclinable
int — interjection
nf — noun, feminine
nm — noun, masculine
phr — phrase
pref — prefix
pron — pronoun
v — verb

स्टैण्डर्ड हिन्दी-अंग्रेजी कोश

HINDI-ENGLISH DICTIONARY

अ

अ the first vowel and the first letter of Devnagri alphabet; a prefix denoting negation as अतुल, अतृप्त, अन्याय

अंक (*nm*) a number; marks; a mark; embrace; an act of a drama; — गणित Arithmetic

अंकन (*nm*) marking; writing

अंकित (*a*) marked; written

अंकुर(*nm*) a sprout

अंकुश (*nm*) a hook; an iron hook with which elephants are driven; control

अंग (*nm*) body; limb; part; portion; — रक्षक a body-guard; — हीन limbless

अंगार, अँगारा (*nm*) a burning charcoal

अँगिया (*nf*) a bodice

अंगी (*nm*) creature in the corporal form

अंगीकार (*nm*) an agreement; acceptance

अँगीठी (*nf*) a portable oven

अँगूठा (*nm*) the thumb

अँगूठी (*nf*) a finger-ring

अंगूर (*nm*) grape

अंगोछा, अँगौछा (*nm*) a towel

अंचल (*nm*) the border of a cloak or that portion of a sari which covers the shoulder; a region

अंजन (*nm*) collyrium

अंजर-पंजर (*nm*) the joints of the body; skeleton

अंजाम (*nm*) result; end; — देना to complete

अंट-शंट (*a*) irrelevant; meaningless, nonsense

अंड-बंड (*a*) see अंट-शंट

अंडा (*nm*) an egg

अंत:करण (*nm*) the inner self, conscience.

अंत: प्रेरणा (*nf*) inspiration; intuition

अंत (*nm*) the end; — हीन endless

अंतत: (*adv*) at last, finally; eventually

अंतरंग (*a*) intimate; internal

अंतर (*nm*) difference; distance; the inner self

अंतरात्मा (*nf*) the soul, spirit, inner self

अंतराल (*nm*) gap; inner space

अंतरिक्ष (*nm*) sky, space; — यात्री an astronaut

अंतरिम (*a*) interim

अंतरीप (*nm*) cape (a land surrounded by water from three sides)

अंतर्गत (*a*) included; hidden

अंतर्जातीय (*a*) inter-caste

अंतर्दृष्टि (*nf*) insight

अंतर्देशीय (*a*) inland; inter-state

अंतर्द्वंद्व (*nm*) inner conflict

अंतर्धान (*nm*) disappearance; (*a*) invisible, vanished; — होना to disappear

अंतर्निहित (*a*) understood; included, implied

अंतर्राष्ट्रीय (*a*) international

अंतिम (*a*) final, last, conclusive, ultimate; — चेतावनी ultimatum

अंदाज़ (*nm*) a guess, an estimate; style; gesture; —न roughly

अंदाज़ा (*nm*) see अंदाज़

अंधकार (*nm*) darkness; cloudiness; gloom

अंधविश्वास (*nm*) superstition

अंधा (*a*) blind; unthinking; careless; thoughtless

अंधाधुंध (*adv*) blindly; at random; ignorantly

अंधापन (*nm*) blindness; folly; carelessness

अंधिया/रा (*a*) dark black; —री (a faminine) dark; black

अंधेर (*nm*) wrong; injustice; outrage; —खाता/गर्दी mismanagement, complete lawlessness

अंधेरा (*nm*) darkness; dimness; —चुप्प black out, pitch dark. -री (nf) dust storm (आँधी)

अंबार (*nm*) bulk, heap, pile

अंश (*nm*) portion, part; share, division; degree

अंशत: (*adv*) partly, partially

अकड़ (*nf*) stiffness; haughtiness; —बाज़ haughty

अकड़ना (*v*) to be stiff; to be haughty

अकर्मक (*a*) intransitive (verb)

अकर्मण्य (*a*) idle

अकस्मात् (*adv*) all of a sudden, suddenly

अकारथ (*a*) useless; (adv.) in vain

अकाल (*nm*) famine; scarcity; (*a*) untimely; —मृत्यु untimely death

अकिंचन (*a*) poor; destitute

अकुलाना (*v*) to feel uneasy

अकेला (*a*) single; solitary;

—पन loneliness, solitude

अक्खड़ (a) rude and rough; haughty; —पन rudeness, fearlessness

अक्ल (nf) wisdom; sense; intellect; —का दुश्मन (nm) a foolish person; —दौड़ाना to reason; —पर पर्दा पड़ना to be stupid

अक्ल/मंद (a) intelligent; sensible; —मंदी intelligence; sensibility

अक्षम्य (a) unpardonable

अक्षय (a) imperishable, durable

अक्षर (nm) the letter of an alphabet; (a) undecaying, permanent

अक्षरशः (adv) literally, word by word, in toto

अक्षुण्ण (a) unbroken, entire, whole

अक्सर (adv) often; usually

अखंड, अखंडित (a) the whole; undivided

अखबार (nm) a newspaper.

अखरना (v) to feel unpleasant

अखरोट (nm) a walnut

अखिल (a) all, entire, whole

अगर (ind) in case, if; —बत्ती incense stick

अगला (a) next, following; yet to come; —भाग front portion

अगवानी (nf) welcome

अगाध (a) bottomless; very deep, profound

अगुआ (nm) a leader; chief, pioneer; —ई leadership

अग्नि (nf) fire; the god of fire; appetite; —बोट a steam boat

अग्र (a) first, chief; —भाग fore part

अग्रणी (a) leading, outstanding

अग्रसर (nm) going ahead

अग्रिम (a) first, chief; (adv) prior, before

अघाना (v) to be satisfied

अचंभा (nm) astonishment, surprise, wonder

अचरज (nm) a miracle, surprise, wonder —भरा wonderful

अचल (a) stationary, immovable; fixed; firm

अचानक (adv) suddenly, all of a sudden

अचार (nm) pickles

अचूक (a) unfailing; sure

अचेत (a) senseless; unconscious; —न unconscious

अच्छा (a) good; fine; healthy; lucky; useful; (adv) well; (int) well done! all right; —ई goodness; merit; —बुराई virtue and vice

अछूत (a) untouchable

अछूता (a) not used; fresh —untouched

अजनबी (a) stranger, unknown; (nm) a stranger

अजब (a) peculiar; strange

अजायबघर (nm) a museum

अजीब (a) (see अजब)

अज्ञात (a) unknown

अज्ञा/न (nm) ignorance; —नी

ignorant

अटपटा (*a*) absurd; odd

अटूट (*a*) unbroken; unbreakable

अट्टहास (*nm*) a horse-laugh, loud laughter

अड़ंगा (*nm*) an obstruction, an obstacle

अड़चन (*nf*) hitch; difficulty; hindrance

अड़ना (*v*) to insist; to halt; to stick

अडिग (*a*) steady; unflinching

अड़ियल (*a*) stubborn; inflexible; obstinate

अड़ोस-पड़ोस (*nm*) neighbourhood

अड्डा (*nm*) meeting place; a stand

अणु (*nm*) atom; (*a*) atomic

अत: (*ind*) therefore; hence; thus

अतएव (*ind*) so; hence

अतल (*a*) bottomless; fathomless

अति (*pref*) a prefix denoting extremity etc.; very much, too much

अतिक्रम (*nm*) violation; deviation

अति/चार (*nm*) violation; transgression; —चारी violator

अतिथि (*nm*) a guest, stranger

अति प्राकृतिक (*a*) supernatural

अति/मानव (*nm*) a superman; — मानवीय superhuman

अति/रंजना (*nf*) exaggeration;

— रंजित exaggerated

अतिरिक्त (*a*) besides; additional; extra

अतिवृष्टि (*nf*) excessive rains; heavy downpour of rain

अतिशय (*a*) excessive

अतिशयोक्ति (*nm*) exaggeration; —पूर्ण exaggerated

अतीत (*a & nm*) past; (*adv*) beyond

अतुल (*a*) immense, unparalleled

अतृप्त (*a*) unfulfilled, unsatisfied

अत्यंत (*adv & a*) very much, extremely; exceedingly

अत्याचा/र (*nm*) tyranny; atrocity; —री atrocious, (*nm*) a tyrant

अथ (*nm*) the beginning, commencement

अथक (*a*) untiring, not fatigued

अथवा (*ind*) or, or even

अथाह (*a*) very deep; bottomless

अदद (*nm*) a number, figure; a piece

अदना (*a*) ordinary; low, inferior

अदब (*nm*) manners; respect; politeness; literature; — क़ायदा good manner

अदम्य (*a*) indomitable; irrepressible. unyielding

अदरक (*nf*) ginger

अदला-बदली (*nf*) exchange, alteration

अदा (*nf*) discharge; performance; —करना to discharge, to pay off

अदायगी (*nf*) payment; fulfilment

अदा/लत (*nf*) a court of law; —लती judicial

अदावत (*nf*) enmity; opposition; hostility

अदृश्य (*a*) out of sight, invisible

अदृष्ट (*nm*) fate; (*a*) unseen; unforeseen

अद्भुत (*a*) fantastic, wonderful

अद्वितीय (*a*) matchless; unparalleled

अघः पतन (*nm*) ruin, downfall

अघकचरा (*a*) half-baked, imperfect, immature

अघम (*a*) low, mean, base, worthless

अघमरा (*a*) half-dead, near dead

अघर (*nm*) lip; underlip

अघ/में (*nm*) sin; vice; —मीं sinful, wicked, immoral

अधार्मिक (*a*) irreligious; impious

अधिक (*a*) surplus; more. —तम maximum. —तर mostly

अधिकांश (*a*) most; majority

अधिकाधिक (*a*) more and more

अधिकार (*nm*) authority; right

अधिकारी (*nm*) an owner; an officer. (*a*) worthy

अधिनायक (*nm*) a dictator

अधिमास (*nm*) a leap month

अधिवेशन (*nm*) a session; meeting

अधीक्षक (*nm*) a superintendent

अधीन (*a*) subordinate; dependent —ता subordination

अधीर (*a*) impatient; nervous; restive; —ता impatience

अधुना (*ind*) at present; now; —तन modern

अधूरा (*a*) unfinished, incomplete

अधेड़ (*a*) middle-aged

अधोगति (*nf*) downfall; misfortune

अध्यक्ष (*nm*) head; president; owner

अध्ययन (*nm*) study; —कक्ष study-room

अध्यवसाय (*nm*) diligence; enterprise

अध्यात्म (*nm*) spiritual contemplation, spiritual knowledge

अध्यादेश (*nm*) an ordinance

अध्या/पक (*nm*) master, a teacher; —पन teaching

अध्याय (*nm*) a canto; a chapter, a lesson

अध्येता (*nm*) a scholar; student

अनंत (*a*) eternal; endless; (*nm*) Vishnu

अनंतर (*ind*) afterwards; soon after

अन (*pref*) in sense of without, (as-बन, —मोल)

अनगढ़ (*a*) unformed, crude; in the natural form

अनगिनत (*a*) countless, numberless

अनजान (*a*) ignorant; unknown

अनदेखा (a) unseen

अनधिकार (a) unauthorised

अनन्नास (nm) pineapple tree or its fruit

अनन्य (a) intimate (as मित्र)

अनपचा (a) undigested

अनपढ़ (a) illiterate, un-educated

अनबन (nf) enmity; discord

अनभिज्ञ (a) ignorant; less informed

अनमना (a) mentally disturbed

अनमिल (a) irrelevant; discordant

अनमेल (a) inharmonious, heterogeneous

अनमोल (a) very costly, price-less

अनर्गल (a) useless; absurd; un-barred

अनर्थ (nm) contrary meaning; grievous wrong; a great loss

अनल (nm) fire

अनवरत (a) always, incessant, continuous

अनशन (nm) fast

अनश्वर (a) eternal, immortal

अनसुना (a) unnoticed, unheard

अनहोनी (nf) the impossible; (a) unusual; impossible

अनागत (a) the future

अनाचार (nm) wrong doing; misconduct

अनाज (nm) corn, grain

अनाड़ी (a) stupid; unskilled

अनाथ (nm) an orphan; (a) helpless

अनाथालय, अनाथाश्रम (nm) an orphanage

अनादर (nm) disrespect; insult

अनादि (a) eternal, having no beginning; an epithet of God

अनाप-शनाप (a & nm) nonsense; meaningless (talk)

अनामिका (nf) the finger between the middle and the little finger; the ring finger

अनायास (adv) suddenly; without effort

अनार (nm) a pomegranate; —दाना dried seeds of pomegranate

अनार्य (nm) a non-Aryan; (a) not respectable; not noble

अनावरण (nm) exposure

अनावर्ती (a) non-recurring

अनावश्यक (a) unimportant

अनावृत (a) open

अनिंद्य (a) faultless, irreproachable

अनिच्छा (nf) unwillingness; reluctance

अनिमेष (a) without a wink

अनियंत्रित (a) uncontrolled

अनियत (a) not fixed, indefinite

अनियमित (a) irregular

अनिर्वचनीय (a) ineffable; indescribable

अनिवार्य (a) compulsory; unavoidable

अनिश्चय (nm) uncertainty; suspense

अनिश्चित (a) undecided,

uncertain

अनिष्ट (*nm*) undesired, harm,
— कारी harmful

अनीति (*nf*) impropriety;
injustice

अनु (*pref*) meaning after,
along with, etc. (as अनुगमन,
अनुचर)

अनुकंपा (*nf*) kindness.

अनु/करण (*nm*) imitation;
— करणीय imitable

अनुकूल (*a*) suitable; agreeable;
— ता suitability

अनुक्रम (*nm*) sequence, succession

अनुक्रमणिका (*nf*) an index, a table
of contents

अनुगत (*a*) succeeding, following, obedient; (*nm*) a
follower

अनुगृहीत (*a*) grateful, obliged

अनुग्रह (*nm*) kindness, help

अनुचर (*nm*) servant; follower

अनुचित (*a*) unsuitable, wrong

अनु/ज (*nm*) a younger brother;
— जा a younger sister

अनुज्ञा (*nf*) permission

अनुताप (*nm*) dissatisfaction;
remorse

अनुदान (*nm*) a grant

अनुदार (*a*) miserly; not liberal

अनुदेश (*nm*) instruction

अनुनय (*nm*) prayer, request

अनुनासिक (*a*) nasalised (*nm*)
a nasalised vowel

अनुपम (*a*) matchless, unequalled; excellent

अनुपयुक्त (*a*) undeserving,
unsuitable

अनुपयो/गी (*a*) useless, unavai-
ling; — गिता uselessness

अनुपस्थित (*a*) absent

अनुपस्थिति (*nf*) absence

अनु/पात (*nm*) ratio, proportion;
— पाती proportional

अनुपूरक (*a*) supplementary

अनुपूर्ति (*nf*) supplementation;
subsidy

अनुप्राणित (*a*) imbued; inspired

अनुप्रास (*nm*) alliteration

अनुबंध (*nm*) contract

अनुभव (*nm*) experience

अनुभवी (*a*) experienced

अनुभूत (*a*) experienced; tried

अनुभूति (*nf*) emotional experience

अनुमति (*nf*) order, assent,
approval

अनुमान (*nm*) supposition,
guess; — त: about

अनुमो/दन (*nm*) approval, — दित
approved

अनुयायी (*nm*) a follower

अनु/रक्त (*a*) attached, fond;
— रक्ति attachment, fond-
ness

अनु/राग (*nm*) affection, love,
— रागी loving, fond

अनुरूप (*a*) fit; like; resembling;
congruent

अनुरोध (*nm*) entreaty; solicitation

अनुवाद (*nm*) translation;
interpretation

अनु/शासन (nm) discipline;
—शासक a disciplinarian

अनुशासित (a) disciplined

अनुशीलन (nm) constant study;
contemplation

अनु/श्रुत (a) traditional —श्रुति
tradition

अनुष्ठान (nm) ceremony,
ritual; undertaking

अनुसं/धान (nm) research;
— धाता a researcher

अनुसार (a & adv) according to;
in confirmity with

अनुस्वार (nm) the mark of nasal
sound used in writing
Devnagri

अनूठा (a) uncommon, unparalleled

अनूदित (a) translated

अनूप (a) unequalled; best

अनेक (a) several, many; more
than one

अनैतिक (a) immoral; —ता
immorality

अनोखा (a) rare; peculiar; —पन
novelty, peculiarity

अनौचित्य (nm) indecency;
impropriety

अनौपचारिक (a) informal,
unofficial

अन् a Sanskrit prefix showing
negation to words begin-
ning with vowels (e.g)
अनर्थ, अनादि (see अ)

अन्न (nm) food, corn

अन्न-जल (nm) bread and butter

अन्नदाता (nm) a supporter, a
patron

अन्य (a) other, diffrent; —पुरुष
the third person

अन्यत्र (ind) in some other
place

अन्यथा (adv) otherwise; (a)
against

अन्यमनस्क (a) unmindful,
absent-minded; —ता
absent-mindedness

अन्याय (nm) injustice, wrong;
—पूर्ण unjust, wrong

अन्यायी (a) lawless, unjust;
(nm) an unjust person

अन्योक्ति (nf) an allegory

अन्योन्य (a) each other, reciprocal

अन्वय (nm) the prose order

अन्वीक्षण (nm) investigation

अन्वेष/ण (nm) exploration;
discovery; —क an explorer

अपंग (a) cripple; maimed

अप (pref) a Sanskit prefix
denoting down & action of
inferiority etc. (as अपमान
अपवाद)

अपकर्ष (nm) downfall

अपकार (nm) damage; harm;
disservice

अपकारी (a) harmful

अपच (nm) stomach derange-
ment; indigeition

अपढ (a) unlettered, illiterate

अपथ्य (a) undigestible

अपदस्थ (a) dismissed, depos-
ed

अपना (a) personal; one's own; mine; —पन cordiality

अपनाना (v) to adopt; to own

अपभ्रंश (nm) one of the middle Indo-Aryan languages

अपमान (nm) disgrace, insult

अपयश (nm) disrepute, infamy

अपरंच (ind) besides, more-over

अपर (a) another, moreover, too

अपराध (nm) fault, crime; —विज्ञान criminology

अपराधी (a) guilty, criminal; offender

अपराह्न (nm) afternoon

अपरिचित (a) unknown; un-acquainted; (nm) a stranger

अपरिमित (a) limitless; infinite

अपरिमेय (a) immeasurable

अपरिष्कृत (a) crude; unrefined

अपरिहार्य (a) indispensible; unavoidable

अपरूप (a) odd, ugly, ill-shaped

अपर्याप्त (a) insufficient, short

अपलक (a & adv) unblinking

अपवाद (nm) censure; excepti-on; defamation

अपविचार (nm) a bad idea; mistrial

अपवित्र (a) unholy

अप/व्यय (nm) expenditure, waste; —व्ययी a wasteful

अपशकुन (nm) bad omen

अपशब्द (nm) a vulgar word, abusive language

अपहरण (nm) kidnapping; usurpation

अपादान (nm) the ablative case

अपार (a) immense; boundless

अपारदर्शी (a) opaque.

अपार्थिव (a) spiritual; un-earthly

अपाहिज (nm & a) disabled; crippled

अपितु (ind) on the other hand, but

अपील (nf) an appeal

अपूर्ण (a) deficient; in-complete

अपूर्व (a) wonderful; novel; unique

अपेक्षा (nf) expectation, neces-sity; की— in comparison with

अपेक्षित (a) expected

अप्रकाशित (a) unexposed; unpublished; kept secret

अप्रचलित (a) out of date, out of currency

अप्रत्यक्ष (a) indirect

अप्रत्याशित (a) sudden; unexpected

अप्रधान (a) minor, secondary

अप्रयुक्त (a) obsolete; unused

अप्रसन्न (a) displeased; un-happy

अप्रस्तुत (a) indirect

अप्राकृ/त —तिक (a) unnatural; uncommon

अप्राप्य (a) rare; unobtainable

अप्रामाणिक (a) inauthentic;

unauthoritative

अप्रासंगिक (a) out of context, irrelevant

अप्रिय (a) unloving, unpleasant

अप्सरा (nf) fairy; nymph

अफरा (nm) swelling of stomach due to over-eating

अफरा-तफरी (nf) hurry-skurry, confusion

अफलातून (nm) a person of overweening pride; the Greek philosopher 'Plato'

अफवाह (nf) a rumour

अफसर (nm) an officer

अफसाना (nm) a tale, story

अफसोस (nm) regret, sorrow

अफीम (nf) opium

अफीमची (nm) an opium-addict

अब (adv.) now; —की/के this time; —जाकर at long last; —से in future

अबरक (nm) mica

अबरी (nf) marble paper

अबला (nf) a woman

अबाध (a) free; without restraint

अबूझ (a) stupid; unintelligible

अबे (ind) to use words of disrespect

अबोध (a) innocent

अभागा (a) unfortunate; unlucky

अभा/व (nm) shortage, lack; —वात्मक negative

अप्रसन्न (a) displeased; unhappy

अभि (pref) a Sanskrit prefix denoting towards, over, above, excessive etc. (as अभिनंदन, अभिमुख)

अभिजात (a) well born; aristocratic; (nm) aristocrat

अभिज्ञ (a) knowing all, well-conversant

अभिधा (nf) denotation, the literal sense of a word

अभिधान (nm) a name

अभिधेय (nm) predicable, literal meaning

अभिनंदन (nm) a ceremonious welcome; greeting

अभिनय (nm) acting

अभिनव (a) new; recent

अभि/नेता (nm) an actor; —नेत्री (nf) an actress

अभिन्न (a) clase; sameness, not different

अभिप्राय (nm) purpose; intention

अभिभावक (nm) a guardian

अभिभाषण (nm) a public speech

अभिभूत (a) overpowered; astonished

अभि/मान (nm) vanity; pride; —मानी arrogant; proud

अभिमुख (ind) facing, directed towards

अभियान (nm) an expedition; a campaign

अभियुक्त (nm & a) an accused

अभियोग (nm) charge, accusation

अभिराम (a) lovely, beautiful

अभिरुचि (nf) taste

अभिलषित (a) longed for,

desired

अभिलाषा (*nf*) desire

अभिवादन (*nm*) greeting

अभिवृद्धि (*nf*) development

अभिव्यंजना (*nf*) expression;
—वाद expressionism

अभिव्यक्ति (*nf*) manifestation;
expression

अभिशाप (*nm*) a curse

अभिसार (*nm*) appointment of
lovers; meeting

अभिसारिका (*nf*) a woman who
goes to meet her lover

अभी (*adv*) this moment, just
now

अभीष्ट (*a*) cherished, desired

अभूतपूर्व (*a*) never existed
before; unprecedented

अभेद (*nm*) absence of difference, identity

अभेद्य (*a*) indivisible

अभ्यर्थना (*nf*) request; welcome

अभ्यागत (*nm*) visitor, a guest

अभ्यास (*nm*) exercise; practice;
habit

अभ्युत्थान (*nm*) elevation; rise

अभ्युदय (*nm*) rising

अमचूर (*nm*) dried mango
parings

अमन (*nm*) tranquillity, peace

अमर (*a*) undying, immortal;
(*nm*) a god

अमरता (*nf*) immortality

अमरूद (*nm*) guava

अमर्त्य (*a*) eternal, deathless

अमल (*a*) pure

अमल (*nm*) conduct, authority, application, —पानी
(*nm*) intoxication

अमलदारी (*nf*) government,
rule

अमला (*nm*) officers, agents,
staff

अमली (*a*) habitual, (*nm*) an
addict

अमानत (*nf*) charge, something
given in trust

अमानुषिक (*a*) devellish;
inhuman

अमावस (*nf*) the last day of the
dark fortnight

अमिट (*a*) fixed, indelible

अमित (*a*) endless, immeasurable; enormous

अमीर (*a*) wealthy, rich;
(*nm*) a noble man

अमीरी (*nf*) richness

अमुक (*a*) a certain person, so
and so

अमूर्त (*a*) abstract

अमूल्य (*a*) costly, valuable;
priceless

अमृत (*nm*) nectar

अमोघ (*a*) effectual, unfailing

अम्माँ (*nf*) mamma, mother

अम्ल (*nm*) acid; (*a*) sour; —ता
acidity, sourness

अयोग्य (*a*) unworthy; un-
qualified, unfit, improper

अरक्षित (*a*) unguarded,
undefended; insecured

अरब (*a*) a thousand million;
(*nm*) the Arab country; an

Arab

अरमान (*nm*) wish, desire, ambition

अरसा (*nm*) a space of time, period; delay

अराजकता (*nf*) the state of being without a king, anarchy

अरारोट (*nm*) arrow-root

अरि (*nm*) an enemy

अरुचि (*nf*) sickness of stomach; dislike; —कर disgusting

अरुणोदय (*nm*) the first appearance of the Sun; day-break

अरे (*int*) O! a form of address

अर्क (*nm*) the Sun; essence

अर्ग/ल—ला (*nm & nf*) a log for fastening a door

अर्घ्य (*nm*) precious, valuable; fit for presentation to a deity, etc

अर्च/न—ना (*nm & nf*) worship, adoration

अर्ज़ (*nm*) prayer, request, solicitation

अर्जित (*a*) gathered, gained, earned

अर्ज़ी (*nf*) petition; an application

अर्ज़ीदावा (*nm*) a plaint submitted in a law-court

अर्थ (*nm*) sense; meaning; money; —गर्भित significant —वत्ता significance

अर्थ-व्यवस्था (*nf*) economy

अर्थ/शास्त्र (*nm*) Economics; the science of wealth; —शास्त्री an economist

अर्थहीन (*a*) moneyless; meaningless

अर्थात् (*ind*) that is to say, namely

अर्थी (*nf*) a bier; (*a*) desirous; (*nm*) a petitioner

अर्दली (*nm*) attendant, an orderly

अर्ध (*a*) half; semi; demi

अर्धचंद्र (*nm*) half moon, the symbol of nasalisation to a vowel

अर्धवृत्त (*nm*) semi-circle

अर्धव्यास (*nm*) radius

अर्धांगिनी (*nf*) wife, better half

अर्पण (*nm*) an offering, —करना to deliver

अर्राना (*v*) to fall down with a violent noise; to rush to

अर्वाचीन (*a*) new, recent; modern, up-to-date

अर्ह (*a*) competent; qualified; —ता (*nf*) competence; qualification

अलंकार (*nm*) ornament; figure of speech

अलक (*nf*) a ringlet of hair

अलकतरा (*nm*) pitch, coal-tar

अलग (*a & adv*) aside, separate, apart

अल/गरज़ (*a*) careless; —गरज़ी (*nf*) carelessness

अलगाव (*nm*) separation;

breach, severance

अलबत्ता (*ind*) certainly, nevertheless

अलबेला (*nm*) hubble -bubble, a dandy; (*a*) dandy

अलभ्य (*a*) unattainable; rare

अलमबरदार (*nm*) a standard-bearer

अलमस्त (*a*) gay; free from anxiety

अलमारी (*nf*) a cupboard; a bookcase

अलसाना (*v*) to be drowsy; to feel lazy

अलसी (*nf*) linseed; —का तेल (*nm*) linseed oil

अलग/ ग (*a*) different, separate, aloof — गी aloofness

अलापना (*v*) to converse, to tune the voice

अलावा (*ind*) moreover, besides, except

अलोना (*a*) without salt

अलौकिक (*a*) heavenly, unearthly

अल्प (*a*) small, few; —ता (*nf*) smallness

अल्लाह (*nm*) God, the Almighty

अल्हड़ (*a*) carefree; —पन inexperience

अव (*pref*) a Sanskrit prefix denoting — downwards, smallness, decay etc. (as — अवगुण, अवतरण, अवमान)

अवकाश (*nm*) leave; recess; leisure

अवगुण (*nm*) fault, defect

अवचेतन (*nm* & *a*) subconscious

अवज्ञा (*nf*) disregard; contempt

अवतरण (*nm*) descent; crossing over; birth; copy —चिह्न quotation marks (" ")

अवतरित (*a*) descended

अवतार (*nm*) exhibition into human form, an incarnation

अवतीर्ण (*a*) manifested, descended

अवधि (*nf*) time; period; limit; duration

अवयव (*nm*) body; limb; a part, portion

अवर (*a*) under; junior; low

अवरुद्ध (*a*) stopped, shut up; hindered; restrained

अवरोध (*nm*) hindrance; restraint

अवर्णनीय, अवर्ण्य (*a*) unspeakable, indescribable

अवलंब (*nm*) a prop and stay; support

अवलोकन (*nm*) beholding, viewing, seeing

अवशिष्ट (*a*) remainder, left; (*nm*) remains, remnant

अवशेष (*nm*) remains, remnant

अवश्य (*adv*) surely, certainly; —मेव undoubtedly

अवसर (*nm*) chance, opportunity, occasion; —वादी

opportunist

अवस्था (*nf*) situation, condition; age

अवहेलना (*nf*) disrespect, neglect, carelessness

अवांछनीय (*a*) undesirable

अवांछित (*a*) undesired

अबाक् (*a*) stunned, wonderstruck; speechless

अविकारी (*a*) permanant condition; immutable

अविचल (*a*) unmoved, steady, motionless

अविनाशी (*a*) everlasting, immortal

अविभाज्य (*a*) indivisible

अविलंब (*adv*) immediately, at once

अविवाहित (*a & nm*) unwedded, bachelor

अविवे/क (*nm*) imprudence; —की stupid

अविश्वसनीय (*a*) incredible; untrustworthy

अविश्वास (*nm*) discredit, distrust; doubt

अविश्वासी (*a*) unfaithful, suspicious; (*nm*) an unbeliever

अवैज्ञानिक (*a*) unscientific

अवैतनिक (*a*) honorary

अवैध (*a*) unlawful, illegal, —ता illegality

अव्यय (*nm*) an indeclinable

अव्यवस्था (*nf*) hotch-potch, disorder, lawlessness

अव्यावहारिक (*a*) impractical

अव्वल (*a*) first

अशक्त (*a*) feeble, weak

अशांत (*a*) unquiet, restless

अशांति (*nf*) disturbance, restlessness

अशिक्षित (*a*) savage, uneducated

अशिष्ट (*a*) indecent; ill mannered; rude; —ता (*nf*) rudeness

अशुद्ध (*a*) impure; incorrect, wrong

अशुभ (*a*) bad, evil, inauspicious

अशोभन (*a*) ugly, unbecoming

अश्रु (*nm*) a tear, —पात shedding of tears

अश्लील (*a*) indecent, vulgar; obscene; —ता obscenity

असंख्य (*a*) countless, untold, numberless

असंग/त (*a*) absurd; irrelevant; —ति absurdity; irrelevance.

असंतुलित (*a*) unbalanced

असंतुष्ट (*a*) discontented, aggrieved, dissatisfied

असंतो/ष (*nm*) discontentment, dissatisfaction; —षी insatiable

असंबद्ध (*a*) disconnected

असंभव (*a*) impracticable, impossible

असंस्कृत (*a*) unrefined; uncultured

असत्य (*nm*) untruth, a lie

असफल (*a*) unsuccessful; —ता failure

असबाब (*nm*) baggage, luggage

असभ्य (*a*) impolite, vulgar, rude; —ता uncivility

असमंजस (*nm*) suspense, a dilemma

असमय (*adv & a*) out of season; untimely

असमर्थ (*a*) unable; —ता inability, incompetence

असमान (*a*) dissimilar; unequal

असर (*nm*) impression; effect

अस/ल—ली (*a*) real; pure

असलियत (*nf*) truth, reality

असहमति (*nf*) disagreement

असहयोग (*nm*) non-co-operation

असहाय (*a*) helpless; single-handed; lonesome

असहिष्णु (*a*) unenduring, peevish —ता intolerance, peevishness

असह्य (*a*) unendurable, intolerable

असाधारण (*a*) unusual, extra-ordinary —ता unusualness

असाध्य (*a*) incurable; impracticable

असामयिक (*a*) untimely, ill-timed, immature

असावधानी (*nf*) negligence, carelessness

असीम (*a*) boundless, limitless

असीमित (*a*) unlimited, unbounded

असुविधा (*nf*) inconvenience

असैनिक (*a*) non-military; civil; (*nm*) a civilian

अस्त (*a*) set; hidden, sunk —प्राय almost set

अस्त-व्यस्त (*a*) scattered; confused

अस्तित्व (*nm*) entity, existence

अस्तु (*ind*) well, however

अस्त्र (*nm*) a weapon, missile

अस्त्र-शस्त्र (*nm*) armament, weapons

अस्त्रागार (*nm*) armoury

अस्थायी (*a*) provisional, temporary

अस्थि (*nf*) a bone

अस्थिर (*a*) unstable, unsteady

अस्पताल (*nm*) a hospital

अस्पष्ट (*a*) vague; dim, obscure

अस्पृश्य (*a*) untouchable; —ता untouchability

अस्वस्थ (*a*) unhealthy

अस्वाभाविक (*a*) artificial, unnatural

अस्वीकृत (*a*) refused; unaccepted; rejected

अहं (*nm*) ego; —वाद egoism

अहंका/र (*nm*) egotism; vanity —री egotist

अहम (*a*) significant, important

अहमियत (*nf*) significance, importance

अहिंसक (*a*) non-violent

अहिंसा (*nf*) benevolence, non-violence

अहित (*nm*) enmity; harm, evil; —कर harmful

आ

आ the second vowel and the second letter of Devnagri alphabet; the long form of अ a Sanskrit prefix denoting the sense upto, through-out etc. (as आजन्म, आजीवन)

आँकड़े (*nm plural*) figures; data; numerals

आँकना (*v*) to assess; to mark

आँख (*nf*) an eye; sight; vision, the eye of a needle; —मिचौली —मिचौनी the game of hide and seek; —डबडबाना to have the eyes filled with tears; —देखा self-witnessed

आँगन (*nm*) a courtyard

आँच (*nf*) fire, the heat of flame

आँचल (*nm*) the end of cloth, sari and shawl etc

आँत (*nf*) intestines

आंतरिक (*a*) innate; internal

आंदोलन (*nm*) an agitation, a movement, campaign; tumult

आँधी (*nf*) a dust-storm, storm; tempest

आंशिक (*a*) fractional; partial

आँसू (*nm*) tear

आइंदा (*adv*) in future

आइना (*nm*) mirror, a looking-glass

आकर (*nm*) source; a mine; treasury

आकर्षक (*a*) attractive, charm-ing, magnetic

आकर्षण (*nm*) charm, attrac-tion, affinity; —शक्ति the power of attraction

आकर्षित (*a*) drawn, attracted

आकस्मिक (*a*) accidental, unexpected, sudden

आकांक्षा (*nf*) wish, aspiration

आकांक्षी (*a & nm*) expectant, aspirant

आकार (*nm*) appearance, form; structure; size; —प्रकार shape and size

आकाश (*nm*) the sky, heavens; —गंगा the milky way; —मंडल the celestial sphere; cosmos

आकाशवाणी (*nf*) an oracle; a proper name given to All India Radio

आकुल (*a*) confounded; un-easy; distressed

आकुलता (*nf*) agitation; mental distress, uneasiness; rest-lessness

आकृति (*nf*) form; structure; features

आक्रमण (*nm*) invasion, attack, thrust

आक्रामक (*nm*) aggressor; attacker

आक्रोश (*nm*) a curse, an abuse; fury

आक्षेप (*nm*) allegation; charge

आखिर (*nm*) end; (*adv*) at last; —कार finally

आगंतुक (*nm*) a new-comer, visitor

आग (*nf*) fire

आगज़नी (*nf*) arson

आगमन (*nm*) precedence; arrival; approach

आगा (*nm*) the fore part of any thing; before; in future

आगामी (*a*) future; about to come; next

आगे (*adv*) before; in future; a head

आग्रह (*nm*) obstinacy, insistence

आघात (*nm*) stroke, blow, shock

आचरण (*nm*) behaviour; conduct; practice

आचार (*nm*) custom; conduct; —विचार morals and manners

आचार्य (*nm*) a professor; the teacher

आज (*adv*) today, now, this day

आजकल (*adv*) now-a-days; —का modern; —में in a couple of days

आज़माइ/श (*nf*) experiment, trial; test —शी experimental

आज़माना (*v*) to test, to try

आज़ाद (*a*) free, independent

आज़ादी (*nf*) liberty, freedom

आजीवन (*adv*) throughout the life

आजीविका (*nf*) profession, livelihood

आज्ञा (*nf*) command, order; —पत्र a written order; a passport

आज्ञाका/री (*a*) obedient; —रिता (*nm*) obedience

आटा (*nm*) flour

आडंबर (*nm*) pomp, ostentation, affectation

आड़ (*nf*) curtain, a cover, shield; block

आड़ा (*a*) transverse; oblique

आतंक (*nm*) fear; terror, panic

आततायी (*nm & a*) an assailant; tyrant; oppressive

आतिथ्य (*nm*) hospitability

आतुर (*a*) restless, distressed; anxious; hasty

आतुरता (*nf*) restlessness, distress; anxiety; hastiness

आत्म (*nm*) one's own, personal; —कथा autobiography; —केंद्रित self-centered; —गौरव self-respect; —घात suicide; —चरित an autobiography; —ज्ञान self-knowledge; —त्याग self-sacrifice; —निंदा self-condemnation; —निरीक्षण introspection —हत्या suicide

आत्मा (*nf & nm*) spirit, soul

आत्माभिमान (*nm*) self-respect

आत्मिक (*a*) spiritual

आवत (*nf*) a habit

आदम (*nm*) Adam (the first man created on earth

according to Islamic, Christian and Jewish mythology)

आदमी (*nm*) human being, man

आदर (*nm*) honour, respect, deference; —षीय respect-able

आदर्श (*nm*) a model, an ideal, norm; pattern; (*a*) model

आदान (*nm*) taking, receiving; —प्रदानexchange, giving and taking

आदाब (*nm*) salutation; manners

आदि (*nm*) a beginning, origin; (*a*) first; —कालीन primitive

आदिक (*ind*) etcetera, and so forth

आदिम (*a*) early, primitive; first

आदिवासी (*nm*) an aboriginal

आदी (*a*) accustomed, habitua-ted

आदेश (*nm*) instruction; command; injunction

आद्यंत (*adv*) from the beginn-ing to the end

आद्य (*a*) first, initial

आद्योपांत (*adv*) from the beginning to the end

आधा (*a*) half; middle; a part

आधार (*nm*) a supporter, basis; —भूत fundamental; —रेखा base; —शिला foundation-stone

आधारित (*a*) based (on)

आधिकारिक (*a*) authoritative, official; —कथानक (*nm*) the main plot or story of a novel, drama or an epic

आधिक्य (*nm*) excess, surplus; abundance.

आधिपत्य (*nm*) lordship, supremacy; power

आधिभौतिक (*a*) caused by animals, material

आधुनि/क (*a*) modern; —कीकरण modernisation

आधृत (*a*) based (on)

आध्यात्मिक (*a*) pertaining to soul, spiritual

आनंद (*nm*) pleasure, delight, joy

आन (*nf*) dignity, honour, prestige

आनन-फ़ानन (में) (*adv*) at once

आना (*v*) to come;

आना-कानी (*nf*) neglect, pro-crastination

आनुवंशिक (*a*) hereditary; —ता heredity

आप (*pron*) one's self; self; you (second person, formal or honorific)

आपत्काल (*nm*) emergency

आपत्ति (*nf*) objection, calamity, trouble

आपदा (*nf*) trouble, distress, adversity

आपस (*pron*) one another, each other

आपसदारी (*nf*) mutual relation-ship

आपसी (a) reciprocal; mutual

आपा (nm) one's own existance; ego, vanity

आपात (nm) an emergency

आपा-धापी (nf) hasty selfserving, a mad race for self-interest

आपेक्षिक (a) relative, comparative

आप्लावन (nm) a dip, a plunge

आफत (nf) trouble, disaster

आब (nf) brilliance, lustre; water — दार brilliant

आबकारी (nf) excise

आबपाशी (nf) irrigation

आबरू (nf) respect, honour

आबहवा (nf) weather; climate of a place.

आबाद (a) populated; inhabited

आबादी (nf) population; habitation

आभा (nf) splendour; beauty; — मंडल a halo

आभार (nm) burden; obligation

आभारी (a) grateful; obliged

आभास (nm) reflection, shadow; false knowledge

आभासी (a) unreal; pseudo

आभूषण (nm) ornaments, jewels; decoration.

आभूषित (a) decorated

आभ्यंतर (nm & a) interior; internal

आमंत्रण (nm) solicitation, invitation

आमंत्रित (a) invited

आम (a) common — आदमी common man

आम (nm) the mango

आमद (nm) coming, approach; income; revenue

आमदनी (nf) revenue, income

आमना-सामना (nm) opposition, coming face to face

आमने-सामने (adv) opposite to one another, face to face

आमरण (ind) till death, throughout one's life

आमादा (a) ready, bent upon

आमाशय (nm) the stomach

आमुख (nm) the prelude of a drama; introduction

आमोद (nm) pleasure, delight, joy; — प्रमोद marriment; orgy

आमोदित (a) happy, delighted

आय (nf) income, receipt

आयत (nf) a rectangle; (a) wide; stretched

आयतन (nm) a resting place; volume

आयताकार (a) rectangular

आया (nf) a female attendant for children, a nurse; (ind) whether, or

आयात (nm) import

आयाम (nm) length; dimension

आयु (nf) age

आयुर्विज्ञान (nm) Medical Science

आयुर्वेद (nm) the Indian medicinal system

आयुष्मान् (a) blessed with a long life (used for youngers)

आयोग (*nm*) a commission

आयोजन (*nm*) arrangement

आरंभ (*nm*) origin; beginning, start

आरजू (*nf*) desire; request

आरती (*nf*) the ceremony performed in the worship of gods by moving a lighted lamp

आर-पार (*adv*) over, across; (*nm*) the two banks of a river

आरा (*nm*) a saw

आराधक (*nm*) a worshipper

आराधना (*nf*) worship; adoration

आराम (*nm*) comfort; rest; relief; —कुर्सी an easy chair

आरामतलब (*a*) lazy, indolent; ease-loving

आरोग्य (*nm*) freedom from disease; health

आरोप (*nm*) charge, allegation; imputation

आरोहण (*nm*) climb; ascension

आर्त (*a*) aggrieved; distressed; afflicted

आर्थिक (*a*) economic, monetary

आर्द्र (*a*) wet; moist; damp; tender

आर्य (*nm*) an Aryan; (*a*) noble

आर्यावर्त (*nm*) the land of Aryans (the country lying between the Himalayas and the Vindhya mountains)

आलंकारिक (*a*) ornamental; rhetorical

आलस (*nm*) idleness, laziness

आलसी (*a*) lazy

आलस्य (*nm*) laziness, lethargy, idleness

आला (*nm*) an instrument; (*a*) excellent; superior

आलिंगन (*nm*) embracing; clasping

आली (*nf*) (a woman's) female friend; range; a row; (*a*) grand; excellent

आलीशान (*a*) magnificent, grand

आलू (*nm*) potato

आलो/क (*nm*) brightness; enlightenment; light; —कित lit, lighted

आलोचक (*nm*) a critic

आलोचना (*nf*) criticism

आलोच्य (*a*) worth criticising

आवभगत (*nf*) hospitality

आवरण (*nm*) covering; envelope

आवर्ती (*a*) recurring

आवश्यक (*a*) important; necessary; essential

आवश्यकता (*nf*) need, requirement, necessity

आवागमन (*nm*) coming and going; transmigration

आवाज (*nf*) voice, sound; echo

आवारा (*nm*) wicked, loafer; (*a*) wandering, vagrant

आवारागर्दी (*nf*) loitering, vagrancy; loafing

आवा/स (*nm*) place of residence, house —सी resident

आवाहन (*nm*) a calling; summoning

आविर्भाव (*nm*) manifestation; advent; emergence

आविर्भूत (*a*) manifested; become visible

आविष्कर्ता (*nm*) an inventor

आविष्कार (*nm*) an invention

आवृत (*a*) covered

आवृत्त (*a*) repeated; turned round

आवृत्ति (*nf*) repetition; frequency; edition

आवेग (*nm*) passion; emotion; impulse; wave

आवेदन (*nm*) petition, an application; —पत्र an application

आवेश (*nm*) intense emotion; wrath

आशंका (*nf*) doubt; fear; alarm

आशय (*nm*) meaning; intention

आशा (*nf*) hope; expectation; —जनक hopeful

आशातीत (*a*) unexpected, beyond hope

आशा/वाद (*nm*) optimism; —वादी optimistic; an optimist

आशिक़ (*nm*) a lover, a suitor; —माशूक़ the lover and beloved

आशिष (*nf*) blessings

आशीर्वाद (*nm*) blessings

आशु (*a*) speedy, swift, prompt, quick, spontaneous

आश्चर्य (*nm*) astonishment, wonder, surprise

आश्रम (*nm*) hermitage, asylum

आश्रय (*nm*) support; shelter, refuge

आश्रित (*a*) enjoying the support of; (*nm*) refugee; a dependent

आश्वस्त (*a*) assured; consoled; encouraged

आश्वासन (*nm*) assurance; guarantee; repose; solace

आस (*nf*) desire; hope

आसक्त (*a*) fond; attached

आसक्ति (*nf*) attachment, addiction

आसन (*nm*) act of sitting, a posture; stage; seat

आस-पास (*adv*) all around, near about

आसमान (*nm*) the sky; heaven

आसमानी (*a*) the colour of sky, light blue; pertaining to the sky

आसरा (*nm*) shelter; reliance; support

आसा/न (*a*) simple; easy; convenient; —नी easiness

आस्तिक (*nm*) a theist

आस्था (*nf*) belief, faith

आह (*int*) ah! (*nf*) a sigh indicating pain, sorrow etc

आहट (*nf*) sound; noise; sound of footsteps

आहत (*a*) wounded, injured

आहार (*nm*) meal, food, diet

आहिस्ता (*adv*) softly, slowly,

gently

आह्लाद (*nm*) delight, gladness, joy

आह्वान (*nm*) a call, a summon

इ

इ the third vowel and the third letter of Devnagri alphabet

इंगित (*nm*) sign, hint; gesture

इंतज़ाम (*nm*) arrangement; management

इंतज़ार (*nm*) expectation; wait

इंतहा (*nf*) extremity; limit

इंद्रजाल (*nm*) trickery; magic

इंद्रधनुष (*nm*) a rainbow

इंद्रिय (*nf*) sense, an organ of sense; —निग्रह self-control; —सुख sensual pleasure

इंसाफ़ (*nm*) equity; justice

इकट्ठा (*a*) gathered, collected; (*adv*) in one lot, together

इकहरा (*a*) single-folded, single

इकाई (*nf*) a unit

इक्का (*nm*) a small one horse carriage; an ace

इच्छा (*nf*) intention; desire; wish; —शक्ति will-power

इच्छित (*a*) willed, desired

इच्छुक (*a*) willing; desirous

इजाज़त (*nf*) consent; permission; sanction

इज़्ज़त (*nf*) prestige; dignity; respect; honour

इठलाना (*v*) to express tenderness by gesture, to act

affectionately

इतना (*a*) so much; this much

इतमीनान (*nm*) assurance; conviction; confidence

इतराना (*v*) to behave in a self-conceited manner

इति (*nf*) conclusion, end; (*ind*) a word denoting conclusion

इतिहास (*nm*) history; —कार a historian

इत्तफ़ाक़ (*nm*) coincidence; friendship, unity; chance; understanding

इत्तला (*nf*) intimation; information; notice

इत्यादि (*ind*) etcetera

इत्र (*nm*) scent; perfume; essence

इधर (*adv*) here; this side, this way

इनकलाब (*nm*) revolution

इनकार (*nm*) denial; refusal; disapproval

इनसान (*nm*) a human being, mankind; man

इनसानियत (*nf*) humanity; human nature; nobility

इनाम (*nm*) reward, prize;

award

इने-गिने (*a*) selected, very few

इमारत (*nf*) structure, building

इम्तहान (*nm*) test; examination; trial

इरादा (*nm*) idea, intention; desire

इर्द-गिर्द (*adv*) about; nearby, around

इलज़ाम (*nm*) allegation, blame, accusation, charge

इलाक़ा (*nm*) area; locality; zone, region

इलाज (*nm*) medical treatment; remedy, cure

इल्म (*nm*) learning, knowledge

इशारा (*nm*) signal; hint; indication

इश्क़ (*nm*) passion, love; amour

इश्तहार (*nm*) poster; advertisement

इस (*pron*) this, it

इस्पात (*nm*) steel

इसलाम (*nm*) the religion of Mohammedans

इस्तरी (*nf*) a smoothing iron; —करना to smooth garment with a heated iron

इस्तीफ़ा (*nm*) resignation

इस्तेमाल (*nm*) use; application

ई

ई the fourth vowel and the fourth letter of Devnagri alphabet

ईंट (*nf*) brick

ईंधन (*nm*) firewood, fuel

ईख (*nf*) sugar-cane

ईजाद (*nf*) an invention

ईमान (*nm*) belief, faith, truth

ईमानदार (*a*) faithful; honest

ईमानदारी (*nf*) faithfulness, honesty

ईर्ष्या (*nf*) jealousy; —लु jealous

ईश्वर (*nm*) God; —वादी a theist

ईश्वरीय (*a*) Godly

ईसवी (*a*) pertaining to Christ; —सन the christian era A.D

ईसा (*nm*) Jesus Christ

ईसाई (*nm*) a Christian

उ

उ the fifth vowel and the fifth letter of Devnagri alphabet

उँगली (nf) a finger

उँडेलना (v) to pour out; to pour into

उऋण (a) free from debt

उकता/ना (v) to be tired of, to fret; —हट weariness, boredom

उकसाना (v) to excite, to instigate; to raise

उक्त (a) spoken, told, mentioned

उक्ति (nf) speech, voice, statement

उखड़ना (v) to be rooted up, to be raised

उखाड़-पछाड़ (nf) ado; manoeuvring

उगना (v) to grow, to rise; to spring up

उगलना (v) to vomit, to spit out; to eject

उग्र (a) sharp; violent; radical; —वादी radicalist, terrorist

उघाड़ना (v) to open, to uncover, to bare

उचकना (v) to leap, to stand on tip-toe

उचक्का (a) a swindler

उचाट (a) mentally wearied, indifferent

उचित (a) reasonable, proper, suitable

उच्च (a) lofty, tall, high; —ता excellence, distinction

उच्चारण (nm) utterance; pronunciation

उच्छिष्ट (a) leavings, waste

उच्छृंखल (a) rude, undisciplined

उच्छ्वास (nm) breath, inspiration; chapter of a book

उछल-कूद (nf) a hopple, jumping

उछलना (v) to jump, to leap, to spring

उजड्ड (a & nm) rash, uncivil

उजबक (a) foolish, stupid, idiot

उजला (a) white; bright; clean; clear

उजागर (a) bright, shining; famous; clear

उजाड़ (a) deserted, ruined; barren

उजाड़ना (v) to lay waste, to root up; to destroy

उजाला (nm) splendour, light, brightness; (a) clear, bright, shining

उज्ज्वल (a) clear, bright, clean; without blemish

उठना (v) to stand up; to rise; to get up (adv)

उठाईगीर (nm) a petty thief

उड़द (nf) black-gram.

उड़ना (v) to fly, to wing; to vanish, to disappear

उड़ाऊ (*a*) squanderer; extravagant

उड़ाकू (*a*) capable of flying; an aviator

उड़ान (*nf*) act of flying, flight

उड़ाना (*v*) to cause to fly, to blow up

उतना (*a*) that much, so much

उतरना (*v*) to come down from a height; to descend

उतार (*nm*) fall, descent

उतार-चढ़ाव (*nm*) rise and fall

उतारू (*a*) determined, bent on

उतावला (*a*) hasty, rash

उतावली (*nf*) haste, rashness

उत् a Sanskrit prefix denoting over, above etc (as उत्क्षेप, उत्थान, उन्नति)

उत्कं/ठा (*nf*) longing; curiosity; craving; —ठित curious

उत्कट (*a*) keen, excessive, intense

उत्कर्ष (*nm*) climax; excellence; prosperity

उत्कृष्ट (*a*) good, superior, excellent

उत्तम (*a*) the best, the greatest; —पुरुष first person (in grammer)

उत्तर (*nm*) an answer, north, response —प्रत्युत्तर reply and counter-reply

उत्तरदायित्व (*nm*) burden, responsibility

उत्तरदायी (*a*) responsive, answerable

उत्तराधिका/र (*nm*) succession, inheritance; —री an heir, inheritor, successor

उत्तरार्ध (*a*) the latter half

उत्तरी (*a*) northern

उत्तरोत्तर (*a & adv.*) continuous; more and more; continuously

उत्तीर्ण (*a*) successful, passed (in test or examination)

उत्तेजक (*a*) exciting; stimulating

उत्तेजना (*nf*) excitement, thrill; stimulation

उत्थान (*nm*) act of rising; progress

उत्पत्ति (*nf*) birth; origin; creation; production

उत्पन्न (*a*) born; produced; originate, —करना to bear, to produce

उत्पात (*nf*) mischief, nuisance, disturbance

उत्पादक (*nm*) an originator; a creator; (*a*) originating; creating

उत्पादन (*nm*) giving birth to; production; —करना to produce

उत्पीड़क (*nm*) an oppressor

उत्पीड़न (*nm*) vexation, oppression

उत्पीड़ित (*a*) oppressed

उत्फुल्ल (*a*) expanded, blossomed

उत्सर्ग (*nm*) abandonment; sacrifice

उत्सव (*nm*) great occasion,

festival, gala

उत्साह (*nm*) enthusiasm, joy, zeal

उत्साही (*a*) zealous; an enthusiast

उत्सुक (*a*) eager, keen

उथल-पुथल (*nf*) state of being capsized or confused

उथला (*a*) shallow

उदय (*nm*) dawn, rise; accent

उदर (*nm*) stomach, abdomen

उदात्त (*a*) generous, sublime

उदार (*a*) bountiful, generous; liberal —ता generosity, liberality

उदास (*a*) dejected, sad, dull, doleful

उदासी (*nf*) sadness

उदासीन (*a*) neutral; indifferent; —ता indifference

उदाहरण (*nm*) example, instance

उदीयमान (*a*) ascending, rising

उदगम (*nm*) appearance, rising; commencement

उदगार (*nm*) feelings (of mind)

उदघाटन (*nm*) opening, inauguration

उदघोष (*nm*) proclamation

उददंड (*a*) arrogant, rude; insolent

उदृदाम (*a*) free from restraint, unchecked, self-willed

उद्दीपन (*nm*) the act of exciting, stimulation

उद्देश्य (*nm*) aim; object; import; purpose

उद्धत (*a*) arrogant, rude, impudent

उद्धरण (*nm*) extract, quotation

उद्धार (*nm*) salvation; restoration; uplift

उद्धृत (*a*) quoted, extracted

उद्बोधन (*nm*) knowledge, awakening

उद्भव (*nm*) origin; birth

उद्यत (*a*) prepared, ready; —होना to be bent on

उद्यम (*nm*) business, enterprise; exertion

उद्यमी (*nm*) active, hardworking, an entrepreneur

उद्योग (*nm*) effort; industry; —धंधा industry; —पति an industrialist

उद्योगीकरण (*nm*) industrialisation

उद्विग्न (*a*) distressed, sulky, troubled

उद्वेग (*nm*) anxiety, restlessness

उधड़ना (*v*) to be unsewn, to be unfold

उधर (*adv.*) thither, on the other side

उधार (*nm*) loan; debt; credit; —खाता credit account; —देना to lend; —लेना to borrow

उधेड़ना (*v*) to unsew, to unfold

उन (*pron*) third person plural, oblique form, those

उनींदा (*a*) sleepy, dozy

उन्नत (*a*) tall, high; improved; progressed

उन्नति (*nf*) increase;

promotion; progress; improvement; development

उन्नयन (nm) development; progress

उन्मत्त (q) crazed; intoxicated

उन्माद (nm) rabidity; insanity; hysteria

उन्मुक्त (a) free; unrestrained

उन्मुख (a) looking upwards, intent, ready

उन्मूलन (nm) ruin; uprooting, destroying; abolition

उन्मेष (nm) twinkling of the eyes; blooming

उप a Sanskrit prefix used in the sense of down, under, near etc (as उपहास, उपमंत्री)

उपकरण (nm) materials; appliance; equipment

उपकार (nm) favour, help, kindness

उपकारी (a) helping, beneficent

उपक्रम (nm) beginning, preparation

उपचार (nm) remedy, medical treatment

उपज (nf) product; crop; fruitfulness; origin

उपजाऊ (a) productive, fertile.

उपदेश (nm) counsel; lesson, advice; preaching

उपद्रव (nm) riot, disturbance, turmoil; —करना to mob

उपनगर (nm) a suburb

उपनाम (nm) a family name, surname, nickname; pen name

उपनिबे/श (nm) a colony; —शीय colonial

उपन्या/स (nm) fiction, novel; —सकार novelist

उपभोक्ता (nm) a consumer; one who enjoys

उपभोग (nm) consuming; enjoyment

उपमा (nf) comparison; a simile

उपयुक्त (a) fit, suitable, proper; used; —ता suitability, propriety

उपयोग (nm) utility, use.

उपयोगिता (nf) service, usefulness

उपयोगी (a) proper; useful; helpful

उपरांत (adv) afterwards, in future

उपरिलिखित (a) above-mentioned

उपर्युक्त (a) above-mentioned; aforesaid

उपलक्ष्य (nm) में on account of

उपलब्ध (a) acquired, received; available

उपलब्धि (nf) acquisition, achievement; availability

उपवास (nm) a fast; starvation

उपसंहार (nm) end, conclusion

उपसर्ग (nm) a prefix

उपस्थित (a) ready; present

उपस्थिति (nf) attendance; presence

उपहार (nm) gift, present

उपहास (*nm*) mockery; sarcasm

उपहासास्पद (*a*) ridiculous,

उपाख्यान (*nm*) a story, narrative

उपादेय (*a*) acceptable, useful

उपाधि (*nf*) attribute, title; qualification

उपाध्यक्ष (*nm*) Vice-President; Vice-Chairman; Deputy Speaker

उपाय (*nm*) measure; remedy; step

उपार्जन (*nm*) acquiring, gain; earning

उपालंभ (*nm*) reviling, complaint

उपासक (*nm*) a worshipper, a devotee

उपासना (*nf*) prayer, worship

उपास्य (*a*) worthy of worship, adorable

उपेक्षा (*nf*) slight, neglect, disregard

उपेक्षित (*a*) slighted, neglected, disregarded

उफनना (*v*) to boil over

उफान (*nm*) a boiling

उबकाई (*nf*) nausea, vomit

उबटन (*nm*) an unguent, a paste for smearing the body with

उबरना (*v*) to be free, to remain over

उबलना (*v*) to boil

उबारना (*v*) to release, to set free

उबाल (*nm*) boiling, seething

उबालना (*v*) to boil

उबासी (*nf*) a yawn

उभय (*a*) both of them, the two

उभरना (*v*) to emerge

उभार (*nm*) swelling, projection

उमंग (*nf*) ambition, aspiration; zeal

उमदा (*a*) fine, excellent, nice

उमस (*nf*) heat, sultry weather

उम्मीद (*nf*) expectation, hope

उम्मीदवा/र (*nm*) a candidate; —री candidature

उम्र (*nf*) time of life, age

उर्फ़ (*ind*) alias

उर्वर (*a*) fertile, fruitful

उलझन (*nf*) tangle, complication

उलझना (*v*) to dispute, to be entangled

उलटना (*v*) to be turned over, to reverse, to overturn

उलट-फेर (*nm*) a change, upsetting

उलटा (*a*) contrary, opposite; reversed

उलटी (*nf*) vomiting, vomit; nausea

उलाहना (*nm*) reproach; complaint

उल्का (*nf*) a flame, fire brand, a falling star

उल्था (*nm*) rendering, translation

उल्लंघन (*nm*) transgression, violation

उल्लास (*nm*) splendour, joy, delight

उल्लू (*nm*) an owl; a fool

उल्लेख (*nm*) description, mention, quotation; —करना to mention, to refer

उल्लेखनीय (*a*) worth mentioning, remarkable, fit for being written

उस(*pron*) the inflexional form of वह

उसाँस (*nf*) long breath, a sigh

उसूल (*nm*) cause, principle

उस्तरा (*nm*) a razor

उस्ताद (*nm*) a tutor, teacher; (*a*) clever, tricky, expert

ऊ

ऊ the sixth vowel and the sixth letter of Devnagri alphabet

ऊँघना (*v*) to slumber, to doze

ऊँच-नीच (*nf*) ups and downs; good and evil

ऊँचा (*a*) tall, high; —सुनना to be hard of hearing

ऊँचाई (*nf*) height, loftiness

ऊँट (*nm*) a camel

ऊँ हूँ (*ind*) denoting refusal, no, never !

ऊटपटाँग (*a*) disorderly; absurd, meaningless

ऊत (*a*) foolish

ऊदा (*a*) violet

ऊघ/म (*nm*) uproar; disturbance; —मी naughty

ऊन (*nf*) wool; (*a*) less, worthless

ऊनी (*a*) wollen

ऊपर (*adv*) upward; upon

ऊपरी (*a*) superficial, showy; upper

ऊब (*nf*) feeling of aversion arising from continuous work

ऊबना (*v*) to feel irked, to be bored

ऊर्जस्वी (*a*) powerful, glorious

ऊर्जा (*nf*) vigour; energy

ऊल-जलूल (*a*) irrelevant, disconnected; rude, foolish

ऊसर (*a & nm*) sandy fallow land

ऊहापोह (*nf*) reasoning, arguing

ऋ

ऋ the seventh vowel and the seventh letter of Devnagri alphabet

ऋचा (nf) a Vedic hymn

ऋजु (a) not crooked; straight; easy

ऋण (nm) debt; minus; loans

ऋणात्मक (a) concerning a debt; negative

ऋणी (a) beholden, indebted; (nm) a debtor

ऋतु (nf) season; menses, menstrual discharge

ऋद्धि (nf) wealth, name of medicinal plant; —सिद्धि wealth and prosperity

ऋषि (nm) a seer; sage

ए

ए the eighth vowel and the eighth letter of Devnagri alphabet

एक (a) an, alone, single, one

एकक (nm) a unit

एकटक (adv) without a wink

एकड़ (nm) an acre

एकतंत्र (nm) autocracy

एकतरफ़ा (a) one-sided; one way

एकता (nf) oneness, unity

एकत्र (a) collected, in the same place, together

एकत्रित (a) gathered, collected; assembled —करना to collect, to assemble

एकदम (ind) in one breath; suddenly; completely

एकबारगी (adv) suddenly; completely; all of a sudden

एकमत (a) agreeing, unanimous

एकमात्र (a) the only one, solitary

एकमुश्त (a & adv) lump; in a lot

एकरंगा (a) not diverse; monochromatic

एकवचन (a) singular

एकसार (a) uniform, even

एकांकी (a & nm) one-act (play); —कार a one-act play-wright

एकांगी (a) one-sided, partial

एकांत (a) alone, solitary; (nm) solitude; privacy

एकांतर (a) alternate (angle)

एका (nm) unity

एकाएक (adv) at once, suddenly

एकाकी (a) alone; solitary

एकाग्र (a) undisturbed, concentrated on the same point

एकाग्रता (nf) intentness, concentration

एकादशी (nf) the eleventh day in the fortnight of a lunar month

एकाधिकार (nm) exclusive right, monopoly

एकीकरण (nm) unification, integration

एकबार (nm) faith; confidence

एतबार (nm) faith; confidence

एतराज़ (nm) objection, opposition

एलान (nm) an announcement

एवज़ (nm) recompense, substitution

एवज़ी (nm) one officiating for another, substitute

एहतियात (nm) caution; warning

एहसान (nm) obligation, gratefulness

एहसानमंद (a) obliged, grateful

एहसास (nm) feeling

ऐ

ऐ the ninth vowel and the ninth letter of Devnagri alphabet

ऐंठ (nf) twist, cramp

ऐंठना (v) to twine, to twist

ऐंद्रिय (a) pertaining to senses

ऐक्य (nm) oneness; unity

ऐच्छिक (a) intentional, voluntary, unrestrained

ऐतिहासिक (a) traditional; historical

ऐन (a) just, exact

ऐनक (nf) an eyeglass; spectacles for weak eyes

ऐब (nm) defect; blemish; vice

ऐबी (a) wicked, defective

ऐयारी (nf) deception, wiliness, fraud

ऐयाश (a & nm) luxurious, licentious person

ऐयाशी (nf) luxurious living

ऐरा-गैरा (a) stranger, unknown

ऐश्वर्य (nm) wealth, fortune; glory

ऐसा (a) so, such, like; —वैसा trifling

ऐहिक (a) pertaining to this world; temporal; worldly

ओ

ओ the tenth vowel and the tenth letter of Devnagri alphabet

ओंकार (*nm*) the mysterious syllable called प्रणव

ओछा (*a*) shallow; narrow-minded

ओज (*nm*) strength; vigour; —स्वी vigorous; powerful —स्विता vigorousness

ओझल (*a*) impediment, out of sight

ओट (*nm*) protection, shelter

ओठ (*nm*) a lip

ओढ़ना (*v*) to cover the body with something

ओढ़नी (*nf*) a woman's mantle

ओत-प्रोत (*a*) full of, well mixed

ओफ़ (*int*) expressing pain and wonder; Ah me !

ओम् (*nm*) the sacred syllable called प्रणव

ओर (*nm*) direction, side

ओर-छोर (*nm*) the beginning and the end; the two ends

ओला (*nm*) hail; hailstone

ओषधि (*nf*) a medicine herb

ओस (*nf*) dew

ओह (*int*) an exclamation of sorrow and wonder, oh !

ओहदा (*nm*) rank, position

ओहो (*int*) expressing regret, Alas ! Heigh-ho !

औ

औ the eleventh vowel and the eleventh letter of the Devnagri alphabet

औंधा (*a*) overturned, with the face downwards

औंस (*nm*) an ounce

औकात (*nf*) capability; status

औचित्य (*nm*) propriety; righteousness

औज़ार (*nm*) tool, an instrument

औटना (*v*) to thicken by evaporation

औद्योगिक (*a*) industrial

औपचारिक (*a*) pertaining to service, formal

औपन्यासिक (*a*) pertaining to a novel

और (*conj*) and, also (*adv*) else; other; more

औरत (*nf*) a woman; one's wife

औरस (*a*) legitimate child

औलाद (*nf*) descendent, progeny, child

औषध (*nm*) a medicine, drug

औषधालय (*nm*) a dispensary, pharmacy

औसत (*a*) average; mean

क

क the first member of the first pentad of consonants in Devnagri alphabet

कंकड़ (*nm*) a small piece of stone; pebble

कंकण (*nm*) a bangle, a bracelet

कंकरीट (*nm*) a mixture of gravel, lime, cement and sand; concrete

कंकाल (*nm*) a skeleton

कंगन (*nm*) a bracelet

कंगाल (*nm*) poor, miserable

कंगाली (*nf*) misery, poverty

कंगूरा (*nm*) tower; parapet wall; ornament on crowns

कंघा (*nm*) a comb

कंचन (*nm*) wealth; gold

कंचुक (*nm*) a bodice, brassieres; skin of a snake

कंजू/स (*a*) parsimonious, miserly —सी niggardliness and miserliness

कंटीला (*a*) prickly, thorny

कंठ (*nm*) neck, the throat; —हार a necklace

कंठस्थ (*a*) learnt by heart

कंठाग्र (*a*) learnt by heart

कंद (*nm*) an esculent tuber root; sugar candy

कंदरा (*nf*) a cave

कंधा (*nm*) a shoulder

कंपन (*nm*) shiver, thrill

कंपायमान (*a*) oscillating, quivering

कंबल (*nm*) a rug, a blanket

ककड़ी (*nf*) cucumber

कक्ष (*nm*) chamber, a room

कक्षा (*nf*) a class room; an orbit

कचरा (*nm*) sweepings, rubbish

कचहरी (*nf*) a court of justice; assembly

कचूमर (*nm*) anything well-crushed

कचोट (*nf*) a lingering agony

कच्चा (*a*) unripe, immature

कछुआ (*nm*) a tortoise, a turtle

कटकटाना (*v*) to grind teeth

कटना (*v*) to be cut; to pass away time; to be ashamed; to complete; to die in battle; to be disconnected

कटाई (*nf*) act of cutting, harvesting

कटाक्ष (*nm*) ogling, a side-look; taunt

कटार (*nf*) a large knife, a dagger

कटु (*a*) sharp; unpleasant; bitter

कटोरदान (*nm*) a brass pot with a lid for keeping articles of food

कटोरा (*nm*) a big bowl, cup

कटौती (*nf*) deduction; reduction

कट्टर (*a*) strict, fanatic; dogmatic

कठघरा (*nm*) a dock; bar

कठपुतली (*nf*) a wooden toy, a puppet

कठमुल्ला (*nm*) a dogmatic Mullah, bigot

कठि/न (*a*) hard, difficult; —नता a difficulty

कठोर (*a*) rough, hard; unkind

कड़वा (*a*) unpleasant; bitter

कड़ा (*a*) stiff; hard; stony; (*nm*) a ring of metal

कड़ाह (*nm*) a big boiling pan

कढ़ाई (*nf*) the art of embroidery

कण (*nm*) jot, particle; a small fragment of rice or wheat

कतई (*adv & a*) altogether, wholly, completely, whole, complete

कतरना (*v*) to cut; to clip, to chip

कतरा (*nm*) portion cutt off, a drop, fragment

कतराना (*v*) to cause to be cut out; to avoid an encounter or coming face to face

कताई (*nf*) spinning

कतार (*nf*) row, a line

कत्ल (*nm*) slaughter; murder

कथन (*nm*) mention, statement; saying

कथनी (*nf*) speech, narration

कथा (*nf*) a tale, fable; a religious discourse

कथानक (*nm*) a small story, the plot

कथोपकथन (*nm*) conversation; the dialogue

कथ्य (*nm*) subject matter

कद (*nm*) height; size

कदम (*nm*) footstep; step, pace

कदाचित् (*adv*) may be, possibly, by chance

कदापि (*adv*) seldom, ever; —नहीं never

कद्दावर (*adj*) of tall stature, giant like

कद्दू (*nm*) gourd, pumpkin

कद्र (*nf*) merit; appreciation; respect —दान patron; just appreciator

कनखी (*nf*) a glance of the eye, ogle, leer

कनस्तर (*nm*) a canister

कनात (*nf*) a screen of canvas, walls of a tent

कनी (*nf*) a small particle; uncooked grain of rice

कन्नी (*nf*) edge; border; ends of kite; a tool of a mason

कन्या (*nf*) a girl; virgin; daughter

कप/ट (*nm*) guile; fraud; hypocrisy; —टी cunning,

trickish

कपड़ा (*nm*) cloth, fabric; —लत्ता wearing fabrics or clothes

कपाट (*nm*) a screen, a door leaf

कपाल (*nm*) the head, skull; a begging bowl; —क्रिया the ceremony of breaking the head of a burning corpse

कपास (*nf*) cotton

कपूत (*nm*) a son of bad character, an undutiful son

कपूर (*nm*) camphor

कप्तान (*nm*) a captain

कफ (*nm*) phlegm, mucus

कफ (*nm*) a cuff

कफन (*nm*) coffin, pall, shroud

कब (*adv*) at what time, when

कबड्डी (*nf*) an Indian outdoor game of boys

कबाड़ (*nm*) worthless articles; rubbish

कबाड़ी (*nm*) one who sells old and broken articles

कबीला (*nm*) a tribe

कबूतर (*nm*) a pigeon; —खाना a pigeon house

कबूल (*nm*) agreement, con-sent; confession; —करना to confess, to admit

कब्ज़ (*nm*) constipation

कब्ज़ा (*nm*) grip, possession; a hinge

कब्र (*nf*) a tomb, a grave

कब्रिस्तान (*nm*) cemetery, a graveyard

कमी (*ind*) seldom, sometimes; — कभी occasionally

कमजो/र (*a*) feeble, weak —री feebleness, weakness

कमबख़्त (*a*) unlucky, illfated, cursed

कमनीय (*a*) desirable, beautiful

कमर (*nf*) the waist

कमरा (*nm*) a chamber, room

कमल (*nm*) a lotus flower

कमाई (*nf*) earnings; wages

कमाऊ (*a*) laborious, earning a livelihood

कमान (*nm*) a bow; an arch; command

कमाना (*v*) to earn; to process

कमानी (*nf*) a spring of steel

कमाल (*nm*) perfection, excellence

कमी (*nf*) decline, deficiency, shortage

कमीज़ (*nf*) a shirt

कमीन (*a*) low-born; mean

कमीना (*a*) mean, wicked —पन vulgarity, meanness

कयामत (*nf*) the day of resurrection, the last day of judgement

कर (*nm*) tusk of an elephant; hand; ray of the Sun or Moon; tax; custom

करतब (*nm*) work, performance, skill, jugglery

करतार (*nm*) master, husband, the creator

करतूत (*nf*) misdeed, evil doing

करना (*v*) to act; to perform; to

use; to do

करनी (*nf*) action, deed

करवट (*nf*) a sleeping on the side, a turning from one side to the other side

करामात (*nf*) a wonderful feat, a miracle

करार (*nm*) a contract, an agreement; —नामा a written agreement

करारा (*a*) hard; rigid; crisp; befitting (reply)

कराहना (*v*) to cry in pain, to moan

करिश्मा (*nm*) a magic, miracle

करीना (*nm*) manner, mode, orderliness

करीब (*adv*) close by, near, almost

करुण (*a*) merciful, touching

करुणा (*nf*) mercy, pity, tenderness of feeling

करोड़ (*a*) ten million; —पती a very rich person, a millionaire

कर्कश (*a*) husky, cruel

कर्ज़ (*nm*) debt; loan; —दार a debtor

कर्ण (*nm*) the ear, hypotenuse, helm of a ship

कर्तव्य (*nm*) duty; (*a*) necessary

कर्ता (*nm*) the creator; doer; —धर्ता all in all

कर्म (*nm*) act, work, occupation, fate, grammatical object —चारी a worker

—फल the outcome of one's deeds; —शील industrious —हीन unlucky; idle

कर्मठ (*a*) active, energetic; —ता hard work

कर्मण्य (*a*) hard working, laborious

कलंक (*nm*) aspersion, blemish

कलंकित (*a*) blemished, defamed

कल (*a*) melodious; (*nm*) yesterday; tomorrow; (*nf*) comfort; a machine or its part

कलई (*nf*) tin; white wash; external grandeur

कलपना (*v*) to grieve, to lament

कलफ (*nm*) starch; a pimple or spot on the face

कलम (*nf*) pen

कलसा (*nm*) a waterpot, a jar

कलह (*nm*) scramble, quarrel

कला (*nf*) a division, moon's phase; art; —कार an artist

कलाई (*nm*) the fore-arm, the wrist

कली (*nf*) bud, a gusset

कलुष (*nm*) impurity, sin; (*a*) dirty, sinful

कलूटा (*a*) of black complextion; sun-burnt

कलेजा (*nm*) heart; the liver

कल्पना (*nf*) supposition; imagination; —शक्ति ingenuity

कल्पनातीत (*a*) beyond imagination, unimaginable

कल्याण (*nm*) welfare, good fortune

कल्लोल (*nm*) frolic, play

कवच (*nm*) armour, helmet

कवयित्री (*nf*) a poetess

कवायद (*nm*) military exercise, drill

कवि (*nm*) a poet

कविता (*nf*) a poem; poetry

कवित्व (*nm*) poetic genius

कश (*nm*) lash, whip, pulling, flogging

कशमकश (*nf*) tension

कशीबा (*nm*) embroidery

कष्ट (*nm*) distress; pain; trouble; —साध्य burdensome

कसक (*nf*) griping pain, strain

कसकना (*v*) to cause a pain (or strain)

कसना (*v*) to tighten, to fix firmly

कसबा (*nm*) a town

कसम (*nf*) an oath

कसर (*nf*) deficiency; draw back

कसर/त (*nf*) physical exercise; —ती athletic

कसाई (*nm*) a butcher

कसाव (*nm*) astringency, tightness

कुसूर (*nm*) error, fault; —वार a guilty person. (see कुसूर)

कसैला (*a*) pungent, astringent

कसौटी (*nf*) an assay, touch stone

कहकहा (*nm*) a boisterous laugh

कहना (*v*) to relate, to say, to utter; (*nm*) saying, order, command

कहा (*nm*) order, precept, saying; —सुनी altercation

कहानी (*nf*) a tale, story

कहावत (*nf*) a saying, proverb

काँच (*nm*) glass

काँटा (*nm*) a thorn; fishing hook

काँटेदार (*a*) prickly; thorny

कांड (*nm*) sectional division; chapter; incident

कांत (*nm*) the lover; husband; (*a*) pleasing; lovely

कांति (*nf*) beauty, loveliness; lustre

काँपना (*v*) to shiver, to shudder

काँसा (*nm*) bronze

काइयाँ (*a*) shrewd, cunning

काई (*nf*) lichen, moss

काक (*nm*) a crow; cunning fellow

कागज़ (*nm*) paper; written document

कागज़ी (*a*) made of paper; delicate

काजल (*nm*) lampblack for use on eyes, soot

काजू (*nm*) the cashew-nut

काट (*nm*) act of cutting, a cut; bite, wound

काटना (*v*) to cut; to bite; to reap; to trim

काठ (*nm*) timber; wood

काठी (*nf*) structure; frame; a saddle

काढ़ना (*v*) to embroider

कातना (*v*) to spin

कातिक (*nm*) the eighth month of the Hindu calender

कातिल (*nm*) a murderer

कान (*nm*) an ear

काना (*a*) one eyed; partly rotten (fruit); —फूसी an inkling, a whisper

कानू/न (*nm*) law; —नन lawfully; —नी legal

कापी (*nf*) an exercise book

काफ़िर (*nm*) a disbeliever in Mohammedanism; cruel; pitiless

काफ़िला (*nm*) a caravan

काफ़ी (*a*) sufficient, enough; (*nf*) coffee

क़ाबिल (*a*) qualified; able

क़ाबू (*nm*) possession, control

काम (*nm*) task; employment; job; desire; —कला the art of love; —देव Cupid, god of love; —बाण the fire of passion, the flowery arrow of Cupid

कामकाजी (*a*) busy; active, laborious

कामगार (*nm*) labourer, worker

कामचलाऊ (*a*) ad hoc

कामचोर (*a*) inactive, lazy; shirker

काम/धंधा (*nm*) occupation; work; —धाम work

कामना (*nf*) wish, desire

कामया/ब (*a*) successful; —बी success

कामिनी (*nf*) a beautiful lady, a lustful woman

कामी (*a*) loving, lustful

कामुक (*a*) sensual, amorous; —ता lewdness

क़ायदा (*nm*) regulation practice; —क़ानून rules and regulations

क़ायम (*a*) settled; established

कायर (*a*) timid, coward —ता timidity

क़ायल (*a*) convinced by argument; —होना to be convinced

काया (*nf*) the body, person

कारख़ाना (*nm*) mill; factory; workshop

कारगर (*a*) effective

कारण (*nm*) cause, purpose, reason

कारतूस (*nm*) a cartridge

कारनामा (*nm*) deed, doing

कारबार (*nm*) business; profession; occupation

कारबाँ (*nm*) a caravan

कारागृह (*nm*) a jail; prison

कारावास (*nm*) imprisonment, captivity

कारिंदा (*nm*) one who works for another, an agent

कारिस्तानी (*nf*) trickery, cunningness

कारीग/र (*nm*) a mechanic, a craftsman, an artisan; —री workmanship

कारोबार (*nm*) occupation; business

कार्य (nm) work; vocation; job

कार्यकर्ता (nm) an employee; a worker

कार्यकुशल (a) efficient; —ता efficiency

कार्यक्रम (nm) programme

कार्यवाहक (a) officiating; acting

कार्यवाही (nf) proceedings

कार्यसूची (nf) agenda

कार्यान्वित (a) executed

कार्यालय (nm) an office

कालकोठरी (nf) solitary cell

काला (a) dark, black; —कलूटा pitch black; —कानून black law —पानी imprisonment for life

कालिख (nf) lampblack, stain, soot; blackness

कालिमा (nf) blemish; blackness

कालीन (nm) a carpet

काल्पनिक (a) unreal, imaginary

काव्य (nm) poetry; —कारa poet

काश (int) Had God willed thus ! May it happen !

काश्त (nf) tenancy, cultivation; —कारa tenant; a cultivator, a farmer

काहि/ल (a) indolent; lazy; —ली indolence, laziness

किंचित (a) somewhat, a little

किंतु (ind) but

किंवदंती (nf) false report, rumour

किचकिच (nf) useless prattling, quarrel

कितना (a) how much

कितने (a) how many

किधर (a) where, whither

किनारा (nm) side, edge; bank; border

किफ़ायत (nf) thrift, economy

किरण (nf) ray of light, a beam

किरायेदार (nm) a hirer, the tenant

किराना (nm) grocery

किराया (nm) hire, rent, fare

किलकना (v) to shout in joy

किलकारी (nf) sound of joy

किला (nm) a castle; fort, tower

किवाड़ (nf) a door-leaf

किशमिश (nf) small stoneless raisins, currants

किशोर (a) youthful; adolescent

किश्ती (nf) a boat

किसान (nm) a peasant, farmer, cultivator

किस्त (nf) a portion of debt, instalment

किस्म (nf) kind; sort; type

किस्सा (nm) tale, a story; dispute; —कहानी fiction

कीचड़ (nm) clay, mud

कीटाणु (nm) a germ

कीड़ा (nm) a worm, an insect

कीम/त (nf) cost, price; worth; /ती valuable, costly

कीर्ति (nf) fame, reputation

कील (nf) a pin, peg, nail

कुँआरा (a) unmarried, bachelor

कुंकुम (nf) saffron

कुँजड़ा (nm) a vegetable vendor

कुंजी (nf) a key

कुंठा (nf) frustration

कुंडल (*nm*) a large ring worn on the ears

कुंद (*nm*) a lotus flower

कुआँ (*nm*) a well

कुकरे (*nm*) trachoma

कुक/र्म (*nm*) sin, misdeed; —र्मी sinner

कुख्यात (*a*) defamed, of bad repute

कुचलना (*v*) to tread, to crush

कुछ (*pron & a*) some, a little, anything

कुटनी (*nf*) procuress, a bawd

कुटिल (*a*) cruel, crooked; —ता crookedness

कुटी (*nf*) a hut, cottage

कुटीर (*nm*) cottage

कुटुंब (*nm*) family

कुढ़ना (*v*) to grudge, to fret

कुतरना (*v*) to nibble; to gnaw

कुतूहल (*nm*) eagerness, curiosity

कुत्ता (*nm*) a dog

कुत्सित (*a*) vile; shabby, contemptible

कुदरत (*nf*) the nature, power, God

कुनबा (*nm*) household, family

कुपित (*a*) angry, offended, irate

कुबड़ा (*a*) crook-backed; bent

कुमक (*nf*) reinforcement; aid; assistance

कुमार (*nm*) a boy; a son; (*a*) unmarried (man)

कुमुद (*nm*) lily, red lotus

कुम्हलाना (*v*) to wither, to shrivel, to fade

कुम्हार (*nm*) a potter

कुरबानी (*nf*) a sacrifice

कुरेदना (*v*) to scratch, to scrape

कुर्सी (*nf*) a chair

कुल (*a*) all, entire, complete; (*nm*) lineage; dynasty —पति Vice-Chancellor; —मर्यादा the dignity of a family; —वधू the virtuous woman of a noble family

कुलटा (*nf*) an unchaste woman

कुलबुलाना (*v*) to rumble, to creep; to be restless

कुली (*nm*) a labourer, a coolie

कुलीन (*a*) well born, of noble descent, of gentle blood

कुल्ला (*nm*) rinsing and washing of mouth, gargle

कुल्हा/ड़ा (*nm*) an axe, hatchet; —ड़ी a small hatchet

कुशल (*a*) expert, skilful; (*nm*) safety, prosperity; —क्षेम good-health; —मंगल welfare

कुशलता (*nf*) trick, skill; well-being

कुशाग्र (*a*) sharp; penetrating —बुद्धि of keen intelligence

कुशासन (*nm*) maladministration

कुश्ती (*nf*) duel, wrestling

कुष्ठ (*nm*) leprosy

कुसुम (*nm*) a flower

कुसूर (*nm*) omission, fault; —वार defaulter

कुहकना (*v*) to twiter; to coo

कुहरा (*nm*) damp, fog, mist

कुहराम (*nm*) uproar, outcry

tumult

कुहासा (*nm*) fog, mist

कूकना (*v*) to cackle, to warble

कूच (*nm*) departure; march

कूचा (*nm*) a narrow path, a lane

कूट (*a*) false; counterfeit; —नीति diplomacy

कूटना (*v*) to macerate; to crush; to beat

कूड़ा (*nm*) sweepings; rubbish; waste; —करकट waste materials

कूढ़ (*a*) dull-headed, stupid; —मग्ज़ a dullard

कूदना (*v*) to leap; to jump

कूबड़ (*nm*) a hunch, hump

कूल्हा (*nm*) the bones of the hip; hip

कृतकृत्य (*a*) successful, fulfilled

कृतघ्न (*a*) thankless, ungrateful

कृतज्ञ (*a*) indebted, grateful

कृतार्थ (*a*) satisfied, gratified; obliged

कृति (*nf*) a work; —कार the author

कृती (*a*) creative, (*nm*) creator

कृत्य (*nm*) duty, performance, work which ought to be done

कृत्रिम (*a*) bogus, artificial, fictitious; laboured

कृदंत (*nm*) participle

कृपण (*a*) stingy, miser; —ता illiberality

कृपया (*ind*) favourably, kindly, please

कृपा (*nf*) grace, kindness; pity; —कांक्षी seeking favour

कृपालु (*a*) compassionate, kind; —ता kindness

कृश (*a*) thin, lean

कृषक (*nm*) a peasant, a farmer

कृषि (*nf*) agriculture, farming

कृष्ण (*a*) dark, black; (*nm*) Sri Krishna; —पक्ष the fortnight of the waning moon

केंचुआ (*nm*) an earthworm

केंचुली (*nf*) the slough of a snake

केंद्र (*nm*) the centre

केंद्र/क (*nm*) a nucleus; —कीय nuclear

केंद्रित (*a*) concentrated; centralised

केंद्रीकरण (*nm*) centralisation

केंद्रीय (*a*) central

केतली (*nm*) a kettle

केला (*nm*) a banana

केलि (*nf*) frolic, pastime, sport

केवट (*nm*) a boat man

केवड़ा (*nm*) the fragrant flower pandanus

केवल (*a & ind*) alone, only, mere; simply

केसर (*nf*) the tendrils of a flower, saffron

केसरी (*nm*) a lion

कैंची (*nf*) scissors, shears

कैंसर (*nm*) cancer

कै (*nf*) vomiting, nausea

कै/द (*nf*) imprisonment; —दी a prisoner

कैफियत (*nf*) statement; description; remarks

कैसा (*a*) of what sort; (*adv*) how

कोंपल (*nf*) a new sprout, a new and tender leaf

कोई (*pron*) anybody; a few; someone; —कोई some one

कोख (*nf*) womb

कोट (*nm*) a fort, citadel; a coat

कोया (*nm*) quota

कोटि (*nf*) rank; category; ten million

कोठरी (*nf*) a small room, cabin

कोठा (*nm*) a big room; a ware house

कोठी (*nm*) a mansion, bungalow

कोड़ा (*nm*) a lash, a whip

कोद (*nm*) leprosy

कोण (*nm*) a corner; an angle

कोतवाली (*nf*) the chief police station in a city

कोताही (*nf*) want, deficiency

कोप (*nm*) anger, wrath

कोफ्त (*nf*) tedium

कोमल (*a*) tender, mild; soft

कोयल (*nf*) a cuckoo

कोयला (*nm*) coal

कौल (*nm*) agreement; contract; promise

कौशल (*nm*) art, welfare, skill

क्या (*pron*) what

क्यों (*ind*) why; —कर how; —कि because

क्रम (*nm*) system; chain, series; —बद्ध consecutive; —हीन out of order

क्रमशः (*adv*) by degrees, respectively

क्रमांक (*nm*) roll number

क्रमिक (*a*) serial, successive

क्रांति (*nf*) a revolution; —कारी revolutionary

क्रिया (*nf*) activity, action, work

क्रियात्मक (*a*) active; functional

क्रियान्विति (*nf*) implementation

क्रियाविधि (*nf*) procedure

क्रियाशील (*a*) active

किस्तान (*nm*) a christian

क्रीड़ा (*nf*) amusement, sport

क्रुद्ध (*a*) infuriated, angry, wrathful

क्रूर (*a*) unkind, ruthless, cruel; —ता savagery, ruthlessness; cruelty

क्रोध (*nm*) fret, anger; —वश out of anger

क्रोधित (*a*) resentful, lofty, angry

क्रोधी (*a*) wrathful, high-tempered

क्लांति (*nf*) fatigue, weariness

क्लिष्ट (*a*) difficult

क्लेश (*nm*) trouble, suffering, pain

क्वार (*nm*) the seventh month of the Hindu calendar

क्षण (*nm*) an instant, a moment

क्षणिक (*a*) momentary

क्षत (*a*) hurt, wounded —विक्षत wounded all over

क्षति (*nf*) harm; injury; wastage

क्षतिपूर्ति (nf) reparation; compensation

क्षमता (nf) fitness, ability; competence

क्षमा (nf) forgiveness; mercy

क्षम्य (a) forgivable

क्षय (nm) decrease, loss; erosion, —रोग tuberculosis

क्षार (nm) alkali, (a) alkaline, salty

क्षितिज (nm) the horizon

क्षीण (a) weak, feeble

क्षुद्र (a) contemptible; small

क्षुब्ध (a) impatient, angry

क्षेत्र (nm) ground, field

क्षेत्रफल (nm) area

क्षेम (nf) protection, welfare

क्षोभ (nm) excitement; agitation, fret

ख

ख the second member of the first pentad of consonants in Devnagri alphabet

खँखारना (v) to hawk; to make effort before spitting

खंज़र (nm) a poniard, dagger

खंड (nm) part, section

खंडन (nm) denial, repudiation; —मंडन repudiation and vindication

खँडहर (nm) debris, the ruins of a house

खंडित (a) destroyed; broken

खंदक (nm) a moat round a fort, a deep ditch

खंभा (nm) a post, pillar

खचाखच (a & adv) overcrowded

खच्चर (nm) a mule

खज़ांची (nm) a treasurer

खज़ाना (nm) treasury; treasure

खटकना (v) to throb; to feel disgusted

खटका (nm) fear; doubt; knocking

खटखटाना (v) to knock, to tap

खटना (v) to spend money, to labour hard

खटपट (nf) strife, wrangling, quarrel

खटमल (nm) a bed bug

खटाई (nf) sourness; tartness

खटाखट (nf) sound of beating constant clicking; (adv) quickly

खटास (nf) tartness, sourness

खट्टा (a) tart, sour

खड़ा (a) erect, standing; upright

खड्ड (nm) a deep pit

खत (nm) a letter; hand-writing

खतरनाक (a) risky, dangerous

खतरा (nm) risk, danger

खता (nf) error, mistake; —वार

a guilty person

खत्म (a) end, complete, finished

खदेड़ना (v) to drive away

खद्दर (nm) hand-spun cloth.

खनकना (v) to clink, to jingle

खनिक (nm) a miner

खनिज (a & nm) a mineral substance

खपत (nf) consumption; sale

खपना (v) to be expended, to be consumed

खफ़ा (a) angry, enraged, displeased

खबर (nf) intelligence; news

खंबरदार (a) careful, cautious

ख्/ब्त (nm) madness, mania; —ब्ती mad, crazy

खमियाज़ा (nm) retribution; loss

खरगोश (nm) hare, rabbit

खरबूज़ा (nm) a musk melon

खरा (a) pure, sincere, candid

खरा/ब (a) spoiled; bad; wicked; defected; —बी defect; badness

खरीद (nf) purchase, buying

खरीदना (v) to purchase, to buy

खरीदा/र (nm) a purchaser, —री purchasing

खरीफ़ (nf) the crop which is reaped in autumn

खरोंचना (v) to scrape, to scratch

खर्च (nm) expenditure, expense

खर्चा (nm) see खर्च

खर्चीला (a) extravagant, lavish; costly, expensive

खर्रा (nm) a long sheet

खर्राटा (nm) snoring

खलबली (nf) alarm, agitation, commotion

खलल (nm) confusion, interruption

खलिहान (nm) a grainary, barn

खसखस (nm) mawseed, poppy seed

खसम (nm) husband, master

खसरा (nm) measles

खसोटना (v) to pull out, to scratch

खस्ता (a) very brittle; crisp

खाँड (nf) unrefined sugar

खाँसना (v) to cough

खाँसी (nf) cough

खाई (nf) a dike, ditch; trench

ख्राक (nf) dirt; ashes; anything trivial; nothing

ख्राका (nm) a map; diagram, sketch

ख्राकी (a) dusky, brown

खाट (nf) a bedstead; cot

खाड़ी (nf) a bay; a gulf

खाता (nm) ledger; account

खातिर (nf) hospitality; (ind) for, for the sake of

खातिरी (nf) hospitality

ख्राद (nf) manure; fertilizer

ख्राद्य (nm) food; (a) eatable

खान (nf) mine

खान/दान (nm) family, —दानी of high family

खाना (v) to live on; to eat

खाना (*nm*) a house; compartment; shelf

खानाबदोश (*nm*) a rover, an idle scamp

खामी (*nf*) a defect

खामो/श (*a*) taciturn, silent; —शी silence

खारा (*a*) salty, brackish; —पन salinity

खारिज (*a*) expelled, dismissed, discharged

खारिश (*nf*) itch, scab

खाल (*nf*) skin; hide

खालिस (*a*) unmixed; pure

खाली (*a*) void, empty, vacant

खास (*a*) peculiar; special; proper

खासा (*a*) good, noble

खासियत (*nf*) quality; characteristic

खिंचना (*v*) to be drawn; to be pulled

खिंचाव (*nm*) tightness; attraction

खिचड़ी (*nf*) a dish prepared from rice and pulse boiled together; a mixture; hotch-potch

खिड़की (*nf*) a window

खिताब (*nm*) a title

खिदमत (*nf*) duty, service

खिन्न (*a*) wearied, sad, glum, gloomy

खिलखिला/ना (*v*) to laugh loudly; —हट laughter

खिलना (*v*) to blow; to blossom

खिलवाड़ (*nf*) pastime, frolic

खिलाड़ी (*nm*) a player, sportsman

खिलाफ़ (*a*) contrary, opposite, against

खिलौना (*nm*) a plaything, toy

खिल्ली (*nf*) jest, joke

खिसकना (*v*) to slip away, to move slowly

खिसिया/ना (*v*) to grin, to giggle; —हट giggle

खींचना (*v*) to wrest; to pull; to haul

खीज/खीफ़ (*nf*) **anger, vexation**

खीरा (*nm*) a cucumber

खुजली (*nf*) itch, eczema

खुजाना (*v*) to scratch

खुद (*pron*) self; (*adv*) of one's own accord

खुदगरज़ (*a*) selfseeking, selfish

खुदरा (*a*) small coins; retail

खुदा (*nm*) God, the Almighty; —ई creation

खुदाई (*nf*) providence, digging

खुफ़िया (*a*) secret; (*nm*) a spy

खुरचना (*v*) to scrape something

खुरदरा (*a*) coarse, rough.

खुराक (*nf*) diet; dose

खुर्दबीन (*nf*) a microscope

खुलना (*v*) to be unravelled; to be opened; to be untied

खुलासा (*nm*) brief, summary, gist; (*a*) brief

खुल्लम-खुल्ला (*a*) without

reservation, publicly

खुश (a) pleased, merry, happy

खुशकिस्मत (a) fortunate

खुशख़बरी (nf) glad findings, happy news

खुशनसी/ब (a) fortunate; —बी good luck

खुशबू (nf) odour, fragrance

खुशमिज़ाज (a) cheerful, good-tempered

खुशहाल (a) prosperous, in good circumstances

खुशामद (nf) false praise, flattery

खुशी (nf) delight, cheerful-ness, happiness

खुश्क (a) withered; dry

खुश्की (nf) drought; dryness

खूँख्वार (a) ferocious, cruel

खूँटी (nf) a peg

खून (nm) murder; blood

खूनी (nm) a murderer, an assassin

खूबसूर/त (a) handsome; beautiful; —ती handsome-ness; beauty

खूबी (nf) goodness; speciality; merit

खेत (nm) a field, farm

खेतिहर (nm) a peasant, a farmer

खेती (nf) agriculture; farming

खेद (nm) sorrow, gloominess; regret

खेमा (nm) a tent, pavilion

खेल (nm) fun, game, sport; -कूद sports

खेलना (v) to sport, to play; to stage

ख़ैर (nf) welfare, happiness; (ind) all right, well

ख़ैरा/त (nf) alms, charity; —ती charitable

ख़ैरियत (nf) safety; welfare

खोखला (a) empty, hollow

खोज (nf) search, investiga-tion; discovery

खोजना (v) to seek, to search, to investigate, to discover

खोटा (a) faulty, defective

खोदना (v) to scratch, to dig

खोना (v) to lose, to squander, to destroy

खोपड़ी (nf) the pate, skull

खोलना (v) to unfold; to open; to unbind

ख़ौफ़ (nm) dread, fear; —नाक fearful

खौलना (v) to bubble; to boil

ख्याति (nf) renown, fame, repute

ख्याल (nm) attention; thought, idea, opinion

ख्वाब (nm) a dream

ख्वाहमख्वाह (ind) without any purpose, uselessly

ख्वाहिश (nf) desire; wish

ग

ग the third member of the first pentad of consonants in Devnagri alphabet

गंज (*nf*) treasure, pile; (*nm*) baldness

गंजा (*a*) scald-headed, bald

गँठबंधन (*nm*) a custom in marriage ceremony in which the skirts of bridegroom's and bride's mantles are tied together

गंदगी (*nf*) impurity, dirtiness

गंदा (*a*) filthy, dirty, nasty

गंदला (*a*) dirty, muddy

गंध (*nf*) odour, smell, scent

गंभीर (*a*) sober; grave, reserved —ता gravity; sobriety; reservedness

गँवाना (*v*) to waste; to lose

गँवार (*a*) vulgar, ill-bred; —पन vulgarity

गँवारू (*a*) rude, rustic

गऊ (*nm*) a cow; (*a*) gentle

गज (*nm*) an elephant, a yard; a yardstick

गज़ब (*nf*) a calamity

गटकना (*v*) to eat, to swallow, to gulp

गट्ठर (*nm*) a big bundle; package

गठन (*nf*) construction

गठरी (*nf*) a parcel, bundle

गठिया (*nf*) a sack; pains in the joints, rheumatism

गठीला (*a*) full of knots, robust

गड़गड़ा/ना (*v*) to rumble, to gurgle; —हट a rumble

गड़पना (*v*) to glut, to swallow

गड़बड़ (*nf*) confusion; shuffling; —झाला bustle, disorder

गड़डी (*nf*) a pack, bundle

गड्ढा (*nm*) ditch; hollow

गढ़ (*nm*) a castle; a battery

गढ़ना (*v*) to form, to mould

गण (*nm*) multitude, union

गणतंत्र (*nm*) a Republic

गणना (*nf*) reckoning, calculation, counting

गणराज्य (*nm*) a government by the people

गणिका (*nf*) harlot, a prostitute

गणित (*nm*) Mathematics; —ज्ञ a mathematician

गति (*nf*) movement; speed; condition

गतिमान (*a*) on the move, moving

गदर (*nm*) a rebellion

गदगद (*a*) overwhelmed, very happy, greatly delighted

गदुदा (*nm*) a bed cushion

गदुदार (*nm & a*) traitor

गदुदी (*nf*) a stuffed pad or cushion

गद्य (*nm*) prose

गधा (*nm*) a donkey; a stupid fellow

गन्ना (*nm*) a sugarcane

गप (*nf*) a gossip, chat; —शप tittle-tattle

गपोड़ (*nm*) a gossiper; —बाज़ी gossiping

गफ़ (*a*) thick, dense, compact

गफ़लत (*nf*) mistake, carelessness

गबन (*nm*) misappropriation of money; embezzlement

ग़म (*nm*) woe, sorrow; —गीन gloomy

गमला (*nm*) a flower-pot

ग़मी (*nf*) the period of observing mourning; death

गरज (*nf*) thunder; roar

ग़रज़ (*nf*) concern; need

गरजना (*v*) to bluster, to roar

गरदन (*nf*) the neck

गरम (*a*) burning, warm, hot; woollen (cloth)

गरमागरम (*a*) heated; hot; fresh

गरमागरमी (*nf*) exchange of hot words

गरमाना (*v*) to be hot; to be in excitement

गरमी (*nf*) heat; anger; summer

गरिमा (*nf*) grace, dignity

गरिष्ठ (*a*) indigestible, heavy

ग़रीब (*a*) mild, meek; poor; —खाना humble dwelling; —परवर supporter of the poor people

ग़रूर (*nm*) pride, vanity

गर्त (*nm*) a pit, crack in a wall

गर्द (*nf*) dust, dirt

गर्दन (*nf*) the neck

गर्दिश (*nf*) circulation; distress

गर्भ (*nm*) pregnancy; the womb; —धारण conception; —पात abortion; —स्राव miscarriage

गर्भाधान (*nm*) conception, impregnation

गर्भाशय (*nm*) uterus; the womb

गर्भिणी (*a*) pregnant

गर्व (*nm*) conceit, pride; elation

गर्हित (*a*) vile, wicked, ignoble

ग़लत (*a*) incorrect, wrong, untrue

ग़लतफ़हमी (*nf*) misunderstanding

ग़लती (*nf*) error, mistake

गलना (*v*) to be dissolved; to decay; to be boiled; to rot

गला (*nm*) throat, neck

गली (*nf*) a lane, street

गलीचा (*nm*) a carpet

गल्प (*nf*) a small tale

गल्ला (*nm*) produce; daily income of a shop kept in a chest

गँवाना (*v*) to waste; to suffer

गवाह (*nm*) a deponent, witness

गवाही (*nf*) testimony, evidence

गवैया (*nm*) a singer

गश्त (*nf*) beat, patrol

गहन (*a*) deep; profound

गहना (*nm*) an ornament; jewellery; (*v*) to handle

गहरा (*a*) profound; deep; bold; sound; intimate

गहराई (*nf*) depth, profoundity

गहराना (*v*) to be deep; to excavate

गाँठ (*nf*) a knob, knot, tie

गांभीर्य (*nm*) gravity; depth; importance

गाँव (*nm*) a village

गाज (*nf*) roar; thunderbolt; lighting

गाजर (*nf*) carrot

गाड़ना (*v*) to lay; to bury; to pitch

गाड़ी (*nf*) a car, a cart, a carriage; —वान a cartman, coachman

गाढ़ा (*a*) dense; thick; close; (*nm*) hand woven cloth

गाना (*v*) to chant, to sing; (*nm*) a song

गाफ़िल (*a*) careless, stupid, negligent

गाय (*nf*) a cow; (*a*) meek and humble

गायक (*nm*) a singer

गायन (*nm*) chant, singing

ग़ायब (*a*) lost; vanished

गाल (*nm*) a cheek

गाली (*nf*) rebuke, abuse

गावदी (*a*) dull-headed, stupid

गाहक (*nm*) a client, a purchaser, a customer

गिचपिच (*a*) not clearly written; illegible

गिड़गिड़ाना (*v*) to implore, to beseech in an humble manner

गिद्ध (*nm*) a vulture

गिनती (*nf*) calculation; reckoning

गिनना (*v*) to figure, to count; regard

गिरगिट (*nm*) chameleon; opportunist

गिरजाघर (*nm*) a church

गिरना (*v*) to come down, to fall, to drop

गिरफ़्ता/र (*a*) seized, arrested; —री an arrest

गिरवी (*a*) pledged, mortgaged

गिरावट (*nf*) lapse, spill

गिरोह (*nm*) a gang

गिला (*nm*) accusation, complaint

गिलाफ़ (*nm*) a pillow-cover

गीत (*nm*) a song

गीदड़ (*nm*) a jackal; (*a*) coward

गीला (*a*) wet

गुंजन (*nm*) humming sound

गुंजाइश (*nf*) capacity; accommodation

गुंजार (*nm*) buzzing

गुंडा (*nm*) a rogue; (*a*) wicked; —गर्दी foppishness, hooliganism

गुंबद (*nm*) vault, dome

गुच्छा (*nm*) a bunch; tuft

गुज़र (*nf*) passing of time; —बसर livelihood; —करना to maintain

गुज़रना (*v*) to cross over; to pass away

गुज़ारना (*v*) to pass time

गुज़ारा (*nm*) livlihood; subsistence

गुट (*nm*) group; a block

गुड़ (*nm*) raw sugar; jaggery

गुड़िया (*nf*) a doll

गुड्डी (*nf*) a kite

गुण (*nm*) quality; attainment

गुणन (*nm*) calculation, multi-plication

गुणा (*nm*) multiplication; —करना to multiply

गुत्थमगुत्था (*nm*) entanglement, a scuffle

गुत्थी (*nf*) entanglement, a knot

गुदगुदा (*a*) fleshy, soft

गुदगुदाना (*v*) to titillate, to tickle

गुनगुना (*a*) slightly warm

गुनगुनाना (*v*) to buzz, to hum

गुनहगार (*a*) guilty, sinful, (*nm*) a criminal

गुना a suffix denoting times or fold

गुनाह (*nm*) guilt; sin, fault

गुप्त (*a*) hidden, concealed, confidential

गुप्त/चर (*nm*) a spy; —चर्या espionage

गुफा (*nf*) a cave

गुबार (*nm*) dust; vexation

गुब्बारा (*nm*) a balloon

गुम (*a*) hidden; missing; lost; —नाम nameless; —राह depraved; —शुदा missing

गुमान (*nm*) imagination, fancy; doubt; pride

गुमाश्ता (*nm*) manager, an agent

गुर (*nm*) a simplified method;

a formula

गुरदा (*nm*) kidney

गुरु (*nm*) a teacher; a spiritual guide

गुरुता (*nf*) weight, heaviness; greatness, gravity

गुरुत्वाकर्षण (*nm*) gravitation

गुरुघंटाल (*a*) very crafty, a great knave

गुर्गा (*nm*) a servant, a spy; low fellow

गुर्राना (*v*) to snarl, to roar, to gnarl

गुलछर्रें (*nm pl*) revelry, merry-making; —उड़ाना to enjoy freely

गुलाब (*nm*) rose; —जल rose-water

गुलाबी (*a*) ruddy, rosy, of light red colour

गुला/म (*nm*) a slave; —मी slavery

गुसलखाना (*nm*) a bathroom

गुस्ता/ख (*a*) rude, arrogant; —खी (*nf*) arrogance, rudeness

गुस्सा (*nm*) rage; anger

गुस्सैल (*a*) choleric, furious

गूँगा (*a*) dumb

गूँज (*nf*) buzzing, echo

गूँजना (*v*) to buzz, to resound; to echo

गूँधना (*v*) to knead

गूढ़ (*a*) obscure, secret

गूदड़ (*nm*) a bundle of old tattered clothes, rags

गूदा (*nm*) pulp; essential

portion of a thing

गृह (*nm*) a house; residence

गृहस्थ (*nm*) a householder

गृहस्थी (*nf*) household; family

गृहिणी (*nf*) wife.

गेरुआ (*a*) red brown

गेहुआँ (*a*) of the colour of wheat

गेहूँ (*nm*) wheat

गैर (*a*) alien, other; —कानूनी unlawful; —ज़िम्मेदार irresponsible

ग़ैरत (*nf*) modesty, emulation; —मंद having a sense of honour

गोंद (*nm*) gum, wood-gum

गो (*nf*) a cow; —दानthe gifting away of a cow; —धन cattle-wealth; —मांस beef; —रक्षा cow protection

गो (*ind*) though

गोचर (*a*) visible

गोता (*nm*) immersion, dive; —मार diver

गोद (*nf*) the lap; —लेना to adopt

गोदना (*v*) to puncture

गोदाम (*nm*) a storehouse, a warehouse

गोदी (*nf*) the lap; a dock

गोपी (*nf*) a cowherd's wife

गोबर (*nm*) cow-dung

गोया (*ind*) as if

गोरा (*a*) fair-skinned, white

गोलंदाज़ (*nm*) a marksman, gunner

गोल (*a*) globular; round; —मटोल vague

गोला (*nm*) a ball; a cannon ball; —ई roundness; —बारी bombardment

गोलार्ध (*nm*) hemisphere

गोली (*nm*) pill; a bullet; tablet

गोशाला (*nf*) cow-shed, enclosure of cattle

गोश्त (*nm*) flesh; —ख़ोर a meat-eater

गोष्ठी (*nf*) assembly, discourse

गौ (*nf*) a cow

गौण (*a*) secondary, inferior

गौर (*a*) white, fair

ग़ौर (*nm*) considration; pondering (*v*) (करना) to ponder; to take note of

गौरव (*nm*) heaviness, pride, glory

ग्रंथ (*nm*) a book, volume; —कार an author

ग्रीष्म (*nm*) the summer

ग्लानि (*nf*) lassitude; repentance

ग्वाला (*nm*) a cowkeeper, a milkman

घ

घ the forth member of the first pentad of consonants in Devnagri alphabet

घंटा (*nm*) a gong, a bell; an hour; —घर a clock-tower

घंटी (*nf*) a small bell

घटक (*nm*) an intermediary, a factor

घटना (*nf*) happening, incident; (*v*) to decrease, to decline; —स्थल scene

घटा (*nf*) a gathering of clouds

घटिया (*a*) low in price, cheap, of bad quality

घड़ा (*nm*) an earthen pot, jug

घड़ी (*nf*) time; a space of 24 minutes; a watch

घन (*nm*) cloud; sledge-hammer, assembly; —घोर roaring of clouds

घना (*a*) thick; close

घनिष्ठ (*a*) most intimate; close.

घपला (*nm*) bungling

घबरा/ना (*v*) to be confused, to be nervous; —हट nervous-ness

घमं/ड (*nm*) pride; conceit; —डी arrogant; vain

घमासान (*a*) a fierce

घर (*nm*) house; home

घराना (*nm*) a family

घरेलू (*a*) domestic; private

घसीटना (*v*) to trail; to drag

घहराना (*v*) to thunder

घाघ (*a*) a shrewd, cunning

घाटा (*nm*) deficit; loss

घात (*nf*) killing; ambush; opportunity; power (like a^x)

घातक (*a*) fatal, savage; (*nm*) a murderer

घायल (*a*) hurt; wounded

घाव (*nm*) injury; wound

घास (*nf*) grass

घासलेट (*nm*) vegetable oil; inferior stuff

घिनौना (*a*) hateful, odious

घिसना (*v*) to be worn out; to rub

घुंघराले (*a pl*) curly

घुग्घू (*nm*) an owl; a fool

घुटना (*v*) to be suffocated, (*nm*) the knee

घुट्टी (*nf*) a medicine which is given to newborn infants to clear out the bowels

घुड़ an allomorph of घोड़ा used as the first member in compound words; —घुड़-सवार a horse rider; —साल a stable for horses

घुड़की (*nf*) a reprimand, a threat, rebuking

घुन (*nm*) wood-worm

घुन्ना (*a*) one who conceals his emotions, reticent, taciturn

घुप्प-अंघेरा (*a*) pitch dark,

obscure

घुमक्कड़ (a) a rover, fond of wandering about; (nm) wanderer

घुमड़ना (v) the gathering up of clouds in the sky

घुमाव (nm) curvature; a turning; twist; —दार circuitous, winding

घुलना (v) to be lean and thin; to be dissolved in a liquid; to be melted

घुसना (v) to pierce; to enter; to thrust into

घुसपैठ (nf) access; entrance; infiltration; —घुसपैठिया an infiltrator

घुसाना (v) to pile; to poke; to penetrate

घुसेड़ना (v) to pierce; to thrust in; to stuff in

घूँसा (nm) buffet; a blow with the fist; boxing

घूँघट (nm) a veil which conceal the face

घूँघर (nm) a curl of hair; —वाले curly

घूँट (nm) a sip, draught

घूमना (v) to wander; to roam, turn; to stroll

घूरना (v) to ogle; to stare; to frown

घूरा (nm) rubbish, sweepings

घूस (nf) emolument; bribe; —खोर bribee; —खोरी bribery

घृणा (nf) hatred, dislike

घृणित (a) despicable, abominable, abhorred

घृत (nm) clarified butter; ghee

घेरना (v) to encircle, to encompass, to enclose

घेरनी (nf) the handle of a spinning wheel

घेरा (nm) circumference; enclosure; fence

घेवर (nm) a kind of sweetmeat

घोंघा (nm) conch, slug, snail, (a) foolish; worthless

घोंसला (nm) a nest

घोटना (v) to rub for smoothening; to cream up; to commit to memory

घोटाला (nm) turmoil; bungling; confusion

घोड़ा (nm) a horse; hammer of a gun

घोड़ी (nf) a mare; a song sung at the time of marriage

घोर (a) horrible, terrible; awful

घोल (nm) a solution

घोलना (v) to mix; to dissolve

घोषणा (nf) announcement; a declaration

ड.

ड. the fifth member of the first pentad of consonants in

Devnagri alphabet

च

च the first member of the second pentad of consonants in Devnagri alphabet

चंगा (*a*) healthy, sound, healed

चंगुल (*nm*) grasp, claw

चंचरीक (*nm*) the buzzing bee

चंचल (*a*) restless; unsteady; flickering

चंचलता (*nf*) unsteadiness; inconsistancy

चंट (*a*) willy, cunning; (*nm*) a cheat, a cunning fellow

चंड (*a*) violent, fierce; powerful

चंडाल (*nm*) a low born; an outcaste; cruel

चंडालिका (*nf*) an epithet of Durga

चंदन (*nm*) sandalwood

चंदराना (*v*) to deceive, to beguile

चंदला (*a*) bald-headed

चंदा (*nm*) the moon; contribution, subscription

चंद्र (*nm*) the moon; —ग्रहण lunar eclipse; —बिंदु the nasal sign represented by a crescent with a dot over it ( ); —बिंब the lunar disc; —मंडल the halo of the moon; — मुखी woman blessed with a moon-like face; —वार Monday; —हार a kind of broad necklace; —लोक the sphere or heaven of the moon

चंद्रमा (*nm*) the moon

चंद्रिका (*nf*) moonlight, moonbeams

चंपत (*a*) disappearing, vanishing; —होना to abscond, to disappear

चंपा (*nm*) the tree *Michelia Champacca* which bears fragrant yellow flowers

चंपू (*nm*) a literary work which is composed in alternations of prose and verse

चँवर (*nm*) a whisk, a flapper made of the tail of a yak

चक (*nm*) a plot of land

चकई (*nf*) a whirling toy like a pulley; the female of a ruddy goose

चकती (*nf*) patch of leather; a round plate of metal

चकता (*nm*) a blotch on the skin

चकनाचूर (*a*) broken into fragments; much weary

चकबंबी (*nf*) marking the boundaries of plots of land

चकमक (*nm*) a kind of hard stone, flint

चकमा (*nm*) deception; trick; —खाना to be tricked; —देना to play a trick

चकराना (*v*) to revolve; to feel dizzy; to be confused

चकल्लस (*nf*) jocularity, fun; —बाज़ी drollery, fun

चकाचौंध (*nf*) the dazzling effects of light on the eyes

चकित (*a*) surprised, astonished, amazed

चक्कर (*nm*) multitude, circle, whirl; a wheel; vertigo; —काटना to revolve

चक्की (*nf*) mill, grinding mill

चक्र (*nm*) a wheel; cycle; disc; — वर्ती (राजा) an universal (monarch); an emperor; —वात a whirlwind; —बुद्धि ब्याज compound interest

चक्राकार (*a*) circular

चक्षु (*nm*) an eye; —गोचर visible

चखना (*v*) to taste

चखाना (*v*) to cause to taste

चचा (*nm*) paternal uncle

चची (*nf*) paternal aunt

चचेरा (*a*) descended from the paternal uncle

चचोड़ना (*v*) to sip by pressing under the teeth

चट (*a*) quickly, instantly; —पट immediately

चटक (*nf*) splendour, brilliance; (*a*) sharp, bright; —दार of bright colour

चटकना (*v*) to snap, to make a sound of breaking up

चटकनी (*nf*) a click, the bolt of a door. (see also चटखनी)

चटक-मटक (*nf*) gaudiness; wantonness; ornamentation

चटकीला (*a*) of rich colour; shining, brilliant; glittering

चटचट (*nf*) a crackig sound

चटखनी (*nf*) tower bolt, a bolt

चटनी (*nf*) sauce, मीठी —, jelly

चटपटा (*a*) delicious, saucy, pungent

चटाई (*nf*) the act of licking; a mat

चटाक (*nf*) a crackling sound

चटुल (*a*) agile; fickle; clever

चटोरा (*a*) fond of spicy food-stuff. greedy

चट्टान (*nf*) cliff, rock, ledge shelf

चट्टा-बट्टा (*nm*) a play thing for children

चढ़ना (*v*) to ascend; to rise; to go up; to attack

चढ़ाई (*nf*) invasion; ascent;

assault; attack

चढ़ावा (*nm*) an offering to a god; exaltation

चणक (*nm*) gram

चतुरंग (*nm*) chess; an army consisting of pedestrians, chariots, horses and elephants

चतुरंगिणी (*a*) having four divisions of an ancient Indian army (see चतुरंग)

चतुर (*a*) dexterous, ingenious, expert, clever; —ता cleverness

चतुर्दिक् (*nm*) the four quarters; (*adv*) on all sides

चतुर्भुज (*a*) quadrilateral; four sided figure

चतुर्भुजी (*nf*) the four armed one; a Vaishnava cult

चतुर्मास (*nm*) the four months of the rainy season

चतुर्मुख (*a*) four faced; (*nm*) the god Brahma

चतुर्विध (*a*) of four types, fourfold

चतुराई (*nf*) ingenuity, cleverness

चना (*nm*) gram

चपटा (*a*) flat

चपड़ा (*nm*) shellac, a kind of red insect

चपत (*nm*) a slap; a push; loss

चपरकनाती (*nm & a*) foolish, stupid

चपरासी (*nm*) a peon

चपल (*a*) a variable; unsteady; wanton

चपलता (*nf*) variability, nimbleness, unsteadiness

चपला (*nf*) the goddess Lakshmi; lighting (*a*) faminine form of चपल

चपाती (*nf*) a thin cake or bread (of the Indian style)

चपेट (*nf*) a blow, a slap; a sudden misfortune

चप्पल (*a*) a sandal, a slipper

चप्पा (*nm*) a fourth part; a small portion; a hand's breadth

चप्पू (*nm*) an oar, a paddle

चबाना (*v*) to masticate; to chew; to munch

चबारा (*nm*) a room in the upper most storey of a house

चबूतरा (*nm*) stand; platform; stage; dais

चमक (*nm*) brilliancy, sheen, flash; —दमक brilliancy, glitter; —दार sheeny, shining

चमकना (*v*) to flash; to sparkle, to glitter

चमकनी (*nf*) an irritable woman

चमकाना (*v*) to burnish, to varnish; to sparkle

चमकीला (*a*) sunny, glossy, clear, splendid

चमगादड़ (*nm*) a bat; a vampire

चमचम (*nf*) a kind of Bengali sweetmeat; (*a*) glittering, bright

चमचमाना (v) to glitter, to shine, to brighten

चमचमाहट (nm) brightness, glow, glitter

चमचा (nm) a large spoon; flatterer

चमड़ा (nm) skin; leather; hide

चमत्का/र (nm) wonder; marvel; surprise; —रिक marvellous; — री marvellous, amazing

चमन (nm) bed of a garden, a small garden

चमर (nm) the tail of a yak used as a flapper to whisk off flies

चमाचम (adv) brightly, shining

चमार (nm) a shoemaker; a skinner; a cobbler

चमेली (nf) the jasmine plant, its fragrant flower

चम्मच (nm) spoon

चयन (nm) work of collecting or picking; selection

चयनिका (nf) a collection

चर (nm) a secret messenger, a spy; sound made when tearing cloth

चरई (nf) manger, trough which is used for feeding cattle

चरक (nm) a spy, a secret messenger; a traveller; a treatise on Indian system of medicine

चरकटा (nm) a chaff-cutter; a non entity

चरका (nm) a slight wound; loss; trick, fraud

चरख़ (nm) a revolving wheel, a lathe

चरखा (nm) a revolving wheel, a spinning wheel.

चरखी (nf) a winch; a reel

चरचराना (v) to crackle, to sputter

चरण (nm) the foot; the line of poetry; root; —चिह्न foot-mark —तल sole of the foot

चरणामृत (nm) ambrosia of the feet

चरपरा (a) hot, pungent, acrid

चरबी (nf) grease; fat; tallow

चरम (a) final, last, ultimate

चरमराना (v) to produce a creaking sound

चरवाई (nf) the work or wages paid for grazing cattle

चरवाना (v) to cause to graze

चरवाहा (nm) a shepherd, a herdsman

चरस (nm) a large bucket of leather used in irrigation; an intoxicating drug prepared from the flowers of hemp

चरसी (nm) one who smokes

चरागाह (nm) a pasturage; meadow

चराचर (a) sentient and lifeless, movable and immovable

चराना (v) to graze; to make a fool of

चरित (nm) conduct; character; biography

चरितार्थ (*a*) gratified, successful

चरित्र (*nm*) conduct; custom; character; —चित्रण characterisation, —हीन character-less

चरित्रांकन (*nm*) characterisation

चर्चा (*nf*) discussion; mention; rumour

चर्चरी (*nf*) a song sung in the spring season; clapping of hands

चर्पटी (*nf*) a kind of thin cake

चर्म (*nm*) skin; leather; —कार shoemaker; a cobbler

चलन (*nm*) motion; use; method; custom

चलना (*v*) to go, to walk, to proceed

चलनी (*nf*) a sieve

चलाऊ (*a*) lasting, durable

चलायमान (*a*) movable, wavering, unsteady

चवर्ग (*nm*) the palatals च, छ, ज, झ, ञ

चश्मा (*nm*) spectacles, eyeglasses; a fountain; a spring

चसका (*nm*) an ardent desire, relish; habit

चस्पाँ (*a*) stuck, fixed, affixed

चहकना (*v*) to warble, to be talkative, to chirp

चहचहाना (*v*) to warble, to chirp

चहलकदमी (*nf*) walking of a person at a slow pace

चहलपहल (*nf*) mirth, merriment, hustle-bustle

चहारदीवारी (*nf*) the four surrounding walls of a palace or house

चहेता (*a*) dear, beloved

चहेती (*nf*) beloved

चाँटा (*nm*) a slap, a blow

चांडाल (*nm*) the untouchable, a sinful person

चाँद (*nm*) the moon

चाँदतारा (*nm*) a kind of kite, a kind of fine muslin on which stars of coloured silk are woven

चाँदनी (*nf*) moonlight, bed-sheet

चाँदी (*nf*) silver; argent

चाँप (*nf*) pressure; a thrust; the lock of a gun

चांसलर (*nm*) the highest officer of a University, Chancellor

चाक (*nm*) a wheel; a potter's wheel; a circular mark

चाकर (*nm*) servant, menial; waiter

चाकरनी (*nf*) a house maid, a female servant

चाकरी (*nf*) service, attendance

चाकू (*nm*) a knife

चा/चा (*nm*) paternal uncle; ची paternal uncle's wife, aunt

चाट (*nf*) a spicy preparation of cut fruits, vegetables etc.

चाटना (*v*) to lap, to lick

चाट्ट (*nm*) favourable conversation; —कार a flatterer; —कारिता false praise, flattery

चाणक्य (*nm*) the famous statesman of ancient India

चातक (*nm*) a kind of cuckoo which is supposed to drink only drops of rain

चातुरी (*nf*) cleverness, art

चातुर्य (*nm*) skill, cleverness

चादर (*nf*) a sheet; plate; bedsheet

चान्द्रायण (*nm*) a fast which is observed for one month

चाप (*nm*) a bow; semi-circle; pressure (*nf*) sound of stepping

चापना (*v*) to press

चापलूस (*a*) servile; flattering; obsequious

चापलूसी (*nf*) adulation, flattery

चापी (*nm*) an archer; the god Shiva

चाबना (*v*) to masticate, to chew (see also चबाना)

चाबी (*nf*) a key;— देना to wind a clock or watch

चाबुक (*nm*) a whip, lash

चाम (*nm*) skin; hide; leather

चामुंडा (*nf*) an apithet of Durga

चाय (*nf*) tea;— घर a tea-house; —दानी a tea pot; —पानी breakfast

चारखाना (*nm*) chequered cloth

चारण (*nm*) a bard, a panogyrist, a wandering minstrel

चारदीवारी (*nf*) an enclosure

चारपाई (*nf*) bedstead, cot, bed

चारपाया (*nm*) a quadruped

चारा (*nm*) food for cattle, fodder, pasture

चारु (*a*) attractive, elegant, beautiful

चारुता (*nf*) beauty

चारों ओर (*adv*) about, around, on all sides

चाल (*nf*) walk; gait, movement; step; —चलन conduct, behaviour; —ढाल gait, air, fashion; —बाज़ deceitful, crafty; —बाज़ी fraud, deception

चालक (*a*) a driver

चाला/क (*a*) sharp, clever, cunning; —की cleverness, craftiness

चालान (*nm*) invoice; a challan

चालू (*a*) tenable; current; prevalent; cunning

चाव (*nm*) ardent desire; eagerness

चावल (*nm*) rice

चाशनी (*nf*) syrup; taste

चाह (*nm*) desire, will; love, liking; want, need

चाहत (*nf*) longing, fondness; affection

चाहना (*v*) to desire; to love; to need, to want

चाहे (*ind*) either or; —कोई whichever; —जो हो come what may

चिउँटा (*nm*) the black ant of bigger species

चिउँटी (*nf*) an ant

चिंघाड़ (nf) a shrillery

चिंघाड़ना (v) to scream, to trumpet like an elephant

चिंतक (a) musing, thinker

चिंतन (nm) study; thinking, reflection

चिंता (nf) anxiety; worry; care

चिंत्य (a) refletive; thinkable

चिकन (nf) embroidered fine muslin

चिकना (a) smooth; glossy; clean, slippery, —चुपड़ा looking smart; full of flattery

चिकनाई (nf) gloss; smoothness; oiliness; fattiness

चिकनापन (nm) greasiness; smoothness

चिकित्सक (nm) a doctor; a physician

चिकित्सा (nf) treatment; medication;—शास्त्र medical science

चिकित्सालय (nm) dispensary, hospital

चिकोटी (nf) pinch; twitch

चिट्ठा (nm) detailed list; account book

चिट्ठी (nf) a letter; —पत्री correspondence

चिड़चिड़ा (a) peevish, irritable; —पन testiness, surliness, peevishness

चिड़िया (nf) a bird

चिढ़ (nf) vexation, irritation; hatred

चिढ़ना (v) to be irritated

चिढ़ाना (v) to tease, to huff

चित (a) supine; (nm) attention; mind; —चोर heart-stealing; beloved

चितकबरा (a) spotted

चितवन (nf) glance, look

चिता (nf) funeral pyre

चितेरा (nm) a painter

चित्त (nm) mind; (a) supine; —चुराना to bewitch, to charm; —देना to attend to

चित्ती (nf) a scar, a spot; —दार spotted

चित्र (nm) painting; picture; —कला the art of painting; —कार an artist; a painter; —शाला a picture gallery

चित्रण (nm) drawing; portrayal

चिथड़ा (nm) a rag, shred

चिथाड़ना (v) to tear to pieces

चिनगारी (nf) a spark, an ember

चिनाई (nf) bilge and cantline, brick-laying

चिपकना (v) to stick, to cling

चिपचिपा (a) waxy, limy, gummy

चिपचिपाना (v) to feel sticky

चिपटना (v) to stick, to adhere to

चिपटा (a) stuck, flat; चिपटी नाक वाला pug-nosed

चिबुक (nm) the chin

चिमटना (v) to embrace, to cling, to hold fast

चिमटा (nm) tongs, pincers

चिमनी (nf) a chimney, a funnel

चिरंजीव (a) blessed with longevity; — (nm) son

चिरंतन (a) ever lasting, perpetual

चिर (a) lasting for a long time; (ind) ever; —काल since a long time; —जीवी immortal; —निद्रा death; — परिचित long known; प्रतीक्षित long-awaited; —स्थायी enduring; permanent; —स्मरणीय adorable

चिरना (v) to be sawed

चिराग़ (nm) a light; lamp;—गुल करना to put out the lamp

चिरौंजी (nf) the tree Chironji, its edible nut

चिलगोजा (nm) fruit of the pine tree of tubular form

चिलचिलाना (v) shine scorchingly; चिलचिलाती धूप (nf) scorching sun

चिलम (nf) the part of a hubble-bubble which contains the fire

चिलमची (nf) a metal basin to wash the hands in

चिल्ल-पों (nf) a scream, a cry, a noise

चिल्लाना (v) to cry out, to shout

चिल्लाहट (nf) clamour, scream, call

चिह्न (nm) sign; mark

चिह्नित (a) marked, stained, spotted

चीं (nf) chirp, —चपड़ speaking something againt; —बोलना to confess helplessness; to own defeat

चींटी (nf) an ant

चीख़ (nf) screech, scream; —पुकार shriek and scream

चीख़ना (a) to shriek, to scream

चीज़ (nf) a commodity; a thing; — बस्त belongings

चीता (nm) a panther; a leopard

चीत्कार (nf) shouting; uproar

चीथड़ा (nm) rag

चीनी (nf) chinese (language); sugar; (a) a chinese; —मिट्टी clay

चीर (nm) cloth; bark of tree; rag

चीरना (v) to rip, to cleave, to tear

चीरा (nm) a surgical operation, incision

चील (nf) a kite, a snap

चुंगल (nm) claw, talon, a handful

चुंगी (nf) cess, octroi; —घर custom-house

चुधियाना (v) to see dimly; to be dazzled

चुंबक (nm) a loadstone; a magnet

चुंबन (nm) kissing, a kiss

चुंबित (a) kissed, loved

चुकंदर (nm) a tuberous vegetable, beet root, beet, sugar beet

चुकाना (v) to settle; to pay off

चुगना (v) to pick up food with beak

चुगल-ख़ोर (nm) a tell tale, a back biter; —ख़ोरी back-biting

चुग़ली (*nf*) whispering, back-biting

चुगाई (*nf*) act of picking

चुगाना (*v*) to cause to peck

चुटकी (*nf*) a pinch

चुटकुला (*nm*) a joke; an anecdote

चुड़ैल (*nf*) a hag, a witch

चुनना (*v*) to extract, to pick, to gather

चुनरी (*nf*) a piece of coloured cloth worn by women

चुनाँचे (*ind*) thus, therefore

चुनाव (*nm*) pick; choice; election; selection; —क्षेत्र constituency;—मंडल electorate

चुनिंदा (*a*) selected

चुनौती (*nf*) a challenge

चुप (*a*) quiet, silent

चुपचाप (*adv*) quietly, silently

चुपड़ना (*v*) to besmear, to flatter

चुप्पा (*a*) secretive

चुप्पी (*nf*) silence

चुमना (*v*) to be pierced; to be fixed in the mind; to feel pain

चुमकारना (*v*) to coax, to fondle, to produce a kissing sound

चुराना (*v*) to steal, to pinch

चुलबुला (*a*) restless, gay, fidgeting; —पन fickleness

चुल्ली (*nf*) a fire place; a chimney of stove

चुल्लू (*nm*) hollowed palm, handful of liquid

चुस्की (*nf*) a suck, a sip

चुसना (*v*) to be sucked

चुसनी (*nf*) a child's coral, feeding bottle for babies

चुसाना (*v*) to cause to be sucked

चुस्त (*a*) tight, narrow, active, smart; —चालाक sharp and smart

चुस्ती (*nf*) agility, smartness

चुहटना (*v*) to crush with feet, to trample

चुहल (*nf*) merriment, jollity; —बाज a jester; a buffoon

चुहिया (*nf*) a small mouse

चूँ (*nm*) chirping of a small bird

चूँकि (*ind*) for this, because

चूकना (*v*) to slip, to err, to miss

चूजा (*nm*) a chicken

चूड़ा (*nf*) the top, crest, a bracelet

चूड़ी (*nf*) ring; a bangle

चून (*nm*) wheat-meal, flour

चूना (*v*) to drap; to leak; (*nm*) mortar, lime

चूमना (*v*) to kiss

चूरन (*nm*) a powder, digestive powder

चूरमा (*nm*) a sweetmeat made of crushed bread

चूरा (*nm*) sawdust, a broken part

चूर्ण (*nm*) digestive powder, powder

चूल्हा (*nm*) a stove, a fireplace, hearth

चूसना (v) to sip, to suck, to drink

चूहा (nm) mouse; a rat;

चूहेदानी (nf) a rat trap

चेचक (nf) small-pox

चेट (nm) a servant

चेटी (nf) a female servant

चेतना (nf) feeling, consciousness; (v) to understand; to think

चेताना (v) to acquaint; to awaken; to tease

चेतावनी (nf) a warning; alarm

चेरी (nf) a female slave

चे/ला (nm) a disciple; a pupil; —ली a female disciple

चेष्टा (nf) bodily action, spirit; effort

चेहरा (nm) face; countenance; front part of a thing

चैत (nm) the first month of the Hindu calender

चैतन्य (a) perceiving, sensitive, conscious; (nm) intelligence

चैन (nm) rest; tranquillity; relief

चोंगा (nm) a funnel, a telephone's receiver

चोंच (nf) neb, bill, beak

चोखा (a) pure; clear; keen; fine

चोगा (nm) a long coat, a gown

चोचला (nf) coquettishness, playfulness

चोट (nf) a hurt; stroke; blow; attack; —करना to strike a

blow

चोटी (nf) braided hair of a woman; an apex; crown; braid

चोर (nm) burglar; a thief

चोरी (nf) burglary, theft

चोली (nf) corset, bodice, brassieres

चौंकना (v) to start up in sleep, to be alarmed

चौंकाना (v) to alarm, to startle

चौंगा (nm) wheedling, bait

चौंधियाना (v) to flash, to daze

चौ an allomorph of चतु: (चार); — कन्ना cautious, alert; —कोर quadrangular; —खटा door-frame; —खाना chequered cloth; —गिर्द all round, on all sides; —गुना fourfold; —तरफा all round; —पाया a quadruped; cattle; neat; —पाल an assembly hall; —मासा the four months of the rainy season beginning from Asharha; —मुखा having four mouths or burners of lamp; —रस flat, plane, square; —राहा a cross road

चौक (nm) a square plot of ground, a courtyard

चौकी (nf) a stool; a bench for sitting; a police station; an outpost

चौकीदार (nm) a sentry, a guard, a watchman

चौकीदारी (nf) the business of a

watchman

चौगान (*nm*) the game of polo

चौड़ा (*a*) wide, broad; —ई width, breadth

चौथा (*a*) the fourth; (*nm*) the fourth lunar day; the fourth day of somebody's death

चौथाई (*a*) the fourth part

चौथापन (*nm*) the fourth stage of life, old age

चौदस (*nf*) the fourteenth day of a lunar month according to Hindu calendar

चौधरी (*nm*) the headman of a village, a foreman

चौपड़ (*nm*) a game like backgammon which is played with three long dices

चौपाई (*nf*) a metre or verse

consisting of four lines

चौबाइन (*nf*) the wife of a choube

चौबारा (*nm*) an open room built on the roof of a house

चौबे (*nm*) a subcaste among Brahmans

चौमंज़िला (*a*) built of four storeys

चौसर (*nm*) a game played with oblong dice

चौहान (*nm*) a caste among Rajputs

च्यवन (*nm*) dripping, oozing, a leak; the name of a sage

च्यवनप्राश (*nm*) an Ayurvedic medicine

च्युत (*a*) dropped, fallen, degraded

च्युति (*nf*) falling, perishing

छ

छ the second member of the second pentad of consonants in Devnagri alphabet

छँटना (*v*) to be separated on being cut, to be removed, to be lean and thin

छँटा हुआ (*a*) selected; cunning

छँटाई (*nf*) the work or wages for cleaning or pruning

छँटनी (*nf*) retrenchment

छंद (*nm*) metre, stazna; —शास्त्र

prosody

छंदोबद्ध (*a*) in the form of a verse

छकड़ा (*nm*) a wooden car; cart

छकना (*v*) to be satisfied; to be intoxicated

छकाना (*v*) to satiate, to intoxicate, to cheat

छक्का (*nm*) a group of six, the sixth at cards; a six in cricket

छगन (*nm*) a baby, a darling

छछूँदर (*nf*) mole, musk-rat

छछूंदरी (*nf*) a vole

छज्जा (*nm*) terrace; a balcony; drip stone

छटंकी (*nf*) a weight of one chhatank

छटकना (*v*) to slip off, to keep aloof

छटपटाना (*v*) to toss; to struggle; to be restless

छटपटी (*nf*) restlessness, struggling

छटाँक (*nf*) one sixteenth of a seer

छटा (*nf*) brilliance, glory, lustre

छटाव (*nm*) separation

छठ (*nf*) the sixth day of a fortnight in a lunar month

छठी (*nf*) the ceremony performed on the sixth day after child birth

छड़ी (*nf*) a rod, a cane, a stick

छत (*nf*) roof; the ceiling

छतरी (*nf*) an umbrella

छत्ता (*nm*) a covered footpath, carridor, bee-hive

छत्र (*nm*) an umbrella, a parasol; —छाया protection, a mushroom

छत्रक (*nm*) a temple, a pavilion

छत्रधारी (*a*) carrying an umbrella; (*nm*) a prince

छद्म (*nm*) pretext, trick, fraud

छद्मी (*a*) crafty, impersonating

छनकना (*v*) to emit a hissing sound

छनना (*nm*) a filter

छनाई (*nf*) percolation

छपाई (*nf*) work of stamping or printing

छपाका (*nm*) the sound produced by striking against water

छपाना (*v*) to cause to be printed

छप्पर (*nm*) a booth, a thatched roof

छबड़ा (*nm*) a shallow basket

छबि (*nf*) aspect, beauty

छबीला (*a*) handsome, graceful

छरहरा (*a*) light, swift, slim and smart

छर्रा (*nm*) a small shot

छल (*nm*) deception, —कपट duplicity, trick

छलकना (*v*) to spill out, to over flow

छलनी (*nf*) strainer; a sieve

छलाँग (*nf*) a spring, a vault, a leap, jumping

छलावा (*nm*) the shadow of a ghost, magic, will-o'-the-wisp

छलिया (*a* & *nm*) artful, crafty, cunning

छल्ला (*nm*) a ring worn on the fingers; a bangle; eye Curl

छवि (*nf*) features; beauty; brilliance

छाँटना (*v*) to sort out, to select; to cut

छांदोग्य (*nm*) an Upanishad of the Samaveda

छाँव (*nf*) shadow; shade

छांह (*nf*) reflection, shadow;

shade; —वार shadowy —से बचना to keep away from shadow

छाछ (nf) butter-milk, whey

छाज (nm) a winnowing basket, a thatch

छाजन (nm) covering, cloth

छाता (nm) an umbrella

छाती (nf) chest, breast; bosom; heart

छात्र (nm) a pupil, a scholar, a student; —वृत्ति scholarship

छात्रावास (nm) a boarding house, hostel

छान (nf) frame work for thatching with straw

छानना (v) to strain, to filter, to investigate

छान-बीन (nf) search, investigation, critical research

छाना (v) to thatch, to cover; to spread; to stay

छाप (nf) stamp; print; impression; brand

छापना (v) to stamp; to imprint; to impress

छापा (nm) impression; stamp; seal, —मार a raider; guerilla

छापाख़ाना (nm) a printing press

छाया (nf) shade; shadow; करना to shade; —वार sunless, shadowy; —पन shadiness; —पूर्ण umbrageous; —मात्र phantom; —तरु a large tree which gives ample shade; —ग्राहिणी a demon who had pulled Hanuman by his reflection while he was crossing the ocean; —वान the giving as a gift of oil in which a person has seen his reflected image; —पथ the Milky way; —पुरुष a reflected image of a person; —छूना to pursue the unreal

छार (nm) ashes; salt; dirt

छाल (nf) rind, bark, skin

छाला (nm) a blister; a pimple

छालिया (nf) betel nut

छावनी (nf) thatch, encampment, cantonment

छावा (nm) a boy, son

छि: (ind) a word used to express contempt, tush

छिंकाना (v) to cause someone to sneeze

छिछला (a) thin, shallow; —पन shallowness

छिछली (nf) the play of ducks and drakes

छिछोरा (v) trivial, petty; —पन meanness

छिटकना (v) to be scattered, to be dispersed

छिटकाना (v) to spread all round, to scatter

छिटकी (nf) a speck

छिड़कना (v) to spill, to sprinkle, to patter

छिड़काव (nm) the act of sprinkling

छिड़ना (v) to begin, to commence

छितरना (v) to be scattered

छिद्र (nm) hole, gap, slot; defect

छिनना (v) to be snatched away; to be taken by force

छिनाल (a & nf) adulterous, sluttish

छिन्न (a) cut; divided; rent; —भिन्न broken up; destroyed

छिपकली (nf) a lizard

छिपना (v) to be concealed, to be hidden

छिपाना (v) to cover; to hide, to conceal

छिपाव (nm) hiding, secrecy

छिलका (nm) rind, crust, peel, skin

छिलना (v) to be rubbed away, to be excoriated

छींक (nf) a sneeze

छींकना (v) to sneeze

छींट (nf) fine drops especially of water

छींटना (v) to scatter, to diffuse

छींटा (nm) a slap, a casual glance, spot made by a drop of water; —कशी ironical utterance

छींका (nm) network of strings for hanging anything in

छीछड़ा (a) tough flesh of an animal

छीछालेदर (nf) embarrassment

छीज (nf) diminution, waste

छीनना (v) to take possession of, to extort, to snatch

छीना-झपटी (nf) extortion, forcible seizing

छीबर (nf) thick calico

छीलना (v) to peel; to pare; to scrap

छुआछूत (nf) untouchability

छुईमुई (nf) the sensitive plant, the mimosa plant

छुगनू (nm) small bells attached to an ornament

छुटकारा (nm) escape; exemption; riddance

छुटपन (nm) infancy, childhood

छुट्टा (a) free, alone, not bound

छुट्टी (nf) leave, vacation; holiday

छुड़वाना (v) to cause to be dismissed from service; to cause someone freed

छुड़ाव (nm) discharge

छुपना (v) to hide oneself

छुरा (nm) a razor; dagger

छुरी (nf) a knife; a small dagger

छुहारा (nm) the date palm

छू (nm) the act of blowing or uttering, an incantation; —मंतर होना to disappear from sight, to fly away, to vanish

छूट (nf) remission, discount; rebate

छूटना (a) to lag; to be dismissed; to get rid of

छूत (nf) touch, infection, contagion

छूना (v) to touch, to feel, to excel

छेक (nm) a hole, a division

छेड़खानी (nf) act of provoking, teasing

छेड़छाड़ (nf) teasing; provocation

छेड़ना (v) to irritate, to excite, to tease

छेद (nm) aperture, breach, hole

छेदक (a) boring or cutting, a divisor

छेदना (v) to perforate, to drill, to bore

छैला (nm) a fap, spark, dandy; (a) dandical

छोकरा (nm) a boy, lad

छोकरी (nf) a girl

छोटा (a) little; narrow; junior; —मोटा minor, ordinary

छोटी इलायची (nf) cardamom

छोड़ना (v) to relinquish, to remit, to let go; to leave

छोर (nm) border; end; the edge

छोरा (nm) a boy, lad

छोला (nm) gram

छौंकना (nm) to fry

छौना (nm) a young one

ज

ज the third member of the second pentad of the consonants in Devnagri alphabet

जंग (nf) battle, fight

जंग (nm) rust

जंगम (a) movable; moving; living

जंगल (nm) a forest; wood; wilderness

जंगली (a) wild; savage; boorish

जंगी (a) military, warlike, martial; large

जंघा (nf) thigh

जंजाल (nm) perplexity, embarrassment; entanglement

जंजीर (nf) a shackle; a chain

जंतु (nm) an animal, a creature

जंभाई (nf) yawning

जकड़ना (v) to tighten, to grasp

जखीरा (nm) a treaxiry; collection; a store-house

जख्म (nm) injury, a wound

जख्मी (a) injured, wounded, hurt

जग (nm) the universe, the world

जगत (nm) the universe, the world; —सेठ a very rich man

जगदंबा (nf) the goddess Durga

जगदीश (nm) the Lord of the universe

जगना (v) to be awakened; to be careful

जगमगा/ना (v) to glint, to shine

to twinkle; —हट glimmer, splendour

जगह (nf) place, locality; space; —जगह everywhere

जगाना (v) to raise; to awake

जघन्य (a) abominable; detested; low

जच्चा (nf) a woman in child-bed; —ख़ाना maternity home

जज़्ब (a) assimilated; absorbed

जज़्बा (nm) feeling, emotion; —ती emotional

जटिल (a) very difficult, intricate

जठ/र (nm) the womb, the stomach; —राग्नि the fire of the stomach which helps to digest food

जड़ (nf) root; (a) senseless, material, inert; —बुद्धि stupid

जड़ता (nf) stupor, immovable-ness, stiffness

जड़ना (v) to fit, to join; to set with jewels

जड़ाऊ (a) studded or set with jewels

जड़ाना (v) to cause to be set

जड़ी (nf) a medicinal root; —बूटी medicinal herbs

जताना (v) to inform, to make known, to remind

जत्था (nm) gang; a band

जन (nm) mankind, a person, people; —गणना census; —जीवन public life; —तंत्र

democracy; —प्रिय popular; —मत public opinion; —श्रुति rumour; —संख्या population; —समूह crowd; —साधारण the commonman; —हित public welfare

जनक (nm) father; originator; the father of Sita —नंदिनी Sita

जनजाति (nm) a tribe

जनता (nm) the public, masses

जननी (nf) mother

जनाना (a) female; (nm) female apartment

जनाब (a & nm) your honour, your highness; mister

जनार्दन (nm) an epithet of Lord Vishnu

जनेऊ (nm) the sacred thread of a Brahman

जनोक्ति (nf) a proverb

जन्म (nm) birth; production; origin

जन्मोत्सव (nm) birthday celebration

जप (nm) the silent repetition of a Mantra

जपना (v) to repeat silently the name of any deity, to mutter prayers

जपमाला (nf) a rosary for counting prayers

जब (adv) when, at whatever time; —कि when; —तब sometime

जबड़ा (nm) a jaw

जबरद/स्त (a) strong, powerful,

violent;—स्त्री injustice, high-handedness

जबरन (adv) forcibly, with force

ज़बह (nm) slaughter

जबहा (nm) spirit, courage

ज़बान (nf) the tongue, language

ज़बानी (a) by word of mouth, vocal; (adv) orally, verbally

जबाब (nm) answer

जवाबदेह (a) accountable, liable; subject

जवाबदेही (nf) liability, responsibility

जबून (a) bad, wicked

ज़ब्त (a) confiscated, forfeited; —करना to impound

ज़ब्ती (nf) forfeiture, forfeit

जब्र (nm) oppression, force, violence

जमघट (nm) throng, crowd, assembly

जमदग्नि (nm) the name of a sage

जमना (v) to be coagulated, to be frozen, to be fixed

जमवट (nf) the wooden foundation of a well

जमहाई (nf) a gaping, yawning

जमा (a) accumulated, collected, stored; —ख़र्च debit and credit;—पूँजी total accumulation

जमाई (nm) a son-in-law

जमात (nm) assembly; a class

जमादार (nm) head of soldiers, a person on guard

ज़मानत (nf) bond; surety; bail

ज़मानती (nm) a surety, guarantor

ज़माना (nm) time; world, (a) age, period

जमाव (nm) crowd, accumulation, collection

ज़मींकन्द (nm) the yam

ज़मीं/दार (nm) a cultivator; a landlord; —दारी an estate, a landed property

ज़मीन (nf) land, the earth; soil; ground

ज़मीनी (a) earthly, pertaining to the earth

जम्बुक (nm) a jackal

जम्बूद्वीप (nm) one of the seven divisions of the world as described in the Puranas

जम्बूरा (nm) a swivel, small pliers

जम्हाई (nf) yawning; —लेना to yawn

जयंत (a) victorious, triumphant; (nm) the name of Indra's son

जयंती (nf) jubilee; Durga

जय (nf) victory, conquest

जयकार (nf) cheers, rejoicings

जयघोषणा (nf) noise of victory

जयद्रथ (nm) brother-in-law of king Duryodhana

जयध्वज (nm) the name of an ancient king of Avanti; banner of victory

जयपत्र (nm) a bond of victory

जयमंगल (*nm*) the elephant on which a king mounts

जयश्री (*nf*) the goddess of victory

जयस्तंभ (*nm*) the monument erected to commemorate a victory

जया (*nf*) an epithet of Durga; green grass

ज़र (*nm*) riches, wealth; —ख़रीद purchased

जरा (*nf*) senility, an old age

ज़रा (*a*) little, less; (*adv*) a little, somewhat; —सा a small amount

जराग्रस्त (*a*) aged, old

जरामीरू (*nm*) cupid

जरासंघ (*nm*) the name of an ancient king of Magadha

ज़रिया (*nm*) connection, means, agency

ज़री (*nf*) a cloth woven with gold thread

जरीब (*nf*) chain used in measuring land

ज़रूर (*adv*) of course, certainly, necessarily

ज़रूरत (*nf*) need, want, necessity

ज़रूरी (*a*) necessary, needful; important

ज़र्क-बर्क (*a*) shining, brilliant

जर्जर (*a*) old, decrepit, worn out

जर्जरित (*a*) tattered, crushed

ज़र्दी (*nf*) yellowness, paleness

ज़र्रा (*nm*) a particle, an atom

जर्राह (*nm*) a surgeon, an anatomist

जर्राही करना (*v*) to operate

जलंधर (*nm*) the name of a demon, dropsy

जल (*nm*) water, aqua; hydro; —मार्ग channel waterways; —यात्रा a voyage; —यान a ship, vessel; boat

जलज़ला (*nm*) an earthquake

जलन (*nf*) inflammation, a burning sensation; jealousy

जलना (*v*) to flame, to burn

जलनिधि (*nm*) sea, ocean

जलपक्षी (*nm*) an aquatic bird

जलपात्र (*nm*) ewer, urn, flagon

जलपान (*nm*) breakfast; light refreshment

जलप्रणाली (*nf*) sluice of water

जलप्रपात (*nm*) a waterfall

जलप्रवाह (*nm*) a torrent; the act of throwing something into water

जलप्रलय (*nm*) the destruction of the world by water

जलप्लावन (*nm*) a flood

जलबेंत (*nm*) a water-cane

जलभँवर (*nm*) a whirl pool

जलभँवरा (*nm*) a water bee

जलमय (*a*) watery

जलमानुष (*nm*) a merman

जलयन्त्र (*nm*) an appliance to raise water, water wheel

जलवायु (*nf*) climate

जलशास्त्र (*nm*) hydromechanics

जलसा (*nm*) a meeting; a function; social gathering

जलसेना (*nf*) navy

जलस्तंभ (*nm*) a lighthouse; a water-sprout

जलाना (*v*) to light, to kindle; to burn; to scold

ज़लालत (*nf*) meanness

जला-भुना (*a*) hot-tempered

जलाई (*a*) moist, wet

जलाल (*nm*) splendour, glory; power

जलावतन (*nm*) exile; (*a*) exiled

जलाशय (*nm*) a tank; lake

ज़लील (*a*) wretched, base, mean

जलूस (*nm*) a procession

जलेबी (*nf*) a kind of sweetmeat

जल्दी (*nf*). quickness, hurry; (*adv*) hastily, quickly

जल्प (*nm*) babbling

जल्पना (*v*) to brag, to boast

जल्लाद (*nm*) an executioner, a cruel person

जवनिका (*nf*) a theatrical screen

जवाँमर्द (*a*) brave, heroic

जवाँमर्दी (*nf*) gallantry, bravery, heroism

जवान (*a*) young, youthful; brave, (*nm*) a youth; a soldier or sepoy

जवानी (*nf*) youth,

जवाब (*nm*) answer; reply; retaliation; —देह answerable; responsible; —देही liability

जवाबी (*a*) requiring a reply; pertaining to answer

जवाहर (*nm*) a jewel, a gem

जश्न (*nm*) merriment, festivity, festival

जस्ता (*nm*) zinc

जहन्नुम (*nm*) hell

ज़हमत (*nf*) affliction, trouble; injury

ज़हर (*nm*) venom, poison; —बाद a carbuncle; septic

ज़हरमोहरा (*nm*) the bezoar, a kind of green stone supposed to be an antidote to poison

ज़हरीला (*a*) poisonous, venomous

जहाँ (*adv*) wherever; —तक as far as; —तहाँ everywhere, here and there

जहाँगीरी (*nf*) a kind of bracelet

जहाँपनाह (*nm*) the protector of the world, His Imperial Majesty

जहाज़ (*nm*) a ship; a vessel, a sail; —रानी shipping, navigation

जहाज़ी (*a*) marine, nautical; (*nm*) a sailor

जहान (*nm*) the world

जहानी (*a*) worldly, terrestrial

जहालत (*nf*) ignorance, barbarity, stupidity

जहीं (*adv*) wherever, at whatsoever place

ज़हीन (*a*) intelligent, sagacious, wise

जहेज़ (*nm*) dowry, gift in marriage; (see also दहेज़)

जह्नु (nm) the name of the sage who adopted the river Ganga as his daughter

जाँघ (nf) thigh

जाँघिया (nm) a lower under-wear, short drawers

जाँच (nm) trial, assay, investigation; — पड़ताल enquiry

जाँचना (v) to ascertain; to examine; to try; to investigate

जागना (v) to get up from bed, to awake; to be careful

जागता हुआ (adv) vigilant, unwinking

जागरण (nm) watch, vigil, wakefulness

जागरित (a) wide-awake, watchful, alert

जागरूक (a) wakeful, vigilant

जागीर (nf) a rent-free grant given by the Government as a reward for some services, grant

जागृति (nf) wakefulness, an awakening

जाज्वल्यमान (a) shining, lustr-ous

जाट (nm) a tribe among Rajputs

जाड़ा (nm) winter; cold

जाड्य (nm) lack of sensation,

जातक (nm) a child, a newborn babe

जात-पाँत (nf) caste and community

जाता (nf) a girl, daughter

जाति (nf) race; sex; caste; community

जाती (a) personal, individual

जातीय (a) pertaining to tribe or caste

जातीयता (nf) communal feeling

जादू (nm) juggling, magic, spell; charm; — टोना socre-ry; voodooism

जादूगर (nm) juggler, magician; conjurer

जादूगरनी (nf) a witch

जादूगरी (nf) magic, sorcery, a charm

जान (nf) understanding; life; spirit; — बीमा life insurance; — व माल life and property

जानका/र (a) conversant; knowing; experienced; — री acquaintance; know-ledge

जानकी (nf) Sita; — नाथ Shri Rama

जानदार (a) animate, having life

जानना (v) to know; to under-stand

जान-पहचान (nf) acquaintance

जानवर (nm) an animal, a beast

जाना (v) to go; to depart; to lose

जानु (nm) the knee

जानी (a) dear, beloved, animate; — दुश्मन a mortal enemy; — दोस्त a fast friend

जाप (nm) a rosary for counting mantras

जापक (nm) one who repeats

the names of a deity on a rosary

जाफ़रान (*nm*) saffron

जाबालि (*nm*) the preceptor of king Dasharatha

ज़ाब्ता (*nm*) regulation, rule; —दीवानी Civil Procedure Code; —फ़ौजदारी Penal Code

जाम (*a*) jammed; (*nm*) jam; a peg; a period of three hours

जामन (*nm*) rennet used in coagulating milk;

जामा (*nm*) a garment, a raiment, a robe

जामाता (*nm*) a son-in-law

जामुन (*nm*) a black plum, jambo

जाम्बवती (*nf*) one of the wives of Lord Krishna

जाम्बवंत (*nm*) a minister of King Sugreeva

ज़ाय/का (*nm*) relish, taste; —केदार tasteful, relishing

जायदाद (*nf*) property

ज़ाया (*a*) waste, ruined

जार (*nm*) a lover, an adulterer

जारण (*nm*) burning, reducing to ashes

जारी (*a*) proceeding, running, in force

जालंधर (*nm*) dropsy

जाल (*nm*) mesh, net, network; plot; —साज़ a deceiver, a cunning person; —साज़ी forgery, deception

जाला (*nm*) a net, cobweb

ज़ालिम (*a*) tyrannical, cruel, oppressive; (*nm*) a tyrant

जाली (*nf*) network, guaze, grating

जासू/स (*nm*) an emissary, a spy; —सी the work of a spy or secret agent

ज़ाहिर (*a*) obvious, clear, plain, manifest

जाहिल (*a*) foolish; ignorant; illiterate; rude

जाह्नवी (*nf*) an epithet of river Ganga

ज़िंदगी (*nf*) duration of life, age

ज़िंदा (*a*) living, alive; —दिल jolly, jovial, merry; —दिली liveliness

ज़िक्र (*nm*) recital, mention

जिगर (*nm*) the liver; the heart

जिगरा (*nm*) courage, bravery

जिगरी (*a*) intimate, friendly; —दोस्त very intimate friend

जिगीषा (*nf*) desire for victory, superiority

जिज्ञासा (*nf*) curiosity

जिज्ञासित (*a*) questioned, enquired

जिज्ञासु (*a*) inquisitive, curious

जित/ना (*a*) as much as, however; ने as many

जितात्मा (*a*) self-controlled

जिताना (*v*) to cause to win

जितेंद्रिय (*a*) having the sense subdued; (*nm*) an ascetic, virtuous person

ज़िद (nf) persistence, obstinacy

ज़िद्दी (a) obstinate

जिधर (adv) whither, wherever

जिन (nm) the Jain Tirthankars; Vishnu; the Sun; the plural form of जिस

जिमाना (v) to feed at a table

जि/म्मा (nm) trust, charge, duty; —म्मेदार responsible; —म्मेदारी responsibility

जिरह (nf) fault-finding, cross-examination

जिला (nm) a district

जिलाना (v) to give life, to bring back to life

जिलाधीश (nm) the district magistrate

जिल्द (nf) skin, leather, binding of a book; —बंदी book-binding work; —साज a bookbinder

जिस (pron) who, whom, which

जिस्म (nm) the body of an animate being or animal

जिहाद (nm) crusade

जिह्वा (nf) the tongue

जिह्वाग्र (nm) the tip of the tongue

जी (nm) soul, spirit, mind; a term of respect — sir, madam etc

जीजा (nm) husband of one's elder sister

जीजी (nf) an elder sister

जीत (nf) mastery; victory, success

जीतना (v) to conquer, to win; to overcome

जीता (a) living, alive; —जागता living

जीना (v) to live, to be alive

जीना (nm) a ladder, staircase

जीभ (nf) the tongue

जीरा (nm) cuminseed; pollen contained in a flower

जीरी (nf) a kind of fine rice

जीर्ण (a) old, ragged, decayed

जीर्णता (nf) triteness, old age

जीर्णोद्धार (nm) restoration, repair of broken objects

जीवंत (a) living, alive

जीव (nm) a creature; life; soul; —जंतु tiny creatures; —धारी having life, animate

जीवट (nm) adventure; courage

जीवन (nm) existence, breath; life; —चरित biography; —चर्या livings —दान sacrifice of life; —वृत्तांत bio-data; —संघर्ष struggle for existence

जीवनी (nf) biography

जीवाणु (nm) microbe; bacteria

जीवात्मा (nm) the vital principle, the spiritual essence in man

जीविका (nf) allowance, livelihood

जीवित (a) animate, alive, living

जुआ (nm) the yoke; gambling

जुआरी (nm) a gambler

जुकाम (nm) a cold, catarrh

जुगाली (nf) the chewing of the

cud

जुगुप्सा (nf) aversion, abuse, censure

जुटना (v) to unite, to be entangled

जुड़वाँ (nm) twins

जुदा (a) separate, different; —ई separation

जुर्म (nm) sin; crime; fault

जुर्माना (nm) penalty, fine

जुर्रत (nf) courage

जुर्राब (nf) socks, stocking

जुलाब (nm) a purgative

जुलाहा (nm) a weaver

जुलूस (nm) a procession

जुल्फ (nf) curling lock of hair, a ringlet

जुल्म (nm) tyranny, oppression, outrage

जुल्मी (a) oppressive, tyrannical

जुहार (nf) salutation

जुहारना (v) to ask for assistance, to be obliged

जुही (nf) a kind of jasmine

जूँ (nf) a louse

जूझना (v) to fight; to quarrel

जूट (nm) jute, matted hair

जूठन (nf) garbage, offal, leavings

जूठा (a) what is left off after eating

जूड़ा (nm) a plait, a tress, a tuft

जूता (nm) shoe; boot; slipper

जूताखोर (a) beaten with shoes; degraded, shameless

जूती (nf) shoes worn by ladies; slippers

जूस (nm) broth, soup

जूही (nf) a kind of jasmine, a kind of fireworks see also जुही

जृम्भक (a) one who yawns; a certain demon

जेठ (nm) the third month of the Hindu year; elder brother of one's husband

जेठा (a) first born, elder

जेठानी (nf) the wife of husband's elder brother

जेतव्य (a) conquerable

जेब (nf) a pocket; —कतरा pickpocket; —ख़र्च pocket money;-घड़ी a pocket watch

जेल (nf) jail, prison

जेलर (nm) a jailor

जेव/र (nm) ornament, jewel, —रात jewellery, ornaments

जेहन (nf) intellect

जैतून (n) olive tree, its fruit

जैमिनी (nm) the founder of the Purva Mimansa school of Hindu philosophy

जैसा (a) like, similar to; (adv) as, according to

जैसे (adv) in the manner, in which; —जैसे as far as; —तैसे some how

जोंक (nf) a leech

जोंकी (nf) a nail which is pointed at both ends

जो (pron) who, which, that; (ind) if; —कुछ whatever, whatsoever

जोखा (*nm*) (mostly used after लेखा-) account

जोखिम (*nm*) enterprise; danger, risk

जोगिया (*a*) ascetic, of reddish colour

जोगी (*nm*) a saint; an ascetic

जोड़ (*nm*) connection; joint; sum; match

जोड़ना (*v*) to rejoin; to supplement; to affix; to mix; to link; to collect

जोड़ा (*nm*) a pair; couple; twin; a pair of shoes; suit of clothes

जोड़ी (*nf*) couple; a pair

जोत (*nf*) the strap of leather or rope; flame

जोतना (*v*) to plough a field, to till; to yoke

जोताई (*nf*) the worker's wages tilling a land

जोबन (*nm*) bloom of youth, lustre, brilliance

ज़ोर (*nm*) force, strength, power; effort

ज़ोरदार (*a*) strong, powerful

जोरू (*nf*) wife, better half

जोश (*nm*) heat; zeal; passion

जोशाँदा (*nm*) a medicinal decoction

जोशीला (*a*) enthusiastic, zealous

जौहर (*nm*) a precious stone, a jewel; excellence; collective sacrifice in fire by Rajput ladies when their husbands die in the battle

जौहरी (*nm*) a jeweller

ज्ञा/त (*a*) acquainted, known, understood; —ता one who knows

ज्ञातव्य (*a*) knowable, worth knowing

ज्ञान (*nm*) knowledge, perception, understanding

ज्ञानी (*a*) experienced; one who has knowledge of self; intelligent

ज्ञानेंद्रिय (*nf*) the organs of perception and intellect

ज्ञापक (*a*) giving information, making known; memo

ज्ञापन (*nm*) memorandum

ज्ञेय (*a*) knowable, fit to be known

ज्या (*nf*) a bow string, the earth; sine - - - - (Maths)

ज्यावृती (*nf*) abundance, excess, increase

ज्यादा (*a*) too much; more

ज्यामिति (*nf*) conic section, geometry

ज्येष्ठ (*a*) best; elder; (*nm*) the third month of the Hindu year

ज्यों (*adv*) as; if; —ज्यों in which order, as much; —त्यों somehow or other; —ही as soon as; —का त्यों precisely the same

ज्योति (*nf*) a flood of light; lustre, brilliance; flame

ज्योतिष (*nf*) astrology; astronomy

ज्योतिषी (*nm*) an astrologer; astronomer

ज्योत्स्ना (*nf*) moonlight

ज्वर (*nm*) fever

ज्वराकुंश (*nm*) a medicine which is used to remove fever; a kind of fragrant grass

ज्वरांश (*nm*) feverishness

ज्वरार्त (*a*) suffering from fever

ज्वलन (*nm*) a burning, inflammation

ज्वार (*nm*) flood tide; — भाटाthe flood tide and ebb -tide

ज्वाला (*nf*) blaze, flame, fire, heat

ज्वालादेवी (*nf*) a goddess whose place of worship is in the Kangra district in Himachal Pradesh

ज्वालामुखी (*nm*) a volcano

झ

झ the fourth member of the second pentad of consonants in Devnagri alphabet

झंकार (*nf*) jingling, tinkling; ringing

झंकारना (*v*) to produce a jingling

झंख (*nf*) wailing, lamenting; a fish

झंझट (*nm*) difficulty; botheration; trouble

झंझोड़ना (*v*) to shake a thing with a violent jerk

झंडा (*nm*) a flag, streamer, banner

झंडी (*nf*) a small flag, a bunting

झक (*nf*) whim, crank; craze; (*a*) clean

झकझक (*nf*) nonsensical talk, chattering

झकझोरना (*v*) to give a violent jerk

झकना (*v*) to prattle, to chatter, to speak inproperly in wrath

झकाझक (*a*) shining, glittering, polished

झक्कड़ (*nm*) a strong wind, hurricane, a gale; (*a*) crazy, cranky

झक्की (*a*) prattling, crazy, daft

झगड़ना (*v*) to quarrel; to altercate

झगड़ा (*nm*) dispute, variance, quarrel

झगड़ालू (*a*) contentious, disputatious, quarrelsome

झट (*adv*) quickly, instantly, immediately

झटकना (*v*) to give a jerk to a

thing, to toss violently

झटका (*nm*) a push, a jolt, a concussion.

झटकारना (*v*) to toss, to give a jerk to

झटपट (*adv*) very soon, quickly, hastily

झड़ना (*v*) to fall off in small fragments, to drop, to be shed off; erosion

झड़प (*nf*) skirmish, quarrel

झड़पना (*v*) to fight, to snatch away something forcibly

झड़पा-झड़पी (*nf*) skirmish, altercation

झड़वाना (*v*) to cause to be swept

झड़ी (*nf*) continued fall of rain

झनक (*nf*) a tinkling sound

झनकना (*v*) to jingle, to tinkle

झपक (*nf*) a wink; a moment, a very short time

झपकना (*v*) to nap, to wink; to twinkle

झपका (*nm*) a gust of wind

झपकी (*nf*) a nap, drowsiness, doze

झपट (*nf*) a rush; a snatch

झपटना (*v*) to pounce upon; to rush; to snap

झपट्टा (*nm*) an assault, a swoop, a snatch

झमेला (*nm*) disturbance, turmoil

झमेलिया (*nm*) one who creates disturbance

झरझर (*nf*) sound of rain or the flowing of water

झरना (*nm*) a spring, fall; a stream; (*v*) to fall off, to flow

झरोखा (*nm*) window; peep-hole; loophole

झलक (*nf*) glitter; glimpse; glance

झलकना (*v*) to sparkle, to glitter, to shine

झलमलाना (*v*) to twinkle; to glitter, to gleam

झल्लाना (*v*) to be displeased, to be fretful, to excite

झाँकना (*v*) to peer, to peep

झाँकी (*nf*) a glance, a look, a scene

झाँझर (*nf*) anklet, a sieve

झाँसना (*v*) to deceive, to pilfer

झाँसा (*nm*) deception, fraud, trickery

झाँसिया (*nm*) a deceiver, a cheat

झाग (*nm*) scum; foam; yeast, —दार yeasty, scumy

झाड़ (*nm*) a shrub, a bush, (*nf*) scolding; —फानूस chandelier, lights

झाड़खंड (*nm*) a jungle, a wood

झाड़दार (*a*) thick, thorny

झाड़न (*nf*) sweepings; duster

झाड़ना (*v*) to brush, to sweep, to clean

झाड़ी (*nf*) covert, brake, thicket

झाड़ू (*nm*) a swab, a broom, a

comet

झपड़ (*nm*) a slap

झालर (*nf*) a frill, fringe, tatting

झिझक (*nf*) hitch, hesitation

झिझकना (*v*) to feel shy; to hasitate

झिड़कना (*v*) to scold, to speak snapishly

झिड़की (*nf*) rebuke, snubbing, snap

झिपना (*a*) to be shut

झिलमिलाना (*v*) to sparkle, to flash, to twinkle

झींकना (*v*) to grumble; to fret

झीना (*a*) very fine; thin; threadbare

झील (*nf*) a lake

झुंझला/ना (*v*) to be fretful, to be peevish; —हट acrimony, bitterness of language

झुंड (*nm*) cluster, flock, crowd

झुकना (*v*) to droop, to bow

झुकाव (*nm*) bent, leaning; tilt

झुटपुटा (*nm*) twilight

झुठलाना (*v*) to falsify, to prove to be false

झुनझुना (*nm*) a child's rattle

झुर्री (*nf*) furrow, wrinkle, blemish

झुलसना (*v*) to be singed; to be charred; to be scorched

झुलाना (*v*) to swing, to rock, to dandle

झूठ (*a*) untrue, false; (*nm*) lie, falsehood, fiction; —मूठ falsely, uselessly

झूठा (*a*) fictitious, dishonest, untrue

झूमना (*v*) to wave, to swing, to toss the head

झूमर (*nm*) an ornament worn on the head; a kind of song

झूलना (*v*) to swing; to linger in suspense; to wobble

झूला (*nm*) a swing, a swinging rope

झेंपना (*v*) to be ashamed

झेलना (*v*) to bear, to endure, to suffer

झोंकना (*v*) to cast something into fire; to push violently

झोंका (*nm*) a blast; puff, gust

झोंपड़ी (*nf*) a small cottage, a hut

झोलदार (*a*) soupy; loose

झोला (*nm*) a bag, knapsack

झोली (*nf*) a small bag; —फैलाना to beg

ञ

ञ the fifth member of the second pentad of conso- nants in the Devnagri alphabet

ट

ट the first member of the third pentad of consonants in Devnagri alphabet

टंकी (nf) a large tub for storing water or oil; tank

टैंगना (v) to be hung; to be suspended; (nm) the rope on which clothes are hung up to be dried

टंटा (nm) quarrel, wrangling, altercation

टकटकी (nf) stare, gaze, fixed look; —बाँधना to gaze intently

टकराना (v) to be knocked or dashed together, to clash

टकसाल (nm) a mint; —में बने सिक्के mintage

टकसाली (a) pertaining to mint; genuine

टका (nm) a rupee; a brass coin worth half an anna

टक्कर (nf) pushing, knocking; a collision

टखना (nm) the ankle joint

टटोलना (v) to touch, to feel with the hand; to sound

टट्टी (nf) latrine; stool; fence; hedge

टट्टू (nm) a pony

टन (nf) a tinkling sound; (nm) ton, a weight of about twenty eight maunds

टपकना (v) to drop; to drip, to gutter

टपना (v) to jump over, to overleap

टपाटप (a) successively, continuously

टब (nm) a tub

टमटम (nm) a gig, a tandem

टमाटर (nm) a tomato

टर (nm) harsh sound, obstinacy, croaking of frogs

टरकना (v) to disappear, to abscond

टरकाना (v) to remove; to postpone; to evade

टरटर (nm) crackle, chattering, murmur

टर्राना (v) to chatter, to quack, to grumble

टलना (v) to vanish, to slip, to disappear

टसक (nf) throbbing or shooting pain in the body

टसर (nm) a kind of coarse silken cloth

टसुआ (nm) tear

टहनी (nf) a spray, sprig, twig

टहल (nm) service, attendance

टहलना (v) to roam, to walk, to stroll

टाँकना (v) to stitch; to cobble; to jot down

टाँका (nm) a solder; a stitch; a patch work

टाँग (nf) the leg

टाँगना (v) to hang

टाँगा (nm) a kind of two wheeled carriage

टाई (nf) neck-tie

टाट (nm) canvas, sack-cloth; floor mat

टाप (nm) sound of a horse's hoof

टापना (v) to be left helpless

टापू (nm) an island

टाल (nf) a heap, a fuel; postponement; —मटोल prevarication; avoidance

टालना (a) to put aside, to postpone

टिकिट (nm) a ticket; stamp; —घर booking-office

टिकड़ा (nm) a disk, a thick bread which is fried on fire

टिकना (v) to stop; to abide; to continue; to stay

टिकाऊ (a) lasting, durable

टिकाना (v) to lodge; to station

टिकिया (nf) a small cake; a tablet

टिक्की (nf) round circular piece; a tablet

टिड्डा (nm) a grasshopper

टिड्डी (nf) a locust; —दल locust swarm

टिपटिप (nf) sound made by the fall of water in drops

टिप्पणी (nf) annotation; a note; comment; critical remark

टिप्पस (nf) manipulation

टिमटिमाना (v) to give a faint light, to glimmer

टीका (nm) annotation; commentary, note; mark made on the forehead with sandal paste; an ornament for the head

टीकाकार (nm) a commentator

टीन (nm) tin, sheet of tinned iron

टीप (nf) pressure; raising of voice in singing; —टाप tip-topping

टीपना (v) to record; to point; to copy

टीम (nm) a team of players

टीमटाम (nf) empty show; ostentation; dressing

टीला (nm) a rising ground, mound, small hill

टीस (nf) a throbbing pain in a part of body

टीसना (v) to throb, to palpitate

टुकड़ा (nm) a piece, fragment, bit; a part, portion

टुकड़ी (nf) a small piece; part of an army

टुच्चा (a) trivial, insignificant

टुटपुँजिया (a) of meagre means

टूटना (v) to break, to fall; to rupture

टूटा (a) broken, decayed

टेंटुआ (nm) neck, throat

टेक (nf) prop, support; habit

टेकना (v) to support; to rest; to lean

टेढ़ा (a) bent, crooked, uneven; difficult; —पन obliquity, crookedness; —मेढ़ा crooked, zigzag

टेव (*nf*) habit, wont

टेवा (*nm*) horoscope, calculation of nativity

टोंटी (*nf*) a tap

टोकना (*v*) to interrogate, to question; to prevent

टोकरा (*nm*) a large wicker work basket

टोकरी (*nf*) a small basket

टोटका (*nm*) spell, charm; remedy for a disease

टोटा (*nm*) deficiency; loss; part (of a cigarette etc.)

टोना (*nm*) spell, magic, enchantment

टोप (*nm*) a hat; a helmet; cover

टोपी (*nf*) a cap

टोल (*nm*) a band, group

टोला (*nm*) part of a town or city

टोली (*nf*) band, group, crowd

टोह (*nf*) search, secret watching

टोहना (*v*) to seek, to be in search of

ठ

ठ the second member of the third pentad of consonants in Devnagri alphabet

ठंड (*nf*) coldness, chilliness; —क coolness

ठंडा (*a*) cold; cool; dull; lifeless; unfeeling

ठंडाई (*nf*) a cooling medicine; an indigenous cold drink prepared from almond

ठक (*nf*) a tapping sound

ठकठक (*nf*) a knock; difficulty, uneasiness

ठकुराइन (*nf*) wife of Thakur; landlady

ठग (*nm*) a cut throat, cheat

ठगई (*nf*) cheating, robbing; theft

ठगना (*v*) to cheat, to swindle; to rob

ठगपन (*nm*) the work of cheating

ठट्ठा (*nm*) fun, jest, joke, gibe

ठठरी (*nf*) a skeleton; a bier

ठठेरा (*nm*) a brazier; a tinker

ठठोली (*nf*) joking, humour, fun

ठनठन-गोपाल (*nm*) a worthless object, a penniless-person

ठप (*a*) reduced; at a standstill

ठपना (*v*) to fix on the mind; to settle anything

ठप्पा (*nm*) a dice, stamp, matrix

ठर्रा (*nm*) a kind of cheap spirituous liquor

ठस (*a*) solid, thick, heavy; dull; miserly

ठसाठस (a) filled up to brim; crowded

ठहरना (v) to stop, to halt; to rest

ठहराव (nm) pause; settlement, agreement

ठहाका (nm) a peal of laughter, explosion

ठाकुर (nm) god; idol; lord; leader

ठाकुरी (nf) mastery

ठाठ (nm) splendour, pomp, magnificence; —बाट pomp, splendour

ठानना (nm) to intend, to determine, to resolve

ठिकाना (nm) place; station, destination

ठिगना (a) dwarfish, short

ठिठकना (v) to step short, to shrink, to hesitate

ठिठोलिया (nm) a jester, a buffoon, a joker

ठिठोली (nf) buffoonery, banter

ठीक (a) accurate; just; fit; right; (adv) accurately; all right

ठीक-ठाक (adv) regularly, properly

ठीकरा (nm) a broken piece of earthen ware

ठुकराना (v) to strike with the toes, to kick off; to reject contemptuously

ठुकवाना (v) to cause to be beaten

ठुड्डी (nf) chin

ठुनकना (nm) sobbing of a child; (v) to sob

ठुमकना (v) to strut, to walk with grace

ठुमका (a) dwarfish, of low stature; (nm) a strutting round in a dance

ठुसाना (v) to feed to the fill, to cause to be stuffed

ठूँठ (nm) stump, snag

ठूँठा (a) leafless; stubby

ठूँसना (v) to stuff, to be crammed

ठेंगा (nm) a thumb

ठेका (nm) support; a contract; —ठेकेबार a contractor

ठेठ (a) genuine; pure; un-mixed

ठेलना (v) to push forward, to shove

ठेलमठेल (nf) hustle and bustle; rush

ठेला (nm) push; stroke; trolley, wheel-barrow

ठेस (nf) shock;

ठोकना (v) to beat, to tap; to hammer

ठोकर (nf) blow, stroke, thump, kick

ठोड़ी (nf) the chin

ठोस (a) dense, solid, hard; sound

थौर (nf) place, —ठिकाना whereabouts

ड

ड the third member of the third
pentad of consonants in
Devnagri alphabet

डंक (nm) the sting of a wasp-
bee

डंका (nm) a big drum, a kettle
drum

डंगर (nm) a beast, cattle

डंठल (nm) stem, a small shoot
or spring of a plant

डंड (nm) a kind of exercise;
—पेलना to take exercise in
the form of डंड

डंडा (nm) a bar, rod, stick

डंडी (nf) thin stick, beam of a
scale

डंसना (v) to bite; to sting

डकार (nf) belch, eructation

डकारना (v) to belch; to swallow
up

डकै/त (nm) a robber, dacoit;
—ती robbery, piracy

डग (nm) pace, step in walking

डगमगाना (v) to stagger, to totter, to falter

डगर (nm) path, road

डटना (v) to stop; to stay; to
stand firmly

डपट (nm) rebuke, objurgation

डपटना (v) to rebuke, to shout
at

डबडबाना (v) to be filled with
tears

डब्बा (nm) a tin box; a railway
wagon

डर (nm) terror, fear, awe,
dread

डरना (v) to be frightened, to
dread

डरपोक (a) timid; shy; cowardly

डरावना (a) awful, horrible,
terrible

डरावा (nm) anything told to
frighten

डाँट (nf) subjugation, intimidation

डाँटना (v) to rebuke, to chide,
to browbeat

डाँड़ी (nf) handle, shaft, beam
of a balance

डाइन (nf) a witch

डाक (nf) post, mail, dak; —खर्च
postage; —खाना post-office

डाका (nm) robbery, plunder,
dacoity

डाकिनी (nf) a hellcat

डाकिया (nm) a postman

डाकू (nm) a robber, bandit,
dacoit

डाट (nf) a plug, a cork

डायरी (nf) a diary

डाल (nf) a branch, a bough

डालना (v) to put in, to throw

डाली (nf) a small branch

डावांडोल (a) unsteady, wandering, fluctuating

डाह (nf) envy; jealousy; spite

डिगना (v) to deviate; to be shaken

डिबिया (nf) a small box or case

डींग (nf) boasting, bragging; —मारना to boast

डीलडौल (nm) figure, stature

डुगडुगी (nf) a small drum

डुबकी (nf) a plunge, a dip

डूबना (v) to dive, to set in the horizon, to sink

डेढ़ (a) one and a half

डेगची (nf) a kettle

डेरा (nm) dwelling, abode, a camp; tent

डैना (nm) a wing of a bird

डोम (nm) the sweeper or scavenger class among the Hindus

डोर (nf) thick cord or thread

डोरा (nm) thread, string

डोल (nm) a bucket, agitation

डोलना (v) to roam, to wander, to swing

डौल (nm) form, mode, shape, manner

ड्यौढ़ा (a) one and a half times

ड्यौढ़ी (nf) the main gate of a house

ढ

ढ the fourth member of the third pentad of consonants in Devnagri alphabet

ढंग (nm) method, mod; manner

ढकना (v) to conceal; to cover; (nm) a cover, a lid

ढकेलना (v) to push, to press against, to ram

ढकोस/ला (nm) affectedness, hypocrisy; —लेबाज़ a hypocrite, humbug

ढक्कन (nm) a cover, lid

ढब (nm) ways, manner

ढर्रा (nm) method; system; path

ढलना (v) to decline, to roll, to flow

ढलाई (nf) casting, moulding

ढलान (nm) a slope, descent

ढहना (v) to fall or tumble down; to be destroyed

ढाँचा (nm) frame; skeleton; sketch; outline

ढाँपना (v) to cover up, to conceal

ढाई (a) two and a half

ढाक (nm) the tree Butea frondosa; a war trumpet

ढाढ़स (nm) comfort, solace, consolation; —बँधाना to console

ढाना (v) to destroy, to pull to the ground, to demolish

ढाबा (nm) a small common hotel

ढाल (nf) buckler, shield; slope

ढालना (v) to pour out, to shape; to found

ढालू (a) descending, sloping

ढिंढोरची (nm) a public crier, one who proclaims by beat of drum

ढिंढोरा (nm) proclamation; —पीटना to proclaim aloud

ढिठाई (nf) impudence, pertness, impertinence

दिबरी (nf) an earthen lamp

ढिलाई (nf) looseness, slug- gishness, laziness

ढीठ (a) impudent, pert

ढीला (a) loose; sluggish; —ढाला loose; sluggish

ढुलमुल (a) unsteady; vacil- lating

ढुलकना (v) to roll down, to let fall

ढूँढना (v) to investigate, to search

ढेर (nm) pile; heap; hoard; lump; (a) abundant, plenty

ढेला (nm) a clod; a lump of earth

ढोंग (nm) trick; fraud, deceit

ढोंगी (nm) deceitful, fraud- ulent, impostor

ढोना (v) to carry; to bear on head or shoulders; to maintain

ढोर (nm) cattle

ढोल (nm) a drum, a kettle- drum

ढोलक (nf) a small drum

ण

ण the fifth member of the third pentad of consonants in Devnagri alphabet

त

त the first member of the fourth pentad of consonants in Devnagri alphabet

तंग (a) narrow; tight; troubled; scarce

तंगदस्त (a) poor

तंगदस्ती (nf) poverty, miser- liness

तंगी (nf) tightness; want; trouble; poverty

तंडुल (nm) rice

तंतु (nm) tendril; thread, yarn

तंतुवादक (nm) one who plays on a stringed musical instrument

तंतुवाय (nm) a weaver of cloth

तंत्र (nm) thread, filament; system; technique

तंत्रिका (nf) nerve

तंत्री (nf) strings or wires which are used in musical instruments

तंदुरुस्त (a) free from illness, healthy

तंदुरुस्ती (nf) good health, healthiness

तंदूर (nm) an oven

तंदूरी (a) fried in an oven

तंद्रा (nf) sleepiness, drowsiness; lassitude

तंद्रालु (a) drowsy, sluggish, sleepy

तंबाकू (nm) tobacco

तंबू (nm) a tent

तंबूर (nm) a kind of a small drum

तंबूरची (nm) one who plays on a Turkish guitar

तंबूरा (nm) a Turkish guitar

तंबोली (nm) the man who sells betel leaves

तअज्जुब (nm) wonder, astonishment

तअल्लुक़ (nm) relation; connection between things

तक (ind) till, until, upto, for, as long as

तक़दीर (nf) fate, destiny, luck

तकना (v) to gaze at, to stare at, to look at

तकरार (nf) dispute, altercation; quarrel

तक़रीबन (ind) nearly, approximately

तक़रीर (nf) speech, lecture

तकला (nm) the spindle of a spinning wheel

तकली (nf) a bobbin of cotton

तकलीफ़ (nf) affliction; difficulty, distress

तकल्लुफ़ (nm) formality, conventionality

तकसीम (nf) distribution; division

तक़ाज़ा (nm) demand; importunity

तकिया (nm) a pillow, cushion

तकिया-कलाम (nm) the favourite phrase which a man is habituated to use repeatedly in his speech

तकियादार (nm) the Mohammedan Fakir who dwells in a तकिया

तक्र (nm) butter milk

तक्षक (nm) one of the eight principal serpents

तक्षण (nm) wood or stone modelling pattern

तक्षणी (nf) a carpenter's jackplane, long plane

तक्षशिला (nf) an ancient city of India

तख़्त (nm) a royal seat, throne; a seat made of planks

तख़्ता (nm) a board; plank;

rack

तख़्ती (nf) a small plank; a school boys' board to write on

तगड़ा (a) robust, strong, sturdy, powerful

तगड़ी (nf) a gold or silver chain worn round the waist

तगमा (nm) a medal

तजना (v) to leave, to quit, to give up

तजुरबा (nm) test, trial; experience; experiment

तजुरबेकार (a) experienced

तट (nm) bank; shore

तटस्थ (a) indifferent; neutral; —ता neutrality

तड़क-भड़क (nm) tawdriness, pompous exhibition

तड़का (nm) dawn, peep of day, early morning

तड़प (nf) throbbing, palpitation, fury

तड़पना (v) to flutter, to palpitate; to writhe in pain

ततैया (nf) a wasp

तत्काल (adv) instantly, immediately

तत्कालीन (a) contemporary

तत्क्षण (adv) at the same time, instantly

तत्त्व (nm) essence; element; principle; truth

तत्त्वज्ञ (nm) a philosopher, a metaphysician

तत्त्वज्ञान (nm) knowledge of the divine, philosophy

तत्त्वत: (ind) essentially, in essence

तत्त्वदृष्टि (nf) intuition, inner sight

तत्त्वप्रकाश (nm) superficial knowledge of the supreme soul

तत्त्वभाषी (a) one who describes the real facts

तत्त्वशास्त्र (nm) metaphysics

तत्त्वावधान (nm) investigation of true knowledge, under the auspices of

तत्पर (a) ready, engaged; clever; —ता readiness, alertness

तत्र (adv) there, at that place

तथा (ind) and, so, thus

तथाकथित (a) so-called

तथापि (ind) too, nevertheless, also

तथाविध (adv) in that manner

तथ्य (nm) truth, reality, fact

तदनंतर (adv) afterwards, hereafter

तदनुसार (ind) accordingly

तदबीर (nf) arrangement, method; effort

तदर्थ (a) ad hoc

तन (nm) body

तनख़्वाह (nf) pay, salary

तनाव (nm) tension; strain

तनिक (a) slight, little, small

तप (nm) devotion, penance, religious austerity

तपन (nf) warmth, heat, burning

तपना (v) to glow; to be heated;

to burn with grief

तपस्या (*nf*) penance, austerity, devotion

तपाक (*nm*) warmth

तपिश (*nf*) mental anguish; heat

तपेदिक (*nf*) tuberculosis

तफ़्तीश (*nf*) an investigation, probe

तफ़रीह (*nf*) recreation, fun

तफ़सील (*nf*) details; particulars

तब (*adv*) then, at that time; afterwards

तबका (*nm*) a class; a group

तबदी/ल (*a*) altered; changed; —ली change

तबाह (*a*) destroyed, ruined

तबाही (*nf*) ruin, destruction

तबियत (*nf*) disposition; temperament; nature

तबेला (*nm*) a stable

तभी (*adv*) at the same moment, on this account

तमंचा (*nm*) a small musket; a pistol

तमग़ा (*nm*) a royal charter, a medal

तमतमाना (*v*) to grow red in the face owing to heat of Sun or wrath

तमतमाहट (*nf*) ardour, heat

तमन्ना (*nf*) an aspiration, longing

तमाचा (*nm*) a slap

तमाम (*a*) whole, entire, complete

तमाशबीन (*nm*) an onlooker, a spectator, a sightseer

तमाशबीनी (*nf*) luxury, libertinism

तमाशा (*nm*) spectacle, show; sport

तमीज़ (*nf*) sense; good manner's

तय (*a*) settled; completed; fixed

तरंग (*nf*) ripple, wave, billow

तरंगिणी (*nf*) a river

तरंगी (*a*) unsteady, whimsical, fantastic

तर (*a*) wet; damp

तरकश (*nm*) a quiver

तरकारी (*nf*) cooked or green vegetable

तरकीब (*nf*) way; tact

तरक्क़ी (*nf*) increase; promotion; progress

तरखान (*nm*) a carpenter

तरजीह (*nf*) priority, preference

तरणि (*nf*) a boat, a raft or float

तरफ़ (*nf*) direction, side, quarter; —दार a follower; — दारी partisanship, bias

तरबूज़ (*nm*) a water-melon

तरल (*a*) liquid, fluid; —ता fluidity

तरस (*nm*) pity, mercy; —खाना to feel pity for

तरसना (*v*) to long, to desire

तरसाना (*v*) to cause to long or desire

तरह (*nf*) kind, sort

तराई (*nf*) marshy ground, a

valley

तराजू (nf) a scale, a balance

तराना (nm) a kind of song

तरावट (nf) moisture, humidity, coolness

तराश (nf) trimming, cutting; paring

तराशना (v) to trim, to cut, to clip; to pare

तरीक़ा (nm) mode, manner; custom; method

तरु (nm) a tree

तरुण (a) young; adult

तरुणाई (nf) youth, puberty

तरुणी (nf) a young woman

तर्क (nm) reasoning; argument; —वितर्क argumentation

तर्जनी (nf) the fore-finger

तल (nm) surface; bottom; under part

तल/ख (a) pungent, bitter; acrid; —ख़ी acridity; bitterness

तलछट (nf) sediment; —संबंधी sedimentary or dregs

तलना (v) to fry

तलब (nf) wages, salary; demand

तलवा (nf) the sole of the foot

तलवार (nf) sabre; a sword

तलहटी (nf) a vale, a valley

तला (nm) bottom; sole of a shoe; support

तलाक़ (nm) a divorce; —शुदा divorced

तलाश (nf) search; investigation

तलाशी (nf) a search

तल्ला (nm) floor; a storey; sole of a shoe

तल्लीन (a) deeply involved; immersed; identified with

तवा (nm) the round plate of iron on which bread is baked, a griddle

तवाज़ा (nf) respect, hospitality, entertainment

तवायफ़ (nf) a harlot, a prostitute; a dancing girl

तशरीफ़ (nf) a term signifying respect; —रखना welcome (your) coming

तशतरी (nf) a tray; a small plate

तसकीन (nf) satisfaction; consolation

तसबीक (nf) attestation; verification

तसल्ली (nf) comfort, solace; satisfaction

तसवीर (nm) portrait, a picture

तस्कर (nf) a thief, a smuggler

तस्करी (nf) the act of smuggling

तह (nf) fold; layer; bottom; —ख़ाना a cell

तहकीक़ात (nm) investigation, enquiry, inquest

तहज़ीब (nf) civilization

तहमद (nf) loin cloth

तहरीर (nf) style of writing, a testimonial

तहलका (nm) agitation, havoc

तहस-नसह (a) destroyed, ruined

तहसील (nf) the office or court

of a Tehsildar, a part of a district

ताँगा (*nm*) a tonga

तांडव (*nm*) a dance, dancing of Shiva

ताँता (*nm*) a row; series

तांबा (*nm*) copper

तांबूल (*nm*) betel leaf

ताई (*nf*) paternal (elder) uncle's wife, aunt

ताईद (*nf*) support, confirmation

ताऊ (*nm*) father's elder brother, uncle

ताकझाँक (*nf*) gazing at intervals

ताकत (*nf*) strength, force, might, power; —वर powerful

ताकना (*v*) to see; to stare at; to view

ताकि (*ind*) therefore, so that

ताकीद (*nf*) instruction

तागा (*nm*) thread

ताज (*nm*) crown; the Taj

ताज़गी (*nf*) greenness; freshness, health

ताज़ा (*a*) new; fresh; green

ताज़िया (*nm*) a model of the tomb of Imam Husain which is buried by Mohammedans under the earth in the Moharram festival

ताज्जुब (*nm*) astonishment, wonder

ताड़ (*nm*) the palmyra tree

ताड़ना (*nf*) whipping, admonition, rebuke; (*v*) to whip; to guess

ताड़ित (*a*) beaten, rebuked, chided

ताड़ी (*nf*) the juice of a toddy tree

तात (*nm*) father; a revered person; dear and younger

तात्कालिक (*a*) immediate, quick

तात्पर्य (*nm*) sense, meaning

तात्त्विक (*a*) essential, real; elementary

तादात्म्य (*nm*) similarity, identity

तादाद (*nf*) number

तानना (*v*) to expand, to stretch; to spread

ताना (*nm*) a taunt

ताना (*nm*) the warp; loom for weaving carpet; —बाना warp and woof

तानाशाह (*nm*) a dictator

तानाशाही (*nf*) dictatorship

ताप (*nm*) warmth, heat; fever; —मान temperature; —मापी a thermometer

तापना (*v*) to warm oneself, to heat

तापस (*nm*) one who performs religious austerities

ताबड़तोड़ (*adv*) incessantly, successively

ताबूत (*nm*) a coffin, a bier

तार (*nm*) thread; wire; chord

तारक (*nm*) a planet, a star; the pupil of the eye; the name of a demon

तारकोल (*nm*) coal-tar, tarmac

तारघर (*nm*) a telegraph office

तारतम्य (*nm*) proportion, comparative value; accordance

तारना (*v*) to free, to deliver from sin

तारा (*nm*) a star; pupil of the eye

तारापथ (*nm*) the sky

तारामंडल (*nm*) the starry sphere, firmament

तारिका (*nf*) cine-actress

तारीख़ (*nf*) a date; an appointed day; — वार datewise

तारीफ़ (*nf*) praise; introduction

तारुण्य (*nm*) youth

तार्किक (*nm*) a logician, a metaphysician

ताल (*nm*) musical measure, rhythm, tune; a pond

तालमेल (*nm*) concordance; co-ordination

ताला (*nm*) a lock; — बंदी a lock-out

तालाब (*nm*) a tank, pool

तालिका (*nf*) key; a list; table

ताली (*nf*) a key; clapping of hands together

तालीम (*nf*) education

तालु (*nm*) the palate

ताल्लुक़ (*nm*) relationship, connection

ताल्लुक़ेदार (*nm*) a landlord

ताव (*nm*) a sheet of paper; heat; anger

तावीज़ (*nm*) an amulet

ताश (*nm*) playing cards

तिकड़म (*nf*) manipulation; unfair means

तिकोन (*nm*) a triangle

तिकोना (*a*) triangular

तिक्त (*a*) pungent; acrid

तिगुना (*a*) triple, three-times

तिजारत (*nf*) trade, commerce

तिजोरी (*nf*) an iron safe

तितर-बितर (*a*) dispersed; diffused; scattered

तितली (*nf*) butterfly, lady-bird; glamour girl

तिथि (*nf*) a date

तिनका (*nm*) a bit of dry grass, straw

तिपाई (*nf*) a three-legged table, tripod, teapoy

तिबारा (*adv*) a third time

तिमंज़िला (*a*) three-storied building

तिमाही (*a*) quarterly

तिमिर (*nm*) darkness; a disease of the eye in which objects are not clearly seen

तिरंगा (*a*) tricolour; (*nm*) the tri-colour flag

तिरछा (*a*) transverse, bent, crooked, oblique

तिरना (*v*) to float on water

तिरपाल (*nm*) tarred canvas, tarpaulin

तिरस्कार (*nm*) disregard, disrespect; insult

तिरस्कारी (*a*) insulting, scorning; disregarding

तिरस्कृत (a) censured, reproached; hidden

तिराहा (nm) a junction of three roads or paths

तिल (nm) a mole; small particle; sesamum plant and its seeds

तिलकना (v) to slip

तिलचट्टा (nm) a cockroach

तिलपट्टी (nf) a kind of sweetmeat which is made of fried sesamum and treacle

तिलमिलाना (v) to dazzle; to be in the grip of impotent anger

तिलस्म (nm) miracle, wonder, spell

तिलहन (nm) oilseed

तिलांजलि (nf) oblations to the dead with sesamum seeds and water; abandonment

तिहाई (a) one-third

तीक्ष्ण (a) sharp; keen

तीक्ष्णता (nf) severity, sharpness

तीक्ष्णदृष्टि (a) hawk-eyed

तीखा (a) harsh; sharp; pungent

तीज (nf) the third day of the each half of a lunar month

तीतर (nm) a partridge

तीन (a) three

तीमारदा/र (nm) a person attending on a patient; an attendant; —री nursing the sick and invalid person

तीर (nm) bank; arrow

तीरंदाज़ (nm) an archer

तीर्थ (nm) a sacred place; a place of pilgrimage; —यात्रा pilgrimage; —यात्री a pilgrim

तीव्र (a) pungent; fast; high; sharp

तीसमारखाँ (nm) a very brave person (said ironically), a sham hero

तीसरा (a) a third

तुंग (a) lofty, high, tall; (nm) a mountain

तुक (nf) part of a song, rhyme, alliteration; —जोड़ना grotesque rhyming of verse; —बंदी poetry of an inferior or grotesque type

तुकांत (a) rhyming

तुक्का (nm) a kind of arrow which is blunt at one end; unsure means, vain bid; —लगाना to make conjecture

तुच्छ (a) trivial; contemptible; insignificant; —ता insignificance, meanness, lowness

तुड़वाना (v) to cause to be broken

तुड़ाई (nf) the work or wages for breaking a thing

तुतलाना (v) to speak indistinctly as a child, to lisp

तुमुल (a) noisy, excited, tumultuous

तुम्हारा (pron) your, yours

तुम्हीं (pron) you alone

तुम्हें (pron) to you, unto you

तुरंग (nm) a horse; mind

तुरंत (adv) rapidly, at once, quickly, soon

तुर्श (a) sour, acid; harsh

तुर्शी (nf) sourness, tartness

तुलना (nf) similarity, comparison; (v) to be weighed; —त्मक comparative

तुला (nf) balance

तुल्य (a) like; equivalent, similar

तुल्यता (nf) parity, balance

तुषार (nm) cold, frost, thin rain

तुष्टि (nf) satisfaction, delight

तूफ़ान (nm) deluge; storm, tempest; false accusation

तूफ़ानी (a) strong, violent; quarrelsome

तूलिका (nf) a painter's brush

तृण (nm) grass, sedge

तृणकुटी (nf) thatched hamlet

तृतीय (a) the third

तृ/प्त (a) satisfied, contented, pleased; —प्ति satisfaction, gratification

तृ/षा (nf) thirst, desire, wish; —षित thirsty, desirous

तृष्णा (nf) thirst; ambition, desire

तेंदुआ (nm) a leopard

तेज (nm) glory, ardour, magnificence; brilliance

तेज़ (a) sharp, keen, pointed; swift; hot; smart

तेजहीन (a) spiritless; muzzy, lack-lustre

तेजपुंज (nm) stream of light

तेजपत्ता (nm) cassia, bay tree and its leaf

तेजवान् (a) glorious, energetic, strong

तेजस्विता (nf) radiance, nobility, lordliness, lustre

तेजस्वी (a) lustrous, glorious, brilliant

तेज़ाब (nm) an acid

तेज़ी (nf) pungency, sharpness, smartness; intelligence

तेरा (pron) thy, thine

तेल (nm) oil; petrol

तेली (nm) an oilman

तेवर (nm) an angry look, the eyebrow

तैनात (a) appointed, engaged

तैया/र (a) ready, prepared; ready-made; —री preparation, readiness

तैरना (v) to swim (for animate); to float. (for inanimate)

तैराई (nf) the act of swimming

तैरा/क (a) an expert swimmer; —की swimming

तैराना (v) to cause some-one to swim

तैश (nm) anger, wrath; passion; — में आना to be provoked

तैसा (a) similar

तैसे (adv) in the same manner, accordingly

तोंद (nf) pot belly, abdomen, paunch

तो (ind) therefore; then; moreover; however

तोड़ (nm) break; rent —फोड़ (nm) breakage; sabotage

तोड़ना (v) to break; to burst, to violate; to pluck

तोतला (a) stammering, lisping

तोतलाना (v) to stutter, to lisp

तोता (nm) a parrot

तोप (nf) a cannon, a gun —खाना the place where cannon and artillery are kept; —ची a gunner

तोय (nm) water

तोल (nf) weight

तोलना (v) to balance; to weigh

तोला (nm) a weight of rupee or twelve Mashas

तोहफ़ा (nm) a gift, a present

तोहमत (nf) false accusation, calumny

तौबा (nf) solemn assertion for not doing a forbidden act in future; — करना to vow never to repeat

तौर (nm) manner, mode, way; —तरीका conduct, manners

तौलिया (nf) a towel

तौहीन (nf) disrespect; insult

त्यक्त (a) abandoned; rejected

त्यजनीय (a) liable to be abandoned

त्याग (nm) avoidance; a abandonment, forsaking

त्यागना (v) to lose, to desert

त्यागी (a) a hermit

त्यों (adv) in like manner, so like

त्योरी (nf) glance; angry look, wrinkles of the forehead

त्योहार (nm) a festival; fete

त्रसित (a) frightened, terrified; trembling

त्राण (nm) protection, shelter; security

त्राता (nm) a protector; a deliverer

त्रास (nm) fear, fright, dread; awe

त्रासदायी (a) terrifying, dreadful

त्रासदी (nf) a tragedy

त्राहि (int) save me, protector;

त्रि (a) three

त्रिकालदर्शी (nm) the omniscient one

त्रिकोण (a) triangular, (nm) a triangle

त्रिगुण (nm) an aggregate of the three principal qualities of human nature

त्रिपथगामिनी (nf) an epithet of the river Ganga

त्रिफला (nf) a mixture of three kinds of myrobalan

त्रिभुज (nm) a triangle

त्रिशूल (nm) a trident

त्रिया (nf) a female; —चरित्र the wiles of a female

त्रुटि (nf) diminution, imperfection; mistake

त्रेता (nm) the second Yuga

त्रैकालिक (a) eternal, permanent

त्रैमासिक (a) quarterly, three-monthly

त्वक (nm) the bark of a tree; skin

त्वचा (nf) the skin

त्वरा (nf) haste, quickness,

speed

क्विकली

quickly

त्वरित (a) swift; (adv) hastily,

थ

थ the second member of the fourth pentad of consonants in Devnagri alphabet

थंबा, थंभ (nm) a pillar; support or prop

थकना (v) to be wearied, to be tired; to be stagnant

थकान (nf) weariness, tiredness, fatigue

थका-माँदा (a) weary, tired

थकावट (nf) fatigue, exhaustion, weariness

थक्का (nm) lump; clot

थन (nm) udder, nipple

थपकना (v) to tap, to pat, to strike gently with the palm

थपकी (nf) a pat, a tap

थपथपाना (v) to tap, to dab

थपेड़ा (nm) a slap; a box; blow, stroke

थप्पड़ (nm) a slap, clap

थमना (v) to stay; to stop; to have patience

थरथर (a) shuddering, trembling

थरथराना (v) to quiver, to tremble, to shake

थरथराहट (nf) shivering, trembling

थर्मामीटर (nm) a thermometer

थर्राना (v) to shake, to shudder, to tremble

थल (nm) a dry land

थलथल (a) undulating owing to flabbiness of flesh

थाती (nf) a thing given in charge, a trust; capital

थान (nm) a long piece of cloth of fixed length

थाना (nm) a police-station

थानेदार (nm) the officer in-charge of a police-station

थामना (v) to assist; to grasp; to hold; to prop

थाल (nm) a large flat dish; basin

थाली (nf) a dish, tray, a plate

थाह (nm) depth of water; bottom, limit

थिगली (nf) a patch which is used for mending holes in cloths

थिरकना (v) to dance with expressive action and gestures

थू (nf) the sound made in spitting; (ind) word of contempt

थूक (nm) spittle; saliva

थूकना (v) to spittle, to spit; to curse

थूथन (nm) the snout of an animal

थैला (nm) a bag, a wallet; a purse

थैली (nf) a small bag; a purse

थोक (nm) a heap; whole-sale

थोड़ा (a) some; little; short; small

थोथा (a) worthless, hollow, blunt

थोपना (v) to heap; to impose

द

द the third member of the fourth pentad of consonants in Devnagri alphabet

दंग (a) astonished, wonder-struck

दंगल (nm) a wrestling

दंगा (nm) mutiny, confusion; disturbance; riot; —दंगेबाज़ quarrelsome

दंड (nm) punishment; a staff; a stick; —विधि the law of crimes

दंत (nm) a tooth; —कथा a legend

दंपती (nm) a (married) couple, husband and wife

दं/भ (nm) boast, pious fraud, deceit; —भी vain-glorious, conceited

दंश (nm) a sting, biting

दकियान/स (a) conservative person; —सी conservative idea or thinking

दक्खि/न (nm) the South; —नी southern

दक्ष (a) able; expert; astute, clever; —ता readiness, expertness

दक्षिण (nm) the South; right; —पंथी rightist

दक्षिणा (nf) reward, present given to Brahman

दखल (nm) interference; authority, possession

दगा (nm) deception; treachery; —बाज़ deceitful, fraudulent

दगाबाजी (nf) treachery, cheating

दढ़ियल (a) having a long beard

दत्तक (पुत्र) (nm) an adopted son

दत्तचित (a) concentrating one's mind in performing a work, fully attentive to do a work

दविहाल (nm) paternal grand father's family

दधि (nm) curd

दनादन (adv) non-stop

दफनाना (v) to entomb; to bury

दफ़ा (nf) one time, one turn —होना (v) to go to hell

दफ़्तरदार (*nm*) an official in the Indian Army

दफ़्तर (*nm*) an office

दफ़्तरी (*nm*) one who is employed in an office for ruling registers; a book-binder

दबंग (*a*) influential; fearless, overbearing

दबकाना (*v*) to check, to threaten

दबदबा (*nm*) state; dignity, sway

दबना (*v*) to be pressed down, to go down, to yield

दब जाना (*v*) to with-draw, to retire

दबाव (*nm*) pressure, compulsion; repression

दबोचना (*v*) to subdue, to seize suddenly

दब्बू (*a*) tame

दम (*nm*) life; breath

दमक (*nf*) brilliance; glimmer

दमकना (*v*) to shine, to glisten, to glow

दमकल (*nf*) a water pump, the fire brigade, fire engine

दमदमा (*nm*) a mound of sand used in warfare, grandeur

दमदार (*a*) strong, enduring; sharp

दमन (*nm*) subdual, suppression, subjugation

दमनशील (*a*) fit to be subdued, restrianable

दमा (*nm*) asthma

दमित (*a*) repressed, suppressed

दयनीय (*a*) inspiring pity, pitiable

दया (*nf*) tenderness, affection, kindness

दयाकर (*a*) generous, benevolent, pitiful

दयादृष्टि (*nf*) favour, kindness

दयावान (*nm*) kind-hearted, merciful

दयानत (*nf*) genuineness; honesty; —दार genuine; honest; —दारी honesty

दयानिधान (*nm*) one who is very generous; an epithet of God

दयार्द्र (*a*) tender-hearted; charitable

दयालु (*a*) tender, kind-hearted, a kind

दर (*nf*) price, rate; (*nm*) door; —असल in reality, in fact; —दर door to door, place to place

दरकार (*a*) necessary, needed; (*nf*) necessity

दरख़्वास्त (*nf*) application, petition; request

दरख़्त (*nm*) a tree

दरगाह (*nf*) a doorsill, a shrine; holyplace; tomb

दरबान (*nm*) a porter, a door-keeper, watchman

दरबार (*nm*) hall of audience, a royal court

दरबारदारी (*nf*) paying visit to a person very often and flattering to please him

दरबारी (*nm*) a courtier

दरमियान (*nm*) a middle; (*adv*) among, during, between

दरमियानी (*nm*) a middle man, an umpire

दरवाज़ा (*nm*) door; doorleaves

दरवेश (*nm*) a beggar, dervish

दराज़ (*nf*) the compartment of a box, a drawer; (*a*) long

दरार (*nf*) leak; gap

दरिंदा (*nm*) a carnivorous, meat-eating beast

दरिद्र (*a*) poor, needy; indigent, poverty-stricken; of low qualities

दरिद्रता (*nf*) poverty, wretchedness

दरिद्रनारायण (*a*) the have-not; the poor

दरिया (*nm*) a river; — दिल liberal, large-hearted

दरियाफ्त (*a*) known; (*nm*) an enquiry

दरी (*nf*) a cotton carpet

दर्ज (*a*) entered, recorded

दर्जन (*nm*) a dozen

दर्जा (*nm*) degree; a class; rank; gradation

दर्जी (*nm*) a tailor

दर्द (*nm*) pain, ache; —नाक painful, tragic

दर्प (*nm*) pride, arrogance, boastfulness

दर्रा (*nm*) a valley, a cleft between hills

दर्शक (*nm*) spectator, a looker

on; visitor

दर्शन (*nm*) seeing, prospect, looking, sight; philosophy

दर्शनीय (*a*) worth seeing, agreeable, handsome, beautiful

दर्शित (*a*) exposed to view

दल (*nm*) leaf; a party

दलबल (*nm*) an army of followers and supporters

दलदल (*nm*) fen, swamp, marsh, mire

दला/ल (*nm*) tout, a broker; an agent; — ली brokerage

दलित (*a*) rent, broken, torn, depressed

दलिया (*nf*) coarse meal, hominy

दलील (*nf*) an argument, proof, plea

दवा (*nf*) medicine, drug; remedy; —ख़ाना a clinic, dispensary; —दारू medical treatment; medicine

दवात (*nf*) an inkpot

दशक (*nm*) a decade

दशमलव (*nm*) a decimal fraction

दशा (*nm*) state, condition; degree

दस (*a*) ten; (*nf*) the number ten

दस्त (*nm*) the hand; loose faeces

दस्तक (*nf*) a tapping noise made with hands, a knock at the door

दस्तकार (nm) craftsman, an artisan

दस्तकारी (nf) handicraft

दस्तखत (nm) signature

दस्ता (nm) handle of an instrument, bunch of flowers, a small band of soldiers

दस्ताना (nm) glove, gauntlet

दस्तावर (a) purgative

दस्तावेज़ (nm) a note of hand; a document; deed

दस्तूर (nm) custom, fashion; regulation

दहकना (v) to burn with a red hot flame, to blaze

दहन (nm) burning, combustion; — शील combustible

दहलना (v) to tremble, to shake, to be terrorised

दहलीज़ (nf) a corridor, gallery, threshold

दहशत (nf) fear, dread; terror; panic

दहाड़ना (v) to roar; to weep loudly, to shout aloud

दही (nm) curd

दहेज (nm) dowry

दाँत (nm) a tooth

दांपत्य (a) pertaining to husband and wife; (nm) conjugal relations

दाँव (nm) a stake, a bet, a wager

दाई (a) pertaining to the right

दाई (nf) a nurse; a midwife

दाखिल (a) entered; admitted; produced

दाखिला (nm) entry; admission

दाग़ (nm) scar; speck; stigma

दाग़ (nm) act of burning

दाग़ना (v) to burn, to brand; to fire a gun

दाढ़ (nf) jaw-tooth, grinder

दाढ़ी (nf) chin; beard

दाता (nm) a donor, benefactor, a generous man

दातुन (nm) a native tooth-brush (made of a spray of a tree)

दाद (nf) shingles, ring worm; praise

दान (nm) the act of giving alms; charity, donation

दान-धर्म (nm) almsgiving; charity

दान-पात्र (nm) a fit person for the bestowal of alms

दानशील (a) charitable, liberal bountiful

दान/व (nm) giant; demon; —वीय giant-like; demonic

दाना (nm) grain; food; seed; corn; —पानी food; seed;

दानी (a &·nm) charitable, generous, liberal

दाब (nf) pressure; force; control

दाबना (v) to suppress, to press down

दाम (nm) price; value; cost

दामन (nm) the skirt of a garment

दामाद (nm) a son-in-law

दामिनी (nf) the lightning; an ornament for the head

वाय (nm) nuptial present, inheritance, heritage

वायरा (nm) a ring; a circle; range

वायाँ (a) right

वायाधिकार (nm) heritage

वायित्व (nm) responsibility; liability

वारा (nf) wife

वारुण (a) horrible; dreadful; difficult

वारू (nf) medicine, drug; liquor

वारोगा (nm) a sub-inspector of police

वार्शनिक (nm) a metaphysician, a philosopher

वाल (nf) pulse

वालान (nm) a lobby; verandah

वाव (nm) chance; stake; a trick; —पेंच strategical moves

वावत (nf) banquet; feast; invitation for a feast

वावा (nm) suit; claim

वावात (nf) an inkpot

वावानल (nm) forest conflagration

वावेदार (nm) a claimant

वास (nm) servant; slave, helot, —ता vassalage, enslavement; —प्रथा slavery

वास्तान (nf) account, narration, story, tale

वाह (nm) inflammation; burning, heat

वाहकर्म (nm) cremation, burning of the dead

वाहिना (a) right

दिक् (nf) quarter, direction

दिक्क़त (nf) trouble; difficulty, perplexity

दिक्सूचक (nm) a compass

दिखना (v) to be seen

दिखाऊ (a) presentable, worth seeing, showy

दिखावट (nf) exhibition; show, display

दिखावा (nm) pomp, ostentation, show

दिग an allomorph of दिक् —विजय the world conquest; —विजयी conqueror of whole of the world

दिग्दर्श/क (nm) a director; —न survey; something exhibited as a sample

दिन (nm) day, time; -ब-दिनday by day

दिनचर्या (nf) daily routine

दिन-भर (adv) all day long

दिनमान (nm) the length of a day

दिनांक (nm) date

दिमाग (nm) mind, brain; pride, arrogance

दिमागी (a) proud, haughty; pertaining to mind, mental

दिया (nm) a lamp; (a) given

दियासलाई (nf) a match box; a match stick

दिल (nm) mind; heart;

courage; spirit; —कश attractive; —वार beloved;
corageous

दिलगीर (a) sorry, afflicted

दिलचस्प (a) attractive, beautiful, interesting

दिलचस्पी (nf) attractiveness,
interest

दिलचोर (a) lazy, slow in doing
a work; a lover

दिलजला (a) greatly afflicted

दिलदरिया (a) bountiful, liberal

दिलाना (v) to cause to be given

दिलावर (a) brave, courageous,
intrepid

दिलासा (nm) comfort, consolation, encouragement,
solace

दिली (a) pertaining to the heart,
hearty; sincere

दिलेर (a) proud, courageous

दिलेरी (nf) daring; boldness;
bravery

दिल्लगी (nf) jest, joke, fun;
—बाज़ a jester, a jocular

दिवंगत (a) deceased, late

दिवस (nm) a day

दिवाकर (nm) the Sun

दिवाचर (nm) a bird

दिवानिश (nf) day and night

दिवावसान (nm) evening, close
or decline of day

दिवाला (nm) insolvency,
bankruptcy

दिवालिया (a) a bankrupt,
insolvent

दिव्य (a) heavenly, divine,

supernatural

दिव्यता (nf) brilliancy, godliness; beauty

दिव्य/वृष्टि (nf) supernatural
power

दिशा (nf) direction, way;
region, quarter

दीक्षा (nf) investiture of sacred
thread; initiation

दीक्षित (a) initiated, consecrat-
ed

दीखना (v) to look, to appear

दीदार (nm) sight, interview,
meeting or conference

दीन (a) badly off, poor,
miserable; (nm) religion

दीनता (nf) distress, want,
poverty

दीन-दुनिया (nf) this world and
the next world

दीनबंधु (nm) friend of the
poor; (nm) an epithet of
God

दीनार (nm) a gold coin used in
Arabic countries, denarius

दीपक (nm) a lamp, a light

दीपगृह (nm) a lighthouse

दीप्त (a) luminous, radiant,
bright

दीप्ति (nf) light, flash, lustre;
splendour

दीप्तिमान (a) shining, glittering

दीमक (nf) white ant, termite

दीर्घ (a) large; long; wide;
huge; —सूत्री a slow coach;
dilatory

दीर्घायु (a) long lived, of long

दीवट (*nf*) a lamp-stand

दीवान (*nm*) a royal court, a court-minister

दीवाना (*a*) mad, insane; —पन insanity, madness

दीवानी (*nf*) the post of minister; (*a*) civil (court)

दीवार (*nf*) a wall

दीवारगीर (*nm*) a bracket fixed in a wall for keeping articles on it

दीवाल (*nf*) a wall

दुंदुभि, दुंदुभी (*nm*) a kettle-drum

दु:ख (*nm*) suffering, distress; sorrow, unhappiness

दु:खदायक (*a*) troublesome, painful, vexatious

दु:खमय (*a*) full of trouble or pain

दु:खांत (*a*) ending in sorrow

दु:खात्मक (*a*) lugubrious; tragic

दु:खित (*a*) unhappy, sorrowful

दु:खी (*a*) sad, sorrowful, unhappy

दु:शील (*a*) wicked, of bad character

दु:सह (*a*) intolerable, unbearable

दु:साध्य (*a*) arduous, difficult, difficult to do

दु:साहस (*nm*) a futile enterprise, rashness

दु:साहसी (*a*) bold; rash, arrogant

दु:स्वप्न (*nm*) a bad dream, a nightmare

दु:स्वभाव (*nm*) evil nature, wickedness

दु an allomorph of दो used as the first member in compound words —गुना double; —तरफ़ा two-sided; —नाली double-barrelled; —पहर noon, midday; —बारा a second time; —भाषिया an interpreter; —मंज़िला double-storeyed; —मुँहा double mouthed; —रंगा two-coloured

दुआ (*nf*) blessings

दुकान (*nf*) a shop; —दार a shop-keeper, a seller; —दारी the business of shopkeeping

दुखड़ा (*nm*) description of one's sufferings, trouble

दुखाना (*v*) to trouble, to inflict pain; to torement

दुखिया (*a*) afflicted with pain, troubled; —रा ill, unwell

दुतकार (*nf*) reproof; reprimand; —ना (*v*) to reprove, to show contempt

दुधमुँहा (*nm* & *a*) still feeding on mother's milk; an infant

दुधारू (*nf*) yielding much milk

दुनिया (*nf*) people; the world; —दार worldlywise; —दारी worldliness

दुनियावी (*a*) wordly

दुबला (*a*) weak, lean, gaunt, thin; —पतला lean and thin

दुम (*nf*) tail; end

दुरभिसंधि (*nf*) a secret plot, stratagem

दुराग्रह (*nm*) prejudice, wilfulness, prejudgement

दुराग्रही (*a*) grumpy, mulish, prejudicial

दुरा/चरण (*nm*) villainy, misbehaviour, bad conduct; —चार crime, misconduct; —चारी (*a*) wicked

दुरात्मा (*a*) (*a*) vile, wicked

दुराव (*nm*) trick, concealment; reservation

दुराशय (*nm*) evil intention; (*a*) wicked, vicious

दुरुपयोग (*nm*) perversion, abuse, misapplication

दुरुस्त (*a*) fit, proper, just, correct

दुरुस्ती (*nf*) exactitude, propriety, fitness

दुरूह (*a*) difficult to understand, hidden, obscure

दुर्गंध (*nf*) bad or offensive smell; stink

दुर्ग (*nm*) castle, fort; citadel

दुर्गति (*nf*) poverty, misfortune, meanness

दुर्गम (*a*) inaccessible, out of the way, deep, difficult

दुर्गुण (*nm*) flaw; defect, blemish, fault

दुर्घटना (*nf*) tragedy, accident; misadventure

दुर्जन (*nm*) a rascal, wicked person, mischief-maker

दुर्जेय (*a*) difficult to be subdued, indomitable, inconquerable

दुर्जत (*a*) wicked, miserable

दुर्द/म (*a*) irrepressible; unyielding; difficult to subdue; —मनीय impregnable; —म्य difficult to be subdued

दुर्दशा (*nf*) adversity, plight, misfortune, calamity

दुर्दिन (*nm*) bad weather, cloudy or rainy day; a bad time

दुर्दैव (*nm*) ill-luck, misfortune, a mishap

दुर्धर्ष (*a*) difficult to subdue, invincible

दुर्नि/वार (*a*) unrestrainable; —वार्य irrepressible; inevitable

दुर्नीति (*nf*) bad policy, injustice, evil behaviour

दुर्ब/ल (*a*) infirm, faint, slight, weak; —लता thinness, feebleness

दुर्बुद्धि (*a*) foolish, senseless, evil-minded

दुर्बोध (*a*) difficult to be understood, hard to conceive

दुर्भाग्य (*nm*) ill-luck, mischance, tragedy

दुर्भाव (*nm*) malice, ill-temper, bad conduct

दुर्भिक्ष (*nm*) scarcity, dearth, famine

दुर्भेद्य (*a*) unable to be penetrated, impregnable

दुर्लभ (*a*) scarce, rare, difficult to be attained

दुर्वचन (nm) abuse, reproach
दुर्व्यवस्था (nf) mismanagement
दुर्व्यवहार (nm) bad treatment, misconduct; misuse
दुर्व्यसन (nm) dissipation, evil habit
दुविधा (nf) fix, dilemma
दुश्चरित्र (nm) an evil purpose, misconduct; (a) bad conduct, deprave
दुश्म/न (nm) foe, enemy; —नी animus, hostility, enmity
दुष्कर (a) difficult to be performed, impossible, arduous
दुष्कर्म (nm) sin, wrong, vice
दुष्ट (a) bad, mean, wicked sly, faulty; (nm) a rascal, scamp, villain
दुष्टता (nf) knavery, guilt, improperiety, wickedness
दुष्टात्मा (a) malicious; (nm) a very wicked person
दुष्प्राप्य (a) difficult to be attained, rare
दुस्तर (a) difficult to cross, insuperable, impassable
दुहना (v) to milk; to squeeze, to extract the essence of
दुहरा (a) double-folded; dual, two-fold
दुहराना (v) to do over again; to repeat; to revise
दुहिता (nf) a daughter
दूत (nm) legate, messenger, envoy
दूतावास (nm) residence of a

foreign embassy
दूध (nm) milk; juice of certain plants
दूधिया (a) milky; white as milk; (nm) an opal
दूभर (a) arduous; difficult
दूरदेश (a) prudent, far-sighted
दूर (adv & a) away, aloof, fro, distant; —गामी gone afar or away; —दर्शक यंत्र a field-glass, a telescope; —दर्शिता prudence, far-sightedness; —बीन a telescope; —संचार telecommunication
दूरी (nf) distance; separation
दूल्हा (nm) a bridegroom; a husband
दूषण (nm) defect, flaw, calumny
दूषित (a) corrupted, defield, sullied
दूसरा (a) other, second, another; next
दृढ़ (a) hard, firm, iron-bound, powerful
दृश्य (nm) a sight, view, scene; (a) visible
दृश्यमान (a) seen, visible
दृष्टांत (nm) illustration, citation, instance
दृष्टि (nf) seeing; sight; vision; view; —कोण point of view; —गोचर visible, perceptible; —पात glance, look; —हीन blind
देखना (v) to look, to see, to behold; to observe; to view

देखभाल (nf) maintenance; care; supervision

देख-रेख (nf) supervision; care, guidance

देन (nf) giving; gift; a prize; —दार a debtor; —दारी indebtedness; due

देना (v) to grant; to give, to afford; to confer

दे/र (nf) delay; —री suspension, delay

देव (nm) a deity, a respectable person, god; a demon; —दूत an angel, a divine messenger; —स्थान a temple

देव/ता (nm) deity, god; —त्व godliness

देवर (nm) husband's younger brother, brother-in-law

देवरानी (nf) wife of the younger brother of a woman's husband

देवांगना (nf) a celestial damsel

देवालय (nm) paradise, the temple of a god

देश (nm) land; country; —ज local; native; —भक्त a patriot; —भक्ति nationalism, patriotism

देश/द्रोह (nm) disloyalty to one's country; —द्रोही a traitor

देशनिकाला (nm) banishment, exile

देशांतर (nm) foreign country, longitude

देशाटन (nm) a wandering through a country

देशी (a) pertaining to a country; local; native

देसावर (nm) marketing centre; a foreign country

देसी (a) native, not foreign

देह (nf) figure, body; person; —धारी possessing a body, corporal, —त्यागना to die; —धरना to be born

देहरी (nf) doorsill, the threshold

देहांत (nm) demise, death

देहा/त (nm) village; country; —ती rural, rustic

देही (nm) the body

दैत्य (nm) giant, a demon, evil spirit

दैनंदिन (a & adv) pertaining to each day; daily

दैनिक (a) daily, quatidian

दैन्य (nm) poverty; humbleness

दैव (nm) destiny, fate, fortune; —गति a supernatural occurrence, misfortune; —ज्ञ an astrologer; —योग chance; —वश luckily, haply; —वाणी the Sanskrit language

दैहिक (a) bodily, physical; material

दो (a) two; (nm) the number two; —गला a bastard; —टूक decisive, crystal clear; —पहर noon; midday

दोज़ख़ (nm) hell

दोष (nm) harm, blemish,

defect, guilt

दोषी (*a & nm*) a criminal, a culprit

दोषारोपण (*nm*) impeachment, charge, imputation

दोस्त (*nm*) a friend

दोस्ताना (*a*) friendly

दोस्ती (*nf*) friendship

दोहनी (*nf*) a milk pail, the act of milking a cow

दोहरा (*a*) twofold, duplicate, double

दोहराना (*v*) to double, to renew, to repeat, to fold

दोहा (*nm*) a couplet (in Hindi)

दोहित्र (*nm*) a daughter's son

दौड़ (*nf*) running; a race, gallop; —धूप hard-labour, tumult

दौड़ना (*v*) to gallop, to run, to go fast

दौना (*nm*) a plant with fragrant leaves; rosemary; a bowl made of leaves

दौर (*nm*) roaming, revaluation, round

दौरा (*nm*) circuit, tour; attack of disease

दौलत (*nf*) wealth, riches, property; —खाना a place of residence; —मंद rich, wealthy; —मंदी wealthiness

दौवारिक (*nm*) a porter, a door keeper

द्यु (*nm*) day; sky; heaven

द्युति (*nf*) glow, radiance

द्यूत (*nm*) playing at dice, gambling

द्योतक (*a*) making manifest, showing, explaining

द्रव (*nm*) fluid, a liquid

द्रवित (*a*) moved by emotion; melted

द्रव्य (*nm*) matter, substance; wealth, property

द्रष्टव्य (*a*) worthy to be seen, attractive

द्रष्टा (*nm*) one who sees, a looker on, spectator

द्रुत (*a*) swift, quick

द्रुति (*nf*) motion

द्रो/ह (*nm*) malice, hostility, rancour —ही (*a*) rancorous, malicious

द्वंद्व (*nm*) a pair; a quarrel; uproar

द्वार (*nm*) gate; door; a doorway; —पाल watchman, a door-keeper

द्वारा (*ind*) by means of, by, through

द्विज (*nm*) a twice born; a bird; a Brahman

द्वितीय (*a*) second

द्विधा (*ind*) in two ways, in two parts

द्वीप (*nm*) an island, isle

द्वे/ष (*nm*) hatred, malice, spite; —षी inimical, hostile

ध

ध the fourth member of the fourth pentad of consonants in Devnagri Alphabet

धंधलाना (*v*) to play a false trick, to make ostentation

धंधा (*nm*) occupation; business, employment; work

धँस (*nm*) a dip into water

धँसना (*v*) to be penetrated; to enter a place; to sink

धक (*nf*) agitation, excitement, palpitation

धकधकाहट (*nf*) palpitation

धकधकी (*nf*) palpitation

धकपकाना (*v*) to be frightened, to be in fear

धकापेल (*nf*) jostling; (*adv*) vigorously, non-stop

धकियाना (*v*) to jostle, to jerk, to elbow

धकेलना (*v*) to push, to thrust

धकैत (*a*) pushing, thrusting

धक्कम-धक्का (*nm*) pushing, jostling

धक्का (*nm*) a shove; a push, concussion, dash; shock; —देना to hustle, to jostle; to shock; —मारना to buffet; —देनेवाला jerky, knocky; —मुक्कीpushing and jostling

धड़ (*nm*) trunk of body or tree, a torso

धड़कन (*nf*) pulsation, palpita-

tion, throbbing

धड़कना (*v*) to pulsate, to throb

धड़धड़ (*nf*) the noise produced by a thing falling from a height, a knocking sound

धड़धड़ाना (*v*) to palpitate, to walk heavily and briskly

धड़ाका (*nm*) crash, thump, explosion

धड़ाधड़ (*adv*) continuously, incessantly, quickly

धड़ाम (*nm*) the sound which is produced by a heavy object falling on the ground

धड़ी (*nf*) a weight of five seers

धत् (*ind*) be off! a word of contempt

धतकारना (*v*) to drive away with contempt, to reprove

धतूर (*nm*) a kind of trumpet

धधक (*nf*) flame, heat of fire

धधकना (*v*) to flare, to blaze, to burn with a flame

धन (*nm*) treasure, wealth, riches, property; —दौलत wealth and affluence; —धान्यall round prosperity; मूल — capital; —वान weal-thy; —हीन moneyless, poor

धनिक (*a*) rich, wealthy; (*nm*) a wealthy person

धनिया (*nm*) coriander seed

धनी (*a*) wealthy, rich, substantial; (*nm*) owner;

—मानी eminent

धनुर्धर (nm) a bowman, an archer

धनुर्विद्या (nf) archery

धनुष (nm) an arch, a bow

धन्य (a & nm) prosperous, lucky, blessed; (ind) well done! how fortunate!

धन्यवाद (nm) expression of gratitude, thanks-giving; (ind) thanks!

धब्बा (nm) spot, speck, blemish, stain, taint

धमकाना (v) to reprimand, to threaten, to intimidate

धमकी (nf) intimidation, threat, bluster; —में आना to be frightened or terrified

धमधमाहट (nm) a stumping over head, a thump

धमनी (nf) an artery; —संबंधी arterial, pertaining to artery

धमाका (nm) a bump, thud, crash; the report of a gun

धमाचौकड़ी (nf) bustle, turmoil, noise

धमाधम (a) with incessant thumping; (nf) sound of stamping on something

धर/णि —णी (nf) the earth, ground

धरती (nf) the earth, ground; the world

धरना (v) to place; to hold, to keep, to apply; (nm) picketing

धरा (nf) earth, soil, the world

धरातल (nm) the earth, area; surface of earth

धराशायी (a) razed to the ground, fallen

धरोहर (nf) trustmoney, deposit

धर्म (nm) religion; faith; duty; —ग्रंथ Holy Scriptures; —च्युत fallen from religion; —ध्वज the name of an ancient king of Mithila; —ध्वजी a hypocrite; —निरपेक्ष secular; —परायण religious, religious-minded; —युद्ध crusade; —रक्षक a protector of religion; —रत dutiful; —शास्त्र theology; —संकट a dilemma; —सुधार reformation

धर्मार्थ (a) for the sake of religion or justice, chartable

धर्मांध (a) fanatic; —ता fanaticism

धर्मात्मा (a) religious, devout

धर्मिष्ठ (a) pious, virtuous

धर्षण (nm) disrespect, attack, assault

धवल (a) clear; white; bright; beautiful

धवलता (nf) whiteness

धसक (nf) a dry cough

धसकना (v) to sink, to fear

धाँधल (nf) turmoil, disturbance, fraud

धाँधली (nf) chaos, outrage

धाँस (nf) the smell of a dry

tobacco leaf which causes constant sneezing

धांसना (*v*) to cough as a horse

धाक (*nf*) pomp, renown, commanding

धागा (*nm*) thread, cord

धाता (*nm*) the creator, an epithet of Brahma

धातु (*nf*) a semen ; a mineral, a metal; root

धात्री (*nf*) mother; a wet nurse

धान (*nm*) the rice plant, paddy

धान्य (*nm*) a measure equal to four sesamum seeds, corn, crop

धाम (*nm*) a house; dwelling; seat of a diety

धार (*nf*) sharp edge; an edge; current; flow

धारण (*nm*) maintaining; holding; wearing

धारणा (*nf*) resolution, impression; concept, idea

धारा (*nf*) a current of water; stream, river; section; —प्रवाह non-stop, fluent

धार्मिक (*a*) virtuous, religious, holy

धार्मिकता (*nf*) piety, virtuousness, sanctity

धावक (*nm*) a harbinger

धावा (*nm*) quick running, incursion, assault, attack; —बोलना to launch an attack

धावित (*a*) cleansed, purified

धिक् (*int*) a word denoting blame, censure, fie ! shame !

धिक्कार (*nm*) contempt, repulse, curse, repudiation

धिक्कारना (*v*) to disdain, to curse, to upbraid

धीमा (*a*) tardy, slow, mild, gentle; —चलने वाला tardigrade; —पन slowness, tardiness; —स्वर undertone

धीर (*a*) grave, solemn, patient, firm

धीरज (*nm*) a consollation, patience, gravity

धीरता (*nf*) patience, satisfaction, solace

धीरे (*adv*) slowly, lazily; —धीरे little by little; gradually; slowly

धीवर (*nm*) a fisherman; a sailor

धुंकार (*nf*) a loud noise, a roar

धुंध (*nf, nm*) haziness, mist, fog

धुंधकार (*nm*) darkness, mistiness, thunder

धुंधलका (*nm*) darkishness, twilight

धुंधला (*a*) dim, misty; faded; foggy

धुआँ (*nm*) smoke, fume, reek; —धार violent; fiery; eloquent

धुकधुकी (*nf*) the middle portio of the heart; fear, throbbi

धुन (*nf*) propensity, assidu

धुनकना (*v*) to card cotton

धुनना (*v*) to comb, to wool

card cotton

धुरंधर (a) one who carries a weight, leading

धुरा (nm) axis, hub, shaft

धुरी (nf) pivat, axis

धुर्रा (nm) a fragment; —उड़ाना to break a thing into small pieces, to destroy

धुलना (v) to be washed or cleaned with water

धुलाई (nf) the work or wages which is paid for washing

धुलाना (v) to cause to be washed

धूर्त (a) wicked cunning; rascal

धू-धू (nm) noise which is made by a flaming fire

धूनी (nf) incense, fire lighted by a Hindu mendicant who sits near it and inhales the smoke; —रमाना to practise austerity

धूप (nf) incense, burnt perfume, the light and heat of the sun; —घड़ी a sun-dial; —छाँह sun and shade; —बत्ती incense-stick

धूम (nm) smoke, vapour; (nf) funfare, tumult; boom; —धाम hustle and bustle; pomp

धूमकेतु (nm) fire, a comet, an epithet of Shiva

धूम-धड़क्का (nm) noise, tumult, pomp

धूमिल (a) smoky, hoary, vague

धूल (nf) dirt, dust

धूलि (nf) dust, dirt

धूसर (a) grey, dusk-coloured

धूसरित (a) full of dirt

धृत (a) held, possessed; sustained, kept up

धृष्ट (a) insolent, impudent; saucy, impertinent

धृष्टता (nf) insolence, impudence; sauce; impertinence

धृष्या (nf) a woman of loose character; (a) shameless

धेनु (nf) a cow

धैर्य (nm) patience, firmness; constancy, endurance

धोखा (nm) deceit, deception; guile; —देना to outwit, to deceive, —खाना to be deceived; —धड़ी cheating; beguilement

धोखेबाज़ (nm) a cheat; a deceitful, fraudulent

धोती (nf) loin cloth worn by Indians

धोना (v) to wash; to launder; to cleanse

धोबिन (nf) a washer-woman

धोबी (nm) a washer-man, a laundry-man

धोवन (nm) work of washing; water in which anything has been washed

धौंकना (v) to blow with bellows

धौंकनी (nf) bellows

धौंस (nf) bluster, threat, awe

धौंसना (v) to frighten, to chide,

to threaten

ध्याता (*nm*) one who thinks on a subject, a contemplator

ध्यान (*nm*) consideration, reflection; attention; meditation — देना to pay attention to; — न देना to ignore; — धरना to contemplate; — लगाना to meditate; to concentrate — से उतरना to forget

ध्यानी (*a*) contemplative, meditative; (*nm*) one who applies himself to religious meditation

ध्येय (*nm*) end, aim

ध्रुव (*nm*) the pole; the polestar; (*a*) fixed, a permanent, firm; — तारा the polestar

ध्वंस (*nm*) destruction; loss

ध्वज (*nm*) a flag, symbol, banner

ध्वजा (*nf*) a flag, banner, ensign

ध्वनि (*nf*) sound; suggested meaning, purport

न

न the fifth member of the fourth pentad of consonants in Devnagri alphabet; (*ind*) no, not

नंग-धड़ंग (*a*) completely naked

नंगा (*a*) undraped, naked, nude; shameless; wicked; — पन nakedness; shamelessness; wickedness

नंदोई (*nm*) the husband of husband's sister

नंबर (*nm*) number; counting, marks

नंबरदार (*nm*) the Zamindar of a village who helps the co-sharers in realising rent

नंबरवार (*adv*) one by one

नंबरी (*a*) numbered, bearing a number; notorious

नई (*a*) new

नकटा (*a, nm*) noseless; a nose-clipped person; shameless

नकद (*a*) hard cash; (*nm*) cash, ready money; (*adv*) in lieu of cash, in cash

नकल (*nf*) imitation; copy, duplicate, transcription; — करना to copy, to duplicate; — करनेवाला (*nm*) a copyist

नकली (*a*) false, counterfeit; artificial, not genuine

नकशा (*nm*) a plan, map; — बनाना to sketch, to plan; — बनाने वाला (*nm*) a draftsman; — नापने का यंत्र (*nm*) pantograph

नकसीर (*nf*) bleeding from the nose

नक़ाब (*nf*) a veil; a mask; visor; —पोश masked, visored

नकार (*nm*) refusal; denial; negation

नकारना (*v*) to deny; to refuse, to decline

नकारा/नाकारा (*a*) useless, worthless

नकाशी (*nf*) see नक्काशी

नकुल (*nm*) a mongoose

नकेल (*nf*) the string fixed in a camel's, ox's or bear's nose to serve as a rein

नक्कारा (*nm*) a huge kettle-drum

नक्काशी (*nf*) carving, engraving; designing; —दार carved; carving designs

नक्श (*nm*) features

नक्षत्र (*nm*) a star

नख (*nm*) nail; claw

नखरा (*nm*) prudery, coquetry

नखरीला (*am*) coquetish, prude

नख-शिख (*nm*) from top to toe

नग (*nm*) a jewel, precious stone; piece; mountain

नगण्य (*a*) insignificant, ordinary; worthless

नगदी (*nf*) hard cash

नग्मा (*nm*) a song; melody

नगर (*nm*) town; city

नगाड़ा (*nm*) a tymbal, kettle-drum, tomtom

नगीना (*nf*) a precious stone, gem

नग्न (*a*) naked, nude; —ता nakedness

नज़दीक (*adv*) near, close, almost, about

नज़र (*nf*) eyesight; glance, look; vision; attention

नज़राना (*nm*) a gift, present

नज़ला (*nm*) cold, catarrh

नज़ाकत (*nf*) tenderness, delicacy

नज़ारा (*nm*) sight, view, scene

नज़्म (*nf*) poem; verse

नट (*nm*) dancer; an acrobat, tumbler, an actor

नटखट (*a*) naughty, mischive-ous

नटखटी (*nf*) trickery, naughti-ness

नटनी (*nf*) an actress, a female of the rope-dancer's class

नत (*a*) twisted, bent, curved; —मस्तक respectful

नतीजा (*nm*) consequence; result

नत्थी (*a*) annexed; attached; tagged

नथ (*nf*) a ring-shaped ornament for the nose

नदारद (*a*) absent, disap-pearing from view

नदी (*nf*) a river

ननद (*nf*) sister-in-law, husband's sister

ननसाल (*nf*) mother's paternal home

नंदिनी (*nf*) daughter; the river Ganga

नन्हा (*a*) small; tiny; wee

नपुंसक (*nm*) a eunuch; a

coward; an impotent person; (*a*) cowardly

नफ़रत (*nf*) contempt; hatred, disgust

नफ़ा (*nm*) gain; profit; advantage

नफ़ासत (*nf*) delicacy, refinement, nicety

नफ़ीस (*a*) excellent, fine, good, clean

नब्ज़ (*nf*) the pulse; — देखना to feel the pulse; — छूटना stopping of the pulse, death

नभ (*nm*) the sky; firmament

नम/क (*nm*) table salt; salt; — कहराम ungrateful; — कीन (*a*) salty

नमस्/कार (*nm*) adieu; salutation; — ते salutation to you

नमाज़ (*nf*) a formal prayer by the muslims

नमी (*nf*) dampness; humidity

नमूना (*nm*) specimen, model; a sample; pattern

नम्र (*a*) humble; polite; submissive

नय/न (*nm*) an eye; — नाभिराम (*a*) charming, beautiful

नया (*a*) fresh; new; modern; young; inexperienced

नर (*nm*) a male; a man; (*a*) male; — बलि human sacrifice; — भक्षी a man-eater

नरक (*nm*) inferno, hell, the infernal regions, a very dirty place

नरकगामी (*a*) one who goes to hell after death

नरगिस (*nf*) narcissus flower

नरम (*a*) delicate; soft; pliant; timid

नरमी (*nf*) delicacy; softness; kindness

नरमेध (*nm*) the sacrifice of a human-being

नराधम (*nm*) a mean person

नराधिप (*nm*) a king

नरेंद्र (*nm*) a king

नरेश (*nm*) a king

नर्त/क (*nm*) a dancer; — की a dancing girl

नर्स (*nf*) a nurse

नल (*nm*) a long pipe; tap; — कूप a tube-well

नलिनी (*nf*) a lotus; a lily

नली (*nf*) pipe; tube; barrel of a gun

नव (*a*) fresh; new; young; recent; — युवक a young man; — युवती a young lady

नवधा (*a*) of nine kinds; — भक्ति the nine ways of devotion

नवनीत (*nm*) butter

नवरंग (*a*) beautiful, of new design

नवरत्न (*nm*) the nine precious stones; the nine gems of the court of Vikramaditya (also in the court of Akabar)

नवल (*a*) fresh; recent; new, modern; young

नवासा (*nm*) a daughter's son; — सी a daughter's daughter

नवी/न (a) novel, new; fresh; youthful; young; —नीकरण renewal; —नता freshness; novelty; modernity

नव्य (a) recent; new; modern

नशा (nm) intoxication; pride; —पानी some intoxication; —बंदी prohibition

नशी/ला (a) inebrient; intoxicating; hence —ली (fam. form of नशीला)

नशे/बाज़ (nm & a) a drunkard, addict; hence —बाज़ी the habit of drinking

नश्तर (nm) surgical knife; a lancet

नश्वर (a) destructible, transient

नश्वरता (nf) destructibility

नष्ट (a) destroyed, annihilated

नष्टचित्त (a) insane, mad

नष्टचेष्ट (a) having lost the power of moving limbs

नष्टचेतना (nf) torpor, trance

नष्टबुद्धि (a) stupid, dull

नष्ट-भ्रष्ट (a) broken asunder, destroyed; —होना to be smashed to wear

नष्टात्मा (nm) a mean fellow, a rogue

नस (nf) vein, sinew; nerve, —चढ़ना to have sprain in a part of the body; नसवार snuff; —बंदी vasectomy

नसल (nf) genealogy, pedigree

नसीब (nm) fortune, fate luck; destiny

नसीहत (nf) advice, instruction, counsel; —देना to counsel

नहर (nf) a channel, canal; waterway

नहरनी (nf) an instrument for cutting the nails

नहलाना (v) to cause to be bathed or washed

नहाना (v) to bathe; to perform ablution

नहीं (ind) not, no; —तो or, else, otherwise, if not

नाँद (nf) an earthen trough; manger

ना (ind) no, not; —इंसाफी injustice; —उम्मीद hopeless; —काबिल undeserving; —कारा good for nothing; idle; —खुश displeased; —गवार unbearable; —चीज़ worthless; trifling; —जायज़ undue; improper; —दान ignorant; —बालिग under age; —मंज़ूर rejected; —मर्द impotent; coward; —मुमकिन impossible; —मुराद ill-fated; —वाक़िफ़ a stranger; ignorant

नाई (ind) like

नाई (nm) a barber

नाक (nf) the nose; honour; pre-eminent person; a symbol of prestige; (nm) the heaven

नाक-नक़्शा (nm) features

नाकाबंदी (nf) posting guards to stop the entry in a place

नाखून (nm) nail, claw

नाग (*nm*) snake; serpent; a cobra; an elephant; (*a*) treacherous

नागर (*a*) pertaining to the city, civil; urban; (*nm*) a civilian

नागरिक (*a*) civilian; urbane; (*nm*) a citizen; civilian; —सभा municipality; —अधिकार की प्राप्ति enfranchisement; —संस्थाbody politic; —ता citizenship

नागलोक (*nm*) the Hades

नागा (*nf*) absence from work

नागिन (*nf*) a female serpent

नाच (*nm*) dance, a ball, a dramatic entertainment; —गाना dance and music, ballet; —घर a dancing hall

नाचना (*v*) to dance; to frisk, to gambol

नाचरंग (*nm*) dancing entertainment, nautch party

नाज़ (*nm*) pride; airs; —उठाना to show coquettishness

नाज़नीन (*nm*) delicate beauty

नाजायज़ (*a*) unlawful, illegal; improper, unjust

नाज़िर (*nm*) a supervisor, a superintendent

नाज़ुक (*a*) soft, delicate, fine, tender; —बदन of a delicate frame; —मिज़ाज one who is unable to bear even a little hardship

नाटक (*nm*) a play; a drama; a dramatic performance; —कार a dramatist, play-wright

नाटकशाला (*nf*) stage, theatre

नाटकीय (*a*) pertaining to a stage or drama, dramatic; —ता dramatic character

नाटना (*v*) to break a promise; to deny; to negate

नाटा (*a*) short, dwarfish; stunted; —मोटा stocky; —मनुष्य a pigmy

नाटिका (*nf*) a short drama consisting of four acts

नाट्य (*nm*) the act of dancing, a mimic play

नाट्यकला (*nf*) stage craft

नाट्यकार (*nm*) a dramatist; an actor; the performer of a drama

नाट्यशास्त्र (*nm*) dramaturgy

नाड़ा (*nm*) untwisted thread, a tape

नाड़ी (*nf*) nerve, vein, pulse

नाता (*nm*) relationship, relation

नाती (*nm*) a son's son; a daughter's son

नाते (*adv*) in relation with, for the sake of some one

नातेदा/र (*adv*) relation; (*nm*) a relative; —री kinship, relationship

नाथ (*nm*) lord, master; husband

नाथना (*v*) to pierce the nose of a cattle and pass a rope through it to have a complete control over it

नाद (*nm*) a sound; noise; music

नादिरशाही (*nf*) great tyranny and injustice; (*a*) very harsh and terrible

नान (*nf*) bread

नानखताई (*nf*) a kind of sweet-meat

नाना (*nm*) maternal grand-father, grandsire; (*a*) different, varied, miscellaneous

नानारूप (*nm*) different shapes

नानी (*nf*) mother's mother, maternal grand mother

नाप (*nm*) measurement; survey; dimension; —जोख/तोल work of measuring something

नापना (*v*) to measure; to survey

नापाक (*a*) polluted, defiled, impure

नाभि (*nf*) the navel; hub

नाम (*nm*) title; name; fame; —करण the ceremony of naming a child; —कीर्तन constant repetition of god's name; —ज़द nominated; -धामname and address; —पट्ट a name-plate; —मात्र को nominal

नामक (*a*) named, bearing the name

नामांकन (*nm*) nomination

नामी (*a*) bearing the name of; famous, reputed

नायक (*nm*) a guide, leader, chief, hero; a military official of a low rank

नायकत्व (*nm*) lead, captainship

नायब (*a*) deputy; (*nm*) an agent, an assistant

नायिका (*nf*) the heroine of drama etc.

नारंगी (*nf*) an orange; (*a*) of orange colour; —का बगीचा orangery

ना/रा (*nm*) a slogan; —रेबाज़ a slogan-monger

नाराज़ (*a*) displeased, dissatisfied

नाराज़गी (*nf*) displeasure

नारियल (*nm*) the coconut

नारी (*nf*) a woman, lady

नाल (*nf*) hollow tubular stalk, a tube; barrel of gun

नाला (*nm*) a canal; a rivulet; a gutter

नालायक़ (*a*) unfit; improper; wretched, worthless

नालिश (*nf*) plaint, law suit

नाली (*nf*) sewer, drain; tube

नाव (*nm*) a boat, a sailing vessel

नाविक (*nm*) a boatman, sailor

नाश (*nm*) damage; ruination; waste

नाशक (*a*) destroying; killing

नाशपाती (*nf*) a pear

नाशवान (*a*) perishable, destructible, liable to decay

नाश्ता (*nm*) breakfast

नासमझ (a) ignorant; stupid; dull

नासमझी (nf) ignorance; stupidity; folly

नासिका (nf) the nose

नासूर (nm) cancer, ulcer, sinus

नास्तिक (nm) an atheist, an unbeliever; —ता atheism, disbelief

नाहक (adv) improperly, unjustly, in a useless manner

निंदक (nm) a calumniator; (a) abusive

निंदना (v) to defame, to calumniate, to abuse

निंदनीय (a) blamable, reprehensible, censurable

निंदा (nf) scorn, blame, slander

निंदिया (nf) sleep

नि:स्पृह (a) free from wish or desire, contented

नि:स्वार्थ (a) unselfish, disinterested, impartial; hence —ता (nf) selfless-ness

निकट (adv & a) close, near, proximate; —वर्ती standing or residing near, ready; (n) a neighbour

निकम्मा (a) worthless, useless, idle, indolent

निकलना (v) to issue; to get out; to rise; to be extracted

निकष (nm) touchstone, emerystone

निकाह (nm) marriage ceremony performed according to Mohammedan rites and customs

निकृष्ट (a) wretched; vile, low, base; —ता wretchedness; baseness

निखट्टू (a, nm) earning nothing; unemployed; lazy, idle

निगरानी (nf) supervision, watch

निगलना (v) to swallow, to gulp

निगाह (nf) look, glance; observation; attention

निगूढ़ (a) secret, hidden, obscure

निगोड़ा (a) supportless, unfortunate, wicked; (nm) an idler

निग्रह (nm) obstruction, restraint

निचला (a) lower; low-lying

निचोड़ (nm) summary, gist, essence; —ना to wring, to press, to squeeze

निजी (a) own, personal; private; unofficial

निठल्ला (a) without employ-ment; idle; (nm) an idler; —पन idleness

निडर (a) fearless, dauntless; daring, intrepid

निढाल (a) languid, wearied; slow

नित (adv) daily, everyday, each day

नितांत (a) complete, excessive,

entire, whole

नित्य (a) perpetual, constant, eternal, permanent; (adv) constantly, for ever; —प्रति every day, daily

नियार (nm) distilled water, decantation

नियारना (v) to decant, to purify, to distil

निदर्शन (nm) illustration; example; evidence

निदान (nm) cause of disease; diagnosis

निदेश (nm) order, command; instruction

निदेशालय (nm) a directorate

निद्रा (nf) sleep, slumber

निघड़क (adv) without reflection, boldly, fearlessly

निधन (nm) death

निधान (nm) receptacle, support, abode

निधि (nf) fund; treasure, hoard

निनाद (nm) a sound

निपट (adv) exceedingly, very, sheer

निपटना (v) to be settled, to be decided

निपटारा (nm) settlement; termination

निपात (nm) fall, ruin; death

निपुण (a) clever, eminent, perfect

निपुणता (nf) adoritness; talent; efficiency

निबंध (nm) an essay, a treatise

निबटना (v) to be settled, to be decided, to be finished

निबल (a) feeble, weak

निबाह (nm) maintenance, accomplishment, arrangement

निबाहना (v) to perform; to achieve; to conduct; to maintain

नि/भना (v) to be accomplished; —भाना to accomplish, to fulfil

निमंत्रण (nm) invitation for feast; —पत्र invitation card

निमग्न (a) drowned; engaged

निमज्जन (nm) dipping bath

निमित्त (nm) motive; cause; account

निमेष (nm) twinkling of an eye, blink

निम्न (a) sunken, depressed, low; — लिखित the following

नियंता (nm) ruler, governor, master

नियंत्रक (nm) a controller

नियंत्रण (nm) fixing up a rule and following it

नियंत्रित (a) restrained, controlled

नियत (a) fixed, prescribed

नियति (nf) fate, destiny, luck

नियम (nm) regulation; principle

नियमावली (nf) rules and regulations

नियमित (a) regulated, regular; —ता regularity

नियुक्त (a) appointed; engaged;

posted

नियुक्ति (*nf*) appointment; posting

नियोजक (*nm*) one who appoints men in different occupations

निरंकुश (*a*) unrestrained, uncontrolled; self-willed

निरंतर (*a*) incessant, ceaseless, continuous

निरपराध (*a*) guiltless, innocent

निरपेक्ष (*a*) without expectation, unconcerned

निरभिमान (*a*) prideless, humble

निरर्थक (*a*) useless, purposeless, insignificant

निरस्त्र (*a*) unarmed, not equipped

निरस्त्रीकरण (*nm*) disarmament

निरा (*a*) mere, single; (*adv*) entirely

निराकरण (*nm*) removing, abrogation

निराकार (*a*) formless, shapeless; (*nm*) God

निरादर (*nm*) disrespect, dishonour, disregard

निराधार (*a*) without support; baseless; groundless

निरापद (*a*) protected, prosperous

निरामिष (*a*) vegetarian

निराला (*a*) strange, excellent, peculiar

निराश (*a*) disappointed; desperate

निराशा (*nf*) hopelessness, disappointment, despondency

निराश्रय (*a*) having no refuge, helpless, shelterless

निराहार (*a & adv*) fasting, without food

निरीक्षक (*nm*) a foreman; an inspector; a superintendent

निरीक्षण (*nm*) observation; supervision

निरीह (*a*) not desiring anything, disinterested

निरुत्तर (*a*) without an answer, unable to answer, wordless

निरुत्साह (*a*) without enthusiasm, cowardly, supine

निरुद्देश्य (*a & adv*) without purpose, aimless

निरोध (*nm*) control; obstruction, restriction, hold

निर्गंध (*a*) devoid of fragrance, without smell

निर्गत (*a*) coming out, departed

निर्गम (*nm*) exit, a going out, departure

निर्गुण (*a*) without qualities; bad

निर्जन (*a*) uninhabited; lonely, solitary

निर्जल (*a*) without water; dry; (*nm*) a desert

निर्जीव (*a*) dead, lifeless, inanimate

निर्णय (*nm*) judgement, conclusion, decision

निर्णायक (*nm*) a judge, umpire; (*a*) critical

निर्दय (*a*) cruel, hard-hearted;

ruthless; —ता cruelty, oppression

निर्दलीय (a) independent

निर्दिष्ट (a) described, pointed out, mentioned

निर्देश (nm) description, order, command; —क director; —न direction

निर्दोष (a) guiltless; correct; harmless; innocent

निर्द्वंद्व (a) carefree

निर्धन (a) moneyless, penniless, indigent, poor; —ता poverty

निर्धारण (nm) settlement; fixation

निर्बल (a) powerless, weak, —ता weakness

निर्बोध (a) ignorent; foolish, stupid

निर्भय (a) fearless, brave, daring

निर्भर (a) dependent, relying on

निर्भीक (a) audacious, fearless; —ता fearlessness, intrepidity

निर्मम (a) ruthless, cruel, heartless; —ता cruelty

निर्मल (a) pure; clear; clean, holy; —ता clearness, cleanness

निर्माण (nm) creation, structure, construction

निर्माता (nm) a builder; creator; constituent; a producer

निर्मित (a) made, constructed, formed

निर्मुक्त (a) free; —करना to unbay, to acquit

निर्मूल (a) rootless, unfounded, baseless; —न ruin, destruction

निर्मोही (a) without affection, cruel, unkind

निर्यात (nm) export

निर्लज्ज (a) immodest, shameless, bare-faced

निर्लज्जता (nf) effrontery; immodesty; shamelessness

निर्लिप्त (a) unconnected, unengrossed, unengaged

निर्लेप (a) sinless, pure

निर्लोभ (nm) absence of greed, unselfishness

निर्वंश (a) without a family, childless

निर्वा/चन (nm) work of selector, election; —चक an elector;

निर्वाचन-क्षेत्र (nm) constituency

निर्वाचित (a) elected

निर्वाण (a) extinguished, liberated from existence

निर्वात (a) without air, unmoving

निर्वासित (a) exiled; expelled, banished

निर्वाह (nm) maintenance; accomplishment

निर्विकल्प (a) fixed; settled

निर्विकार (a) unaltered, passionless, immutable

निर्विघ्न (a) unchecked, unimpeded, uninterrupted; (adv) freely; —ता

immunity, exemption

निर्विरोध (*a & adv*) uncontested, unanimous, unanimously

निर्विवाद (*a*) incontestable, indisputable

निवारक (*a*) hindering; prohibitive; deterrent

निवारण (*nm*) prohibition, hinderance

निवास (*nm*) dwelling, abode, residence; house

निवासी (*a*) inmate, inhabitant, resident

निवेदक (*nm*) applicant; informant

निवेदन (*nm*) a petition; tender

नि:शंक (*a*) dauntless, fearless

निशा (*nf*) night; —कर the moon; —चर a demon

निशान (*nm*) mark, spot, sign; flag; signal

निशा/ना (*nm*) aim; target; —नेबाज़ a marksman; —नेबाज़ी marksmanship

निशानी (*nf*) sign; token; memorial

निश्चय (*nm*) certainty, determination; trust; (*adv*) undoubtedly, really

निश्चिंत (*a*) free, careless; —ता carelessness

निश्चित (*a*) assured, carefree

निश्चेष्ट (*a*) devoid of motion; in a trance; powerless

निश्छल (*a*) without wiles; simple

निश्शंक (*a*) dauntless, intrepid, fearless

निषिद्ध (*a*) prohibited; forbidden; banned

निषेध (*nm*) prohibition; prevention; negation; denial

निष्कर्ष (*nm*) conclusion, substance; essence

निष्काम (*a*) free from any wish; disinterested

निष्का/सन (*nm*) expulsion; —सित expelled

निष्क्रिय (*a*) doing no work, idle —ता idleness

निष्ठा (*nf*) faith, belief; devotion

निष्ठावान् (*nm*) one who fulfils his religious duties, loyal, sincere

निष्ठुर (*a*) harsh, brutal, merciless, cruel; —ता brutality, severity

निष्णात (*a*) very learned; competent; adept

निष्पक्ष (*a*) unbiased, unprejudiced, neutral; —ता neutrality

निष्पाप (*a*) innocent; sinless

निष्प्रभ (*a*) deprived of light; obscure

निष्फल (*a*) unproductive; of no avail, vain

निसर्ग (*nm*) nature, creation of universe

निसार (*a*) sacrificed

निस्तब्ध (*a*) immovable, quiet; —ता silence

निस्तार (*nm*) a passing out,

quittance

निस्तेज (a) spiritless; powerless, cold

निस्पंद (a) motionless, still object

निस्पृह (a) free from desire, contented

निस्संकोच (a) without hesitation

निस्संदेह (adv) certainly, undoubtedly, of course

निस्सहाय (a) helpless; —ता helplessness

निस्सार (a) worthless, having no essence, of no value

निस्स्वार्थ (a) unselfish, selfless; —ता selflessness

निहंग (a) naked, shameless

निहत्था (a) unarmed; —करना to disarm

निहारना (v) to look, to see, to behold

निहित (a) inherent, under-stood, implied

नींद (nf) sleep, slumber

नींव (nf) base; foundation; ground

नीच (a) vulgar, mean, vile; —ता lowness, meanness

नीचा (a) low, down,

नीचे (adv) below, under, down, beneath

नीति (nf) morality; policy; —ज्ञ a statesman, a politi-cian; —मान a moral person; —शास्त्र the science of ethics

नीबू (nm) lime, lemon, citron; —का शर्बत lemonade

नीम (nm) the margosa tree; (a) half, semi; —हकीम (a) quack

नीयत (nf) intention, motive

नीर (nm) water; —ज lotus

नीरव (a) without sound, silent; —ता silence

नीरस (a) devoid of juice or sap, dry, dry flat; uninteresting; hence —ता

नीरोग (a) hale, healthy; free from disease

नील (a) blue; (nm) indigo, woad; mark made on the body by bruise

नीलम (nm) a sapphire

नीला (a) blue, azure

नीलाथोथा (nm) sulphate of copper, blue vitriol

नीलाम (nm) public sale, auction

नीहार (nm) mist, fog

नुकसान (nm) loss; harm; dis-advantage

नुकीला (a) sharp, pointed

नुक्कड़ (nm) a point, a pointed end, protruding corner

नुक्स (nm) flaw, defect; fault

नुमाइंदा (nm) a representative

नुमाइ/श (nf) show, display, exhibition; —शी gaudy, showy, boastful

नुसख़ा (nm) recipe; prescrip-tion

नूतन (a) new; fresh; recent; modern

नूपुर (nm) an ornament for the

ankles, an anklet

नूर (nm) splendour, light

नुत्य (nm) dancing; a dance, —शाला a ball room

नुशंस (a) cruel, tyrannical, harmful; —ता cruelty

नेक (a) gentle, good; —दिल gentle; virtuous; —नीयत of good intentions, honest

नेकी (nf) virtue, goodness

नेता (nm) a pioneer; a leader; —गीरी leadership

नेतृत्व (nm) leadership

नेम (nm) religious practice; routine

नेस्ती (a) lazy; ominous; —पन ominousness

नैतिक (a) pertaining to duty, moral; —ता morality

नैसर्गिक (a) spontaneous; natural

नैहर (nm) a woman's paternal home

नोक (nf) tip; point; end; forepart; —झोंक taunt, mutual repartee

नोचना (v) to pluck; to pinch; to scratch

नोट (nm) paper money; bank note; draft

नोटिस (nm) a notice; a bill

नौ (a) nine; new; (nm) the number nine; (nf) a boat; —जवान a young man; —निहाल the growing generation; —सिखिया a learner, a novice, not well-trained; —सेना navy

नौकर (nm) servant; an employee; —शाही bureaucratic

नौकरी (nf) service, labour for another

नौबत (nf) turn, condition; kettle-drum

न्याय (nm) justice; fairness; logic

न्यायाधीश (nm) justice; judge

न्यायालय (nm) a court of justice, judicature

न्यायोचित (a) equitable, just, fair

न्यारा (a) separate, different; uncommon; unique, peculiar

न्यास (nm) deposit; a trust; —धारी a trustee

न्यून (a) deficient, lacking; less; low

न्यूनता (nf) want, shortage; weakness

न्योता (nm) invitation

न्यौछावर (nm) sacrifice

प

प the first member of the fifth pentad of consonants in Devnagri alphabet

पंक (*nm*) mire, mud, bog, sin

पंकज (*nm*) a lotus

पंक्ति (*nf*) row, line; series; rank

पंख (*nm*) feather; wing; fin

पंखड़ी (*nf*) blade, petal

पंखा (*nm*) fan

पंगु (*a*) lame, crippled

पंच (*a*) five; (*nm*) the number five; council, arbiter, assembly, a juror

पंचकोण (*nm*) a pentagon

पंचफैसला (*nm*) arbitration

पंचायत (*nf*) village assembly; arbitration

पंछी (*nm*) a bird

पंजर (*nm*) a skeleton, the ribs, the bones of human body

पंजा (*nm*) an aggregate of five; claw; paw; palm of hand

पंडित (*nm*) learned, literate, wise, skilful

पंथ (*nm*) a path, a sect; a custom, a religious order

पंथी (*nm*) a traveller; a sectarian, the follower of a sect

पंसारी (*nm*) a grocer

पकड़ (*nf*) hold; seizure; catch; grasp; — धकड़ holding and seizing

पकड़ना (*v*) to seize; to take hold of; to grasp, to catch

पकना (*v*) to be cooked; to ripen

पकवान (*nm*) dressed food, pudding, victuals which are fried in clarified butter

पकाना (*v*) to cook; to fry; to bake; to ripen

पक्का (*a*) strong; prepared, boiled or cooked; expert, clever

पक्ष (*nm*) side; alternative party; a fortnight; wing

पक्ष/पात (*nm*) bias, partiality, partisanship; — पाती a partisan, partial

पक्षाघात (*nm*) palsy, hemiplegia

पक्षीशाला (*nf*) an aviary

पक्षी (*nf*) a bird; aves

पक्ष्म (*nf*) the eye-lashes

पखवाड़ा (*nm*) a period of fifteen days, one half of a lunar month, a fortnight

पखारना (*v*) to wash, to cleanse

पखेरू (*nm*) a bird

पग (*nm*) pace; foot; step; — पग पर at every step

पगडंबी (*nf*) a path, track, foot-path

पगड़ी (*nf*) a turban

पगला (*a*) mad

पगार (*nf*) salary, wages

पचड़ा (*nm*) wrangling, quarrel, disturbance, trouble

पचना (*v*) to be digested; to be

consumed

पचनीय (*a*) digestible

पछताना (*v*) to rue, to repent, to regret, to grieve

पछतावा (*nm*) penitence; repentance, remorse

पछाड़ (*nf*) falling down in a trance; —खाना to fall sense-less on the ground

पछाड़ना (*v*) to throw down, to defeat in wrestling

पट (*nm*) a piece of cloth, a garment; a screen, covering

पटकना (*v*) to knock, to let fall with a jerk, to overthrow

पटकाना (*v*) to dash or beat against a thing

पटना (*v*) to be covered; to be levelled; roof to be made over a well

पटरा (*nm*) a plank, the board of a washerman

पटरानी (*nf*) the queen who is installed with the king, the head queen

पटरी (*nf*) rail; pavement

पटल (*nm*) screen; board; layer

पटवाना (*v*) to have the work of roofing done by some one

पटवारी (*nm*) a person who keeps a record of village accounts

पटसन (*nm*) jute

पटाक (*nm*) a crash, a thump, an explosion

पटाक्षेप (*nm*) curtain fall, ringing down of the curtain;

closing of an affair

पटाखा (*nm*) a cracker; explosion

पटाना (*v*) to level a floor, to repay in full

पटिया (*nf*) a slab of stone, slate; a board

पटु (*a*) clever, smart, skilful

पटुत्व (*nf*) cleverness, dexterity

पटिटका (*nf*) a small board; ribbon

पट्टी (*nf*) a slip, strip, ban-age; wooden plate; —पढ़ाना to misguide; to persuade for selfish motives

पट्ठा (*nm*) full grown youth, a wrestler; flesh, muscle

पठनीय (*a*) able to read, readable

पठान (*nm*) people inhabiting the hilly country in Afghanistan

पठाना (*v*) to send, to dispatch

पठित (*a*) read, recited, studied

पड़ताल (*nf*) survey; investi-gation; search

पड़तालना (*v*) to survey; to investigate; to examine

पड़ना (*v*) to drop, to fall down; to lie on bed

पड़ाव (*nm*) a halting place, a camp

पड़ो/स (*nm*) vicinity, environment, neighbour-hood; —सी a neighbour

पढ़ना (*v*) to study; to read; to recite

पढ़वाना (v) to cause to be read

पढ़ाई (nf) teaching; education; study

पढ़ा (a) well-read, learned; —लिखा literate, educated

पतंग (nm) a bird; a grasshopper; a kite

पतंगा (nm) a moth

पतझर (nm) the fall of leaves, autumn, defoliation

पतन (nm) fall; down fall; decline; ruin, deterioration

पतला (a) thin; slim; lean; weak; —पन thinness; weakness, slimness

पतलून (nf) pantaloon; trousers

पतवार (nf) helm, rudder

पता (nm) address; information

पताका (nf) flag; banner

पति (nm) husband; lord; owner; —त्व ownership, —व्रता faithful, virtuous wife, chaste

पतित (a) degraded; fallen, corrupt, wicked

पतीली (nf) a pan, a kettle, a vessel for boiling

पतोहू (nf) daughter-in-law, son's wife

पत्तल (nf) a plate made of leaves (food served on such a plate)

पत्ता (nm) leaf, blade of grass

पत्ती (nf) a leaf, foliage; share; —दार co-sharer

पत्थर (nm) stone; heartless; hard-hearted

पत्नी (nf) wife, better-half; —व्रत attachment for one's wife only

पत्र (nm) a leaf; a piece of paper; letter; newspaper; —कार the editor of a newspaper; journalist; —वाहक the bearer or carrier of a letter, postman —व्यवहार correspondence

पथ (nm) way, path, road

पथरी (nf) a whetstone; stone in the kidney or bladder

पथ्य (nm) regimen, diet

पद (nm) a word, a foot, a step; rank, status

पदक (nm) a badge, a medal

पदवी (nf) rank, dignity; surname, degree

पदार्थ (nm) stuff, material, a thing

पदोन्नति (nf) promotion

पद्धति (nf) a way, method, system

पद्म (nm) a lotus, a kind of tree like the almond

पधारना (v) to proceed, to arrive at a place; to take leave

पनघट (nm) a quay from which people draw water

पनचक्की (nf) a water-mill

पनडुब्बी (nf) a submarine ship

पनपना (v) to prosper, to flourish, to revive

पनवाड़ी (nm) a seller of betel leaves

पनाला (nm) a drain, a gutter

पनाह (nf) protection, shelter, refuge

पनीर (nm) cheese

पनीला (a) mixed with water

पन्ना (nm) leaf of a book; page; emerald

पपड़ी (nf) the upper hard surface of a thing

पपीहा (nm) the sparrow hawk

पपीता (nm) the papaya fruit

पपोटा (nm) the eyelid

पयोद (nm) a cloud

पयोधर (nm) cloud; udder, female breasts

परंतु (ind) however; but

परंपरा (nm) order, succession; tradition; —गत traditional; —वादी traditionalist; traditional

पर (ind) yet; but; even so; after; (a) distant; other, separate; (nm) feather; —पुरुष a man other than a woman's husband

परकार (nf) a compass

परकोटा (nm) a rampart constructed around a fort

परख (nf) examination, test, inspection

परखना (v) to examine, to assay

परचून (nm) flour, rice etc., grocery; (a) retail

परचूनी (nm) a grocer

परछत्ती (nf) a thatch made over mud-walls

परछाई (nf) shade; shadow; reflection

परजीवी (nm) a parasite; (a) parasitic

परतन्त्र (a) subdued, dependent; —ता reliance; dependence; heteronomy

परत (nf) fold; layer; scale

परती (nf) uncultivated waste land, fallow land

परदा (nm) a screen; a curtain; veil; obstruction

परदादा (nm) great grandfather (paternal)

पर/देश (nm) a country other than one's native land, foreign country; —देशी an alien; stranger, foreigner

परदु:ख (nm) trouble of others

परधाम (nm) Heaven, Paradise

परनाना (nm) great grand father (maternal)

परनाला (nm) a drain, a gutter, a kennel

परपीड़क (nm) one who afflicts pain on others

परम (a) best; supreme; uttermost

परमल (nm) a kind of fried cereal used as food

परमाणु (nm) an atom, —बम an atom bomb; —युद्ध atomic warfare

परमात्मा (nm) the Supereme Spirit, the oversoul; God

परमानंद (nm) the highest pleasure; the blissful soul, God

परमार्थ (nm) the best end, the

subtle truth

परमार्थी (a) one in search of the highest truth; a philosopher

परमेश्वर (nm) God, the Almighty

परराष्ट्र (nm) foreign land, another country

परला (a) of the other side; —सिरा the other end

परलोक (nm) the next world; the other world;—गमन death

परवरदिगार (nm) the Almighty

परवरिश (nf) fostering; protection; patronising

परवर्ती (a) subsequent, later

परवश (a) subservient; dependent; —ता dependence, submission

परवाह (nf) care; concern, anxiety

परशु (nm) an axe, a battle axe

परसना (v) to touch

परसर्ग (nm) a postposition

परसों (ind) the day before yesterday; the day after tomorrow

परस्पर (ind) reciprocal; mutual; (a) each other, one another; —भिन्न diametrically opposed; —मिलन to intermingle; —विरुद्ध inconsistent, irreconcilable; —व्यवहार reciprocity

परहित (nm) beneficence, benevolence

परहेज़ (nm) abstinence; temperance, sobriety

परांठा (nm) a kind of fried cake made in several layers

पराकाष्ठा (nf) the end; the highest degree, climax, peak

पराक्रम (nm) strength, might, power

पराक्रमी (a) valiant, strong, brave, bold

पराग (nm) the pollen of a flower; a fragrant powder used before bathing

पराड्मुख (a) disinclined; backward, averse

पराजय (nf) repulse, defeat

पराजित (a) defeated

पराधीन (a) dependent; subjugated, subjugative —ता dependence

पराभव (nm) disregard, defeat

पराभूत (a) vanquished; defeated; ruined

परामर्श (nm) consultation; discussion, inference; advice; — दाता an advisor

परायण (a) wholly occupied, intent, devoted

पराया (a) pertaining to another; foreign, strange

परार्थ (nm) other's work or business

पराश्रित (a) dependent

परास्त (a) vanquished; defeated; ruined

पराह्न (nm) the afternoon

परिंदा (nm) a bird

परिक्रमा (*nf*) circumambulation; a going round an idol as a mark of reverence

परिचय (*nm*) acquaintance; introduction; —पत्र a letter of introduction; identity-card

परिचर्या (*nf*) service, attendance, tending a sick person

परिचायक (*a*) introductory; (*nm*) one who makes an introduction to a person

परिचा/रक (*nm*) a servant, an attendant, a retainer; —रिका (*nf*) a nurse

परिचित (*a*) known, acquainted with, familiar

परिणति (*nf*) ripeness, end; development

परिणय (*nm*) marriage ।

परिणाम (*nm*) result; effect, issue; —स्वरूप as a result of

परितप्त (*a*) hot, ardent

परिताप (*nm*) heat; affliction; pain

परितापी (*a*) causing pain or sorrow, teasing

परि/तुष्ट (*a*) much pleased, very satisfied, hence —तुष्टि much satisfaction, much pleasure

परितोष (*nm*) gratification, satisfaction; pleasure

परित्यक्त (*a*) abandoned, left off

परित्याग (*nm*) repudiation, abandonment, desertion

परित्रस्त (*a*) terrified

परित्राण (*nm*) a shelter, a protection; deliverance, salvation

परित्राता (*nm*) a saviour, a protector, deliverer

परिधान (*nm*) a dress, a garment, a clothing

परिधि (*nf*) compass, circumference, boundary

परिपक्व (*a*) perfectly ripe; developed, matured

परिपाक (*nm*) digestion; perfection, maturity

परिपाटी (*nf*) a convention; tradition

परिभव (*nm*) disrespect, disregard

परिभाषा (*nf*) definition

परिभाषित (*a*) explained, defined

परिभ्रमण (*nm*) travel, tour, stroll; circulation

परिभ्रष्ट (*a*) degraded, corrupted, sinful

परिमंडल (*nm*) circumference, circle, orbit

परिमल (*nm*) fragrance, sweet scent

परिमाण (*nm*) quantity; measure, size, volume

परिमार्जक (*nm*) one who washes or cleanses

परिमा/र्जन (*nm*) the work of cleansing or washing a thing; —र्जित cleansed, washed

परिमित (a) finite, limited

परिमिति (nf) measure, quantity

परिमेय (a) able to be measured or weighed, limited

परिरक्षण (nm) thorough protection from injury or harm

परिलिखित (a) surrounded by lines

परि/वर्तन (nm) alteration, chang; revolution; —वर्तित changed, altered

परिवर्धन (nm) increase in quantity or number of a thing

परिवहन (nm) transportation

परि/वाद (nm) reproach, abuse; censure, slander; —वादी (a) calumnious, abusive; —वादक one who plays on a guitar

परिवार (nm) family

परिवृत (a) covered, concealed; surrounded

परिवेश (nm) boundary; environment

परिशीलन (nm) a touch, reading a book with attention and thought

परिश्रम (nm) pain; work, labour

परिश्रमी (a) laborious, painstaking

परिषद (nf) an assembly, a meeting, congregation

परि/ष्कार (nm) purification, cleanness, initiation; —ष्कृत cleansed, purified, adorned

परिस्थिति (nf) surroundings, circumstances

परिहार (nm) remedy; avoidance

परिहास (nm) jest, joke, fun, humour; —प्रिय humorous

परी (nf) a fairy, elf, nymph; a very beautiful lady

परीक्षक (nm) an examiner; an experimenter; a judge

परीक्षण (nm) examining; trial

परीक्षा (nf) an examination, test

परीक्षार्थी (nm) an examinee

परुष (a) hard-hearted, cruel, harsh; pitiless

परे (ind) on the other side, apart, above

परेशान (a) troubled, distressed, harassed

परेशानी (nf) distress, perplexity, trouble

परोक्ष (nm) absence; invisibility, (a) invisible, out of sight

परोपकार (nm) charity; beneficence, benevolence

परोपकारी (a) hospitable, benevolent; kind

परोसना (v) to serve food

पर्जन्य (nm) cloud, Indra

पर्चा (nm) a question paper

पर्ची (nf) a slip of paper

पर्यंक (nm) a bed, bedstead

पर्यंत (ind) upto, till, until

पर्यटन (nm) wandering from place to place; roaming; trip

पर्याप्त (a) ample, adequate;

पाटंबर (*nm*) silken cloth

पाटना (*v*) to cover with earth; to roof; to heap

पाटल (*a*) rose-coloured, red; (*nm*) the tree of trumpet flowers

पाठ (*nm*) reading, study, a chapter of a book; recital; —पढ़ाना to teach a lesson

पाठक (*nm*) a reader

पाठन (*nm*) the work of teaching, instructing

पाठशाला (*nf*) a school

पाठांतर (*nm*) variant, version

पाठार्थी (*nm*) a student

पाठित (*a*) taught, instructed

पाठ्य (*a*) worth studying; legible; —पुस्तक a text book; —क्रम syllabus prescribed for certain examinations

पाणि (*nm*) the hand, —ग्रहण act of marriage, a wedding

पातक (*nm*) guilt, sin, misdeed, crime

पातकी (*a*) sinful, peccable; a criminal

पाताल (*nm*) the lower regions, hades, hell

पातिव्रत्य (*nm*) chastity

पात्र (*nm*) a vessel, can, pot; character; a deserving person

पात्रता (*nf*) fitness, capacity, worthiness, propriety

पाथेय (*nm*) provisions stored up for a journey

पाद (*nm*) the foot; a leg; verse; —तल sole of a foot; foot; —प a plant

पादरी (*nm*) padre, clergy, christian priest

पान (*nm*) drinking; liquid food; betel, betel-leaf

पानगोष्ठी (*nf*) a band of drunkers

पानदान (*nm*) a box of metal, in which betel leaf, lime etc. are kept

पाना (*v*) to acquire, to get, to obtain, to receive

पानी (*nm*) water; liquid substance; temper

पाप (*nm*) guilt, sin, evil; crime

पापकर्म (*nm*) a sinful act

पापग्रह (*nm*) an inauspicious planet

पापड़ (*nm*) a thin crisp cake which is made of several kinds of pulse

पापत्व (*nm*) impiety, criminality, sinfulness

पापदर्शी (*a*) one who sees with a wicked intention

पापबुद्धि (*a*) wicked, depraved, sinful

पापात्मा (*a*) unholy, sinful; (*nm*) a sinner, an unholy person

पापाशय (*a*) wicked, sinful

पापी (*a*) evil, immoral, sinful, criminal (*nm*) a sinner, a criminal

पाबंद (*a*) tied, bound, dependent

पाबंदी (*nf*) restriction, restraint

पामर (a) low, wicked, vile, sinful

पायजामा (nm) trousers, pantaloons

पायजेब (nf) an anklet, an ornament for the ankles (see पाजेब)

पायदार (a) strong, steady; durable

पायदारी (nf) stability, durability

पायल (nf) an ornament for the ankles

पाया (v) past tense of the verb पाना, to get, to obtain; (nm) a leg of a piece of furniture

पारंगत (a) conversant or versed in a subject; proficient

पार (nm) end, limit, extremity; opposite side of a river

पारखी (nm) an examiner

पारतंत्र्य (nm) dependence, subordination, reliance

पारदर्शक (a) clear, transparent; —ता transparence

पारदर्शी (a) seeing the opposite shore; farseeing, shrewd, skilful

पारमार्थिक (a) pertaining to spiritual object, immortal

पारलौकिक (a) relating to the next world, ultramundane

पारस (nm) the philosopher's stone which is believed to convert a baser metal into gold by a mere touch; (a) healthy

पारस्परिक (a) concomitant, mutual, reciprocal

पारा (nm) mercury, quicksilver

पारायण (nm) work of finishing, end, completion; reading a book from the beginning to the end

पारावार (nm) limit; boundary; the ocean

पारिजात (nm) the coral tree; a tree of Paradise obtained from the churning of the ocean

पारितोषिक (nm) reward, prize

पारिभाषिक (a) technical; —शब्द technology, technical terms

पारिवारिक (a) pertaining to the family

पारिश्रमिक (nm) remuneration, allowance

पारिषद (nm) a councillor, a senator

पारी (nf) turn, time; shift

पारु (nm) fire; the Sun

पारुष्य (nm) roughness of speech, abuse

पार्थक्य (nm) separation, difference

पार्थिव (a) earthen, made of earth; material

पार्श्व (nm) nearness; neighbourhood; part of the body below the armpit

पार्षद (nm) a servant, a courtier

पाल (nm) the process of ripening fruits by keeping

them under the layers of straw; the sail

पालक (nm) protector, a guardian; a kind of spinach

पालकी (nf) a sedan; —गाड़ी a coach

पालतू (a) domesticated, tame

पालन (nm) protection, cherishing, tending; —पोषण support, nurture

पालना (v) to tame; to foster; to feed; to bring up

पालना (nm) a swing, a cradle, a cot

पाला (nm) hoar frost; (a) brought up

पालिश (nf) polish

पाली (nf) shift; turn

पाँव (nm) leg; foot

पावक (a) purifying, pure; (nm) fire, heat, the Sun

पावन (a) holy, pure; —ता purification

पाश (nm) a net or noose, tie; snare, trap

पाशविक (a) beast-like, brutal, savage

पाश्चात्य (a) belonging to the west, western

पाषाण (nm) stone

पास (nm) side, nearness, proximity; —जाना to go near

पासा (nm) a die; dice

पाहुना (nm) a guest, a newcomer

पिंगल (a) yellow, tawny; (nm) science of prosody

पिंजड़ा (nm) a cage, trap

पिंजर (nm) a cage; skeleton of body

पिंड (nm) a round mass, lump

पिंडली (nf) the calf of a leg

पिघलना (v) to dissolve, to thaw, to be melted; to flow

पिघलाना (v) to dissolve, to cause to be melted

पिघलाव (nm) melting

पिचकना (v) to be squeezed, to be dented

पिचकारी (nf) a syringe, a pump

पिचपिचा (a) flabby, watery

पिछड़ना (v) to remain behind, to lag, to be left behind

पिछलगा (nm) the work of following a person

पिछला (a) hinder, hind; back, previous; latter

पिछवाड़ा (nm) back part of the house, the rear or hinder part

पिटना (v) to be defeated; to be beaten; to flop

पिटरिया (nf) a small box

पिटाई (nf) beating; stroke; work or wages for beating

पिटारा (nm) a large basket

पिटारी (nf) a small basket

पिट्ठू (a & nm) helper, follower, supporter; toady

पितर (nm) forefather, parents, ancestors

पिता (nm) father, dad

पितामह (nm) grand father

पितामही (nf) grand mother

पितृ (*nm*) father; —ऋण one of the three debts on a man from which he is freed when he begets a son; —कुल paternal family; —भक्ति filial attachment

पित्त (*nm*) gall, bile; bilious, humour

पिपासा (*nf*) craving, thirst; greediness; desire

पियक्कड़ (*nm*) a drunkard

पिरोना (*v*) to string, to thread

पिल्ला (*nm*) a puppy, a pup

पिशाच (*nm*) demon, devil, evil spirit

पिस्ता (*nm*) pistachio-nut

पिस्तौल (*nf*) revolver, pistol

पिस्सू (*nm*) a flea

पीकदान (*nm*) a cuspidor

पीछ (*nm*) the back; the rear; —करना to chase, to hunt, to follow; —छुड़ाना to get rid of

पीछे (*adv*) afterwards, after; in the absence of

पीटना (*v*) to thrash; to beat; to strike; to flog; to defeat

पीठ (*nf*) the back; (*nm*) a seat, bench

पीठिका (*nf*) background; seat, base

पीड़ा (*nf*) anguish, aching, woe, trouble, pain

पीड़ित (*a*) oppressed; sick; ill

पीतल (*nf*) brass

पीतांबर (*nm*) yellow silk cloth; yellow silk clothes worm at the time of worship; Lord Vishnu

पीना (*v*) to drink; to smoke; to conceal a secret; to absorb

पीप (*nm*) pus, purulent matter coming from a wound

पीपा (*nm*) tub, a cask, a barrel

पीपल (*nm*) the pipal tree

पीर (*nf*) pain, trouble, ache; (*nm*) a muslim saint

पीला (*a*) yellow; pale, pallid; ashen; —पन yellowness

पीलिया (*nm*) chlorosis, jaundice

पी लेना (*v*) to drink; to swallow

पीसना (*v*) to pound, to grind; to reduce to powder; to gnash the teeth

पीहर (*nm*) the father's family of a married woman, maternal kins-folk

पुंगीफल (*nm*) the betel-nut

पुं/ज (*nm*) mass; heap; collection; —जीभूत heaped together, massed together

पुंडरीक (*nm*) white lotus; a lion; a white elephant

पुंस्त्व (*nm*) manhood, virility

पुआ (*nm*) a sweet cake

पुआल (*nm*) straw of paddy

पुकार (*nf*) call; cry, shout; invitation

पुकारना (*v*) to call out; to exclaim, to shout

पुखराज (*nm*) topaz

पुख्ता (*a*) durable; strong; firm

पुचकार (*nf*) encouragement

पुचकारना (*v*) to produce a hissing sound from lips, to

fondle, to love

पुच्छल तारा (*nm*) a comet

पुजारी (*nm*) a worshipper, a Hindu priest

पुण्य (*nm*) meritorious action, happiness, merit, virtue; —काल auspicious moment; —कर्म meritorious action; — क्षेत्र a holy place

पुण्यात्मा (*a*) pious, virtuous, religious, saintly, holy

पुतला (*nm*) an idol, an image; an effigy, a lay figure

पुतली (*nf*) a doll, a puppet; pupil of the eye

पुताई (*nf*) white washing, the wages paid for white washing

पुत्र (*nm*) a son; —वधू son's wife, daughter-in-law of a person

पुत्री (*nf*) daughter

पुदीना (*nm*) garden mint, mint

पुन: (*a*) again, also, on the contrary, afterwards; —कथन repetition; —पुन: again and again; —स्थापना re-instatement

पुनरागमन (*nm*) recurrence, return

पुनरा/वृत्ति (*nf*) repetition, revision of statement; —वृत्त told a second time

पुनर्गठन (*nm*) reorganisation

पुनर्जागरण (*nm*) restoration; renaissance

पुनर्निर्माण (*nm*) reproduction, reconstruction

पुनर्वास (*nm*) rehabilitation

पुनीत (*a*) pure, clean; holy

पुरज़ा (*nm*) a piece, fragment; bill; part of a machine

पुरस्कार (*nm*) reward, prize

पुरस्कृत (*a*) rewarded, respected

पुराण (*a*) old, ancient; (*nm*) tale of by-gone ages; an ancient literature of Hindu mythology

पुरातत्त्व (*nm*) archaeology

पुरातन (*a*) old, ancient, aboriginal, mythological

पुराना (*a*) ancient, old, old-fashioned; antiquated

पुरी (*nf*) a city; the city of Jagannath

पुरुष (*nm*) male, man; mankind; —त्व manhood; virility, masculinity

पुरुषार्थ (*nm*) labour, energy, exertion

पुरुषार्थी (*a*) energetic; industrious; strong, vigorous

पुरुषोत्तम (*nm*) an epithet of the god Vishnu

पुरोहित (*nm*) a family priest of Hindus

पुरोहिताई (*nf*) the functions of a family priest

पुल (*nm*) a bridge

पुलक (*nm*) horripilation, thrill

पुलकित (*a*) rejoiced; —होना to thrill, to bristle

पुलटिस (*nm*) poultice

पुलाव (*nm*) a kind of dish made of rice boiled in soup and spices

पुलिंदा (*nm*) a bundle; a parcel; a sheaf of corn

पुलिया (*nf*) a culvert

पुलिस (*nf*) police; —मैन a constable

पुश्त (*nf*) back portion; back side of generation, ancestry

पुश्तैनी (*a*) ancestral, hereditary, traditional

पुष्कर (*nm*) a pond; a lotus; the fore part of an elephant's trunk, holy place of Hindus

पुष्टता (*nm*) lustiness, strength

पुष्टि (*nf*) nourishment; maintenance; confirmation

पुष्ट (*a*) able-bodied, strong; nourished, stiff

पुष्टिकर (*a*) causing growth, nourishing; —ओषधि nutriment

पुष्टिवर्धक (*a*) nutritious

पुष्प (*nm*) a flower, a blossom; —केसर stamen; —मय flowery; —राग pollen

पुष्पित (*a*) flowering, blossomed, filled with flowers

पुष्पोद्यान (*nm*) a garden of flowers

पुस्तक (*nf*) a book

पुस्तकालय (*nm*) a library, —का अध्यक्ष librarian

पुस्तिका (*nf*) a pamphlet

पूँछ (*nf*) tail of a beast, the back part of an object

पूँजी (*nf*) capital; investment; —पति a capitalist

पूँजी/वाद (*nm*) capitalism; —वादी a capitalist

पूछ (*nm*) inquiry, investigation; respect; —ताछ investigation, inquiry

पूछना (*v*) to ask; to enquire; to question

पूजक (*nm*) a votary, worshipper, an adorer

पूजन (*nm*) worship, adoring

पूजना (*v*) to adore, to worship, to respect

पूजनीय (*a*) venerable, respectable, fit for being worshipped

पूजा (*nf*) homage, reverence, worship, —करना to adore, to worship, to glorify

पूजित (*a*) venerated, adored, respected, worshipped

पूज्य (*a*) worthy, sacred, respected, venerable; —पाद one whoose feet are worth adoring, very respectable

पूत (*nm*) a son; (*a*) clean, pure; sincere, true

पूतात्मा (*nm*) a saint, an ascetic, one who is purified by ablution

पूनी (*nf*) a roll of cotton prepared for spinning thread

पूरक (*nm*) a supplement; (*a*) completing, supplementary

पूरना (v) to complete, to fill; to make up a deficiency

पूरब (nm) the east quarter

पूरबी (a) eastern

पूरा (a) all, entire, complete; full; total

पूरी (nf) unleavened cake fried in clarified butter

पूर्ण (a) perfect; complete, whole; full; finished; —कालिक whole-timer; —विराम full stop; —काम having the desire fulfilled or satisfied

पूर्णत: (adv) fully, completely, entirely

पूर्णत्व (nf) completeness; perfection; totality

पूर्णांक (nm) maximum marks; an integer

पूर्णिमा (nf) a full-moon day

पूर्ति (nf) completion

पूर्व (nm) the east; (a) previous, fore, former; (adv) before; —अधिकार preoccupation; —अवस्था में लाना to renew; —कथित aforesaid; —कालीन whilom, formerly; —गामी preceding, prior; —ज ancestor (s), fore-father (s); —रूप previous form; —वर्ती previous, prior, happening before

पूर्वानुमान (nm) estimate; forecast

पूर्वार्द्ध/पूर्वार्ष (a) the first/former half

पूर्वावस्था (nf) pre-stage; initial stage

पूर्वी (a) eastern

पूर्वोक्ति (a) mentioned above, aforesaid

पृथक् (a) irrespective; peculiar; separate; diverse; —भाग fragment; unit; —करण separation

पृथु (a) wide, large; innumerable

पृथ्वी (nf) the earth, ground, land; —नाथ a king

पृष्ट (a) asked, enquired

पृष्ठ (nm) page; the back; the rear, the hind part of anything; —भाग back surface, —त: from behind; —पोषक a helper, one who backs, supporter

पेंग (nf) oscillation of a swing; —मारना to be tossed from one side to the other, to swing

पेंडल (nm) a pendant

पेंदा (nm) base; the bottom

पेच (nm) coil, screw, part of a machine; intricacy

पेचदार (a) screwed; intricate, complex

पेचिश (nf) dysentery

पेचीदगी (nf) perplexity; intricacy; complexity

पेचीदा (a) coiled, twisted; difficult, intricate

पेट (nm) abdomen, belly, stomach; —भर (a) belly-

full; —भरना (v) to be
satiated —पालना to subsist

पेटी (nf) a small box; a chest, a
belt

पेटीकोट (nm) a petticoat

पेटू (a) varacious, ravenous,
gluttonous; (nm) a glutton

पेठा (nm) a kind of gourd

पेड़ (nm) a tree; —पौधे trees
and plants

पेड़ा (nm) a kind of sweetmeat
made of milk; a globular
mass of kneaded flour

पेय (nm) a beverage; (a)
drinkable

पेरना (v) to press something in
a machine, to crush; to
torment

पेलना (v) to push, to thrust in;
to press

पेश (adv) before, in front of;
—करना to present

पेशगी (nf) advance, advance
money

पेशतर (ind) formerly, before,
heretofore

पे/शा (nm) trade; profession, a
work, occupation; —शेवर
an artisan, a workman

पेशानी (nf) brow, forehead; lot,
fate

पेशाब (nm) urine, —खाना urinal

पेशी (nf) a muscle, hearing of a
law suit

पैंतरा (nm) see पैतरा

पैगम्बर (nm) a prophet, an
apostle, a messenger of
God

पैगाम (nm) a message, a
mission

पैठ (nf) penetration; access;
enterance

पैठना (v) to enter; to pierce; to
rush in, to access

पैड़ी (nf) a ladder, a staircase

पैतरा (nm) the preparatory
movements of a wrestler;
counter move

पैतरे/बाज़ (nm) a strategist,
dodger; —बाज़ी dodge,
strategy

पैताना (nm) the foot part of
any thing

पैतृक (a) paternal; ancestral,
hereditary; —धन patri-
mony; —भूमि fatherland;
—सम्पत्ति inheritance

पैदल (a) walking on foot;
(nm) infantry; —चलनेवाला
pedestrian, —सिपाही kern,
infantry; —यात्रा tramp

पैदा (a) born; produced;
created; discovered; (nm)
gain, income

पैदाइश (nf) birth, existence;
production; creation

पैदाइशी (a) inborn, natural,
innate, implanted by
nature

पैदावार (nf) produce of land,
crop, harvest; production

पैना (a) fine-pointed, sharp;
(nm) the goad of a
ploughman

पैबंद (*nm*) a patch

पैमाइश (*nf*) surveying, measurement or survey of land

पैमाना (*nm*) an instrument for measuring, a scale, a meter

पैयाँ (*nf*) the foot

पैर (*nm*) leg, foot; footprint; step

पैरवी (*nf*) pleading; advocacy; —करना to advocate; to pursue; to support; —कार a supporter, a follower

पैशाचिक (*a*) infernal, demoniacal, horrible

पैसा (*nm*) pice; wealth; पैसेवाला a wealthy person

पोंछना (*v*) to rub out; to wipe; to efface; to clean

पोच (*a*) mean, worthless, weak

पोटली (*nf*) a bale, a small bundle, a package

पोत (*nm*) a ship; a big boat

पोतना (*v*) to white-wash; to coat

पोता (*nm*) grandson, son's son; a white washing

पोती (*nf*) grand daughter. son's daughter

पोथा (*nm*) a book of large size; manuscript written on long separate leaves

पोथी (*nf*) a book

पोदीना (*nm*) mint

पोपला (*a*) toothless; (*nm*) a toothless person

पोर (*nm*) the space which lies between two joints, a gnarl; अंगुली का— knuckle

पोल (*nf*) an empty space, hollowness, agate; —खुलना disclosure of a secret

पोला (*a*) hollow, empty

पोशाक (*nf*) dress, clothes, raiment, garment, habiliment

पोशीबा (*a*) concealed, hidden

पोषक (*a*) a nourisher; a supporter

पोषण (*nm*) nourishing, cherishing, nutrition; assistance; supporting

पोषित (*a*) reared, nourished

पोसना (*v*) to pet, to rear, to nourish

पोस्त (*nm*) poppy plant; poppy seed

पोस्ती (*a*) one who intoxicates himself with infusion of poppy heads; idle (man)

पोस्तीन (*nm*) a garment which is made of leather covered with fine hairs

पौ (*nf*) early dawn; a ray of light

पौत्र (*nm*) a son's son, a grand son

पौत्री (*nf*) a son's daughter, a grand daughter

पौद (*nf*) a small plant; a transplanted seedling, a sapling

पौधा (*nm*) a young plant, a sapling

पौन (nm) three-fourth, three quarters

पौना (nm) a ladle with a long handle; (a) three quarters; three fourth

पौनी (nf) a low caste people who get tips on festive occasion; a small ladle

पौर (a) pertaining to a city

पौराणिक (a) old, pertaining to tradition; —कथा legend, mythological tales, —ता mythology

पौरुष (nm) manhood, masculinity; vigour

पौरुषेय (a) manly, performed by man; vigorous

पौष्टिक (a) tonic; nutritive

प्याऊ (nf) a waterbooth

प्याज़ (nm) onion

प्याज़ी (a) of light rosy colour

प्यादा (nm) a foot-soldier, a messenger

प्यार (nm) love; affection; attachment

प्यारा (a) dear, beloved, lovely

प्याला (nm) a cup

प्याली (nf) a small cup

प्यास (nf) thirst; eager; desire; —बुझाना to quench thirst; —लगना to be thirsty

प्यासा (a) thirsty, athirst

प्रकंप (nm) trembling, shivering

प्रकट (a) clear; manifest; apparent; evident

प्रकटित (a) displayed, manifested, evident

प्रकंपन (nm) quivering

प्रकंपित (a) quivered, trembled

प्रकरण (nm) subject, context; topic

प्रकर्ष (nm) superiority, excellence, eminence

प्रकांड (a) eminent; leading

प्रकार (nm) kind, quality; method, mode

प्रकारंतर (nm) a different method or manner

प्रकाश (nm) light; splendour, lustre

प्रकाशक (nm) an illuminator, discoverer; a publisher

प्रकाशन (nm) illuminating; publication

प्रकाशमान (a) shining, resplendent, brilliant, radiant

प्रकाशित (a) manifest; evident; apparent; published

प्रकाश्य (a) requiring to be manifested or published

प्रकीर्ण (a) extended, exposed; scattered; miscellaneous

प्रकीर्ति (nf) celebrity, fame

प्रकुपित (a) extremely angry; enraged; agitated

प्रकृत (a) true, real genuine; natural, —वादी a naturalist

प्रकृति (nf) nature; habit, disposition, temprament; —वाद naturalism; —वादी a naturalist; naturalistic; —शास्त्र the study of nature; —सिद्ध natural

प्रकोप (nm) excessive wrath;

agitation; disturbed condition of the body

प्रकोष्ठ (*nm*) a side room near, the main gate of a house, a big court yard; a bracket

प्रक्रम (*nm*) beginning; series

प्रक्रिया (*nf*) manner, observance, method of performance

प्रक्षालन (*nm*) cleansing, washing

प्रक्षालित (*a*) washed, cleansed

प्रक्षिप्त (*a*) cast forth; thrown; projected

प्रक्षेप (*nm*) throwing; scattering; mixing, adding

प्रखर (*a*) fierce, sharp; keen; hot

प्रख्यात (*a*) renowned, well-known, illustrious, famous, reputed

प्रगटना (*v*) to be manifested; to appear, to come to view

प्रगति (*nf*) development; progress; —वाद progressivism; —वादी progressivist, —शील progressive

प्रगल्भ (*a*) bold, impertinent, active

प्रगाढ़ (*a*) much, excessive, profound, deep

प्रचंड (*a*) furious, violent, terrible, fierce; daring, bold

प्रचंडता (*nf*) violence, fierceness

प्रचलन (*nm*) prevalence; custom; movement; usage

प्रचलित (*a*) prevailing, current, common, in usage

प्रचार (*nm*) propaganda; publicity; use

प्रचारक (*nm*) a propagator; a herald, a proclaimer

प्रचारित (*a*) proclaimed, made known

प्रचुर (*a*) abundant, plentiful, enough

प्रचुरता (*nf*) plenty, abundance

प्रचोदित (*a*) agitated; excited

प्रच्छन्न (*a*) concealed; covered, hidden; secret

प्रच्छादन (*nm*) a cover, covering; concealing

प्रच्छेद्य (*a*) fit to be lopped off

प्रजनन (*nm*) birth, midwifery

प्रजा (*nf*) a subject; public; —तंत्र democracy; —तांत्रिक democratic; —पति lord of creation; a king

प्रज्ञप्ति (*nf*) hint, suggestion

प्रज्ञा (*nf*) wisdom, intellect; understanding

प्रज्ञात (*a*) understood, known

प्रज्वलन (*nm*) the act of burning a thing

प्रज्वलित (*a*) blazing, burning

प्रण (*nm*) a pledge, vow; resolution, promise

प्रणम्य (*a*) fit to be reverenced

प्रणय (*nm*) love between man and woman, sexual love; affection

प्रणयी (*nm*) a lover, a husband

प्रणयन (*nm*) composition,

writing

प्रणव (nm) God, the holy monosyllable Om; absolutely new

प्रणाम (nm) salutation; bowing with respect; a term used in greeting elders

प्रणाली (nf) a method, system

प्रणेता (nm) creator; author

प्रताप (nm) dignity, glory; splendour

प्रतापी (a) glorious, powerful, famous, dignified

प्रति (nf) a copy; an inseparable prefix used in the following senses — instead of, each, every, equal, again, likeness

प्रतिकार (nm) retaliation, revenge; return

प्रतिकूल (a) opposite; contrary; inverted; unfavourable

प्रतिकृति (nf) an image, a picture; reflection

प्रति/क्रिया (nf) return, reaction; —क्रियात्मक reactivative; —क्रियावादी reactionary

प्रतिक्षण (adv) at every moment, constantly

प्रतिक्षेप (nm) obstruction

प्रतिघात (nm) a counter blow, concussion

प्रतिघाती (nm) foe, an enemy; a hostile person

प्रतिच्छाया (nf) a reflected image, shadow; a picture

प्रतिज्ञा (nf) a vow; promise;

resolution; —पत्र a bond, a written contract

प्रतिदान (nm) returning a thing deposited, an exchange

प्रतिदिन (ind) daily, every day

प्रतिद्वंद्व (nm) mutual struggle; contest; conflict

प्रतिद्वंद्वी (nm) a competitor; a rival; an opponent; an enemy

प्रतिध्वनि (nf) echo of a sound, repetition

प्रतिनिधि (nm) a deputy, an agent to a person; —त्व agency, substitution

प्रतिपक्ष (nm) rival side, opposition, contesting party

प्रतिपक्षी (nm) an adversary, an opponent, a competitor

प्रतिपादक (nm) one who makes a demonstration

प्रतिपादन (nm) ascertainment, thorough knowledge, proof, donation

प्रतिपादित (a) established; ascertained

प्रतिपालक (nm) a benefactor, a patron, a guardian

प्रतिपालन (nm) fostering, rearing, nourishing, protection

प्रतिफल (nm) result, conclusion

प्रतिबंध (nm) obstruction, impediment, restriction

प्रतिबिंब (nm) a shadow; an image; a reflection in a

looking glass

प्रतिभा (nf) intellect, sharpness of understanding, genius —शाली endowed with genius, most intelligent

प्रतिमा (nf) an image, an idol of a deity

प्रतिमान (nm) a pattern, example; standard

प्रतियोगिता (nf) rivalry, competition, emulation; contest; match

प्रतियोगी (nm) a competitor, rival

प्रतिरूप (nm) an image, a picture

प्रति/रक्षा (nf) defence; —रक्षात्मक defensive

प्रतिरोध (nm) obstruction, hindrance; opposition

प्रतिलिपि (nf) a copy of something, a facsimile

प्रतिलोम (a) inverted, reverse; opposite

प्रतिवाद (nm) a controversy, counter-statement

प्रतिशत (ind) percent

प्रतिशोध (nm) retaliation, revenge

प्रतिषेध (nm) rejection, prohibition, forbiddance

प्रतिष्ठा (nf) installation; honour; dignity, prestige

प्रतिष्ठित (a) established, respected

प्रतिस्पर्धा (nf) emulation, competition, rivalry

प्रतिस्पर्धी (nm) a rival, a competitor

प्रतिहिंसा (nf) retaliation, revenge

प्रतीक (nm) a mark, a sign; a symbol; —वाद symbolism; —वादी symbolical

प्रती/क्षा (nf) expectation; wait; —क्षालय a waiting room

प्रतीत (a) appeared; known

प्रत्यक्ष (a) cognizable by sight, visible, tangible; apparent

प्रत्यय (nm) credit; concept; suffix; —पत्र letter of credence

प्रत्याख्यान (nm) refutation, contradiction

प्रत्यावर्तन (nm) a return, a coming back

प्रत्याशा (nf) hope, expectation

प्रत्याशी (nm) an expectant; a candidate

प्रत्याह्वान (nm) recall, calling back

प्रत्युत (ind) but, contrary to, against

प्रत्युत्तर (nm) reply to an answer, a rejoinder, a retort

प्रत्युत्पन्न (a) reproduced, prompt

प्रत्युपकार (nm) return of service for a kindness

प्रत्येक (a) every, one by one

प्रथम (a) first, chief; initial; —तः firstly; previously

प्रथा (nf) custom, rule

प्रदक्षिणा (nf) walking round a

revered person or temple

प्रदत्त (a) granted, bestowed

प्रदर्शन (nm) display, exhibiting, demonstrating

प्रदर्शनी (nf) a public exhibition

प्रदर्शित (a) exhibited; displayed; showed

प्रदहन (nm) burning completely

प्रदाता (nm & a) a bestower, giver

प्रदान (nm) a gift, a giving in marriage

प्रदीप्त (a) lighted; resplendent

प्रदीप्ति (nf) light, brightness

प्रदेश (nm) a country; a territory, a region

प्रदोष (nm) evening, sunset; guilt or sin

प्रधान (nm) a chief, president; (a) principal, head; —मंत्री the prime minister

प्रधानता (nf) superiority; leadership; pre-eminence

प्रपंच (nm) fraud; the world, creation

प्रपंची (a) artful; deceitful, fraudulent, cunning

प्रपात (nm) a waterfall; a falling down of something

प्रपौत्र (nf) a great grandson

प्रबंध (nm) arrangement; management; —कर्ता a manager

प्रबल (a) strong, mighty; violent; powerful

प्रबुद्ध (a) awake, roused, expanded, wise, learned; —ता thorough knowledge

प्रबोध (nm) awakening from sleep, wakefulness

प्रभात (nm) the time of early morning, dawn

प्रभा (nf) light, lustre, radiance

प्रभाव (nm) effect; influence; might, power

प्रभावित (a) influenced; impressed

प्रभु (nm) lord, God, master, owner

प्रभुत्व (nm) superiority, lordship; dignity

प्रभूत (a) abundant, plentiful, over, much

प्रभृति (ind) the rest, and so forth

प्रभेद (nm) difference; sort, kind

प्रमाण (nm) proof; authority; —पत्र a certificate

प्रमाणित (a) authentically proved; certified

प्रमाद (nm) negligence, an error, a mistake; —पूर्ण careless

प्रमादी (a) negligent, careless; erring, confused

प्रमुख (a) first, best, chief

प्रमुदित (a) delighted, pleased, glad, very happy

प्रमेय (nm) fit to be used as a universal statement

प्रमोद (nm) pleasure, hilarity, delight, happiness

प्रयत्न (nm) an exertion; an effort; an action, attempt

प्रयाण (nm) voyage, departure; attack

प्रयास (nm) attempt; effort; labour, exertion

प्रयुक्त (a) used, applied

प्रयोक्ता (nm) user; an employer for a work

प्रयोग (nm) an experiment; exercise

प्रयोगत: (adv) practically

प्रयोजक (nm) one who performs an action, a stimulator

प्रयोजन (nm) motive, purpose; occasion

प्रयोज्य (a) suitable, fit to be used

प्रलंब (a) hanging, dilatory

प्रलय (nf) dissolution, final destruction of the universe

प्रलाप (nm) useless talk, useless gossip

प्रलेप (nm) an ointment

प्रलेपन (nm) the work of an ointing or besmearing

प्रलोप (nm) ruin, destruction

प्रलोभन (nm) temptation, allurement; attraction

प्रलोभित (a) enticed

प्रवंचना (nf) cheeting, fraud, deceipt

प्रवक्ता (nm) an eloquent speaker, a propounder of sacred texts

प्रवचन (nm) an explanation of the text

प्रवचनीय (a) explainable

प्रवर (a) eminent, chief, superior

प्रवर्त्तक (nm) a founder, an instigator

प्रवर्तन (nm) resolution, establishment, persuasion

प्रवर्तित (a) commenced, begun

प्रवाद (nm) rumour; false accusation

प्रवास (nm) residence in a foreign land, dwelling abroad; migration

प्रवासी (nm) a migrant

प्रवाह (nm) a stream of water, a current; flow

प्रविष्ट (a) entered, engaged in

प्रवीण (a) expert, competent, skilful

प्रवीणता (nf) proficiency

प्रवृत्त (a) inclined, determined; engaged in a work

प्रवृत्ति (nf) tendency; a continuous flow, inclination of mind; activity

प्रवेक्षण (nm) forseeing

प्रवेक्षित (a) anticipated

प्रवेश (nm) entrance, admission; —पत्र an admission ticket;—शुल्क admission fee

प्रशंसक (nm) one who praises; (a) praising

प्रशंसनीय (a) worthy of praise, laudable

प्रशंसा (nf) applause; praise; eulogy

प्रशस्त (a) vest; wide

प्रशस्ति (*nf*) praise, excellence; inscription on copper plates

प्रशांत (*a*) calm; peaceful, quiet

प्रशाखा (*nf*) a twig or small branch of a tree

प्रशास/न (*nm*) rule; administration; —क ruler; administrator

प्रशिक्षण (*nm*) training

प्रश्न (*nm*) a question; an enquiry; a problem; —कर्ता an interrogator; —पत्र a question paper; —माला questionnaire

प्रश्नोत्तर (*nm*) question and answer

प्रश्रय (*nm*) a place of shelter, an object of support

प्रष्टव्य (*a*) enquirable, enquiring

प्रसंग (*nm*) context, connection; occasion; sexual intercourse

प्रसक्त (*a*) attached, devoted

प्रसन्न (*a*) delighted, pleased, rejoiced

प्रसन्नता (*nf*) happiness, joy, pleasure

प्रसव (*nm*) child-birth, delivery, progeny

प्रसाद (*nm*) boon; blessing; gift, kindness

प्रसाधन (*nm*) make-up; cosmetics

प्रसार (*nm*) extent, scattering, expansion

प्रसारण (*nm*) spreading; broadcasting; extending outwardly

प्रसारित (*a*) spread, extended, broadcast

प्रसिद्ध (*a*) renowned, famous, well-known

प्रसिद्धि (*nf*) fame, reputation, renown

प्रसुप्त (*a*) sleeping, asleep

प्रसूत (*a*) born, delivered, produced

प्रसून (*nm*) a blossom, flower

प्रस्ताव (*nm*) a preliminary discourse, a suggestion, resolution; proposal

प्रस्तावना (*nf*) prologue to a play; introduction

प्रस्तावित (*a*) projected, proposed

प्रस्तुत (*a*) mentioned, declared; praised

प्रस्थान (*nm*) a journey, departure

प्रस्थापन (*nm*) establishment

प्रस्थापित (*a*) well-established

प्रस्फुटन (*nm*) manifest; blooming

प्रस्फुरण (*nm*) coming out, emanation

प्रहर (*nm*) the eighth part of a day, a period of three hours

प्रहरी (*nm*) a guard, watchman

प्रहर्षित (*a*) merry, delighted

प्रहसन (*nm*) a comedy; mockery

प्रहार (*nm*) a blow, a stroke

with fist; a kick

प्रहास (nm) a loud laughter

प्रहेलिका (nf) a riddle, an enigma

प्रांगण (nm) the courtyard in the middle of a house

प्रांजल (a) straight, plain; true; —ता clarity; refinement

प्रां/त (nm) territory; country; —तीय provincial, territorial

प्राकार (nm) a rampart; a surrounding wall

प्राकृत (a) low, unrefined, common

प्राकृतिक (a) nature made; unrefined

प्रागैतिहासिक (a) pre-historical

प्राची (nf) the east, the orient

प्राचीन (a) old, ancient; antique; outdated; —तर older; earlier; —तम most ancient; earliest; —ता antiquity, ancientness

प्राचुर्य (nm) abundance, plenty

प्राच्य (a) east, eastern; oriental

प्राज्ञ (a) intelligent, brilliant; prudent

प्राण (nm) one of the five vital-airs; breath, life; vitality; soul; —का ग्राहक a seeker after one's life; —दण्ड punishment of death; —दाता lifegiver; —धन beloved, as dear as life; —धारी a living being, a creature; —नाथ master of life; —शक्ति vitality; —हानि loss of life;

—हीन lifeless, inanimate

प्राणवान (a) animated, full of vitality; powerful

प्राणांत (nm) the end of life, death

प्राणी (nm) a sentient being, a creature; a man

प्राणेश्वर (nm) darling, beloved; husband

प्रात: (nm) dawn, early in the morning

प्राथमिक (a) elementary; primary, initial

प्रादुर्भाव (nm) appearance, coming into existence; manifestation; birth, rise

प्रादुर्भूत (a) born, manifested

प्रादेशिक (a) pertaining to a place or country; regional, territorial

प्रादेशिकता (a) regionalism

प्राधान्य (nm) superiority, supremacy

प्राध्यापक (nm) lecturer

प्रांत (nm) province; end, border

प्राप्त (a) gained, acquired, got, obtained

प्राप्ति (nf) gain; profit; benefit; income; receipt

प्राप्य (a) obtainable; attainable; available

प्राबल्य (nm) predominence; intensity

प्रामाणिक (a) reliable, authentic; established by proof; credible

प्राय: (*adv*) usually, often, generally; mostly

प्रायश्चित्त (*nm*) penance, atonement, expiation; —विधि rules prescribed in Shastra for expitation

प्रायोगिक (*a*) practical; experimental

प्रारंभ (*nm*) commencement; beginning; the starting point

प्रारंभिक (*a*) primary; first; elementary

प्रारब्ध (*nm*) fate, destiny, lot

प्रारूप (*nm*) a draft

प्रार्थना (*nf*) prayer; request, solicitation; petition; —पत्र an application

प्रार्थनीय (*a*) fit to be petitioned

प्रार्थित (*a*) solicited, requested; asked

प्रार्थी (*nm*) a petitioner; an applicant; one who submits a request

प्रासंगिक (*a*) pertaining to a topic under discussion; relevant; incidental; —ता relevance

प्रासाद (*nm*) a mansion, a palace

प्रियंवद (*a*) sweet speaking

प्रिय (*a*) darling, beloved, dear; pleasing, favourite; (*nm*) a lover; husband; —जन near and dear ones; —तम dearest; husband; —दर्शी showing love to all, —भाषी speaking sweet words; —वर much beloved, very dear

प्रिया (*a & nf*) darling, beloved; wife; sweet heart

प्रीतम (*nm*) husband, master, beloved person

प्रीति (*nf*) affection; love; enjoyment, satisfaction; —पूर्वक with love and kindness; —भाव courtesy, —भोज a feast in which friends and relatives dine together, a social party

प्रेक्षक (*nm*) a beholder; an onlooker; spectator

प्रेक्षण (*nm*) the work of seeing, looking, sight

प्रेक्षणीय (*a*) able to be seen or beheld

प्रेत (*nm*) a ghost, an evil spirit, a frightful person; —लोक the world of dead persons

प्रेतनी (*nf*) feminine form of प्रेत

प्रेम (*nm*) affection, love, kindness; —कहानी a love tale; —करना to love; —गीत a love song; —पत्र a love-letter; —पात्र beloved, dear; —भाव emotion of love, love

प्रेमालिंगन (*nm*) embracing in love

प्रेमाश्रु (*nm*) tears of joy falling in love

प्रेमिका (*nf*) a beloved

प्रेमी (*nm*) a lover

प्रेयसी (*nf*) darling, a beloved

प्रेरक (*nm*) a promptor, an

instigator, an inducer; inspirer

प्रेरणा (nf) drive; motive; inspiration, exitement; —शक्ति motive force, inspiration

प्रेरणार्थक क्रिया (a) a causative verb

प्रेरणीय (a) able to be impulsed or instigated

प्रेरित (a) induced, inspired; prompted

प्रेषक (nm) a sender, a dispatcher

प्रेषण (nm) the act of sending or dispatching a thing

प्रेषित (a) directed, dispatched, sent

प्रोक्त (a) declared; said, uttered

प्रोत्साहक (nm) an instigator

प्रोत्साहन (nm) instigation, stimulation

प्रोत्साहित (a) excited, stimulated, incited

प्रौढ़ (a) full grown, adult; mature

प्रौढ़ता (nf) full growth, adulthood, maturity

प्रौढ़ा (nf) an elderly woman

प्लवन (nm) leaping, swimming, plunging

प्लेग (nf) plague

फ

फ the second member of the fifth pentad of consonants in Devnagri alphabet

फंदा (nm) a loop; a knot; noose;

फंदेदार (a) loopy; having a knot

फँसना (v) to be entrapped, to be involved in a difficulty

फँसाना (v) to entrap, to ensnare; to bait

फक (a) white, clean, pale, —पड़ना to turn pale; to be scared out of wits

फकीर (nm) a beggar, a hermit; a poor person

फकीरी (nf) beggary; poverty; the life of a hermit

फक्कड़ (a) carefree; a rough fellow, a base person, —पन carefreeness, carefree manner; indigence

फख्र (nm) pride

फजीहत (nf) infamy, disgrace, insult

फजूल (a) worthless, useless; futile; —खर्च dissipating; extravagant; —खर्ची dissipation; extravagance

फज्ल (nm) favour, kindness, grace

फट (adv) at once; (nf) the

sound made by the fall of a light object, a crack; —फट an auto -rickshaw

फटकना (v) to knock off, to shake; to winnow

फटकार (nf) a reprimand, rebuke, chiding

फटकारना (v) to chide, to rebuke, to scold

फटना (v) to burst; to be torn; to be cracked; to be cut

फटफटाना (v) to make a fluttering noise; to flap

फटा (a) rent; torn; —पुराना old and shattered, shabby

फटीचर (a) shabbily dressed, shabby

फट्टा (nm) a long piece of split bamboo, a plank

फड़क उठना (v) to be thrilled

फड़कन (nf) throbbing; palpitation, pulsation

फड़कना (v) to throb, to be thrilled; to pulsate

फड़फड़ाना (v) to flap, to flutter, to throb

फड़फड़ाहट (nf) flutter, flapping, throbbing

फणि (nm) the expanded hood of a snake, —धर snake

फषी (nm) a snake

फ़तवा (nm) a judicial judgement or decree passed by a Mohammedan judge

फ़तह (nf) victory, triumph, conquest; —करना (v) to conquer

फ़तूर (nm) defect, flaw; craze

फन (nm) snake's hood

फ़न (nm) skill; art, draft, artifice

फनकना (v) to move about in the air with a hissing sound

फ़नकार (nf) an artist

फ़ना (nf) ruin, destruction; died

फफूँदी (nf) mildew, fungus

फफोला (nm) a blotch, a blister; a scald

फबती (nf) a sarcasm, a jest, banter

फबना (v) to seem beautiful; to suit; to become an occasion

फ़रज़ी (nm) the queen in the play of chess; a minister; (a) artificial, unnatural

फ़रमा (nm) a frame; a shoe-maker's last; a full sheet of paper folded several times on which book is printed

फ़रमाइश (nf) an order, a command; a royal edict; an imperative request

फ़रमाइशी (a) prepared or made according to order

फ़रमान (nm) a royal edict or command

फ़रमाना (v) to order, to command

फ़रशी (nf) a hubble-bubble

फ़रसा (nm) an axe, halberd, a poleaxe

फ़रार (a) absconding (person), a culprit at large; (nm) an

outlaw

फ़रियाद (nf) complaint; a petition; a request

फ़रियादी (a) a petitioner; a complainant

फ़रिश्ता (nm) a messenger of god, an angel

फ़रीक (nm) an opponent, an adversary, a section

फ़रेब (nm) duplicity, fraud, trick, wiliness

फ़रेबी (a) deceptive, fraudy, fraudulent

फ़र्क (nm) difference, distance

फ़र्ज़ (nm) moral duty; obligation; —करना to assume, to suppose

फ़र्ज़ी (a) fictitious; assumed; (nm) a minister, a vazir; the queen in the game of chess

फ़र्द (nf) a piece of cloth or paper, a roll, a catalogue

फ़र्राटा (nm) the sound of something fluttering in the air, rattling sound

फ़र्राश (nm) a servant who spreads carpets, lights, candles

फ़र्राशी (a) pertaining to the work of farrash

फ़रोश (nm) a seller, a vendor

फ़र्श (nm) a floor, a carpet

फ़र्शी (nf) a kind of large hubble bubble

फल (nm) a fruit; effect; gain; —त: therefore; thus; —दायक

fruitful, advantageous

फलक (nm) the sky

फलक (nm) a board, a bench, a sheet

फलना (v) to be fruitful, to bear fruit, to be useful; —फूलना to thrive

फलाँ (a) such and such; so and so

फलाहार (nm) fruitarian diet; subsisting on a diet of fruits alone

फलाहारी (nm) pertaining to fruitarian diet, one who subsists on fruits alone

फलालेन (nf) flannel

फलार्थी (nm) one who desires favourable consequences

फलित (a) full of fruits; successful, fulfilled; —ज्योतिष astrology

फली (nf) pod of a leguminous plant, a bean

फलीभूत (a) fructified, resulted in success

फव्वारा (nm) a fountain

फसल (nf) season time; crop, harvest; —काटनेवाला a harvester

फसली (a) pertaining to a season or crop; —बुखार seasonal fever

फसाद (nm) revolt, agitation, quarrel, disturbance, dispute

फ़सादी (a) revolting, rowdy, quarrelsome, mischieveous, one who initiates an altercation

फ़साना (*nm*) a long narrative, a story

फ़सील (*nf*) battlement, para- pet; a boundary wall

फहराना (*v*) to wave; to flutter in the air, to flap

फाँक (*nf*) a cleft; a cut slice, a slit, fragment; —करना to pare

फाँकना (*v*) to put something powdered into the mouth, to chuk 'some powdery thing into the mouth; धूल —to knock about, to run from pole to post

फाँट (*nm*) the distance bet- ween the two banks of a river, the width

फाँटना (*v*) to divide something into equal parts

फाँद (*nf*) a leaping, spring; jumping

फाँदना (*v*) to leap over; to jump across; to skip; to spring; to cross

फाँस (*nf*) the splinter of a noose, a trap, knot

फाँसना (*v*) to catch in a trap, to ensnare

फाँसी (*nf*) a noose; execution, hanging; —चढ़ना to be hang- ed; —देना to hang by the neck; —देने वाला a hangman; —लगाना to commit suicide by means of hanging

फ़ाक़ा (*nm*) a fast; starvation; —कशी starving

फ़ाक़ा/मस्त (*a*) one who is merry even in extreme poverty, one whose spirit is not damped even though starved; carefree; —मस्ती carefreeness even though starved; maintenance of undamped spirit even in affliction

फ़ाख़्ता (*nf*) a dove

फाग (*nm*) the Holi festival; a typical song sung collecti- vely during the Holi festival

फ़ाज़िल (*a*) proficient, extra; learned

फाटक (*nm*) main gate; ent- rance; door

फाट/का (*nm*) speculation; —बाज़ a speculator —केबाज़ी speculation

फाड़ना (*v*) to rend; to tear off; to crack; to split

फानूस (*nm*) large candles, a chandelier to burn candles

फ़ायदा (*nm*) profit; gain; use, utility; advantage

फ़ायदेमंद (*a*) useful; profitable; advantageous; beneficial

फ़ारख़ती (*nf*) the deed of release or acquittance

फ़ारसी (*nf*) the Persian languge; (*a*) persian

फ़ारिग़ (*a*) free from work, freed

फ़ार्म (*nm*) an agricultural farm

फाल (*nm*) a piece of betel nut; ploughshare; measure of one pace

फ़ॉल (*nm*) a fall of sari

फ़ालतू (*a*) spare; sufficient; surplus, extra

फ़ालसई (*a*) brownish red

फ़ालसा (*nm*) a tree and its round tiny fruit — *Grewia asiatica*

फ़ालिज़ (*nm*) paralysis; palsy

फावड़ा (*nm*) a spade, mattock

फ़ाश (*a*) evident, exposed, uncovered; manifest; — करना to disclose a secret that undermines some-body's prestige

फासला (*nm*) interval; space; a distance; gap; difference

फ़ाहा (*nm*) a flock of cotton used as a lint for dressing a wound, a plaster of medicine

फ़िकरा (*nm*) a sentence; taunt, phrase; — कसना to taunt

फ़िक्र (*nf*) care; anxiety, worry; thought; concern

फ़िक्रमंद (*a*) concerned; worried

फिटकिरी (*nf*) alum

फ़ितूर (*nm*) a defect, unsound-ness; craze

फ़िरंगी (*a*) English (man); (*nm*) a white man

फिर (*adv*) again; then; more-over, afterwards; in future; — आना to come back, to return; — जाना to go back; — कहना to encore; — से anew, afresh; — फिर again and again; — भी not with-standing; — क्या what then

फ़िरका (*nm*) a tribe, a sect; community; — परस्त a communalist; sectarian; — परस्ती communalism

फिरकी (*nf*) a spool; whirligig; a reel of thread

फिरना (*v*) to ramble; to walk about; to travel; to go round; to return

फ़िराक (*nf*) looking for, waiting for, keeping a watch for

फ़िलहाल (*adv*) for the present, for the time being

फ़िल्म (*nf*) a movie, film

फ़िल्मी (*a*) cinematographic

फिसड्डी (*a*) always lagging behind; doing nothing; sluggish

फिसलन (*nf*) the act of slipping, slipperiness; skid

फिसलना (*v*) to slide; to slip; to skid

फिसलाहट (*nf*) slipperiness

फ़ी (*ind*) every, each; — सदी percent, per hundred

फीका (*a*) insipid, tasteless; dull coloured; dim; — पन vapidity

फ़ीता (*nm*) a tape; tag; a lace; ribbon

फ़ीरोज़ी (*a*) violet-blue

फ़ील (*nm*) an elephant; a piece in the game of chess

फ़ीस (*nf*) tution fee; fee

फूँकना (*v*) to burn, to be reduced to ashes, to be destroyed

फुंकार (*nf*) hiss of a snake

फुंसी (*nf*) a pimple, whelk

फुट (*nm*) a foot

फुटकर (*a*) miscellaneous; retail, — चीज़ें odds and ends, miscellaneous articles

फुदकना (*v*) to leap, to jump

फुनगी (*nf*) tip, top, summit, upper extremity

फुफ्फुस (*nm*) a lung

फुफकार (*nf*) the hissing of a snake

फुफकारना (*v*) to hiss like a snake

फुर्ती (*nf*) quickness, smartness, promptness

फुर्तीला (*a*) quick, smart; prompt, alert

फुरसत (*nf*) spare time; leisure; respite; — पाना to get time

फुलका (*nm*) a thin bread

फुलझड़ी (*nf*) a kind of fire-work which emits flower-like sparks

फुलवाड़ी (*nf*) a flower garden

फुलाना (*v*) to cause to swell; to cause to become proud; to inflate

फुलेल (*nm*) scented oil

फ़व्वारा (*nm*) a fountain

फुसफुसा (*a*) weak; hollow, fragile; not sturdy

फुसफुसाना (*v*) to speak in a hushed up voice or low tone, to whisper

फुसफुसाहट (*nf*) a whisper

फुसलाना (*v*) to allure, to coax; to entice

फुसलाहट (*nf*) allurement

फुहार (*nf*) fine dense drops of rain, drizzle; spray

फुहारा (*nm*) a spray of water, a fountain, shower

फूँक (*nf*) a blowing; a puff

फूँकना (*v*) to burn; to blow; to set on fire

फूट (*nf*) enmity; disunion, disagreement, discord; — डालना to sow the seeds of a discord

फूटना (*v*) to crack; to break; to be broken, to burst; to sprout

फूफा (*nm*) husband of one's father's sister

फूफी (*nf*) father's sister

फूल (*nm*) a blossom, a flower; flower in embroidery; post-cremation ashes; a very light thing; — कारी embroidering of flowers; embroidery; — गोभी cauliflower; — दान a flower-pot; — दार embroidered; flowery; — माला a flower-garland

फूलना (*v*) to puff, to flower; to bloom; to feel proud; — फलना to flourish, to prosper

फूस (*nm*) dry grass, straw, hay

फूहड़ (*a*) unmannerly; (*nm*) a slattern

फूही (*nf*) a light shower of rain, drizzle

पेंकना (*v*) to cast, to throw; to waste; to toss

पेंटना (*v*) to beat up into froth, to batter, to mix by trituration

पेंटा (*nm*) a small turban; the part of the धोती rolled and tucked up round the waist

फेन (*nm*) froth, foam, lather

फेनिल (*a*) frothful, full of lather

फेफड़ा (*nm*) a lung

फेर (*nm*) a turning, a twist; doubt

फेरा (*nm*) a return, circuit, going round; coming and going back

फेरी (*nf*) round; going round; hawking

फेल (*a*) unsuccessful, plucked; (*nm*) action; misdeed; doings

फेहरिस्त (*nf*) an inventory, list

फैक्टरी (*nf*) a factory

फैलना (*v*) to spread, to expand; to extend; to be famous

फैलाव (*nm*) spread; scattering, dispersion

फैशन (*nm*) fashion; —परस्त fashionable; —परस्ती fashionableness

फैशनेबल (*a*) fashionable

फैसला (*nm*) decision; judgement, settlement

फोकट (*a*) worthless, of no value; —में without payment

फोटो (*nm*) a photograph; —ग्राफर a photographer

फोड़ना (*v*) to break; to split, to burst

फोड़ा (*nm*) an ulcer; a boil

फोरमैन (*nm*) a foreman

फौज (*nf*) a multitude; an army, regiment

फौजदार (*nm*) a military officer

फौजदारी (*nf*) a criminal court; —करना to commit a criminal offence

फौजी (*a*) pertaining to the army, martial; (*nm*) a soldier; —कानून martial law; —अदालत a military court

फौरन (*adv*) at once, immediately, there and then

फौलाद (*nm*) steel

फौलादी (*a*) made of steel, sturdy

फ्राक (*nm*) a frock

फ्रेम (*nm*) a frame

ब

ब the third member of the fifth pentad of consonants in Devnagri alphabet

बंकिम (*a*) curved, bent; oblique

बंका (*a*) bent, curved, powerful

बंगला (*nm*) a bungalow; (*nf*) the Bengali language

बंगाली (*a*) the language spoken in Bengal

बंजर (*a*) unproductive, barren, fallow

बंजारा (*nm*) nomad, a gypsy

बँटवारा (*nm*) a division, partition, separation

बंटाढार (*nm*) devastation, undoing, ruination

बंडल (*nm*) a bundle

बंडी (*nf*) waistcoat, a jacket

बंद (*a*) shut; locked; stopped, discontinued; —गोभी cabbage

बंदगी (*nf*) salutation; service, worship, prayer

बंदनवार (*nf*) an ornamental arch, festoon of flowers and green leaves

बंदर (*nm*) harbour; monkey

बंदरगाह (*nf*) a harbour, port

बंदा (*nm*) a slave, servant; humble self used by a speaker for himself out of modesty

बंदिश (*nf*) forestalling; a restriction; musical pattern

बंदी (*nm*) a bard; prisoner; captive; —करना to catch, to arrest —गृह a prison, a jail

बंदूक़ (*nm*) a gun

बंदूक़ची (*nm*) a musketeer, a gunman, gunner

बंदोबस्त (*nm*) an arrangement, settlement; management

बंध (*nm*) a tie, a knot; a bond; —पत्र a bond

बंधक (*nm*) pawn; surety; —रखना to mortgage, to pawn

बंधन (*nm*) the act of binding; restriction; a bond

बँधना (*v*) to be bound; to be arrested; to be kept under restraint

बंधु (*nm*) a brother; a relation, kinsman; friend; —बांधव relatives, kinsfold; —त्व relationship, kinship, cognation

बंध्या (*nf*) a barren woman; childless woman; —पन barrenness; —पुत्र something which is impossible

बंब (*nm*) a bomb

बंबा (*nm*) waterpipe; a hydrant

बंसी (*nf*) a pipe, flute; fishing hook

बक (*nm*) a heron

बकझक (*nf*) gabble, babbling, —करना to jabber

बकना (v) to chatter, to babble, to make senseless talk

बकबक (nf) raving; twaddle

बकरा (nm) a he-goat

बकरी (nf) a she-goat

बकवाद (nf) chatter, twaddle, gabble

बकवादी (a) an idle talker, tattler, twaddler

बकसुआ (nm) fibula, a buckle

बक्स (nm) a box

बकाना (v) to cause some-one to gabble

बकाया (nm) amount of arrears, balance; (a) remaining, payable

बख्रान (nm) exposition; description; praise

बख्रानना (v) to relate, to dwell in details, to sing the praises

बख्रार (nm) a store-house, a barn in a village

बखिया (nf) back-stitching; a kind of strong stitching with needle; —उधेड़ना to expose thoroughly

बखुद (ind) by self, by oneself

बखूबी (ind) very well, in good manner, thoroughly

बखेड़ा (nm) complication; difficulty; broil

बखेरना (v) to scatter, to spread; to diffuse

बख्त (nm) fortune, fate; lot; कम — ill-fated, unfortune; नेक— fortunate, lucky

बख्तर (nm) an armour; —बंद armoured

बख्शना (v) to grant, to bestow; to pardon

बख्शीश (nf) grant, gift; tip

बग़ल (nf) flank; an arm-pit; a side; (adv) by the side, closy by

बगला (nm) a heron —भगत a hypocrite

बगावत (nf) mutiny, rebellion, revolt

बगिया (nf) a small garden

बग़ीचा (nm) a garden, a small park

बगुला (nm) a heron

बगूला (nm) a whirlwind

बगैर (ind) excluding, without

बग्घी (nf) a four wheeled carriage drawn by horses

बघार (nm) spices which are used to season food

बघारना (शेखी) (v) to boast; to show off; to talk tall

बचकाना (a) fit for a child, puerile

बचत (nf) saving; gain

बचना (v) to escape; to recover; to be saved; to remain; बाल-बाल— to have a hair-breadth escape

बचपन (nm) childhood

बचपना (nm) childishness

बचाना (v) to defend; to save; to retain; to protect

बचाव (nm) defence, safety, protection

बच्चा (*nm*) a kid; a child; baby; infant; (*a*) inexperienced

बच्ची (*nf*) a small girl

बछड़ा (*nm*) a he-calf

बछिया (*nf*) a she-calf

बछेड़ा (*nm*) a colt

बछेड़ी (*nf*) a filly

बजना (*v*) to sound, to be struck

बजरंग (*a*) very stout and strong

बजरबट्टू (*a & nm*) stupid, fool, block-head

बजवाना (*v*) to cause a person to sound an instrument

बजा (*a*) fit, right, proper, true

बजाज (*nm*) a cloth merchant

बजाजा (*nm*) a cloth market

बजाजी (*nf*) the work of a draper

बजाना (*v*) to play on a musical instrument; to beat a drum; to accomplish a work

बजाय (*ind*) instead of, in place of

बटन (*nm*) switch; a button

बटना (*v*) to twist rope etc.

बटलोही (*nf*) a wide mouthed pot which is used for cooking food

बटवारा (*nm*) an assignation; partition; division

बटाई (*nf*) partition, division

बटाऊ (*nm*) a traveller

बटालियन (*nf*) a battalion

बटुआ (*nm*) moneybag, a purse

बटेर (*nf*) a quail; —बाज one who tames quails

बटोई (*nf*) a small cooking jar

बटोरना (*v*) to accumulate; to collect; to gather

बटोही (*nm*) a traveller, a wayfarer

बट्टा (*nm*) deficit, loss, damage; a stone pestle, a discount

बट्टाखाता (*nm*) dues which are unrealisable

बट्टी (*nf*) a small pestle or muller

बड़ (*nm*) a banyan tree; —पन greatness, eminence

बड़बोला (*a*) one who brags or boasts

बड़भागी (*a*) fortunate

बड़बड़ (*nf*) muttering, tattle, useless talk

बड़बड़ाना (*v*) to jabber, to grumble, to gabble, to babble

बड़बड़ाहट (*nf*) a rattle, a mutter

बड़वानल (*nm*) submarine fire

बड़ा (*a*) great; large; big; important, elder; grown up; (*adv*) very; (*nm*) ground pulse-formed into small round cakes and fried; —दिन the Christmas day; —बाबू head clerk; —बूढ़ा elderly

बड़ाई (*nf*) greatness, praise

बढ़ई (*nm*) a carpenter; —गीरी carpentry

बढ़ती (*nf*) abundance; growth; enhancement

बढ़ना (*v*) to grow; to surpass; to

proceed; to progress

बढ़ाना (v) to promote, to increase, to extend

बढ़ावा (nm) excitement, encouragement

बढ़िया (a) superior, nice, fine, excellent

बढ़ोतरी (nf) gradual increment; bonus; progress; addition

बतख़ (nf) a duck

बताना (v) to inform; to point out, to signify, to tell

बतासा (nm) a semi-spherical cake which is made of sugar and is very light and spongy

बतियाना (v) to talk, to converse with

बतौर (ind) just like; like; as

बत्ती (nf) a candle; a lamp, a light

बथुआ (nm) the common herb *chenopodium album*

बद (a) wicked, bad, mean, depraved; —अमनी disturbance, breach of peace; —इंतज़ामी bad management; —कार wicked, licentious; —कारी wickedness; —क़िस्मत unfortunate, unlucky, ill-fated; —ख़त bad hand-writing, —गुमान one who looks with suspicion at a person; —गुमानी a false suspicion; —चलन depraved, of immoral character, licentious; —चलनी bad

character; —ज़बान ill-speaking; —ज़ात mean, wicked, depraved; —ज़ायक़ा tasteless; —तमीज़ vulgar, uncivilised; —तर worse, more wicked; —दिमाग़ arrogant; —दुआ curse, malediction; —नसीब ill-fated, unfortunate; —नाम infamous, calumniated, notorious; —नामी a slander, a disrepute, a scandal; —नीयत of ill-intention; —नीयती a deception; —नुमा ugly, grotesque; —परहेज़ी an immoderate indulgence in diet, intemperance; —बख़्त unfortunate; —बू a foul smell, bad odour

बदन (nm) the body, physical frame

बदना (v) to settle, to bet

बदमाश (a) wicked; immoral; (nm) a man of bad character

बदमाशी (nf) wickedness, dissoluteness

बदमिज़ाज (a) of wicked nature

बदनसीबी (nf) lucklessness

बदल (nm) change, exchange

बदलना (v) to alter; to turn; to shift

बदला (nm) revenge, retaliation; return

बदली (nf) exchange; cloudiness; transfer, —करना to transfer

बदले में (*adv*) inspite of, in lieu of, instead of

बदशक्ल (*a*) deformed, ugly

बदसलूकी (*nf*) ill-behaviour

बदसूरत (*a*) deformed, ugly

बदस्तूर (*adv*) in the ordinary way; as usual; in the customary manner

बदहज़मी (*nf*) indigestion

बदहवास (*a*) in a fit of coma, perplexed, confused, thrown in disorder

बदा (*a*) fated, destined

बदी (*nf*) wickedness, evil, harm; the dark half of a lunar month

बदौलत (*ind*) by virtue of; by means of; for; due to; through; by the kindness of

बद्ध (*a*) tied up; bound; fixed

बधाई (*nf*) congratulation; — देना to congratulate, to felicitable

बधिक (*nm*) a slayer, a hunter

बधिया (*nm*) a castrated animal (bull)

बधिर (*a*) deaf, hard of hearing

बन (*nm*) a wood, forest

बनचर (*nm*) a wild beast, a forester

बनचारी (*a*) one who lives or wanders about in a forest

बनजारा (*nm*) a grain dealer, a grocer

बनना (*v*) to be made or prepared; to be constructed; to be fit for use; to seem beautiful

बनवास (*nm*) residing in forest, an exile

बनवासी (*a*) inhabiting in a forest

बनबिलाव (*nm*) a wild cat

बनमानुस (*nm*) a wild animal resembling a man

बनमाला (*nf*) a garland made of several kinds of flowers

बनराज (*nm*) a lion

बनवाई (*nf*) the work or wages paid for preparing a thing

बनाना (*v*) to construct; to make; to form

बनाम (*ind*) as against, versus

बनाव (*nm*) preparation, formation, ornamentation; — सिंगार make-up

बनावट (*nf*) construction; composition; frame, structure, get up

बनावटी (*a*) artificial, unnatural, showy, unreal; — बोली बोलना to mince; — रूप personation; — भक्ति sanctimony

बनिया (*nm*) a merchant, a grocer, a trader, a shop-keeper

बनियाइन (*nf*) a trader's wife; a kind of undergarment

बनैला (*a*) wild of forest

बपौती (*nf*) patrimony, heritage

बबर (*nm*) a lion; — शेर a lion

बबुआ (*nm*) a word of endearment used for a son, a child

बबूल (*nm*) mangrove, *acacia* tree

बबूला (*nm*) a bubble; आग — very enraged, fiery

बम (*nm*) a shell, a bomb

बया (*nm*) a weaver-bird, a tailor-bird

बयान (*nm*) a narration, a description or statement, an account

बयाना (*nm*) money which is given in advance, earnest money, advance money

बर/वर (*nm*) a bridegroom; (*a*) good, excellent, complete; (*ind*) on the other hand; beyond; on, upon; —करार fixed, established, effective; —ख्वास्त dismissed, discharged; dissolved; — ख्वास्तगी dismissal; dissolution; discharge

बरकत (*nf*) blessing, abundance, gain, profit

बरखा (*nf*) rain

बरगद (*nm*) a banyan tree

बरछा (*nm*) a lance, a dart

बरछी (*nf*) a pike, a spear, a dart

बरजना (*v*) to obstruct; to forbid, to prohibit

बरजोरी (*nf*) tyranny, force

बरत (*nm*) a fast

बरतन (*nm*) a pot, utensil

बरतना (*v*) to behave; to use

बरताव (*nm*) treatment, behaviour

बरदाश्त (*nf*) endurance; forbe-

arance; patience

बरफ़ (*nf*) ice

बरबस (*adv*) forcibly, all of a sudden

बरबाद (*a*) destroyed, ruined; wasted

बरमा (*nm*) an auger, a drill

बरस (*nm*) an year; —गाँठ birthday

बरसना (*v*) to shower, to rain; to be spread all round

बरसात (*nm*) the rainy season; the rains

बरसाती (*a*) pertaining to rains; (*nm*) a raincoat

बरसी (*nf*) the first death anniversary

बराँडा (*nm*) a verandah

बरात (*nf*) a marriage party

बराती (*nm*) people comprising a marriage party

बराबर (*a*) level; equal, plain, matching; (*adv*) constantly; —करना to make even; to ruin; to leave nothing

बराबरी (*nf*) parity, equality, similarity

बरामद (*a*) recovered; exposed

बरामदा (*nm*) a balcony, a corridor, a gallery

बरौनी (*nf*) the eyelashes

बर्ताव (*nm*) treatment, behaviour

बर्फ़ीला (*a*) snowy, icy; glacial

बर्फ़ी (*nf*) a kind of rectangular sweetmeat, a lozenge

बर्बर (*a*) savage, barbarian;

—ता savagery

बल (*nm*) power; strength; vitality; —वान powerful; —हीन weak

बलगम (*nm*) phlegm

बलवा (*nm*) riot; rebellion; —ई a rioter; riotous

बलवान् (*a*) potent, vigorous, strong, stout

बलशाली (*a*) strong, powerful

बला (*nf*) calamity; an evil spirit

बलात् (*ind*) all of a sudden; forcibly

बलात्कार (*nm*) ravishment, rape; violence; oppression

बलि (*nf*) an oblation; an offering, sacrifice; the victim offered to a deity; —चढ़ाना to sacrifice

बलिदान (*nm*) offering a sacrifice to god, an immolation; —करना to sacrifice, to immolate

बलिष्ठ (*a*) very strong; strongest, having tremendous vigour

बलिहारी (*nf*) sacrifice

बली (*a*) powerful, robust, strong

बलैया (*nf*) trouble, disease, calamity

बल्कि (*ind*) moreover; on the contrary; but; rather

बल्लम (*nm*) a spear or lance; —दार a spearman

बल्ला (*nm*) racket; a bat

बल्ली (*nf*) a prop or pole

बवंडर (*nm*) a violent storm, a cyclone, a typhoon

बवासीर (*nf*) piles; खूनी— bleeding piles, haemorrhoids

बशर्ते (*ind*) —कि with the provision that, provided that, only if

बसंत (*nm*) the spring season

बस (*nm*) will; control; a bus; (*adv*) sufficient, enough; (*ind*) that's all, that'll do; enough; sufficiently

बसना (*v*) to live, to dwell, to settle, to stay

बसर (*nf*) maintenance

बसाना (*v*) to inhabit; to colonize; to rehabilitate

बसेरा (*nm*) a dwelling; an abode; short stay

बस्ता (*nm*) a bag; a bundle; a portfolio

बस्ती (*nf*) an inhabited place, a dwelling; colony

बहँगी (*nf*) a sling for carrying things on shoulders

बहक (*nf*) raving, rave

बहकना (*v*) to talk incoherently; to rave; to be intoxicated; to be enticed

बहकावा (*nm*) allurement, enticement; instigation

बहन (*nf*) a sister

बहना (*v*) to float, to flow, to glide, to blow

बहनोई (*nm*) the sister's

husband, brother-in-law

बहरहाल (*ind*) however, at any rate, nevertheless

बहरा (*a*) deaf, hard of hearing

बहलाना (*v*) to recreate, to amuse; to divert one's mind

बहलाव (*nm*) recreation, diversion, amusement, entertainment

बहलावा (*nm*) enticement, allurement; false hope

बहस (*nf*) an argument, a discussion, debate

बहादुर (*a*) brave, valiant; courageous; bold

बहादुरी (*nf*) bravery; courage; boldness

बहाना (*nm*) a pretence, false colours, an excuse; make believe; (*v*) to cause to flow, to set afloat; to ruin, to destroy

बहार (*nf*) the spring season; merriment; joviality

बहाल (*ind*) reinstated

बहाली (*nf*) restoration to former post

बहाव (*nm*) a flow, flood, ebb in water, outflow

बहिष्कार (*nm*) a proscription, reprobation, exile

बहिष्कृत (*a*) expelled from society, boycotted

बही (*nf*) an account book; —खाता a ledger

बहु (*a*) many, several, much; —ज्ञ well-informed, very experienced; master of many trades; —धंधी multipurpose; variously occupied; —मुखी multifarious; —मूल्य precious, invaluable; —रूपिया one who assumes various forms; —संख्यक majority

बहुत (*a*) very, abundant, too, plentiful

बहुतायत (*nf*) abundance, plenty

बहुतेरा (*a*) much, abundant; (*adv*) in various ways, fully

बहुतेरे (*a*) numerous, several

बहुदर्शी (*a*) learned, experienced

बहुधा (*ind*) in various ways; usually; generally, mostly

बहुभाषी (*a*) polyglot

बहुमत (*nm*) opinion of the majority

बहुलता (*nf*) amplitude, manifoldness

बहुवादी (*a*) very talkative

बहू (*nf*) a son's wife, a daughter-in-law; wife; a newly married woman

बहेड़ा (*nm*) the fruit of the tree —*belleric myrobalan*

बहेलिया (*nm*) a fowler, hunter

बाई (*a*) left

बाँका (*a*) curved, crooked, foppish, dandy

बांग (*nf*) the call of Mohammedans to worship; the crowing of a cock

बांचना (v) to read aloud; to read

बाँझ (nf) a barren woman; (a) barren, unfertile

बाँट (nf) allotment, division; deal; share

बाँटना (v) to divide; to distribute; to deal

बाँदी (nf) a bondmaid, a slave girl

बाँध (nm) a dike; dam; lock; barrage

बाँधना (v) to attach; to tie; to pack; to wrap around

बांधव (nm) relation, kindred; friend; brother

बांबी (nf) an ant-hill; a snake's hole

बाँस (nm) a bamboo; pole

बाँसुरी (nf) a flute, pipe; reed

बाँह (nf) a sleeve; an arm

बा a prefix to nouns meaning-having; —अदब respectful; humble; —क़ायदा regularly, duly; according to rules

बाक़ी (a) left over, remaining; (nf) balance; remainder

बाग (nm) a garden; (nf) the reins; —मोड़ना to turn in a direction; —डोर the reins, a halter

बाग़बान (nm) a gardener

बाग़बानी (nf) gardening, the act of cultivating, horticulture

बाग़ान (nm) gardens

बाग़ी (nm) a rebel; a mutineer

बाघ (nm) a tiger, a lion

बाज़ (nm) a hawk, falcon, kestrel

बाजरा (nm) Indian corn, millet

बाजा (nm) a muscial instrument of any kind

बाज़ार (nm) a market, market place; —भाव market-rate

बाज़ा/री —रू (a) belonging to the market place; vulgar; cheap

बाज़ी (nf) a wager, bet; play; turn

बाज़ीगर (nm) a conjurer; a juggler, a magician

बाज़ीगरी (nf) jugglery

बाज़ू (nm) the arm; overside; wing of bird; flank of an army

बाट (nf) way, path, course; (nm) a weight; —जोहना to wait for

बाड़ (nf) a hedge; a fence

बाड़ी (nf) an enclosure; a small orchard; house

बाढ़ (nf) freshet, a flood

बाण (nm) an arrow

बात (nf) talk; a discourse, a conversation, saying, statement; —काटना to interrupt

बातूनी (a & nm) talkative; great talker; a chatter-box

बाद (ind) subsequently, after, later

बादल (nm) a cloud; —फटना the clouds to be scattered; —छाना the sky to be overcast with clouds

बादशाह (nm) a ruler, a king

बादशाहत (nm) rule, kingdom, government

बादशाही (a) kingly, royal

बादाम (nm) an almond

बादामी (a) of the colour of almond

बादी (a) windy, flatulent; (nf) flatulence, fat; wind

बाधक (a) obstructing, troubling; hindering; —ता obstruction, impediment

बाधना (v) to obstruct, to impede

बाधा (nf) an impediment, **obstruction, hinderance**

बाधित (a) impeded, hindered obstructed

बाध्य (a) compelled, forced; obliged; —करना to obligate

बान (nm) an arrow; (nf) a structure, a custom

बानगी (nf) a sample, a specimen; an example

बानर (nm) a monkey; an ape

बाना (nm) dress

बानी (nf) speech

बाप (nm) father; —दादा fore-fathers, ancestors

बापुरा (a) mean, helpless; needy

बाबत (nf) connection, affair

बाबा (nm) father, dad, papa; grandfather; an old man; ascetic; —आदम the most primitive man

बाबुल (nm) father

बाबू (nm) a word used for a gentleman; father; middle class man

बायाँ (a) left, adverse

बायें (ind) to the left; in the opposite camp

बारंबार (ind) time and again, again and again; repeatedly

बार (nf) turn; time; (nm) a gate, a door, a place of shelter; —बार again and again

बारदाना (nm) the commodities of a trader, goods, wares

बारहखड़ी (nf) the consonants of the Devnagri alphabet combined with the twelve vowels

बारहदरी (nf) a summer-house with several indoors

बारहमासा (nm) a kind of song which is sung in all the seasons of the year

बारहमासी (a) flowering all round the year; —पौधा a perennial plant

बारहसिंगा (nm) a reindeer, stag, gnu or wild beast

बारात (nf) a marriage procession; —सम्बन्धी processional

बाराती (a) member of a wedding party

बारिश (nf) the rainy season

बारिस्टर (nm) a barrister

बारी (nf) millet; a turn; (nm) a low Hindu caste in the traditional caste set up;

—बारी से in turns

बारीक (a) thin; slender; subtle; very small

बारीकी (nf) thinness; excellence; subtleness

बारूद (nf) gun-powder

बारे में (ind) with regards to

बाल (nm) a boy; hair; (a) young of tender age; not mature —बुद्धि childishness; childish; —ब्रह्मचारी a life-long celibate; —रोग children's disease; —विधवा child widow; —विवाह early marriage; —बराबर hair-breadth, very narrow

बालक (nm) a young child, a lad, a boy; —के सदृश boyish, —पन का juvenile; —त्व purility; —हत्या infanticide

बालकपन (nm) infancy, boyhood

बालकाल (nm) boyhood, infancy

बालचरित्र (nm) childish pranks and freaks

बालटी (nf) a bucket, pail

बाला-बच्चे (nm) children, family

बालभाव (nm) infancy

बालभोग (nm) offering made to Lord Krishna in the morning

बालम (nm) a lover; a husband, a beloved person

बालरोग (nm) diseases of children

बाललीला (nf) childish pranks

बालसूर्य (nm) Sun appearing in the sky in the early morning

बाला (nm) an ear-ornament; (nf) young woman; an adolescent girl

बालिका (nf) a girl, a daughter, a female child

बालिग (a) a youth who has attained the age of maturity; a major; adult; —होना to come of age

बालिग मताधिकार (nm) adult franchise

बालिश (nf) a pillow; (a) ignorant; stupid

बालिश्त (nm) a hand span

बाली (nf) an ear-ring; ear of corn

बालुका (nf) sand

बालू (nf) sand, gravel; —दानी a sand box

बालूशाही (nf) a kind of sweet-meat

बाल्य (nm) childhood, infancy, boyhood; (a) belonging to a boy; —काल childhood

बाल्यावस्था (nf) childhood, tender age, immaturity

बावड़ी (nf) a tank of water

बावजूद (adv) nevertheless, in spite of, against

बावरची (nm) a Mohammedan cook; —ख़ाना kitchen

बावला (a) insane; crazy, mad; —पन insanity; craziness

बावली (nf) an insane woman; a large well in which there

are flights of stairs to descend up to the water

बाशिंबा (*nm*) an inhabitant of a place, a resident

बाष्प (*nm*) vapour; tears

बास (*nf*) foul smell, bad adour

बासा (*a*) kept overnight, stale; (*nm*) a dwelling place

बासी (*a*) not fresh, stale, dried up

बाहर (*ind*) outside, without; beyond

बाहरी (*a*) exterior, outward; superficial, alien

बाहु (*nf*) an arm; —पाश an arm-embrace; —बल strength of one's arms, valour

बाहुल्य (*nm*) plenty, abundance

बाह्य (*ind*) beyond; outside; (*a*) external, outward, exterior; superficial

बिंदी (*nf*) a dot; a point; zero, cipher

बिंदु (*nm*) a spot; a point, dot; zero, cipher

बिंधना (*v*) to be entangled in something, to be pierced

बिंब (*nm*) a shade, reflection, glimmer, image; a shadow of something

बिकना (*v*) to be sold

बिकवाना (*v*) to cause to be sold

बिकाऊ (*a*) saleable, for sale

बिक्री (*nf*) sale, marketing; disposal

बिखरना (*v*) to be dispersed, to be scattered

बिखेरना (*v*) to scatter; to diffuse

बिगड़ना (*v*) to be spoiled; to be damaged; to be enraged, to lose temper

बिगाड़ (*nm*) friction, discord; quarrel

बिगाड़ना (*v*) to destroy; to spoil; to put out of order; to cause to go astray

बिगाना (*a*) foreign, alien

बिगुल (*nm*) a bugle

बिचकाना (*v*) to make mouths at, to balk, to wry the mouth

बिचरना (*v*) to loiter, to roam; to travel

बिचला (*a*) situated in the middle, mid; central

बिचारा (*a*) helpless, poor; —पन helplessness

बिच्छू (*nm*) a scorpion, a prickly plant

बिछना (*n*) the spreading of a bed

बिछाना (*v*) to spread out a bed, to scatter, to extend

बिछावन (*nm*) a bed, bedding

बिछुड़ना (*v*) to be separate, to be separated from a person

बिछोह (*nm*) bereavement, deprivation

बिछौना (*nm*) a bed, bedding

बिजली (*nf*) lightning; electricity; thunderbolt; —घर a power-station

बिटिया (*nf*) a daughter

बिड़ाल (*nm*) a cat

बिताना (*v*) to spend time

बित्ता (*nm*) a span

बिदकना (*v*) to split asunder, to be provoked

बिदाई (*nf*) a farewell, a send off, an adieu

बिनती (*nf*) an earnest request, an entreaty

बिनना (*v*) to weave, to knit, to pick up, to select

बिना (*ind*) but, without, in the absence of

बिनाई (*nf*) work or wages for knitting, work of picking

बिनौला (*nm*) cotton-seed

बिफरना (*v*) to revolt, to be displeased, to be unhappy

बियाबान (*nm*) a desert, a wilderness, a jungle; (*a*) uninhabited; deserted

बिरता (*nm*) strength, power; capability

बिरला (*a*) rare, uncommon, scarce

बिरह (*nm*) separation from one's beloved; love-sickness

बिरही (*a & nm*) a lover who is suffering from the pangs of separation from his beloved

बिराजना (*v*) to take one's seat; to grace by one's presence

बिरादरी (*nf*) fraternity; brotherhood, community

बिराना (*a*) strange, alien; (*v*) to offend by making wry faces, to jeer, to make mouths at

बिरोज़ा (*nm*) tar, turpentine

बिल (*nm*) a hole; burrow; cavity; bill

बिलकुल (*a & adv*) all, quite, wholly, completely; utter, sheer

बिलखना (*v*) to sob, to weep, to lament

बिलग (*a*) separate

बिलगना (*v*) to be separated

बिलगाना (*v*) to detach, to disjoin, to separate

बिलगाव (*nm*) separation; detachment; aloofness

बिलटी (*nf*) a railway way-bill, railway receipt; —काटना to despatch

बिलबिलाना (*v*) to be tormented, to be restless with pain

बिला (*ind*) without, unless

बिलाना (*v*) to be ruined; to disappear, to vanish

बिलार (*nm*) a he-cat

बिलाव (*nm*) a tom-cat, big cat

बिलोना (*v*) to churn milk; to stir

बिलौटा (*nm*) a kitten

बिल्ला (*nm*) a tom-cat

बिल्ली (*nf*) a cat

बिल्लौर (*nm*) a pebble, a crystal

बिल्लौरी (*a*) pertaining to a crystal or pebble

बिवाई (*nf*) chilblain; —फटना to have chilblain

बिसात (*nf*) ability, capacity; a chess-board; —के बाहर beyond one's capacity

बिसातख़ाना (*nm*) a general

merchandise shop

बिसाती (*nm*) a pedlar, a haberdasher

बिसारना (*v*) to forget, not recollect or keep in mind

बिसूरना (*v*) to lament, to wail; to sob

बिस्कुट (*nf*) a biscuit

बिस्तर (*nm*) a bed; —बंद a hold - all

बिस्मिल्लाह (*nf*) beginning, commencement; (*ind*) with the name of God, a word used by Muslims at the commencement of a work; —करना to commence, to make a beginning; —ही गलत होना to misfire at the very outset, to have a wrong beginning

बिहा/र (*nm*) an eastern state of the Indian Union; a Buddhist monastery; र—री belonging or pertaining to बिहार

बींधना (*v*) to bore a hole into, to pierce

बीघा (*nm*) a land measure which is five-eighths of an acre

बीच (*nm*) centre, middle part; —का intermediate; central; —बचाव mediation

बीचोंबीच (*adv*) exactly in the middle or centre of things

बीज (*nm*) seed; germ; origin; cause; nucleus

बीजक (*nm*) list; a bill of purchase, invoice

बीजगणित (*nm*) Algebra

बीट (*nf*) the dung of birds

बीड़ी (*nf*) a packet of betel leaves; crude form of a cigarette

बीतना (*v*) to be spent; to expire; to pass; to happen

बीन (*nf*) a lute, a flute; a classical Indian stringed instrument called बीणा

बीनना (*v*) to pluck; to choose; to pick up

बीबी (*nf*) a respectful word used by a woman for a younger sister of her husband; a respected lady

बीभत्स (*a*) loathsome, disgusting

बीमा (*nm*) an insurance

बीमार (*a*) diseased; ill; unwell; (*nm*) a patient

बीमारी (*nf*) illness; disease; sickness

बीर (*a*) intrepid; brave; (*nm*) brother

बीवी (*nf*) wife

बीहड़ (*a*) rugged; dense, thick; (*nm*) a dense forest

बुंदा (*nm*) an ornament in the form of a pendant which is worn in the ear

बुआ (*nf*) father's sister

बुखार (*nm*) fever

बुजदि/ल (*a*) timid, coward; —ली timidness

बुजुर्ग (a) old, elderly; venerable; (nm) forefathers, ancestors

बुजुर्गाना (a) befitting elders; elderly

बुझना (v) to be extinguished, to be quenched; to be dejected

बुझाना (v) to put out; to extinguish; to quench; to talk in riddles

बुड़बुड़ाना (v) to murmur, to gabber

बुड्ढा (a) aged, old

बुढ़ापा (nm) old age

बुढ़िया (nf) an old woman

बुत (nm) a statue, an idol, image; (a) dumb and lifeless; —परस्त idol-worshipper; —परस्ती idol-worship

बुदबुदाना (v) to jabber; to mutter

बुद्ध (nm) Lord Buddha

बुद्धि (nf) wisdom, intellect; sense; mind

बुद्धिमत्ता (nf) prudence, intelligence

बुद्धिमान (a) wise; intelligent; brilliant

बुद्धू (a) block-headed, stupid

बुध (a) wise

बुनकर (nm) a weaver

बुनना (v) to knit, to weave

बुनवाई (nf) charges for weaving

बुनाई (nf) wages paid for weaving

बुनिया/द (nf) base, foundation; basis; —दी fundamental

बुरक़ा (nm) a mantle, a veil

बुरा (a) wicked; bad; evil; —व्यवहार misbehaviour; —भला bad and good, abuse; —मानना to feel bad

बुराई (nf) vice, evil; defect; fault

बुर्ज (nm) pinnacle; a tower

बुलं/द (a) lofty, high; —दी loftiness, height

बुलबुल (nf) a nightingale

बुलबुला (nm) a bubble; (a) transient, transitory

बुला/ना (v) to summon, to call, to invite; —वा call, invitation, summons

बुवाई (nf) sowing

बुहारना (v) to broom, to sweep

बुहारी (nf) a broom

बूँद (nf) a drop

बूँदाबाँदी (nf) light shower, a drizzle

बू (nf) foul smell; a disagreeable odour

बूचड़ (nm) a butcher; —खाना butchery; a slaughterhouse

बूझना (v) to make out; to enquire; to solve

बूट (nm) a boot; green pod of gram

बूटा (nm) a large sized embroidered

बूटी (nf) medicinal plant, a herb

बूढ़ा (a) aged, old

बूता (nm) capability; capacity

बूरा (nm) unrefined powdered sugar

बृह/त (a) big; huge; large; —तर bigger

बेंत (nm) a stick, a cane

बे (pref) without, out of, void of, a vocative particle used to express contempts; —अक्ल foolish, stupid; —अदब rude, impudent; —आब without lustre, worthless; —आबरू disgraced; —इंसाफी injustice, tyranny; —इज़्ज़त disgraced, dishonoured; —इज़्ज़ती dishonour, disgrace; —इल्म illiterate; —ईमान dishonest, treacherous; —ईमानी improbity; dishonesty, —कद्र disrespect; —करार restless, uneasy, perplexed; —करारी restlessness, perplexity; —कल disturbed in mind; —कली uneasiness, restlessness; —कस humble, mean, shelterless; —कसूर innocent, faultless; —काबू uncontrolled; —काम unemployed; idle; —कायदा contrary to rule or law, illegal; —कार useless, unemployed; idle; —कारी unemployment; —खटके without apprehension, freely; —खबर uninformed, senseless; —खबरी the state of being out of senses;

—गरज़ी carelessness; —गाना foreign, alien; —गार the act of forcing a person to work for less wages; —गुनाह faultless, innocent; —घर homeless; —चारा helpless, poor; —चैन restless; —जान lifeless, feeble; —जोड़ unparalleled, matchless; —टिकिट ticketless; —डौल ugly; —ढंगा silly; —ढब unmanageable; —तकल्लुफ informal; —तरतीब disorderly; —तहाशा at top speed; —तार wireless; —तुका absurd; —परवा unveiled, exposed; —फिक्र careless; un-worried; —फिक्री un-mindful; —बस helpless; —बसी helplessness; —मन unspirited; —मानी useless, —मेल mismatched; —रहम cruel; —रुखी disregard; —रोक-टोक without any hitch; —रोज़गार unemployed; —वफा faithless, —शक of course; —शर्म shameless; —शुमार countless; —सबी impatience; —सुध senseless, careless; —सुरा out of tune; —हया shameless; —हाल miserable; —हिसाब unlimited, very much; —होश unconscious, fainted

बेचना (v) to sell; to dispose of

बेटा (nm) a son

बेटी (nf) a daughter

बेठिकाने (a) in the wrong place,

out of place

बेड़ा (nm) a raft; fleet

बेड़ी (nf) iron fetters for the legs, shackles

बेडौल (a) incongruous; ugly

बेतकल्लुफ़ (a) frank, without observing formalities

बेतमीज़ (a) rude, unmannerly

बेताब (a) perplexed

बेतौर (a) in a bad way

बेदख़ल (a) ejected, dispossessed from holdings

बेदर्दी (nf) hard-heartedness

बेधड़क (adv) fearlessly, unhesitatingly

बेधना (v) to pierce; to puncture

बेनसीब (a) unfortunate

बेपरवाह (a) unmindful, careless

बेबुनियाद (a) without a foundation

बेर (nm) a plum, a jujube

बेल (nm) the wood apple; (nf) a creeping plant, a flowery decoration made on walls

बेलदार (nm) a labourer who digs with a spade

बेलदारी (nf) working with a pick-axe; labour job

बेलन (nm) cylinder; a roller

बेलना (nm) a pastry roller; (v) to roll kneaded flour into flat bread

बेला (nm) a jasmine flower; a kind of violin, a house-hold utensil; (nf) time

बेवकूफ़ (a) foolish, unintelligent, stupid

बेवक़्त (adv) untimely, inopportunately

बेवा (nf) a widow

बेशक़ीमत (a) precious, costly

बेशक़ीमती (a) costly, of great value

बेसन (nm) gram flour

बेस्वाद (a) insipid, tasteless

बेहतर (a) better; (ind) very well

बेहतरी (nf) goodness, excellence

बेहद (a) boundless, unlimited

बेहूदा (a) rude, impolite, mean, uncivilised

बैंगन (nm) brinjal

बैंजनी (a) purple, reddish blue, violet-coloured

बैकुंठ (nm) the paradise

बैठक (nf) meeting; sitting; drawing room; base; —ख़ाना a drawing room

बैठना (v) to occupy a seat; to sit; to sink; to be adjusted; to appear; to ride on

बैरंग (a) bearing letter

बैर (nm) hostility, enmity, ill-will

बैरा (nm) a bearer

बैराग (nm) renunciation, disownment

बैरागी (nm) a recluse

बैरी (nm & a) a foe; an enemy; an opponent

बैल (nm) a bullock, an ox

बैसाखी (nf) a crutch

बोआई (nf) the work or wages

paid for sowing seeds in a field

बोझ (nm) load; a burden

बोझा (nm) same as बोझ

बोझिल (a) very heavy; burdensome

बोटी (nf) a slice of flesh

बोतल (nf) a bottle

बोदा (a) dull; lazy; timid; meek

बोदापन (nm) laziness; dulness

बोध (nm) sense; perception; knowledge; understanding

बोधक (a) informing, indicating

बोधगम्य (a) fit to be comprehended

बोधिसत्त्व (nm) an epithet of Gautama Buddha

बोना (v) to sow seeds, to set, to scatter

बोरा (nm) a canvas bag, a sack

बोरिया (nf) a small sack; a mat, a bedding

बोरी (nf) a small bag or sack

बोल (nm) speech; taunt

बोलचाल (nf) conversation, talk; friendly relation

बोलना (v) to speak, to utter; to pronounce

बोलवाना (v) to cause to speak up

बोलबाला (nm) overbearing influence, sway

बोली (nf) speech; dialect; language; a bid

बोवाई (nf) sowing

बोवाना (v) to cause seeds to be sown by another

बोहनी (nf) the first sale of the day of a trader

बौखला/ना (v) to be terribly enraged; to be insane or mad; —हट rage, fury

बौछार (nf) a shower, a splash; spray

बौड़म (a & nm) silly, stupid; hance —पना (nm)

बौद्ध (a & nm) a follower of Gautam Buddha, a Buddhist; —मत Buddhism; —विहार a Buddhist monastery

बौद्धिक (a) intellectual; —ता intellectuality

बौना (a & nm) pigmy; dwarf; dwarfish

बौर (nm) the small flowers that grow on mango or neem trees

बौरा (a) mad; ignorant; foolish; —ई madness; ignorance; foolishness; —या mad, insane

बौराना (v) to be mad or insance

ब्याज (nm) interest; —ख़ोर a usurer; —ख़ोरी usury; —दर-ब्याज compound interest

ब्याना to calf, to foal, to give birth to (in animals)

ब्यालू (nf) supper; dinner

ब्याह (nm) wedding, marriage ceremony

ब्याहता (a & nf) married to a person

ब्याहना (v) to wed, to marry; to

give or take in marriage

ब्यौंत (nf) an arrangement; a method; an opportunity; cutting of a cloth in tailoring

ब्यौंतना (v) to cut cloth for preparing garments

ब्यो/रा (nm) detail; particulars; description; —रेवार systematic, detailed

ब्यौरा (nm) see ब्योरा

ब्रह्म (nm) God; the divine source of the universe; ego; — घाती killer of a Brahman. — ज्ञानी theologian — भोज the collective feeding of the Brahmans — विद्या theosophy

ब्रह्मचर्य (nm) celibacy, chastity

ब्रह्मचारिणी (nf) a woman who observes celibacy

ब्रह्मचारी (nm) a religious student who observes celibacy

ब्रह्मांड (nm) the universe, cosmos

भ

भ the fourth member of the fifth pentad of consonants in Devnagri alphbet

भंग (nm) fracture; dissolution; split; breach

भंगिम (nf) posture, pose; obliquity

भंगी (nm) a sweeper

भंगुर (a) brittle, perishable; —ता brittleness, perishableness

भंजन (nm) demolition, breaking; ruination

भंडा (nm) a secret; a utensil

भंडार (nm) a store house, a store; the place where household goods are stored

भँवर (nm) a whirlpool

भँवरा (nm) the black bee

भक्त (nm) a follower; devotee

भक्ति (nf) worship; devotion

भक्षक (nm) an eater, eating

भक्षण (nm) feeding; devouring; eating

भक्ष्य (a) eatable, edible

भगंदर (nm) fistula in the anus

भग (nf) the female genital

भगदड़ (nf) fleeing, stampede

भगवती (nf) a goddess, an epithet of Durga or Saraswati

भगवा (a) saffron (coloured)

भगवान् (nm) God, Lord

भगाना (v) to cause to run away, to drive off, to put to flight

भगिनी (nf) a sister, sisterly relation

भगोड़ा (*nm & a*) run away, deserter

भग्न (*a*) broken, defeated, vanquished

भग्नावशेष (*nm*) the broken fragments of something, the ruins of building

भजन (*nm*) a prayer; worship; adoration; a hymn

भजना (*v*) to adore; to worship; to repeat the name of God

भट (*nm*) a warrior, a soldier

भटकना (*v*) to lurk, to meander; to go astray

भटिया/र (*nm*) an innkeeper; —रिन (*nf*) a female inn-keeper

भट्ट (*nm*) a title of Brahmans,

भड़क (*nf*) show, pomp; gaud; splendour; —दार gaudy; splendid; shining

भड़कना (*v*) to be startled

भड़काना (*v*) to blow up into a flame; to excite

भड़कीला (*a*) showy; gaudy; —पन gaudiness, vividness

भड़मड़ाना (*v*) to tap, to thump

भड़भूँजा (*nm*) a man who parches grain

भड़ास (*nf*) accumulated grudge

भड़ुआ (*nm*) one who lives on the earnings of prostitutes

भती/जा (*nm*) a nephew (brother's son); —जी (*nf*) a niece (brother's daughter)

भत्ता (*nm*) an allowance

भदंत (*a*) reverend, honourable; adored

भदेस (*a*) unsophisticated; clumsy

भद्द (*nf*) humiliation, disgrace

भद्दा (*a*) gawky; ugly; vulgar; —पन deformity; vulgarity; ugliness

भद्र (*a*) educated; gentle; pious worthy, noble. —जन a gentle man

भनक (*nf*) a low sound; rumour, hearsay

भनभनाना (*v*) to buzz, to hum, to drone

भनभनाहट (*nf*) buzz, whizzing

भभक (*nf*) a sudden burst of flame, sudden blaze

भभकना (*v*) to inflame, to kindle fire

भभका (*nm*) a still, a retort

भभकी (*nf*) a threat

भभूका (*nm*) flame, blaze

भभूत (*nf*) the ashes of cowdung smeared on the forehead by ascetics

भयंकर (*a*) fierce, fearful, dreadful, terrible

भय (*nm*) a fright, fear; danger; risk. —ग्रस्त frightened; —शून्य dauntless

भयभीत (*a*) frightened, afraid; alarmed

भयाकुल (*a*) terrified, frightened

भयानक (*a*) fearful, frightened, dreadful, horrible

भयावह (*a*) terrible, fearful

भर (a) complete, full, entire, whole; —पाई quittance, payment in full, —पूर full, full to the brim; —पेट to the fullest satisfaction

भरण (nm) cherishing, a nourishing, the act of bearing; —पोषण maintenance, support

भरती (nf) admission, an enlistment, a recruitment; enrolment

भरना (v) to fill; to load

भरम (nm) doubt, suspicion

भरमाना (v) to delude, to deceive, to create an illusion

भरमार (nf) plenty, abundance

भरसक (adv) to the best of one's ability

भराई (nf) the work or wages paid for filling a thing

भराव (nm) stuffing; filling

भरोसा (nm) hope; trust; confidence

भर्ता (nm) lord; husband; Vishnu

भर्त्सना (nf) reproach; abuse; denunciation

भर्राना (v) to be choked; to whizz; to turn hoarse

भलमनसाहत (nf) nobility

भला (a) good, well, gentle, noble; (nm) well-being; good; —चंगा healthy, in good health; —मानस a gentleman

भलाई (nf) goodness; weal, well-being

भव/दीय (ind) your, yours; —दीया feminine form of भवदीय

भवन (nm) mansion; a house, a palace

भवानी (nf) an epithet of Durga

भविष्य (nm) the future; —दर्शी, द्रष्टा a seer, one who can see through into the future; —वक्ता a prophet, an augur; —वाणी oracle, prediction

भविष्यत् (a) that is yet to come, future

भव्य (a) beautiful, grand; divine

भस्म (nf) ash; —सात् burnt to ashes

भस्मीभूत (a) burnt to ashes; ruined

भहराना (v) to crash down

भाँग (nf) the intoxicating hemp; —खाना to be intoxicated; —छनना to drink भाँग

भाँजना (v) to fold; to twist something; to brandish

भाँजी (nf) interruption, impediment; niece (sister's daughter)

भांड (nm) a jester, clown

भाँड़ (nm) buffoon

भाँड़ा (nm) a pot, utensil, equipment

भांडागार (nm) a treasure-house

भांडार (nm) a store-house, a

treasure-house

भाँति (*nf*) kind; mode; method

भाँपना (*v*) to look into; to guess the truth

भाँय-भाँय (*nm*) sound produced in a lonely place

भाई (*nm*) a brother; —चारा fraternity; —बंद् kith and kin; —भतीजावाद nepotism

भाग (*nm*) a share; a portion, a division

भाग-दौड़ (*nf*) strenuous effort; running about

भागना (*v*) to run away, to flee; to escape

भागी (*a & nm*) fortunate, lucky; —दार a sharer, partner

भागीरथी (*nf*) the river Ganga

भाग्य (*nm*) destiny, fate, fortune, lot, luck; —दोष fault of fortune; —परायण, वादी a fatalist; —लक्ष्मी goddess of fortune; —वशात् luckily; —वाद fatalism; —विधाता fortune-maker; —शाली fortunate; —हीनता star-crossed

भाग्य/वान् (*a*) happy, lucky; —वती fortunate lady

भाजक (*nm*) a divisor in mathematics; (*a*) dividing

भाजन (*nm*) a pot; a fit or suitable person

भाज्य (*nm*) a factor, divisor; (*a*) divisible

भाट (*nm*) a bard, a minstrel, a flatterer

भाटा (*nm*) low tide, falling tide

भाड़ (*nm*) a parcher's oven

भाड़ा (*nm*) fare; hire; rent; freight

भात (*nm*) boiled rice

भानजा (*nm*) the sister's son

भानजी (*nf*) sister's daughter

भाना (*v*) to fit, to suit; to be liked, to be pleasing

भाप (*nf*) steam; damp; fume; vapour

भामी (*nf*) brother's wife, a sister-in-law

भामिनी (*nf*) a woman

भार (*nm*) load; burden; weight; —क्षमता carrying capacity; —वाहक a carrier; porter

भारत (*nm*) India; —माता Mother India; —वर्ष India, the Indian sub-continent; —वासी an Indian; —विद्या Indology

भारती (*nf*) speech, the name of the goddess Saraswati

भारतीय (*a & nm*) Indian; an Indian

भारी (*a*) big; heavy, weighty; —पन weight; heaviness; —भरकम of massive structure

भार्या (*nf*) a married woman; wife, better half

भाल (*nm*) the forehead

भाला (*nm*) a spear, lance

भालू (*nm*) a bear

भाव (*nm*) rate; emotion, feeling; idea, —ताव bargain-

ing; —प्रधान emotional;
—व्यंजक expressive; —शून्य
unattached; —हीन cold

भावज (nf) brother's wife,
sister-in-law

भावना (nf) wish, fancy, desire,
motive

भावात्मक (a) emotional

भावबोधक (a) sentimental

भाववाचक (a) infinitive; (nm)
an abstract noun

भावानुवाद (nm) free translation

भावार्थ (nm) purport; sense

भावी (a) future, coming

भावुक (a) emotional; sentimental; reflecting; hence—
ता (nf) emotion, sentiment

भाव्य (a) possible, probable

भावोत्कर्ष (nm) emotional
excellence

भावोन्मत्त (a) emotion-crazy,
overwhelmed by emotion

भावोन्मेष (nm) emergence of an
emotion or sentiment

भाषण (nm) talk, speech;
address; —कर्ता a speaker

भाषांतर (nm) rendition,
translation; —कार a tran-
slator; interpreter

भाषा (nf) speech, language,
tongue; —विज्ञान philology;
—शास्त्र glossology; —बद्ध
written in current dialect

भाषाई (a) linguistic

भाषित (a) spoken, uttered, told

भाषी (nm) a speaker

भाष्य (nm) a commentary,

annotation; —कार an-
notator

भास (nm) light, ray, —मंत
brilliant, —मान appearing

भासना (v) to glean; to appear,
to be known

भासित (a) glittering, appeared

भिंडी (nf) the vegetable called
lady's finger

भिक्षा (nf) begging; —वृत्ति a
beggar's occupation

भिक्षार्थी (nm) a beggar

भिक्षु (nm) a beggar; Buddhist
mendicant

भिक्षुक (nm) a beggar

भिखारिन (nf) a female beggar

भिखारी (nm) a beggar

भिगोना (v) to sop, to soak, to
drench

भिड़ंत (nf) clash; encounter,
confrontation

भिड़ (nf) a wasp; —का छत्ता a
cluster of wasps

भिड़ना (v) to quarrel, to collide,
to clash; to skirmish

भित्ति (nf) a wall; the board on
which a painting is made

भिदना (v) to enter into; to
penetrate; to be pierced

भिनकना (v) to hum as bees, to
create disgust, to buzz

भिनभिनाना (v) to make a
buzzing sound

भिन्न (a) separate, various;
—ता discordance, diversity,
difference

भिन्नार्थक (a) having a different

meaning or significance

भिन्नाना (v) to feel giddy

भिश्ती (nm) one who carries water in a large leather bag

भिषज् (nm) a physician

भींचना (v) to pull, to tighten

भी (ind) also; too; even

भीख (nf) begging; alms

भीगना (v) to be wet, to be drenched

भीड़ (nf) multitude; crowd; mob

भीड़-भड़क्का (nf) hustle and bustle

भीत (a) terrified; afraid; (nf) a wall

भीतर (ind) in, within, inside, into; —ही भीतर within one-self

भीतरी (a) inner, inward; internal; secret

भीति (nf) terror; awe; trembling

भीनी (a) pleasant, sweet smell

भीम (a) awful, terrible

भीरु (a) coward; shy; timid

भीरुता (nf) timidity; cowardice

भील (nm) a wild mountainous tribe dwelling on the banks of the river Nurmada

भीषण (a) awful, terrible, fearful

भीषणता (nf) awfulness

भीष्म (a) terrible, frightful; —पितामह Grand-uncle of the Pandavas & Kauravas

भुक्खड़ (a) hungry, gluttonous; poor

भुक्त (a) eaten; enjoyed

भुक्ति (nf) food, meal; enjoy-ment

भुख/मरा (a) starved, hungry; gluttonous; —मरी famine; starvation

भुगतना (v) to suffer pain; to undergo

भुगतान (nm) payment in full settlement, decision

भुगताना (v) to finish; to pay; to deliver; to accomplish

भुजंग (nm) a snake, sarpent

भुजा (nf) arm; side

भुजिया (nf) dried and parched vegetable

भुट्टा (nm) maize-corn

भुनना (v) to be parched or fried

भुनभुनाना (v) to mutter, to speak in an indistinct way

भुनाना (v) to encash; to get parched; to change

भुरभुरा (a) friable; crisp; dry and powdery

भुलक्कड़ (a) forgetful; negligent

भुलाना (v) to cause to forget, to coax, to neglect

भुलावा (nm) deception, delusion

भुवन (nm) the universe; world

भुवनपति (nm) a king

भुस (nm) chaff, straw, husk

भूँकना (v) to bark, to yap, to bay, to yelp

भूँजना (v) to parch, to trouble

भू (nf) the earth; the world; ground; soil; — धर a mountain; — मंडलthe globe, the earth; — विद्‌a geologist; — विद्या geology

भूकंप (nm) an earthquake

भूख (nf) appetite, hunger; desire, necessity; — हड़ताल hunger strike

भूखा (a) hungry; needy, desirous

भूगर्भ (nm) the internal part of the earth

भूगोल (nm) geography, globe; — वेत्ता a geographer

भूघन (nm) material, matter

भूचर (nm) an animal living on the earth

भूचाल (nm) an earthquake

भूचित्र (nm) map of the world

भूटानी (a) pertaining to Bhutan; (nm) a resident of Bhutan

भूत (a) gone, past, bygone; (nm) an evil spirit, a ghost; — काल the past (tense); — पूर्व ex, previous, former

भूतल (nm) the surface of the earth, the world

भूदान (nm) gift of land

भूनना (v) to roast; to parch; to fry; to toast

भूपति (nm) an emperor, a king

भूपाल (nm) a king

भूमंडल (nm) the earth

भूमध्येरेखा (nf) equator

भूमध्यसागर (nm) the mediter-ranean sea

भूमि (nf) land; the earth, globe, soil; — गत underground

भूमिका (nf) foreward, preface; introduction; back-ground; — बाँधनाto prepare the back-ground

भूरा (a) brown, hoary, grey

भूरि (a) very much; — भूरिvery much

भूल (nf) a mistake; negligence; slip, — करना to slip; — से amiss; — चूक a lapse, a miss; — सुधार correction

भूलना (v) to mistake; to err; to be forgotten

भूलभुलैयाँ (nf) a maze

भूलाभटका (a) stray

भूषण (nm) an ornament, jewels

भूषित (a) decorated, dight, adorned

भूसा (nm) chaff, husk, straw

भूसी (nf) chaff, bran, husk

भुंग (nm) the large black bee

भृकुटी (nf) eyebrow; a frown

भृत्य (nm) a slave; a servant; an employee

भेंगा (a) squint-eyed

भेंट (nf) an interview; meeting; gift, present; an offering

भेंटना (v) to visit

भेजना (v) to send; to transmit; to send forth

भेजवाना (v) to cause to despatch

भेजा (nm) the brain

भेड़ (nf) sheep; timid person

भेड़ा (*nm*) a ram

भेड़िया (*nm*) a wolf

भेद (*nm*) difference; secret

भेदक (*a*) piercing, breaking through

भेदभाव (*nm*) a difference

भेदिया (*nm*) a spy, an emissary

भेष (*nm*) an assumed appearance; a disguise; a counterfeit dress

भेषज (*nm*) medicine, medicament; remedy

भेस (*nm*) appearance; dress; guise; —बदलना to disguise

भैंस (*nf*) a female buffalo; an extra-fat woman

भैंसा (*nm*) a he-buffalo; stout and sturdy man

भैया (*nm*) a brother

भैरवी (*nf*) a Raga which is sung in the early morning

भोंकना (*v*) to pierce, to poke

भोंड़ा (*a*) ugly, illshaped; —पन insolence

भोंदू (*a*) stupid, foolish, silly

भोंपू (*nm*) a wind-instrument, horn, siren

भोक्ता (*a*) one who eats or enjoys; (*nm*) a licentious person

भोग (*nm*) the experience of pleasure or a pain; pleasure, enjoyment

भोगलिप्सा (*nf*) evil habit

भोगलोलुप (*a*) sybarite

भोगना (*v*) to suffer; to enjoy; to undergo

भोगी (*nm*) one who enjoys a thing, one who is always engaged in the pursuit of pleasure

भोग्य (*a*) worthy of being enjoyed or experienced, fit to be used

भोज (*nm*) a feast; banquet

भोजन (*nm*) meals, food; diet; —भट्ट a glutton

भोजनशाला (*nf*) a kitchen

भोजनालय (*nm*) a restaurant; mess

भोजपत्र (*nm*) the leaf and bark of birch tree

भोर (*nm*) the early morning, dawn

भोला (*a*) simple, innocent; foolish; —पन innocence, simplicity; —भाला very simple, artless

भौं (*nf*) an eyebrow

भौंकना (*v*) to bark like a dog; to talk too much

भौंरा (*nm*) a black bee, beetle

भौगोलिक (*a*) pertaining to the terrestrial globe, geographical; —ता geographicality

भौचक्का (*a*) non-plussed, dumb-founded

भौजाई (*nf*) brother's wife

भौतिक (*a*) material; physical, elemental; —वाद materialism; —वादी a materialist; —विज्ञान physics

भौतिकी (*nf*) physics

भौमवार (*nm*) Tuesday

भ्रंश (*nm*) falling, declining

भ्रम (*nm*) suspicion, confusion; —जाल illusion; चित्त— crack-brained

भ्रमण (*nm*) going round; excursion; travel

भ्रमर (*nm*) large black bee; beetle

भ्रष्ट (*a*) spoilt; corrupt; fallen

भ्रष्टता (*nf*) corruption, degradation

भ्रष्टाचार (*nm*) wantonness, depraved behaviour

भ्रष्टाचारी (*a*) of loose morals

भ्रांत (*a*) mistaken, fallen into error

भ्रांति (*nf*) a mistake, an error; delusion, a doubt

भ्राता (*nm*) a brother

भ्रातृत्व (*nm*) brotherhood

भ्रातृभाव (*nm*) brotherly affection

भ्रामक (*a*) causing to whirl, causing to err, deceiving

भू (*nm*) an eyebrow; —भंगिमा attractive movement of eyebrows

भ्रूण (*nf*) a child in the womb; —हत्या murder of a foetus

म

म the fifth member of the fifth pentad of consonants in Devnagri alphabet

मंगता (*nm*) a beggar

मंगनी (*nf*) engagement; a borrowed thing

मंगल (*nm*) auspiciousness; Mars; welfare; Tuesday; (*a*) auspicious; —कामना good wishes; —कार्य an auspicious ceremony; —सूचक auspicious; —सूत्र the lucky thread worn by a married woman

मंगलाचरण (*nm*) the worship of Ganesha at the commencement of an undertaking, a benediction

मंगाना (*v*) to ask for, to send for, to cause to bring

मंगेतर (*nm & nf*) fiance or fiancee; (*a*) one to whom a man or a women is betrothed (for marriage)

मंच (*nm*) a bed; a dais, a raised platform

मंजन (*nm*) tooth-powder

मंजना (*v*) to be cleansed, to be rinsed

मंजरी (*nf*) a new shoot, a sprout

मंजाई (*nf*) act of cleansing

मंज़िल (*nf*) a halting-place in a journey; a storey of a house; destination

मंजु (a) good, beautiful, pleasing, lovely; —भाषी sweet-speaking (man) —भाषिणी sweet-speaking (women)

मंजुल (a) see मंजु

मंजूर (a) accepted; granted; bestowed; approved

मंजूरी (nf) acceptance; approval; sanction

मंजूषा (nf) a small chest, a case, a box

मंझधार (nf) see मझधार

मंझला (a) intermediate; middle

मंझोला (a) middling, of average size

मंडन (nm) ornamentation, decoration; support through argumentation

मंडप (nm) a shelter; a canopy raised for ceremonial purposes; a pavilion

मंडराना (v) to hover, to circumambulate, to flutter about

मंडल (nm) circumference; ring; territory; board; orbit

मंडलाकार (a) circular, annular

मंडली (nf) corporation, association, party, society; ring

मंडलेश्वर (nm) a ruler over twelve kingdoms

मंडवा (nm) canopy

मंडित (a) ornamented; decorated; filled

मंडी (nf) a big market; a bazar

मंडूक (nm) a frog

मंतव्य (nm) a view, opinion

मंत्र (nm) advice; a counsel; a secret consultation

मंत्रणा (nf) a counsel; advice; view, opinion

मंत्रविद्या (nf) the science of spells; magic, jugglery

मंत्रसंहिता (nf) part of the Veda which contains hymns

मंत्रालय (nm) ministry

मंत्रिमंडल (nm) cabinet, ministry

मंत्री (nm) a minister; a secretary; an adviser; a counsellor

मंथन (nm) agitating, stirring; churning, a churning stick

मंथर (a) slow, lazy, stupid, dull

मंद (a) feeble, idle, dull

मंदता (nf) slowness, tardiness, lassitude

मंदप्रकाश (nm) dimlight, glimmer

मंदबुद्धि (a) dull, blunt

मंदभाग्य (a) wretched, ill-fated; unlucky, unfortunate

मंदमति (a) feather-brained

मंदा (a) slow, tardy; weary, bad

मंदाकिनी (nf) celestial Ganga

मंदाग्नि (nf) indigestion

मंदिर (nm) a temple

मंदी (nf) a fall in price

मंशा (nf) wish, desire; wild

intention; purpose

मंसूख (a) repealed, cancelled

मँहगा (a) costly, expensive, high in price; see also महँगा

मकई (nf) Indian corn, maize

मकड़ी (nf) a spider

मकनातीस (nm) a loadstone, a magnet

मकबरा (nm) a large building containing a tomb

मकसद (nm) desire, intention

मकान (nm) a house, a residence, a dwelling place; —मालिक house-owner, landlord

मकोड़ा (nm) any small insect

मक्का (nm) maize, corn

मक्कार (a) deceitful, crafty, cunning

imposture

मक्खन (nm) butter; —बाज़ a flatterer; —बाज़ी flattery

मक्खी (nf) a fly; a bee; —मारना an idle fellow

मक्खीचूस (nm) skinflint, miser, a niggardly person

मखमल (nm) velvet, plush

मखमली (a) velvety

मखाना (nm) a kind of dry fruit

मखौल (nm) a joke, a jest

मगज़ (nm) brain; kernel, pith; —पच्ची too much of brain-taxing

मगज़ी (nf) welter, edging, hem, frill

मगर (nm) a crocodile; (ind)

but, except

मगरमच्छ (nm) a crocodile

मगरूर (a) proud, arrogant

मग्न (a) drowned, sunk, engaged

मचलना (v) to persist, to insist

मचला (a) insisting, obstinate

मचली (nf) nausea; —आना to feel like vomitting, to nauseate

मचान (nm) a raised platform, a stage, a scaffold; —बाँधना to prepare a scaffold

मच्छर (nm) a mosquito; gnat

मच्छरदानी (nf) a mosquito net

मछंदर (nm) a buffoon, a dunce

मछली (nf) a fish; pisces

मछुआ (nm) a fisherman, a fishmonger

मज़दूर (nm) a labourer, worker; —वर्ग the working class; —दल the Labour Party

मज़दूरी (nf) price which is paid for work or labour, wages; remuneration; stipend

मजनूँ (nm) the celebrated lover of Laila; a mad or insane man

मज़बूत (a) strong, compact, firm, vigorous, sturdy

मज़बूती (nf) firmness, strength, vigour; durability

मजबूर (a) helpless; obliged; compelled

मजबूरी (nf) helplessness, compulsion

मजबूरन (ind) under pressure,

being compelled

मज़मून (nm) subject, topic; article; composition

मजलिस (nf) an assembly, a meeting, a congregation

मज़हब (nm) sect, creed, religion

मज़हबी (a) religious

मज़ा (nm) flavour, relish; taste; pleasure

मज़ाक (nm) a joke, jest, humour

मज़ाकिया (a) humorous, witty, pranky; (nm) a jester, buffoon

मज़ाल (nf) power, strength

मजिस्ट्रेट (nm) a magistrate

मज़ेदार (a) relishing, tasteful; giving pleasure; delicious

मज्जन (nm) a bathing, a bath

मज्जा (nf) marrow

मझधार (nf) the current in the middle of a river

मझला (a) intermediate; middling

मझोला (a) middle, middle-most, of average size

मटकना (v) to conquet, to strut, to swagger

मटकाना (v) to cause to twinkle, to conquet

मटका (nm) a large earthen pitcher

मटकी (nf) a small pitcher

मटकीला (a) moving the body in ogling or winking eyes

मटमैला (a) muddy, dusty, dusky

मटर (nm) a pea

मटरगश्ती (nf) a stray walking, a ramble, a stroll

मटियामेट (a) almost destroyed or ruined

मटियाला (a) muddy, dusty, dirty

मट्ठा (nm) churned curd, butter milk

मट्ठी (nf) a kind of small bread which has been cooked in oil or clarified butter

मठ (nm) a monastery, a hermitage; —धारी the head of a monastery, an ascetic

मढ़ना (v) to envelop; to wrap, to frame; to impose

मणि (nf) a jewel, a gem, a precious stone

मणिधर (nm) a snake

मणिबंध (nm) the wrist, the corpus

मतंग (nm) an elephant; cloud

मत (nm) dogma, belief; an opinion; faith; vote; —दान poll, polling, casting of votes; —दाता a voter, an elector

मतभेद (nm) disagreement

मतलब (nm) purport, meaning; relation

मतलबी (nf) selfish, self-concerned

मतलाना (v) to feel like vomitting, to feel sick

मतली (nf) nausea, a feeling like vomitting

मतवाला (a) drunk, intoxicated; insane

मताधिकार (nm) a right to vote, suffrage, franchise; वयस्क— adult franchise

मताधिकारी (nm) one who is authorised to vote

मतनुयायी (nm) the follower of a tenet, a theorist

मति (nf) sense, intellect; understanding; opinion; —हीन stupid, foolish; —भ्रम confusion

मतैक्य (nm) agreement; unanimity

मत्त (a) drunk, mad, intoxicated; happy

मत्था (nm) the forehead; head

मत्स्य (nm) a fish

मत्स्यावतार (nm) an incarnation of Vishnu in the form of a fish

मथना (v) to churn, to batter; to agitate

मद (nm) passion; intoxication, arrogance; —मत्त intoxicated; passionate

मदद (nf) aid; help; assistance, support; relief

मददगार (nm) a helper; a supporter; an assistant

मदन (nm) the god of love

मदरसा (nm) a school

मद/होश (a) dead drunk; rendered senseless; —होशी drunkenness; intoxicatedness

मदारी (nm) a snake-charmer, a juggler

मदिरा (nf) wine, spirit

मदोन्मत्त (a) intoxicated; arrogant

मद्धिम (a) dim; slow; moderate

मद्य (nm) liquor, spirit, wine; —निर्माणशाला a distillery; —पान drinking

मधु (nm) honey; juice of flowers; liquor; the spring; —कोष a honey comb, —कर the large black bee; —करी alms given in the form of cooked food only; —मक्खी honey-bee, bee; —मेह diabetes; —शाला a bar

मधुर (a) pleasant; sweet; —ता sweetness; melodiousness

मधुरिमा (nf) sweetness, softness, melodiousness

मध्य (a) central, middle; intermediate; (nm) the middle part, the centre; —काल interval; mediaeval period; —भाग heart; —युग the Middle Ages; —पूर्व middle-east; —वर्ग middle class; —वर्ती central

मध्यम (a) middle, intermediate of moderate strength or size

मध्यमा (nf) the middle finger

मध्यस्थ (a) intermediate, medial; (nm) a mediator; —ता mediation

मध्यांतर (nm) an interval

मध्याह्न (*nm*) midday, noon

मन:शास्त्र (*nm*) psychology

मन (*nm*) heart; mind; desire; disposition; a weight equal to forty seers; —गढ़ंत imaginary; —चाहा desired, wished for, favourite; —बहलाव amusement, entertainment, recreation; —भावन beloved; attractive; —माना arbitrary; self-willed; —मौजी self-willed

मनका (*nm*) a bead

मनन (*nm*) brooding; meditation; thinking deeply over something; —शील thoughtful

मनश्चिकि/त्सा (*nf*) psychological treatment; —त्सक a psychotherapist

मनसूबा (*nm*) design; plan; intention; idea

मनस्ताप (*nm*) mental agony, regret, remorse, sorrow

मनस्वी (*a*) wise, strong-minded

मनहू/स (*a*) inauspicious, ill-fated; gloomy; —सियत (*nf*) gloominess, sombreness, inauspiciousness

मनहूसी (*nf*) gloominess, sombreness

मना (*a*) prohibited, forbidden

मनाही (*nf*) a prohibition, a restraint, forbiddance

मनाना (*v*) to persuade

मनिहार (*nm*) one who sells or makes glass bangles

मनीऑर्डर (*nm*) a money order

मनीषी (*a*) wise, learned

मनुष्य (*nm*) a man, human being; —लोक the world

मनुष्यत्व (*nf*) humanity

मनुहार (*nf*) persuasion

मनोकामना (मन:कामना) (*nf*) desire, wish

मनोगति (*nf*) mental disposition

मनोज (*nm*) an epithet of cupid-the god of love

मनोनीत (*a*) approved; nominated

मनोबल (*nm*) morale, moral strength

मनोयोग (*nm*) concentration

मनोरंजक (*a*) attractive, pleasing to the mind

मनोरंजन (*nm*) recreation, amusement

मनोरथ (*nm*) wish, desire; longing

मनोरम (*a*) attractive, beautiful, lovely

मनोवांछित (*a*) desired, wished

मनोविकार (*nm*) emotion of mind, feeling

मनोविज्ञान (*nm*) psychology

मनोविनोद (*nm*) amusement, pastime; hobby

मनोविलास (*nm*) musing, fancy

मनोविश्लेषण (*nm*) psycho-analysis

मनोवृत्ति (*nf*) mentality; mental attitude

मनोवेग (*nm*) impulse; a

passion

मनोवैज्ञानिक (*a & nm*) psychol-ogical; a psychologist

मनोव्यथा (*nf*) mental agony; affliction

मनोव्यापार (*nm*) thought, conception, mental work

मनोहर (*a*) beautiful, lovely

मनौती (*nf*) an assurance, a vow to offer something to a deity after the fulfilment of one's desire

मंतव्य (*nm*) thought

मन्नत (*nf*) same as मनौती

मन्मथ (*nm*) cupid

मम/ता (*nf*) —त्व (*nm*) affec-tion, attachment

मयूर (*nm*) a peacock

मयूरी (*nf*) a peahen

मरकत (*nm*) emerald

मरघट (*nm*) a cremation ground, a place for burning the dead

मरज़ (*nm*) a disease, a malady, a bad habit

मरण (*nm*) death, dying, mortality, expiration

मरणासन्न (*a*) on the death bed

मरतबा (*nm*) an order; a turn

मरदानगी (*nf*) bravery, valour, courage

मरदाना (*a*) masculine, male

मरना (*v*) to die, to decease, to pass away

मरम्मत (*nf*) mending, repair

मरहम (*nm*) an ointment; an unction; —पट्टी bandage

मरहूम (*a*) deceased, late, dead

मराल (*nm*) a goose, swan

मरियल (*a*) lean and thin, weak

मरीचिका (*nf*) mirage, sunbeam

मरीज़ (*a*) sick; ill; diseased; (*nm*) an ailing person, a patient

मरीना (*nm*) a kind of soft fine woollen cloth

मरु (*nm*) a desert, a barren soil

मरुत् (*nm*) wind, the deities of the wind

मरुद्वीप (*nm*) a fertile land in a desert, an oasis

मरुस्थल (*nm*) a desert

मरोड़ (*nm*) sprain, wrench, twist

मरोड़ना (*v*) to wring, to twist, to tease

मरोड़ा (*nm*) a gripe in the stomach

मर्कट (*nm*) a monkey, an ape

मर्ज़ (*nm*) a disease; ailment

मर्तबान (*nm*) an enamelled earthen pot which is used for holding oil or ghee

मर्ज़ी (*nf*) will, desire; pleasure

मर्त्य (*a*) dying, earthly; (*nm*) a mortal; —लोक the earth; —धर्म mortality, human nature

मर्द (*nm*) a man; a brave person

मर्दन (*nm*) rubbing; massage

मर्दानगी (*nf*) bravery; masculi-nity

मर्दाना (*a*) masculine; male

मर्म (*nm*) a secret, core, a vital organ

मर्मज्ञ (*a*) having a deep insight into a subject; (*nm*) a learned man, one who knows the secret

मर्मभेदक (*a*) fatal

मर्ममेदी (*a*) stinging, heart-rending

मर्म/पीड़ा (*nf*) intense mental agony; —स्पर्शी touching, poignant, heart-rending

मर्मर (*nm*) rustling; marble; —ध्वनि rustling noise

मर्यादा (*nf*) limit, dignity; rank

मल (*nm*) rubbish, filth; dirt; - —मूत्र urine and faeces, excrement

मलना (*v*) to press hard; to rub; to smear; to massage

मलबा (*nm*) rubbish, debrish

मलमल (*nf*) muslin, linen

मलहम (*nm*) see मरहम

मलाई (*nf*) the cream of milk

मलाल (*nm*) sadness, dejection

मलिन (*a*) foul, dirty, filthy, sad; —पदार्थ filth

मलिनता (*nf*) nastiness, pollution

मलेरिया (*nm*) malaria

मल्ल (*nm*) an ancient tribe of wrestlers; an athlete; —भूमि a place for wrestling; —युद्ध a duel, a hand to hand fight

मल्लाह (*nm*) a boatman; a sailor, mariner, seamar

मवाद (*nm*) purulent matter, pus secreted from body

मवेशी (*nm*) cattle, quadrupeds, beast; —ख़ाना a cattle pond

मशक (*nm*) a mosquito; (*nf*) a leathern water bag

मशक्कत (*nf*) labour, toil, pains

मशगूल (*a*) busy, engaged, employed

मशविरा (*nm*) counsel, advice, consultation

मशहूर (*a*) well-known, famous, celebrated

मशाल (*nf*) a torch; —ची a torch-bearer

मश्क़ (*nf*) exercise; practice

मस (*nf*) ink; the hairs on the upper lip appearing in early youth

मसकना (*v*) to split, to press, to tear asunder

मसख़रा (*a*) humoursome; waggish; funny (*nm*) a joker, a buffoon, jester, funnyman

मसख़री (*nf*) a joke, a jest

मसजिद (*nf*) a mosque

मसनद (*nf*) a very big pillow

मसल (*nf*) a fable, an allegory, an example

मसलन (*adv*) pressing; rubbing; crushing; (*ind*) for example, for instance

मसलना (*v*) to crush, to press hard, to rub

मसला (*nm*) a proverb, a maxim, a saying

मसविदा (nm) a plaint of a suit, draft

मसहरी (nf) a mosquito curtain, a bedstead which is fitted with such a curtain

मसा (nm) a wart, mole

मसान (nm) a place for burning the dead, a cremation ground

मसाला (nm) spices; condiments; मसालेदार spiced

मसि (nf) writing ink; — शोषक blotting paper; — दानी an inkpot

मसीहा (nm) Jesus Christ; a religious leader

मसूड़ा (nm) the gum of the teeth

मसूर (nf) lentil, a kind of pulses

मसोसना (v) to repress; to subdue

मसौदा (nm) a draft

मस्जिद (nf) see मसजिद

मस्त (a) intoxicated, drunk, happy

मस्तक (nm) the head; forehead

मस्ताना (a) intoxicated, drunk; (v) to be lustful, to be overjoyed

मस्तिष्क (nm) head, brain, cerebrum

मस्ती (nf) intoxication, drunkenness, carefreeness

मस्तूल (nm) the mast of a boat or ship

मस्सा (nm) a wart

महँगा (a) expensive; dear; costly, high-priced

महँगाई (nf) dearness; expensiveness; costliness

महंत (nm) head priest of a temple, a monk; self-willed leader

महक (nf) odour, fragrance, scent, perfume; — दार sweet-smelling, fragrant

महकना (v) to give out fragrance or sweet smell, to perfume

महकमा (nm) the department for the performance of a work

महज़ (a) mere, pure, unmixed, only; (adv) only, entirely, merely, wholly

महताब (nm) the moon; (nf) moonlight

महतारी (nf) mother

महत् (a) big; great; excellent

महत्तर (a) greater, bigger

महत्ता (nf) significance, importance; greatness

महत्त्व (nm) greatness; — पूर्ण important, significant

महत्त्वाकां/क्षा (nf) ambition; — क्षी ambitious

महफिल (nf) a private assembly, recreational assembly

महबूब (a) dear, beloved

महर्षि (nm) a great saint

महल (nm) a palace, a stately mansion

महसूल (nm) custom, duty,

levy

महसूस (*a*) felt; experienced; perceived

महा (*a*) great, large, very, most; —कवि a great poet; an epic poet; —काल an epithet of Shiva; —काव्य a poetical composition of great length, an epic; —देव an epithet of Lord Shiva; —देवी an epithet of goddess Parvati; —नगर/नगरी cosmopolitan city; —पातक a great sin; —पातकी a great sinner; —पुरुष a great man; —प्रलय the great deluge; —प्रस्थान death; the final journey; —रथी a great warrior

महा/जन (*nm*) money lender; —जनी money lending

महात्मा (*a*) lofty-minded, high-souled; noble, generous; (*nm*) a great sage

महादान (*nm*) a great gift which attains heaven

महाद्वीप (*nm*) a continent, a mainland

महान् (*a*) great; eminent; big; —ता nobility; greatness

महानुभाव (*a*) illustrious, glorious, grand, eminent

महापुरुष (*nm*) a great personage, a saint

महाप्रलय (*nm*) the total destruction of the world

महाबली (*a*) extremely powerful, very strong

महाबाहु (*a*) having very long arms; very powerful

महामारी (*nf*) plague, an epidemic

महायज्ञ (*nm*) a great sacrifice

महायुद्ध (*nm*) a world-war, a war

महारत (*nm*) practice, expertise

महा/राज (*nm*) a great king; a term of respect used for Brahmans; a cook; —राजा a ruler, king; —राजाधिराज a king of kings; —रानी the queen

महावत (*nm*) the driver of an elephant

महावर (*nm*) red colour which is prepared from lac with which ladies whose husbands are alive paint their feet

महाविद्यालय (*nm*) a college

महावीर (*a*) lion-hearted, a very brave, heroic

महाशय (*a & nm*) a term of respect, sir, master, mister

महाशालीन (*a*) very humble and meek

महिमा (*nf*) dignity, greatness, worship, magnitude

महिला (*nf*) a lady

महिष (*nm*) a he-buffalo

महिषी (*nf*) a she-buffalo; a queen

महीन (*a*) thin, fine, not coarse, soft

महीना (*nm*) a month; menses;

महीने से in menses

महोत्सव (*nm*) great festival, a big celebration

महोदय (*a*) sir; hence महोदया madam

माँ (*nf*) mother, mamma

माँग (*nf*) a demand, a request, requirement

माँगना (*v*) to demand, to call for; to claim; to invite

मांगलिक (*a*) prosperous, auspicious

माँजना (*v*) to cleanse, to scrub; to polish

माँझी (*nm*) a seaman, a boatman, sailor

माँड (*nm*) boiled rice-water, rice-starch

माँडना (*v*) to rub, to knead flour

माँद (*nf*) a lair, den, barrow

माँदा (*a*) tired, ill, sick

मांस (*nm*) flesh; meat; —पेशी a muscle; —ल fleshy

मांसाहारी (*nm*) non vegetarian

माई (*nf*) a maid servant; an old woman; mother

माचिस (*nf*) a match-box, safety matches; match stick

मातम (*nm*) mourning; grief; —पुरसी expression of condolence

मात/हत (*a*) subordinate, under; hence —हती

माता (*nf*) mother; small-pox

मातामह (*nm*) mother's father, maternal grandfather

मातृ (*nf*) mother; —त्व mother-hood; —भाषा mother-tongue; —भूमि mother land

मात्र (*ind*) merely; only; barely; sheer

मात्रक (*a*) a certain size, magnitude or measure

मात्रा (*nf*) quantity, magnitude, a dose; scale

मात्सर्य (*nm*) jealousy, malice

माथा (*nm*) the forehead; forepart

मादक (*a*) inebriant; intoxi-cating; fascinating

मादकता (*nm*) drunkenness

मादा (*a*) female, of female sex

मादुबा (*nm*) essence; capability; pith; element

माधुर्य (*nm*) sweetness, grace-fulness

माध्यम (*a*) medium, middle, central

माध्यमिक (*a*) intermediary; secondary

मान (*nm*) weight; measure, dignity; —चित्र a map; —दंड a standard; —पत्र an address of welcome

मान/क (*a & nm*) standard, norm, —कीकरण standardi-zation

मानता (*nf*) recognition; importance

मानना (*v*) to accept; to agree, to confess; to respect; to suppose

माननीय (*a*) respectable;

honourable; revered; worthy

मानव (nm) human being, a man; mankind

मानवता (nf) mankind; humanity; —वाद humanism; —वादी a humanist

मानवीय (a) humane

मानस (nm) the mind; thought, the psyche; heart

मानसरोवर (nm) a large lake in the north of the Himalayas

मानसिक (a) mental, fanciful, psychic

मानहानि (nf) defamation

मानिनी (a) amorously sulking

मानी (a) haughty, proud, arrogant; (nm) purport

मानीटर (nm) a monitor

माने (nm) meaning, purport

मानो (ind) as though, as if, supposing

मान्य (a) respectable; considerable; —ता recognition

माप (nm) size; measurement; dimensions; —दंड touchstone; standard

मापक (nm) measurer, one who measures a quantity

मापना (v) to measure; to weigh

माफ़ (a) pardoned; forgiven; excused

माफ़िक (a) suitable; agreeable, favourable

माफ़ी (nf) pardon; forgiveness; exemption; rent-free land

मामला (nm) a business; an affair; a case; matter

मामा (nm) a maternal uncle, mother's brother

मामी (nf) a maternal aunt; mother's brother's wife

मामूली (a) common; ordinary; usual

मायका (nm) maternal house of a married woman

माया (nf) illusion, unreality; riches; phantom; —मोह illusion and attachment

मायावी (a) deceitful, illusive, phantasmic

मायूस (a) disappointed, frustrated

मार (nm) thrashing, beating, the cupid; —काट bloody encounter; —धाड़ fighting and killing

मारक (a) destroying, killing, putting to death

मारकीन (nm) a kind of coarse jaconet, unbleached cloth

मारना (v) to beat; to kill; to hit, to strike; to punish

मारफ़त (ind) through; by; care of

मार्का (nm) a sign, a mark, a trade-mark

मार्ग (nm) a path, passage, way; road, route; —प्रदर्शक a guide; pioneer; —प्रदर्शन guidance

मार्गरक्षक (nm) a watch, a sentry

मार्जक (nm) a cleaner,

washerman

मार्जनी (*nf*) a broom

माफ़त (*ind*) by; through; C/o (care of)

मार्मिक (*a*) affecting the vital parts, influential to a great degree, touching

मार्मिकता (*nf*) the quality of having a thorough know-ledge; heart-touching

माल (*nm*) goods; commodity; merchandise; stock; produce; riches; —ख़ाना a store house, a ware house; —गाड़ी a goods train; —गुज़ारी rent paid for land;—गोदाम the store house at a Rail-way station; —दार rich, wealthy; —पुआ a sweet cake; —मत्ता assets, riches, wealth

माला (*nf*) a row, series; a garland of flowers

मालाकार (*nm*) a garland-maker

मालामाल (*a*) immensely rich, very rich or wealthy

मालिक (*nm*) owner; master; a proprietor; husband

मालिकिन (*nf*) a matron, a mistress, housewife

मालिकाना (*nm*) ownership, a landed property; (*a*) pro-prietary

मालिकी (*nf*) ownership

मालिन (*nf*) wife of a gardener

मालिन्य (*nm*) dirtiness, impu-rity, foulness

मालिश (*nf*) rubbing oil on the body, massage

माली (*nm*) a gardener; gar-lander

मालूम (*a*) known

मावा (*nm*) essence, pith

माश (*nm*) black gram

माशा (*nm*) a weight of eight Rattis or eighteen grains

माशूक़ (*nf*) a beloved

मास (*nm*) a month

मासिक (*a*) monthly; per mensem; (*nm*) menstrua-tion; a monthly magazine; —धर्म menstruation, month-ly course

मासी (*nf*) the mother's sister

मासूम (*a*) harmless; innocent; hence —मियत

माह (*nm*) a month; —ताब the moon; —वार monthly, —वारी pertaining to every month, monthly

माहात्म्य (*nm*) glory, greatness

माहिर (*a*) expert

मिकदार (*nf*) quantity

मिचकाना (*v*) to wink, to blink

मिचना (*v*) to close, to shut

मिचलाना (*v*) to feel sick, to nauseate

मिचली (*nf*) feeling like vomitting, nausea

मिज़ाज (*nm*) temperament, habit; pride

मिज़ाजदार (*a*) arrogant, proud

मिज़ाज़ी (*a*) arrogant; fasti-dious

मिटना (v) to be erased, to be destroyed; to be ruined

मिट्टी (nf) earth; dust; soil; —का तेल kerosene oil; —के मोल damn cheap

मिट्ठू (nm) a parrot

मिठबोला (nm) a sweet-speaking person

मिठाई (nf) sweets, sweetmeat; confectionery

मिठास (nf) sweetness

मितभाषी (nm) one who is moderate in speech

मितव्यय (nm) economy, frugality

मितव्ययी (a) spending sparingly, frugal

मिताई (nf) friendship

मित्र (nm) a friend; an ally; —ता friendship; intimacy

मित्रद्रोही (nm) one who is on bad terms with his friends

मिथ्या (a) false, untrue, sham; (nm) untruth, falsehood; illusion

मिनमिनाना (v) to speak through nasal sounds

मिन्नत (nf) supplication; entreaty, request

मिमियाना (v) to bleat as sheep or goats

मियाँ (nm) master; husband; sir; a Mohammedan; —बीवी husband and wife; —मिट्ठू a sweet-spoken person; a parrot

मिरगी (nf) epilepsy

मिर्च (nf) pepper; chillies

मिलता-जुलता (a) resembling, having resemblance, like

मिलन (nm) union; a meeting; contact; —सार sociable

मिलना (v) to meet; to be mixed; to encounter; to merge

मिलान (nm) a comparison; verification, authentication

मिलाना (v) to compare; to unite; to mix

मिलाप (nm) an agreement, meeting; union

मिलावट (nf) blend, mixing; alloy adulteration

मिल्कियत (nf) estate; property; landed property

मिश्र (a) blended; mixed; combined; —ण a mixture, blend; combination

मिश्रित (a) mixed, compounded, complex

मिश्री (nf) sugar candy

मिश्रीकरण (nm) an admixture

मिष्टान्न (nm) sweetmeat, confectionery

मिसरी (nf) sugar candy

मिसाल (nf) an example, a comparison, a maxim

मिस्त्री (nm) a mechanic, mistry; technician; artisan

मींचना (v) to close, to shut

मीठा (a) pleasant; sweet; (nm) sweetmeat

मीन (nm) a fish; the twelfth sign of zodiac

मीना (nm) a valiant tribe of Rajputana; a kind of precious stone of blue colour

मीनाक्षी (nf) having eyes like those of a fish

मीनार (nf) a tower, a spire

मीमांसक (nm) one who reflects deeply on a subject

मीमांसा (nf) one of the six systems of Hindu Philosophy

मीर (nm) a leader, a chieftain, a religious promulgator

मीरासी (nm) a sect of Mohammedans who earn their living by buffoonery and singing

मील (nf) a mile

मुँगरा (nm) a wooden hammer, mallet

मुंज (nf) a kind of stiff grass which is used in making ropes (see also मूँज)

मुंडन (nm) the shaving of the head, the shaving of hairs of a child's head for the first time

मुँडना (v) to be head shaven; to be robbed

मुँडेर (nm) a parapet

मुँदना (v) to be closed or covered, to be shut up

मुंशी (nm) a scribe, a writer, a clerk; —गीरी the work or profession of a clerk/scribe

मुसिफ़ (nm) a judge of the civil court who is subordinate to a civil judge

मुँह (nm) the mouth; face; forepart; an opening; outlet; source; —काला disrespect, infamy; —ज़बानी verbal, oral; —दर-मुँह face-to-face; —देखी superficial; —फट loose-tongued; —बोला adopted; —माँगा fully answering one's wish; —लगा allowed too much liberty

मुहाँसा (nm) the pimples which appear on the face on the advent of youth

मुअत्तल (a) suspended from work for some time

मुअत्तली (nf) suspension

मुआ (a) dead; good-for-nothing

मुआफ़िक़ (a) suitable; agreeable, favourable (see also माफ़िक़)

मुआयना (nm) inspection; visit

मुआवज़ा (nm) compensation; remuneration

मुक़दमा (nm) a law suit; a case

मुक़दमेबाज़ (nm) a litigant

मुक़द्दर (nm) luck, fate, destiny

मुक़द्दस (a) pure, holy

मुकम्मल (a) finished; ready

मुक़र्रर (a) fixed, appointed, employed

मुक़ाबिला (nm) an opposition; competition; a comparison

मुक़ाम (nm) a halting place,

halt; a place, site

मुकुट (*nm*) a diadem, crown

मुकुर (*nm*) a looking-glass, a mirror

मुकुल (*nm*) a bud, a blossom

मुकुलित (*a*) blossoming, half-opened and half-shut; twinking of eyes

मुक्का (*nm*) a blow with the fist, buffet, thump

मुक्केबाज़ (*nm*) a boxer

मुक्केबाज़ी (*nf*) boxing

मुक्त (*a*) liberated, released from bondage, set free, let loose; —कंठ one who speaks very loudly, one who speaks up without any reserve; —चेता one who is desirous of attaining salvation; —वसन naked; —संशय whose doubts have been removed

मुक्ता (*nf*) a pearl

मुक्तावली (*nf*) a string of pearls

मुक्ति (*nf*) salvation; redemption, release, deliverance

मुख (*nm*) the mouth; face; forepart; entrance; —ज produced from mouth; —पृष्ठ the cover-page; —मंडल the face

मुखड़ा (*nm*) the mouth, face

मुख़तार (*nm*) an agent, a deputy, an attorney; —नामा power of an attorney

मुख़तारी (*nf*) the profession of a Mukhtar, attorneyship

मुखप्रक्षालन (*nm*) the washing of the mouth

मुखबंध (*nm*) a preface, an introduction or foreword to a book

मुख़बिर (*nm*) an informer

मुख़बिरी (*nf*) the work of a reporter or informer

मुखमंडल (*nm*) face, look, countenance, visage

मुखर (*a*) talkative, noisy

मुखरित (*a*) resonant, out-spoken

मुख़ातिब (*a*) with whom a person talks, conversable

मुखापेक्षी (*nm*) one who is dependent on others

मुख़ालिफ़ (*a*) opposing, an enemy, a foe

मुख़ालिफ़त (*nm*) enmity

मुखिया (*nf*) a leader, a chief, the headman of a village

मुखौटा (*nm*) a mask

मुख्य (*a*) premier, chief; main, capital; —त: primarily, chiefly, mainly

मुख्यालय (*nm*) headquarters

मुगदर (*nm*) a club which is used in physical exercise

मुगालता (*nm*) illusion, mistake; misconception

मुग्ध (*a*) beautiful, infatuated; charmed

मुचलका (*nm*) a bond, binding agreement

मुजरा (*nm*) a deduction, allowance, salutation

मुजरिम (*nm*) an offender, a criminal

मुज़ायका (*nm*) worry, anxiety; obstruction

मुजाहिद (*nm*) a crusader

मुझ (*pron*) an inflective case of मैं

मुझे (*pron*) to me

मुटाई (*nf*) sturdiness; thickness

मुटापा (*nm*) plumpness, fatness

मुट्ठी (*nf*) a clutch, a grip; fist; a handful

मुठभेड़ (*nf*) conflict; an encounter, a confrontation

मुड़ना (*v*) to be turned back; to be bent; to be twisted

मुतआल्लिक (*a*) concerning, belonging to

मुताबिक (*ind*) agreeable to, corresponding, in accordance with

मुदित (*a*) delighted, pleased, rejoiced, happy

मुद्दई (*nm*) a complainant; a plaintiff, a prosecutor

मुद्दत/त (*nf*) a space of time, duration, time-limit; —ती old, antiquated

मुद्दा (*nm*) intention, theme, purport

मुद्रक (*nm*) a printer

मुद्रण (*nm*) the act of printing; —कला typography

मुद्रांकित (*a*) stamped, sealed

मुद्रणालय (*nm*) a printing press

मुद्राक्षर (*nm*) a printing type

मुद्रा (*nf*) a seal; stamp; money, coin

मुद्रित (*a*) stamped; printed; sealed

मुनक्का (*nm*) a large-size dried grape, big currant

मुनसिफ (*nm*) a judge, an administrator of justice

मुनादी (*nf*) a proclamation by beat of drum

मुनाफ़ा (*nm*) a profit, deal, a bargain, gain; —ख़ोर a profiteer; —ख़ोरी profiteering

मुनासिब (*a*) proper, suitable, fit, convenient

मुनि (*nm*) a pious and religious person, an ascetic, a saint

मुनीम (*nm*) an assistant, an accountant, a syndic

मुफ़लिस (*a*) indigent, poor, penniless

मुफ़लिसी (*nf*) poverty, indigence

मुफ़स्सल (*a*) detailed; (*nm*) the suburb of a town

मुफ़ीद (*a*) beneficial, profitable, useful

मुफ़्त (*a*) without price, free of charge; —ख़ोर one who enjoys the wealth of others

मुबारक (*a*) auspicious, blessed, happy; —बाद congratulations

मुमकिन (*a*) feasible, possible

मुमुक्षु (*a*) wishing salvation

मुरझाना (*v*) to fade, to wither; to lose lustre

मुरदा (*nm*) a dead person, a

corpse; (*a*) lifeless, dead,
—दिल lifeless, melancholic

मुरब्बा (*nm*) a jam, candy, a
preserve, a sweetmeat, (*a*)
square

मुरली (*nf*) a pipe, flute

मुरव्वत (*nf*) politeness, benevolence, affability

मुराद (*nf*) a desire, wish;
purport, craving

मुरीद (*nm*) a follower, a pupil,
a disciple

मुर्गा (*nm*) a cock, fowl

मुर्गी (*nf*) a hen

मुर्दनी (*nf*) a death-like stillness

मुर्दा (*nm*) corpse, dead body;
—घर mortuary

मुलज़िम (*nm*) a convict, an
accused

मुलम्मा (*nm*) the covering of an
article with gold or silver

मुलहठी (*nf*) liquorice

मुलाकात (*nf*) a visit, a meeting,
an interview

मुलाकाती (*nm*) an acquaintance

मुलाज़मत (*nf*) employment,
service

मुलाज़िम (*nm*) a servant, an
attendant

मुलायम (*a*) soft; tender, gentle

मुलायमियत (*nf*) softness,
gentleness, tenderness

मुलाहज़ा (*nm*) notice, inspection, regard

मुल्क (*nm*) a country, kingdom,
realm

मुल्की (*a*) belonging to one's
country, civil, national

मुल्तवी (*a*) postponed; adjourned

मुल्ला (*nm*) a Muslim priest

मुवक्किल (*nm*) a pleader's
client

मुशायरा (*nm*) a poetic
symposium

मुश्किल (*a*) difficult, intricate,
(*nf*) difficulty, hardship

मुसकराना (*v*) to smile, to titter

मुसकराहट (*nm*) smile, a laugh,
a beam

मुस्कान (*nf*) a smile

मुसन्निफ (*nm*) the compiler or
writer of a book

मुसम्मात (*nf*) a woman, a
female; a title which is
affixed to the name of a
female

मुसलमान (*nm & a*) a Mohammedan; Muslim

मुसाफिर (*nm*) a traveller, a
passenger; —ख़ाना a halting
place for passengers; an
inn; a waiting room at a
railway station

मुसीबत (*nf*) misery, misfortune,
disaster, —का मारा afflicted

मुस्टंडा (*a*) stout, robust,
wicked

मुस्तकिल (*a*) firm, strong,
settled, permanent

मुस्तैद (*a*) prompt, ready

मुस्तैदी (*nf*) promptness,
readiness

मुहताज (*a*) needy, poor,

necessitous, indigent

मुहताजी (nf) poverty, indigence

सुहब्बत (nf) love, affection, fondness

सुहर (nf) seal; a gold coin; stamp; — बंद sealed

सुहरा (nm) the front part, face

सुहर्रम (nm) the first month of the Arabic year-which is held sacred by Mohammedans

सुहर्रमी (a) pertaining to Moharrum; melancholy

सुहर्रिर (nm) a scribe, a clerk

सुहर्रिरी (nf) the work of a scribe or clerk, the work of writing

सुहलत (nf) grace period; extra time

सुहल्ला (nm) a locality

सुहाना (nm) the mouth of a river

सुहाफ़िज़ (a) a protector, guard, keeper

सुहाल (a) impossible, difficult; (nf) facade

सुहावरा (nm) idiom; practice, phraseology

सुहिम (nf) an arduous task, an expedition, compaign

सुहर्मुंह (ind) again and again

सुहूर्त (nm) a division of time, auspicious moment

सुहैया (a) available, procured

मूँग (nm) the kidney-bean or black gram, green lentil

मूँगफली (nf) ground nut

मूँगा (nm) coral

मूँगिया (a) of dark-green colour

मूँछ (nf) moustaches, whiskers

मूँज (nf) a kind of red long reed of which ropes are made

मूँड़ना (v) to shave, to shave the hair of one's head

मूँदना (v) to cover, to shut up, to close the upper portion of a thing

मूक (a) speechless, dumb, wordless

मूठ (nf) a staff, stock, a handle

मूढ़ (a) ignorant, stupid, foolish, silly; —ता foolishness, stupidity; silliness

मूत्र (nm) urine, piss

मूत्राशय (nm) urinary bladder

मूर्ख (a) foolish, stupid, idiot, silly; —मंडली an assembly of fools, a group of idiots

मूर्खता (nf) folly, ignorance, stupidity

मूर्छा (nf) fainting, fit; state of unconsciousness

मूर्च्छित (a) fainted, swooned; unconscious

मूर्त (a) tangible; formal

मूर्ति (nf) statue, an idol; image; —कला sculpture; statuary; —कार sculptor, statuary

मूर्तिमान (a) incarnate, personified

मूर्धन्य (a) pertaining to the head, top-ranking

मूल (nm) the root of a tree; an edible tuber; principal; origin, source; the original

text; (a) chief, original;
—त: basically, fundamen-
tally, primarily; essentially;
—तत्त्व the essential; —धन
the principal; —पाठ text,
original text; —भूत fundamental, essential, basic;
original; —स्रोत main source

मूली (nf) a radish, rootlet

मूल्य (nm) price; rate;
worth

मूल्यवान (a) precious, costly;
valuable, expensive

मूल्यांकन (nm) assessment,
evaluation

मूषक (nm) a mouse, a rat

मूसल (nm) a pestle; a pounder;
a rammer

मूसलाधार (a) heavy rain

मूसली (nf) a plant, the roots of
which are used in medicine

मूसा (nm) the founder of
Jewish religion

मृग (nm) a beast of the forest,
a deer; —चर्म the skin of an
antelope; —छाला deer-skin;
—जल waves seen in a
mirage; —तृष्णा mirage;
—नाभ musk

मृगया (nm) sport, hunting

मृगलोचना/नी (a) deer-eyed or
fawn-eyed (women)

मृगांक (nm) the moon

मृणाल (nf) the root of a lotus
plant

मृणालिनी (nf) a lotus plant

मृत (a) dead, late, no more

मृतक (nm) a dead person, a
corpse, a defunct person;
—कर्म funeral rites

मृतकल्प (a) almost dead

मृतगृह (nm) a cemetery, a
burying place

मृतजीवनी (nf) the art of
restoring a dead body to
life

मृत्तिका (nf) clay, earth

मृत्युंजय (nm) one who has
conquered death; (a)
deathless; an epithet of
Lord Shiva

मृत्यु (nf) death, demise,
decease; quietness, the end

मृत्युलोक (nm) the world of the
dead, the mortal world

मृत्युशय्या (nm) death-bed

मृत्युशोक (nm) mourning

मृदंग (nf) a drum, a tabor, a
timbrel

मृदु (a) cool; soft, mild; sweet;
tender; gentle

मृदु/ता (nf) softness; sweetness,
tenderness; —भाषी soft-
spoken; —हृदय pitiful,
tender-hearted

मृदुल (a) sweet; soft; tender;
mild; —ता softness; sweetness; mildness

मृषा (ind) falsely, uselessly, in
vain; (a) false, untrue

में (ind) in, into; among; between

मेंगनी (nf) the orbicular dung
of sheep or goat

में-में (nf) the bleating of sheep or goat etc.

मेंढक (nm) a frog; toad

मेंह (nm) rain

मेंहदी (nf) myrtle

मेख (nf) a peg; nail

मेखला (nf) a girdle, waist bend, a sword-belt

मेघ (nm) a cloud, a musical mode

मेघनाद (nm) the rumbling of clouds, thunder

मेज़ (nf) a table

मेज़पोश (nm) a table-cover

मेज़बान (nm) one who entertains a guest, a host

मेट (nm) a supervisor of labourers in a factory

मेथी (nf) a small plant the leaves of which are used as vegetable

मेदा (nm) the stomach

मेधा (nf) sense, intellect, prudence, understanding

मेधावी (a) wise; sagacious, intelligent

मेम (nf) an European lady, madam

मेमना (nm) a lamb, a kid, a species of horse

मेरा (pron) my, mine

मेरी (pron) faminine form of मेरा

मेरु (nm) a mythological mountain which was supposed to be made of gold

मेरुदंड (nm) backbone, spine; spinal cord

मेल (nm) connection; treaty; relation; match; mixture —जोल intimacy; union

मेला (nm) crowd, assemblage; fair; procession

मेवा (nm) dry fruit

मेह (nm) rain, rainfall; diabetes (see also मेंह)

मेहतर (nm) a sweeper of public lanes, a scavenger

मेहतरानी (nf) a female sweeper

मेहनत (nf) toil, labour; hard work; —कश a labourer

मेहनताना (nm) wages, price paid for a work

मेहनती (a) hardworking; laborious; industrious

मेहमान (nm) a guest; —खाना a guest house; —वार a host; —दारी hospitality, kindness to strangers

मेहमानी (nf) hospitality

मेहर (nf) kindness, compassion, favour

मेहरबान (a) kind, compassionate

मेहरबानी (nf) favour, kindness

मेहराब (nm) an arch, vault

मेहरी (nf) a woman who works as household utensil cleaner

मैं (pron) I; — स्वयं myself

मैका (मैके) (nm) a woman's paternal house

मैत्री (nf) friendship, cordiality

मैथुन (nm) sexual intercourse

मैदा (nm) fine flour

मैदान (nm) an open field; plain; battle-field

मैदानी (a) pertaining to plains; even

मैना (nf) blackbird

मैया (nf) mother

मैल (nm) filth, dirt, dross

मैलखोरा (a & nm) absorbing dirt, an apron

मैला (a) dirty, foul, unclean

मैला-कुचैला (a) filthy, dirty, dingy

मोढ़ा (nm) a stool which is made of basket

मोक्ष (nm) final liberation, salvation

मोच (nf) sprain, twist

मोची (nm) a shoe-maker, a cobbler, a saddler

मोज़ा (nm) stocking, socks

मोटर (nf) a motor-car

मोटा, (a) fat, plump; coarse, rough; —ई fatness, thickness; —ताज़ा fleshy; robust; मोटे तौर पर roughly speaking

मोटापा (nm) fatness, plumpness

मोड़ (nm) a bend, a twist; the winding of a river

मोड़ना (v) to twist; to turn back or in another direction

मोतिया (nm) a kind of jasmine flower; (a) light red or yellow, pearly-coloured

मोतियाबिंद (nm) a disease of the eye, cataract

मोती (nm) a pearl; —झरा typhoid

मोदी (nm) a grocer; —खाना a provision store

मोम (nf) wax; —जामा oil-cloth; —बत्ती a candle-stick

मोमी (a) made of wax

मोर (nm) a peacock; —नी a peahen; —पंख a peacock-feather

मोरचा (nm) rust on iron; a battle front; —बंदी entrenchment

मोल (nm) price

मोह (nm) ignorance; delusion, illusion; affection; spell; —पाश the snare of worldly illusion; —भंग disillusionment; —ममता affection and attachment

मोहक (a) charming, fascinating; producing ignorance

मोहन (a) attractive, charming; tempting; (nm) enchantment; an epithet of Lord Krishna

मोहनी (nf) enchantment; delusion; a spell

मोहब्बत (nf) love, affection

मोहर (nf) a seal; a stamp; a guinea, gold coin

मोहल्ला (nm) a locality, ward, street

मोहलत (nf) fixed time

मोहित (a) charmed, spellbound; fallen in love; deceived

मोहिनी (a) charming, bewitching, fascinating; (*nf*) delusion, an incarnation of the god Vishnu

मौका (*nm*) occasion; chance; situation; location; site of occurrence; मौके पर at the appropriate time; on the spot; मौके से duly, just in time

मौखिक (*a*) oral, verbal; —परीक्षा *viva voce*

मौज (*nf*) caprice, a whim; delight; a wave

मौज़ा (*nm*) a village

मौजी (*a*) working according to one's whim, whimsical, merry

मौजूद (*a*) existing; present; ready, at hand

मौजूदगी (*nf*) presence; existence

मौजूदा (*a*) present, ready, current, existing

मौत (*nf*) demise, death, mortality

मौन (*a*) silent, taciturn, mum, quiet, speechless; (*nm*) quiescence; —व्रत a vow to keep quiet, to adopt silence

मौनी (*a*) taciturn, reticent

मौर (*nm*) a crown which is worn by a bridegroom during the marriage cere- mony; blossom of a mango tree

मौलवी (*nm*) a learned Mohammedan

मौलिक (*a*) ultimate, original; fundamental; essential; —ता originality

मौली (*nf*) untwisted red coloured thread which is used in worship

मौसम (*nm*) season; weather

मौ/सा (*nm*) the husband of mother's sister; —सी mother's sister; —सेरे born of mother's sister

म्याऊँ (*nf*) mewing of a cat

म्यान (*nf*) a sheath

म्लान (*a*) faded, weak, withered; dirty; —ता state of being faded

म्लेच्छ (*nm*) a barbarian, a man of low birth; (*a*) unclean, shabby

य

य the first of the य, र, ल, व series of Devnagri alphabet, traditionally called अंत:स्थ (semi-vowels.)

यंत्र (*nm*) an engine, a machine; an instrument; mystical diagram; —चालित mechani- zed; —वत् like a machine; —कार a machinist, an engineer

यंत्रणा (*nf*) torment, torture

यंत्रशाला (*nf*) an observatory

यंत्रीकरण (*nm*) mechanization

यकीन (*nm*) faith; confidence; trust

यकृत (*nm*) the liver

यक्ष (*nm*) a kind of demi-god, attendant on Kuvera

यक्ष्मा (*nm*) tuberculosis, consumption

यजमान (*nm*) a host, one who performs a sacrifice

यजुर्वेद (*nm*) the third of the four Vedas

यज्ञ (*nm*) a religious sacrifice, an oblation; —कुण्ड the alter on which a sacrifice is made; —करने वाला a sacrificer; —कर्म a sacrificial ceremony; —पति he who makes a sacrifice; —पशु an animal which is slain in a sacrifice; —पुरुष an epithet of the God Vishnu; —भूमि the place where a sacrifice is performed

यज्ञोपवीत (*nm*) the sacred thread which is mostly worn by three upper classes of Hindus, the initiation ceremony among Hindus

यति (*nf*) a pause, check; (*nm*) an ascetic, an anchorite who has completely subdued his passions

यतीम (*nm*) an orphan, a foundling or deserted infant; —खाना an orphanage

यतींद्रिय (*a*) one whose passions and senses are under his control

यत्किंचित (*adv*) somewhat, a little

यत्न (*nm*) effort; exertion; attempt; labour

यत्नवान् (*a*) making effort; laborious; energetic; strenuous

यत्र (*adv*) where; —यत्र wheresoever; —तत्र hither and thither; —तत्र-सर्वत्र here, there and everywhere

यथा (*adv*) in whatever manner, as for example, for instance, as per; thus; —अवसर according to opportunity; — क्रम systematically, in order; —तथा in every way, by some means or other; —तथ्य as it is; —नियम as per rule; —निर्दिष्ट as directed; —पूर्व as existed before; —योग्य proper, suitably; —रुचि according to one's liking or taste; —वत as before; —विधि according to rule; —शक्ति according to one's capacity or power; —शीघ्र as early as possible; —संभव as far as possible; —समय in due course; —स्थान at the proper place

यथार्थ (*a*) actual, real

यथार्थता (*nf*) really, actually; —वाद realism; —वादिता realism; —वादी a realist; realistic

यथेच्छ (*adv*) according to one's wishes or desire

यथेष्ट (*a*) enough, sufficient; adequate

यथोक्ति (*a*) as already stated, above mentioned

यथोचित (*a*) proper; rightful; reasonable; due; (*adv*) justly; properly; duly

यदा (*a*) while, when, —कदा sometimes or other

यदि (*ind*) provided that, if, in case

यद्यपि (*ind*) although, though, however

यदृच्छा (*nf*) free will

यम (*nm*) the god of death; —दूत the messenger of Yama, the god of death; —लोक hell

यमक (*nm*) an alliteration in different meanings

यमुना (*nf*) one of the most important Indian rivers

यवन (*nm*) a Mohammedan; a Greek

यवनिका (*nf*) a curtain; drop scene

यश (*nm*) reputation, fame; name; glory

यशस्वी (*a*) renowned, reputed; glorious

यष्टि (*nf*) a stick, a twig, the branch of a tree

यह (*pron*) it, this

यहाँ (*adv*) here, hither

यहीं (*adv*) at this very place

यहूदी (*nm*) a Jew

या (*ind*) or, whether

याचक (*nm*) a suppliant; a beggar

याचना (*nf*) solicitation, begging; asking for something

याचिका (*nf*) a petition

याजक (*nm*) one who performs a sacrifice, a sacrificing priest

यातना (*nf*) agony, anguish, torment, torture

यातायात (*nm*) traffic

यात्रा (*nf*) a travel, journey; trip; tour

यात्री (*nm*) a pilgrim; a traveller; a passenger; a tourist

याद (*nm*) recollection; remembrance, memory

यादगार (*nf*) a monument; memorial; memento

याददाश्त (*nf*) memory

यादव (*nm*) a descendant of Yadu

यान (*nm*) vehicle; a van

यानी (*ind*) that is, that is to say

यापन (*nm*) spending time, passing away of time

यामिनी (*nf*) night

यार (*nm*) a companion; a friend; a lover; —बाश a friend of friends, good companion

यारान (nm) friendship

यारी (nf) friendship; illegal love affair

यावत् (adv) until, as long as, as far as

यीशु (nm) Jesus Christ; —मसीह Jesus Christ

युक्त (a) combined, united; joined; fit, proper

युक्ति (nf) tact, skill, device; argument; —संगत reason-able, logical

युग (nm) era; period; times; age; epoch; couple

युगांत (nm) the end of a Yuga, cosmic destruction

युगांतर (nm) a new era, another age; —कारी revolutionary

युग्म (nm) couple; pair; (a) two

युद्ध (nm) a war, warfare, battle; fight; hostilities; —क्षेत्र battle-field; —नीति strategy; —पोत warship, —बंदी a prisoner of war; —विराम cease-fire

युयुत्सा (nf) an intention to wage war

युवक (nm) a young man; a youth

युवती (nf) a young woman, a youthful lady

युवराज (nm) a prince

युवराज्ञी (nf) a princess

युवा (a) young, vigorous; —अवस्था prime of life, youth

यूँ (adv) in this way, in this manner

यूथ (nm) a group, company, band

यूनिवर्सिटी (nf) a university

यूनानी (a) Greek; (nm) a Greek

ये (pron) these

येन-केन-प्रकारेण (adv) somehow, by fair or foul means; by hook or by crook

यों (adv) thus, in this way, like this, in this manner

योग (nm) sum, total; combination; addition; joining together; mixture; —क्षेम possessions, —तत्त्व the name of an Upanishad; —दर्शन one of the six schools of Hindu philosophy; —दान contri-bution; —निद्रा Vishnu's sleep which comes after the annihilation of the world —फल the sum total of numbers; —बल the power which is derived from continuous meditation; —रूढ़ि a compound word which is used in a sense quite different from the meanings of its component parts

योगात्मा (nm) an ascetic

योगाभ्यास (nm) the practice of योग

योगासन (nm) posture of body which is proper for pro-found meditation of a Yogi

योग्य (a) suitable, fit; qualified; eligible

योग्यता (nf) eligibility; talent; aptitude; capacity

योजक (a) uniting, joining; (nm) one which combines

योजन (nm) union, joining, uniting; a measure of distance

योजना (nf) joining, uniting; a planning scheme; —आयोग Planning Commission

योद्धा (nm) a combatant, warrior, fighter, soldier

योनि (nf) source, origin; vagina, female organ of generation

यौगिक (a) pertaining to the practice of yoga; proper, suitable

यौवन (nm) youth, manhood, youthfulness

र

र the second amongst the series य, र, ल, व of Devnagri alphabet, tradi-tionally called as अंत:स्थ (Semi vowels)

रंक (a) penniless, poor, pauper; (nm) a beggar, penniless person

रंग (nm) dye; colour; complexion; paint; beauty; influence; whim; kind; stage; —ढंग ways, manners; —बिरंगा multi-coloured; —भूमि theatre; —मंच stage; —रंगीला colourful; —रूप physical appearance; —शाला theatre; —साज़ a painter; —साज़ी painting

रंगत (nf) complexion; colour, delight; colour of face

रँगना (v) to dye; to paint, to colour

रँगरूट (nm) a newly recruited soldier or police man

रँगरेज़ (nm) a dyer of clothes

रँगवाई (nf) the price paid for colouring or dyeing

रैंग/रेली —रेलियाँ (nf) (usually used in plural form) rejoi-cing, merriment

रँगाई (nf) dying charges; dyeing

रंगावट (nf) colouring, dyeing

रंगीन (a) coloured, dyed; painted; gay; luxury-loving; —मिज़ाज gay, colourful; mirthful; luxury loving

रंगीनी (nf) mirthfulness;

colourfulness

रँगीला (a) gaudy, showy; beautiful, colourful, gay

रंचक (a) a little, slight; a small quantity (of a thing)

रंज (nm) grief, sorrow; anxiety; trouble

रंजक (a) delighting, gladdening; a dyer; a painter

रंजित (a) painted; dyed; coloured; happy, delighted

रंजिश (nf) enmity; displeasure; ill-feeling

रंजीदा (a) sorry, grieved; sad, gloomy

रंजीदगी (nf) sadness, sorrow, displeasure

रँडापा (nm) widowhood

रंडी (nf) a harlot, prostitute

रँडुआ (nm) a widower

रंदना (v) to smoothen with a plane

रंदा (nm) a carpenter's smoothing instrument

रँधना (v) to cook food

रंध्र (nm) a hole, an aperture

रंभा (nf) the name of a fairy; (nm) a crow-bar, a lever

रँभाना (nm) the bellowing of a cow or bull

रका/र (nm) the letter र (ra) and its sound; —रांत (word) ending in र

रईस (nm) a noble man; a rich person; (a) rich, wealthy; hence —ज़ादा

रईसी (nf) wealthiness; nobility;

richness

रकम (nf) an amount, a sum, wealth

रकाब (nm) a stirrup

रक्त (nm) blood; (a) red, saffron; attached; —क्षीणता anaemia, —पात a bloodshed, a bloody fight, slaughter; —पिपासा blood-thirst; —पिपासु blood-thirsty; —रंजित bloody; causing bloodshed

रक्षक (nm) a guard; a rescuer, defender; protector; (a) preventive

रक्षण (nm) a defence, protection; an insurance

रक्षणीय (a) tenable

रक्षा (nf) protection; safety; care; defence; guarding; —सेना defence force

रक्षात्मक (a) safeguarding; defensive; protective

रख/ना (v) to set; to put; to hold; to keep; to possess; to employ; —रखाव maintenance; safe-keeping

रखवाला (nm) a guard, a guardian; a watchman

रखवाली (nf) care, guardianship, custody; protection

रखाना (v) to cause to keep, to give in charge

रग (nf) a vein, an artery, a nerve

रगड़ (nm) a rub, friction, concussion

रगड़ना (v) to rub, to chafe, to scrub, to bruise

रगड़ा (nm) friction; toil, a rub

रचना (nf) work; production; structure; composition; (v) to create; to form, to construct

रचयिता (nm) an author; creator; composer

रचित (a) composed; made; compiled; formed

रजक (nm) a washerman

रजत (nf) silver; (a) silvery; white; bright; —जयन्ती silver jubilee

रजनी (nf) night

रजवाड़ा (nm) a former princely state of India

रज(स) (nm) menstruation; —कण dust particle

रज़ा (nf) consent, permission; will; —मंद consenting, willing; —मंदी will; consent, agreement

रज़ाई (nf) a quilt

रजिस्ट्री (nf) registration

रजोगुण (nm) the passion of love and pleasure, one of the three constituent qualities of living-beings which is the cause of vice

रज्जु (nf) a rope; a cord; a string

रट (nm) repetition, iteration

रटना (v) to repeat, to iterate; to learn by heart

रण (nm) a combat; a war; a battle; —क्षेत्र the battle-field; —नीति strategy; —बाँकुरा a great fighter

रति (nf) the wife of Cupid; affection, love, beauty; a very pretty woman

रतौंधी (nf) night-blindness, the disease called nyctalopia

रत्ती (nf) a weight equal to eight grains of rice

रत्न (nm) a gem, jewel, precious stone, ruby

रत्नाकर (nm) the ocean; a heap of jewels

रत्नावली (nf) a necklace of gems

रथ (nm) a chariat; —यात्रा the chariot festival of Jagannath

रथी (a) riding a chariot; (nm) a fighter, warrior

रद्द (a) refuted, rejected; cancelled

रद्दी (a) worthless, of inferior quality; rough; (nf) waste paper

रद्दोबदल (nf) alteration, change; modification

रनिवास (nm) an apartment allotted to females in a palace, a harem

रपट (nf) hard labour; slipperiness; a report

रपटना (v) to slide, to slip, to skid

रफ़ा (a) removed, settled; pacified —दफ़ा settled

रफू (nm) darn; —गर a darner

रफूचक्कर (a) disappeared, run away

रफ्तार (nf) speed, pace

रफ्ता-रफ्ता (adv) by degrees, slowly

रबड़ (nm) a rubber

रबड़ी (nf) milk which is thickened by boiling and mixing sugar in it

रबी (nf) the crop reaped in the spring season

रब्त (nm) practice, custom; —ज़ब्त intimacy, acquaintance

रमज़ान (nm) the ninth month of the Mohammedan year in which they observe fast from early morning to sunset

रमणी (nf) a young woman, a pretty woman; —क beautiful

रमणीय (a) pretty, beautiful, charming

रमता (a) wandering, moving about

रमना (v) to make merry, to enjoy; to roam, to wander about

रम्य (a) pretty, beautiful, elegant, pleasant, delightful

रम्यता (nf) elegance, amenity

रड़कना (v) to smart, to produce a painful sensation

रव (nm) noise, cry, tumult

खानगी (nf) a setting out, a departure, a start

खाना (a) proceeded, departed, sent out; —होना to depart, to set out

रवि (nm) the Sun

खैया (nm) attitude, behaviour; practice, custom

रश्क (nm) malice, jealousy, spite

रश्मि (nf) a ray or beam of light; a horse's rein

रस (nm) taste, flavour, juice; —दार juicy, tasty, relishing; —भरी raspberry; —मीना full of flavour

रसगुल्ला (nm) a kind of Bengali sweetmeat

रसज्ञ (a) competent in appreciating literature; a poet who understands the various sentiments; one who appreciates the beauty of literature

रसद (nf) provision, supplies

रसना (nf) the tongue; relish; cord

रसवंत (a) full of relish; juicy; having aesthetic sense

रसा (nf) tongue; soup; juice

रसातल (nm) the nether world, hell

रसायन (nm) chemistry; (a) chemical; —ज्ञ well versed in chemistry; —विज्ञान/शास्त्र chemistry

रसास्वाद (*nm*) relish, emotive, relish

रसिक (*nm*) admirer, lover, one who appreciates beauty or excellence; (*a*) amorous, sharp, humorous

रसिकता (*nf*) taste, joviality

रसिया (*nm*) amorist, having aesthetic relish

रसीद (*nf*) the acknowledgement of a sum, receipt

रसीदी (*a*) regarding to a receipt

रसीला (*a*) tasteful; juicy; delicious; inspired by love

रसूल (*nm*) divine messenger, prophet

रसोइया (*nm*) a cook

रसोई (*nf*) cooked food; kitchen; —घर a kitchen

रसौली (*nf*) a disease attended with glandular swellings, a tumour

र/स्म (*nf*) a custom; practice; a ceremony; formality; —स्मी formal

रस्सा (*nm*) a thick rope; a cable; —कशी tug of war

रस्सी (*nf*) a cord; rope

रहट (*nf*) an appliance for lifting water from a well, a water-wheel

रहन (*nm*) manner, a pawn, mortgage; —सहन living

रहना (*v*) to reside; to remain; to stay; to live; to continue

रहम (*nm*) mercy, pity; compassion, kindness, —दिल merciful

रहमत (*nf*) pity, compassion

रहस्य (*nm*) a secret; a mystery

रहस्योद्घाटन (*nm*) disclosure of mystery

रहित (*adv*) without, devoid of, destitute of

राँड (*nf*) a widow; a term of abuse

राई (*nf*) mustard; a very small quantity

राक्षस (*nm*) monster, a demon; a wicked person

राक्षसी (*nf*) monstress; (*a*) monstrous

राख (*nf*) ashes

राग (*nm*) mental affectation, desire, —द्वेष love and hatred

रागिनी (*nf*) modification or a musical mode

राज (*nm*) rule, administration; government; kingdom; —काज affairs of the state; —कुमार a prince; —कुमारी a princess; —कीय royal, regal, —गद्दी the royal throne; —गृह a royal palace; —तिलक the coronation ceremony of a king; —दूत a royal ambassador; —द्रोह sedition; —द्रोही disloyal; —द्वार the door of a palace; —धर्म the duties of a sovereign or king; —पथ a highway; —पाट reign, royal throne; —प्रासाद a palace; —भक्त a loyalist; —भक्ति

loyalism; —मर्मज्ञ a statesman; —यक्ष्मा tuberculosis; —वंश a dynasty; —वैद्य royal physician; —व्यवस्था polity; —सत्ता royal authority; —सभा a royal court; —सिंहासन the royal throne

राज़ (nm) a secret

राजकीय (a) royal; official

राजधानी (nf) a capital

राजनीति (nf) politics

राजनैतिक (a) political

राजनीतिज्ञ (nm) a politician

राजनीतिशास्त्र (nm) political science

राजप/त्र (nm) a gazette; —त्रित gazetted

राजभवन (nm) governor's house; palace

राजभाषा (nf) the official language

राजसी (a) royal, kingly, princely

राजस्व (nm) a royal tax or duty, revenue

राजहंस (nm) a male swan

राजा (nm) a king, lord, a monarch, darling; —बेटा good boy

राजाज्ञा (nf) the order of a king, a royal mandate

राजाधिराज (nm) an emperor, overlord

राज़ी (a) willing; healthy, happy; —खुशी welfare; —नामा agreement; writ of compromise which is filed in a court

राजीव (nm) a lotus flower

राजेश्वर (nm) a king of kings, an emperor

राज्ञी (nf) a queen

राज्य (nm) kingdom; state; —च्युत dethroned; —त्याग abdication; —द्रोह sedition; —पाल a governor; —सभा the Upper House of the Indian Parliament

राज्याभिषेक (nm) accession to the throne

राज्याधिकार (nm) the right to a kingdom

रात (nf) the night; —का राजा an owl; —दिन day and night; always

रातिब (nm) food for cattle

रात्रि (nf) night

रानी (nf) a queen; a king's wife; beloved

राम (nm) the eldest son of Dasharath, God; —कहानी narration of events of one's own life; —लीला the folk drama in which the deeds of king Rama are enacted for a number of days; —बाण very efficacious

राय (nf) view, opinion; advice; (nm) a king

रायता (nm) vegetables pickled and spiced in curd

रार (nf) a quarrel, a dispute; wrangling

राशन (nm) ration

राशि (nf) a sum; amount; heap; sign of the zodiac; —चक्र the zodiac

राष्ट्र (nm) a kingdom; a nation; —गीत the national anthem; —चिह्न the national emblem; —ध्वज the national flag; —नीति national policy; —पति President; —भाषा the national language; —वाद nationalism; —वादी a nationalist; —संघ the United Nations Organisation —हीन stateless

राष्ट्रिक (a & nm) national

राष्ट्रीय (a) national; —करण nationalisation; —ता nationality

रास (nm) the circular dance performed by Krishna

रासधारी (nm) a person who acts in रासलीला

रासलीला (nf) the amorous pastime of Lord Krishna with cowherdesses

रासायनिक (a) chemical; (nm) a chemist

रास्ता (nm) a path; street; road; route, course; passage

राह (nf) a way, a path; a road; method; manner; —खर्च travelling expenses; —गीर a traveller; —ज़नी robbery on the highway; —चलता a stranger

राहत (nf) relief; comfort, ease; —कार्य relief operations

राहदारी (nf) duty which is imposed on roads, toll-tax

राही (nm) a traveller, wayfarer

राहु (nm) one of the nine principal planets, the mythological dragon's head which is supposed to devour the Sun during an eclipse

रिंगाना (v) to cause to crawl, to help a child to walk

रिंद (nm) a freewilled person, (a) passionate, intoxicated

रिंदा (a) unrestrained, impudent, rash, headstrong

रिआयत (nf) concession; favour, softness

रिआयती (nm) a favoured person; concessional

रिआया (nf) a subject

रिकार्ड (nm) a record; gramophone record; —तोड़ना to break a record

रिक्त (a) empty, void; evacuated; —ता vacancy; vacuum

रिक्थ (nm) legacy

रिक्शा (nm) a rickshaw

रिझाना (v) to please, to entice, to captivate, to charm

रिझाव (nm) the act of being happy or pleased

रिटायर (a) retired

रिपु (nm) a foe, an enemy

रिमझिम (nf) the drizzling of rain

रियाज़ (*nm*) exercise; practice

रियासत (*nf*) dominion, estate, a state

रिरियाना (*v*) to whimper, to cry as a child

रिवाज (*nm*) custom; practice

रिश्ता (*nm*) affinity; relation-ship; connection

रिश्तेदार (*nm*) a relation, a relative; kith and kin

रिश्तेदारी (*nf*) relationship, kinship

रिश्वत (*nf*) a bribe; —ख़ोर a bribee; —ख़ोरी bribery

रिसना (*v*) to leak in drops, to drizzle

रिसवाना (*v*) to cause to get angry

रिसालदार (*nm*) an officer of Indian infantry

रिसाला (*nm*) a journal; cavalry

रिहा (*a*) set at liberty, released, discharged

रिहाई (*nf*) release, deliverance, liberation

रिहाइ/श (*nf*) residence; —शी residential

री (*ind*) a vocative particle used in addressing a female

रीछ (*nm*) a bear

रीझना (*v*) to be pleased; to be charmed to be satisfied

रीठा (*nm*) soap-wart, soap-nut

रीढ़ (*nf*) the backbone, spine

रीता (*a*) empty; void

रीति (*nf*) method; manner; custom; —रिवाज traditions

रील (*nf*) a reel

रुँधना (*v*) to be choked; to be obstructed

रुआँ (*nm*) fuzz; wool

रुई (*nf*) cotton

रुकना (*v*) to halt; to stop; to stay; to stand

रुकावट (*nf*) obstacle, hurdle, hindrance; blockade; bar; resistance

रुक्का (*nm*) a small letter, a note; a chit, slip; promis-sory note

रुक्षता (*nf*) harshness, rough-ness

रुख़ (*nm*) direction; attitude; face; (*a*) in the direction

रुख़सत (*nf*) permission; departure; leisure from work

रुख़सती (*nf*) a departure

रुख़ाई (*nf*) indifference, harshness, roughness

रुग्ण (*a*) sick, unwell; ill

रुचना (*v*) to be gratifying, to be agreeable

रुचि (*nf*) taste; liking; relish; wish, desire; —कर full of taste; interesting; relishing; —कारक relishing

रुचिर (*a*) beautiful; agreeable, pleasing

रुचिवर्धक (*a*) appetising, increasing relish or hunger

रुझान (*nm*) proclivity; natural tendency

रूतबा (*nm*) dignity; rank; respect

रुदन (*nm*) weeping, wailing

रुद्ध (*a*) obstructed, hindered; choked

रुधिर (*nm*) blood

रुनझुन (*nf*) the tinkling of small bells

रुपया (*nm*) wealth; money; rupee; —पैसा money; रुपये वाला rich, wealthy

रुपहला (*a*) silvery, made of silver

रुलाई (*nf*) weeping, a cry

रुष्ट (*a*) angry, displeased; vexed; enraged

रुष्टता (*nf*) anger, displeasure, sulkiness

रू (*nm*) face; —ब-रू face to face; —रियायत considera-tion; leniency

रूखा (*a*) dry; crude; rough; inconsiderate; —सूखा plain and simple

रूखापन (*nm*) roughness, acrimony, indifference

रूठना (*v*) to be displeased

रूढ़ (*a*) established; popular; traditional

रूढ़ि (*nf*) usage, convention, —वाद conventionalism; —वादी a conventionalist

रूप (*nm*) form, shape, appear-ance; beauty

रूपरेखा (*nf*) a synopsis, an out-line

रूपवान (*a*) good looking, hand-some

रूपसी (*nf*) a beauty

रूपांतर (*nm*) transformation; variation; adaptation

रूपी (*a*) similar to

रूमानी (*a*) romantic

रूमाल (*nm*) a handkerchief

रूह (*nf*) soul; spirit; essence

रेंकना (*v*) to bray, to sing badly, to shout hoarsely

रेंगना (*v*) to crawl; to creep

रेंड़ी (*nf*) the castor seed

रेखां/कन (*nm*) lineation, lining, under-lining; —कित lined, under-lined

रेखा (*nf*) a straight line, line-ament; mark; —गणित geometry; —चित्र a sketch

रेगिस्तान (*nm*) a sandy desert

रेचक (*a*) laxative, purgative; (*nm*) a purgative

रेज़गारी (*nf*) smaller coins

रेड (*nf*) destruction; ruination

रेषु (*nf*) dust, dirt, sand

रेत (*nm*) sand

रेतना (*v*) to file, to polish by rubbing or filing

रेताई (*nf*) the work or wages paid for filing an object

रेती (*nf*) sandy soil; a file, a rasp

रेतीला (*a*) sandy, gritty

रेल (*nf*) a railway train or carriage; —पेल (*nf*) plenty; abundance, overcrowding; rush

रेला (*nm*) a rush, a flood,

huge wave, influx

रेवड़ (*nm*) a flock of sheep or goats

रेवड़ी (*nf*) a kind of crisp sweetmeat

रेशम (*nm*) silk; —का कीड़ा silkworm

रेशमी (*a*) made of silk, silken, silky

रेशा (*nm*) fibre, filament, crude fibre; grain

रेहन (*nm*) pawn, mortgage

रैयत (*nf*) a subject; a tenant

रोंगटा (*nm*) the hairs on the entire body

रोआँ (*nm*) small and soft hair on the body

रोक (*nf*) restraint, bar, ban, check; barrier; —टोक restriction; obstruction; —थाम prevention; check

रोकड़ (*nf*) ready money, cash, —जमा opening balance; —बाकी cash balance in hand

रोकड़िया (*nm*) a cashier, a treasurer; a financier

रोकना (*v*) to stop; to shut; to detain; to prevent; to ban; to forbid

रोग (*nm*) a disease; sickness; illness; —ग्रस्त ailing, diseased, ill; sick

रोगन (*nm*) paint, varnish; oil; polish

रोगी (*nm*) a patient, diseased; (*a*) ailing

रोचक (*a*) pleasing, interesting

रोज़ (*nm*) day; (*adv*) everyday; —ब-रोज़ everyday, daily; —मर्रा everyday, daily

रोज़गार (*nm*) an occupation, a profession; trade; a business; employment

रोज़नामचा (*nm*) a book of daily accounts, diary, journal

रोज़मर्रा (*a*) daily, always

रोज़ा (*nm*) the fast observed by Mohammedans in the month of Ramzan

रोज़ाना (*a*) daily

रोज़ी (*nf*) livelihood; living; —रोटी livelihood

रोटी (*nf*) bread; loaf; meals; food; —कपड़ा means of sustenance; —दाल plain and simple food

रोड़ा (*nm*) a fragment of stone or brick-bat; a pebble

रोदन (*nm*) weeping, lamentation

रोना (*v*) to weep, to cry, to lament; (*nm*) weeping, crying, lamenting; —धोना/पीटना to weep and wail

रोपना (*v*) to plant, to sow, to obstruct

रोब (*nm*) dignity, influence; terror; —दाब awe, influence; sway

रोबदार (*a*) imposing; awe-inspiring; commanding

रोम (*nm*) the small hair on the body; —रोम से throughout the body; —रोम में with heart and soul

रोमकूप (*nm*) the pores on the surface of the skin

रोमांच (*nm*) titillation, standing of hairs on the end

रोमांचित (*a*) thrilled in rapture; horripilant

रोयाँ (*nm*) the small hair on the body

रोली (*nf*) a powder prepared from a mixture of turmeric and lime used in painting the forehead

रोवेंदार/रोपैंदार (*a*) fleecy, fluffy, feathery

रोवाँसा/रोआँसा (*a*) about to weep

रोशन (*a*) burning; lighted, bright; shining, glittering,

—दान ventilator

रोशनाई (*nf*) ink

रोशनी (*nf*) brightness, light, illumination

रोष (*nm*) rage, wrath, anger, resentment

रोषी (*a*) angry, wrathful

रौंदना (*v*) to trample, to tread, to crush

रौ (*nf*) flow of water, impulsive mood

रौद्र (*a*) formidable, terrible, fearful, violent

रौनक (*nf*) splendour, elegance, brightness; —दार gay, splendid

रौला (*nf*) noise

ल

ल the third of the semi-vowel series य, र, ल, व of Devnagri alphabet

लँगड़ा (*a*) lame, crippled, limp; (*nm*) a lame person

लँगड़ाना (*v*) to limp, to walk lamely or limpingly

लँगड़ा-लूला (*nm*) crippled

लंगर (*nm*) an anchor; an alms-house

लंगूर (*nm*) an ape, a kind of black-faced monkey with a stiff long tail

लँगोट (*nm*) loin cloth, a piece

of cloth tucked to the waist to cover the privities

लंघन (*nm*) passing beyond limit, jumping over, fast

लंठ (*a*) foolish, impertinent

लंपट (*a*) sensual, licentious, wanton, lustful

लंपटता (*nf*) wantonness, sensualism

लंबा (*a*) lenghty, long; tall; large; huge; —चौड़ा vast, tall and well-built; —तड़ंगा tall and tough

लंबाई (*nf*) length; tallness;

largeness

लंबी (*a*) tall; long; great

लँहगा (*nf*) a gown, petticoat

लकड़बग्घा (*nm*) a hyena

लकड़हारा (*nm*) a woodcutter

लकड़ी (*nf*) wood; timber; firewood; stick

लकवा (*nm*) palsy, paralysis

लकीर (*nf*) a line

लक्ष (*a*) one hundred thousand

लक्षण (*nm*) a characteristic mark, a symbol, sign

लक्षणा (*nf*) a metaphor

लक्षित (*a*) observed, marked, seen

लक्ष्मी (*nf*) the goddess of wealth, prosperity, fortune

लक्ष्य (*nm*) a mark; an aim; objective; (*a*) indicated, implied

लक्ष्यार्थ (*nm*) the metaphorical meaning or significance

लखना (*v*) to behold, to see, to look

लखपती (*nm*) a very wealthy person, a millionaire

लगन (*nf*) an attachment, love, devotion; —पत्री a letter sent by the bride's father to the father of the bridegroom for informing the day of marriage

लगना (*v*) to be attached; to be applied; to be affixed to, to be employed; to seem, to appear; to be engaged

लगभग (*ind*) about, almost, thereabouts, nearly, approximately; roughly

लगवाना (*v*) to cause to be placed or applied, to cause to be fixed

लगा (*a*) attached, occupied in, connected with, related

लगातार (*adv*) continuously, consecutively, incessantly; (*a*) continuous; continual

लगान (*nm*) land revenue, the work of fastening or attaching one thing to another

लगाना (*v*) to attach; to apply; to stick; to join; to engage; to employ

लगाम (*nf*) reins, bridle, check

लगालगी (*nf*) affection, attachment; love; a connection

लगाव (*nm*) attachment; love; affection; connection

लगे (*ind*) until

लग्गा (*nm*) a long bamboo, a pole used to propel a boat, the commencement of a work

लग्घी (*nf*) a rod, a fishing rod

लग्घड़ (*nm*) a kind of hawk; a kind of leopard

लग्न (*nm*) the rising of a sign of the zodiac above the horizon, the sun's entrance into a sign of the zodiac; an auspicious moment for the performance of a work; (*a*) attached, connected with, —पत्र (see लगनपत्री)

लघिमा (*nf*) smallness, little-
ness

लघु (*a*) short; small; light; low;
mean; —तम minimum,
lowest; —तर smaller; lower

लघुता (*nf*) insignificance; smallness; meanness

लघुमति (*a*) foolish, a fool

लघुशंका (*nf*) urinating, urine;
making water

लघुकरण (*nm*) reduction in
weight, commutation

लचक (*nf*) flexibility, elasticity;
—दार flexible, elastic

लचकना (*v*) to bend; to spring

लचकाना (*v*) to bend; to jolt

लचर (*a*) week, loose; (*nm*) a
foolish person

लचीला (*a*) elastic, flexible,
limp, soft; —पन spring,
elasticity

लच्छा (*nm*) a bundle of thread,
a hank; बालों का— tress

लच्छी (*nf*) a small skein of
thread

लच्छेदार (*a*) pleasant to hear
interesting; fascinating

लजाना (*v*) to feel shy, to put to
shame, to be ashamed

लजीला (*a*) shy

लज़ीज़ (*a*) tasty, tasteful

लज़्ज़त (*nf*) deliciousness; taste;
relish

लज्जा (*nf*) dishonour, shame,
shyness; modesty

लज्जालु (*a*) sheepish, shy

लज्जावती (*a*) bashful woman

लज्जावान् (*a*) modest, bashful,
shy

लज्जित (*a*) bashful; blushing;
ashamed

लट (*nf*) tangled hair, a lock of
hair, a ringlet.

लटक (*nf*) the work of hanging,
a bend; an affected motion

लटकना (*v*) to overhang, to
hang; to lop; to suspend, to
be in a suspense; to be
delayed

लटका (*nm*) tip; device; trick

लटकाना (*v*) to suspend; to hang

लट्टू (*a*) top; bulb

लट्ठ (*nm*) a long stick, —बाज a
cudgel, player, a fencer;
—मार one who fights with a
cudgel; harsh and cruel
person

लट्ठा (*nm*) a long, raft, pile

लठैत (*a & nm*) skilled in
wielding cudgel

लड़ (*nf*) a string of pearls;
chain

लड़कपन (*nm*) boyhood; childhood; frivolity

लड़का (*nm*) a boy, a lad; male
child; son; an inexperienced person

लड़की (*nf*) a girl; a daughter

लड़खड़ाना (*v*) to falter; to
stagger; to stutter

लड़खड़हट (*nm*) stagger; totter

लड़ना (*v*) to fight; to quarrel; to
struggle; —भिड़ना to pick up

quarrel

लड़ाई (nf) a war; fight; a quarrel; encounter; enmity; —झगड़ा quarrel

लड़ाका (a) quarrelsome, hostile

लड़ाना (v) to cause to fight or quarrel

लड़ी (nf) chain; row

लड्डू (nm) comfit, a sweetmeat of the shape of a ball

लत (nf) a bad habit, whim, addiction

लता (nf) a creeping plant, tender branch of a tree; vine

लताड़ (nf) insult, scolding

लताड़ना (v) to rebuke; to trample under feet

लतीफ़ा (nm) a joke, jest, anecdote

लत्ता (nm) a scrap of cloth, rag

लथपथ (a) wet, drenched

लदना (v) to be laden, to be loaded

लपक (nf) flash, radiance, flame; swiftness

लपकना (v) to stretch out the hand for snatching; to rush

लपट (nf) flame; a blast of fragrance

लपलपाना (v) to be bent; to glitter

लपेट (nf) a fold, twist; envelopment

लपेटना (v) to coil; to roll up; to fold; to involve

लपेटवाँ (a) folded; rolled up; twisted

लप्पड़ (nm) a slap with the hand

लफंगा (nm) a loafer, a vagabond, a man of loose character

लफंगेबाज़ी (nf) roguery

लफ़्ज़ (nm) a word or expression

लब (nm) a lip; brim; edge

लबड़ना (v) to speak a lie, to speak absurdly

लबादा (nm) a gown, a cloak; a heavy overall

लबार (nm) a liar; a babbler

लबालब (adv & a) brimful, spilling; full to the brim

लब्ध (a) obtained, got, received; —प्रतिष्ठ renowned, honoured

लब्धपुत्र (nm) an adopted son

लब्धि (nf) acquirement, achievement

लभ्य (a) attainable, available, within the reach of

लमहा (nm) a moment

लय (nf) tune; rhythm; —बद्ध rhythmic, attuned

ललक (nf) intense desire; ardour; longing, yearning

ललकना (v) to desire intensely, to long for, to be greedy

ललकार (nf) a challenge, bawl

ललकारना (v) to call out insultingly, to challenge, to hold out

ललचना (v) to feel greedy, to be enticed, to be impatient owing to an intense desire

ललचाना (v) to allure, to temp, to charm; जी— to feel tempted

ललना (nf) a woman

लला (nm) a beloved son

ललाई (nf) redness

ललाट (nm) the forehead, front part, bow; fortune; —पटल the surface of the forehead; —रेखा lines on the forehead supposed to indicate good or bad fortune

ललित (a) lovely, beautiful, attractive, pretty; elegent, —कला fine arts

लल्ला (nm) a boy

लव (nm) a very small division of time; a bit, a portion, a particle; —लीन absorbed; —लेश a very small quantity

लवण (nm) salt

लश्कर (nm) an encampment; a crowd

लश्करी (adv) pertaining to an army or navy

लसलसा (a) adhesive, viscous; glutinous

लसीला (a) adhesive, viscous, glutinous

लस्सी (nf) a drink made of churned curd and water with sugar or salt added to it

लहकना (v) to wave, to quaver, to blow, to flash

लहजा (nm) tone of voice, speech, accent

लहमा (nm) a moment

लहर (nf) a large wave, surf, ripple; caprice, whim; — दार wavy, sinuate

लहराना (v) to fluctuate; to wave

लहरिया (nm) the total effect of wavy lines

लहलहाना (v) to be full of green leaves, to be verdant, to be pleased, to be delighted

लहसुन (nm) garlic

लहसुनिया (nm) a precious stone of grey colour; cat's eye

लहू (nm) blood; —लुहान covered with blood, blood-stained

लाँघना (v) to pull through, to go over, to cross, to jump over

लांछन (nm) a stigma, stain, blemish, blame

लांछित (a) blamed, reproached

लाइलाज (a) irremediable, incurable

लाइसेंस (nm) a licence; —दार licensed, licence holder

लाक्षणिक (a) symbolic; metaphorical; allegorical

लाक्षा (nf) lac; —गृह a house which is made of lac

लाख (nf) sealing lac; lac; (nm) the number one lac; (a) a hundred thousand, a large number

लाग (nf) competition; hostility;

connection, —झट rancour,
rivalry; competition

लागत (nf) expenditure, prime
cost of a commodity; cost

लागू (a) adhering to, applicable, desirous, enforceable

लाघव (nm) minuteness, skill;
smartness

लाचार (a) forlorn; helpless;
compelled; obliged; (adv)
being helpless

लाचारी (nf) helplessness,
pressing necessity

लाज (nf) shyness; shame;
—वंत/वंती a very sensitive
plant called 'touch me not'

लाजवाब (a) matchless; silent,
speechless

लाज़िमी (a) inevitable, essential,
compulsory

लाट (nm) a lord, governor; a
thick lofty pillar

लाठी (nf) a stick, a club, a
cudgel; —चलना fighting
with sticks

लाड़ (nm) endearment, fondling, affection

लाड़ला (a) dear, a darling

लात (nf) leg, foot, a kick;
—मारना to kick, to spurn; to
abandon

लादना (v) to burden, to load; to
freight; to heap one upon
another

लानत (nf) reproach, reproof,
censure, condemnation;
rebuke

लाना (v) to fetch; to bring; to
present; to introduce

लापता (a) disappeared;
missing, gone underground

लापरवाह (a) listless, careless,
negligent; headless

लापरवाही (nf) negligence, carelessness

लाभ (nm) an advantage; profit;
gain; benefit; dividend

लाभकारी (a) beneficial; gainful;
profitable

लाभांश (nm) bonus; dividend

लाम (nm) a host, an army;
war-front; —बंदी mobili-
sation

लामा (nm) a Buddhist monk of
Tibet or Mongolia

लायक (a) fit, able; competent;
proper, capable

लायकी (nf) nobility; ability

लार (nf) saliva, sputum

लारी (nf) a lorry

लाल (a) red, angry; commu-
nist; (nm) darling, dear
boy; ruby

लालच (nm) temptation, greed,
greediness, covetousness;
avarice

लालची (a) covetous, greedy,
avaricious

लालटेन (nm) lantern

लालन (nm) coaxing, caressing,
fondling; —पालन nurturing

लालमिर्च (nf) pepper, chilly

लालसा (nf) longing, an ardent
desire, yearning

लालसी (a) wishful, desirous, eager

लाला (nm) a term of address used for a Kayastha and certain other Hindu castes, like Bania

लालायित (a) coveted, eager; tempted

लालित्य (nm) beauty, gracefulness, delicacy

लालिमा (nf) redness; ruddiness

लाली (nf) redness, ruddiness; honour, respect

लाव (nf) —लश्कर an array of followers, army with civilian support and material

लावण्य (nm) saltness; loveliness, grace, extreme beauty

लावा (nm) parched rice, fried gram; lava, hot mud of a volcano

लावारिस (a) heirless

लाश (nf) a dead body, a carcass

लासा (nm) a glutinous substance

लिंग (nm) a sign, a mark; male genital organ

लिए (ind) with a view to, for the sake of, for, on account of; (a) carrying, bearing

लिखना (v) to write; to note down; to record; —पढ़ना to study; writing and reading, studying

लिखाई (nf) work of writing, composition; —पढ़ाई study, education

लिखा-पढ़ी (nf) written agreement; correspondence

लिखावट (nf) handwriting; writing

लिखित (a) written; recorded

लिटाना (v) to cause to lie down, to lay on bed

लिपटना (v) to adhere to, to embrace, to coil around

लिपाई (nf) the act of smearing or plastering; —पुताई plastering and whitewashing

लिपि (nf) writing; a script; —बद्ध recorded; written

लिपिक (nm) a clerk

लिप्त (a) absorbed; deeply attached; involved

लिप्यंतरण (nm) transcription; transliteration

लिप्सा (nf) greed, lure, an earnest desire for a thing

लिफ़ाफ़ा (nm) a wrapper; an envelope; cover

लिफ़ाफ़िया (a) showy

लिबास (nm) garment, dress, attire, clothes

लिबासी (a) false, counterfeit

लियाकत (nf) merit; ability, fitnes, skill; qualification

लिहाज़ (nm) sense, respect, considerateness; point of view

लिहाज़ा (ind) therefore, thus, accordingly

लिहाफ़ (nm) a quilt

लीक (nf) mark, track, track-way; rut

लीचड़ (a) slow, sluggish, mean, one who is not prompt in the payment of dues

लीची (nf) the fruit of the tree *seytalia lichi*

लीडर (nm) a leader

लीद (nf) dung of horse

लीन (a) immersed, absorbed, rapt; merged

लीपना (v) to coat; to plaster; to smear; —पोतना to clean and tidy up

लीलना (v) to gulp, to swallow

लीला (nf) a sport, play; amorous sport; fun and frolic

लुंगी (nf) a piece of cloth which is wrapped round the waist

लुंज (a) without hand and feet, crippled; leafless tree; —पुंज having no muscles

लुठन (nm) robbing, plunder-ing; the act of stealing

लुगदी (nf) pulp

लुगाई (nf) a woman; wife

लुच्चा (a & nm) wanton; vile, a scoundrel, black sheep

लुटना (v) to be robbed; to be undone; to be sacked

लुटिया (nf) a small jug

लुटेरा (nm) a plunderer, a bandit, a robber

लुढ़कना (v) to tumble down, to roll down

लुत्फ़ (nm) pleasure, fun

लुनाई (nf) beauty

लुप्त (a) concealed, hidden, disappeared, missing

लुभाना (v) to charm; to lure; to attract; to captivate

लू (nf) the hot wind of summer, warm air; sunstroke; —लगना to have a sunstroke

लूट (nf) a spoil; a plunder; booty; —खसोट plunder, pillage; —मार plundering and killing or murder

लूटना (v) to rob, to plunder, to spoil, to maraud

लूला (a) maimmed, crippled, handless; —लँगड़ा crippled, disabled

लेई (nf) paste, starch, mortar

लेकिन (ind) but; on the other hand

लेख (nm) writing; an essay, an article; writ

लेखक (nm) an author, a writer

लेखन (nm) the work or art of writing, writing, —कला art of writing; —शैली style of writing; —सामग्री stationery, writing material

लेखनी (nf) a pen

लेखा (nm) record, account; —जोखा calculation; estimate

लेखिका (nf) a female author

लेटना (v) to lie down; to rest

लेन (nm) the act of taking or receiving anything; —दार a creditor; a money-lender; —देन transaction, exchange; dealings

लेना (v) to accept; to take, to receive; to borrow; to buy, to hold

लेप (nm) a plaster, an ointment; a paint; smearing

लेपना (v) to apply plaster to, to coat; to smear

लेश (a) very small; (nm) a small portion, smallness, a whit; —मात्र a shadow of

लैंगिक (a) phallic; sexual

लैस (a) ready, equipped

लोंदा (nm) a ball of wet powder etc.

लोक (nm) the world, the universe; people, folk; public; (a) popular, public; —कथा a folk tale; —कल्याण public welfare; —गीत a folk song; —तंत्र democracy; —तांत्रिक democratic; a democrat; —निंदा public slander; —नृत्य folk dance; —प्रिय popular; —मत public opinion; —सभा House of the People; —सम्मत enjoying popular support; —सेवा public service; —हित public welfare

लोकाचार (nm) a popular custom, fashion; convention; popular tradition

लोकाचारी (nm) a man of the world; (a) worldly wise

लोकप्रवाद (nm) a public slander

लोकोक्ति (nf) a popular saying,

a proverb

लोकोत्तर (a) supernatural, extraordinary

लोग (nm) the public; people; men; —बाग people; men in general

लोच (nf) elasticity, flexibility; tenderness

लोचन (nm) the eye

लोट (nf) lying, rolling; —पोट rolling; resting; bursting with laugh

लोटना (v) to lie in bed; to roll; to toss

लोथ (nf) a carcass; a corpse

लोथड़ा (nm) a lump of flesh

लोन (nm) salt; charm, beauty

लोप (nm) disappearance; elimination

लोभ (nm) greed, attraction; avarice, lure; covetousness

लोभी (a) covetous, greedy

लोम (nm) the hair on the body

लोमड़ी (nf) a fox

लोरी (nf) an Indian lullaby; —देना to lull a baby to sleep

लोलुप (a) greedy, voracious, covetous

लोहा (nm) iron; (a) very hard, very strong

लोहार (nm) a hammersmith, an ironsmith, a blacksmith

लोहारी (nf) the blacksmith's profession

लोहित (a) red, reddened

लोहिया (nm) an iron-monger

लोहू (nm) blood

लौंग (nf) the clove; an ornament in the form of a pin or stud worn on the nose

लौंडा (nm) a boy, a lad, a slave boy

लौंडी (nf) a servant girl, a slave girl, a girl

लौंडिया (nf) a girl

लौ (nf) the flame, the light of a lamp; glow; attachment; —लगाना to be deeply attached to

लौकिक (a) earthly, secular; worldly

लौकी (nf) a pumpkin

लौट (nf) returning; —फेर substantial change; modification

लौटना (v) to return, to come back

लौटाना (v) to send back, to return, to refund, to withdraw

लौह (nm) iron; (a) made of iron; —पुरुष an iron man; —युग iron age

व

व the last of the traditional semi-vowel set य, र, ल, व of Devnagri alphabet

वंग (nm) the province of Bengal, Indian state of Bengal

वंचना (nf) a deception, a fraud, sham

वंचित (a) cheated, deceived

वंदन (nm) adoration, obeisance

वंदना (nf) salutation, obeisance, worship

वंदनीय (a) adorable, fit to be worshipped

वंध्या (a) unfertile, barren; unproductive

वंश (nm) a bamboo, family; stock; dynasty; —गत pertaining to family

वंशज (nm) a descendent

वंश-परंपरा (nf) lineage, family tradition

वंश-वृक्ष (nm) a bamboo tree, lineage

वंशी (nf) a pipe, a flute; a fishing hook

वकालत (nf) delegation, pleadership, advocacy; —नामा a writ for the appointment of a lawyer to plead in a case, power of attorney

वकील (nm) pleader, a lawyer, an advocate

वक्त (nm) time; opportunity; circumstance; —का पाबंद punctual

वक्तव्य (nm) a speech, a statement (a) proper to be

spoken or told

वक्ता (*nm*) spokesman; speaker

वक्तृता (*nf*) a speech, an oration

वक्तृत्व (*nm*) eloquence, art of speaking

वक्र (*a*) crooked, curved, oblique; cunning; —गति crooked gait, zigzag motion; —गामी a fraudulent person; —दृष्टि an angry look; —रेखा curved line

वक्रता (*nf*) crookedness; dishonest dealings

वक्ष (*nm*) the breast, chest

वगैरह (*ind*) and so forth, etcetera

वचन (*nm*) speech, utterance; number (in grammar) commitment, pledge; —तोड़ना to break a promise; —देना to make a promise, —बद्ध committed; —ग्राही obedient, submissive

वजन (*nm*) weight; burden; value; —दार heavy; important, weighty

वज़नी (*a*) weighty, heavy; important

वजह (*nf*) reason, cause

वज़ीफ़ा (*nm*) stipend; scholarship

वज़ीर (*nm*) a minister of state; the queen in chess

वज़ीरी (*nf*) the office of a minister

वजूद (*nm*) presence; existence

वज्र (*nm*) the thunderbolt of Indra, lightning; a fatal weapon; (*a*) very hard

वज्रपात (*nm*) the stroke of lightning

वज्राघात (*nm*) an astounding calamity or misery

वट (*nm*) a banyan tree

वटी (*nf*) a pill, tablet

वणिक् (*nm*) a merchant, a trader, a shopkeeper

वतन (*nm*) the native country

वत्स (*nm*) a calf; dear boy

वत्सल (*a*) tender, affectionate, child-loving

वत्सलता (*nf*) fondness, tenderness

वदन (*nm*) the mouth, face

वध (*nm*) slaughter; murder, killing

वधिक (*nm*) a hunter; a murderer

वधू (*nf*) wife, a bride; son's wife

वध्य (*a*) fit to be killed or murdered

वन (*nm*) a wood, jungle, forest; —चर a woodman, —राज a lion; —रोपण afforestation; —लक्ष्मी forest-goddess; —वास dwelling in a forest; —स्थली a heath

वनस्पति (*nf*) a tree or plant, vegetable; —घी hydrogenated oil of groundnut etc.; —विज्ञान Botany

वनिता (*nf*) a beloved woman;

mistress; wife

वनौषधि (*nf*) the herbs of a forest

वन्य (*a*) produced in a forest; wild, savage

वपु (*nm*) the body

वफ़ा (*nf*) the fulfilment of a promise, fidelity, sincerity; —दार faithful, loyal

वबाल (*nm*) a curse, calamity

वमन (*nm*) puke, vomitting

वय (*nm*) the duration or period of time; age

वयस्क (*a*) pertaining to age, adult; major

वयस्कता (*nf*) adulthood

वयस्य (*nm*) a friend, a companion

वयोवृद्ध (*a*) old, aged

वर (*nm*) a blessing; bride-groom; (*a*) excellent, beautiful, better

वरक़ (*nm*) the leaf of a book, a gold or silver leaf

वरज़िश (*nf*) physical exercise

वरण (*nm*) selecting or choosing; a promise of marriage

वरदान (*nm*) a boon

वरदी (*nf*) the uniform

वरन् (*ind*) on the other hand

वराह (*nm*) pig, a boar

वरिष्ठ (*a*) best, most preferable or excellent, respected, senior; most preferable

वरीय (*a*) senior; —ता seniority

वरुण (*nm*) the deity of the

waters

वरुणालय (*nm*) the ocean

वर्ग (*nm*) a multitude of similar objects, a class, a kind, group; a square; a square number; निम्न— the lower class; निम्नमध्य — lower middle class; —फल square; —भेद class distinction; —संघर्ष class-struggle; —हीन classless

वर्गीकरण (*nm*) a classification; —करना to square, to classify

वर्गीकृत (*a*) classified

वर्जन (*nm*) inhibition, prohibition

वर्जनीय (*a*) fit to be avoided; wicked

वर्जित (*a*) avoided, inhibited, prohibited

वर्जना (*nf*) a taboo, an inhibition; (*v*) to inhibit, to taboo

वर्ण (*nm*) colour; caste; dye; a letter of the alphabet; —क्रम colour scheme, alphabetical order; —माला the alphabet; —विचार orthography; —विन्यास spelling; —व्यवस्था the caste system; —संकर a mixture of castes; —हीन casteless; colourless

वर्णन (*nm*) narration, description

वर्णनातीत (*a*) indescribable

वर्णनीय (*a*) describable

वर्णाश्रम (*nm*) the caste to which

a person belongs

वर्ण्य (a) fit for being described; (nm) the topic of a description

वर्तनी (nf) spelling

वर्तमान (a) present, existing, living; current; (nm) the present

वर्तुल (a) round, circular, spherical

वर्धन (a) increasing, growing, growth

वर्ष (nm) a year

वर्षण (nm) the falling of rain

वर्षा (nf) rain, rainfall

वलय (nm) circle, a ring; fold

वली (nm) a master; a ruler; a guardian; —वारिस guardian or heir, kith and kin

वल्कल (nm) the bark of a tree, cloth made of bark

वल्गा (nf) a rein, a bridle

वल्लरी (nf) a creeper

वल्लभ (a) dear, beloved; (nm) a lover; husband

वश (nm) control; power

वशीकरण (nm) conjuration, bewitchment, glamour

वशीभूत (a) subdued, overpowered, fascinated

वसंत (nm) the spring season

वसीयत (nf) a testament, a will, a legacy; —नामा a will

वसुंधरा (nf) the earth

वसूल (a) obtained, realised, collected; —करना to collect

वसूली (nf) the realisation or collection of dues

वस्तु (nf) an item, an article, a substance, an object

वस्तुत: (ind) strictly, in fact, rather, actually

वस्त्र (nm) cloth, textile; fibre

वस्ल (nm) lover's union

वह (pron) that; he; she; it

वहन (nm) carrying, conveying, bearing

वहम (nm) false notion, doubt, suspicion

वहमी (a) whimsical, suspicious

वहशत (nf) rudeness, savagery; incivility

वहशी (a) rude, uncivilised, savage; —पन savagery, barbarousness

वहाँ (adv) there, thither

वहीं (ind) at that very place, on the spot

वही (pron) the same

वह्नि (nm) fire

वांछनीय (a) desired, desirable, worth wishing for

वांछित (a) desirable, wished

वा (ind) or; or else; either, whether

वाक् (nm) a word, speech, language

वाकई (ind) actually, infact

वाक़िफ़ (a) conversant; acquainted

वाकफ़ियत (nf) conversance; knowledge, acquaintance

वाकया (nm) event, incident

वाक़ (nf) voice, speech;

goddess of speach; —पटु eloquent in speech

वाक्य (nm) a sentence, —रचना syntax, construction of sentence; —शैली a mode of expression

वाक्यार्थ (nm) the meaning of a sentence

वाग्जाल (nm) an equivocation, circumlocution, an empty talk

वाग्दान (nm) betrothal, engagement

वाग्देवी (nf) the goddess Saraswati, the power of speech

वाड.मय (nm) literature

वाचक (nm) a speaker, a reader

वाचन (nm) speaking; reading

वाचनालय (nm) a reading room

वाचाल (a & nm) talkative, gobbling, chattering

वाच्य (a) expressible in words, predicable; (nm) voice (in grammar)

वाच्यार्थ (nm) the denotative meaning

वाजिब (a) fit, suitable, proper

वाजिबी (a) reasonable, necessary

वाटिका (nf) a garden

वाणिज्य (nm) trade, commerce

वाणी (nf) voice; speech; an epithet of the goddess Saraswati

वात (nm) wind; air; breeze; one of the humours of the body; —प्रकोप the disorder of wind which creates diseases of various kinds

वातानुकूल (nm) airconditioning

वातायन (nm) a ventilator

वातावरण (nm) atmosphere

वात्सल्य (nm) fondness, affection, a parent's love towards progeny

वाद (nm) cause, a suit; discussion; dispute; theory; —प्रतिवाद controversy; —विवाद dispute, discussion

वादा (nm) a promise, an agreement (see also वायदा)

वादी (nm) a speaker, an arguer, a disputant, a plaintiff in a suit, a prosecutor; —प्रतिवादी the plaintiff and the defendant

वाद्य (nm) a musical instrument; —वृंद the orchestra

वानर (nm) a monkey; an ape

वापस (a) given back; returned; come back; reverted

वापसी (a) returned; (nf) a withdrawl, refund

वाम (a) left; reverse; inverted, opposite

वामन (nm) dwarfish, a dwarf; a pigmy

वायदा (nm) commitment; a promise; —खिलाफ़ी breach of a promise

वायस (nm) a crow

वायवीय (a) windy, airy; aerial

वायु (nf) air, wind; windy

humour; —मंडल atmosphere; —मार्ग airways; —सेना air force

वायुयान (nm) an aeroplane, aircraft

वारंट (nm) a warrant; voucher

वारंवार (ind) again and again; repeatedly

वार (nm) a stroke; an assault; a day of the week; —पार full expanse; this side and the other

वारदात (nf) unfortunate event; a mishap

वारना (v) to dedicate, to sacrifice; to make an offering of

वारनिश (nf) varnish

वारांगना (nf) a prostitute, a harlot

वाराणसी (nf) the old name of Kashi or Banaras

वारा-न्यारा (nm) decision, a settlement, gain

वारि (nm) water

वारिज (nm) lotus, conch

वारिस (nm) a successor, an heir

वारुणी (nf) wine, liquor

वार्डन (nm) a warden

वार्ता (nf) talks, a talk; negotiation; —कार a talker; negotiator

वार्तालाप (nm) conversation, a dialogue, a discourse, parley

वार्तिक (nm) an explanatory, commentary, gloss

वार्धक्य (nm) old age, senility

वार्षिक (a) yearly, annual; per annum

वार्षिकोत्सव (nm) anniversary

वालंटियर (nm) a volunteer

वालिद (nm) father

वालिदा (nf) mother

वाबैला (nm) uproar, turmoil, weeping, lamentation

वाष्प (nm) vapour; tears

वास (nm) residence, habitation; odour, fragrance; —स्थान a house

वासना (nf) passion, intense desire, fancy

वासर (nm) a day

वासी (nm) an inhabitant, a dweller

वास्तव (a) real, factual; genuine; substantial

वास्तविक (a) factual, real, true, solid, bonafide; —ता reality, truth

वास्ता (nm) connection, relation

वास्तु (nm) the site of a building, house, a building, —विद्या the science or art of building a house; —कला/शिल्प architecture

वास्ते (ind) for the purpose of, for the sake of, in order to; in the name of

वाह (int) denoting admiration or contempt, Well done! Ah! Bravo! excellent!

fine ! hurrah

वाहक (nm) a porter, carrier, bearer; a charioteer, horse-man

वाहन (nm) a conveyance of any kind, a vehicle

वाहवाही (nf) praise, applause

वाहिनी (nf) an army; —पति the commander of any army

वाहियात (a) worthless, useless; nonsense; ridiculous

विकट (a) huge, horrible, ghastly, frightful; difficult

विकराल (a) terrible, horrible, dreadful; frightful; hideous; monstrous

विकर्षण (nm) repulsion; detachment

विक/ल (a) agitated, restless, mutilated; —लांग crippled, disabled

विकल्प (nm) an option, alternative

विकसित (a) opened; bloomed; developed

विकार (nm) a defect, alternation, deformation, defilement; disorder

विकास (nm) expansion, development, evolution, growth; —वाद theory of evolution; —शील developing

विकीर्ण (a) scattered, diffused, renowned

विकृत (a) altered, changed, deformed, mutilated, disordered; oblique

विकृति (nf) a change of form or nature, a defect, a deformed appearance

विक्रम (nm) heroism, strength, mettle; (a) best, excellent

विक्रमी (a) pertaining to Vikramaditya; heroic, valiant

विक्रय (nm) sale, selling

विक्रयी (nm) a seller, vendor

विक्रांत (a) valiant, heroic, mighty

विक्रेता (nm) a seller, vendor

विक्षत (a) injured, wounded

विक्षिप्त (a) crazy, mad; perplexed

विक्षिप्तता (nf) madness

विक्षुब्ध (a) bewildered, perplexed, confused

विक्षेपण (nm) scattering, confusion, disturbance

विक्षोभ (nm) the agitation of mind

विख्यात (a) notable, renowned, famous, distinguished

विख्याति (nf) fame, renown, celebrity

विगत (a) gone away, passed, departed, disappeared

विग्रह (nm) a struggle, strife, quarrel, form

विग्रही (nm) a fighter, one who quarrels with another

विघटन (nm) a breaking up, destruction, disintegration, disorganisation; decomposition

विघ्न (nm) an obstacle, an interruption; meddling, interference

विचक्षण (a) far-sighted, extremely sagacious

विचर (a) wandered, strayed; —ण wandering, strolling, movement; variation

विचल (a) unsteady, movable, unfixed

विचलन (nm) deviation; moving about

विचलित (a) unsettled, unsteady, not fixed

विचार (nm) thinking, thought; idea; observation; pondering; reflection; —क a thinker; —गोष्ठी a seminar, —विमर्श discussion; —धारा ideology; —शील thoughtful

विचारणीय (a) noteworthy, noticeable, dubious, questionable

विचारना (v) to think, to consider

विचाराधीन (a) under consideration, under trial

विचित्र (a) surprising; strange; wonderful; curious

विचित्रता (nf) strangeness, diversity

विच्छिन्न (a) cut off; divided, separated

विच्छेद (nm) disjunction; separation, division; breaking up

विच्छेदन (nm) separation, destruction

विच्छोह (nm) separation

विजय (nf) mastery; victory, conquest, triumph; —देवी the goddess of victory; —ध्वज the banner of victory; —लक्ष्मी the goddess of victory

विजया (nf) an intoxicating herb 'भाँग' — दशमी Dushahra

विजयोत्सव (nm) the festival on the विजयादशमी or Dushahra day

विजाति (nf) another caste or class

विजेता (nm) a conqueror

विज्ञ (a) wise, clever; skilful, experienced; learned

विज्ञता (nf) wisdom; learning, knowledge

विज्ञप्ति (nf) an information, notification, a communique

विज्ञान (nm) science; —वेत्ता a scientist, man of science;

विज्ञानी (nm) a scientist

विज्ञापन (nm) an advertisement; announcement; a poster

विटप (nm) a tree; a plant

विडंबन (nm) mimicry, disguise

विडंबना (nf) mockery

विडंबित (a) troubled, distressed; mocked

वितरण (nm) a gift, a donation; a distribution; delivery

वितर्क (nm) reasoning, discussion; a doubt

वितृष्णा (nf) repulsion, repugnance

वित्त (nm) wealth, riches; property

वित्तीय (a) financial

विदग्ध (nm) a libertine, a clever person

विदग्धता (nf) cleverness, shrewdness, learning

विदा (nf) a taking leave, farewell, adieu; a departure

विदाई (nf) sending off, farewell; departure

विदित (a) known, understood

विदीर्ण (a) split, torn, opened; killed

विदुषी (nf) a learned woman

विदूषक (nm) a jester, a buffoon; a humorous companion of the hero in a sanskrit drama

विदूषण (nm) reviling, corruption

विदेश (nm) a foreign country, a distant land

विदेशी (a) foreign, alien; (nm) a foreigner

विद्यमान (a) extant, present, still existing

विद्यमानता (nf) presence

विद्या (nf) knowledge, learning, study; —दान teaching, imparting knowledge; —देवी Saraswati, the goddess of learning; —पीठ a school

विद्याभ्या/स (nm) pursuit of learning; study; —सी studious

विद्यार्थी (nm) a pupil, a student; a scholar

विद्यालय (nm) a school

विद्युत (nm) lightning, electricity

विद्रूप (a) ugly, distorted, hideous, monstrous; (nm) monstrosity; irony

विद्रोह (nm) revolt, uprising, rebellion, insurrection

विद्रोही (a) mutinous, revolting, a rebel

विद्वत्ता (nf) learning, knowledge; scholarship

विद्वान् (a & nm) learned, wise, well-read, a scholar

विद्वेष (nm) enmity; hatred, contempt; malice

विद्वेषी (a) inimical, malicious, spiteful

विधना (nm) the god Brahma, Providence

विधर्म (nm) a religion different from one's own; heresy; (a) unjust, inequitable

विधर्मी (nm) a man who follows a religion different from one's own

विधवा (nf) widow

विधवाश्रम (nm) a refuge or home for widows

विधा (nf) form, type; device

विधाता (nm) the creator — Brahma

विधान (nm) an arrangement, legislation, rule; methold; —परिषद legislative council;

—सभा legislative assembly

विधायक (nm) a legislator, a prescriber, a manager

विधायी (a) legislative

विधि (nf) an order, command; manner, process; law; method, system; direction; rule; —पूर्वक duly; methodically, systematically; —वत् duly, methodically, systematically; —विधान method and manner; —वेत्ता a jurisconsultant; —शास्त्र jurisprudence; —शास्त्री a jurisprudent

विधु (nm) the moon

विधुर (nm) widower; (a) widowed

विधेय (a) what is required; to be accomplished, governable

विधेयक (nm) a bill

विध्यात्मक (a) positive

विध्वंस (nm) ruin, destruction, devastation

विध्वंसी (nm) one who ruins or demolishes, a destroyer

विध्वस्त (a) destroyed, demolished

विनत (a) bent, humble, bowing, modest

विनती (nf) request; prayer; humility; solicitation

विनम्र (a) bent, humble, modest, meek; respectful, courteous

विनय (nf) politeness, modesty, humility, humbleness; good behaviour

विनयी (a) mild, courteous, humble, modest, polite

विनश्वर (a) transitory, not lasting for ever, perishable

विनष्ट (a) ruined, destroyed, spoiled; dead, perished

विनायक (nm) an epithet of the god Ganesha

विनाश (nm) ruin, destruction, down fall, disaster, wreck

विनाशक (nm) a spoiler, a destroyer annihilator

विनाशी (a) destructive, baneful

विनिमय (nm) exchange, substitution, permutation; —करना to exchange, to permute

विनियोग (nm) the use of an object for attaining a special end or purpose

विनीत (a) gentle, humble, modest; polite, submissive, meek

विनोद (nm) fun, amusement, recreation, entertainment; a joke; wit, humour

विनोदी (a) jovial, witty, jolly, humorous

विन्यास (nm) laying down, an adjustment; structure, disposition, arrangement

विपक्ष (nm) the opposition

विपक्षी (a) opposition; rival; hostile; (nm) an opponent, an enemy

विपत्काल (nm) the time of distress or disaster, misfortune

विपत्ति (nf) a calamity, a disaster; misfortune, hardship; —ग्रस्त afflicted, distressed

विपथ (nm) a bad road

विपद् (nf) affliction, distress, hardship, calamity, crisis; —ग्रस्त in distress, afflicted

विपन्न (a) fallen into a calamity; distressed, afflicted

विपरीत (a) contrary; opposed; reverse

विपर्यय (nm) a change, perverseness of disposition, reversal

विपिन (nm) a jungle, a forest

विपुल (a) broad, large, big, deep, extensive; mammoth

विपुलता (nf) magnitude, plentitude

विप्र (nm) a Brahman

विप्रलंभ (nf) separation of lovers; deception, a trick

विप्रलब्ध (nm) the man whose desires are not fulfilled; separated

विप्लव (nm) disorder, insurrection; insurgency, revolt

विफल (a) vain, useless, failed, unsuccessful; fruitless, futile

विभंजन (nm) the act of breaking up into component parts

विभक्त (a) separated, partitioned; divided

विभक्ति (nf) a separation, partition; division

विभव (nm) wealth, riches, dignity

विभाग (nm) division, department; portion, part

विभागीय (a) departmental

विभाजक (a) dividing, parting; (nm) a division

विभाजन (nm) partition, division

विभाजित (a) divided; distributed

विभाज्य (a) divisible, fit to be divided or distributed

विभावरी (nf) night

विभिन्न (a) various; quite different; disunited; —ता variety, diversity

विभीषण (a) terrible, fearful; a brother of Ravana

विभीषिका (nf) a show of fear, a dreadful sight; horror, terror

विभु (a) huge, powerful; (nm) God, Vishnu

विभूति (nf) majesty; ash

विभूषित (a) decorated; adorned, ornamented; beautified

विभेद (nm) separation, division

विभ्रम (nm) doubt; blunder, error; motion

विभ्रांति (nf) an error; a confusion; mistake

विमंडन (nm) ornamentation, decoration

विमंडित (a) decorated; beautified

विमत (a) contrary opinion,

counter principle

विमर्दन (*nm*) crushing, killing

विमर्श (*nm*) a trial, an investigation; consultation, consideration, examination

विमल (*a*) clean; clear; dirtless; pure

विमाता (*nf*) step-mother

विमान (*nm*) aircraft, an aeroplane; —चालक a pilot; —पत्तन airport; —परिचारिका air-hostess

विमार्ग (*nm*) an evil course

विमुक्त (*a*) released, liberated, set free

विमुक्ति (*nf*) liberation

विमुख (*a*) disinclined, indifferent, having a sense of aversion

विमुग्ध (*a*) fascinated, attracted, charmed

विमूढ़ (*a*) very foolish or stupid; senseless, unconscious

विमोक्ष (*nm*) release, salvation

विमोचन (*nm*) untying, liberation, acquittal

विमोह (*nm*) ignorance, suspicion, seduction

विमोही (*a*) alluring, fascinating; cruel, hard-hearted

वियुक्त (*a*) abandoned, separated, deserted

वियोग (*nm*) disunion, a separation; bereavement

वियोगिनी (*nf*) a woman separated from her husband or lover

वियोगी (*nm*) a lover/husband separated from his beloved/wife

विरंचि (*nm*) creator, Brahma

विरक्त (*a*) free from worldly attachment; disaffected; indifferent

विरचित (*a*) prepared; composed; written

विरत (*a*) free from worldly attachment; indifferent, stopped

विरति (*nf*) the absence of desire, indifference

विरल (*a*) fine; rare, scarce

विरलता (*nf*) tenuity; scarcity

विरह (*nm*) parting, separation

विरहिणी (*nf*) one separated from her lover/husband

विरहित (*a*) deserted, exempt, devoid

विराग (*nm*) absence of desire or passion, renunciation, detachment

विरागी (*a*) averse to worldly pleasures

विराजना (*v*) to enjoy oneself, to grace; to take seat

विराजमान (*a*) shining, brilliant, handsome; seated, looking glorious

विराट् (*a*) very big, huge, colossal, gigantic

विराम (*nm*) interval, pause; stop; stoppage; rest; halt; —चिह्न punctuation mark

विरासत (*nf*) inheritance, legacy

विरुद्ध (a) contrary; against; opposite; adverse, hostile

विरुद्धता (nf) hostility, opposition

विरूप (a) variegated, multi-coloured, ugly, ill-shaped

विरेचक (a) purgative

विरेचन (nm) a purgative medicine, purging

विरोध (nm) hostility, opposition, antagonism; resistance; objection; protest

विरोधाभास (nm) a paradox

विरोधी (a) hostile, inimical, disputant, an adversary, rival; opponent

विलंब (nm) tardiness, delay; lag

विलंबित (a) hanging, late, delayed, tardy

विलंबी (a) tardy, laggard

विलक्षण (a) uncommon; queer, strange, wonderful; remarkable, extra-ordinary, fantastic

विलक्षणता (nf) imparity, queerness

विलग (a) separated, detached

विलय (nm) merger; annihilation; dissolution

विलाप (nm) crying, weeping, lamentation

विलायत (nm) a foreign country, a distant land

विलायती (a) foreign, European

विलास (nm) merriment, enjoyment; luxury; amorous, playfulness

विला/सी (a & nm) amorous, playful, lustful; luxury-loving; —सिता debauchery; —सिनी a beautiful woman, a harlot, a flirt

विलीन (a) hidden, vanished, disappeared, invisible

विलोकन (nm) the act of seeing

विलोकित (a) beheld, looked at, viewed

विलोचन (nm) the eye

विलोड़न (nm) stirring, whirling, moving

विलोम (a) converse; reverse; contrary; antonym

विलोल (a) unsteady; beautiful

विवक्षित (a) desired, intended, signified

विवरण (nm) explanation, description, statement

विवरणिका (nf) a brochure

विवर्ण (a) of low caste; of bad colour, faded; colourless

विवर्त (nm) illusion, falsity

विवश (a) compelled, helpless; under compulsion; forced

विवस्त्र (a) devoid or destitute of clothes, naked

विवाद (nm) dispute, argument; quarrel, altercation; discussion

विवादास्पद (a) controversial

विवादी (nm) a wrangler

विवाह (nm) wedding, marriage, matrimony; —संबंध matrimonial relation

विवाहित (*nm*) married man
विवाहिता (*nf*) married woman
विविध (*a*) various, different, multiform; —ता variety, variation
विवृत (*a*) expanded, opened
विवेक (*nm*) discretion, reason; wisdom, intelligence
विवेकी (*a*) judicious, prudent, wise
विवेचन (*nm*) a thorough investigation, judgement, critical appreciation
विवेचित (*a*) discussed; critically appreciated; evaluated, investigated
विशद (*a*) elaborate, detailed; clear-cut
विशारद (*nm*) a very learned man; (*a*) learned, wise, clever, competent
विशाल (*a*) extensive; huge, large, big; grand; gigantic
विशिष्ट (*a*) special; particular; prominent; typical
विशिष्टता (*nf*) speciality, qualification
विशुद्ध (*a*) pure, unmixed, unadulterated; true, genuine
विशुद्धि (*nf*) greater purity, genuineness
विशूचिका (*nf*) the disease called cholera
विश्रृंखल (*a*) disorderly, disintegrated, disarrayed
विशेष (*a*) special, peculiar, specific, distinctive, chara-cteristic; typical
विशेषज्ञ (*nm*) an expert, a specialist; (*a*) skilful; —ता specialisation
विशेषण (*nm*) attribute; adjective; — पद attributive
विशेषता (*nf*) peculiarity
विशेषांक (*nm*) a special number of a newspaper or a magazine
विशेषाधि/कार (*nm*) privilege; —कारी a special officer; privileged person
विशेष्य (*nm*) a substantive, that which is qualified
विश्रब्ध (*a*) calm and quiet; confidential; fearless
विश्रांत (*a*) calm; at ease; reposed
विश्रांति (*nf*) rest, repose, recess
विश्राम (*nm*) recreation, repose, relaxation, rest
विश्रुत (*a*) famous, renowned
विश्लिष्ट (*a*) analysed, disunited, separated
विश्लेषण (*nm*) analysis
विश्लेषित (*a*) analysed
विश्व (*nm*) the world, universe; —कोश an encyclopaedia; —विद्यालय a university; —विख्यात world known; —विजयी world-conqueror; —व्यापी pervading the universe
विश्वसनीय (*a*) trustworthy, bonafide, reliable, dependable, believable, credible

विश्वस्त (a) reliable, confidential; solid, responsible,
truthful

विश्वास (nm) trust, credit,
belief, faith; confidence;
assurance; —घात betrayal,
treachery, violation of trust;
—घातीtreacherous, a traitor;
—पात्र a reliable person;
—भंग a breach of faith

विश्वासी (a) honest, faithful,
steady

विष (nm) poison, venom; —धर
a snake; —मंत्र a charm for
curing snake-bite

विषण्ण (a) gloomy, melancholic

विषम (a) uneven, rough, odd;
adverse, dissimilar; dis-
agreeable

विषमता (nf) irregularity,
disproportion, enmity

विषय (nm) topic, a subject;
matter; content; an affair;
object; —रत sexy; —लोलुप
lustful, sexy, sensual;
—वासना sexuality and lust;
sensuality; —वस्तु theme;
—सुख sexual pleasure;
—सूची a list of contents,
table of contents

विषयक (ind) concerning,
relating to

विषयांतर (nm) another topic;
digression

विषयासक्त (a) lustful, sensual,
given to sexual indulgence

विषयी (nm & a) a sensualist,
an amorous person, rich,
wealthy

विषाक्त (a) poisonous, toxic

विषाद (nm) sorrow, sadness,
gloom, dejection, melan-
choly

विषैला (a) poisonous,
venomous, viperous

विसंग/त (a) illogical, irrelevant; —ति irrelevance

विसर्जन (nm) departure;
dispersion

विसर्जित (a) dispersed

विस्तार (nm) spread, elabora-
tion, expanse, span; extent;
enlargement; details;
volume; —पूर्वक extensively;
in details; elaborately

विस्तीर्ण (a) spread wide,
extended; spacious; elaborate

विस्तृत (a) expanded;
voluminous; elaborate,
detailed; lengthy

विस्था/पन (nm) displacement;
—पित displaced

विस्फारित (a) spread

विस्फोट (nm) explosion, blast;
burst

विस्फोटक (nm) a poisonous
boil, an explosive substance

विस्मय (nm) astonishment,
wonder, surprise

विस्मयाकुल (a) wonderstruck

विस्मयादिबोधक (nm) an interjection

विस्मरण (nm) forgetting,

oblivion; — शील forgetful;
— शीलता forgetfulness

विस्मित (a) amazed, astonished, surprised

विस्मृत (a) forgotten

विस्मृति (nm) forgetting, oblivion

विहंगम (nm) a bird

विहंगावलोकन (nm) a bird's eye view

विहग (nm) a bird

विहसित (nm) a laugh which is neither too loud nor too slow

विहान (nm) day-break

विहार (nm) pastime, merry-making; wandering, roaming; a Buddhist monastery

विहित (a) arranged; instituted, performed

विहीन (a) abandoned, deserted; deprived of; (adv) without

विह्वल (a) confused, agitated; perplexed; impatient

वीक्षण (nm) the act of seeing

वीचि (nf) a wave, ripple

वीणा (nf) Indian lute, lyre; —वादिनी an epithet of goddess सरस्वती, —वादक a lute player

वीत (a) abandoned, left off, released; —राग one who is free from worldly attachment

वीथि, वीथी (nf) a path, passage, way, a road

वीर (a) brave, valiant, plucky, daring; —गति the attainment of heaven which a warrior slain in war is supposed to get; —पूजा hero-worship; —हृदय stout-hearted

वीरता (nf) bravery, valiancy, heroism, daring

वीरा/न (a) devastated, desolate; uninhabited; —नी desolateness, desertedness

वीरासन (nm) a special posture of body befitting a warrior

वीर्य (nm) semen; potency, valour; virility; heroism

वुजूद (nm) existence, being

वृंत (nm) nipple, leaf

वृंद (nm) an assembly, multitude, a collection; —गान chorus; —गायक the chorus

वृक्ष (nm) a tree

वृत्त (nm) ring; circle; account; news; verse, meter

वृत्तांत (nm) a report, narrative, account; news

वृत्ति (nf) subsistence, instinct; mentality; vocation; stipend; —कार a commentator

वृथा (a) fruitless, useless; ineffective; (adv) vainly, in vain

वृद्ध (a) aged, old; (nm) aged man, oldman

वृद्धता (nf) senility, old age

वृद्धा (nf) an old woman

वृद्धावस्था (*nf*) old age

बुद्धि (*nf*) progress, increase; growth; enlargement; magnification

वृषभ (*nm*) a bull, bullock

वृष्टि (*nf*) rain, shower; —काल rainy season

बृहत् (*a*) large, great, much, big

बे (*pron*) they, those

वेग (*nm*) momentum, speed

वेगवान् (*a*) swift, rapid, quick, hasty

वेणी (*nf*) a woman's braided hair falling down on her back like a tail

वेणु (*nf*) bamboo, a flute, a pipe

वेतन (*nm*) wages, salary; —भोगी salaried; —वृद्धि increment

वेताल (*nm*) a sentinal, a porter, a goblin

वेत्ता (*nm*) one who knows, (*a*) understanding, knowing, acquainted with

वेद (*nm*) the most ancient and sacred scripurates of the Hindus; the divine knowledge; —ज्ञ one who knows the Vedas, conversant with the scriptures

वेदना (*nf*) pain, ache, agony, distress, affliction, torment

वेदांग (*nm*) the six subordinate branches of Vedas; —शिक्षा rules for correct pronunciation of Vedic Mantras; —कल्प details of religious ceremonies

वेदांत (*nm*) one of the six systems of Hindu philosophy which is particularly based on the Upanishads, theology; —सूत्र the ophorisms on Vedanta compiled by the sage Vadarayan

वेदांती (*nm*) a follower of the Vedanta philosophy, a theologian

वेदाभ्यास (*nm*) the study of the Vedas

वेदी (*nf*) an altar, a platform; terrace

वेदोक्त (*a*) enjoined by the holy writ, scriptural, taught in the scriptures, or Vedas

वेध (*nm*) a hole, perforation, piercing; the observation of planets by means of a telescope

वेला (*nf*) time; an hour; coast, shore

वेश (*nm*) dress, costume, guise; —भूषा apparel; get-up, appearance

वेश्या (*nf*) a harlot, a prostitute; —वृत्ति profession of prostitution

वेष्टन (*nm*) enclosure, fence

वेष्टित (*a*) enclosed, surrounded

वैकल्पिक (*a*) alternative, optional

वैकुंठ (*nm*) paradise, heaven

वैचित्र्य (nm) queerness, peculiarity, strangeness

वैजयंती (nf) a banner; a garland of five colours of Lord Vishnu

वैज्ञानिक (nm) a scientist; (a) scientific

वैतनिक (a) salaried, on salary-basis

वैतालीय (a) pertaining to a goblin

वैदेशिक (a) foreign, external

वैद्य (nm) a physician; —शास्त्र medical science, medicine

वैद्यक (nm) the Indian system of medical science, Ayurveda

वैध (a) legal, valid; tenable, regular

वैधर्म्य (nm) heresy, atheism

वैधव्य (nm) widowhood

वैभव (nm) greatness, majesty; wealth; grandeur, glory

वैभवशाली (a) rich, magnificent, royal

वैमनस्य (nm) enmity, hostility, malice, rancour

वैयक्तिक (a) personal; individual; private; —ता individuality

वैयाकरण (nm) a grammarian

वैर (nm) enmity, hostility, opposition

वैरागी (a & nm) detached; one who has subdued his passions

वैराग्य (nm) freedom from worldly desires; renunciation

वैरी (nm) a foe, an enemy, an adversary

वैरूप्य (nm) difference of form

वैवाहिक (a) matrimonial, married

वैशिष्ट्य (nm) peculiarity; speciality

वैषम्य (nm) difference, irregularity

वैषयिक (a) pertaining to a subject

वैष्णव (nm) a devotee of Vishnu; (a) pertaining to Vishnu

वैष्णवी (nf) the personified energy of Vishnu

वैसा (adv) so, such, like that; (a) of that kind, such as that

वैसे (ind) in that manner, that way; in the same manner

व्यंग्य (nm) joke, irony, sarcasm, caricature; —चित्र a cartoon; —चित्रकार a cartoonist

व्यंग्यार्थ (nm) suggestion; connotative meaning

व्यंजक (a) making clear or manifest; (nm) a mark, a symbol

व्यंजन (nm) a consonant; rich cooked food

व्यंजित (a) conveyed through suggestion, suggested

व्यक्त (a) manifest, apparent,

clear; expressed

व्यक्ति (*nm*) a person, an individual; subject; —गत subjective; individual, personal; —त्व personality; individuality; —वादी an individualist; individual-istic

व्यग्र (*a*) impatient, restless; concerned

व्यग्रता (*nf*) perplexity, solici-tude, anxiety

व्यतिक्रम (*nm*) contrariety, converse

व्यतिरेक (*nm*) negation, exclu-sion, an exception

व्यतीत (*a*) gone, passed; past

व्यथा (*nf*) anguish, pain, suffering, misery, distress

व्यथित (*a*) troubled, distressed pained, afflicted

व्यभिचार (*nm*) following an improper or sinful course, debauchery; adultery

व्यभिचारिणी (*nf*) a wanton woman, an adulteress

व्यभिचारी (*a & nm*) unchaste, immoral; a debauchee; an adulterer; lewd

व्यय (*nm*) expense, cost, expenditure; consumption

व्यर्थ (*a*) to no purpose, fruit-less, useless; futile, in-effective; unprofitable

व्यवच्छेद (*nm*) separation, division, contrast

व्यवधान (*nm*) hindrance, interruption

व्यवसाय (*nm*) an occupation; profession; vocation; practice

व्यवसायी (*nm*) a man of business

व्यवस्था (*nf*) form; an adjustment, order, system, arrangement; provision

व्यवस्थापक (*nm*) a regulator; a director; an organiser; a manager

व्यवस्थित (*a*) regular, systematic; settled; provi-ded

व्यवहार (*nm*) dealings, treat-ment; behaviour; transac-tion; practice; usage, use

व्यवहार्य (*a*) usual, practicable, feasible

व्यवहृत (*a*) followed in practice, employed, used, applied; adjusted

व्यष्टि (*nm*) individual

व्यसन (*nm*) calamity, misfortune, addiction

व्यसनी (*a & nm*) vicious; (*nm*) a person who is addicted to a vice

व्यस्त (*a*) perplexed, engaged in some work, busy, occupied

व्याकरण (*nm*) grammar

व्याकुल (*a*) upset, perturbed, restless, distempered

व्याकुलता (*nf*) distraction, agitation, confusion

व्याख्या (nf) a description, interpretation; explanation; commentary; exposition; —कार a commentator

व्याख्याता (nm) a speaker, a lecturer

व्याख्यान (nm) an explanation, speech, lecture; interpretation

व्याघात (nm) an obstacle, interruption; hindrance, obstruction

व्याघ्र (nm) a lion, a tiger

व्याज (nm) fraud, deception, interest

व्याध (nm) a fowler, a hunter

व्याधि (nf) a malady, disease, an ailment

व्यापक (a) extensive, comprehensive, circumambient

व्यापकता (nf) prevalence, diffusion, extensiveness

व्यापार (nm) profession, trade, business; traffic; function; phenomenon

व्यापारिक (a) mercantile, commercial

व्यापारी (nm) a trader, merchant, business man

व्याप्त (a) diffused; pervaded, spread; extended

व्याप्ति (nf) pervasion, omnipresence

व्यामोह (nm) ignorance, illusion, bewilderment

व्यायाम (nm) exercise, physical exercise; gymnastics; —शाला a gymnasium

व्यावसायिक (a) vocational, professional

व्यावहारिक (a) customary; practical

व्यास (nm) calibre, diameter; diffusion; —शैली diffused style

व्युत्क्रम (nm) irregular arrangement of a thing, disorder

व्युत्पत्ति (nf) origin, derivation, etymology of words

व्युत्पन्न (a) literate, well-read, learned

व्यूह (nm) a military array, an army; —रचना logistic strategy

व्योम (nm) the sky

व्रण (nm) a tumour, boil, wound

व्रत (nm) a fast; vow; pledge

व्रती (nm) one who observes a religious vow, an ascetic, a devotee

ब्रीड़ा (nf) bashfulness; shyness

श्र

श्र the first of the conventional sibilant trio (श, ष, स) of Devnagri alphabet

शंका (*nf*) suspicion; mistrust; doubt; — शील suspicious

शंकालु (*a*) mistrustful; of suspicious nature

शंकित (*a*) filled with doubt; alarmed

शंकु (*nm*) a cone

शंख (*nm*) conchshell; a number equal to 10,000,000,000 crores

शऊर (*nm*) decency; manner-liness

शक (*nm*) suspicion, doubt

शक संवत् an era introduced by emperor Shalivahan of India (in 78 A.D.)

शक्ति (*nf*) strength, energy; power, — मान strong

शक्ल (*nf*) form; shape, — सूरत appearance; looks

शख्स (*nm*) a human being; an individual; person

शख्सियत (*nf*) individuality; personality

शगल (*nm*) recreation; a pastime, hobby

शत (*nm*) one hundred; — प्रति शत cent percent

शतक (*nm*) one hundred,a century

शता/ब्दि, ब्दी (*nf*) century

शती (*nf*) a century

शत्रु (*nm*) an enemy, a foe; — ता enmity, hostility

शनि (*nm*) Saturn — वार Saturday

शनै: (*ind*) slowly; gradually, — शनै: little by little

शपथ (*nf*) swearing; an oath, — पत्र an affidavit

शफ़ा (*nf*) health; recovery; curative power; — ख़ाना a dispensary, clinic

शबनम (*nf*) dew

शब्द (*nm*) a word; voice, sound; noise; tone, — कोश a dictionary; — रचना word-formation, — सूची concor-dance

शब्दश: (*ind*) word by word

शमन (*nm*) quenching; suppres-sion; pacification

शमा (*nf*) a candle, flame (of fire)

शयन (*nm*) sleep, (the act of) sleeping, — कक्ष a bedroom

शय्या (*nf*) a bed, bedstead

शरण (*nf*) protection; shelter, refuge

शरणार्थी (*nm*) a refugee

शरद् (*nf*) the autumn

शरबत (*nm*) syrup; beverage

शराफत (*nf*) nobility; civility; politeness

शराब (*nf*) wine, liquor; — ख़ाना

a bar, wine shop

शराबी (*nm & a*) a drunkard, intoxicated, drunk

शरारत (*nf*) wickedness; mischief

शरीफ़ (*n*) a gentleman; noble, virtuous, pure, holy

शरीर (*nm*) physique, body; —और आत्मा body and soul; —क्रिया विज्ञान Physiology; —रचना शास्त्र Anatomy

शर्त (*nf*) provision; bet; a condition; term

शर्तिया (*a & adv*) positively, definitely, without fail; sure

शर्म (*nf*) shame; shyness; —नाक shameful, disgrace-ful

शर्माना (*v*) to feel shy, to blush; to be ashamed

शर्मि/दा (*a*) ashamed; —दगी shame

शर्मीला (*a*) shy, modest, bashful —पन shyness, modesty

शल्य (*nm*) a surgical instru-ment; a thorn; —क्रिया/चिकित्सा surgery/surgical operation

शव (*nm*) a corpse, dead body; —दाह cremation; —परीक्षा post-martem

शशि (*nm*) the moon

शस्त्र (*nm*) an arm, weapon; tool

शस्त्रागार (*nm*) an armoury

शहंशाह (*nm*) a king of kings

शहद (*nm*) honey

शहर (*nm*) a town; city

शहादत (*nf*) martyrdom; evidence

शहीद (*a & nm*) martyr

शांत (*a*) peaceful; still; slient, quiet

शांति (*nf*) peace; calmness, quiet; silence

शाक (*nm*) vegetable

शाकाहा/र (*nm*) vegetarian diet; —री a vegetarian

शाखा (*nf*) a branch; sect

शागिर्द (*nm*) a pupil, disciple; an apprentice

शादी (*nf*) wedding, marriage

शान (*nf*) splendour, pomp, magnificence, grandeur —दार grand; splendid, pompous; magnificent —शौकत pomp and show

शाप (*nm*) a curse

शाबा/श (*int*) bravo! well-done!, excellent; —शी praise, applause

शाम (*nf*) evening, dusk

शामत (*nf*) misfortune, ill-luck, affliction

शामियाना (*nm*) a canopy

शामिल (*a*) included; connected, associated; united

शाय/र (*nm*) a poet; —राना poetic —री poetry

शारीरिक (*a*) physical, bodily; concrete

शाला (*nf*) a house, residence

शालीन (a) modest, gentle; cultured, well-behaved

शाश्वत (a) permanent, eternal, immortal

शास/क (nm) a ruler; king; —कीय governmental

शासन (nm) administration, government; rule; command

शासित (a) administered, governed; ruled

शाहंशाह (nm) an emperor, a monarch; (a) very liberal

शाही (a) regal, majestic, royal

शिकंजा (nm) a clamp, pressing appliance; clasp

शिकस्त (nf) defeat

शिकायत (nf) a complaint; grievance; accusation

शिकार (nm) a prey; victim

शिकारा (nm) a long, partly covered boat

शिकारी (a & nm) hunting; huntsman, a hunter

शिक्षक (nm) a teacher

शिक्षण (nm) teaching, education; instruction; —कला the art of teaching

शिक्षा (nf) teaching; moral; education; instruction

शिक्षार्थी (nm) a pupil, student

शिक्षालय (nm) a school, educational institution

शिखर (nm) a peak; top; summit, pinnacle

शिथिल (a) loose; slow; slack; weary; —ता looseness; weariness; slackness

शिनाख्त (nf) indentification

शिला (nf) a rock, foundation stone; cliff; —न्यास laying of the foundation stone

शिल्प (nm) architecture; craft; —कला technology; craft; —कार a craftsman

शिव (nm) one of the divine trio of the Hindus; welfare; well-being

शिविर (nm) a camp, tent

शिशिर (nm) the winter

शिशु (nm) an infant; a baby, child; —ता childhood

शिश्न (nm) penis, male genital organ

शिष्ट (a) civilised, polite, courteous, civil

शिष्टता (nf) civility, gentleness, decency

शिष्टाचार (nm) etiquette; courtesy, decency

शिष्य (nm) a pupil, disciple; student

शीघ्र (adv) soon, urgently; immediately, quickly, hurriedly, speedly; —ता quickness, rapidity, hurry

शीतल (a) cold, frigid; cool; —ता coldness, frigidness; coolness

शीतला (nf) small-pox

शीतोष्ण (a) moderate, temperate

शीर्ष (nm) the head; top, summit

शीर्षक (*nm*) a heading, title

शील (*nm*) modesty; virtue, piety

शीलवान् (*a*) well-behaved; modest; hence शीलवती feminine form

शीश (*nm*) the head; the front part of the head

शीशा (*nm*) a mirror, looking glass; glass

शीशी (*nf*) a small bottle

शुक्र (*nm*) semen; venus; Friday

शुक्र (*nm*) thanks, an expression of gratitude —गुज़ार grateful, thankful; —गुज़ारी gratefulness

शुक्रिया (*nm*) gratefulness, gratitude, thankfulness

शुक्ल (*a*) white; —पक्ष the bright half of a lunar month

शुगल (*nm*) hobby; fun

शुचि (*a*) free from fault; pure, virtuous; sacred

शुद्ध (*a*) pure; sacred; unadulterated; uncorrupt; correct; amended; clean; —ता, —त्व purity; sacredness; correctness; cleanliness

शुभ (*a*) auspicious; good; (*nm*) the good, well-being; —कामनाएँ good wishes; —चिंतक a well-wisher; —मुहूर्त an auspicious moment

शुभाकांक्षी (*a*) well-wisher

शुभागमन (*nm*) welcome

शुभाशुभ (*a*) good and evil

शुमार (*nm*) accounting; counting

शुरू (*nm*) beginning, commencement

शुरुआत (*nf*) beginning, commencement

शुल्क (*nm*) fee; subscription; duty

शुश्रूषा (*nf*) attendance, nursing

शुष्क (*a*) dried; withered; tedious (as काम); dull; hard

शून्य (*a*) empty, void; zero; (*nm*) the empty space

शूर (*a & nm*) brave, gallant, heroic, mighty; a warrior; hero

शृंखला (*nf*) a chain, fetters; order; belt; —बद्ध systematic, orderly

शृंग (*nm*) peak; pinnacle; horn of an animal

शृंगार (*nm*) elegant make-up; adornment

शेखी (*nf*) boasting, bragging; —बाज़ boastful; —बाज़ी boastfulness

शेरवानी (*nf*) a typical long-tight coat

शेष (*a & nm*) rest, remaining; balance; remainder

शेषांश (*nm*) the remaining part; remainder; residue

शैक्षिक (*a*) academic, educational

शैतान (*nm*) devil, the Satan; a mischief-monger; (*a*) mischievous, naughty

शैतानी (*nf*) mischievousness, wickedness; naughtiness

शैल (*nm*) a rock; mountain

शैली (*nf*) style; —कार a stylist

शोक (*nm*) sorrow, grief; condolence; —संदेश a condolence message; —सभा a condolence meeting

शोख (*a*) insolent; bright, of deep shining colour

शोखी (*nf*) insolence; playfulness, brightness

शोचनीय (*a*) critical; miserable

शोणित (*nm*) blood; (*a*) bloody, red

शोध (*nf*) research; purification, refinement; setting right; cleaning; correction

शोधना (*v*) to purify; to correct; to refine

शोभा (*nf*) grace, glory, beauty; splendour

शोभित (*a*) splendid; adorned; beautiful

शोर (*nm*) noise; tumult, hue and cry

शोरबा (*nm*) soup, broth

शोला (*nm*) a flame of fire

शोषक (*nm*) an exploiter, an absorbent

शोषण (*nm*) exploitation; soaking

शोहरत (*nf*) celebrity, fame

शौक (*nm*) an eager desire; hobby; fondness

शौकिया (*a & adv*) amateurish; fondly, fashionably; as a hobby

शौकी/न (*a*) fashionable; fond of fine things; —नी fashionableness, fondness

शौच (*nm*) toilet; cleanliness

शौचालय (*nm*) a latrine, lavatory

शौर्य (*nm*) valour, heroism, bravery

शौहर (*nm*) husband

श्याम (*a*) black, dark-coloured; dark-blue

श्याम/ल (*a*) dark-coloured, of blue-black colour; hence —लता (*nf*)

श्रद्धांजलि (*nf*) homage, tribute

श्रद्धा (*nf*) faith, trust, veneration; reverence

श्रद्धालु (*a*) having faith, trustful

श्रद्धास्पद (*a*) venerable, deserving faith

श्रद्धेय (*a*) venerable, worthy of faith

श्रमण (*nm*) a Buddhist monk

श्रमिक (*nm & a*) a labourer; labour

श्रमी (*a & nm*) hard-working, laborious

श्रव/ण (*nm*) an ear; audition; —णीय audible, hearing

श्रव्य (*a*) audible; able to be heard

श्रांत (*a*) exhausted; fatigued,

tired, wearied

श्री (a) Mr.; (nf) the goddess of wealth — Lakshmi

श्रेष्ठ (a) good; —तर, better; —तम best, topmost

श्रोता (nm) a listener; —गण audience

श्लथ (a) loose, weary, languid, slothful; feeble

श्लाघा (nf) praise, applause

श्लील (a) clean, nice, not vulgar

श्लेष्मा (nm) mucus, phlegm

श्वास (nm) breath, respiration; —क्रिया the act of breathing

श्वेत (a) white; bright; spotless

ष

ष the second of the sibilant-trio (श ष स) of Devnagri alphabet

षट् (a) six; (nm) the number six; —कोण six angled

षट्पद (nm) a large black bee; having six legs

षट्पदी (nf) a female bee

षट्शास्त्र (nm) the six schools of Indian philosophy (viz न्याय, सांख्य, योग, वैशेषिक, पूर्व-मीमांसा and उत्तरमीमांसा)

षड् (a) an allomorph of षट् (six) appearing as the first member in some compound words —अंग the six supplementary branches of sacred science (viz शिक्षा, कल्प, व्याकरण, निरुक्त, छंद and ज्योतिष); the six parts of body (viz. two arms, two legs, the head and the waist); —ऋतु the six seasons of the year (viz. ग्रीष्म, वर्षा, शरत् हेमन्त,

शिशिर, वसंत)

षड्भुज (nm) a hexagon

षड्रस (nm) six prominent tastes (viz salt, sour, astringent, pungent, bitter and sweet —लवण, अम्ल, तिक्त, कषाय, कटु और मधु)

षड्राग (nm) the six main ragas in Indian music (viz. भैरवी मल्हार, श्रीराग, हिंडोल, मालकोस and दीपक)

षड्रिपु (nm) the six internal enemies of man according to Indian tradition (viz. काम, क्रोध, मद, लोभ, मोह, मत्सर)

षड्यंत्र (nm) a conspiracy, an intrigue; —कारी a conspirator, an intriguer, plotter

षष्टि (a) sixty; (nm) the number sixty

षष्ठ (a) sixth

षष्ठी (nf) the sixth day of a fortnight, the sixth day from the day of child birth

षोडश (*a*) sixteen (*nm*) the number sixteen

षोडशी (*nf*) a girl of sixteen years of age

स

स the last of the sibilant trio (श, ष, स) of Devnagri alphabet

संकट (*nm*) misfortune, risk, crisis; hazard, danger

संकर (*nm*) hybrid; a mixed caste; intergrade; —ता (*nf*) hybridization

सैंकरा (*a*) narrow

संकर्षण (*nm*) attraction; ploughing; Balram, brother of Krishna

संकलन (*nm*) a collection; compilation; —कर्ता a compiler

संकलित (*a*) compiled, collected; assembled

संकल्प (*nm*) resolve, determination; solemn promise, will; vow —करना to resolve

संकीर्ण (*a*) narrow; mean; crowded; —ता narrowness

संकुचित (*a*) narrow; mean; limited

संकुल (*a*) confused; congested; crowded

संकेत (*nm*) a sign; signal; hint; symbol; —करना to hint, to suggest

संको/च (*nm*) hesitation, hitch; shame, shyness; contraction; —ची shy, hesitant, reserved, bashful

संक्रमण (*nm*) motion, transition; —काल transition period

संक्रामक (*a*) contageous, infectious; —रोग an epidemic

संक्षिप्त (*a*) abridged; short, brief; —करना to abbreviate; —रूप में summarily

संक्षेप (*nm*) brief, summary; brevity; —करना to shorten, to summarize, to curtail; to abbreviate

संक्षेपत: (*a*) briefly, in short

संखिया (*nm*) arsenic

संख्या (*nf*) a number; numeral; figure; —की गणना score, बड़ी — multitude; सैनिकों की — strength; —सूचक numerical

संग (*nm*) a union, association, company, attachment; stone; —तराश a stone-carver; —तराशी stone-carving —मरमर marble

संगठन (*nm*) a league; an organization; an act of organization

संगठित (a) organised

संगत (nf) company, party; (a) logical; relevant; appropriate, harmonious; —करना to keep company with; —होना to hold good

संगति (nf) association, company; relevance, relation; sexual intercourse; —प्रिय social

संगम (nm) junction, union, meeting; federation

संगिनी (nf) a female companion

संगी (nm) a comrade, a friend, an ally, a companion and associate; —साथी companions and friends

संगीत (nm) the art of music and dancing; playing on musical instruments; — नाटक a musical drama, an opera; —शास्त्र music

संगीतज्ञ (nm) a musician

संगीताचार्य (nm) a master of music

संगीन (nf) a bayonet; (a) serious; —भोंकना to bayonet

संगृहीत (a) gathered; amassed; collected; compiled

संग्रह (nm) collection; compilation; storage; deposit; —करना to gather; to amass; to collect; to compile, to store —कर्ता collector

संग्रहण (nm) collection

संग्रहणी (nf) a chronic disorder of bowels, acute form of chronic diarrhoea, sprue

संग्रहणीय (a) worthy of collecting, fit to be acquired

संग्रहालय (nm) a museum

संग्राम (nm) battle, war; fight; —योग्य warlike

संग्राह्य (a) worthy of collecting, fit to be acquired

संघ (nm) a club, society; corporation, federation; union, league; an assembly

संघटन (nm) formation; constitution; organization

संघटक (a) constituent, component

संघर्ष (nm) rubbing; conflict, struggle, strife

संघीय (a) federal; union

संचय (nm) collection; deposit, reserve; hoard; —करना to hoard; to deposit

संचरण (nm) act of going; movement of a body etc.; —करना to go, to move

संचार (nm) motion, movement; communication; transmission

संचालक (nm) a leader, director; conductor

संचालन (nm) management; direction; conduction

संचित (a) collected, gathered; hoarded; —करना to gather

संजी/वा (a) serious; sober; wise, intelligent —वगी

intelligence

संजीवनी (a) reanimating, restoring; (nf) a kind of medicine which is supposed to restore a dead man to life

सैजोना (v) to arrange; to put things in order

संज्ञा (nf) a noun (gram); name; consciousness; sign; जातिवाचक— a common noun; भाववाचक— an abstract noun; व्यक्तिवाचक— a proper noun; —हीन unconscious, senseless

सैझरला (a) younger than the middle brother

संडास (nm) a latrine, lavatory, sink

संत (nm) a saint; saintly; a devotee

संतत (adv) perpetually, continuously, ever, eternally

संतति (nf) descendant, progeny, generation succession, issue

संतप्त (a) grieved, troubled; burnt; afflicted

संतरण (nm) swimming; salvation, emancipation

संतरा (nm) an orange

संतरी (nm) a watchman, a sentry, a door-keeper

संतान (nm) children, progeny, issue

संताप (nm) sorrow, torment, distress, grief

संतु/लन (nm) equilibrium, balance; —लित balanced

संतुष्ट (a) complacent, content, satisfied, gratified, acquiescent, —करना to satisfy, to suffice, to meet, to gratify

संतृ/प्त (a) gratified, saturated; hence —प्ति gratification

संतोष (nm) satisfaction; contentment; —जनक satisfactory

संतोषी (a & nm) a contented person

संदर्भ (nm) a context, reference, —ग्रंथ a reference book

संबल (nm) sandal wood

संदिग्ध (a) dubious, uncertain, doubtful; ambiguous, suspicious

संदूक (nm) a chest, a box; —चा a box; —ची a little box (feminine form)

संदूकड़ी (nf) a small box or chest

संदेश (nm) a message; information, word; a kind of Bengali sweet; —भेजना to send word

संदेह (nm) suspicion, doubt; distrust

संधि (nf) union; joint; a treaty; articulation; —पत्र a treaty

संध्या (nf) evening, twilight

संन्यास (nm) asceticism, renunciation

संपत्ति (nf) wealth, richness, property, estate

संपदा (nf) property, wealth

संपन्न (a) rich, prosperous; —ता prosperity, wealthiness

संपर्क (nm) contact

संपादक (nm) one who performs a certain action; an editor; —त्व act of editing

संपादकीय (nm & a) an editorial

संपादन (nm) performing; executing, editing

संपूर्ण (a) all, total; completed

सँपेरा (nm) a snake-charmer

संप्रदाय (nm) a religious society, a community; sect

संप्रेष/ण (nm) communication; —णीय communicable

संबंध (nm) connection, relation, link; terms; association, —रखना to regard, to belong

संबंधित (a) related; affiliated; connected

संबद्ध (a) attached to, jointed, connected; bound; related; affiliated

संबल (nm) backing, support

सँभलना (v) to be alert; to maintain; to save one self from a fall

संभव (a) probable, possible; practicable

संभवत: (adv) probably, possibly; perhaps

सँभालना (v) to help; to support; to manage; to take care of; to hold

संभावना (nf) probability, possibility, likelihood

संभावित (a) likely, probable

संभाव्य (a) possible, probable

संभाषण (nm) conversation, dialogue, talk

संभ्रांत (a) respectable

संभ्रांति (nf) confusion

संयत (a) suppressed, tied up, guarded; controlled, restrained; sober

संयम (nm) a check, restraint; moderation, control

संयुक्त (a) joint; united; mixed

संयुत (a) fitted, mixed together

संयोग (nm) chance, coincidence; luck; mixture

संयोजक (nm) a convener

संयोजन (nm) composition; conjugation; attachment

संरक्षक (nm) protector, patron; guardian

संरक्षण (nm) safeguard, protection; guardianship

संलग्न (a) joined; attached; engaged; enclosed

संवत् (nm) an era, a year

संवत्सर (nm) a year

सँवरना (v) to be mended; to be arranged; to be tip-top; to be decorated

संवर्धन (nm) increase; protection; nourishment

संवाद (nm) conversation;

dialogue; news; message; —वाता a pressman, a correspondent

सँवारना (v) to adorn; to dress; to make up; to decorate; to arrange; to mend

संवेग (nm) emotion, passion, momentum

संवेदन (nm) feeling, sensation —शील sensitive

संवेदना (nf) sensibility, sensation, feeling

संशय (nm) doubt, suspicion; uncertainty

संशयी (a) doubting, sceptic, uncertain

संशोधक (nm) a mender; purifier

संशोधन (nm) correction; amendment; purification; revision

संशोधित (a) amended, corrected; improved; revised

संश्रय (nm) alliance; refuge, protection

संश्रयण (nm) taking refuge; shelter, protection

संश्लेषण (nm) uniting, joining together; synthesis

संस/द (nf) parliament; —दीय parliamentary

संसर्ग (nm) connection, relation, contact; company, association

संसार (nm) the world; the mortal world; domestic life

संसारी (nm & a) a mortal being; belonging to the world

संसृष्ट (a) joined together, mixed up, muddled

संसृष्टि (nf) an intermixture

संस्करण (nm) correction; an edition of a printed book

संस्कर्ता (nm) the person who corrects or purifies

संस्कार (nm) ceremony, rite; sacrament; purification

संस्कृत (a) purified, cleansed, refined; (nf) Sanskrit language

संस्कृति (nf) purification; culture; civilisation

संस्था (nf) an organisation, institution; concern

संस्थान (nm) an organisation, institute

संस्थापक (nm) a founder

संस्थापन (nm) setting up, establishing

संस्मरण (nm) memoirs

संहत (a) collected, gathered

संहति (nf) union, collection

संहार (nm) completion; destruction, slaughter

संहारक (nm) destroyer; slaughterer, murderer

सइयां (nm) husband; lover

सकना (v) may; can; to be competent

सकपकाना (v) to wonder, to be amazed; to hesitate, to totter

सकर्मक (a) transitive; —क्रिया a transitive verb

सकल (a) all, whole, entire

सकाम (a) inspired by a desire; desirous, lustful

सकुचाना (v) to intimidate, to hesitate

सक्षम (a) capable; competent

सखा (nm) a friend, an associate

सखी (nf) a female friend

सखी (a) liberal, open-handed

सख्त (a) hard; strong; stiff; strict

सख्ती (nf) strictness; stiffness; hardness; harshness

सगा (a) born of the same parents

सगाई (nf) an engagement, betrothal

सगापन (nm) near relationship

सगोत्र (a) allied by blood; a kin, relative

सघन (a) thick, dense, cloudy

सच (a) real, true; right; —मुच actually; truly, really

सचाई (nf) truthfulness; truth; integrity

सचित्र (a) illustrated, pictorial

सचिव (nm) secretary

सचिवालय (nm) secretariat

सचेत (a) wakeful; careful, alert; attentive

सचेतक (nm) a whip

सचेतन (a) conscious

सचेष्ट (a) active, zealous, alert; energetic

सच्चरित्र (a) honest, virtuous, of moral character

सच्चा (a) genuine; loyal; real, sincere

सचाई (nf) sincerity, reality, truth

सच्चिदानंद (nm) an epithet of the supreme soul of Brahma

सजग (a) cautious; careful; watchful, alert

सजधज (nf) paraphernalia, ornamentation

सजन (nm) a respectable person, a gentleman; a husband; a lover

सजना (v) to prank; to be made up; to be decorated; to be neatly arranged, (nm) a lover/husband

सजनी (nf) sweetheart; wife; beloved

सजल (a) containing water; full of tears, tearful

सजवाई (nf) the work or wages paid for decorating

सज़ा (nf) penalty; punishment; —देना to punish; —पाना to be chastised or punished; —याफ़्ता convicted

सजाति (a) belonging to the same class, homogeneous

सजातीयता (nf) homogeneity

सजान (a) knowing, clever, adept

सजाना (v) to adorn, to decorate; to furnish; to arrange; to dress neatly

सजाव/ट (nf) ornamentation,

decoration; make up; display; —टी decorative

सजीला (a) beautiful; handsome, graceful, attractive

सजीव (a) lively, quick, living, active

सज्जन (nm & a) noble, gentle; a gentleman; —ता nobility

सज्जा (nf) equipment; decoration

सज्जित (a) adorned, decorated; equipped

सज्ञान (a) intelligent, wise; careful, sagacious

सटना (v) to stick; to be in close proximity

सटपट (nf) astonishment, suspense; doubt; wonder

सटपटाना (v) to be surprised, to wonder

सट्टा (nm) a written agreement or contract; speculation

सड़क (nf) a road; street; lane

सड़न (nm) decay; rottenness, rot

सड़ना (v) to rot; to decay; to perish, to fall in misery

सड़ाना (v) to addle, to rot; to decompose

सड़ाँध (nf) stench; rot, rottenness; mustiness

सड़ियल (a) rotten; decomposed; bad, good for nothing, worthless

सत (nm) juice, essence; strength; truth; virtue

सतगुना (a) sevenfold, septuple

सतगुरु (nm) a good preceptor; God

सतजुग (nm) the golden age or period

सतत (adv & a) always; continuous, incessant, incessantly

सतफेरा (nm) the ceremony of going round the sacred fire seven times at the time of wedding

सतर्क (a & adv) cautions, alert, careful

सत/ह (nf) upper surface; level; —ही superficial

सताना (v) to torment, to oppress, to torture

सती (nf) a faithful woman, a woman who willingly burns herself on her husband's funeral pyre; daughter of Daksha who was married to Shiva

सत् (a) pious, good; virtuous; true

सत्कार (nm) welcome; hospitality; salute

सत्कार्य (nm) virtue, a pious action

सत्कीर्ति (nf) fame, reputation

सत्कुल (nm) a high family, a person of noble birth

सत्त (nm) extract, essence; truth

सत्ता (nm) existence, being; power, authority

सत्ताधारी (*nm*) an officer of state, administrator

सत्पथ (*nm*) a good way; virtuous action

सत्पात्र (*nm*) a worthy person, a man of good character

सत्फल (*nm*) good result

सत्य (*a*) veritable, true, real, right, (*nm*) truth, virtue, —काम a lover of truth; —त: really, truly

सत्यपुरुष (*nm*) a gentleman

सत्ययुग (*nm*) the first of the four Hindu ages, the golden age

सत्यवान (*nm*) the husband of Savitri

सत्याग्रह (*nm*) civil disobedience

सत्यानाश (*nm*) total destruction, complete ruin

सत्यानाशी (*a*) ruining devastating; destructive

सत्वर (*ind*) soon, immediately, swiftly; —ता quickness

सत्संग (*nm*) intercourse with pious men

सदन (*nm*) dwelling, a house; place of rest, chamber

सदमा (*nm*) a stroke, emotional stroke; sorrow, a blow

सदय (*a*) kind, merciful, compassionate

सदर (*a*) chief, principal; (*nm*) president

सदस्य (*nm*) a fellow, a member; —ता membership

सदा (*adv*) constantly, always,

ever; (*nf*) echo, voice, call; —चरण good behaviour

सदाचार (*nm*) probity, morality, virtuous conduct

सदाबहार (*a*) evergreen

सदी (*nf*) a century

सदुपयोग (*nm*) good or proper use

सदृश (*a*) alike, similar, like

सदेह (*a*) with a body, in an embodied form

सदैव (*adv*) ever, always

सद्गति (*nf*) salvation; emancipation

सद्गुरु (*nm*) a good tutor; God

सद्भाव (*nm*) courtesy, amiability, kind feeling

सद्य: (*adv*) immediately; recently; afresh

सघना (*v*) to be completed; to be habituated, to be tamed; to hit the mark

सघवा (*a & nf*) a woman whose husband is alive

सन (*nm*) year; ईस्वी— the christian era

सनक (*nf*) caprice; craze

सनकी (*a & nm*) crazy; capricious

सनद (*nf*) a certificate, testimonial; deed

सनसनाना (*v*) to rustle; to tingle; to faint, to thrill

सनसनी (*nf*) excitement; thrilling sensation

सनातन (*a*) continual; ancient; eternal

सनेह (*nm*) love, (see also स्नेह)

सन्न (*a*) stupefied, stunned, dumb-founded

सन्नद्ध (*a*) tied up, attached; ready, equipped

सन्नाटा (*nm*) loneliness, silence, still

संन्या/स (*nm*) renunciation, monasticism; —सी a monk

सपत्नीक (*a*) along with wife

सपना (*nm*) a dream

सपरिवार (*a & adv*) with family

सपरेटा (*a & nm*) separated (milk)

सपाट (*a*) smooth, even; flat

सपूत (*nm*) a dutiful son, the son who performs his filial duty

सप्तद्वीप (*nm*) the seven continents of the world

सप्ता/ह (*nm*) a week; —हांत week-end

सफर (*nm*) journey, travel; —नामा a travelogue

सफल (*a*) effective; successful; fruitful; —ता success; achievement; —होना to succeed

सफा (*a & nm*) clean, a page; —चट perfectly clean

सफाई (*nf*) purity; cleanliness; defence; clarification

सफाया (*nm*) a clean sweep, end; ruination

सफीर (*nm*) an envoy, ambassador

सफेद (*a*) blank, not written upon; white; —पोश dressed in white

सफेदा (*nm*) white lead

सफेदी (*nm*) whitewash; whiteness

सब (*a*) entire, whole, total; all —कुछ all; all in all, —डिवीज़न a sub-division

सबक (*nm*) a moral; a lesson

सबब (*nm*) a cause; reason

सबर (*nm*) patience, (see also सब्र)

सबल (*a*) forcible; strong, powerful

सबूत (*nm*) testimony, evidence, a proof

सबेरे-सबेरे (*adv*) in the early morning

सबेरा (*nm*) dawn, the time of early morning

सब्ज़ (*a*) green; good

सब्ज़ी (*nf*) herbage; vegetable; —मंडी a vegetable market

सब्बल (*nm*) a crowbar

सब्र (*nm*) contentment, patience

सभा (*nf*) association, assembly; meeting; society; —गार/गृह an assembly hall; —पति chairman; —सद member of an assembly

सभ्य (*a*) civilised; polite, genteel, decent; —ता civilization, courtesy, decency

समंजन (*nm*) co-ordination,

adjustment

सम (a) equal; level, even; similar; —कक्ष equal, similar

समकालिक (a) contemporary; contemporaneity

समकालीन (a) contemporary, living, —ता contemporaneity

समकोण (nm) a right angle; (a) having equal angles

समक्ष (adv) in front of, before

समग्र (a) entire, whole, total; all

समझ (nf) intellect, understanding; —दार intelligent; sensible; wise

समझ/ना (v) to grasp, to know, to understand, to catch, to follow; —बूझकर deliberately

समझाना (v) to persuade; to explain; —बुझाना to persuade

समझौता (nm) the settlement of a dispute; compromise, understanding; an agreement

समतल (a & nm) even, level, plain

समता (nf) similarity, likeness; equality

समतुल्य (a) equivalent; hence —ता equivalence

समदर्शी (a) impartial, dispassionate; equanimous

समधिन (nf) mother-in-law of son or daughter

समधी (nf) father-in-law of son or daughter

सम/न्वय (nm) harmony, co-ordination; —न्वित harmonized, co-ordinated

समय (nm) period; time; occasion; leisure

समर (nm) a battle; a war; conflict; —नीति strategy; —भूमि field of battle

समरस (a) harmonious, equanimous; —ता harmony, equanimity

समर्थ (a) competent, capable

सम/र्थक (nm) vindicator, supporter; —र्थन vindication, support; —र्थित supported

समर्पक (nm) assigner, dedicator

सम/र्पण (nm) surrender; sacrifice; dedication, assignment; —र्पित surrendered, dedicated

समवा/य (nm) Company, collection; concomitance, —यी concomitant, inseparable

समवेत (a) collective

समवेदना (nf) condolence

समशीतोष्ण (a) temperate, moderate

समशक्ति (nf) equal power

समष्टि (nf) aggregate, collectiveness

समसामयिक (a) contemporary

समस्त (a) whole, entire, complete; all

समस्या (nf) a problem

समाँ (nm) time; season, weather; occasion

समागत (a) arrived, approached

समाचार (nm) information; message; news; report

समाज (nm) community; society; —वाद socialism; —वादी a socialist; —सेवी a social worker

समादृत (a) honoured, respected

समाधान (nm) solution, answer

समाधि (nf) a tomb; intense meditation, devotion

समान (a) alike, similar; equal, —ता equality, similarity

समानांतर (a) parallel, equidistant

समाना (v) to penetrate; to fill, to fit, to enter

समानार्थक (a) of similar meaning, synonymous

समापन (nm) work of finishing, completion, conclusion

समाप्त (a) completed, ended, finished; concluded; terminated; —प्राय almost finished

समाप्ति (nf) termination; conclusion; completion

समारोह (nm) function, celebration

समालोचक (nm) a critic, reviewer

समालोचन (nm) criticism

समाविष्ट (a) entered, included; pervaded

समावेश (nm) entry, inclusion, pervasion

समास (nm) abridgment, a compound, curtailment, contraction; —शैली terse style

समाहित (a) concentrated, collected

समिति (nf) a committee; meeting; society

समीकरण (nm) the act of equalizing, equation, —करना to equate

समीक्षक (nm) a reviewer

समी/क्षा (nf) a review; search; commentary; —क्षाकार a reviewer

समीप (a) beside; near; about

समीपता (nf) proximity, congruity; vicinity

समीर (nf) wind, breeze, air

समुचित (a) right; proper, useful, fit

समुच्चय (nm) collection, assemblage, heap

समुदाय (nm) collection; group, assemblage; community

समुद्र (nm) sea, brine, ocean

समुद्री (a) marine, maritime, oceanic

समूचा (a) whole, entire; all

समूह (nm) community; collection; group

समृ/द्ध (a) wealthy, rich; prosperous, successful; flourish; —द्धि prosperity;

richness

समेटना (v) to collect; to wind up; to rally; to wrap up

समेत (a & adv) mixed up, with, together with, along with

सम्मत (a) approved, agreed upon

सम्मति (nf) consent; opinion; advice

सम्मान (nm) honour, respect; prestige

सम्माननीय (a) respectable, honourable

सम्मानित (a) respected, revered, esteemed, honoured

सम्मिलित (a) mixed; united; included; —करना to inter-mix; to interblend; to federate

सम्मुख (a) in front of, before; facing; opposite

सम्मेलन (nm) meeting; conference; assembly

सम्मो/ह (nm) fascination; hypnosis; —हन fascinating, hypnotising

सम्यक (adv & a) wholly; duly, thoroughly

सम्राज्ञी (nf) an empress

सम्राट् (nm) an emperor

सयाना (a) clever; grown up

सरंजाम (nm) arrangements; preparations; accomplish-ment

सरकना (v) to glide; to slip; to creep; to slide

सरकस (nm) circus

सरकार (nf) government, administrator

सरकारी (a) governmental; official; administrative

सरपट (a & adv) apace; galloping

सरमा/या (nm) capital; —येबार a capitalist; —येदारी capita-lism

सरल (a) simple easy; direct; straight; light; —ता simpli-city; easiness

सरस (a) sweet; juicy; tasteful, delicious; relishable

सरसना (v) to prosper, to flourish; to be in full bloom

सरसरी (a) hurried, cursory

सरसों (nf) mustard

सरस्वती (nf) name of a river; speech; the goddess of learning

सरह/द (nf) border, boundary; frontier; —दी pertaining to boundary

सरा/फ (nm) a dealer in gold and silver jewellery; —फा gold and silver exchange market

सराफी (nf) banking, money changing

सराबोर (a) quite wet, drenched with water; soaked

सरासर (adv) entirely, altogether; sheer

सराह/ना (v) to laud, to applaud, to praise, to commend.

(*nf*) praise, applause, appreciation; —नीय praise-worthy

सरिता (*nf*) stream, a river

सरीखा (*a*) resembling, like

सरोवर (*nm*) a large pond, pool; a lake

सर्दी (*nf*) cold weather, winter; coldness; catarrh

सर्प (*nm*) snake, serpent

सर्पिणी (*nf*) a female snake

सर्व (*a*) whole, complete, entire; all; —गत eternal —नाश complete ruin; —प्रिय dear to all; —व्यापक omnipresent; universal; —व्यापी omnipresent; universal; —शक्तिमान omnipotent; —श्रेष्ठ the best, —साधारण the common man

सर्वत्र (*ind*) always, every-where; in very case

सर्वथा (*ind*) thoroughly, entirely

सर्वदा (*ind*) at all times, always

सर्वस्व (*nm*) entire property, everything

सर्वहारा (*nm*) the proletariat

सर्वात्मा (*nm*) the supreme spirit; the god Brahma

सर्वाधिकार (*nm*) full power; general control

सर्वेक्ष/ण (*nm*) survey; —क surveyor

सर्वेसर्वा (*a*) all powerful, all-in-all

सर्वोत्तम (*a*) paramount, foremost, excellent, the best

सर्वोदय (*nm*) uplift of all

सर्वोपरि (*a*) above all, on the whole, supreme, ahead of all

सर्वोच्च (*a*) highest, best, supreme; —ता supremacy

सलज्ज (*a*) modest; shy, bashful

सलहज (*nf*) wife's brother's wife

सलाई (*nf*) thin wire; needle; stick, a knitting needle

सलाख (*nf*) a rod

सलाम (*nm*) good bye, salutation; adieu

सलामी (*nf*) salute, salutation

सलाह (*nf*) counsel, advice; opinion, reconciliation

सलाहकार (*nm*) counsellor; an adviser

सलीका (*nm*) manners; etiquette

सलीब (*nm*) cross

सलूक (*nm*) conduct, behaviour, favour

सलोना (*a*) winsome, charming; saltish; —पन winsomeness, charm; saltishness

सवर्ण (*a*) homogeneous, of the same caste or colour

सवार (*nm*) horseman; rider

सवारी (*nf*) riding, carriage, vehicle; passenger

सवाल (*nm*) a question; an exercise; demand; —जवाब question and answer

सविनय (a) courteous, modest, polite, civil

सवेरा (nm) dawn, morning, daybreak

सशंक (a) sceptic, suspicious

सशक्त (a) strong, forceful, powerful

सशस्त्र (a) equipped with arms, armed

ससुर (nm) father-in-law

ससुराल (nf) father-in-law's house

सस्ता (a) of little value, cheap; trivial; trash

सस्ती (a) cheap

सस्य (nm) crop; —क्रांति green revolution

सह (ind) together, along with, with; —कारिता co-operation, —कारी co-operative

सहज (a) easy, simple, natural

सहधर्म (nm) congeniality

सहधर्मी (a) congenial

सहन (nm) tolerance, forbearance; —शक्ति forbearing, endurance; tolerance, —शील tolrant, enduring, forbearing

सहपाठी (nm) a fellow student

सहभोज (nm) taking food together

सहम (nm) dread, fear, terror, hesitation

सहम/त (a) of one mind, agreed; —ति agreement, consent

सहयोग (nm) help, co-operation, assistance; —करना to co-operate with others

सहयोगी (nm) a helper, an assistant; a co-operator, one who works with others

सहल (a) simple, easy

सहलाना (v) to rub-to tickle; to rub gently

सहसा (ind) all of a sudden, suddenly, unexpectedly

सहानुभूति (nf) sympathy, fellow-feeling, — शील sympathetic

सहायक (nm) a helpmate, an assistant, a supporter

सहायता (nf) assistance; help; aid; relief; —करना to contribute; —देना to assist, to support

सहार (nm) endurance, tolerance —ना to endure, to tolerate

सहारा (nm) backing; support, help

सहित (ind) together with, along with, with

सहिष्णु (a) enduring, patient; tolerant; —ता endurance tolerance, forbearance

सही (a) right; accurate; correct; true; —सलामत safe and sound, hale and hearty; faultless

सहूलियत (nf) facility; convenience

सहृदय (a) kind, gentle, humane; considerate

सहेजना (v) to keep with care; to

entrust

सहेली (nm) a female companion

सहोदर (nm) a real brother

सह्य (a) endurable, tolerable

सांकेतिक (a) allusive; token;
nominal

सौंझ (nf) dusk, evening

सौंझा (nm) partnership, share
in business

साँड़ (nm) a bull

साँड़नी (nf) a she-camel used
for riding

सांत्वना (nf) pacification,
solace, consolation

साँप (nm) a serpent, a snake

सांप्रदायिक (a) communal; —ता
communalism

साँवला (a) blue-black, dark
complexioned

साँस (nf) breath; sigh; asthma

साँसत (nf) affliction, trouble,
distress

सांसारिक (a) earthly, worldly,
mundane

साकार (a) concrete, formal

साक्षर (a) literate; —ता literacy

साक्षात् (adv) within sight of,
before, visibly; —कार an
interview

साक्षी (nm) an eye-witness,
evidence, deponent

साक्ष्य (nm) testimony, evidence

साख (nf) credit; reputation;
trust; —पत्र credit-note

साग (nm) greens; vegetable;
—पात vegetables and herbs;

—सब्जी vegetables

सागर (nm) sea, the ocean

साज़ (nm) musical instru-
ments

साजन (nm) lover, husband,
lord

साज़िश (nf) plot, conspiracy

सा/झा (nm) partnership;
share; —झेदार a partner,
shareholder; —झेदारी
partnership

साड़ी (nf) a sari

साढ़ू (nm) the husband of
wife's sister

सादे (a) plus half

सातत्य (nm) continuity

सात्त्विक (a) righteous, virtuous;
—ता righteousness

साथ (adv) together, with,
along with, by, (nm)
association, company,
support

साथी (nm) an associate,
friend; a fellow, a
companion

सादगी (nf) simplicity, plainness

सादर (adv) with regards,
respectfully

सादा (a) plain, simple; artless;
—पन simplicity, plainness;
artlessness

साधन (nm) means; medium,
device; equipment

साधना (nf) practice; devotion;
spiritual endeavour; (v) to
aim; to practise

साधारण (a) simple; ordinary; common; usual

साधु (nm) saintly person; a saint; hermit; (a) noble, good, virtuous

साधुवाद (nm) applause

साध्य (nm) the end; —ता feasibility

साध्वी (a) chaste woman, virtuous wife

सानंद (a & adv) happy with pleasure, happily

सान (nf) whetting; whetstone

सानी (nf) food for cattle consisting of chaff and oilcake mixed together with water

सान्निध्य (nm) nearness, proximity

सापराध (a) guilty, faulty; offending; criminal

सापेक्ष (a) conditional, qualified; relative; —ता relativity

साप्ताहिक (nm) a weekly journal; (a) weekly

साफ (a) pure; clean; frank; —करना to purify, to cleanse, to kill; —कहना to speak plainly; —सुथरा prim, trim

साफल्य (nm) success; fruitfulness

साबित (a) complete, entire, unbroken; proved; steady

साबुत (a) complete, entire

साबुन (nm) a soap

साबूदाना (nm) sago

साभार (adv) gratefully

सामंजस्य (nm) harmony

सामंत (nm) a warrior, landlord; —वाद feudalism

सामंती (a) feudal

साम (nm) Sam (Veda)—one of the four Vedas; conciliation

सामग्री (nf) material; matter; stuff, things; —जुटाना to provide; —भंडार में रखना to put in store

सामना (nm) meeting; encounter; opposition, confrontation —करना to face; to confront, to oppose

सामने (ind) before, face to face; —का frontal, opposite; —से from before one's face

सामयिक (a) timely, temporal, provisional; modern; upto date; —पत्र a newspaper

सामरिक (a) pertaining to war; strategic; military

सामर्थ्य (nf) capacity; competence; strength

सामवेद (nm) the third Veda

सामवेदीय (adj) pertaining to Samaveda; (nm) one who has studied this Veda

सामाजिक (a) pertaining to an assembly, social; —जीवन social life; —स्थिति status

सामाजिकता (nf) sociability

सामान (nm) luggage, goods; stock, stuff, tools; —घर luggage-office

सामान्य (a) ordinary, general; common; normal; usual; —प्रकृति का of the common nature —बातचीत table talk; —बुद्धि mother wit; —भोजन simple diet; —मूल्य से अधिक above par; —मूल्य से कम below par; —रूप से usually —वार्ता common talk; —व्यक्ति common man; —वर्णन an outline

सामान्यत: (ind) usually, generally; normally; ordinarily, on an average

सामिष (nm) non-vegetarian

सामीप्य (nm) nearness; proximity

सामुदायिक (a) pertaining to an assembly; collective

सामूहिक (a) collective

साम्य (nm) similarity, equality; resemblance, identity

साम्राज्य (nm) reign, sovereignty, empire; —वाद the theory of imperialism

सायं (a) pertaining to the evening; (nm) the evening; —काल the eve, the evening, dusk

सा/या (nm) shelter, shade; influence, —येदार shady

सारंग (nm) a hawk; a peacock; a deer; a snake, a sword; —पाणि an epithet of Vishnu

सारंगी (nf) a lute, a typical stringed Indian musical instrument

सार (nm) gist, substance; essence; —गर्भित full of pith or marrow; —तत्त्व extract, substance; —भूत essential; substantial; —वान significant, useful, substantial, meaningful

सारणी (nf) schedule; a table

सारथि, सारथी (nm) a charioteer

सारस (nm) a crane, species of heron

सारना (v) to complete, to finish, to mend

सारनाथ (nm) a place near Banaras where lord Buddha first preached his new religion

सारस्वत (nm) sub-sect of Brahmans originally inhabiting in the punjab

सारांश (nm) gist, abstract, summary, purport, substance

सारा (a) all; whole, entire

सारिका (nf) an Indian (मैना) bird

सारूप्य (nm) identity; likeness, similarity, uniformity

सार्थक (a) meaningful; effective, useful; —ता meaningfulness

सार्घ (a) one and a half

सार्वकालिक (a) pertaining to all times, everlasting, eternal; universal

सार्वजनिक (a) public, relating to people in general

सार्वत्रिक (a) universal

सार्वदेशिक (a) pertaining to all countries, universal

सार्व/मौम, मौमिक (a) universal

सार्वलौकिक (a) cosmopolitan, universal

साल (nm) pain; year; the sal tree

सालगिरह (nf) birthday

सालना (v) to tease, to torment, to pierce

सालस (nm) an arbitrator or umpire

सालसी (nf) arbitratorship, arbitration

साला (nm) wife's brother, brother-in law; a term of abuse (directed to man)

सालाना (a) annual, yearly

सालिम (a) whole, complete, entire

साली (nf) wife's sister, sister-in-law; a term of abuse (directed to women)

सालू (nm) a kind of red sari

सावधान (a) aware, alert; attentive, careful; (ind) attention

सावन (nm) the fifth month of the Hindu year

सावनी (a) pertaining to the month of sawan or shravan

साष्टांग (a) in conjunction with eight limbs; —प्रणाम prostration before a person on the ground as a mark of high esteem

सास (nf) mother-in-law, mother of (one's) wife or husband

साहचर्य (nm) company, association

साहब (nm) lord, the master, gentleman, —ज़ादा son of a gentleman —ज़ादी daughter of a gentleman

साहबी (nf) sway, eminence, grandeur, lordliness

साह/स (nm) rashness, boldness; courage, —सिक/—सी courageous, daring; adventurous, enterprising; —सहीन courageless; coward

साहि/त्य (nm) literature, —त्यकार writer, a litterateur; —त्यिक literary —त्यिकता literariness

साहिब (nm) see साहब

साहूकार (nm) a capitalist, money-lender; a richman; साहू/कारा, कारी banking, money lending business

साहेब (nm) see साहब

साहेबा (nf) a mistress; a lady

सिंकना (v) to roast on open fire

सिंगार (nm) ornamentation; make up

सिंगी (nm) a kind of trumpet; a kind of pipe with which village surgeons suck up bad blood from the body

सिंघाड़ा (nm) water chestnut, a waternut

सिंचन (nm) irrigation; sprinkling of water

सिंचना (v) to sprinkle water on an object; to irrigate a field

सिंचाई (nf) irrigation

सिंचाना (v) to cause to be irrigated

सिंचित (a) drenched; irrigated

सिंदूर (nm) vermilion red lead; minium; —रंग scarlet; —वृक्ष oak

सिंदू/रिया, री (a) deep red, scarlet; very red in colour

सिंघ (nm) the province of Sindh. (nf) the Sindh river which flows in the Punjab

सिंघी (a) belonging or pertaining to Sindh

सिंधु (nm) a river; sea, ocean; the province of Sindh; —जा the goddess of wealth

सिंह (nm) a lion; leo, the fifth sign of the zodiac; —द्वारthe main gate of a palace —नाद the roaring of a lion, war cry

सिंहल द्रीप (nm) name of an island in the south of India

सिंहवाहिनी (nf) an epithet of the goddess Durga

सिंहावलोकन (nm) a retrospect

सिंहासन (nm) a throne

सिंहिनी (nf) a lioness

सिकंदर (nm) Alexander

सिकता (nf) sand, sandy soil

सिकुड़न (nf) wrinkle; shrinkage, shrivel

सिकु/ड़ना (v) to shrink; to

wrinkle; —ड़ हुआ shrunk; —ड़ने योग्य shrinkable

सिकोड़ना (v) to contract, to draw, to compress, to shrivel

सिक्का (nm) a medal; a coin, coinage

सिक्ख, सिख (nm) a sikh, a follower of Guru Nanak

सिक्त (a) wet, drenched; irrigated; watered

सिखलाना, सिखाना (v) to teach; to school; to train; to instruct; to show, to guide; to educate

सिगरा, सिगरी (a) entire, full, complete; all

सिजदा (nm) salutation, prostration

सिटपिटाना (v) to hesitate, to be stupefied, to be in a flux

सिटृटी (nf) bragging

सिड़ (nf) insanity, madness, eccentricity, whim

सिड़ी (a) mad, insane, eccentric

सित (a) white; clear, shining, bright; —ता whiteness, brightness

सितम (nm) violence; injustice, tyranny, oppression; —गर tyrannical, unjust, troublesome

सितार (nm) a kind of guitar

सितारा (nm) planet, star, fate

सिद्ध (a) accomplished; proved, perfect; (nm) a saint, one who has acquired supernatural powers

सिद्धांत (*nm*) theory, principle, rule, doctrine

सिद्धांती (*a & nm*) dogmatic, theoretician; a demonstrator

सिद्धार्थ (*a*) whose desires are attained; (*nm*) Gautama Buddha

सिद्धि (*nf*) success, proof; fulfilment, acquisition

सिद्धेश्वर (*nm*) a great saint, an epithet of Shiva

सिधाना (*v*) to help acquire practice; to tame

सिधारना (*v*) to depart; to expire, to die

सिनकना (*v*) to expel mucus from the nose; to snot

सिपहसालार (*nm*) the commander of an army

सिपाही (*nm*) sepoy, a constable, a policeman; a soldier

सिपुर्द (*a*) entrusted

सिप्पा (*nm*) approach; influence; means; —जमाना to make an approach, to fulfil an aim

सिफ़त (*nf*) quality, nature; characteristic

सिफर (*nm*) zero; a cipher; blank

सिफ़ा/रिश (*nf*) recommendation; —रिशी recommendatory

सिमटना (*v*) to contract; to shrink; to shrivel; to be complete

सिमेटना (*v*) to gather; (*adv*) together

सियन (*nf*) a stitch, seam

सियापा (*nm*) weeping over a death, mourning

सियार (*nm*) a jackal; cunning fellow

सियाह, स्याह (*a*) black

सिया/सत (*nf*) politics; —सतदां (*nm*) a politician

सिर (*nm*) head; top, highest part or point; —के बल headlong; —खपाई (too much of) mental exertion; —ताज crown; —नामा form of address

सिरकटा (*nm & a*) with head cut off; one who does evil to others

सिरका (*nm*) vinegar

सिरजन (*nm*) creation; —हार the creator

सिरजना (*v*) to produce, to create

सिरमौर (*nm*) a coronet

सिरा (*nm*) head; extremity; end, beginning

सिर्फ़ (*a*) only, merely, alone, mere, unmixed

सिलना (*v*) to sew, to stitch

सिलवाना (*v*) to cause to be sewn or stitched by somebody

सिलसि/ला (*nm*) series; a chain; line; system; —लेवार serial, systematic

सिलाई (*nf*) stitching charges,

the act or process of sewing

सिलाना (v) same as सिलवाना

सिल्ली (nf) a whetstone

सिवा (ind) except, but, without

सिवाय (ind) without, but, save

सिसकना (v) to sob

सिसका/रना (v) to hiss, to produce a hissing sound; —री hissing sound

सिसकी (nf) sobbing, a sob

सिहरन (nf) shiver, thrill

सिहरना (v) to shiver; to be thrilled, to be afraid

सींक (nf) wicker, spit

सींकचा (nm) window-bars

सींग (nm) a horn

सींचना (v) to drench, to wet; to irrigate

सी (ind) similar; equal; hissing sound

सीकर (nm) a drop of water, sweat

सीख (nf) counsel, ‘teaching, advice; instruction; moral

सीखना (v) to acquire knowledge; to learn

सीझना (v) to be roasted or fried; to boil

सीटी (nf) a pipe, whistle; a whistling sound

सीठा (a) tasteless, insipid

सीठी (nf) dregs, a worthless object

सीढ़ी (nf) a ladder

सीता (nf) a furrow made by a plough; the daughter of Janaka who was married to Ram

सीताफल (nm) the custard-apple

सीध (nf) straightness; alignment

सीधा (a & adv) simple, straight, direct, gentle, good, upright, plain, calm and quiet

सीधी (a & adv) feminine form of सीधा; —राह a straight path

सीधे (adv) without a halt; straight

सीना (v) to stitch, to sew, to seam; (nm) the chest —पिरोना stitching etc

सीप (nf) mother pearl

सीमंत (nm) the parting of hairs on the head

सीमा (nf) a landmark; extremity; limit; —चिह्न landmark, terminus; —प्रांत verge; —रहित limitless, —रेखा border line

सीमित (a) limited, restricted, bounded

सीरा (nm) molasses

सील (nf) damp/dampness; a seal

सीलन (nf) moisture, dampness

सीवन (nm) sewing, stitching, a seam, a joint

सीसमहल (शीश महल) (nm) a house which is fitted with mirrors

सीसा (nm) lead

सुँघनी (nf) a snuff

सुँघाना (v) to cause to smell

सुंदर (a) pretty; lovely; beautiful; fancy; —ता beauty; prettiness

सु (pref) a prefix showing the meanings of good, excellent beautiful, easy, well etc. (just as in सुप्रभात, सुभाष, सुकुमारी, सुगम etc.)

सुअर (nm) a pig, a boar, a swine

सुकर (a) easy, practicable

सुकर्म (nm) a pious action, a good deed

सुकुमा/र (a) delicate, tender, gentle, soft; —री of tender body

सुकून (nm) comfort; peace, consolation

सुकृत (a) pious, virtous, auspicious

सुकोमल (a) soft, very delicate;

सुख (nm) pleasure; comfort; happiness; contentment; —चैन happiness and comfort; —द pleasant, happy, pleasurable; —दा a female who affords pleasure; —दायक affording pleasure; —पूर्वक comfortably, happily; —शांति happiness and peace; —से at ease, happily —सौभाग्य pleasure and plenty

सुखी (a) well; glad; pleasant; happy; contented

सुख्यात (a) famous, reputed

सुगंध (nf) perfume, scent, smell

सुगंधि (nf) fragrance, perfume

सुगंधित (a) fragrant, odourous, sweetscented

सुगठित (a) wellbuilt, muscular; well-organised

सुगति (nm) happy condition, salvation

सुगम (a) plain, practicable, easy, accessible, simple

सुगम्य (a) easily accessible, attainable

सुघड़ (a) beautiful, elegant, clever, competent, dextrous; —ता elegance, beauty; —पन competency, cleverness, ability

सुघड़ाई (nf) shapeliness, elegance; dexterousness

सुचारु (a) very beautiful, pretty, charming

सुचेत (a) careful, attentive, clever, alert

सुजन (nm) a respectable person, a gentleman

सुजान (a) intelligent, wise, learned

सुझाना (v) to propose, to suggest, to show

सुझाव (nm) proposal, suggestion

सुड़कना (v) to sniff up; to drink noisily

सुडौल (a) shapely, well-shaped, well-built

—पन symmetry

सुत (*nm*) a son

सुतली (*nf*) thin rope, twine

सुता (*nf*) a daughter

सुथरा (*a*) pure, clean; neat; tidy —पन neatness and tidiness; cleanliness; refinement

सुदर्शन (*a*) elegant, beautiful, attractive

सुदी (*nf*) the bright half of a lunar month

सुदूर (*a*) at a long distance, far

सुदृढ़ (*a*) very firm, very strong, very powerful

सुदेश (*nm*) a beautiful country; (*a*) elegant, beautiful

सुध (*nf*) attention; conscious- ness, senses, care; memory; —बुध memory; conscious- ness, senses

सुधरना (*v*) to be corrected; to be mended; to be reformed

सुधर्मी (*a*) pious, virtuous

सुधांशु (*nm*) the moon

सुधा (*nf*) nectar, ambrosia water

सुधाकर (*nm*) the moon

सुधार (*nm*) reform; correction; repair; improvement, amendment; —कa reformer

सुधारना (*v*) to refine; to amend; to adjust; to improve; to correct, to reform, to revise

सुधि (*nf*) see सुध

सुधी (*a*) wise, learned, pious; (*nm*) a learned man

सुनना (*v*) to listen, to hear; to pay heed

सुनवाई (*nf*) listening, hearing, hearing of a law-suit

सुनसान (*a*) lonely; desolate; barren

सुनह/रा, —ला (*a*) golden; —रापन goldenness

सुनाना (*v*) to relate, to cause to hear; to recite; to read out

सुनाम (*nm*) fame, reputation, good name

सुना/र (*nm*) a goldsmith; —रिन a goldsmith's wife

सुनारी (*nf*) the profession of a goldsmith

सुनीति (*nf*) name of Dhruva's mother; good policy, morality

सुन्न (*a*) benumbed; senseless, lifeless

सुपच (*a*) easily digestible

सुपथ्य (*a*) salubrious; (*nm*) salubrious diet

सुपरिचित (*a*) intimate

सुपात्र (*nm*) a worthy person, a respectable man

सुपारी (*nf*) the betel nut

सुपुर्द (*a*) entrusted, committed, —गी trust; charge, care

सुप्त (*a*) asleep, shut up

सुप्रतिष्ठित (*a*) very respectable, far renowned, highly distinguished

सुप्रसिद्ध (*a*) very famous reputed, renowned

सुफल (*nm*) good result

सुबह (nf) dawn, early morning

सुबास (nf) fragrance, sweet smell (see also सुवास)

सुबुद्धि (nf) wisdom, good sense; (a) intelligent, wise

सुबूत (nm) proof, authenticity

सुबोध (a) intelligent, intelligible

सुभ/ग (a) beautiful, fortunate, beloved, —गा beautiful woman, having her husband alive

सुभट (nm) a great warrior

सुभद्रा (nf) name of lord Krishna's sister married to Arjuna; an epithet of goddess Durga

सुभाषित (a) well-said, well-spoken, eloquent

सुभीता (nm) opportunity, convenience, leisure

सुमति (nf) good understanding

सुमन (nm) a flower; (a) beautiful, benevolent, kind

सुसुखी (a & nf) pretty faced, beautiful

सुयोग (nm) a happy chance, good opportunity

सुयोग्य (a) able, worthy

सुरंग (nf) mine, a tunnel

सुर (nm) a god; a note in music; tone, —मिलाना to tune

सुर/क्षण (nm) क्षा (nf) protection, security —क्षित protected, safe; reserved

सुरखाब (nm) an ostrich

सुरखी (nf) brick-dust which is used in masonry; redness; lipstick

सुरभि (nf) aroma, fragrance, scent, purfume; —त fragrant, aromatic, scented

सुरमा (nm) antimony ground into fine powder, collyrium

सुरा (nf) liquor, wine

सुराख (nm) an aperture, hole

सुराग (nm) trace, clue

सुराही (nf) longnecked earthen water-pot, pitcher

सुरीला (nm) melodious, sweet; lyric, —पन symphony, sweetness

सुरुख, सुर्ख (a) red; happy, compassionate

सुरुचि (nf) good taste, refined taste

सुरूपा (a) beautiful (woman)

सुर्खी (nf) a headline, redness, lipstick

सुर्ता (a) clever, wise, intelligent

सुल/क्षण (a) auspicious; fortunate, lucky, —क्षणा beautiful female, attractive

सुलगना (v) to burn, to be kindled; to be sorry

सुलगाना (v) to light, to kindle fire, to inflame

सुलझना (v) to be solved, to be unravelled

सुलझाना (v) to disentangle a thing, to unravel

सुलझाव (nm) disentanglement, solution

सुलटा (a) straight, unopposed

सुलतान (*nm*) an emperor, king

सुलभ (*a*) accessible; handy, —ता feasibility

सुलह (*nf*) treaty, agreement, truce; —नामा a deed of compromise

सुलाना (*v*) to cause to sleep, to put to sleep, to lull

सुलूक (*nm*) treatment, behaviour

सुलेख (*nm*) calligraphy

सुलेमान (*nm*) Solomon, the name of a mountain situated in the west of Punjab

सुवर्ण (*nm*) good colour; higher caste; gold

सुवा/स (*nm*) sweet smell, fragrance, —सित fragrant

सुविधा (*nf*) comfort, facility, convenience, benefit, gain

सुव्यव/स्था (*nf*) orderliness, good organisation; —स्थित well-organized

सुशिक्षित (*a*) well-educated

सुशील (*a*) good, gentle, modest, polite

सुशोभित (*a*) graceful, adorned

सुश्री (*a*) very beautiful, very rich (used for ladies)

सुषमा (*nf*) exceptional prettiness, beauty, charm, excellent beauty

सुषु/प्त (*a*) fast or sound asleep, in deep slumber —प्ति deep sleep

सुष्ठु (*a*) appropriate, elegant

सुसंगति (*nf*) good society, good company

सुसंस्कृत (*a*) refined, cultured

सुसज्जित (*a*) well-equipped, well-adorned

सुसमय (*nm*) season of plenty, good times

सुसमाचार (*nm*) the gospel, good news

सुसर, सुसरा (*nm*) (see ससुर) a term of abuse (directed to man)

सुसाध्य (*a*) easily accomplished

सुस्त (*a*) indolent; languid; lazy; spiritless

सुस्ताना (*v*) to rest, to relax

सुस्ती (*nf*) laziness; depression; idleness; indolence

सुस्थिर (*a*) stable, resolute, firm

सुस्पष्ट (*a*) very intelligible, distinct or clear

सुस्वादु (*a*) delicious, flavoury

सुहबत (*nf*) association, company

सुहाग (*nm*) good fortune; husband

सुहागा (*nm*) borax

सुहागिन (*nf*) a female whose husband is alive

सुहाना (*v*) to look charming, to be pleasing

सुहावना (*a*) charming, pleasing

सुहृत, सुहृद् (*nm*) a friend (*a*) friendly, loving

सूँघना (*v*) to scent; to smell; to sniff

सूँघनी (*nf*) a snuff

सूँड (*nf*) the trunk of an

elephant

सूअर (*nm*) pig, boar, swine, a word of abuse

सूआ (*nm*) a parrot; big needle

सूई (*nf*) the hand of a watch, a needle

सूक्ति (*nf*) an epigram, maxim, good saying

सूक्ष्म (*a*) thin; subtle, minute; fine; —ता subtlety, fineness, thinness; —दर्शक यंत्र a microscope; —दर्शी nice-sharp-sighted

सूखना (*v*) to parch, to dry, to wither, to fall away

सूचक (*a*) a pointer, an informant

सूचना (*nf*) notice; information; intimation, —पत्र a notification, circular; —देने वाला an informer, a reporter

सूचिका (*nf*) a needle; the trunk of an elephant

सूचित (*a*) intimated; informed; indicated, —करना to refer, to attribute

सूची (*nf*) list; —पत्र a catalogue; —बनाना to list

सूजन (*nf*) a swelling, —संबंधी inflammatory, फेफड़े की— bronchitis

सूजना (*v*) to swell

सूज़ाक (*nm*) the veneral disease called gonorrhoea

सूजी (*nf*) coarse ground flour

सूझ (*nf*) vision, insight, perception; —बूझ imagina-

tion, intelligence

सूझना (*v*) to appear, to be visible; to be understood; to be intelligible

सूत (*nm*) thread, yarn, —कातना to spin yarn

सूतिका गृह (*nm*) a lying-in-chamber

सूत्र (*nm*) a thread, fibre, formula —मय thready; —पात beginning

सूथनी (*nf*) trousers

सूद (*nm*) interest; —खोर usurer; —खोरी usury; —दर सूद compound interest

सूना (*a*) lonely; empty; —पन loneliness; emptiness

सूप (*nm*) a cook; broth; a winnowing basket

सूबा (*nm*) a province

सूबेदार (*nm*) the governor of an Indian province

सूम (*a*) miser; niggardly; (*nm*) a miser; the hoof of a horse

सूर (*a*) blind; brave; (*nm*) the sun; a wise man; blind man

सूरज (*nm*) the Sun; —मुखी the sunflower, *albino*

सूरत (*nf*) looks, face; appearance; means; method; figure

सूरमा (*nm*) a hero, warrior

सूराख़ (*nm*) a hole; a puncture; a passage

सूर्य (*nm*) the Sun; —कांत a magnifying glass; —ग्रहण

solar eclipse; —घड़ी a sun dial; —पूजा heliolatry; —मणि jasper; —मुखी a sunflower

संक्रांति (nf) the enterning of the Sun from one sign of zodiac to the other

सूर्यास्त (nm) the time of sunset, the evening

सूर्योदय (nm) the time of sunrise, the morning

सूली (nf) gibbet, gallows

सृजन (nm) the work of creation, creation; —शील creative

सृष्टि (nf) creation; the World; construction; —कर्ता the creator

सेंकना (v) to roast; to foment; to bake

सेंध (nf) a hole made in a wall by a thief; burglary

सेंधना (v) to make a hole in the wall of a house as a burglar

सेंवई (nf) vermicelli

सेज (nf) richly decorated bed; sofa; a bed

सेठ (nm) a great merchant; a wealthy person; lender

सेतु (nm) a bridge; causeway

सेना (v) to hatch an egg

सेना (nf) an army; a troop; a regiment; military, —ध्यक्ष, the commander of an army, —नायक a brigadier —नायक (समुद्री) an admiral

सेब (nm) an apple; खट्टा—

crab

सेम (nf) kidney-bean, bean

सेमल (nm) the silk-cotton tree

सेव (nm) a sweet meat prepared from the meal of gram

सेवक (nm) a servant; attendant; a worshipper; —गण suite

सेवकाई (nf) service; attendance

सेवन (nm) use; serving; taking (as medicine etc.)

सेवा (nf) service; attendance; homage; —टहल service, servitude; —धर्म servitude; —वृत्ति servitude

सेविका (nf) a female servant

सेवित (a) used, enjoyed; served; employed

सेवी (a) serving, enjoying

सेव्य (a) deserving to be served; worthy of being protected —सेवक the master and the servant

सेहत (nf) good health; relief from illness; comfort; happiness

सैंधव (nm) rock salt; a resident of Sindh; (a) pertaining to Sindh

सैकड़ा (nm) a group of hundred; one hundred

सैकड़ों (a) several hundred; numerous

सैद्धांतिक (a) theoretical; (nm) a learned man

सैनिक (nm) a soldier; troop; sentry; —क्रांति military

revolution —शासन martial law

सैन्य (a) an army; military; —बल platoon; —समूह lavy of warriors

सैयाँ (nm) lord; master; husband; lover

सैर (nf) rample; a walk for the sake of amusement; stroll

सैलानी (nm) wanderer; tourist; (a) roaming at pleasure

सैला/ब (nm) flood. —बी wet, drenched, damp

सैलून (nm) a saloon; barber's shop

सोंटा (nm) a truncheon, mace, baton

सोंठ (nf) dry ginger

सोंधा (a) fragrant, odorous; sweet-smelling

सो (adv) thus, therefore; (pron) that, he

सोखना (v) to absorb, to merge, to dry up

सोख्ता (nm) blotting paper

सोच (nm) thought; anxiety; reflection; repentence; regret; —विचार considera- tion, pondering, reflection

सोचना (v) to consider; to suppose, to think, to ponder, to imagine, to conceive, to reflect

सोज़िश (nf) swelling; inflam- mation

सोया (nm) same as सोंटा

सोता (nm) a spring, a fountain, brook; current; source, (see स्रोत)

सोषना (v) to amend, to correct; to purify, to refine; to investigate

सोषाना (v) to cause to be amended, purified or refined

सोनहला (a) see सुनहला or सुनहरा

सोना (nm) gold; an excellent thing; (v) to lie, to sleep; —चढ़ाना to gild; —चाँदी gold and silver; wealth

सोनार (nm) goldsmith

सोपान (nm) a staircase, stair

सोफ़ा (nm) a sofa; —सेट a sofa set

सोफ़ियाना (a) attractive, gaudy; fashionable; sophisticated

सोम (nm) the moon; Yama; nectar; —पान the drinking of the Soma juice —पायी one who drinks Soma juice —रस the juice of the Soma plant; —वार Monday

सोयाबीन (nm) soyabean

सोहन हलवा (nm) a kind of nice sweetmeat

सोहना (v) to look attractive or beautiful, to be pleasing, to shine; to be glorious

सोहनी (nf) a broom; (a) beautiful

सोहबत (nf) intercourse, coition, copulation; company, association

सोहम (phr) (Sanskrit) I am

the same i.e. I am none other but the Brahma

सोहागिन (nf) see सुहागिन

सोहागा (nm) borax

सोहाना, सोहावना (v) to be agreeable or pleasant

सौंदर्य (nm) beauty, charm, attractiveness, prettiness

सौंधा (a) odorous, pleasing, excellent

सौंपना (v) to give in charge, to hand over, to give; to surrender, to assign

सौंफ (nf) anise; fennel; aniseed

सौंह (nf) an oath, swearing

सौ (nm) the number hundred, century; (a) hundred; —गुना hundred times —वाँ hundredth —वर्ष century

सौकुमार्य (nm) youth; delicacy, tenderness

सौख्य (nm) happiness, pleasure; comfort, relief; ease, joy, delight; good health

सौगंध (nf) an oath, swearing; —खाना to take a vow, to swear; —टूटना breaking of a vow

सौगात (nf) a present, gift; a present for a friend etc; brought from a distant place

सौगाती (a) given to someone as a gift or present

सौजन्य (nm) goodness; courtesy; generosity; compassion, kindness, gentility

सौत (nf) a rival wife, co-wife; —तिया डाह malice as between co-wives

सौते/ला (a) begotten from a step-mother

सौतेला भाई a step-brother

सौतेली बहन a step-sister; —ली माता a step-mother

सौदा (nm) a bargain; negotiation; goods; commodity; —गर a merchant, trader

सौदाई (nm & a) mad; insane

सौदामिनी (nf) lightning

सौभाग्य (nm) fortune, good luck, prosperity, auspiciousness —वती fortunate in having one's husband alive

सौम्य (a) gentle; amiable, mild, lunar, auspicious

सौर (a) produced by the Sun; solar; —परिवार solar system — मास a solar month a solar month

सौर/भ (nm) aroma, saffron, fragrance —भित odorous; fragrant

सौष्ठव (nm) elegance, excellence, shapeliness

सौहार्द (nm) friendship; amity; attraction, love

स्ख/लन (nm) stumbling; a mistake, a slip, —लित fallen, slipped, dropped down, mistaken

स्तंभ (nm) a pillar, a column; —लेखक a columnist

स्तंभन (*nm*) stoppage, retention, obstruction

स्तंभित (*a*) stupefied, wonder-struck; benumbed

स्तन (*nm*) the breast; udder; —पान sucking of breast

स्तब्ध (*a*) stupefied; stilled, stagnant; —ता stupefaction, firmness

स्तर (*nm*) level; a fold; grade; standard

स्तरीय (*a*) stratified; levelled

स्तव (*nm*) a hymn of praise spoken to a deity

स्तवक (*nm*) a bunch of flowers

स्तव/न (*nm*) praise; eulogy —नीय praise worthy

स्तुति (*nf*) invocation; praise, prayer, orison

स्तुत्य (*nm*) praiseworthy, laudable, admirable

स्तूप (*nm*) a Buddhistic tope

स्तोत्र (*nm*) a hymn of praise, eulogism

स्त्री (*nf*) a woman; female; wife, dame; (*pron*) she. —गमन sexual intercourse; —जाति fair sex; —त्व womanhood; —रोग a female disease; —सुख sexual enjoyment; —हरण kidnapping of a woman

स्त्रैण (*a*) effeminate; womanish

स्थ/गन (*nm*) adjournment; postponement; —प्रस्ताव adjournment motion; —गित adjourned, postponed, suspended

स्थल (*nm*) place, site; spot, region; opportunity; — डमरु-मध्य isthmus; —मार्ग roadway —सेना army

स्थली (*nf*) dry land, soil

स्थविर (*nm*) a Buddhistic monk

स्थान (*nm*) a place; space, room, site; post; —च्युत/ —भ्रष्ट displaced; demoted

स्थानांत/र (*nm*) different place, situation or position. —रण displacement; trans-location; transfer —रित displaced; translocated; transferred

स्थानापन्न (*a*) officiating, acting; substitute

स्थानीय (*a*) local; colloquial; positional

स्थापक (*a*) founder, erector, moulder

स्थापत्य (*nm*) architecture; —कला architecture

स्था/पन (*nm*) foundation, erection; —पित founded, erected, situated; settled

स्थापना (*nf*) founding, establishing; propounding

स्थायित्व (*nm*) permanency; durability; stability

स्थायी (*a*) permanent; lasting; stable; stationary. —करण confirmation; stabilisation; —कृत confirmed

स्थावर (*a*) stationary;

immovable; —जंगम immovable and movable

स्थित (a) residing; situate; —प्रज्ञ firm in judgment

स्थिति (nf) condition; status; location; position

स्थिर (a) motionless; firm; steady; inflexible; stable —ता motionlessness; firmness, steadiness; stability

स्थूल (a) thick; fat; bulky; gross; rough. —ता thickness; fatness; bulkiness; grossness; roughness

स्नात/क (nm) a graduate; —कोत्तर postgraduate

स्नान (nm) bath, bathing —गृह bathroom, a bath

स्नानागार (nm) bathroom, a bath

स्नायविक (a) nervous, ligamentary

स्नायु (nm) nerves, ligament

स्निग्ध (a) oily, greasy, lubricant; affectionate; —ता oiliness, greasiness, lubricity; affection

स्नेह (nm) love, liking, affection; —पान object of love

स्नेहिल (a) of loving disposition, loving

स्नेही (a) loving, kind; (nm) a friend; a lover

स्पं/दन (nm) trembling; vibration, pulsation; —दित vibrated, pulsated

स्पर्धा (nf) rivalry; competition

स्पर्धी (a) rival; competitor

स्पर्श (nm) touch; contact

स्पष्ट (a) clear; simple, vivid; obvious; apparent; plain, —त: clearly; simply; obviously etc.;—तया vividly; apparently etc.;—ता clarity; obviousness; vividness; —वक्ता straight forward

स्पष्टीकरण (nm) clarification; explanation; ellucidation

स्पृश्य (a) touchable

स्पृहणीय (a) desirable, coveted

स्फटिक (a) crystal, quartz

स्फुट (a) miscellaneous, apparent, obvious; separate

स्फुटन (nm) becoming apparent; blossoming

स्फु/रण (nm) pulsation; spurt —रित pulsating; spurting

स्फूर्ति (nf) promptness; inspiration —दायक imparting promptness

स्फोटक (a) explosive —ता explosiveness

स्मरण (nm) recollection; memory; —शक्ति memory

स्मरणीय (a) notable; memorable

स्मारक (nm) memorial, a monument; (a) reminding

स्मारिका (nf) a souvenir

स्मित (nf) a smile; (a) smiling

स्मिति (nf) a smile

स्मृति (nf) remembrance, memory

स्यापा (nm) mourning

स्यार (nm) jackal

स्याह (a) black; dark

स्याही (nf) ink; darkness, blackness

स्रष्टा (nm) creator of the universe (i.e. Brahma)

स्राव (nm) secretion; abortion

स्रोत (nm) source, a current, stream; resource

स्व (pron) personal; self; —त्व one's due; —शासन self-rule

स्वगत (a) to oneself; —कथन/भाषण aside, soliloquy

स्वचालित (a) automatic

स्वच्छंद (a) free; independent; spontaneous; unobstructed; —ता freedom; spontaneity; —तावाद Romanticism

स्वच्छ (a) clean; clear; pure; transparent; —ता cleanliness; clarity; purity; transparency

स्वजन (nm) a kinsman, a relative

स्वजातीय (a) co-racial

स्वतंत्र (a) free, independent; self-willed; separate —ता freedom, independence; —लेखन free lance writing

स्वत: (adv) voluntarily, spontaneously; —सिद्ध self evident

स्वत्व (nm) ownership; monopoly; copyright

स्वदेश (nm) country, homeland motherland; —त्याग emigration; —प्रेम patriotism; —भक्ति patriotism

स्वदेशी (a) pertaining to one's own country

स्वनाम (nm) one's own name

स्वप्न (nm) a dream; —दर्शी a dreamer; —दोष emission; —मय dreamy

स्वप्निल (a) dreamy

स्वभाव (nm) nature; habit; —त: naturally; habitually

स्वयंवर (nm) self-choice of her husband by a bride

स्वयं/सेवक (nm) a (male) volunteer; —सेविका (nf) a female volunteer; —सेवा self-service

स्वयम् (pron) self (adv) personally; by oneself

स्वर (nm) voice; tone, note; a vowel; —बद्ध rhythmic —भंग hoarseness of throat; —मधुरता melody

स्वराज्य (nm) autonomy, home-rule, self-government

स्वराष्ट्र (nm) one's own country, home land

स्वरूप (nm) form, shape; appearance; nature

स्वर्ग (nm) heaven, paradise, abode of gods —वास heavenly abode i.e. death; —वासी late; —सिधारना to die

स्वर्गिक (a) divine, paradisaic,

celestial

स्वर्गी/य (a) late, dead; divine; —या (fem. form) late, dead

स्वर्ण (nm) gold; —कार goldsmith; —जयंती golden jubilee —मुद्रा a gold coin; —युग the golden age

स्वर्णाक्षर (nm) a golden letter

स्वर्णिम (a) golden, of gold

स्व/ल्प (a) very small, very little; —ल्पाहार light refreshment

स्वशासन (nm) self-government, home-rule

स्वस्थ (a) hale, healthy; sound; —चित्त sane; —चित्तता sanity —ता healthiness; health; ease

स्वाँग (nm) mimicry; sham; —बनाना to mimic

स्वागत (nm) reception, welcome; acceptation; —कक्ष reception room —समिति reception committee —समारोह a reception

स्वातंत्र्य (nm) liberty, independence; freedom —सेनानी a freedom fighter

स्वाद (nm) taste, savour; flavour; swallow

स्वादिष्ट (a) tasty, delicious, relishable

स्वाधीन (a) independent, free —ता independence, freedom

स्वाध्या/य (nm) study; regular study; —यी studious

स्वाभाविक (a) natural; inborn; —ता naturality

स्वाभिमा/न (nm) self-respect; —नी self-respecting

स्वामित्व (nm) proprietorship, ownership

स्वामिनी (nf) a female master; the mistress of a house

स्वा/मी (nm) master, owner; lover, —मिभक्त loyal, faithful —मिभक्ति loyalty, faithfulness

स्वायत्त (a) under one's control, autonomous

स्वार्थ (nm) self-interest; —परायण selfish; self-seeking; —परता selfishness —साधक a self-seeker; —हीन liberal

स्वार्थी (a) self-seeking; selfish; interested

स्वावलंबन (nm) self-reliance

स्वास्थ्य (nm) health; sound state of body; —प्रद useful to health; —संबंधी regarding to health

स्वी/करण (nm) granting; sanctioning; —कर्ता one who grants or sanctions

स्वीकार (a) granted; accepted; agreed; admitted; (nm) grant; acceptance; agreement —ना to accept; to admit; to agree; to acknowledge; to accede

स्वीकृ/त (a) accepted; approved; acknowledged;

confessed; —ति acceptance; confession; consent

स्वेच्छया (*adv*) voluntarily

स्वेच्छ (*nf*) free will; —चारिता autocracy —चारी wilful, arbitrary; —पूर्वक voluntarily

स्वेद (*nm*) prespiration, sweat

स्वैच्छिक (*a*) voluntary; arbitrary

स्वैर (*a*) free, sluggish; —चारिता self-willedness; —चारी a self-willed person

स्वैराचा/र (*nm*) self-willed conduct; —री a self-willed person

स्वैरिणी (*nf*) a wanton woman

ह

ह the thirty third letter of Devnagri alphabet

हंगामा (*nm*) tumult, uproar

हँडिया (*nf*) a small earthen pot

हंता (*nm*) a murderer, a slayer

हंस (*nm*) a swan, goose; a duck; —गामिनी a female with a graceful gait; —वाहिनी the goddess Saraswati

हँस/ना (*v*) to laugh, to smile; to joke; to ridicule; —ने योग्य amusing, laughable

हँसमुख (*a*) cheerful, jolly; having a smiling face

हँसली (*nf*) collar-bone

हँसाई (*nf*) ridicule; —कराना to cause ridicule

हँसाना (*v*) to tickle, to make to laugh

हंसिनी (*nf*) a female goose

हँसिया (*nm*) a sickle

हँसी (*nf*) laughter; joke; ridicule; —खुशी happily

—खेल fun

हँसोड़ (*a*) merry; humarous, jolly

हक़ (*nm*) right, due; —दार a claimant; —नाहक़ right and wrong

हकबकाना (*v*) to be confused

हकला (*nm*) a stammerer; —हट stammering

हकलाना (*v*) to falter in speech, to stutter, to stammer

हकारत (*nf*) contempt

हक़ीकत (*nf*) reality, fact; —बयानी statement of truth

हक़ीकतन (*ind*) in fact

हक़ीकी (*a*) factual; real

हकीम (*nm*) a (Unani) physician

हकीमी (*nf*) the Unani system of medicine

हक्का-बक्का (*a*) confused, thunderstuck

हगना (*v*) to go to stool, to

discharge faeces

हगाना (v) to cause to evacuate

हचकोला (nm) a jolting

हज (nm) a pilgrimage to Mecca (by Muslims)

हज़म (a) digested; —करना to digest; to mis-appropriate

हज़रत (nm) an eminent person; a naughty person

हजामत (nf) shaving; hair-cutting; —करना to shave

हज़ार (a) one thousand; innumerable

हजूर (nm) same as हुजूर

हज्जाम (nm) a barber

हटक (nf) prevention, obstruction

हटकना (v) to prohibit, to forbid, to restrain

हटना (v) to step back, to withdraw; to give way; to move away

हटवाना (v) to cause to be removed

हटाना (v) to remove; to push aside; to obstruct

हट्टा-कट्टा (a) vigorous, strong, robust

हट्टी (nf) same as हाट

हठ (nm) obstinacy; disobedience; stubbornness

हठधर्मी (a) obstinate, fanatic; (nm) a bigot

हठात् (ind) all of a sudden, suddenly

हठी (a) obstinate, wilful, arrogant, headstrong, stiff-necked

हठीला (nm) same as हठी

हठीली (nf) same as हठी

हड़कंप (nm) a great agitation

हड़क (n) eager; longing, yearning

हड़काना (v) to estrange

हड़ताल (nf) a strike; —करना to strike

हड़ताली (nm) a striker

हड़प (a) swallowed; illegaly taken

हड़पना (v) to swallow up, to gulp, to misappropriate

हड़बड़ (nf) a confusion

हड़बड़ाना (v) to be perplexed, to be in a hurry; to cause some-one to be in a hurry

हड़बड़िया (a) hasty, rash

हड़बड़ी (nf) haste, rashness; confusion; uproar

हड्डी (nf) a bone

हतक (nf) disrespect, dishonour —करना to dishonour, to defame

हतबुद्धि (a) stupid, foolish, unintelligent

हतभागा (a) unlucky, unfortunate, ill-fated

हतभाग्य (a) unfortunate

हताश (a) hopeless

हताहत (a) slain and wounded

हतोत्साह (a) disheartened, depressed, discouraged

हत्था (nm) the handle of an instrument

हत्थी (nf) the (small) handle

of a small instrument

हत्थे (ind) in hand — आना to be under subjugation

हत्या (nf) murder, slaughter, assassination

हत्या/रा (nm) a murderer, an assassin — री (nf)

हथ contraction of हाथ used as a prefix; — कड़ sleight of hand; — कड़ी handcuff; — गोला a hand-grenade; — चक्की a hand-mill; — बुना hand-woven

हथिनी (nf) a female elephant

हथियाना (v) to seize, to occupy, to pocket

हथियार (nm) a tool; a weapon, arms

हथेली (nf) the palm, the palm of hand

हथौड़ा (nm) a hammer

हथौड़ी (nf) a small hammer

हद (nf) limit; boundary; limitation; — बंदी delimitation

हदीस (nf) the traditional saying of Mohammad

हदूद (nf) (see हद)

हनन (nm) murder, killing, assassination

हनुमान् (a) having big jawbones; (nm) the Monkey God

हफ्ता (nm) a week

हबशी (nm) a negro

हम (pron) we, plural form of first person मैं

हम (a) similar, equal; — जोली a companion; — दर्द sympathetic; — दर्दी sympathy; — नाम name sake; — पेशा co-professional; — राज़ a confidant; — राही a co-traveller; — वतन a compatriot; — सफ़र a co-traveller — साया a neighbour

हमला (nm) attack, assault — वर an assailant

हमवार (a) even, level

हमारा (pron) our, ours

हमें (pron) to us

हमेशा (ind) always, ever

हया (nf) shame, modesty

हयात (nf) existence, life

हर (a) each, every; (nm) Lord Shiva; — दम always; — रोज़ daily

हरकत (nf) movement, motion, action; naughtiness; wickedness

हरकारा (nm) a postman

हरगिज़ (a) at any time, ever; — नहीं never

हरज (nm) see हर्ज

हरजाई (a) a wanderer, flirt; (nf) disloyal (woman)

हरज़ाना (nm) damages, compensation; — देना to compensate

हरण (nm) carrying off, taking away by force

हरना (v) to take away by force

हरम (nm) female apartments; (nf) a kept women, wife, a

handmaid

हरमज़दगी (nf) wickedness; misbehaviour

हरवाना (v) to cause to lose money in gambling

हरषाना (v) to please; to be pleased

हरा (a) green; fresh; unripe (fruit) —पन viridity —भरा fresh, verdant

हराना (v) to defeat, to beat; to counteract

हराम (a) polluted; unlawful; improper —खोर lazy —खोरी slothfulness; —ज़ादा bastard, rascal

हरामी (a & nm) wicked; rascal

हरारत (nf) slight fever; feverishness; warmth

हरिजन (nm) an untouchable

हरि/ण (nm.) a deer; an antelope, –णी a hind

हरित (a) green

हरियाना (v) to turn green; to be delighted; (nm) one of the northern states of the Union of India

हरियाली (nf) verdure; green grass

हर्ज़ (nm) obstruction; harm; loss

हर्ता (nm) kidnapper; stealer

हर्ष (nm) joy, pleasure, glee, delight, mirth, gladness, happiness

हर्षित (a) joyous, pleased, delighted, glad, happy, cheerful

हल, हलंत (nm) a consonant

हल (nm) a plough; solution; —जोतना to plough a field

हलक़ (nm) throat

हलकई (nf) lightness; silliness; meanness

हलकना (v) to toss about

हलका (a) light in weight; cheap; careless; —पन (nm) lightness; cheapness

हलकान (a) perplexed, disturbed; tired

हलचल (nf) tumult, commotion; agitation, turmoil, —मचना commotion to be caused

हलदी (nf) turmeric

हलधर (nm) the farmer having a plough

हलफ़ (nm) an oath —उठाना to take an oath; —नामा an affidavit, a declaration on oath

हलवा (nm) a kind of sweet-meat

हलवा/ई (nm) a confectioner —इन a female confectioner

हलवाहा (nm) a ploughman

हलाक (a) murdered, killed; —करना to murder, to kill; to torment

हलाल (a) lawful, right, sanctioned by law

हलाहल (nm) a very deadly poison

हल्दी (nf) see हलदी

हवन (nm) a fire sacrifice, an

offering

हवस (nf) yearning, longing; thirst; desire

हवा (nf) wind, air, breeze; reputation; —ख़ोरी a walk; —पानी climate; —बाज़ an airman; —बाज़ी airmanship, —भर/सा very flimsy

हवाई (a) airy, aerial; false; —अड्डा aerodrome; —किला imaginary things; —छतरी an air umbrella; —जहाज़ an aeroplane; —डाकairmail; —मार्ग airways —यात्रा air journey

हवा/ला (nm) reference; example; custody, trust; —ले करना to yield, to hand over (to)

हवा/लात (nf) (police) custody —लाती under (police) custody

हवास (nm) senses (used as होश-हवास)

हवेली (nf) a mansion

हम्र (nm) ultimate result

हसद (nf) jealousy, malice; envy

हसरत (nf) craving, longing; desire; —भरा wistful

हसीन (nm) pretty, beautiful, charming

हस्त (nm) the hand; the hand-writing; —कला handicraft; —क्रिया masturbation; —कौशल manipulation; —क्षेप interference; —मैथुन masturbation; —रेखा the line appearing on hand; —रेखा-विशेषज्ञ a palmist

हस्तलिखित (a) handwritten

हस्तलिपि (nf) handwriting

हस्ताक्षर (nm) signature; autograph; —करना to sign; to endorse; to initial; —करने वाला signatory; —युक्त signed

हस्तिनी (nf) a female elephant

हस्ती (nm) an elephant

हस्पताल (nm) a hospital; an asylum

हहरना (v) to tremble; to be embarrassed

हहराना (v) to tremble; to terrified

हाँ (adv) yea, yes; indeed; —करना to assent, to agree

हाँक (nf) calling aloud; —लगाना to call aloud

हाँकना (v) to drive; to push away; to goad

हाँडी (nf) a small earthern pot

हाँपना, हाँफना (v) to heave, to breathe heavily

हाकिम (nm) a governor, ruler; an officer

हाजत (nf) desire; need; pressure in the bowels

हाज़मा (nm) digestion, digestive power

हाज़िर (a) present; ready; —जवाब ready-witted; —करना to cause to appear; —रहना to be present; —होना

to attend a court

हाज़िरी (nf) presence; attendance; —लेना to take attendance

हाजी (nm) one who has made a pilgrimage to Mecca

हाट (nf) a market, bazar; a periodic market; —करना to go for shopping

हाड़ (nm) a bone; —मांस bones and flesh

हातिम (a) competent, proficient; (nm) an ancient chief of Arab, a generous person

हाथ (nm) a hand; handle —खर्च personal expenses

हाथा-पाई (nf) a tussle, scuffle

हाथी (nm) an elephant; —दाँत ivory

हादसा (nm) an accident, mishap, calamity

हानि (nf) a loss, harm; an injury; damage; —कर/कारक/कारी harmful, inhygienic; —पहुँचाना to injure, to damage, to harm

हाफ़िज़ (nm) the Mohammedan who learns the whole of the Quran by heart; a protector

हामिला (a) pregnant (woman)

हामी (nf) acceptance, assent; (nm) supporter; —भरना to give assent

हाय (int) alas! alack! lack-a-day; —तोबा uproar, havoc; —हाय करना to be afflicted

हार (nf) defeat, loss; (nm) necklace, wreath; —मानना to acknowledge defeat; —जीत defeat and victory

हारना (v) to lose, to fail, to be unsuccessful

हार्दिक (a) affectionate, hearty, cordial

हाल (nm) condition, state; news, narratives; (a) recent, current; —चाल general condition; —का fresh, recent

हालत (nf) condition, state

हालात (nf) circumstances, conditions (plural of हालत)

हालाँकि (adv) though, although

हाला (nf) wine, liquor

हालाहल (nm) a deadly poison

हाव-भाव (nm) blandishments; gestures

हावी (a) dominant; —होना to dominate

हाशिया (nm) margin, border

हास (nm) laughter, fun; joke, ridicule; —परिहास fun and humour

हासिल (a) obtained, acquired; what is carried forward; —जमा total; —करना to obtain; —होना to be acquired

हास्य (nm) laughter, a laugh; joke; ridicule; —जनक humorous; —चित्र a cartoon; —चित्रकार cartoonist —व्यंग्य humour and satire

हास्यास्पद (a) funny, ridiculous

हाहा (nf) loud laughter; — हीही fun and humour

हाहाकार (nm) sound of distress, an uproar

हिंग, हिंगु (nf) same as हींग

हिंडो/रा/ला (nm) a sway, cradle

हिंद (nm) India, Hindustan

हिंदवी (nf) Hindi language

हिंदसा (nm) a number, digit

हिंदी (a) Indian, pertaining to India; (nm) a resident of Hindustan; (nf) Hindi language

हिंदुत्व (nm) Hinduism

हिंदुस्तान (nm) India

हिंदुस्तानी (nm) Indian

हिंदुस्थान (nm) same as हिंदुस्तान

हिंदू (nm & a) Hindu

हिंदोस्तान (nm) same as हिंदुस्तान

हिंसक (a) murderous, savage; (nm) a murderer — जंतु fierce animal; — पक्षी carnivorous bird

हिंसा (nf) violence, murder, slaying, slaughter; — त्मक destructive; — रत violent

हिंस (a) fierce, violent; murderous; hard-hearted

हिकमत (nf) Unani medical practice; method; — ती clever, dexterous

हिकायत (nf) a tale, a narration

हिकारत (nf) contempt, scorn

हिक्का (nf) hiccup

हिचक (nf) hitch, hesitation; suspense, doubt

हिचकना (v) to hitch, to hesitate; to shrink

हिचकिचा/ना same as हिचकना; — हट hitch, hesitation

हिचकी (nf) hiccup

हिचकोला (nm) a jolt, jerk

हिजड़ा (nm) eunuch; (a) impotent

हिजरी (nf) the Mohammedan era

हिज्जे (nm) spelling; — करना to spell a word

हिज्र (nm) separation

हित (a) well-being; benefit, gain; — कर/कारक/कारी beneficial, advantageous; — चिंतक well-wisher; — चिंतन well-wishing

हिताहित (nm) good and bad

हितेच्छा (nf) well-wishing

हितेच्छु (a & nm) well wishing; a well-wisher

हितैषी (a & nm) same as हितेच्छु

हिदायत (nf) instruction — नामा a letter of instructions

हिनहिना/ना (v) to whinny, to neigh — हट whinnying, neighing

हिफाज़त (nf) safety, protection; — करना to protect, to safeguard

हिब्बा (nm) a present, gift

हिम (nm) ice, snow; frost; — कण icicle; — कर the moon; — गिरि Himalaya; — नदी a glacier; — पात snow-fall; — मानव snow-man; — युग

the ice-age; —वर्षा snow-
fall; —शिखर ice-cap — सागर
ice-sea

हिमवान् (nm) the Himalayas

हिमांशु (nm) the moon

हिमाकत (nf) stupidity, foolishness

हिमाचल (nm) the Himalayas;
—प्रदेश a northern state of
India

हिमानी (nf) a glacier

हिमाय/त (nf) support, backing;
help, protection; —ती
protector, helper, sup-
porter

हिमालय (nm) the Himalaya
mountains

हिम्मत (nf) courage; bravery;
boldness

हिम्मती (a) courageous; brave;
bold

हिया (nm) heart; courage;
breast, bosom

हिरण्मय (a) of gold, golden

हिरण्य (nm) gold

हिरन (nm) a deer, an antelope

हिराना (v) to disappear; to
forget

हिरासत (nf) custody;
imprisonment

हि/स (nf) ambition, ardent
desire; envy; —सी
ambitious; envious

हिलकोर (nf) हिलकोरा (nm) a
wave, billow

हिलना (v) to rock, to move; to
swing; —डोलना to wander;

to move; —मिलना to have
intimate connection with

हिलाना (v) to move, to wave, to
quaver, to shake, to swing

हिलोर (nf) हिलोरा (nm) a
wave, billow

हिल्लोल (nf) a wave, billow

हिसाब (nm) calculation;
account; rate; arithmetic;
—किताब accounts —करना to
account, to work out;
—चुकाना to clear off the old
dues

हिसाबी (a) calculative

हिस्सा (nm) share; part; portion;
lot

हिस्से/दार (nm) shareholder,
partner; —दारी partnership;
participation

हींग (nf) asafoetida

हीं-हीं (nf) sound of laughter

ही (ind) only, alone, solely;
none but

हीक (nf) a slight bad smell

हीन (a) inferior, low; deprived;
free from; —ग्रंथि inferiority
complex; —चरित of bad
character; —ता inferiority;
—भावना feeling of inferiority

हीरक (nm) a diamond; —जयंती
diamond jubilee

हीरा (nm) adamant, a diamond

हीला (nm) pretence; pretext;
evasion; —हवाला pretence;
evasion

ही-ही (nf) laughing loudly

हुँ (int) a word of assent, yes

हुंकार (*nm*) roar, bellowing

हुंडी (*nf*) a bill of exchange, draft; cheque; —सकारना to honour a bill

हुकुम (*nm*) same as हुक्म

हुकूमत (*nf*) government, rule, authority; —करना to govern, to rule; —चलाना to run a government

हुक्का (*nm*) a hubble-bubble; —भरना to flatter

हुक्म (*nm*) permission; order; command; —उदूली disobeyance; —नामा a decree; —बरदार a loyal servant; —बरदारी loyalty; —रान ruling authority

हुजूम (*nm*) a crowd

हुजूर (*nm*) sir, a title of respect, your majesty, presence

हुजूरी (*nm*) a special attendant

हुज्ज/त (*nf*) controversy, argument; —ती fractious, altercating

हुड़क (*nf*) longing, pining

हुड़कना (*v*) to fret, to pine

हुड़द/ग (*nm*) tumult, uproar, riot; —गी riotous, commotive

हुतात्मा (*nm*) a martyr

हुनर (*nm*) skill; craft, art; —मंद skilful; crafty

हुमकना (*v*) to stretch forward, to leap

हुलसना (*v*) to look pretty

हुलसाना (*v*) to cause to be made merry

हुलास (*nm*) delight, joy, hilarity

हुलिया (*nf*) appearance, shape; —बिगाड़ना to harass

हुल्लड़ (*nm*) uproar, outbreak, tumult; —बाज़ tumultuous; —बाज़ी tumultuousness; —मचाना to make a tumult

हुश (*int*) be silent ! hush !

हुस्न (*nm*) beauty, elegance, prettiness; —परस्ती love of beauty

हूँ (*ind*) yes; (*v*) am

हूक (*nf*) pain, ache, sorrow

हूबहू (*a*) similar, alike

हूर (*nf*) a fairy of paradise; a fairy, beautiful woman

हृत (*a*) stolen, taken away; —बुद्धि stupefied

हृदयंगम (*a*) understood

हृदय (*nm*) the heart; core (of the heart); mind; —ग्राही attractive; —स्थ taken to heart; —स्पर्शी heart-touching; —हारी bewitching, charming —हीन hard-hearted

हृदये/श, श्वर (*nm*) the dear one; husband; lover —श्वरी (*nf*) the beloved; dear wife

हृदगत (*a*) internal, pertaining to the heart

हृदरोग (*nm*) heart disease

हृष्ट (*a*) delighted, glad, pleased; —पुष्ट lusty, robust, stout

हें-हें (*nm*) the low sound of laughter

हे (*ind*) a vocative particle O !

हेकड़ी (*nf*) rudeness, arrogance; —दिखलाना to show arrogance

हेच (*a*) insignificant, mean, trifling

हेठा (*a*) mean, low, trivial; —पन meanness, lowness

हेठी disrespect, insult, humiliation; —होना to insult, to humiliate

हेतु (*nm*) purpose, motive, cause, reason

हेमंत (*nm*) cold season, winter

हेम (*nm*) gold; —गिरि the Sumeru mountain

हेमाद्रि (*nm*) the Sumeru mountain

हेय (*a*) fit to be abandoned, insignificant, worthless

हेरना (*v*) to search; to persue; to spy

हेर-फेर (*nm*) disorder; interchange —करना to make unlawful changes; to make amendments

हेराफेरी (*nf*) interchange; manipulations; —करना to interchange; to make unscrupulous changes

हेलमेल (*nm*) intimacy; familiarity; friendship

हैं (*v*) are, plural of है (*ind*) a particle showing wonder or negation

है (*v*) is

हैज़ा (*nm*) cholera

हैरत (*nf*) astonishment, wonder; —अंगेज़ astonishing

हैरान (*a*) disturbed; perplexed, worried

हैरानी (*nf*) disturbance; perplexity, weariness, harassment

हैवा/न an animal; foolish person; —नियत brutality —नी rustic, brutal

हैसियत (*nf*) ability; status; capacity

हों (*v*) plural of the verb होना (in condition)

होंठ (*nm*) the lip, same as ओठ

होठ (*nm*) see ओठ

होड़ (*nf*) bet; race; competition; —लगाना to bet; to compete, to contest

होनहार (*nm*) fate; destiny, ultimate lot; (*a*) promising, hopeful

होना (*v*) to be; to born; to pass; to happen; to occur; to exist; to become

होनी (*nf*) destiny, a would-be incident

होम (*nm*) a burnt offering, a sacrifice

होलिका (*nf*) the festival of Holi; —दहन burning of the heap of wood on Holi

होली (*nf*) a great Hindu festival; —खेलना to throw coloured water on each other

होश (nm) sense, sensibility, consciousness; —आना to come to senses; —करना to be alert; —में आना to come to senses; —रखना to be watchful; —हवास see होश

होशियार (a) attentive; cautious; smart, clever; intelligent, careful

होशियारी (nf) attentiveness; caution; smartness, cleverness; intelligence, carefulness

हौंस (nf) longing

हौआ (nm) a bugbear, a bogey; a word used to frighten children

हौज़, हौद (nm) a reservoir of water etc.

हौल (nm) dread, fear; —दिली terrified; —नाक dreadful

हौले-हौले (adv) slowly; gently; quietly

हौवा (nm) same as हौआ

हौसला (nm) courage; dare; morale; enthusiasm —पस्त होना loss of energy, —अफ़ज़ाई encouragement

ह्रद (nm) a lake, large pond

ह्रस्व (a) small; short; worthless (nm) a short vowel

ह्रास (nm) decrease; decline; deficiency; downfall; —मान decreasing; decaying

ह्रसोन्मुख (a) decaying —ता decadence

ह्वेल (nf) a whale fish

हिन्दी लोकोक्तियाँ

अंत भला तो सब भला—All is well that ends well.

अंधों में कनवा राजा—A figure among cyphers.

अकल बड़ी कि मैंस — Knowledge is more powerful than mere strength.

अधजल गगरी छलकत जाए, भरी गगरिया चुपके जाए।—Deep rivers move with silent majesty. Shallow brooks are noisy.

अपने पूत सबको प्यारा—Every potter praises his own pot.

अपनी इज्ज़त अपने हाथ—Respect yourself and you will be respected.

अपनी गली में कुत्ता भी शेर होता है—Every cock fights best on his own dunghill.

अपने दही को कोई खट्टा नहीं कहता—Every potter praises his own pot.

अपने मुँह मियाँ मिट्ठू—Self-praise is no recommendation.

अभी दिल्ली दूर है—Make not your sauce till you have caught your fish.

अशर्फियाँ लुटें, कोयले पर मुहर—Penny wise, Pound foolish.

आगे दौड़ पीछे छोड़—Haste makes waste.

आदत प्रकृति बन जाती है—Habit is the second nature.

आप भला तो जग भला—Good mind good find.

आप मरे जग लोप—Death's day is Doom's day.

आम के आम गुठली के दाम—Earth's joys and heaven's combined.

आवश्यकता में सभी कुछ उचित है—Necessity knows no law.

इलाज से परहेज अच्छा—Prevention is better than cure.

इस हाथ दे, उस हाथ ले—Early sow early mow.

उतावला सो बावला—Merry in haste repent at leisure.

उतने पाँव पसारिए जितनी चादर होए—Cut your coat according to your cloth.

उधार स्नेह की कैंची है—He that does lend does lose a fore-friend.

उलटे बाँस बरेली को—To carry coal to New Castle.

ऊँची दुकान फीका पकवान—Great cry little wool.

ऊँट के मुँह में जीरा—A drop in the ocean.

एक अनार सौ बीमार—One post and one hundred candidates.

एक पंथ दो काज—To kill two birds with one stone.

एक परहेज़ सौ इलाज—Diet cures more than doctors.

एक म्यान में दो तलवारें नहीं समातीं—Two of a trade seldom agree.

एक हाथ से ताली नहीं बजती—It takes two to make a quarrel.

एक ही थैले के चट्टे-बट्टे—Cast in the same mould.

एका बड़ी शक्ति है—Union is strength.

ओस चाटे प्यास नहीं बुझती—A fog cannot be dispelled by a fan.

औरत की बात का क्या विश्वास—A winter's wind and a woman's heart oftenest change.

कर बुरा हो बुरा—Do evil and look for the like.

कल किसने देखा है—Tomorrow never comes.

कहीं बूढ़े तोते भी पढ़ते हैं—Can you teach an old woman to dance ?

काठ की हँडिया एक ही बार चढ़ती है—It is the silly fish that is caught with the same bait.

कानी के ब्याह को सौ सौ जोखिम—There is many a slip between the cup and the lip.

काम प्यारा होता है चाम नहीं—Handsome is that handsome does.

काम ही कारीगर बनाता है—Practice makes perfect.

कुछ न होने से थोड़ा अच्छा है—Something is better than nothing.

कूड़े के भी दिन फिरते हैं—Every dog has his day.

कोई सुख ऐसा नहीं जिसमें दुख न होय—No joy without alloy.

कौन है जिससे ग़लती नहीं होती—Even a good horse stumbles.

क्या अक्ल चरने गई है—Wits have gone wool-gathering.

क्या बूढ़े तोते भी पढ़ते हैं—An old dog will learn no tricks.

खाने में भी क्या शर्माना—Never feel shy to eat your meal.

खेती खसम सेती—The master's eye makes the mare fat.

गँवार गन्ना न दे भेली दे—Penny wise Pound foolish.

गया वक़्त फिर हाथ नहीं आता—Time and tide wait for no man.

गरीब की जोरू सबकी भाभी—A light purse is a heavy curse.

गरीबी में आटा गीला—Misfortunes seldom come alone.

गेरुए वस्त्रों से साधु नहीं बनता—Cowl does not make a monk.

गेहूँ के साथ घुन भी पिस जाता है—When the buffaloes fight crops suffer.

घर का जोगी जोगना आन गाँव का सिद्ध—A prophet is not honoured in his own country.

घर का भेदी लंका ढाए—Traitors are the worst enemies.

घर की आधी भली, बाहर सारी नहीं—Dry bread at home is better than sweetmeat abroad.

घायल की गति वैद्य क्या जाने—The wearer best knows where the shoe pinches.

चार दिन की चाँदनी फिर अँधेरी रात—A nine day's wonder.

चोर का साथी गिरहकट—Birds of same feather flock together.

चौबे गए छब्बे होने दूबे होकर आए—An ass went to ask for horns but lost his ears.

जब अपनी उतारी तो दूसरे की उतारते क्या देर—Beware of him who regards not his reputation.

जब तक साँस तब तक आस—As long as there is life, there is hope.

ज़बाने ख़ल्क नक्कारा-ए-खुदा—Public voice is God's voice.

ज़र, ज़मीन और औरत लड़ाई की जड़ है—Money, women and land are the roots of all troubles.

ज़रूरत के वक़्त गधे को बाप बनाना पड़ता है—The needy stoops to every-thing however mean.

जल्दी का काम अच्छा नहीं होता—Quick and well do not go well together.

जहाँ चाह वहाँ राह—Where there is a will, there is a way.

जहाँ फूल वहाँ काँटा—No rose without a thorn.

जाको राखे साइयाँ मार सके ना कोय—Whom God keeps, no frost can kill.

जितना धन उतनी चिंता—Much coin, much care.

जिसके पैर न फटी बेवाई, वह क्या जाने पीर पराई—He laughs at scars who never felt a wound.

जैसा आया वैसा गया—Evil got, evil spent.

जैसा देश वैसा भेष—When you go to Rome, do as the Romans do.

जैसा बाप वैसा बेटा—Like father like son.

जैसा राजा वैसी प्रजा—As the king so are the subjects.

जैसी करनी वैसी भरनी—As you sow, so shall you reap.

जैसे काली कामरी चढ़ै न दूजो रंग—Black will take no other hue.

जैसे को तैसा—Tit for tat.

जो आता है अपना सिक्का चलाता है—New lords, new laws.

जो गरजते हैं वे बरसते नहीं—Barking dogs seldom bite.

डंडा सबका पीर—Rod tames every brute.

डौला-डौल की मिट्टी ख़राब—A rolling stone gathers no moss.

तुरत दान महा कल्याण—He gives thrice who gives in a trice.

तेते पाँव पसारिए जेती लाम्बी सौर—Cut your coat according to your cloth.

तेल देखो तेल की धार देखो—See which way the wind blows.

थोथा चना बाजै घना—Empty vessels make much noise.

दान की बछिया का दाँत नहीं देखा जाता—Beggars and borrowers could not be choosers.

दाम करावे काम—Money makes the man run.

दीवाल के भी कान होते हैं—Hedges have eyes and walls have ears.

दुख भोगे बिना सुख कहाँ—No meat without some sweat.

दुर्बल में क्रोध अधिक होता है—A little pot is soon hot.

दुविधा में दोनों गए माया मिली न राम—Between two stools one falls to the ground.

दूध का जला छाछ फूँककर पीता है—A burnt child dreads the fire.

देखिए ऊँट किस करवट बैठता है—Let us see which way the wind blows.

दो मुल्लाओं में मुर्ग़ी हराम—Too many cooks spoil the broth.

धूप में बाल नहीं पकाए हैं—Wisdom is the daughter of old age.

नक्ल में अक्ल क्या!—Imitation has no intelligence.

न नौ नगद न तेरह उधार—A bird in hand is worth two in bush.

न नौ मन तेल होगा न राधा नाचेगी—If the sky falls, we shall gather larks.

नाच न जाने आँगन टेढ़ा—A bad workman quarrels with his tools.

निरन्तर कार्यशील जीतता है—Slow and steady wins the race.

नीम हकीम ख़तर-ए जान—A little knowledge is a dangerous thing.

नेकी कर दरिया में डाल—Do good and cast it into the river.

नौकरी की क्या जड़—Service is no inheritance.

पढ़े न लिखे नाम विद्यासागर—An ignorant man keeping a great fuss.

पहिले अपने को सम्हालो—Sweep before your own door.

पहिले तौलो फिर बोलो—Think before you speak.

पाँचों अँगुलियाँ घी में—Bread is buttered on both sides.

पानी में रहकर मगर से वैर—To live in Rome and strife with the Pope.

पूत कपूत पालने में ही पहचाने जाते हैं—The child is the father of the man.

पेट की खातिर टोकरी उठानी पड़ती है—Want goads to industry.

प्रत्येक कार्य मनुष्य नहीं कर सकता—No living man can do all things.

प्रश्न गेहूँ उत्तर जौ—Your answer is besides the question.

प्राण बचे लाखों पाए—Life is better than bags of gold.

फ़जूल खर्ची पर कमर कसी है—He burns the candles at both ends.

बगल में छुरी मुख में राम राम—A wolf in lamb's skin.

बड़ी है चिन्ता जो जीते जी भी खाती है—Anxiety is the canker of the heart.

बड़े मियाँ सो बड़े मियाँ छोटे मियाँ सुभान अल्ला—The younger is even worse than the elder.

बद अच्छा बदनाम बुरा—A bad man is better than a bad name.

बातों से पेट नहीं भरता—It is money that buys the land.

बिन बुलाये मान नहीं होता—Uninvited guests sit on thorns.

बिना सेवा मेवा नहीं मिलता—No pain, no gain.

बिल्ली ने शेर पढ़ाया बिल्ली को खाने को आया—My foot my tutor.

बीती ताहि बिसार दे—Let the past bury its dead.

बुरा कर हो बुरा—Do evil and look for the like.

बूँद-बूँद से तालाब भर जाता है—Many a pickle makes a mickle.

बेकार से बेगार भली—Forced labour is better than idleness.

बेकारी में शैतानी सूझती है—An idle brain is a workshop of devil.

बोए पेड़ बबूल के आम कहाँ से खाय—Gather thistles and expect pickles.

भय और प्रेम एक जगह नहीं रहते—Dread and affection never exist together.

भलाई से न चूको—Never be weary of doing good.

भाग्य के लिखे को कौन मेट सकता है—What is lotted, cannot be blotted.

भिड़ों के छत्तों को मत छेड़ो—Let sleeping dogs lie.

भूख में चने भी बादाम—Hunger is the best sauce.

भूखा सो रूखा—A hungry man is an angry man.

मक्खी खांड पर गिरती है—Daub your mouth with honey and you will get plenty of flies.

मरता क्या न करता—The desperate man does all things.

मरे-मुर्दे मत उखाड़ो—Let by-gones be by-gones.

महँगा रोए एक बार, सस्ता रोए बार-बार—The cheaper buyer takes no meat.

माया को माया मिले कर-कर लम्बे हाथ—Money begets money.

माया बादल की छाया—Riches have wings.

माले-मुफ्त दिले बेरहम (हराम का माल बेकार चला जाता है)—Ill-got, ill-spent.

मित्र वही जो समय पर काम आए—A friend in need is a friend indeed.

मुँह पर झूठ नहीं बोला जाता—Face to face, the teeth comes out.

मुल्ला की दौड़ मस्जिद तक—The priest goes no further from the church.

मेहनत का फल मीठा होता है—No roses without thorns.

मौन आधी स्वीकृति है—Silence is half consent.

यथा राजा तथा प्रजा—As king, so are his subjects.

यहाँ तुम्हारी दाल नहीं गल सकती—Your schemes won't take here.

राई को पर्वत बनाना—To make a mountain of a mole hill.

राम राम जपना, पराया माल अपना—A robber in the garb of a saint.

लातों के देवता बातों से नहीं मानते—Rod is the logic of fools.

लालच बुरी बला है—No vice like avarice.

लोहे को लोहा काटता है—Diamond cuts diamond.

वीरता का काम न चाहे नाम—Good deeds need no show.

वे दिन गये जब जनाब फ़ाख़्ता उड़ाते थे—Gone is the goose that was golden.

शक्करख़ोरे को ईश्वर शक्कर देता है—Spend and God will send.

सबको अपना ही मतलब प्यारा है—Every one knows his interest best.

समझदार को इशारा काफ़ी—Word to the wise is enough.

समय को दुर्लभ जानो—Make hay while the Sun shines.

साझे की हँड़िया चौराहे पर फूटती है—A common horse is worst shod.

सारा जाता देखिए आधा लीजे बाँट—Better give the wool than the whole sheep.

सावन के अंधे को हरा ही हरा दिखाई देता है—Everything looks yellow to a jaundiced eye.

स्याना कौवा कूड़े पर—Positive men are often in error.

हथेली पर सरसों नहीं जमती—Rome was not built in a day.

हरफ़न मौला, हरफ़न अधूरा—Jack of all trades and master of none.

होनहार बिरवान के होत चीकने पात—Coming events cast their shadows before.

हिंदी मुहावरे

अंग-अंग मुस्कराना to be beaming and buoyant.

अंग फूले न समाना to be in a rapture.

अंग लगाना to embrace.

अंगारे उगलना to be fierce in speech.

अंगारे बरसना to be excessively hot (weather).

अंगारों पर पैर रखना to invite trouble.

अंगारों पर लोटना to burn within (on account of jealousy).

अँगूठा दिखाना to reject forcibly.

अंगूर खट्टे होना to decry something that has proved inaccessible.

अंतिम साँसें गिनना to be breathing one's last.

अंधा होना to be lost to realities.

अंधे की लाठी a helpless man's only support.

अँधेरे में छलाँग लगाना to leap into the dark.

अँधेरे में रखना to keep in dark.

अक़्ल के घोड़े दौड़ाना to indulge in mental gymnasium.

अक़्ल चरने जाना to be out of one's head.

अक़्ल ठिकाने लगाना to set one right.

अक़्ल पर पत्थर to be out of one's head.

अधर में लटकना to hang in mid-air.

अनसुना करना not to pay any attention.

अपना-सा मुँह लेकर रह जाना to face discomfiture.

अमली जामा पहनाना to put into practice.

अरमान रह जाना not to have one's aspirations materialised.

आँख का तारा darling.

आँख का पानी उतर जाना to be lost to shame.

आँख चुराना to avoid being sighted by.

आँख बदलना to withdraw favour or regard all of a sudden.

आँख लड़ाना to meet stare with stare.

आँखें दिखाना to look at angrily.

आँखें बिछाना to give a very cordial welcome.

आँखों पर परदा पड़ना to be under an illusion.

आँखों में धूल झोंकना to cheat.

आकाश-पाताल एक करना to make a Herculean attempt.

आकाश से बातें करना to be as lofty as the sky.

आग बरसाना to bombard.

आग में घी डालना to add fuel to the fire.

आगे-पीछे कोई न होना to be without any kith and kin.

आटे के साथ घुन पिसना to undergo an undeserved.

आटे-दाल का भाव मालूम होना to be confronted with unwelcome realities of practical life.

आड़े वक्त पर काम आना to do a good turn when one is in difficulty.

आपे से बाहर होना to lose self-control.

आफ़त मोल लेना to own unnecessary botheration.

आवाज़ कसना to pass unwelcome remarks.

आशाओं पर पानी फिरना to have one's hopes shattered.
आस टूटना to be disappointed.
आसन डोलना to be allured or tempted.
आस बँधाना to extend assurances.
आसमान पर थूकना to puff against the wind.
आसमान सिर पर उठा लेना to create a tumult.
आसमान से बातें करना to vie with the sky.
आस लगाना to look hopefully to.

इधर-उधर की हाँकना to gossip.
इधर की उधर लगाना to indulge in back-biting.

उड़न छू होना to disappear all of a sudden.
उन्नीस-बीस होना to be slightly better or worse.
उफ़ न करना to endure quietly.
उम्मीदों पर पानी फेरना to dash all hopes to the ground.
उलटा पाठ पढ़ाना to misguide.
ऊँचा सुनना to be hard of hearing.
ऊपर होना to be senior in status or office.

एक न चलना all efforts to prove in vain.
एहसान मानना to feel obliged.

ऐसी की तैसी करना let it go to hell.

ओखली में सिर देना to take up a difficult challenge.

कंधा देना to lend a shoulder in carrying a dead body.
कंधे से कंधा छिलना to be over-crowded.
कंधे से कंधा मिलाना to lend full co-operation.
कंधों पर उठाना to give a rousing welcome.
कच्चा पड़ना to prove ineffective.
कच्ची गोली नहीं खेलना to have learnt the tricks of the trade.
कटे पर नमक छिड़कना to add insult to injury.
कठघरे में खड़ा करना to bring before the bar.
कदम उठाना to make progress.
कन्नी काटना to fight shy of.

कबाड़ा होना to be ruined.
कमर कसना to be all set for action.
कमर झुकना to become old.
कमर तोड़ना to break one's back.
कमर सीधी करना to relax for a while.
करम फूटना to be unfortunate.
करवट बदलते रात बीतना to spend a restless night.
कलाई खुलना to be exposed.
कलम तोड़ना to work wonders in (one's) writing.
कलम फेरना to strike out or delete what is written.
कलेजा कड़ा करना to prepare oneself for a shock.
कलेजा ठंडा होना to be fulfilled.
कलेजा मुँह को आना to be restless on account of grief.
कलेजे पर साँप लोटना to be struck with jealousy.
कलेजे से लगाना to embrace fondly.
कसर न उठा रखना to leave no stone unturned.
काँटे बोना to sow seeds of misfortune.
काठ का कलेजा होना to be hard-hearted.
काठ मार जाना to be stunned.
कान खड़े करना to get alert.
कान धरना to listen attentively.
कान न देना to turn a deaf ear to.
कान पर जूँ न रेंगना to turn a deaf ear to.
काम तमाम करना to put an end to.
काम रखना to mind one's (own) business.
कायल करना to convince (by argument).
कायल होना to be convinced.
किए-कराए पर पानी फेरना to undo what has been achieved.
किया-कराया मिट्टी में मिलाना to undo what has been accomplished.
कुएँ में धकेलना to ruin the life of.
कुछ कहना to show anger on.
कुछ न सूझना to be in a fog.
कुर्सी तोड़ना to occupy a chair idly.
कैंची-सी ज़बान चलना to talk nineteen to the dozen.
कोई कसर उठा न रखना to leave no stone unturned.
कोठे पर बैठना to turn into a prostitute.
कौड़ी के मोल damn cheap.

खतरे से खेलना to play with fire.

खरी-खरी सुनाना to call a spade a spade.

खरी-खोटी सुनाना to take to tasks.

ख़स्ता हाल हो जाना to go to grass.

खाक में मिलना to fall to the ground.

खाट से लगना to be reduced to skeleton.

खाते में डालना to debit to the account (of).

खाने के लाले पड़ना to be hard up for each meal.

(अपनी) खिचड़ी अलग पकाना to go one's own queer way.

खिलवाड़ करना to treat lightly.

खिल्ली उड़ाना to ridicule.

खुलकर खेलना to indulge in misdeeds openly.

खुशी से पाँव ज़मीन पर न पड़ना to be over-whelmed with joy.

खून चूसना to exploit.

खून सफ़ेद होना to become inhumane.

खेल बिगड़ना to have a business spoilt.

गड़े मुर्दे उखाड़ना to rake up the long lost past.

गत बनाना to give a thorough beating.

गधे को बाप बनाना to flatter a fool for expediency.

गप मारना to indulge in boastful gossip.

गरदन नापना to insult.

गरदन फँसना to be involved in a difficulty.

गला दबाना to exercise undue pressure.

गवारा करना to tolerate.

गाँठ बाँधना to make a note of.

गाली खाना to endure foul language.

गुज़र जाना to pass away.

गुज़र होना to sustain.

गुस्सा थूक देना to forgive and forget.

गोद सूनी होना to lose the only child.

गोली मारना to ignore.

घड़ियाँ गिनना to await keenly.

घर के घर रहना to be even in a bargain.

घर भरना to amass wealth.

घात लगाना to lie in ambush.

घाव पर नमक छिड़कना to add insult to injury.

घी-शक्कर होना to become inseparably.

घोड़े बेचकर सोना to go into a deep care-free sleep.

चकमा खाना to be tricked.

चकमा देना to play a trick.

चपेट में आना to sustain injury/loss.

चमड़ी उधेड़ना to beat bare.

चलता बनना to slip away.

चाँद-सा मुखड़ा lovely face.

चार आँखें करना to come face to face.

चार सौ बीस deceitful.

चिड़िया का दूध a non-existent commodity.

चीं बोलना to accept defeat.

चूल्हे में जाना to go to hell.

चेहरे पर हवाइयाँ उड़ना to be **dispirited.**

छक्के छुड़ाना to put out of gear.

छप्पर फाड़कर देना to give as a windfall.

छाती ठंडी करना to assuage one's feelings.

छाती ठोककर कहना to take a pledge.

छाती पर पत्थर रखना to endure patiently.

छाती पर साँप लोटना to burn with jealousy.

छाती से लगाना to embrace.

छू-मंतर होना to vanish.

ज़ख्म पर नमक छिड़कना to add insult to injury.

ज़बान पर ताला लगाना to be rendered speechless.

ज़बान हिलाना to make an utterance.

ज़मीन चटाना to throw flat.

जले पर नमक छिड़कना to add insult to injury.

जान के लाले पड़ना to be under the shadow of death.

जान छुड़ाना to get rid of.

जान निकालना to be in great agony.

जान पर खेलना to put one's life in peril.

जान में जान आना to feel relieved.

जी खट्टा होना to be disgusted.

जी चुराना to shirk work.

जी छोटा होना to lose heart.
जी बहलाना to recreate.
जोर पर होना to be in full swing.

झंडा गाड़ना to achieve a victory.

टका-सा जवाब देना to say a flat 'no'.
टक्कर लेना to set one's face against.
टुकड़ों पर पलना (किसी के) to thrive on leavings.
टेक निभाना to fulfil one's resolve.
टोपी उछालना to expose publicly.

ठंडी साँस लेना to heave a sigh.
ठोकर खाते फिरना to wander aimlessly.

डंड बजाना to idle away time.
डकार न लेना to assimilate another's due quietly.
डकार लेना to assimilate another's due.
डेरा डालना to come to stay.
डोरे डालना to allure.

ढिंढोरा पीटना to proclaim aloud.
ढेर हो जाना to pass away.

तकदीर खुलना to be in luck.
तकदीर फूटना to be under the spell of ill-luck.
तकल्लुफ़ में पड़ना to be formal.
तड़ी मारना to give oneself airs.
तबियत आना to fall in love with.
तलवे चाटना to fawn upon.
तशरीफ ले जाना to depart.
तहलका मचाना to cause a havoc.
ताना मारना to taunt.
तारीख़ पड़ना a date to be fixed.
तारे गिनना to keep awake the whole night.
नालू से जीभ न लगाना to go on chattering.
तिनका तक न तोड़ना not to stir even a finger.

तिल का ताड़ करना to make a mountain of a mole.
तीर निशाने पर बैठना to hit the mark.
तीसमारखाँ a sham hero.
तुक होना to make a sense.
तुक्का लगाना to take a chance.
तूफ़ान खड़ा करना to work havoc.
तेवर बदलना to frown.
तैयारी पर होना to be in form.
तैश में आना to be provoked.
तोता पढ़ाना to teach over and over again.
तौबा करना to vow never to repeat.

थककर चूर होना to be dead tired.
थप्पड़ जड़ना to slap on the cheek.
थाह लेना to unearth the reality.
थूककर चाटना to eat one's own words.

दत्तचित्त होकर सुनना to be all ears.
दबी ज़बान से कहना to say in a hushed manner.
दबाव डालना to influence.
दम घुटना to be suffocated.
दम घोटना to suffocate.
दम टूटना to be exhausted.
दम न होना to have no guts.
दम निकलना to pass away.
दम लगाना to smoke.
दमड़ी भी न होना (पास में) to be penniless.
दर-दर की ठोकरें खाना to knock at one door after another.
दर्शन दुर्लभ होना to be seen rarely.
दाँत खट्टे करना to force the enemy into a tight corner.
दाँत तोड़ना to render powerless.
दाँतों तले उँगली दबाना to stand amazed.
दामन फैलाना to beg.
दाल न गलना to affect little.
दाल में काला होना to have something wrong.
दिन को तारे दिखाना to put in a very tight corner.
दिन को रात कहना to reverse the truth.

दिन दूना रात चौगुना बढ़ना to grow by leaps and bounds.

दिनों का फेरा run of good luck to be changed.

दिमाग आसमान पर होना to be very much conceited.

दिमाग की खिड़कियाँ खुली होना to have an open mind.

दिमाग लड़ाना to exercise one's brain.

दिल खट्टा होना to feel repulsed.

दिल छोटा करना to feel dejected.

दिल बाग-बाग होना to be extremely delighted.

दिल में घर करना to be taken to heart.

दिल से निकाल देना to forget and forgive.

दुआ देना to wish well.

दुआ मांगना to pray for somebody's well-being.

दुकान उठाना a business to be closed for good.

दुकान जमाना to firmly establish a business.

दुनिया की हवा लगना to acquire worldly wiles.

दुनिया से कूच कर जाना to pass away.

दुम दबाकर भागना to turn tails.

दुःख का पहाड़ टूटना to be in terrible distress.

दूसरों का मुँह ताकना to look to others for help.

दृश्य देखते बनना a sight worth seeing.

दृष्टि फेरना to withdraw one's favour.

दृष्टि रखना to keep uner observation.

देह में आग लगना to get enraged.

दो की चार सुनाना to pay in the same coin along with interest.

दो रोटी कमाना to earn one's livelihood.

दोहरी चाल चलना to play a double game.

धक से रह जाना to be stunned.

धक्के खाना to be tossed about.

धाक जमना to command overwhelming influence.

धूप में बाल सफेद होना to age without experience.

धूल चटाना to knock down.

धूल फाँकना to wander without a job.

धूल में लट्ठ मारना to make a random effort.

धोखा देना to play false.

धौंस जमाना to bluster.

ध्यान में न लाना to ignore.

ध्यान में उतरना to forget.

नकेल डालना to tame.
नज़र करना to offer.
नज़र दौड़ाना to look around.
नज़र बचाना to try to evade.
नज़रों से गिरना to be in bad books of.
नथने फुलाना to be in rage.
नशा उतरना vanity to be knocked off.
नस-नस पहचानना to know through and through.
नसीब सीधा होना to be in luck.
नाक काटना to defame.
नाक बचाना to safeguard one's honour.
नाक में दम करना to harass.
नाक रखना to save one's honour.
नाच नचाना to harass.
नानी मर जाना to feel lost.
नाम आसमान पर होना to be very famous.
नाम कमाना to acquire renown.
नाम डुबाना to lose one's reputation.
निगाहें चार होना to exchange glances.
निशाना बनाना to aim at.
निशाना बाँधना to take an aim.
नींद-भर सोना to have one's fill of sleep.
नींद हराम करना to disturb one's sleep.
नुकसान पहुँचना to suffer a loss.
नुकसान भरना to make good the loss.
नौ दो ग्यारह होना to turn tails.

पत्ता न हिलना everything around to be still.
पत्थर पिघलना a stony heart to be moved.
पर काट देना to render ineffective.
पलड़ा भारी होना to have a stronger case.
पसीने-पसीने होना to perspire profusely.
पहाड़ से टक्कर लेना to cross swords with a giant.
पाँव फूँक-फूँककर रखना to advance every step with care.

पाँव फैलाकर सोना to enjoy a carefree sleep.

पानी उतारना to disgrace.

पानी-पानी होना to be overwhelmed with shame.

पाप कटना to get rid of.

पास तक न फटकना to keep away absolutely.

पासा पलटना the tide to be turned.

पीछे पड़ना to harass continuously.

पीठ दिखाना to flee from the battle field.

पेट काटना to save money by imposing self-restraint.

पेट की आग बुझाना to fill the stomach.

पेट गिरना to commit abortion.

पेट पालना to earn one's living somehow.

पेश आना to treat.

पैर जमना to consolidate one's position.

पैर भारी होना to be in the family way.

प्राण हथेली पर लिए फिरना to face all sorts of risk.

प्राणों से हाथ धोना to lose life.

फंदे में पड़ना to be caught in a trick.

फूट-फूटकर रोना to weep bitterly.

फेर में पड़ना, निन्यानबे के to be unseemly crazy to amass wealth.

बखिया उधेड़ना to expose thoroughly.

बगलें झाँकना to be rendered witless.

बगलें बजाना to be exceptionally happy.

बदन में आग लगना to fret and fume.

बला मोल लेना to own up a trouble.

बहती गंगा में हाथ धोना to make hay while the Sun shines.

बाछें खिलना to be very happy.

बात न पूछना to care nothing for.

बात बनाना to talk much.

बातों में आना to be taken in.

बाल धूप में पकाना to age without experience.

बाल-बाल बचना to have a hair-breadth escape.

बेड़ा पार होना to achieve the end.
बोरिया समेटना to leave.

भाग जागना to have a run of good luck.
भाग फूटना to have a run of ill-luck.
भौं सिकोड़ना to frown.

मनसा वाचा कर्मणा through the mind, speech and deed.
मसें भीगना to be on the threshold of youth.
माँग उजड़ना to be widowed.
मिट्टी पलीद होना to be in a miserable plight.
मिट्टी में मिलाना to be ruined.
मिट्ठू बनना, अपने मुँह to indulge in self-praise.
मुँह काला करना to be disgraced.
मुँह खोलना to speak out.
मुँह देखते रह जाना to be taken aback.
मुँह फेरना to abstain (from).
मुँह बनाना to look displeased.
मुँह में ज़बान न रखना to be tongue tied.
मुट्ठी गरम करना to bribe.
मूँछ नीची होना to be disgraced.
मूँछ पर ताव देना to care for nothing in the world.
मूसलचंद, दाल भात में a wrong man in a wrong place.

यकीन आना to feel assured.
यकीन दिलाना to assure.
येन-केन-प्रकारेण by hook or by crook.

रंग उतरना to fade.
रंग चढ़ना to be in high spirits.
रंग जमना to be held in esteem.
रंग फीका पड़ना to fade out.
रंग में भंग करना to mar a happy occasion.
रग-रग से वाकिफ़ होना to know through and through.

रगों में खून दौड़ना to be excited.
रफूचक्कर होना to make good one's escape.
राई का पहाड़ बनाना to make a mountain 'of a mole.
राशि मिलना agreeably inclined to each other by temperament.
रोयें खड़े होना to be thrilled.

लंबी-चौड़ी हाँकना to talk tall.
लंबी तानकर सोना to enjoy a carefree sleep.
लकीर पीटना to follow the tradition.
लगाना-बुझाना to back-bite.
लहू पीना to trouble constantly.
लहू सफ़ेद हो जाना to become inhumane.
लाड़ लड़ाना fondle.
लेना एक न देना दो for no purpose at all.
लेने के देने पड़ना to lose while expecting to profit.

वक़्त-बेवक़्त at all times.
वचन पालना to implement one's promise.
वचन भंग करना to break a promise.
वास्ता देना to invoke the name of.
वास्ता पड़ना to be concerned with.
विपत्ति मोल लेना to own up avoidable calamity.
वीरगति को प्राप्त होना to achieve a heroic end.

शंख फूँकना to make a declaration of war.
शक्ल न दिखाना not to turn up.
शक्ल बनाना to wear a strange look.
शान मारना to boast.
शान में बट्टा लगना a fair name to be tarnished.
शामत आना to be in the grip of misfortune.
शेर होना to be encouraged too far.

सब्ज़-बाग दिखलाना to arouse high hopes in vain.
सर करना to conquer.

साँप सूँघ जाना to be rendered still.

साथ देना to keep company with.

साथ निबाहना to continue.

साथ लेकर डूबना to involve someone in a sure tragedy.

साफ़ छूटना to go scot free.

सामने आना to confront.

साये की तरह साथ-साथ रहना to shadow somebody.

सिट्टी-पिट्टी गुम हो जाना to be nervous.

सिर उठाना to rebel.

सिर ऊँचा करना to be proud.

सिर खाना to go on bothering.

सिर चकराना to feel giddy.

सिर चढ़ना to take too much liberty.

सिर थोपना to impose (upon).

सिर न उठाने देना to give no opportunity to rise against.

सिर पर आसमान उठाना to create a havoc.

सिर पर चढ़ाना to pamper a bit too much.

सिर पर पाँव रखकर भागना to show a clean pair of heels.

सिर पर सवार रहना to keep bullying.

सिर पैर न होना to make no sense.

सिर फिरना to be out of senses.

सिर लेना to own up.

सुख लूटना to enjoy.

सुहाग उजड़ना to be widowed.

सेहरा बँधना to get the credit for.

स्वाहा करना to ruin.

हँसकर बात उड़ाना to laugh away.

हँसी उड़ाना to make fun of.

हक पर लड़ना to fight for one's right.

हक मारना to usurp one's due.

हड्डी-पसली एक करना to thrash thoroughly.

हरा होना to be gay.

हराम कर देना to make (things) impossible.

हलका पड़ना to prove lesser.

हवा के घोड़े पर सवार होना to be in a great hurry.

हवा खाना to go for a walk.

हवा बँधना a reputation to be earned.

हवा से बातें करना to be moving at a terrible speed.

हवा हो जाना to disappear.

हस्ती होना to be existent.

हाँ में हाँ मिलाना to keep on flattering.

(किसी पर) हाथ उठाना to beat.

हाथ उतरना the arm-bone to be dislocated.

हाथ ऊँचा रहना to have an upper hand.

हाथ कट जाना to be helpless.

हाथ खाली न होना to be busy.

हाथ खींचना to withdraw support.

हाथ खुलना to be a spendthrift.

(किसी काम में) हाथ डालना to undertake a work.

हाथ तंग होना to be tight.

हाथ धो बैठना to lose.

हाथ-पाँव चलना to capable to work

हाथ-पाँव बचाना to keep oneself secure.

हाथ फैलाना to beg.

हाथ बँटाना to co-operate.

हाथ बिकाना to be a slave to.

हाथ मँजना to acquire a fineness (in doing a work).

हाथ में हाथ देना to give away in marriage.

हाथ से जाना to lose.

हाथ होना to have a hand in.

हाय पड़ना a curse to come true.

हिसाब देना to render accounts.

हिसाब साफ़ करना to clear off the account.

हेकड़ी जताना to show arrogance.

होश सँभालना to come of age.

वर्गीकृत सामान्य शब्दावली

अन्न तथा भोज्य पदार्थ

अचार - pickle
अरारूट - arrowroot
आटा - meal
कढ़ी - curry
कहवा - coffee
कुल्फ़ी - ice-cream
गेहूँ - wheat
घी - clarified butter
चटनी - sauce
चना - gram
चपाती - cake
चावल - rice
चाय - tea
चीनी - sugar
जलपान - breakfast
जई का आटा - oatmeal
जौ - barley
तरकारी - vegetable
तिल - sesame
तेल - oil

दलिया - mash
दही - curd
दाल - pulse
दिन का भोजन - lunch
दूध - milk
धान - paddy
पनीर - cheese
पावरोटी - loaf
बरफ़ - ice
बाजरा - millet
बिसकुट - biscuit
भुट्टा - maize
भोज - feast
मकई - maize
मक्खन - butter
मट्ठा - whey, butter milk
मलाई - cream
मांस गाय का - beef
मांस बकरे का - mutton
मांस सुअर का - pork
मिठाई - sweetmeat
मिश्री - sugar-candy

मुरब्बा - jam
मूँग - kidney-bean
मैदा - flour (fine)
मेथी - fenugreek
रात का भोजन - supper, dinner
रेंड़ी - castor-seed
रोटी - bread
शक्कर - loaf-sugar
शर्बत - syrup
शराब - wine
शहद - honey
सरसों - mustard

औजार

आरी - saw
करघा - loom
कुतुबनुमा - compass
कुदाली - shovel
कुल्हाड़ी - axe
कैंची - scissors
कोल्हू (तेली) - oil mill
कोल्हू (ईख पेरने का) - sugar mill
गुनिया - trying-angle
गोलची - gauge
चोसा - rasp
छुरा - razor
छैनी - cold chisel
डिबरी - nut
तराजू - balance
परकाल - divider
पिचकारी - syringe
पेंच - bolt
पेंचकस - screw-driver
फावड़ा - spade
फर्मा (मोची का) - last
बरमा - auger

बरमी - drill
बंसी - fishing-angle
रंदा (छोटा) - trying-plane
रंदा (बड़ा) - jack-plane
रेती - file
रंभा - lever
लंगर - anchor
सबरी - jemmy
सिल्ली - hone
साहुल - plumbline
हथकल - spanner
हथौड़ी - hammer
हल - plough
हल का फाल - ploughshare
हाथ बाँक - hand-vice

खनिज पदार्थ

अभ्रक - mica
काँसा - bell-metal
कोयला (पत्थर का) - coal
खड़िया - chalk
खान - mine
गंधक - sulphur
गेरू - ochre
चकमक पत्थर - flint
चाँदी - silver
जस्ता - zinc
ताँबा - copper
तूतिया - blue vitriol
पक्का लोहा (इस्पात) - steel
पारा - mercury
पीतल - brass
राँगा - tin
शिलाजीत - bitumen
सुरमा - antimony
संखिया - arsenic

सज्जीखार - natron
सिंगरिफ - cinnabar
सीसा - lead
सफेदा - white lead
सिंदूर - vermilion
संगमरमर - marble
लोहा - iron

गृहस्थी की सामग्री

अलमारी - almirah
कनस्टर - canister
कंघी - comb
कुरसी - chair
ओखली - mortar
गगरा - jar
चकला - pastry-board
चटाई - mat
चमचा - spoon
चलनी - sieve
चादर - bed-sheet
चाभी (ताली) - key
चारपाई - bed
चिमटा - tongs
चिमनी - chimney
चूल्हा - stove
छड़ी - stick
छाता - umbrella
टेबुल - table
टोकरी - basket
डिब्बा - box
ढकना - lid
तंदूर - oven
तकिया - pillow
तराजू - balance
तार - wire
ताला - lock

तिजोरी - safe
थाली - plate
दर्पण - mirror
दियासलाई - match
पलंग - bedstead
पीकदानी - spittoon
बक्स - box
बढ़नी (झाड़ु) - mroomstick
बत्ती - wick
बर्तन - pot
बालटी - bucket
बेलन - pastry-roller
बेंच - bench
बोतल - bottle
मथानी - churn
मोमबत्ती - candle
रकाबी - dish
रस्सा - rope
रस्सी - string
लोटा - a small round metal pot
शीशी - phial
संदूक - box
सलाई - match
साबुन - soap
सिंगारदान - casket
सुराही - pitcher, jug
सुई - needle

कीड़े, मकोड़े इत्यादि

अजगर - boa
कछुवा - turtle
केंचुवा - earthworm
केकड़ा - crab
खटमल - bug
गिरगिट - chameleon
घोंघा - snail

छिपकली - lizard
जहर - poison
चींटी - ant
जुगनू - firefly
जूँ - louse
जोंक - leech
झींगुर - cricket
टिड्डी - locust
तितली - butterfly
बिच्छू - scorpion
मछली - fish
दीमक - white ant
मधुमक्खी (नर) - drone
मधुमक्खी (मादा) - bee
मेढक - frog
मेढक का बच्चा - tadpole
फन - hood
मकड़ा - spider
मकड़े का जाला - web
मक्खी - fly
मगर - crocodile
मच्छर - mosquito
बर्रे - wasp
रेशम का कीड़ा - silkworm
साँप - snake
शंख - conch
सीप - oyster

पक्षी

अबाबील - Swallow
अंडा - egg
उल्लू - owl
कठफोड़वा - wood-pecker
कबूतर - pigeon
काला (डोम) कौवा - raven

कोयल - cuckoo
कौवा - crow
गरुड़ - eagle
गिद्ध - vulture
गौरैया - sparrow
घोंसला - nest
चमगादड़ - bat
चील - kite
चोंच - beak
डैना - wing
तीतर - partridge
नीलकंठ - magpie
पर - feather
पिंजड़ा - cage
पंख - plume
पंडुकी - dove
बतख़ - drake
बतख़ी का बच्चा - duckling
बतख़ी - duck
बुलबुल - nightingale
बया - weaverbird
बटेर - quail
बाज़ - falcon
मुर्गा - cock
मुर्गी - hen
मुसैंचा - eagle
मुर्ग - fowl
मुर्गी का बच्चा - chicken
मोर - peacock
मोरनी - peahen
लवा - lark
शुतुमुर्ग़ - ostrich
सारस - crane
सुग्गा - parrot
हिरामन तोता - macaw
हंस - swan

पशु

ऊँट - (camel)
कुत्ता - dog
कुतिया - bitch
खच्चर - mule
खरगोश - rabbit
खरहा - hare
गदहा - ass
गाय - cow
गिलहरी - squirrel
गैंड़ा - rhinoceros
घोड़ा - horse
घोड़ी - mare
चीता - panther
चूहा - mouse
छछूंदर - mole
जंगली सुअर - boar
झबरा कुत्ता - spaniel
टट्टू - pony
तेंदुआ - leopard
नेवला - mongoose
दुम - tail
पशु - beast
पंजा - claw
पिल्ला - puppy
बकरा - he-goat
बकरी - she-goat
बकरी का बच्चा - kid
बछड़ा - calf
बछिया - she-calf
बछेड़ा - colt
बिल्ली - cat
बिल्ली का बच्चा - kitten
बंदर - monkey
बैल - ox
बारहसिंगा - stag

बारहसिंगी - hind
भालू - bear
भेड़ - sheep
भैंसा - buffalo
माँद - den
मेढ़ा - ram
मेमना - lamb
मूसा - rat
मृग - stag
लोमड़ी - fox
लकड़बग्घा - hyena
लंगूर - ape
व्याघ्र - tiger
शिकारी कुत्ता - hound
साँड़ - bull
सियार - jackal
सिंह - lion
सींग - horn
सुअर - hog pig
सुअरी - swine
हरिन - deer
हाथी - elephant

फल-फूल और वनस्पतियाँ

अखरोट - chestnut
अनन्नास - pine-apple
अनार - pomegranate
आम - mango
आलू - potato
अंगूर - grape
अंजीर - fig
इमली - tamarind
ककड़ी - cucumber
कटहल - Jack-fruit
कमल - lotus
कमलिनी - lily

कद्दू - pumpkin
काजू - cashewnut
कुकुरमुत्ता - mushroom
केला - plantain
खजूर - date
ख़रबूजा - musk melon
खीरा - gourd
खुबानी - apricot
गन्ना - sugar cane
गाजर - carrot
गुलमेहँदी - balsam
गुलबहार - daisy
गुलाब - rose
गेंदा - marigold
घास - grass
चंपा - magnolia
चकोतरा - citron
चमेली - jasmine
चिड़चिड़ा - snake-gourd
चुकंदर - beet
जामुन - blackberry
जैतून - olive
तमाखू - tobacco
तरबूज़ - watermelon
दाख - currant
नारियल - coconut
नारंगी - orange
नाशपाती - pear
नींबू - lemon
पपीता - papaya
पान - betel
पालक - spinach
पिस्ता - pistachio
पुदीना - mint
पोस्ता - poppy
पौधा - plant
प्याज़ - onion

फूलगोभी - cauliflower
बादाम - almond
बनफ़शा - violet
बंदगोभी - cabbage
बबूल - acacia
बेर - plum
बेंत - cane
बैंगन - brinjal
भिंडी - lady finger
मिरचा - chilli
मुनक्का - raisin
मूंगफली - ground nut
मूली - radish
मेहँदी - myrtle
रुई - cotton
लता - creeper
लहसुन - garlic
शरीफा - custard apple
शहतूत - mulberry
शकरकंद - sweet-potato
साबूदाना - sago
सुपारी - betel-nut
सेब - apple
सेम - bean

भवन तथा इनके सामान

अटारी - attic
अनाथालय - orphanage
अँगीठी - fireplace
आँगन - courtyard
ईंट - brick
कमरा - room
क़िला - fort
खपरैल - tile
खलिहान - granary
खिड़की - window

खूँटी - peg	मीनार - steeple
खंड - storey	मेहराब - arch
गिरजाघर - church	रसोईघर - kitchen
गुंबज - cupola	शहतीर - rafter
चबूतरा - platform	सराय - inn
चूना - lime	स्नानगृह - bathroom
चौखट - door-frame	सिरमिट - cement
छड़ - bar	सीढ़ी - stair
छत - roof	
छप्पर - shed	**मसाले और औषधियाँ**
जाली (पत्थर की) - lattice	
ज़ंज़ीर - chain	अजवाइन का सत्त - thymol
झरोखा - peep-hole	अदरक - ginger
झोपड़ी - cottage	अफ़ीम - opium
ड्योढ़ी - ante-chamber	इलायची - cardamom
तहख़ाना - cell	कपूर - camphor
दरवाज़ा - door	कस्तूरी - musk
दफ़्तर - office	काली मिर्च - black-pepper
देहलीज़ - corridor	केसर - saffron
धुवाँकश - chimney	खमीर - yeast
नाबदान - drain	कत्था - catechu
नींव - foundation	चंदन - sandal
पत्थर - stone	जायफल - nutmeg
परनाला - gargoyle	जावित्री - mace
पलस्तर - plaster	तुलसी - basil
पाठशाला - school	तेजपात - cassia
पागलख़ाना - lunatic asylum	दालचीनी - cinnamon
पुस्तकालय - library	फिटकिरी - alum
पेशाबख़ाना - urinal	नमक - salt
फ़र्श - floor	मजीठ - madder
बरसाती - portico	माजूफल - gall-nut
बरामदा - verandah	मिर्च - pepper
बोरसी - fireplace	रीठा - soap-nut
बंगला - bungalow	लवंग - cloves
मंदिर - temple	शोरा - saltpetre
मसजिद - mosque	सज्जीखार - alkali
महल - palace	सुपारी - betel-nut

सिरका - vinegar
संखिया - arsenic
सोंठ - dry ginger
सौंफ़ - aniseed
साबूदाना - sago
हल्दी - turmeric
हींग - asafoetida

युद्ध सामग्री

अणुबम - atom bomb
आक्रमण (चढ़ाई) - aggression
आक्रमण(धावा) - attack, offensive
कवच - armour
कारतूस - cartridge
खाई - trench
गोली-बारूद इत्यादि - ammunition
गोली - bullet
घरेलू युद्ध - civil war
घुड़सवार सेना - cavalry
घेरा - seige
जल सेना - navy
जंगी जहाज़ - battleship
तोप - cannon
तोप का गोला - cannon-ball
धमाके से फटने वाला बम - explosive bomb
नाकाबंदी - blockade
पनडुब्बी - submarine
परमाणु युद्ध - atomic warfare
पेंदी तोड़ गोला फेंकने वाली नौका - torpedo-boat
पैदल सेना, स्थल सेना - land force
प्रस्थान (कूच) - expedition
बम - bomb
बम वर्षा - bombardment
बमवर्षक विमान - bomber

बारूद - gunpowder
बारूदख़ाना - magazine
भोजन सामग्री - provisions
मनोबल - morale
युद्ध - battle, war
युद्ध के शस्त्र - armaments
युद्ध कौशल - strategy
युद्ध विराम - cease-fire
युद्ध बंदी - prisoners of war
रंगरूट की भर्ती - recruitment
रक्षा - defence
रक्षा कोष - defence fund
लड़ाकू वायुयान - fighter plane
विद्रोह - mutiny, rebellion
विमान भेदी तोप - anti-aircraft gun
विध्वंसक पोत - destroyer
संधि - treaty
सेना - army, troops
सेनागति - operation
सेनापति - commander general, commander-in-chief
शत्रु - enemy
शीत युद्ध - cold war

रत्न और आभूषण

अँगूठी - ring
कंगन - bracelet
कड़ा - bangle
कड़ी - link
कफ़ का बटन - stud
कर्ण फूल - ear-ring
काँटा (बाल का) - hairpin
काँटा(साड़ी का) - brooch
कील नाक की - nose-pin
चिमटी - clip
चूड़ी - bangle

जवाहिरात - gems
तमग़ा - medal
नथुनी - nose-ring
नीलम - sapphire
पन्ना - emerald
पेटी - belt
पैजनी - anklet
पुखराज - topaz
पोलकी - opal
फ़ीरोज़ा - turquoise
बाजू - armlet
बिल्लौर - pebble
मानिक - ruby
माला - garland
मुकुट - tiara
मूँगा - coral
मोती - pearl
लटकन - locket
लोलक - pendant
हार - necklace
हीरा - diamond
हँसुली - neckband

वस्त्रादिक

अँगरखा - tunic
अँगिया - bodice
अँगोछा - napkin
अस्तर - lining
आस्तीन - sleeve
ऊन - wool
कंबल - blanket
कपड़ा - clothes
कमरबन्द - belt
कमीज - shirt
किनारा - border
किमख़ाब - brocade

कोट - coat
गद्दा - cushion
गुलूबंद - muffler
घूँघट - veil
चादर - sheet
छींट - chintz
जाली - gauze
जाँधिया - half-pant
जीन - drill
जेब - pocket
टोपी - cap
तागा - thread
तौलिया - towel
दस्ताना - gloves
दुपट्टा - scarf
दुशाला - shawl
पतलून - pantaloon
पायजामा - trousers
फ़तुही - waistcoat
फ़ीता - tape
बटन - button
मख़मल - velvet
मलमल - linen
मोज़ा - stockings
रफ़ू - darning
रुई - cotton
रूमाल - hand-kerchief
रेशम - silk
लबादा - cloak, gown
लहँगा - petticoat
साटन - satin
साफ़ा - turban
सूत - yarn

वृक्ष, पौधे, अंग

अंकुर - germ
अमरूद - guava
आम - mango
इमली - tamarind
कली - bud
काठ - wood
काँटा - thorn
गुठली - stone
गोंद - gum
चीड़ - pine
छाल - bark
छिलका - skin
जटा (नारियल की) - coir
जड़ - root
जीरा - stamen
टहनी - branch
डाल - branch
धड़ - stem
नस - fibre
पत्ती - leaf
फूल - flower
बरगद - banyan
बबूल - acacia
बीज - seed
बाँस - bamboo
रस - juice
रेशा - pulp
शाखा - branch
सरो - cypress
सागवान - teak

व्यवसाय

अख़बारवाला - news-agent
अध्यापक - professor

अहीर - milkman
इंजीनियर - engineer
कसाई - butcher
कारीगर - artisan
किसान - farmer
कुली - coolie
ख़ज़ांची - treasurer
खुदरा फ़रोश - retailer
गंधी - perfumer
गाड़ीवान - coachman
ग्रंथकार - author
जर्राह - surgeon
जहाज़ी - sailor
जादूगर - magician
जाँचने वाला - inspector
जिल्दसाज़ - book-binder
जुलाहा - weaver
जूता बनाने वाला - shoe maker
जौहरी - jeweller
टाइप बैठाने वाला - compositor
ठठेरा - brasier
डाकिया - postman
डॉक्टर - doctor
तेली - oil-man
दर्ज़ी - tailor
दलाल - broker
दवा विक्रेता - druggist
दाई - midwife
दाँत चिकित्सक - dentist
दुकानदार - shopkeeper
धाय - nurse
धोबिन - washerwoman
धोबी - washerman
नानबाई - baker
परीक्षक - examiner
पहरेदार - watchman
प्रकाशक - publisher

प्रबंधकर्ता - manager	**शरीर के अंग**
फेरीवाला - hawker	
फोटो उतारनेवाला - photographer	अँगुली (पैर की) - toe
बढ़ई - carpenter	अँगुली (हाथ की) - finger
बज़ाज़ - draper	अँगूठा (हाथ का) - thumb
बारिस्टर - barrister	आँख - eye
भिक्षुक - beggar	आँत - intestine
भंडारी - butler	ओठ - lip
मछुवा - fisherman	एड़ी - heel
मरम्मत करने वाला - repairer	कंधा - shoulder
मल्लाह - boatman	कनपटी - temple
मालिक - proprietor	कमर - waist
माली - gardener	कलाई - wrist
मुनीम - agent	कान - ear
मुद्रक - printer	कोहनी - elbow
मुंशी - clerk	खोपड़ी - skull
मेहतर - sweeper	गर्दन - neck
मोची - cobbler	गर्भ - womb
मोदी - grocer	गर्भाशय - uterus
रसोइयादार - cook	गला - throat
रोकड़िया - cashier	गाल - cheek
रंगसाज़ - painter	गुदा - anus
रंगरेज़ - dyer	घुटना - knee
लादनेवाला - carrier	चमड़ी - skin
लेखक - writer	चूचुक - nipple
लोहार - blacksmith	चूतड़ - buttock
वकील - pleader	चेहरा - face
वैद्य - physician	छाती (पुरुष की) - chest
शिक्षक - teacher	छाती (स्त्री की) - breast
सोनार - goldsmith	जाँघ - thigh
सौदागर - merchant	जिगर - liver
संगतराश - sculptor	जीभ - tongue
संपादक - editor	जोड़ - joint
हज्जाम - barber	ठुड्डी - chin
हलवाई - confectioner	तलवा - sole
	तालु - palate
	दाढ़ - jaw

दाढ़ी - beard
दाँत - tooth
दिमाग - brain
धमनी - artery
नख - nail
नथुना - nostril
नस - vein
नाक - nose
नाभि - navel
पलक - eyelid
पसली - rib
पीठ - back
पेट - stomach
पेड़ू - abdomen
पुतली (आँख की) - eyeball
पेशी (पुट्ठा) - muscle
पैर - foot
फेफड़ा - lung
बगल - arm-pit
बरौनी - eyelash
बाल - hair
बाँह - arm
भौंह - eyebrow
मसूढ़ा - gum
मुट्ठी - fist
मुख - mouth
मूँछ - moustach
मूत्राशय - kidney
योनि - vagina
रक्त - blood
रीढ़ - backbone
रोमकूप - pore
ललाट - forehead
शिश्न - penis
हड्डी - bone
हथेली - palm (of hand)
हृदय - heart

शरीर के विकार तथा रोग

अंधा - blind
अल्पदृष्टि - short-sight
अम्लपित्त - acidity
अतिसार - diarrhoea
आतशक - syphilis
आँत उतरना - hernia
आँसू - tears
उबासी - yawn
कद - stature
कफ़ - phlegm
कय करना - vomit
कास - bronchitis
काना - one-eyed
कुबड़ा - hunch-backed
कोढ़ - leprosy
कोष्ठबद्धता - constipation
कृमि - worms
खाँसी - cough
खून की कमी - anaemia
गठिया - rheumatism
गर्भपात - abortion
गरमी - syphilis
गला बैठना hoarseness
गाँठ - tumour
गिलटी - tumour
गूँगा - dumb
गंजा - bald
घाव - wound
चक्कर - giddiness
चर्बी बढ़ना - obesity
चोट - hurt
छींक - sneeze
जुकाम - coryza
जूड़ी - ague
जंभाई - yawn

ज्वर - fever
ठंड - chill
डकार - belch
थूक - spittle
दमा - asthma
दर्द - pain
दर्द सिर - headache
दस्त - stool
दाद - ringworm
दुबला - lean
दूरदृष्टि - long-sight
नस चटकना - sprain
नींद - sleep
नींद न आना - insomnia
पथरी - stone
पसीना - sweat
पागल - mad
पागलपन - insanity
पित्त - bile
पीब - pus
पेचिश - dysentery
प्रदर - leucorrhoea
फुंसी - pimple
फोड़ा - boil
बलगम - phlegm
बवासीर - piles
बहुमूत्र - diabetes
बुखार - fever
बौना - dwarf
भगंदर - fistula
भूख - hunger
मस्सा - mole
मिरगी - epilepsy
मूत्र - urine
मोतियाबिंद - cataract
मोहासा - acne
लकबा - paralysis

लार - saliva
विष्ठा - stool
रोग - disease
लँगड़ा - lame
लू लगना - sunstroke
शीतला - small-pox
श्वेत कुष्ठ - leucoderma
साँस - breath
सूजन - swelling
सूज़ाक - gonorrhoea
संग्रहणी - sprue
स्वर - voice
हिचकी - hiccough
हैज़ा - cholera
क्षय - tuberculosis

- संगीत के वाद्य

चंग - harp
झाँझ - cymbal
डफ़ - tambourine
डुगडुगी - drum
ढोलक - tomtom
तुरही - bugle
नगाड़ा - drum
पियानो - piano
बाँसुरी - flute
बेला - violin
मसक बाजा - bagpipe
शहनाई - clarion
सितार - guitar
सीटी - whistle
हारमोनियम - harmonium

सम्बन्धी

अम्मा - mamma
उपपत्नी - co-wife
चाचा - uncle
चाची - aunt
जेठानी/देवरानी - sister-in-law
दत्तक पुत्र - adopted son
दत्तक कन्या - adopted daughter
दादा - grand father
दादी - grand mother
दामाद - son-in-law
नाना - grand father
नानी - grand mother
पति - husband
पत्नी - wife
पतोहू - daughter-in-law
परीक्षक - examiner
परीक्षार्थी - examinee
पिता - father
पुत्र - son
पुत्री - daughter
बहिन - sister
भतीजा - nephew
भतीजी - niece
भाई - brother
भांजा - nephew
भांजी - niece
माता - mother
मामा - maternal uncle
मामी - maternal aunt
मौसी - mother's sister
ससुर - father-in-law
सास - mother-in-law
संबंधी - relative
सौतेली कन्या - step-daughter
सौतेला पुत्र - step-son

सौतेला पिता - step-father
सौतेली बहन - step-sister
सौतेला भाई - step-brother
सौतेली माता - step-mother

लिखने-पढ़ने तथा दफ्तर के सामान

अख़बार - newspaper
अलमारी - almirah
आधी रसीद - counterfoil
आराम कुर्सी - easy chair
आलपीन - pin
आलपीन गद्दी - pin cushion
कलम - pen
कलमतराश - pen-knife
कागज़ - paper
कार्ड - card
काली स्याही - black ink
कोश - dictionary
खाता - register
गड्डी - file
गोंद - gum
चिट्ठी का कागज़ - letter paper
चिमटी - clip
चौकी - bench
जेबी पोथी - pocket books
टिकट (स्टाम्प) - postage stamp
टेबल - table
तार - wire
तिपाई - stool
दावात - inkpot
नकल करने का काग़ज़ - carbon paper
नकल करने की स्याही - copying ink
नकल करने की पेंसिल - copying pencil

नक्शा - map
निब - nib
निमंत्रणपत्र - invitation card
नीली स्याही - blue ink
परकाल - divider
पुकारने की घंटी - call-bell
पेंसिल - pencil
फ़ाइल - file
फ़ीता - tape
बंधना - fastener
भेंट करने का कार्ड - visiting card
मोहर - seal
रबड़ - eraser
रबड़ की मोहर - rubber stamp

रद्दी की टोकरी - waste paper-basket
रूलर - ruler
रोशनाई - ink
लपेटने का कागज़ - packing paper
लाल रोशनाई - red ink
लिखने की पट्टी - writing pad
लिफ़ाफ़ा - envelope
लेखा बही - ledger
सरेस - glue
साद्या कागज़ - blank paper
सोखता - blotting paper
सैंड़सी, छेदने की - punch
होल्डर - holder

संख्याएं
NUMERALS

1	एक	One	I
2	दो	Two	II
3	तीन	Three	III
4	चार	Four	IV
5	पाँच	Five	V
6	छ:	Six	VI
7	सात	Seven	VII
8	आठ	Eight	VIII
9	नौ	Nine	IX
10	दस	Ten	X
11	ग्यारह	Eleven	XI
12	बारह	Twelve	XII
13	तेरह	Thirteen	XIII
14	चौदह	Fourteen	XIV
15	पंद्रह	Fifteen	XV

16	सोलह	Sixteen	XVI
17	सत्रह	Seventeen	XVII
18	अठारह	Eighteen	XVIII
19	उन्नीस	Nineteen	XIX
20	बीस	Twenty	XX
21	इक्कीस	Twenty one	XXI
22	बाईस	Twenty two	XXII
23	तेईस	Twenty three	XXIII
24	चौबीस	Twenty four	XXIV
25	पच्चीस	Twenty five	XXV
26	छब्बीस	Twenty six	XXVI
27	सत्ताईस	Twenty seven	XXVII
28	अठाईस	Twenty eight	XXVIII
29	उनतीस	Twenty nine	XXIX
30	तीस	Thirty	XXX
31	इकत्तीस	Thirty one	XXXI
32	बत्तीस	Thirty two	XXXII
33	तैंतीस	Thirty three	XXXIII
34	चौंतीस	Thirty four	XXXIV
35	पैंतीस	Thirty five	XXXV
36	छत्तीस	Thirty six	XXXVI
37	सैंतीस	Thirty seven	XXXVII
38	अड़तीस	Thirty eight	XXXVIII
39	उनतालीस	Thirty nine	XXXIX
40	चालीस	Forty	XL
41	इकतालीस	Forty one	XLI
42	बयालीस	Forty two	XLII
43	तैंतालीस	Forty three	XLIII
44	चौवालीस	Forty four	XIV
45	पैंतालीस	Forty five	XLV
46	छियालीस	Forty six	XLVI
47	सैंतालीस	Forty seven	XLVII
48	अड़तालीस	Forty eight	XLVIII
49	उनचास	Forty nine	XLIX

50	पचास	Fifty	L
51	इक्यावन	Fifty one	LI
52	बावन	Fifty two	LII
53	तिरपन	Fifty three	LIII
54	चौवन	Fifty four	LIV
55	पचपन	Fifty five	LV
56	छप्पन	Fifty six	LVI
57	सत्तावन	Fifty seven	LVII
58	अट्ठावन	Fifty eight	LVIII
59	उनसठ	Fifty nine	LIX
60	साठ	Sixty	LX
61	इकसठ	Sixty one	LXI
62	बासठ	Sixty two	LXII
63	तिरेसठ	Sixty three	LXIII
64	चौंसठ	Sixty four	LXIV
65	पैंसठ	Sixty five	LXV
66	छियासठ	Sixty six	LXVI
67	सरसठ	Sixty seven	LXVII
68	अरसठ	Sixty eight	LXVIII
69	उनहत्तर	Sixty nine	LXIX
70	सत्तर	Seventy	LXX
71	इकहत्तर	Seventy one	LXXI
72	बहत्तर	Seventy two	LXXII
73	तिहत्तर	Seventy three	LXXIII
74	चौहत्तर	Seventy four	LXXIV
75	पचहत्तर	Seventy five	LXXV
76	छिहत्तर	Seventy six	LXXVI
77	सतहत्तर	Seventy seven	LXXVII
78	अठहत्तर	Seventy eight	LXXVIII
79	उन्यासी	Seventy nine	LXXIX
80	अस्सी	Eighty	LXXX
81	इक्यासी	Eighty one	LXXXI
82	बयासी	Eighty two	LXXXII
83	तिरासी	Eighty three	LXXXIII

84	चौरासी	Eighty four	LXXXIV
85	पच्चासी	Eighty five	LXXXV
86	छियासी	Eighty six	LXXXVI
87	सत्तासी	Eighty seven	LXXXVII
88	अट्ठासी	Eighty eight	LXXXVIII
89	नवासी	Eighty nine	LXXXIX
90	नब्बे	Ninety	XC
91	इक्यानबे	Ninety one	XCI
92	बानबे	Ninety two	XCII
93	तिरानबे	Ninety three	XCIII
94	चौरानबे	Ninety four	XCIV
95	पंचानबे	Ninety five	XCV
96	छियानबे	Ninety six	XCVI
97	सतानबे	Ninety seven	XCVII
98	अट्ठानबे	Ninety eight	XCVIII
99	निन्यानबे	Ninety nine	XCIX
100	सौ	Hundred	C

अंशबाचक गिनती

1/2 आधा—Half (हॉफ़)

3/4 तीन चौथाई—Three fourth (थ्री फ़ोर्थ)

2/3 दो तिहाई—Two third (टू थर्ड)

1/4 एक चौथाई—One fourth (वन फ़ोर्थ)

1/5 पाँचवाँ भाग—One fifth (वन फ़िफ़्थ)

1/6 छठा भाग—One sixth (वन सिक्स्थ)

1/7 सातवाँ भाग—One seventh (वन सेवंथ)

1/8 आठवाँ भाग—One eighth (वन एटथ्य)

1/9 नौवाँ भाग—One ninth (वन नाइंथ)

1/10 दसवाँ भाग—One tenth (वन टेंथ)

क्रमबाचक गिनती

पहला — First (फ़र्स्ट)

दूसरा — Second (सेकंड)

तीसरा — Third (थर्ड)

चौथा — Fourth (फ़ोर्थ)

पाँचवाँ — Fifth (फ़िफ़्थ)   आठवाँ — Eighth (एट्थ)

छठा — Sixth (सिक्स्थ)   नौवाँ — Ninth (नाइंथ)

सातवाँ — Seventh (सेवन्थ)   दसवाँ — Tenth (टेंथ)

गुणवाचक गिनती

एक गुना — Single (सिंगल)   छह गुना — Six fold (सिक्स फ़ोल्ड)

दुगना — Double (डबल)   सात गुना — Seven fold (सेवन फ़ोल्ड)

तिगुना — Three fold (थ्री फ़ोल्ड)   आठ गुना — Eight fold (एट फ़ोल्ड)

चौगुना — Four fold (फ़ोर फ़ोल्ड)   नौ गुना — Nine fold (नाइन फ़ोल्ड)

पाँच गुना — Five fold (फ़ाइव फ़ोल्ड)   दस गुना — Ten fold (टेन फ़ोल्ड)

ENGLISH-HINDI
DICTIONARY

Udayanarayan Tiwari
Editor

दो शब्द

यह पॉकिट अंग्रेज़ी-हिन्दी कोश बाज़ार में बिकनेवाले अन्य कोशों से कई माने में भिन्न है तथा सामान्य पाठकों और विद्यार्थियों के लिए विशेष रूप से तैयार किया गया है । इसमें अंग्रेज़ी के साहित्यिक, सामाजिक, कानूनी, वैज्ञानिक और सरकारी कामकाज के ऐसे लग-भग सभी महत्त्वपूर्ण शब्दों को सम्मिलित करने का प्रयास किया गया है जो हमारे दैनिक व्यवहार में आते हैं । इन शब्दों के अर्थ देते समय प्रामाणिकता के साथ ही सुगमता का भी बराबर ध्यान रखा गया है । अन्य भाषाओं की तरह अंग्रेज़ी भाषा के शब्दों में भी अनेक अर्थ होते हैं । इस कोश में अंग्रेज़ी शब्दों के ऐसे अर्थों को प्रमुखता दी गई है जो अधिक प्रचलित हैं । परिणामस्वरूप इस छोटे से कोश में अधिक से अधिक संख्या में शब्दों का समावेश हो सका है, और इस प्रकार इसकी उपादेयता बढ़ गई है । प्रचलित पारि-भाषिक शब्दों और उनके नये प्रामाणिक अर्थों को भी विशेष स्थान दिया गया है । अहिन्दी-भाषी पाठकों की सुविधा के लिए हिन्दी के स्त्रीलिंग शब्दों को चिह्नित किया गया है । परिशिष्ट में प्रशासनिक शब्द, अंग्रेज़ी और हिन्दी की चुनी हुई कहावतें, महत्त्वपूर्ण पद और मुहावरे, दैनिक व्यवहार की आवश्यक शब्दावली आदि सम्मिलित हैं । इससे इस कोश की उपयोगिता और भी बढ़ गई है ।

—सम्पादक

पॉकेट अंग्रेज़ी-हिन्दी कोश

POCKET ENGLISH-HINDI DICTIONARY

A

a *a.* एक ; कोई

A one, (A No. 1) सर्वोत्तम

aback *adv.* पीछे की ओर taken aback चकित, भौंचक्का

abandon *v.t.* त्याग देना

abandonment *n.* पूर्ण त्याग

abase *v.t.* अपमानित करना

abasement *n.* अपमान

abash *v.t.* लज्जित करना

abate *v.t. & i.* कम करना या होना ; रोक-थाम करना

abatement *n.* कमी*, छूट*

abbey *n.* ईसाई मठ

abbreviate *v.t.* संक्षिप्त करना

abbreviation *n.* संक्षेप

abdicate *v.t. & i.* सत्ता त्यागना

abdication *n.* राजत्याग

abdomen *n.* पेट

abdominal *a.* पेट-संबंधी

abdominous *a.* तोंद वाला

abduct *v.t.* अपहरण करना

abduction *n.* अपहरण

abed *adv.* बिस्तर पर

abelmosken गंधमूल

aberration *n.* मतिभ्रम, पतन

abet *v.t.* उकसाना

abetment *n.* उकसाव

abeyance *n.* दुविधा, ठहराव

abhor *v.t.* घृणा करना

abhorrence *n.* घृणा*

abhorrent *a.* घृणित, घिनौना

abide *v.t. & i.* रहना, टिकना

abiding *a.* टिकाऊ ; स्थायी

ability *n.* कुशलता* ; योग्यता*

abinitio *adv.* नये सिरे से

abject *a.* अधम, नीच

abjection *n.* नीचता*

abjuration *n.* शपथपूर्वक त्याग

---

*कोश में चिह्नित शब्द हिन्दी में स्त्रीलिंग में प्रयुक्त होते हैं ।

abjure *v.t.* शपथपूर्वक त्यागना

ablative *n.* पंचमी विभक्ति*

ablaze *a.* जलता हुआ; उत्तेजित

able *a.* योग्य, निपुण

ableness *n.* निपुणता*

ablepsy *n.* अंधापन

ablution *n.* स्नान, अभिषेक

abnegate *v.t.* अस्वीकार करना

abnegation *n.* अस्वीकार

abnormal *a.* असामान्य

aboard *adv.* नौका पर, समीप

abode *n.* घर, डेरा

abolish *v.t.* समाप्त करना

abolition *n.* उन्मूलन, अन्त

abominable *a* घृणित, घिनौना

abominate *v.t.* घृणा करना

aboriginal *a.* आदिम, मूल; *n.* आदिवासी

aborigines *n.* मूलनिवासी

abortion *n.* गर्भपात

abortive *a.* निष्फल, अधूरा

about *adv.* चारों ओर, प्रायः; *prep.* समीप, विषय में; to bring about पूर्ण करना; to come about घटित होना; to go about करने की तैयारी करना; to turn about घुमा देना या घूम जाना

above *adv.* ऊपर; *prep.* विशेषकर, बढ़कर; above all सर्वोपरि; above board

निष्कपट

abreast *adv.* बराबर में

abridge *v.t.* संक्षेप करना

abridgement *n.* संक्षेप, सार

abroad *adv.* विस्तृत, *n.* विदेश

abrogate *v.t.* अभिनिषेध करना

abrogation *n.* अभिनिषेध

abscond *v.i.* फरार होना

absence *n.* अनुपस्थिति

absent *a.* अनुपस्थित; *v. i.* जानबूझकर काम से हटना

absolute *a.* पूर्ण, असीम

absolutely *adv.* पूर्ण रूप से

absolve *v.t.* दोषमुक्त करना

absorb *v.t.* खपाना

abstain *v.i.* अलग रखना

abstinence *n.* संयम, परहेज

abstract *a.* अमूर्त, भाववाचक; *n.* तत्त्व, सारांश; *v.t.* हटाना, अलग करना

abstraction *n.* अमूर्तीकरण

absurd *a.* असंगत, विवेकहीन

absurdity *n.* मूर्खता*

abundance *n.* आधिक्य

abundant *a.* प्रचुर

abuse *v.t.* गाली देना, दुरुपयोग करना; *n.* गाली

abusive *a.* अपमानजनक

abysmal *a.* अथाह

abyss *n.* रसातल

academic *a.* शैक्षणिक, विद्यामूलक, शास्त्रीय

academy *n.* अकादमी*, विद्ध-
त्परिषद्*

accede *v.i.* मान लेना

accelerate *v.t.* गति बढ़ाना

acceleration *n.* गतिवृद्धि,*
तेज़ी*, वेग-वर्धन

accent *n.* स्वर, उच्चारण,
स्वरचिह्न; *v.t.* स्वरोच्चारण
करना

accentuation *n.* स्वरांकन,
स्वरोच्चारण

accept *v.t. & i.* स्वीकार
करना, लेना

acceptable *a.* स्वीकार्य, प्रिय,
रुचिर

acceptance *n.* स्वीकृति*

access *n.* पहुंच*, प्रवेश

accessory *n. & a.* सहायक,
साथी; प्रतिरिक्त

accession *n.* संविलयन, राज्या-
भिषेक

accidence *n.* शब्दरूप

accident *n.* दुर्घटना*, प्राक-
स्मिक घटना, दुर्योग

accidental *a.* प्राकस्मिक

acclaim *v.t.* जयकार करना;
n. जयकार*

acclamation *n.* अभिनन्दन,
समर्थन, स्तुति*

acclimatise *v.t.* जलवायु का
आदी बनाना

acclivity *n.* चढ़ान*

accommodate *v.t.* अनुकूल
बनाना, भगड़ा तय करना,
स्थान देना

accommodation *n.* गुंजाइश*,
निवास, मेल, ठौर, सुविधा*,
समझौता

accompaniment *n.* सहायक
वस्तुएं*; साथ; संगत, साज

accompany *v. t.* साथ देना;
संगत करना

accomplice *n.* अपराध का
साथी

accomplish *v.t.* पूरा करना,
साध लेना

accomplished *a.* पूरा, पारंगत

accomplishment *n.* पूर्णता*,
सिद्धि*

accord *v.i. & t.* मिलान
करना, मिलना; सुर मिलाना;
n. आपसी मेल; तालमेल,
of one's own accord
अपनी इच्छा से

according as *adv.* जैसे कि

accordingly *adv.* तदनुसार

according to *adv.* के अनुसार

account *n.* गणना*, हिसाब,
लेखा; कारण; वर्णन; *v.t.*
& *i.* हिसाब लगाना; कारण
बताना

accountable *a.* उत्तरदायी

accountancy *n.* मुनीमी*

account, audited, *n.* प्रंकेक्षित

लेखा

accountant *n.* मुनीम, प्रकाउंटेंट

accountant general *n.* महालेखापाल

accountantship *n.* मुनीमी*

account-book *n.* लेखाबही*

accredit *v.t.* विश्वास करना, अधिकार देना, मान्यता देना या दिलाना

accrue *v.i.* निकलना, देय होना, बढ़ना, उठना

accruement *n.* निकास; बढ़ती*

accumulate *v.t.* जमा होना या करना, ढेर लगाना

accumulation *n.* ढेर, संचय

accuracy *n.* यथार्थता*, खरापन

accurate *a.* शुद्ध, ठीक, यथार्थ, खरा

accurse *v.t.* शाप देना, कोसना

accursed *a.* शापित, अभागा ।

accusation *n.* दोष, आरोप, अभियोग

accuse *v.t.* दोषारोपण करना, अपराधी ठहराना

accused *n. & a.* अभियुक्त, प्रतिवादी

accuser *n.* वादी

accustom *v.t.* आदी बनाना

accustomed *a.* आदी

ace *n.* इकाई*, पासे या ताश का एक्का

ache *n.* पीड़ा*; *v.i.* पीड़ा होना

achieve *v.t.* हासिल करना, जीतना

achievement *n.* प्राप्ति*, सिद्धि*

acid *a.* अम्ल, खट्टा, तीखा ; *n.* अम्ल, तेज़ाब

acidity *n.* खट्टापन, अम्लता*

acknowledge *v.t.* मान लेना, पहुंच लिखना, रसीद देना

acknowledgement *n.* स्वीकृति*, रसीद*

acorn *n.* बलूत का फल

acoustic *a.* श्रवणेन्द्रिय-सम्बन्धी

acoustics *n. pl.* ध्वनिशास्त्र

acquaint *v.t.* परिचय कराना, सूचना देना

acquaintance *n.* परिचय, परिचित व्यक्ति

acquainted *a.* परिचित

acquiesce *v.i.* सन्तुष्ट होना, सम्मत या राज़ी होना

acquiescence *n.* मौन स्वीकृति*, रज़ामंदी*

acquire *v.t.* प्राप्त करना, अधिकार में करना

acquirement *n.* उपार्जन, अर्जित विद्या*

acquisition *n.* अभिग्रहण,
प्राप्ति*, लाभ, अर्जन,
कमाई ।

acquit *v.t.* बरी या रिहा
करना, कर्तव्य पूरा कर
लेना

acquittal *n.* दोष-मुक्ति*,
रिहाई*

acquittance *n.* बेबाकी*, भर-
पाई*

acre *n.* एकड़, ४८४० वर्ग-
गज़

acreage *n.* एकड़ों में नाप*,
एरूड़ पीछे लगान

acrid *a.* तीखा, चरपरा

acridity *n.* तीखापन, चरपरा-
हट*

acrimonious *a.* रूखा, उग्र,
चिड़चिड़ा

acrimony *n.* रूखापन, उग्रता*,
चिड़चिड़ापन

acrobat *n.* नट, कलाबाज़

acrobatic *a.* क़लाबाज़ी का

across *prep. & adv.* आरपार,
आगे को, बेड़ा; to come
across सामना होना

act *n.* कृति,* नियम, विधि,*
नाटक का अंक; *v.t.* करना,
व्यवहार करना, अभिनय
करना

acting *n.* अभिनय *a.* कार्य-
कारी

action *n.* कार्य, लड़ाई*,
नालिश*, नाटक में घटनाक्रम
या मुद्रा या भाव

actionable *a.* कानूनी कार्रवाई
करने योग्य

action, direct, *n.* प्रत्यक्ष
कार्रवाई*

active *a.* सक्रिय, उद्यमी, तेज़

active voice *n.* कर्तृ वाच्य

activity *n.* सक्रियता*, कर्म-
ठता,* फुर्ती* (ब० व० में)
हलचल*, कार्यकलाप

actor *n.* अभिनेता

actress *n.* अभिनेत्री*

actual *a.* यथार्थ, ठीक, चालू

actually *adv.* वस्तुतः

acumen *n.* सूक्ष्म दृष्टि* या
बुद्धि*, कुशाग्रता*

acute *a.* पैना, विकट, कर्कश

acute angle *n.* न्यून कोण

acute disease *n.* भयंकर या
सांघातिक रोग

adage *n.* सूक्ति*

adamant *n.* (अपनी बात या
हठ पर) अटल

adapt *v.t.* अनुकूल बनाना,
मेल बिठाना

adaptation *n.* अनुकूलन, मेल;
नाटक आदि का रूपान्तर

add *v.t.* जोड़ना, जुटाना

addition *n.* जोड़

additional *a.* अतिरिक्त

addendum *n.* जोड़, परि-शिष्ट

addict *v.t.* निरत होना, व्यसन में पड़ना

addiction *n.* व्यसन, आसक्ति*

addle *a.* सड़ा; *v.t. & i.* सड़ाना

address *v.t.* पता लिखना, संबोधित करना, निवेदन करना, व्याख्यान देना; *n.* पता, व्याख्यान, बोलने का ढंग

addressee *n.* पत्र पानेवाला ।

adduce *v.t.* प्रस्तुत करना, निष्कर्ष निकालना

adept *n. & a.* प्रवीण

adequate *a.* पर्याप्त

adhere *v.i.* लग जाना, मत पर दृढ़ होना

adherence *n.* लगाव, समर्थन, पक्षपात

adherent *a. & n.* अनुयायी, समर्थक, पक्षपाती

adhesion *n.* लगाव, चिपकाव, संलग्नता*

adhesive *a.* चिपकनेवाला, चिपकाने वाला (जैसे गोंद), चिपचिपा, लसलसा

ad hoc committee *n.* तदर्थ समिति*

adieu *n. & interj.* अलविदा

adjacent *a.* समीपवर्ती

adjective *n. & a.* विशेषण; अधीन

adjoin *v.i. & t.* जुड़ा होना, जोड़ना, समीप होना, संयुक्त करना या होना

adjourn *v.t. & i.* स्थगित करना या होना, टालना टलना

adjournment *n.* स्थगन

adjournment motion *n.* कार्यस्थगन-प्रस्ताव

adjudge *v.t.* निर्णय करना

adjudicate *v t.* निर्णय करना

adjunct *n.* अधीन या जुड़ी हुई वस्तु, सहायक, अनुलग्न

adjure *v.t.* शपथ लेकर कहना

adjust *v.t.* अनुकूल बनाना, ठीक जमाना, संवारना, समंजन करना

adjustment *n.* समंजन, समन्वय

adjutant *n.* सेनापति का विशेष सहायक

adjutant general *n.* (सेना का) महासहायक

administer *v.t. & i.* प्रबन्ध करना, शासन करना, शपथ दिलाना, सुख पहुंचाना

administration *n.* प्रशासन

administrative *a.* प्रशासन-संबंधी

administrator *n.* प्रशासक

admirable *a.* प्रशंसनीय

admiral *n.* नौसेनाध्यक्ष

admiralty *n.* नौसेनाध्यक्ष का कार्यालय या पद, नौवाहन-विभाग

admiration *n.* प्रशंसा, आदर

admire *v.t.* प्रशंसा करना, गुण गाना, समादर करना

admissible *a.* ग्राह्य

admission *n.* प्रवेश, पैठ*

admission card *n.* प्रवेश-पत्र

admit *v.t. & i.* प्रवेश करना या कराना, प्रवेश की अनुमति देना, अंगीकार करना, मान लेना

admittance *n.* प्रवेश का अधिकार

admonish *v. t.* धिक्कारना, चेताना

admonition *n.* धिक्कार*, चेतावनी*, झिड़की*

ado *n.* झमेला

adolescence *n.* किशोरावस्था

adolescent *a. & n.* किशोर

adopt *v.t.* गोद लेना, ग्रहण करना, पसन्द करना

adoption *n.* अंगीकरण, गोद लेने का संस्कार

adorable *a.* पूजनीय

adoration *n.* पूजा*, भक्ति*, अति प्रेम

adore *v.t.* पूजा करना, अधिक प्रेम करना

adorn *v.t.* सजाना, श्रृंगार करना

adornment *n.* सजावट, श्रृंगार

adrift *adv.* इधर-उधर बहते हुए, बेठिकाने, भटकते हुए

adroit *a.* निपुण, चतुर

adulation *n.* चापलूसी*

adult *n. & a.* वयस्क, बालिग

adult franchise, adult suffrage, *n.* वयस्क मताधिकार

adulterate *v.t.* मिलावट करना, अशुद्ध करना, भ्रष्ट करना

adulteration *n.* मिलावट*

adultery *n.* पर-स्त्री-गमन, व्यभिचार

ad valorem *a. & adv.* मूल्यानुसार

advance *v.i. & i.* आगे बढ़ना या बढ़ाना, पद में उन्नति करना, पेशगी देना; *n.* पेशगी*, उधार, बढ़ती*, उन्नति*

advancement *n.* वृद्धि,* उन्नति* पेशगी भुगतान

advantage *n.* लाभ, बड़ाई*, *v.t.* लाभदायक होना

advantageous *a.* उपयोगी, लाभदायक

advent *n.* आगमन, अवतार

adventure *n.* साहसिकता*; *v.t.* साहसिक कार्य करना

adventurer *n.* साहसिक, धुनी

adventurous *a.* साहसी

adverb *n.* क्रियाविशेषण

adversary *n.* वैरी

adverse *a.* विपरीत, विरुद्ध

adversity *n.* दुर्दिन, प्रभाग्य

advertise *v.t.* प्रचारित करना, विज्ञापन देना

advertisement *n.* विज्ञापन

advice *n* परामर्श, उपदेश

advisable *a.* अनुमोदनीय, उचित

advise *v t. & .* परामर्श देना, उपदेश करना, समझाना, सूचना देना

advisedly *adv.* समझ-बूझकर

advisory *a.* परामर्श देने की क्षमता या अधिकार या कर्त्तव्य से युक्त

advisory committee *n.* परामर्शदात्री समिति*

advocacy *n.* वकालत*, हिमायत*

advocate *n.* एडवोकेट, वकील, समर्थक; *v.t.* वकालत करना, हिमायत करना

advocate general *n.* महाधि-वक्ता

aerial *a.* हवाई; प्रसार; कल्पित; *n.* आकाश-तार

aerial bombardment *n.* हवाई बमबारी*

aerobatics *n.* हवाई जहाज की क्लाबाजी*

aerodrome *n.* हवाई अड्डा

aeronautical wireless service *n.* वैमानिक बेतार व्यवस्था*

aeronautics *n.pl.* हवाई जहाज चलाने की विद्या* विमान-चालन-विज्ञान

aeroplane *n.* हवाई जहाज

aesthetics *n.pl.* सौन्दर्य-शास्त्र

afar *adv.* दूर से, दूर पर

affable *a.* सुशील, मिलनसार

affair *n.* मामला

affairs *n.pl.* कारबार, लेन-देन*

affect *v.t.* व्यवहार करना, भेस बनाना, ढोंग या दिखावा करना, बहाना करना

affectation *n.* आडम्बर

affected *a.* कपटी, ढोंगी, दिखावटी

affection *n* अनुराग, प्यार

affectionate *a.* प्रीतिमय

affective *a.* भावात्मक

affidavit *n.* शपथपत्र, हलफनामा

affiliate *v.t.* मिलाना, सम्बद्ध करना, प्रबंध संतान का रितु-संबंध बताना

affiliation *n.* संबंधन, संवद्धी-करण, रितु-संबंध का निश्चय, दत्तक-प्रहण

affinity *n.* सम्बन्ध, साहृश्य,

आकर्षण

affirm v.t. पुष्टि करना, दावे से कहना

affirmation n. पुष्टीकरण, दृढ़-वचन

affirmative a. & n. स्वीकारा-त्मक; हामी

affix v.t. जोड़ना, मिलाना; n. प्रत्यय

afflict v.t. पीड़ा देना, सताना

afflicted a. पीड़ित, सताया हुआ

affliction n. पीड़ा*, संताप, मुसीबत*

affluence n. समृद्धि*, प्रचुरता*, बहाव

affluent a. घनी, प्रचुर, प्रबाही; n. सहायक नदी

afford v.t. देना, कर सकना

affray n. कलह, झगड़ा, बलवा

affront v.t. तिरस्कार करना; n. प्रत्यक्ष अपमान

aflame adv. ज्वालामय

afloat adv. बहता हुआ

afoot adv. पैदल

aforesaid a. पूर्व-कथित

afraid a. भयभीत

afresh adv. नये सिरे से

after a. बाद का, पीछे का; prep. & adv. बाद में, पीछे, अनुसरण में, विषय में ; conj. तो भी

afternoon n. अपराह्न, तीसरा पहर

afterwards adv. बाद में

again adv. फिर, प्रतिरिक्त; again and again बार-बार

against prep. प्रतिकूल, सामने, विरुद्ध

agape adv. मुख खोले हुए, भौंचक्का

age n. आयु*, वय*, अवस्था*, युग ; to come of age बालिग होना

aged a. वयोवृद्ध

agenda n.pl. कार्यसूची*

agency n. प्रतिनिधि का पद या काम, एजेंसी*, आढ़त*

agent n. एजेन्ट, प्रतिनिधि, आढ़तिया, आम मुख्तार

aggrandize v.t. पद, शक्ति अथवा प्रतिष्ठा में बढ़ाना

aggravate v.t. छेड़ना, भड़-काना, गम्भीरता बढ़ाना

aggravation n. छेड़छाड़*, भड़-काव, प्रकोप, प्रतिरेक

aggregate v.t. & i. इकट्ठा करना या होना, कुल जोड़ निकालना; a. कुल जमा; n. कुल जोड़

aggression n. आक्रमण, चढ़ाई*

aggressive a. आक्रमणशील, दुर्व्यवहारी, झगड़ालू

aggressor n. आक्रामक

aggrieve v.t. पीड़ा देना, सताना

aggrieved a. पीड़ित

aghast a. भौंचक्का, त्रस्त

agile a. चुस्त, फुर्तीला

agility n. चुस्ती*, फुर्ती*

agitate v.t. क्षुब्ध या उत्तेजित करना, आन्दोलन करना

agitation n. व्याकुलता*, विवाद, आन्दोलन

aglow adv. दमकता हुआ

ago a. & adv. पहले

agonize v.t. & i. तड़पाना, तड़पना

agony n. संताप, यातना*

agrarian a. कृषि-संबंधी, भूमि-धारिता-संबंधी

agree v.i. & t. अनुकूल होना, सहमत हो जाना, एक मत होना, निभना

agreeable a. अनुकूल, सुखद

agreement n. समझौता, क़रार, मेल, स्वीकारपत्र

agricultural a. कृषि-सम्बन्धी

agriculture n. कृषि*, खेती*

agriculturist n. कृषि-विशेषज्ञ, खेतिहर, किसान

ahead adv. आगे, बढ़कर

aid n. सहायता*, सहारा; v.t. सहायता देना

aide-de camp n. अंगरक्षक, सैन्यादेशवाहक

ail v.t. & i. दुःख देना या भोगना

ailment n. रोग, पीड़ा*

aim n. लक्ष्य, उद्देश्य, निशाना; v.t. & i. लक्ष्य करना, निशाना लगाना

aimless a. लक्ष्यहीन, निरुद्देश्य, बेतुका

air n. हवा*, वायुमण्डल, हाव-भाव, तान*, सुर; v.t. हवा लगाना, सुखाना

air-conditioned a. ताप-नियन्त्रित

aircraft n. वायुयान, हवाई जहाज़, गुब्बारा

aircraft carrier n. विमान-वाहक पोत

airgraph n. हवाई चित्र

airgun n. हवाई तोप*

airless a. वायुरहित, शान्त, दमघोंटू

airman n. विमान-चालक

air-raid n. हवाई हमला

air-raid alarm n. हवाई खतरे का भोंपू

air-raid precautions (A. R. P.) n. हवाई हमले से हिफ़ाज़त* (ह० ह० हि०)

air-raid shelter n. हवाई आश्रय

airship n. हवाई जहाज़

air-tight a. वायु-रोधक

338

airy *a.* हवाई, हवादार

ajar *adv.* अधखुला

akin *a.* सगोत्र, सगा, संबंधी

alabaster   *n.* संगमरमरी खड़िया*

alacrity *n.* तत्परता*, धातु-रता*, उत्साह

alarm *n.* भय, बेचैनी*, खतरे की सूचना*, जगाने का यन्त्र; *v.t.* डराना, चौंकाना

alas *inter.* हाय ! अरे !

albeit *adv.* यद्यपि, तथापि

album *n.* चित्राधार, अलबम

alchemy *n.* रस-विद्या*, कीमि-यागरी*

alcohol *n.* मद्यसार

alderman *n.* उप-नगरपाल

alert *a.* सावधान, चंचल

algebra *n.* बीजगणित

alias *n. & adv.* उपनाम, उर्फ

alibi *n.* अन्यत्र उपस्थिति*

alien *a.* परदेशी, गैर, प्रतिकूल, भिन्न स्वभाव का; *n.* विदेशी

alienate *v.t.* अलगाना, हटाना

alight *v.i.* उतरना, नीचे आना या बैठना; *a. & adv.* जलता हुआ, प्रकाशमय

align, aline *v.t. & i.* पंक्ति में करना या होना

alignment *n.* पंक्ति-बन्धन, मार्गरेखा*, सीध*

alike *a. & adv.* सहृश, समान, उसी प्रकार से

alive *a.* जीवित, सचेत, परि-पूर्ण

alkali *n.* क्षार, सज्जीखार

alkaline *a.* क्षार के गुणवाला

all *a. & pron.* सम्पूर्ण, सब ; *adv.* बिलकुल, समूचा; *n.* सभी लोग, सरबस, सब कुछ all along निरन्तर; all but प्रायः; all in all सब मिला-कर ; all over सर्वत्र; all of a sudden एकाएक; once for all सर्वदा के लिए

allay *v.t.* शान्त करना, निरा-करण करना

allegation *n.* अभियोग, आरोप

allege *v.t.* अभियोग लगाना, आरोप लगाना, दलील देना

allegiance   *n.* राजभक्ति*, निष्ठा*

allegoric(al)   *a.* अन्योक्ति-सम्बन्धी, रूपक-सम्बन्धी

allegory *n.* रूपक, दृष्टान्त-कथा*, अन्योक्ति*

alleviate *v.t.* कम या धीमा करना

alley *n.* संकरी गली*

all fools' day *n.* अप्रैल मास का पहला दिन

allfours *n.* ताश का एक खेल; on all fours बकवा, हाथों और घुटनों के बल

alliance *n.* मैत्री-संधि*, मैत्री*; समझौता, एकरूपता*, संबंध, नाता, मेल

allied power *n.* मित्र-शक्ति*

alligator *n.* घड़ियाल

alliterate *v.t.* अनुप्रास लगाना

alliteration *n.* अनुप्रास

alliterative *a.* अनुप्रास का, अनुप्रास-सम्बन्धी, अनुप्रासमय

allocate *v.t.* बांटना, ठहराना, नियत करना

allocation *n.* बंटवारा, निर्धारण

allopathy *n.* सामान्य डाक्टरी चिकित्सा*

allot *v.t.* बांटना, जिम्मे करना, निर्धारित करना

allotment *n.* अंश, बांट*, भाग्य, निर्धारण

allow *v.t. & i.* आज्ञा देना, स्वीकार करना, अनुमति देना, गुंजायश होना

allowable *a.* अनुमोदन के योग्य

allowance *n.* आज्ञा*, अनुमोदन, मुजरा, अनुमति*, भत्ता; *v.t.* भत्ता देना, छूट देना

alloy *n.* मिश्रधातु*, खोट*, भरन*; *v.t.* खोटा करना, मिलावट करना, धातुमिश्रण करना, खोट मिलाना

allude *v.i.* संकेत करना, परोक्ष-निर्देश करना

allure *v.t.* ललचाना, फुसलाना

allurement *n.* प्रलोभन, लालच

alluring *a.* मनोहर

allusion *n.* संकेत

allusive *a.* गूढ़-संकेतमय

ally *v.t.* सम्बन्ध करना, मैत्री करना, मिलाना; *n.* मित्र व्यक्ति या राज्य

alma mater *n.* अपना विद्यालय या विश्वविद्यालय

almanac *n.* पञ्चाङ्ग, जन्त्री*

almighty *a.* सर्वशक्तिमान

almond *n.* बादाम

almost *adv.* लगभग

alms *n.* भिक्षा*

aloft *adv.* ऊपर, ऊपर की ओर

alone *a.* अकेला, एक; *adv.* अकेले, केवल

along *adv. & prep.* एक ओर से दूसरी ओर तक, आगे को, सीधे, लंबान में

aloof *adv.* दूर, पृथक्, परे, न्यारा

aloofness *n.* उदासीनता*, दुराव

aloud *adv.* ऊंचे स्वर से, चिल्लाकर, प्रकट रूप से, खुल्लमखुल्ला

alpaca *n.* ऊनदार ऊंट या

उसकी ऊन का कपड़ा
alphabet n. वर्णमाला*
alphabetical a. अकारादि क्रम में लगा हुआ
already adv. पहले ही, पहले से, अभी तक
also adv. भी, साथ ही
altar n. वेदी*
alter v.t. & i. बदलना
alteration n. परिवर्तन, अदल-बदल
altercate v.i. झगड़ना, विवाद करना
altercation n. विवाद, रार*, झगड़ा, हुज्जत*
alternate a. एवज़ी, परस्परानुवर्ती ; v.t. बारी-बारी से करना या रखना या बदलना
alternative n. पक्षान्तर, विकल्प, पर्याय
although conj. यद्यपि, मानो, हालांकि
altitude n. ऊंचाई*
altogether adv. सर्वथा, पूर्ण रूप से
aluminium n. अलमीनियम
always adv. सर्वदा, निरन्तर
am v.t. & i. हूं
A. M., a.m., n. मध्याह्नपूर्व (म०पू०)
amalgamate v.t. & i. धातु में पारा मिलाना, मिलाना,

मिलना
amalgamation n. पारद-मिश्रण, मिश्रण, जाति-मिश्रण
amass v.t. संग्रह करना, ढेर लगाना
amateur n. शौकीन, कलाप्रेमी
amaze v.t. विस्मित करना, अचम्भे में डालना
amazement n. विस्मय, आश्चर्य
ambassador n. राजदूत
ambiguity n. सन्दिग्धता*, वक्रोक्ति*
ambiguous a. अनिश्चित
ambition n. महत्त्वाकांक्षी*, अभिलाषा*, लालसा*
ambitious a. महत्त्वाकांक्षी, लालसी, उमंगी
ambulance n. एम्बुलेंस*, रोगी-वाहक गाड़ी*, सैनिक चल-चिकित्सालय
ambush n. सिपाहियों की घात*, घात का स्थान
ameliorate v.t. & i. सुधारना, सुघरना, उन्नति करना या देना
amen interj. एवमस्तु, आमीन
amenable a. आज्ञाकारी, वश्य
amend v.i. & t. भूल-सुधार करना, शोधना, सुधारना, सुघरना
amendment n. संशोधन, सुधार

amends *n.pl.* प्रतिफल, हर-जाना

amiability *n.* सुशीलता*, सौजन्य, रमणीयता*

amiable *a.* सुशील, प्रियदर्शन

amicable *a.* मित्रभाव-पूर्ण, शान्तिशील

amid *prep.* में, के बीच, संबंध में

amiss *a. & adj.* बेतुका, ग़लत, भूल से

amity *n.* मैत्री, मेल-जोल

ammunition *n.* गोला-बारूद*, युद्धसामग्री*

amnesty *n.* आम माफ़ी*, सर्व-क्षमा*

among, amongst *prep.* में, के बीच, मिलकर

amorous *a.* प्रेमशील, रसिक

amount *n.* राशि*, मात्रा*, कुल जोड़; *v.t.* बराबर होना, परिणाम होना

ampere *n.* बिजली की धारा की इकाई*

amphitheatre *n.* गोल रंग-भूमि* अखाड़ा

ample *a.* पर्याप्त, विस्तृत, प्रचुर

amplification *n.* विस्तार

amplifier *n.* ध्वनि-विस्तारक

amplify *v.t. & i.* विस्तार करना, बढ़ाना

amuck *adv.* अंधाधुंध, पगला-कर

amuse *v.t.* मन बहलाना

amusement *n.* मनबहलाव

an *a.* एक, कोई

anachronism *n.* काल-भ्रम

anaemia *n.* रक्तहीनता का रोग

anaesthesia *n.* बेहोशी*, संज्ञा-हीनता*

analogous *a.* तुल्य, समरूप, अनुरूप

analogy *n.* समरूपता*, समा-नता*, तुल्यता*, उपमान, अनु-रूपता*

analyse *v.t.* सूक्ष्म विश्लेषण करना, परीक्षा करना

analysis *n* विश्लेषण

analyst *n.* रासायनिक विश्लेषण में निपुण, विश्लेषक

analytic (-al) *a.* विश्लेषणा-त्मक

anarchist *n.* अराजकतावादी

anarchy *n.* अराजकता*, विप्लव

anatomy *n.* शरीर-रचना-शास्त्र

ancestor *n.* पूर्वज, पूर्वपुरुष

ancestral *a.* पैतृक

ancestry *n.* पितरावली*

anchor *n.* लंगर, सहारा *v.t.* लंगर डालकर जहाज़ ठहराना

anchorage *n.* लंगरवानी*, लंगरगाह*

ancient *a.* प्राचीन

and *conj.* और, तथा

anecdote *n.* छोटी-सी कहानी*, उपाख्यान, छोटी-सी घटना का विवरण

anew *adv.* नये सिरे से, पुनः, फिर से, दुहराकर

angel *n.* देवदूत, फ़रिश्ता

anger *n.* कोप, क्रोध; *v.t.* कुद्ध करना

angle *n.* कोण, कोना, बंसी*

angler *n.* बंसी से मछली पकड़ने वाला, कांटेबाज़

angling *n.* बंसी से मछली का शिकार

anglo-Indian *n.* एंग्लो-इंडियन

angry *a.* कुद्ध, क्रोधी, कुपित

anguish *n.* व्यथा*, पीड़ा*, वेदना*

angular *a.* कोणयुक्त

animal *n.* जन्तु, प्राणी, पशु, जीवधारी; *a.* प्राणि-सम्बन्धी, पाशविक, कामुक

animal husbandry *n.* पशु-पालन

animate *v.t.* जीवित करना, उत्तेजित करना; *a.* सजीव, चेतन

animated *a.* प्रफुल्ल, प्रसन्न, सजीव, तेजस्वी

animation *n.* उत्साह, हुलास, सजीवता*, जीव - संचारण,

स्फुरण, जान*

animosity *n.* वैर

ankle *n.* टखना, गुल्फ-संधि*

anklet *n.* नूपुर, पायल*, पाय-जेब*

annalist *n.* वर्षक्रमिक, इतिहास-लेखक

annals *n.pl.* वार्षिक वृत्तान्त, वर्षक्रमिक इतिहास

annex *v.t.* हड़प कर लेना

annexation *n.* राज्यहरण, परिशिष्ट

annex(e) *n.* पूरक अंश, उप-भवन

annihilate *v.t.* लोप करना, मिटा देना

annihilation *n.* विनाश, प्रलय

anniversary *n.* वार्षिकोत्सव

announce *v.t.* घोषणा करना, सूचना देना

announcement *n.* घोषणा*

annoy *v.t.* झुंझला देना, उद्विग्न करना

annoyance *n.* चिढ़

annual *a.* वार्षिक

annuity *n.* वार्षिक वेतन या भत्ता या वृत्ति* या विनियोग

annul *v.t.* अन्त करना, मिटा देना

anomalous *a.* नियमविरुद्ध, विलक्षण

anomaly *n.* अनियम, अव-

घता* गति-विरोध

anonymous *a.* गुमनाम, नाम-रहित, अज्ञात-कृत

another *a. & pron.* दूसरा, भिन्न, दूसरा कोई; one after another एक के बाद दूसरा

answer *n.* उत्तर, प्रतिवचन; *v.t.* उत्तर देना, काम देना

answerable *a.* उत्तरदायी, जवाबदेह, अनुकूल

ant *n.* चींटी*, ant-hill वल्मीक; white ant दीमक*

antagonism *n.* विरोध, शत्रुता*

antagonist *n.* शत्रु, प्रतिपक्षी

antagonistic *a.* विपक्षी, विरोधी

antarctic *a.* दक्षिणी-ध्रुवीय, दक्षिणी

antecedent *a.* पूर्वगामी; *n.* पूर्ववृत्त, पूर्वपद

ante-chamber *n.* ड्योढ़ी*

antennae *n. pl.* कीड़ों के 'स्पर्शसूत्र' या 'मूंछें'*

anteroom *n.* गलियारा, ड्योढ़ी*

anthem *n.* भजन, गान

anthology *n.* पद्यावली*, गद्यावली*

anthropoid *a.* मानवाकार; *n.* वनमानुष

anthropophagi *n.pl.* नरभक्षी

लोग

anti-air-craft gun विमानवेधी तोप*

antic *a.* विलक्षण; *n.* विलक्षण आकृति॰ या स्थिति*, विदूषक

anticipate *v.t. & i.* पहले से सोच रखना, प्रत्याशा करना

antidote *n.* विषहर औषध, मारक

antimony *n.* सुरमा

antipathy *n.* सहज-विरोध, घृणा*, चिढ़

antipathetic *a.* सहज-विरोधी स्वभाव या लक्षणों वाला

antiquarian *n. & a.* पुराविद्, पुरातात्त्विक

antiquary *n.* पुरातात्त्विक शोधकर्त्ता

antiquated *a.* पुरानी रीति का

antique *a.* पुराना, अनोखा

antiquity *n.* पूर्वकाल के अवशेष; प्राचीन रीति*

antiseptic *a. & n.* सड़न रोकने वाली दवा*

antithesis *n.* विलोम, विप-रीतता*

anti-venom serum *n.* विषरोध रस

antler *n.* बारहसिंगे के शाखादार सींग

anvil *n.* निहाई*

anxiety *n.* चिन्ता*, उत्कण्ठा*,

ब्यग्रता*

anxious *a.* चिन्तित, उत्कंठित, ब्यग्र

any *pron. & a.* कोई, कोई एक, एक, थोड़ा-सा, बिलकुल; *adv.* किसी तरह ; anyhow किसी न किसी प्रकार से, जैसे-तैसे ; anywhere कहीं न कहीं, सर्वंत्र

apace *adv.* झटपट

apart *adv.* पृथक्

apartment *n.* मकान का एक कमरा

apartheid policy *n.* रंगभेद-नीति*

apathetic *a.* उदासीन, निरु-त्साह, निठुर

apathy *n.* उदासीनता*, निठु-राई*

ape *n.* पुच्छहीन बंदर, अनुकरण करनेवाला; *v.t.* अनुकरण करना

apery *n.* अनुकरण, वानर-लीला*

apex *n.* शीर्षबिन्दु, चोटी*, सिरा

apiculture *n.* मधुमक्खी-पालन

apiece *adv.* पृथक्-पृथक्, एक-एक करके

apish *a.* बंदर-सा, नटखट, बुद्धू

apologetic *n.* भूल-चूक मानने वाला

apologize *v.t.* क्षमा मांगना

apology *n.* क्षमा-याचना*, दोष-स्वीकार, सफ़ाई*, समर्थन

apoplectic *a.* मिरगी या लक़वा-सम्बन्धी, मिरगी या लक़वा से ग्रस्त

apoplexy *n.* मूर्छा*, मिरगी*, लक़वा

apostle *n.* देवदूत, ईसाई धर्म का प्रचारक

apostrophe *n.* वर्णंलोप या सम्बन्ध कारक का चिह्न (') परोक्ष-सम्बोधन

appal *v.t.* डराना, व्याकुल करना

apparatus *n.* उपकरण, उप-करण-समूह, औज़ार

apparent *a.* प्रकट, प्रत्यक्ष, स्पष्ट; heir apparent राज्य का उत्तराधिकारी, युवराज

appeal *v.t. & i.* पुनर्विचार की प्रार्थना करना, आकर्षक होना; *n.* पुनर्विचार-प्रार्थना*, अपील*

appear *v.i.* दिखाई पड़ना, जान पड़ना, प्रकट होना

appearance *n.* आभास, पेशी* सूरत*, दृष्टिभ्रम, आकृति*, रूप

appease *v.t.* शांत करना,

मनाना, तुष्ट करके चुप करना

appellant *n.* अपील करनेवाला

appellate *a.* अपील-संबंधी

appellate tribunal *n.* अपीली अदालत*, पुनर्विचार न्यायाधिकरण

appellation *n.* नाम, पदवी*

append *v.t.* मिलाना, जोड़ना

appendage *n.* अनुबंध, उपकरण, परिशिष्ट, पिछलगुआ

appendix *n.* परिशिष्ट, शेषसंग्रह

appertain *v.i.* सम्बन्ध रखना

appetite *n.* भूख*, रुचि*, चाव

appetizer *n.* क्षुधावर्धक पदार्थ

applaud *v.t. & i.* प्रशंसा करना, सराहना, ताली बजाना, वाहवाही देना

applause *n.* प्रशंसा*-घोष, वाहवाही*, ताली*, स्तुति*

apple *n.* सेब; आंख का तारा

appliance *n.* उपकरण

applicable *a.* अनुकूल, उचित, उपयुक्त

application *n.* प्रयोग, प्रार्थना*, उपयुक्तता*, प्रार्थना-पत्र

applicant *n.* प्रार्थी

apply *v.t. & i.* प्रार्थना-पत्र देना या भेजना, लागू करना या होना

appoint *v.t.* नियुक्त करना, नियत करना

appointment *n.* नियुक्ति*, समयादेश, नौकरी*

apportion *v.t.* भाग करना, बांटना

apposite *a.* योग्य, ठीक

appraise *v.t.* मूल्य ठहराना, आंकना, कूतना

appreciable *a.* विवेचनीय, प्रशंसनीय

appreciate *v.t. & i.* गुण जानना, मान करना, दाम बढ़ाना, मूल्यांकन करना, सराहना, रस-ग्रहण करना, सहृदय होना

apprehend *v.t.* पकड़ना, अनुभव करना, गिरफ्तार करना, आशंका करना

apprehension *n.* बोध, डर, हिरासत*

apprehensive *a.* समझदार, सशंक, भयभीत

apprentice *n.* नवसिखुआ, चेला; *v.t.* काम सिखाना

apprise *v.t.* सूचना देना, बतलाना

approach *v.t. & i.* निकट आना, प्रस्ताव करना, बढ़ना; *n.* निकटता* प्रवेश, पहुंच*

approbation *n.* समर्थन, स्वीकृति*, प्रशंसा*

appropriate *v.t.* अपनाना, हड़पना; *a.* उपयुक्त, ठीक

appropriation *n.* स्वायत्ती-
करण, विनियोग

appropriation bill *n.* विनि-
योग-विषेयक

approval *n.* अनुमोदन, पसन्द*

approve *v.t.* अनुमोदन करना,
प्रशंसा करना, पसन्द करना,
ठीक समझना

approver *n.* अनुमोदक, सर-
कारी गवाह

approximate *a.* प्रायः शुद्ध,
लगभग

apricot *n.* खूबानी*

April *n.* अप्रैल

apron *n.* पेशबंद

apt *a.* तत्पर, उद्यत, योग्य,
संगत, उपयुक्त

aptitude *n.* सहज रुझान,
उपयुक्तता*, योग्यता*, कौशल

arable *a. & n.* कृषि-योग्य
(भूमि)

arbiter *n.* मध्यस्थ, पञ्च

arbitral tribunal *n.* पंच-
न्यायाधिकरण

arbitrary *a.* मनमाना, विवेका-
धीन

arbitrate *v.t.* पंचायत करना

arbitration *n.* पंच-निर्णय

arbitrator *n.* पंच

arc *n.* वृत्त-चाप

arcade *n.* वृक्षों से ढका हुआ
मार्ग, वीथिका*

arch *n.* वृत्तखण्ड, मेहराब* ;
v.t. & i. मेहराब लगाना
या बनाना; *a.* धूर्त, दुष्ट,
छंटा हुआ, परले दरजे का

archaic *a.* प्राचीन, आदिम

archangel *n.* प्रधान देवदूत

archbishop *n.* मुख्य धर्माध्यक्ष,
लाटपादरी

architect *n.* वास्तुकार

architecture *n.* वास्तुविद्या*,
घर बनाने की कला*

archive *n.* पुरालेख

archives *n.pl.* पुरालेखागार,
अभिलेखागार

archivist *n.* पुरालेखपाल

arctic *a.* उत्तरी ध्रुव सम्बन्धी,
उत्तरी

ardent *a.* उत्साही, परितप्त,
उत्कट, उत्सुक

ardour *n.* उत्कंठा*, उत्सुकता*,
ललक*, प्रगाढ़भाव

arduous *a.* कर्मठ, दुःसाध्य,
कठिन

area *n.* क्षेत्रफल, चौरस भूमि*.

arena *n.* रंगभूमि*, प्रखाड़ा,
रणभूमि*

argent *n. & a.* चांदी*,
रुपहला

argentine *a.* रुपहला

argue *v.t. & i.* तर्क करना,
सिद्ध करने का प्रयत्न करना

argument *n.* तर्क, शास्त्रार्थ

arid *a.* शुष्क, सूखा, बंजर

Aries *n.* मेष राशि*

arise *v.i.* उगना, उठना, दिखना

aristocracy *n.* शिष्टजन, कुलीनतंत्र, रईसवर्ग

aristocrat *n.* रईस, श्रमीर, कुलीन

aristocratic *a.* कुलीनतंत्रीय, भव्य, प्रतापी

arithmetic *n.* अंकगणित

arithmetical *a.* अंक-सम्बन्धी, अंकगणित संबंधी

arm *n.* बांह*, भुजा*

armaments *n.pl.* युद्धसामग्रा*, सज्जसेना*

armature *n.* हथियार, कवच, बिजली के डायनेमो का घात्र

armistice *n.* अस्थायी संधि*

armlet *n.* बाजूबन्द

armour *n.* कवच

armoured car *n.* बख्तरबंद गाड़ी*

armoury *n.* शस्त्रशाला*

arms *n. pl.* अस्त्रशस्त्र

army *n.* सेना*, दल-बल

army-headquarters *n.* सेना का प्रधान कार्यालय

aroma *n.* सुगन्ध*

around *adv.* चारों ओर, सब ओर

arouse *v.t.* जगाना, उकसाना, उत्तेजित करना

arrange *v.t. & i.* क्रम में रखना, ठीक करना, व्यवस्था करना

arrangement *n.* प्रबन्ध, व्यवस्था*

array *n.* क्रम, व्यूह; *v.t. & i.* क्रम में रखना, सजाना, व्यूह रचना

arrear *n.* बक़ाया

arrears *n. pl.* ऋणशेष, बक़ाया

arrest *v.t.* गिरफ्तार करना, रोकना, पकड़ना; *n.* गिरफ़्तारी* रुकावट*

arrival *n.* आगमन, उपस्थिति*, पहुंच*, आया हुआ माल

arrive *v.t.* आना, पहुंचना, लक्ष्य प्राप्त करना, नाम कमाना

arrogance *n.* उद्दण्डता*, गर्व, हेकड़ी*

arrogant *a.* हठी, अभिमानी, हेकड़

arrogate *v.t.* सगर्व या अनुचित दावा करना

arrow *n.* बाण, तीर

arrowroot *n.* अरारोट, शिशु-मूल

arsenal *n.* शस्त्रगृह, हथियारघर

arsenic *n.* संखिया, हरताल*

arson *n.* आग लगाने का अपराध

art *n.* कला*, कौशल, चातुरी*;

black arts जादू, टोना;
fine arts ललित कलाएं*

artery *n.* रुधिरवाहिनी
नलिका*, धमनी*

artful *a.* धूर्त, कपटी

arthritis *n.* जोड़ों की सूजन*,
गठिया*

article *n.* अनुच्छेद, लेख,
वस्तु*, विषय, सामान्य वाक्य

articles of association *n.*
संस्था के नियम

articulate *a.* स्पष्ट, व्यक्त *v.t.*
साफ़-साफ़ बोलना

articulation *n.* ग्रंथन, जोड़-
बंदी*, गांठ*, स्पष्ट उच्चारण

artificial *a.* शिल्पनिर्मित,
कृत्रिम, बनावटी

artillery *n.* तोपें*, तोपख़ाना

artisan *n.* शिल्पी, शिल्पकार

artist *n.* कलाकार

artistic *a.* कलात्मक, सुन्दर

artless *a.* simple, सीधा,
अकृत्रिम, भोला, निश्छल,
अनाड़ी

as *adv., conj., & pron.* उसी
प्रकार से, वैसे ही, जैसे, ज्योंही,
इतना, जितना, ऐसा, जैसा,
जैसे कि, मानो, जभी, जबकि,
की तरह, इसलिए कि, ताकि,
कि, चूंकि, जब; जो, जो
कुछ; as yet अब तक;
as well as और भी

ascend *v.t. & i.* चढ़ना, बढ़ना,
ऊपर जाना

ascendancy (-ency) *a.* अधि-
कार, प्रभुत्व

ascent *n.* उदय, चढ़ाव, उभार,
जीना

ascertain *v.i.* निश्चित करना,
जांचना, पता. चला या पा
लेना

ascetic *n.* तपस्वी, योगी

asceticism *n.* संन्यास, वैराग्य

ascribe *v.t.* लगाना, मढ़ना,
कारण या संबंध बताना

aseptic *a.* सड़न रोकनेवाला,
कीटाणु-नाशक

ash *n.* भस्म, राख*, सून का
पेड़

ashamed *a.* लज्जित

ashen *a.* भस्मवर्ण, सून की
लकड़ी का

ashore *adv.* तट पर

Asiatic *a.* एशियाई

aside *adv.* एक ओर, अलग;
n. स्वगत कथन

asinine *a.* गदहे का, मूर्खवत्

ask *v.t.* पूछना, पूछताछ करना,
याचना करना, मांगना

askance *adv.* तिरछी दृष्टि से,
कनखियों से

asleep *adv. & a.* निद्रा में,
सोते हुए, सुप्त

asp *n.* पहाड़ी पीपल, मिस्री

सांप

aspect *n.* पहलू, स्वरूप

aspersion *n.* आक्षेप, कलंक

asphalt *n.* अलकतरा और बालू मिला हुआ मसाला

aspirant *a.* आकांक्षी, अभ्यर्थी

aspiration *n.* आकांक्षा*, लालसा*

aspire *v.t.* महत्त्वाकांक्षा करना

ass *n.* गदहा

assail *v.t.* आक्रमण करना, धावा बोलना, पिल पड़ना

assailant *n.* आक्रमण करने-वाला, पिल पड़नेवाला

assassin *n.* हत्यारा

assassinate *v.t.* हत्या करना, कपटवध करना

assassination *n.* हत्या*, कपट-वध

assault *n.* धावा, चढ़ाई*, अवंध मारपीट* या गाली* ; *v.t.* आक्रमण करना, धावा करना, घर्षण करना

assemblage *n.* जमाव, जमावड़ा

assemble *v.i. & t.* एकत्र होना या करना

assembly *n.* विधान सभा*, सभा*

assent *v.t.* अनुमति देना, स्वीकार करना, मान लेना; *n.* अनुमति*, सम्मति*,

समर्थन

assert *v.t. & i.* दृढ़तापूर्वक कहना, दावा करना, हक़ जमाना

assess *v.t.* कर निर्धारित करना, कूतना, आंकना, लागू करना

assessment *n.* कर-निर्धारण, मूल्यांकन, लगान

assessor *n.* कर-निर्धारक

assets *n.pl.* सम्पत्ति*, वैभव

assets and liabilities *n.* देना-पावना, देयादेय

assign *v.t.* निर्दिष्ट करना, नियुक्त करना, बांटना, सौंपना

assignee *n.* सम्पत्ति-भागी

assignment *n.* समर्पण, सौंपा गया काम

assimilate *v.t. & i.* आत्मसात् करना

assimilation *n.* परिपाक

assist *v.t. & i.* सहायता करना, साथ होना, हाथ बंटाना

assistance *n.* सहायता*

assistant *n.* सहायक, सहकारी

associate *v.t. & i.* मिलाना, मिलना, जुटना ; *a.* मिला-जुला, सहकारी, संघिबढ ; *n.* साथी, सहकारी

association *n.* संघ, सभा*, मण्डली*

assonance *n.* स्वरों की एकता*

assort *v.t. & i.* छांटना

assuage *v.t.* मृदु करना, शांत करना

assume *v.t.* कल्पना करना, मान लेना, हक़ मारना

assumption *n.* कल्पना*, मानी हुई बात*, गर्व

assurance *n.* विश्वास, बीमा

assure *v.t.* भरोसा दिलाना

asterisk *n.* तारे का (*) चिह्न, फुली*

asthma *n.* दमा

asthmatic *a.* दमे का रोगी, दमा-संबंधी

astonish *v.t.* चकित करना

astonishment *n.* आश्चर्य, अचम्भा

astound *v.t.* चकित करना, घबरा देना

astray *adv.* भटका हुआ, गुम-राह

astrologer *n.* ज्योतिषी

astrology *n.* फलित ज्योतिष

astronomer *n.* खगोल-विद्, गणित-ज्योतिषी

astronomy *n.* गणित-ज्योतिष, खगोल-विद्या*

astute *a.* चतुर, दक्ष, शठ

asunder *adv.* अलग-अलग

asylum *n.* आश्रय, शरणस्थान, अस्पताल

at *prep.* में, से, और, पर ; at

all बिलकुल ; at once तुरंत, एकाएक

atheism *n.* अनीश्वरवाद

athlete *n.* योद्धा, पहलवान

athletics *n.pl.* व्यायाम, मल्ल-विद्या*, दंगल

atlas *n.* मानचित्रों की पुस्तक*

atmosphere *n.* वायुमंडल, हवा*, व्याप्ति*

atom *n.* परमाणु, कण

atone *v.t.* हरजाना देना, प्राय-श्चित्त करना, मेल करना, सुलझाना

atonement *n.* हरजाना, प्राय-श्चित्त

atrocious *a.* अति दुष्ट, घृणित, घोर, पापिष्ठ, नृशंस

atrocity *n.* दुष्टता*, नृशंसता*, अत्याचार

attach *v.t. & i.* बांधना, लगाना, जोड़ना, कुर्क करना

attache *n.* कागज़ात रखने का छोटा बक्स, राजदूत का सह-कारी

attachment *n.* बंधन, कुर्की*, अनुराग, प्रीति*

attack *v.t.* आक्रमण करना ; धावा करना ; *n.* आक्रमण, आक्षेप

attain *v.i. & t.* पहुंचना, प्राप्त करना, सिद्ध कर लेना

attainment *n.* accomplish-

ment लाभ, गुए, सिद्धि*

attar *n.* इत्र

attempt *v.t.* प्रयत्न करना, आज़माना; *n.* प्रयत्न

attend *v.i. & t.* उपस्थित होना, ध्यान देना, सेवा करना

attendance *n.* उपस्थिति*

attendant *n.* अनुचर, सेवक

attention *n.* ध्यान

attentive *a.* सावधान, सचेत

attest *v.t. & i.* संपुष्टि करना

attire *n.* पोशाक*; *v.t.* वस्त्र पहनाना

attitude *n.* रुख, मनोभाव

attorney *n.* मुख्तार

attract *v.t.* आकर्षित करना, खींचना

attribute *v.t.* आरोपित करना, मत्थे मढ़ना; *n.* गुए

auction *n.* नीलाम; *v.t.* नीलाम करना

audible *a.* सुनाई देने योग्य

audience *n.* श्रोतागए, दर्शक

audit *n., v.t.* ऑडिट, हिसाब-किताब की जांच (करना)

auditor *n.* ऑडिटर, लेखा-परीक्षक

auditor general *n.* महालेखा परीक्षक

auditorium *n.* सभा-मण्डप

augment *v.t. & i.* बढ़ना, बढ़ाना; *n.* वृद्धि*, आगम

augury *n.* शकुन, भविष्य-वाएी*

august *n.* अगस्त महीना; *a* प्रतापी, श्रद्धास्पद

aunt *n.* फुआ*, मौसी* चाची*, मामी*

auspices *n.pl.* तत्वावधान

auspicious *a.* शुभ, अनुकूल

austere *a.* सीधा-सादा, सादगी-पसन्द

author *n.* रचयिता, लेखक

authoritative *a.* आधिकारिक, प्रामाएिक

authority *n.* अधिकार, अधिकारी व्यक्ति

authorize *v.t.* अधिकार देना, स्वीकृति देना

autobiography *n.* आत्मकथा*

autocracy *n.* निरंकुश राज्य-शासन, एकतंत्र

autocrat *n.* अनियन्त्रित शासक, अत्याचारी

autocratic *a.* निरंकुश

autograph *n.* स्वाक्षर, अपने हस्ताक्षर, ग्रंथकार की निजी पांडुलिपि*

automatic *a.* स्वचालित

automaton *n.* स्वचालित यंत्र

automobile *n.* मोटर-गाड़ी*

autonomy *n.* स्वराज्य, स्व-शासित जाति* या समाज

autumn *n.* शरद् ऋतु*

auxiliary *a. & n.* सहायक, सहाय

avail *v.t. & i.* उपयोगी होना, काम आना, लाभ उठाना; *n.* प्रयोजन, उपयोग, लाभ, सहायता*

available *a.* सुलभ, उपयोगी

avenge *v.t.* बदला लेना

average *n.* औसत ; *v.t.* औसत निकालना; *a.* औसत दरजे का, सामान्य, मध्यम

averse *a.* प्रतिकूल, पराङ्मुख

aversion *n.* घृणा*, विरोध, विमुखता*, अरुचि*, विरक्ति*, द्वेष

avert *v.t.* हटाना, टालना, फेर देना, रोक देना

aviation *n.* विमान-वहन, विमान-वहन-विद्या*, हवा-बाजी*

aviator *n.* विमान-चालक, हवा-बाज

avoid *v.t.* न करना, टालना

avoidance *n.* परिहार, वर्जन, आनाकानी*, टालमटोल, बचाव

avow *v.t.* खुलकर कहना, स्वीकार करना

avowedly *adv.* खुल्लमखुल्ला, डंके की चोट पर

await *v.t.* प्रतीक्षा करना, प्रत्याशा करना, आसरा ताकना

awake *v.t. & i.* जगना, जगाना, सचेत होना या करना; *a.* जाग्रत, सचेत, चौकन्ना

awaken *v.t.* जगाना

awakening *n.* जागृति*, उत्ते-जना*

award *v.t.* निर्णय करना, फ़ैसला देना; *n.* पंचाट, पंच-निर्णय, विचार, पुरस्कार

aware *a.* सचेत, सावधान, अव-गत, जानकार

away *a. & adv.* दूर, निरन्तर; to go away चले जाना

awe *n.* त्रास, आदर, अभियुक्त भय; *v.t.* भय उत्पन्न करना, रोब जमाना

awful *a.* भयंकर, महिमामय

awhile *adv.* क्षण भर के लिए

awkward *a.* भद्दा, कुरूप, अनाड़ी, फूहड़

axe *n.* फरसा, कुल्हाड़ी*

axis *n.* अक्षरेखा*, धुरी*, आधार, तना

axis country *n.* धुरीराष्ट्र

axle *n.* धुरा

axle-tree *n.* गाड़ी का अचल धुरा

B

babble *v.t.* बड़बड़ाना, कलकल शब्द करना, बकने में भेद खोल देना; *n.* बकवाद, कल-कल शब्द, प्रलाप

babe *n.* बच्चा

baby *n.* बच्चा

bachelor *n.* कंम्रारा, स्नातक

back *n.* पीठ* *v.t. & i.* समर्थन करना, साथ देना, पीछे जाना; *a.* पिछला, बकाया; *adv.* दूर, पीछे की ओर

backbite *v.t.* चुगली खाना, पीठ पीछे निंदा करना; *n.* चुग़ली*

backbone *n.* रीढ़*, आधार-स्तम्भ

background *n.* पृष्ठभूमि*

backward *a.* पिछड़ा; *adv.* पिछला, पीछे का

backwards *adv.* पीछे को

bacon *n.* सुअर के मांस का अचार

bacteria *n.pl.* जीवाणु

bad *a.* बुरा, खोटा, अशुभ, सदोष; *n.* बुराई*, बट्टा-खाता, नाश

badge *n.* बिल्ला

badminton *n.* बैंडमिंटन

baffle *v.t.* विफल करना, मात देना, चकरा देना; *n.* गति-रोधक

bag *n.* बोरा, थैला, थन; *v.t.* थैले में रखना, शिकार मारना, लटकाना, फंसाना

baggage *n.* यात्री का सामान

bag-pipe *n.* मशक-बाजा

bail *n.* जमानत; *v.t. & i.* जमानत पर छोड़ना या छुड़ाना

bailable *a.* जमानती

bailiff *n.* कुर्क-अमीन, कारिंदा

bait *n.* चारा, प्रलोभन; *v.t.* चारा लगाना या डालना, फसाना

baker *n.* नानबाई

bakery *n.* नानबाई की भट्टी*

balance *n.* शेष, संतुलन, तराजू, रोकड़ बाक़ी*, तुला राशि*; *v.t.* तौलना, रोकड़-बाक़ी ठीक करना

balanced diet *n.* संतुलित भोजन

balance of payment *n.* भुगतान-तुला*

balance of power *n.* शक्ति-संतुलन

balance of trade *n.* व्यापाराधिक्य

balance sheet *n.* चिट्ठा, देया देय फलक

balcony *n.* छज्जा, बारजा

bald *a.* गंजा, चटियल, नीरस

bale *n.* गट्ठा, गांठ*, विपदा ;
v.t. गट्ठा बनाना

baleful *a.* कष्टमय

ball *n.* गेंद, गोला, सामाजिक
नृत्य - विशेष, नृत्यशाला*,
नृत्यसभा*

ballad *n.* गाथा*, गाथागीत

ballet *n.* बैले, नृत्य-नाटक

balloon *n.* गुब्बारा

ballot *n.* गुप्त मतदान या
उसका मतपत्र ; *v.t.* गुप्त
मतदान करना

ballot box *n.* मतपेटी*

ballot paper *n.* मतपत्र

balm *n.* मलहम

bamboo *n.* बाँस

ban *n.* रोक*, निषेध, शाप ;
v.t. रोकना, निषेध करना,
अवैध घोषित करना

banal *a.* सामान्य, तुच्छ

banana *n.* केला

band *n.* तसमा, बन्धन, पट्टा,
सशस्त्र जत्था, बैंड बाजा,
वादक-मंडली*

bandage *n.* घाव की या आंख
की पट्टी ; *v.t.* पट्टी बांधना

bandit *n.* डाकू

bang *v.t.* पीटना, ठोंकना,
घड़ाका करना ; *n.* धमाका

bangle *n.* कंकण, चूड़ी*

banish *v.t.* निर्वासित करना,
देश निकाला देना

banishment *n.* निर्वासन, देश-
निकाला

banjo *n.* बैंजो, पंचतंत्री*

bank *n.* किनारा, बैंक *v.i.*
भरोसा करना

banker *n.* साहूकार, बैंक का
संचालक या साझीदार

bankrupt *n. & a.* दिवालिया ;
v.t. दिवाला निकालना

bankruptcy *n.* दिवालियापन,
दिवाला, सत्यानाश

banner *n.* झंडा

banquet *n.* भोज ; *v.t. & i.*
भोज देना, पेट भरना

banter *v.t.* हंसी उड़ाना, छेड़ना ;
n. हंसी*, छेड़*

banyan *n.* बरगद

baptism *n.* बपतिस्मा, ईसाई
दीक्षा या नामकरण संस्कार

baptize *v.t.* ईसाई बनाना,
बपतिस्मा देना, नाम धरना

bar *n.* डंडा, रोक*, छड़*, घेरा,
शराबखाना, वकील-संघ ; *v.t.*
रोकना

barbarian *a.* अशिष्ट, गंवार,
बर्बर, ग़ैर-ईसाई

barbaric *a.* असभ्य, गंवारू

barbarism *n.* असभ्यता*,
गंवारपन, बर्बर अवस्था*

barbarity *n.* क्रूरता, गंवारू
रुचि

barbarous *a.* क्रूर, बर्बर, अपढ़

barbed *a.* कंटीला

barber *n.* नाई

bard *n.* भाट, चारण, कवि

bare *a.* नंगा, छूछा, मात्र, अरक्षित; *v.t.* नंगा करना, खोलना

barely *adv.* केवल, मात्र, मुश्किल से

bargain *n.* मोलतोल, सौदा, लाभ का सौदा; *v.t.* सौदा करना

barge *n.* बजरा

bark *n.* वल्कल, छाल*, तीन मस्तूलों का जहाज, भूंक*; *v.t.* भूंकना, छाल छुड़ाना

barley *n.* जौ

barm *n.* खमीग

barn *n.* खलिहान, बखार

barometer *n.* बैरोमीटर, वायु-मान यंत्र

barrack *n.* सेनावास

barrage *n.* नदी-बांध, आड़*

barrel *n.* पीपा, बन्दूक की नली*, 31½ गैलन मदिरा

barren *a.* बांझ, ऊसर, व्यर्थ, मंद

barricade *n.* क़िलेबंदी*, आड़*

barrier *n.* आड़, सीमागुल्म, रुकावट*, प्रतिबंध

barrister *n.* बैरिस्टर, बड़ा वकील

barter *v.t.* माल बदलना, घाटे का सौदा करना; *n.* अदल-बदल का व्यापार, वस्तु-विनिमय

base *n.* आधार, अड्डा, मूल; *a.* नीच, छोटा; *v.t.* नींव डालना

baseless *a.* निराधार

basement *n.* तहखाना

bashful *a.* विनीत, लज्जालु

basic *a.* मौलिक, बुनियादी; ～ education बुनियादी शिक्षा*

basis *n.* मूल, आधार

basket *n.* टोकरी*, डलिया*

bastard *n.* हरामी

bastion *n.* बुर्ज, गरगज

bat *n.* चमगादड़, बल्ला

batch *n.* दल, जत्था

bath *n.* स्नान

bathe *v.t. & i.* नहलाना, नहाना

battalion *n.* बटालियन, पलटन*

battery *n.* बैटरी

battle *n.* लड़ाई*; *v.t.* लड़ाई करना; battle-field रण-भूमि; battle-plane समर विमान

bayonet *n.* किरिच, संगीन; *v.t.* संगीन भोंकना

beach *n.* समुद्र-तट

beacon *n.* प्रकाश, प्रकाशस्तम्भ

bead *n.* गुरिया, मनका

bear *n.* भालू; great~सप्तर्षि (तारे) *v.t. & i.* सहना

beard *n.* दाढ़ी*

bearer *n.* बैरा, वाहक

bearing *n.* बर्ताव

beast *n.* जानवर

beastly *a.* जानवर की तरह

beat *v.t. & i.* पीटना, हराना, फड़कना; *n.* चोट*, थाप*, गश्त, धड़कन*

beauty *n.* रूप, शोभा*, सुन्दर स्त्री*

because *adv. & conj.* क्योंकि, इसलिए

beckon *v.t. & i.* संकेत करना, संकेत से बुलाना

become *v.t. & i.* होना, फबना

becoming *a.* उपयुक्त

bed *n.* बिस्तर, खाट*, क्यारी*; *v.t. & i.* सोना, पौद लगाना

bedeck *v.t.* सजाना

bedevil *v.t.* पैशाचिक बर्ताव करना

bee *n.* मधुमक्खी*

beef *n.* गोमांस

beer *n.* बियर, जौ की शराब*

befall *v.t.* आ पड़ना, बीतना

befool *v.t.* मूर्ख बनाना

before *adv. prep. & conj.* पहले, सामने, आगे

beforehand *adv.* पहले ही

befriend *v.t.* मित्रवत व्यवहार करना, मित्र बनाना

beg *v.t. & i.* भीख मांगना, गिड़गिड़ाना

beget *v.t.* जनना, उत्पन्न करना

begin *v.t. & i.* आरम्भ करना

beguile *v.t.* मोहना, छलना

behalf *n.* पक्ष

behave *v.i.* आचरण करना

behaviour *n.* आचरण

behead *v.t.* सिर काट लेना

behest *n.* आज्ञा*

behind *adv., prep.* पीछे, बाद को

beholden *a.* आभारी

behove *v.i.* फबना, कर्त्तव्य या योग्य होना

being *n.* अस्तित्व, जीव

belabour *v.t.* बुरी तरह पीटना

beleaguer *v.t.* घेरा डालना, घेर लेना

belie *v.t. & i.* झुठलाना, पूरा न उतरना

belief *n.* विश्वास, श्रद्धा*, मत

believe *v.t. & i.* विश्वास करना, मानना, विचार रखना

believer *n.* विश्वासी, स्वधर्म-विश्वासी, आस्तिक

bell *n.* घंटा, घंटी*, घुंघरू

belle *n.* सुन्दरी

bellicose *a.* लड़ाका, झगड़ालू

belligerency *n.* युद्ध में रत

होने की दशा*

belligerent *a. & n.* युद्धरत (राज्य)

bellows *n.* भाथी*, धौंकनी*

belly *n.* पेट, तोंद*

belong *v.i.* संबद्ध होना

belongings *n.pl* सम्पत्ति*, माल-ग्रसबाब

beloved *a.* प्रिय, माशूक़

below *adv. & prep.* नीचे

belt *n.* पेटी*, कमरबन्द; *v.t.* पेटी बांधना

bench *n.* बेंच, न्यायपीठ

bend *v.t. & i.* मोड़ना, मुड़ना, नम्र होना; *n.* झुकाव, मोड़

beneath *adv. & prep.* नीचे, नीचे की ओर

beneficial *a.* लाभदायी

benefit *n.* लाभ; *v.t. & i.* लाभ उठाना

benevolence *n.* दया*, उदारता*

benevolent *a.* दयालु, उदार

bequeath *v.t.* वसीयत में देना

bereave *v.t.* वंचित या वियुक्त होना

bereavement *n.* शोक दशा*

beset *v.t.* घेर लेना, धावा करना

bestow *v.t.* प्रदान करना

betel *n.* पान; **betelnut** सुपारी

betray *v.t.* विश्वासघात करना

betrothal *n.* सगाई*

betterment *n.* उन्नति*, सुधार

between *prep. & adv.* बीच में, के बीच

beverage *n.* पेय, मदिरा*

beware *v.i.* सावधान होना, सचेत रहना

bewilderment *n.* घबराहट*, हैरानी*

bewitch *v.t.* जादू डालना, मोहित करना

beyond *adv. & prep.* से अधिक, के परे, के पार

Bible *n.* बाइबिल, इंजील

bibliography *n.* ग्रन्थसूची*

bicycle *n.* साइकिल

bid *v.t. & i.* नीलाम में बोली बोलना

bidding *n.* आज्ञा*

biennial *a.* द्विवार्षिक

bier *n.* टिकठी*, अर्थी*

bifurcate *v.t.* दो शाखाओं में बांटना

big *a.* बड़ा, महान

bigamy *n.* दो विवाहों की प्रथा*

bigotry *n.* कट्टरता*

bilingual *a.* द्विभाषिक

bill *n.* बिल, विधेयक, बीजक

billion *n.* दस खरब

billow *n.* तरंग*, बड़ी लहर*

bind *v.t. & i.* बांधना

binding *n.* जिल्द*; *a.* बाध्य-कारी

binocular *n.* दूरबीन

biographer *n.* जीवनी-लेखक

biography *n.* जीवनी*

biology *n.* जीव-विज्ञान

biologist *n.* जीव-विज्ञानी

bioscope *n.* बाइस्कोप

bird *n.* चिड़िया*

birth *n.* जन्म

birthright *n.* जन्मसिद्ध अधि-कार

biscuit *n.* बिस्कुट

bishop *n.* बिशप, बड़ा पादरी

bite *v.t.* काटना; *n.* दांत की काट*

bitter *a.* कड़वा, पीड़ाकर

black *a.* काला, अन्धकारमय; *n.* कालिमा* हब्शी, black art जादू; black-board श्यामपट्ट

olackmail *n.* भेद छिपाने या खोलने की घूस* या धमकी*

blacksheep *n.* कुलकलंक

bladder *n.* मूत्राशय

blade *n.* ब्लेड, पत्ती*, शस्त्र का फल

blasphemy *n.* ईश्वर-निन्दा*

blast *n.* आंधी का भकोरा, विस्फोट; *v.t.* विस्फोट से उड़ा देना

blaze *n.* प्रभा*, ज्वौ*

bleak *a.* आनन्द-रहित, बेरंग

bleed *v.i. & t.* खून बहना या बहाना, लहू चूसना

blend *v.t. & i.* मिश्रित करना; *n.* सम्मिश्रण

bless *v.t.* आशीर्वाद देना

blind *a.* अन्धा, अज्ञ

blindfold *v.t.* आंखों पर पट्टी बांधना

bliss *n.* परम सुख

block *n.* कुन्दा, छपाई का ब्लाक

blockade *n.* नाकाबंदी*

blockhead *n.* मूर्ख

blood *n.* खून, वंश

bloodshed *n.* रक्तपात

bloom *n.* फूल; *v.t.* फूल का या (की तरह) खिलना

blossom *n.* बौर; *v.t.* बौर आना

blow *v.t. & i.* बहना, बहाना; blow out बुझाना; *n.* घूंसा, चोट*

blue *n.* नीला रंग; *a.* नीला; blue-book संसद की रिपोर्ट, blue print मूल योजना*

blunder *n.* भारी भूल

blunt *a.* भुथरा, मन्द बुद्धि

blush *n.* लालिमा*; *v.i.* लजाना

board *n.* बोर्ड, मंडल; *v.t.* जहाज पर चढ़ना; above board ईमानदारी से

boast *v.i.* डींग हांकना; *n.* झूठा गर्व

boat *n.* नाव*

bodice *n.* चोली*

body *n.* शरीर, शव, समुदाय

bodyguard *n.* अंगरक्षक

bog *n.* दलदल

boggy *a.* दलदली

bogus *a.* बनावटी, निकम्मा

boil *n.* फोड़ा ; *v.t. & i.* उबालना

boiler *n.* भट्ठी, बायलर

boisterous *a.* उद्दाम, ऊधमी

bold *a.* साहसी, मोटा (टाइप)

bolt *n.* पेंच; *v.t. & i.* पेंच कसना, चटकनी लगाना

bomb *n.* बम; *v.t.* बमबारी करना

bombard *v.t.* बमबारी करना

bombardment *n.* बमबारी*, गोलंदाजी*

bomber *n.* बममार, बममार विमान

bonafide *a. & adv.* यथार्थ

bond *n.* बंधन

bondage *n.* दासता*

bone *n.* हड्डी*; bone of contention झगड़े की जड़*

bonfire *n.* होलिका*, विजयाग्नि*

bonus *n.* बोनस

book *n.* पुस्तक*, बही*, *v.t.* दर्ज करना, माल बुक करना

bookish *a.* किताबी

book-keeping *n.* बहीखाता, हिसाब-किताब

boon *n.* वरदान, लाभ

boost *n.* बढ़ोतरी*: *v.t.* आगे बढ़ाना

boot *n.* बूट जूता

booty *n.* लूट का माल

border *n.* सीमा*, किनारा; *v.t.* किनारी लगाना

borrow *v.t.* उधार लेना

bosom *n.* हृदय

boss *n.* बॉस, अधिपुरुष

botany *n.* वनस्पतिशास्त्र

bother *v.t. & i.* खीझना या खिझाना

botheration *n.* खीझ*, झंझट*

bottle *n.* बोतल*; *v.t.* बोतल में भरना

bottom *n.* तल, पेंदा

bountiful *a.* यथेष्ट, उदार-हृदय

bounty *n.* उदार उपहार

bouquet *n.* फूलों का गुच्छा

bow *v.t. & i.* झुकाना, *n.* धनुष

bowels *n.pl.* आंत*, आंतड़ियां*

bowl *n.* कटोरा, प्याला

box *n.* बक्स

boxing *n.* मुक्केबाजी*

boy *n.* लड़का

boycott *v.t.* बहिष्कार करना

brain n. दिमाग

brake n. ब्रेक

branch n. शाखा*

brandy n. ब्रान्डी*

brave a. वीर, दिलेर

bravery n. वीरता*

breach n. दरार*, संबंध-विच्छेद; v.t. & i. दरार या व्यवधान डालना

bread n. रोटी*, आहार, जीविका*

breadth n. चौड़ाई*, विस्तार

breadthwise adv. चौड़ाई में

break v.t. & i. तोड़ना, टूटना, सेंध लगाना

breakage n. तोड़फोड़ या उसका हरजाना

breakdown n. दुर्घटना-जनित रुकावट* या ठहराव

breakfast n. नाश्ता; v.t. & i. नाश्ता करना

breast n. सीना, छाती*, स्तन

breath n. सांस*

breathe v.t. & i. सांस लेना

breathless a. बेदम, हांफता

breed v.t. & i. जनना, नस्ल बढ़ाना; n. नस्ल*

breeding n. शिष्टाचार

breeze n. मंद पवन

brevity n. संक्षेप

brew v.t. मदिरा बनाना

brewery n. शराब की भट्टी* या कारखाना

bride n. दुल्हन*

bridegroom n. दूल्हा

bridge n. पुल; v.t. पुल बांधना

brief a. संक्षिप्त

brigade n. ब्रिगेड

brigadier n. ब्रिगेडियर

bright a. उज्ज्वल, स्पष्ट, प्रसन्न

brilliance n. प्रतिभा*; चमक-दमक*

brilliant a. प्रतिभावान, चमकीला

bring v.t. लाना; bring about घटित करना, bring out प्रकाशित करना, bring over सहमत करना, bring round मना लेना, bring up पालन-पोषण करना

brink n. तट, किनारा

brittle a. शीशे की तरह टूटने वाला

broad a. चौड़ा, उदार

broadcast n. प्रसारण; v.t. प्रसारित करना

brochure n. ब्रोचर

broker n. दलाल

brother n. भाई; brother-in-law साला, बहनोई, देवर, जेठ

brotherhood n. बन्धुत्व

brutal a. क्रूर

bud *n.* कली*, कोंपल; *v.t.* अंकुर लगना

buffalo *n.* भैंस*, भैसा

buffoon *n.* भांड, विदूषक

build *v.t.* निर्माण करना, बनाना

building *n.* इमारत*, भवन

bulb *n.* बल्ब, बिजली का लट्टू

bulk *n.* ढेर, थोक

bulky *a.* बड़ा, भारी, महाकाय

bull *n.* सांड, बैल

bulldog *n.* 'बुलडॉग' कुत्ता

bullet *n.* बंदूक या पिस्तौल की गोली*

bulletin *n.* बुलेटिन, अधका-रिक विज्ञप्ति*

bullion *n.* सोना-चांदी*, सोने या चांदी की ठोस ईंट*

bullock *n.* बैल

bully *n.* दंगाई, *v.t.* डरा-धमकाकर कुछ कराना

bulwark *n.* परकोटा

bunch *n.* गुच्छा

bundle *n.* गट्ठा, गठरी*

bungalow *n.* बंगला

bungle *v.t. & i.* गोलमाल करना, विफल होना; *n.* गोल-माल

bunker *n.* तलघर

buoyancy *n.* प्रसन्नचित्तता*

buoyant *a.* प्रसन्नचित्त

burden *a.* बोझ, कविता की टेक*; *v.t.* बोझ लादना

burdensome *a.* भारी, कष्ट-कर

bureaucracy *n.* नौकरशाही*

bureaucrat *n.* नौकरशाह

burglar *n.* सेंधमार*, सेंध-चोर

burglary *n.* सेंधमारी*, सेंध-चोरी*

burgle *v.t.* सेंध मारना

burial *n.* समाधि,* अर्थी*

burial ground कब्रिस्तान

burly *a.* मुस्टंडा

burn *v.t. & i.* जलाना, जलना; *n.* दाह, जलन*

burst *v.t. & i.* फट पड़ना

bury *v.t.* गाड़ना, दफ़न करना

bus *n.* बस*

bush *n.* झाड़ी*, झाड़ी-झुरमुट

bushel *n.* 'बुशल' (तौल में 8 गैलन)

business *n.* कार्य, व्यापार, सरोकार

businessman *n.* व्यवसायी

busy *a.* व्यस्त

busybody *n.* पराए काम में बाधा डालने या टांग अड़ाने वाला

but *prep., conj., adv.* किन्तु, मात्र, सिवा, भी; *n.* आपत्ति, आरोप; *v.t.* अगर-मगर करना

butcher *n.* कसाई; *v.t.* नृशंस-हत्या करना

butter *n.* मक्खन, चाटु-

कारिता*; *v.t.* चुपड़ना, चाप-
लूसी करना

butterfly *n.* तितली

buttermilk *n.* मट्ठा, छाछ*

buttock *n.* चूतड़

button *n.* बटन

buy *v.t.* मोल लेना

buyer *n.* खरीदार, एजेंट

buzz *v.t. & i.* भनभनाना ; *n.*
भनभनाहट*, चहल-पहल*

by *prep.* से, द्वारा, में, की ओर,
के पास, साथ, में, से, का, की
शपथ लेकर, के विषय में;

adv. पास से, से होकर;
by the by प्रसंगवश,
विषयांतर से

byelection, bye-election *n.*
उपनिर्वाचन, उपचुनाव

bylaw, bye-law *n.* उपनियम

bypass *v.i.* बचकर या बचाकर
निकल जाना

byproduct *n.* उपोत्पाद, गौण
उत्पादन

byre *n.* गोशाला*

byword *n.* लोकोक्ति*, कहावत*

C

cab *n.* किराये की गाड़ी*

cabbage *n.* करमकल्ला

cabin *n.* कैबिन, जहाज की
कोठरी*

cabinet *n.* मंत्रिमंडल, छोटा
कमरा

cable *n.* समुद्री तार; *v.t.*
समुद्री तार भेजना

cactus *n.* कैक्टस, नागफनी

cadet *n.* कैडेट, सैनिक छात्र

cafe *n.* कैफे, काफ़ीघर

cage *n.* पिंजड़ा

cake *n.* केक, मालपुवा

calamity *n.* विपत्ति*, दैवी
प्रकोप

calculate *v.t.* हिसाब लगाना,
अनुमान करना

calculation *n.* हिसाब, गणना

calendar *n.* कैलेण्डर

calf *n.* बछड़ा, बछिया*

call *v.t. & i.* पुकारना; *n.*
पुकार*

calling *n.* पेशा

callous *a.* कठोर हृदय

calm *a. & n.* शान्त, शान्ति*;
v.t. शान्त करना

calumny *n.* झूठा अभियोग,
आक्षेप

camel *n.* ऊंट

camera *n.* कैमरा, एकांत या

अंधेरा कक्ष

camouflage *n.* छलावरण

camp *n.* शिविर, पड़ाव

campaign *n.* सैनिक कार्य-वाही*, व्यवस्थित आन्दोलन

camphor *n.* कपूर

can *n.* कनस्तर; *v.t.* डिब्बा बंद करना; *v. aux.* सकना

canal *n.* नहर*

cancel *v.t.* रद्द या मंसूख करना

cancellation *n.* मंसूखी*

cancer *n.* कसर, नासूर

candid *a.* खरा, सरल

candidate *n.* उम्मीदवार

candidature *n.* उम्मीदवारी*

candle *n.* मोमबत्ती*

candour *n.* खरापन

candy *n.* मिसरी; *v.t. & i.* पागना, पगना

cane *n.* बेंत, छड़ी; *v.t.* बेंत लगाना, बेंत से बुनना

canopy *n.* चंदोवा, शामियाना

canteen *n.* कन्टीन

cantonment *n.* छावनी*,

canvas *n.* कनवस, चित्रफलक

canvass *v.t. & i.* वोट मांगना

cap *n.* टोपी*, *v.t & i.* टोपी पहनना

capability *n.* सामर्थ्य

capable *a.* गुणी, योग्य, समर्थ

capacious *a.* विशाल, लंबा-चौड़ा

capacity *n.* क्षमता*

capital राजधानी*, पूंजी*

capital goods *n.* पूंजीगत माल

capital levy *n.* पूंजीकर

capitalist *n.* पूंजीपति

capitalise *v.t.* पूंजी की भांति बरतना, पूंजी में परिणत करना, मूल बनाना

capitation tax *n.* प्रतिव्यक्ति-कर

capitulate *v.t.* किसी शर्त पर हथियार डाल देना

capricious *a.* चपल, सनकी, मनमौजी

capricorn *n.* मकर राशि*

capsize *n*, *v.t. & i.* नाव या जहाज का/को उलटना या औंधा करना

capstan *n.* लंगर की चरखी*

captain *n.* कप्तान

captaincy, captainship *n.* कप्तानी*, सरदारी*, जमादारी*

caption *n.* शीर्षक

captivate *v.t.* बंदी बनाना

captivating *a.* लुभावना, मनोहर

captive *n. & a.* बंदी, बंदी का

captivity *n.* बंदी-दशा*, कारावास

capture *v.t.* बंदी बनाना, अधिकृत करना

car *n.* गाड़ी*, मोटरगाड़ी*, डब्बा

carat *n.* क़िरत (=1 रत्ती 6 चावल 7-$\frac{7}{15}$ खसखस), सोने की शुद्धता का मान 'कैरट' (पूर्ण शुद्ध=24 'कैरट')

caravan *n.* कारवां

carbolic acid *n.* धूने का तेज़ाब

carbon *n.* कार्बन

card *n.* ताश, कार्ड

cardboard *n.* गत्ता, दफ़्ती*

cardamom *n.* इलायची*

cardinal *a.* प्रधान, मूल; *n.* पोप-निर्वाचक धर्माधिकारी

care *n.* चिंता*, दायित्व, मारफ़त*

career *n.* जीवन-यात्रा*, आजीविका*

careful *a.* सावधान

careless *a.* असावधान

caress *v.t.* लाड़ करना, चूमना

cargo *n.* जहाज का खेप

caricature *n. & v.t.* भोंडी नक़्ल* (बनाना)

carnival *n.* आनन्दोत्सव

carpenter *n.* बढ़ई

carpentry *n.* बढ़ईगिरी*

carpet *n.* दरी*, गलीचा; *v.t.* गलीचे से ढंकना

carriage *n.* ढुलाई*

carrier *n.* वाहक

carrot *n.* गाजर*

carry *v.t. & i.* ढोना, पहुंचाना

cart *n.* छकड़ा

cartage *n.* छकड़े की लदाई* या भाड़ा

cartoon *n.* कार्टून, व्यंगचित्र

cartridge *n.* कारतूस

cartridge paper *n.* मोटा खुरदुरा कागज

carve *v.t. & i.* टांकना

carving *n.* तराश*, संगतराशी*

cascade *n.* झालर*

case *n.* घटना*, कांड, पेटी*; *v.t.* खोल चढ़ाना

cash *n.* रोकड़*; *v.t.* भुनाना

cashier *n.* खजांची

cast *v.t. & i.* फेंकना, सांचे में ढालना; *n.* निक्षेप, सांचा, अभिनेता-वर्ग

caste *n.* जाति*

castigate *v.t.* दंड देना, फटकारना

casting vote *n.* निर्णायक मत

castle *n.* गढ़

castor oil *n.* रेंड़ी का तेल

castrate *v.t.* बधिया करना

casual *a.* आकस्मिक

casualty *n.* आकस्मिक दुर्घटना*

cat *n.* बिल्ली*

catalogue *n.* सूचीपत्र

catch *v.t. & i.* पकड़ना, बंदी करना; *n.* पकड़*

catchment *n.* जलग्रह, बहेत*

categorical *a.* सुनिश्चित, स्पष्ट

category *n.* श्रेणी*, पद

caterer *n.* भोजनादि का व्यव-स्थापक

cathedral *n.* प्रधान गिरजा

catholic *a.* उदार

Catholic *n.* रोमन कैथोलिक ईसाई

cattle *n.* ढोर, गोधन

cauliflower *n.* फूलगोभी*

cause *n.* कारण, अभियोग, कार्य; *v.t.* कारण होना

caustic *n. & a.* दाहक, दाहक क्षार, तीखा

caution *n.* सावधानी*, चौक-सी*; *v.t.* चेताना, झिड़कना

cavalcade *n.* घुड़सवार-दल

cavalier *n.* घुड़सवार

cavalry *n.* घुड़सवार, सेना या सैनिक

cave *n.* गुफा*; *v.t* गुफा बनाना

cavern *n.* गुहा*, कन्दरा*

cavity *n.* पोला भाग, छेद

caw *n. & v.i.* कांव-कांव (करना)

cease *v.t. & i.* समाप्त करना या होना; *n.* समाप्ति*

ceaseless *a.* निरंतर

ceiling *n.* भीतरी छत*, ऊपरी सीमा*

celebrate *v.t. & i.* उत्सव मनाना

celebrated *a.* यशस्वी, सुप्रसिद्ध

celebration *n.* समारोह

celebrity *n.* यशस्वी या सुप्रसिद्ध व्यक्ति, प्रसिद्धि*

celibacy *n.* क्वांरापन, ब्रह्मचर्य

cell *n.* बैटरी की इकाई*, जीवकोश, जेल का एकांत कमरा ('तन्हाई'*)

cellar *n.* तलघर

cement *n.* सीमेंट; *v.t.* सीमेंट से जोड़ना

cemetery *n.* कब्रिस्तान

cense *v.t.* धूप जलाना, धूपदान से पूजना

censer *n.* धूपदानी*

censor *n. & v.t.* सेंसर (करना)

censure *n. & v.t.* निंदा* (करना)

census *n.* जन-गणना*

cent *n.* सौ, सैंकड़ा, $\frac{1}{100}$ डालर

centenarian *a. & n.* सौ वर्ष का (व्यक्ति)

centenary *n.* शतवार्षिकी*; *a.* शतवार्षिक

centesimal *a.* शतमिक

centigrade *a.* सेंटीग्रेड, सौ अंशों में बंटा

centigramme *n.* सेंटीग्राम, $\frac{1}{100}$ ग्राम

central *a.* केंद्रीय, प्रधान

centralize *v.t. & i.* केंद्रीय या

केंद्रस्थ करना या होना

centre *n.* केंद्र

centrifugal *a.* केंद्र से दूर जाने वाला, 'अपकेंद्र'

centripetal *a.* केंद्र की ओर जानेवाला 'अभिकेंद्र'

century *n.* शतक, सदी*

cereal *n.* अनाज; *a.* अनाज-संबंधी

ceremonial *a.* शिष्टाचार-युक्त, अनुष्ठानिक

ceremonious *a.* शिष्टाचारी

ceremony *n.* समारोह, संस्कार

certain *a.* निश्चित, अवश्यं-भावी, कोई

certainly *adv.* निस्संदेह

certainty *n.* निश्चयता*

certificate *n. & v.t.* प्रमाण-पत्र (देना)

certify *v.t.* प्रमाणित करना

cess *n.* चुंगी*, उप-कर

cessation *n.* समाप्ति*, विराम

cesspool *n.* नाबदान, चहबच्चा

chain *n. & v.t.* बेड़ी* (डालना), हथकड़ी* (पह-नाना), लड़ी*, जरीब*

chair *n.* कुरसी*, विश्व-विद्यालय की पीठिका

chalk *n. & v.t.* खड़िया* (से लिखना या चिह्न करना)

challenge *n. & v.t.* चुनौती* (देना)

chamber *n.* मंडल, प्रकोष्ठ

champagne *n.* 'शैंम्पेन' मदिरा*-विशेष

champion *n.* वीर, पक्षधर; *a.* सर्वजयी; *v.t.* लक्ष्यरक्षा या समर्थन करना

chance *n.* संयोग; *v.t.* अकस्मात घटित होना

chancellor *n.* कुलपति

chandelier *n.* झाड़-फानूस

change *v.t. & i.* बदलना भुनाना; *n.* परिवर्तन, रेज-गारी*

chaos *n.* गड़बड़ी*, उथल-पुथल*, विप्लव की देवी*

chaotic *a.* अस्त-व्यस्त

chapel *n.* छोटा गिरजा

chapter *n.* अध्याय

character *n.* चरित्र

charge *v.t.* खर्च या दाम मांगना या लगाना, धावा बोलना, दोषी या दायी ठहराना, दायित्व या काम सौंपना; *n.* लागत*, दाम

chariot *n.* रथ

charioteer *n.* सारथी, (ज्यो-तिष में) प्रजापति

charitable *a.* धर्मार्थ, दानी

charity *n.* धर्मदान, भिक्षा*

charlatan *n. & a.* मायावी, ढोंगी

charm *n.* जादू, मोहकता; *v.t.*

मोहना, जादू करना

chart *n. & v.t.* रेखाचित्र या लेखाचित्र या मानचित्र (बनाना)

charter *n.* राज-पत्र

chase *v.t.* पीछा करना; *n.* पीछा, शिकार

chaste *a.* अछूता, मार्जित

chastity *n.* विशुद्धता*, सादगी*

chat *n. & v.i.* गप* (लड़ाना)

chatter *n. & v.t.* बकवास* (करना)

chauffeur *n.* मोटर-चालक

cheap *a.* सस्ता, सुलभ, निकम्मा

cheapen *v.t. & i.* सस्ता या सुलभ करना या होना

cheat *v.t.* छलना, धोखा या बेईमानी करना; *n.* ठग, धूर्त

check *v.t.* रोकना, जांचना; *n.* रोक*, चारखाना

checkmate *n. & v.t.* शह* (देना), मात* (करना), शह-मात*

cheek *n.* गाल

cheer *n., v.t. & i.* जयकार* या वाहवाही* (करना)

cheerful *a.* प्रफुल्ल

cheerless *a.* निरानंद

cheese *n.* पनीर

chemical *a.* रासायनिक; *n.* रसायन

chemise *n.* शमीज़*, कुरती*

chemistry *n.* रसायनशास्त्र

cheque *n.* हुंडी, चेक*

cherish *v.t.* लौ लगा रखना, संजोना

cheroot *n.* चुरुट

chess *n.* शतरंज

chessmen *n. pl.* मोहरे

chest *n.* पिटारी*, छाती*

chestnut *n.* बलूत

chew *v.t. & i.* चबाना; *n.* चर्वण

chick *n.* चूज़ा

chicken *n.* चूज़ा, चूज़े का मांस

chide *v.t. & i.* डांटना, बुरा-भला कहना

chief *a.* मुख्य; *n.* मुखिया, सरदार, शासक

chiefly *adv.* मुख्यतः

chieftain *n.* कबीले या डाकू दल का सरदार

child *n.* बच्चा, बच्ची*

childhood *n.* बचपन

childish *a.* बचकाना, बालोचित

chill *n.* ठंड*, ठिठुरन*

chilli *n.* लाल मिर्च*

chilly *a.* सर्द, जड़वत्

chimney *n.* चिमनी*

chimpanzee *n.* अंगोला-वानर, चिंपांज़ी

chin *n.* ठुड्डी*, चिबुक

china *n. & a.* चीनी मिट्टी
(का बना), चीनी का बरतन

chirp *n., v.t. & i* कूजन
(करना), चहक* (-ना)

chisel *n. & v.t.* टांकी* या
छेनी* (से गढ़ना)

chivalrous *a.* शूरोचित,
सुसभ्य, उदार

chivalry *n.* शूरता

chloroform *n.* क्लोरोफार्म

choice *n.* चुनाव, पसंद* *a.*
बढ़िया

choir *n.* गायक-मंडली*

choke *v.t. & i.* गला या दम
घोंटना या घुटना; *n.* श्वास-
रोध

cholera *n.* हैज़ा

choose *v.t.* चुनना, छांट लेना

chop *v.t. & i.* बोटियां काटना

chord *n.* तांत*, बाजे का तार

chorus *n.* सहगान, कोरस

Christ *n.* ईसा मसीह, मसीहा

christen *v.t. & i.* बप्तिस्मा
करना, नाम देना

Christendom *n.* ईसाई-जगत्

Christian *n. & a.* ईसाई

Christianity *n.* ईसाई धर्म,
ईसाइयत*

Christmas *n.* ईसा का जन्म-
दिन, 'बड़ा दिन'

chromatic *a.* चटकीला

chronic *a.* चिरकालिक

chronicle *n.* वृत्तांत, इतिहास,
कालक्रम से अभिलेखन

chronological *a.* कालक्रमबद्ध

chronology *n.* कालक्रम-
निर्णय-विद्या*

chronometer *n.* बिलकुल ठीक
समय बतानेवाली घड़ी*

chrysanthemum *n.* गुलदाऊदी

chubby *a.* हृष्ट-पुष्ट, गलफुल्ला

chum *n.* लंगोटिया यार

church *n.* गिरजा

churchyard *n.* गिरजे का
कब्रिस्तान

churl *n.* कंजूस, असभ्य

churlish *a.* अशिष्ट, अक्खड़,
गंवार

churn *v.t. & i.* मथना; *n.*
मंथन

cigar *n.* चुरुट, सिगार

cigarette *n.* सिगरेट*

cinema, cinematograph *n.*
चलचित्र, चलचित्र दिखाने
का यंत्र, सिनेमा, सिनेमाघर

cinnamon *n.* दालचीनी*

cipher, cypher *n.* शून्य

circle *n.* वृत्त, मंडली*; *v.t. &*
i. घेर लेना, परिक्रमा करना

circuit *n.* सर्किट, परिधि*, गश्त

circular *a.* वृत्तीय, चक्करदार

circulate *v.t. & i.* घुमाना,
संचारित करना या होना

circulation *n.* दौरा, बिकी या

बंटी प्रतियों की संख्या*, मुद्रा-
चलन

circumference *n.* परिधि*,
मण्डल

circumscribe *v.t.* घेरा बनाना

circumspect *a.* चौकस,
चौकन्ना

circumstance *n.* घटना*
(ब॰व॰) परिस्थिति*

circus *n.* सरकस

citadel *n.* किला, नगरकोट

cite *v.t.* उद्धरण देना, तलब
करना

citizen *n.* नागरिक

citizenship *n.* नागरिकता*

city *n.* नगर, शहर

civic *a.* नागरिक

civics *n.* नागरिकशास्त्र

civil *a.* नागरिक, असैनिक,
सभ्य, दीवानी

civil war *n.* गृहयुद्ध

civilization *n.* सभ्यता*.

civilize *v.t.* सभ्य बनाना

civilized *a.* सभ्य

claim *n.* & *v.t.* मांग*
(जताना); दावा (करना)

claimant *n.* दावेदार, हकदार

clamour *n.* कोलाहल; *v.t.*
& *i.* शोर मचाना या मचना

clan *n.* गोत्र, परिजन, कबीला

clarify *v.t.* & *i.* स्पष्ट करना

clarion *n.* तुरही*, ललकार*

clash *n.* टक्कर*; *v.t.* टकराना,
संघर्ष करना

clasp *n.*, *v.t.* & *i.* अंकवार*
(भरना), पकड़* (-ना)

class *n.* & *v.t.* वर्ग (-निर्धारण
करना), श्रेणी* (देना), कक्षा*

classic *n.* क्लासिक, गौरव ग्रंथ

classic, classical *a.* क्लासिकी,
शास्त्रीय, श्रेष्ठ

classification *n.* वर्गीकरण,
श्रेणीविभाजन, क्रमविन्यास

classify *v.t.* वर्गविभक्त या
श्रेणीबद्ध या क्रमबद्ध करना

clause *n.* खंडवाक्य, वाक्यखंड,
विधान की धारा*, दफ़ा*

claw *n.* चंगुल, पंजा

clay *n.* चिकनी या लसदार
मिट्टी*

clean *a.* & *v.t.* स्वच्छ या शुद्ध
(करना), निर्दोष; *n.* सफ़ाई*,
झाड़पोंछ*

cleanliness *n.* स्वच्छता*

cleanly *a.* स्वच्छ, सफ़ाई-
पसंद; *adv.* सफ़ाई से

cleanse *v.t.* स्वच्छ या पवित्र
करना, मांजना, शोधना

clear *a.* & *v.t.* शुद्ध या निर्मल
(करना), खाली या साफ़
(करना), बरी (करना),
बेबाक़ (करना); *adv.* साफ़-
साफ़

clearance *n.* सफ़ाई*, भुगतान*

clearly *adv.* स्पष्टतः, अवश्य

cleft *n.* दरार*, फांक*

clemency *n.* राजदया*, मृदुता*, क्षमा*

clement *a.* सदय, कृपाशील

clench, clinch *n., v.t. & i.* बंदिश*, जकड़*(-ना), अंतिम रूप से तय करना या पटाना

clergy *n.* पादरी-वर्ग

clerical *n. & a.* संसद् का पादरी सदस्य, पादरी या लिपिक संबंधी

clerk *n.* क्लर्क, मुंशी, सहायक पादरी

clever *a.* चतुर, दक्ष, फुर्तीला

client *n.* मुवक्किल, असामी

cliff *n.* खड़ी चट्टान*

climate *n.* जलवायु*

climax *n.* पराकाष्ठा*, उत्कर्ष; *v.t. & i.* पराकाष्ठा पर पहुंचना

climb *v.t. & i.* चढ़ना, उन्नति करना; *n.* चढ़ान*, चढ़ाव

climber *n.* आरोही, लता*

cling *v.i.* चिमटना, अडिग या कृतज्ञ या वफादार रहना

clinic *n.* दवाख़ाना

cloak *n.* लबादा

clock *n.* बड़ी घड़ी*, घंटा-घड़ी*

close *n.* अंत; *a.* गुप्त, पास, घना, बंद; *v.t. & i.* समाप्त या बंद करना या होना, सटकना, भिड़ना

closet *n.* गुप्त कोठरी*, बरतनों की आलमारी*

closing balance *n.* रोकड़ बाकी*

closure *n.* समापन, घेर

clot *n., v.t. & i.* थक्का या पिंड (बनाना या बनना)

cloth *n.* कपड़ा

clothe *v.t.* कपड़े पहनाना या देना, ढकना, उढ़ाना

clothes *n.pl.* पोशाक*

clothing *n.* पहनावा, आवरण

cloud *n. & v.t.* बादल (छाना), अंधेरा (छाना)

clouded, cloudy *a.* मेघमय, मलिन, धूमिल, उदास

clown *n.* विदूषक, भांड़, नक्काल, गंवार, उजड्डु

club *n. & v.t.* गदा या डंडा (मारना), क्लब, सभा, संघ; गड्डमड्ड कर लेना, इकट्ठा करना या हो जाना

clue *n.* संकेत, सूत्र, सुराग

clumsy *a.* भद्दा, बेढंगा

cluster *n.* गुच्छा, भुंड; *v.t. & i.* इकट्ठा करना या होना

clutch *v.t. & i.* चंगुल या झपट्टा मारना, मुट्ठी में भींचना; *n.* पंजा, शिकंजा

clutter *n.* हुल्लड़, हल्ला

coach n. बग्घी*, गृह-शिक्षक; v.t. & i. घर पर, या परीक्षा की तैयारी में पढ़ाना

coachman n. कोचवान

coal n. कोयला

coaltar n. अलकतरा

coalesce v.i. सम्मिलित या एक होना, साथ बढ़ना

coalescence n. सम्मिलन, संश्लेप

coalition n. संस्थाओं का अस्थायी मिलाप, संघिमेल; coalition govt. संयुक्त सरकार*

coarse a. घटिया, खुरदुरा, भद्दा

coarsen v.t. & i. भद्दा या खुरदुरा बनाना या होना

coast n. तट, समुद्रतट; v.i. (जहाज़ का) किनारे-किनारे चलना

coat n. कोट, समूर, मुलम्मा; v.t. मुलम्मा या कलई करना

coating n. कोट का कपड़ा, रंग आदि का पोट

coat of mail n. कवच

coax v.t. & i. फुसलाना, पटाना, दम-दिलासा देना

cobbler n. मोची

cobra n. करैत सांप

cobweb n. मकड़े का जाला

cock n. मुर्गा

cockatoo n काकातुआ

cock-pit n. मुर्गों के लड़ने का अखाड़ा

cockroach n. तिलचट्टा

coconut n. नारियल

code n. संहिता*, संकेतावली*

co-education n. सहशिक्षा*

coerce v.t. जबरन कराना

coercion n. जबरदस्ती*, दबाव

co-exist v.t. एक समय में होना, एक साथ होना

co-existence n. सहअस्तित्व

coffee n. कॉफ़ी*, कहवा

coffin n. ताबूत

cognizance n. पहचान*, हस्तक्षेप का अधिकार

coherent a. संगत

coin n. सिक्का

coinage n. सिक्का, धन, गढ़े हुए शब्द

colic n. उदरशूल

collaborate v.i. मिलकर काम करना

collapse v.i. भहराना, दिल के दौरे से मर जाना

collar n. कॉलर, गला

colleague n. सहकर्मी

collect v.t. & i. संग्रह करना, जमा या वसूल करना या होना

collected a. संग्रहीत

collective a. सामूहिक

collector n. संकलनकर्ता, संग्रहकर्ता, जिलाधीश

college *n.* कॉलेज, महाविद्यालय

collide *v.t.* टक ।ना, परस्पर विरोधी होना

colliery *n.* कोयलरी, कोयले की खान*

collision *n.* टक्कर*, टकराव

colloquial *a.* बोलचाल का

colloquy *n.* बातचीत* ग्राम बोलचाल*

colonel *n.* कर्नल

colonial *a.* उपनिवेशी, ग्रौप-निवेशिक

colonist *n.* उपनिवेशवासी

colonization *n.* उपनिवेश की स्थापना*

colonize *v.t.* उपनिवेश स्थापित करना या बसाना

colony *n.* कालोनी, उपनिवेश, नई बस्ती*

colossal *a.* प्रकांड, चमत्कार-पूर्ण

colossus *n.* प्रकांड या भीमा-कार मूर्ति* या व्यक्ति या साम्राज्य

colour *n.* रंग, (*pl.*) रंग के द्रव्य, पताका; *v.t.* रंगना

colourless *a.* फीका, बेरंग

column *n.* स्तंभ

coma *n.* अचेत दशा*

comb *n.* & *v.t.* कंघी* (करना), कलग़ी*, मधुछत्ता

combat *n.* & *v.t.* संग्राम या सामना (करना)

combatant *n.* & *a.* योद्धा, लड़नेवाला

combination *n.* संयोग, मेल

combine *v.t.* & *i.* संघटित करना या होना; *n.* दंबरी-मशीन*

combustible *a.* & *n.* शीघ्र जलनेवाला या दहनशील (पदार्थ)

combustion *n.* ज्वलन, दाह

come *v.i.* ग्राना, पहुंचना

comedy *n.* सुखांत नाटक

comet *n.* धूमकेतु

comfort *n.* & *v.t.* सुख या ग्राराम (पहुंचाना)

comfortable *a.* ग्रारामदेह

comic *a* & *n.* हास्यकर, हास्य-पत्रिका*

comical *a.* हास्यकारक, ग्रनीखा

command *n.* & *v.t.* कमान (में रखना), हिदायत*

commandant *n.* क़िलेदार, सेनानायक

commander *n.* सेनापति, कमांडर

commanding *a.* प्रभावशाली

commemorate *v.t.* स्मरण करना, ग्रभिनंदन करना

commence *v.t.* & *i.* ग्रारंभ करना या होना, उद्भूत होना

commencement *n.* ग्रारंभ

commend *v.t.* रक्षार्थ सौंपना, प्रशंसा करना

commendable *a.* प्रशंसनीय

commendation *n.* प्रशंसा*, सिफ़ारिश*

comment *v.t.* टीका या व्याख्या करना *n.* टीका*, टिप्पणी*, व्याख्या*, समीक्षा*, विवेचना*

commentary *n.* टीका*, समीक्षा*

commentator *n.* टीकाकार, समीक्षक

commerce *n.* वाणिज्य

commercial *a.* व्यापारिक

commission *n.* आयोग, आयुक्त-पद, कमीशन, दलाली* ; *v.t.* आयुक्त करना, अभियान का आदेश देना

commissioner *n.* आयुक्त, कमिश्नर

commit *v.t.* कर डालना, फंस या बंध जाना

committee *n.* कमेटी* समिति*

commodity *n.* जिंस*, उपयोगी वस्तु*

common *a.* सामान्य, उभय-निष्ठ, दोनों पक्षों को ग्राह्य

common noun *n.* जातिवाचक संज्ञा*

common sense *n.* समझ*, सामान्यबोध, व्यावहारिक ज्ञान

commoner *n.* सामान्यजन

commonwealth *n.* राष्ट्रमंडल

commotion *n.* क्षोभ, हल-चल*, विद्रोह

communal *a.* सांप्रदायिक, सार्वजनिक, पंचायती

communicate *v.t. & i.* सूचना देना, बताना, संचार करना

communication *n.* संपर्क, सूचना*, संचार

communism *n.* साम्यवाद

community *n.* संप्रदाय, समुदाय

commutation *n.* विनिमय, एकराशिदान, भुनाई*

companion *n.* साथी

company *n.* कंपनी, सेना का गुल्म

comparative *n. & a.* तुलना-त्मक, आपेक्षिक

compare *v.t.* तुलना या मिलान करना

comparison *n.* तुलना*, उपमा*

compartment *n.* विभाग, दरजा, डिब्बा

compassion *n.* करुणा* दया*, कृपा*, तरस*

compassionate *a.* कारुणिक, कृपालु

compatriot *n.* देशभाई

स्वदेशवासी

compel *v.t.* विवश करना, ढकेलना

compensate *v.t. & i.* हरजाना या मुझाविज़ा देना, क्षतिपूरण या प्रत्युपकार करना

compensation *n.* मुझाविज़ा क्षतिपूर्ति*

compete *v.t.* प्रतिस्पर्धा करना, बराबरी करना

competence *n.* कार्यनिर्वाह-क्षमता*, अर्हंता* (पात्रता*), संपन्नता*

competent *a.* सुयोग्य, निपुण

competition *n.* प्रतियोगिता*

competitive *a.* प्रतियोगिता-मूलक

compilation *n.* संग्रह, संकलन

compile *v.t.* संकलित करना, संग्रह तैयार करना

complacence, complacency *n.* तृप्ति*, आत्मतृप्ति*, प्रसन्नता*, शालीनता*

complacent *a.* आत्मतृप्त, प्रसन्न

complain *v.t.* अभियोग करना, असंतोष प्रकट करना, दुखड़ा रोना

complainant *n.* अभियोक्ता (मुद्दई)

complaint *n.* शिकायत*, अभियोग

complement *n. & v.t.* पूरक (जोड़ना)

complementary *a.* पूरक

complete *a. & v.t.* पूरा (करना)

complex *a.* जटिल

complexion *n.* रंगरूप, रंग-ढग

complexity *n.* उलझन*, पेचीदगी

complicate *v.t.* फंसाना, उलझाना

complication *n.* जटिल स्थिति*, गुत्थी*

compliment *n. & v.t.* प्रशंसा* या अभिनंदन या समादर (करना), स्तुतिवाद, (*pl.*) नमस्कार

comply *v.t.* आज्ञापालन करना, इच्छा पूरी करना, मानना

compose *v.t.* कंपोज़ करना, रागबद्ध करना, उद्वेग शांत करना

compositor *n.* कंपोज़ीटर, छापे के कांटे जमानेवाला

compost *n.* कूड़े की खाद*, मिलावट*

composure *n.* मानसिक संतुलन या शांति*

comprehend *v.t.* समझना, अंतर्भूत करना

comprehensible *a.* सुबोध

comprehension *n.* ज्ञान, बोध

comprehensive *a.* विस्तृत, बोध-संबंधी

compress *v.t.* दबाना, संक्षिप्त करना

comprise *v.t. & i.* से युक्त होना

compromise *n. & v.t.* समाधान या समझौता (करना)

compulsion *n.* विवशता*, दबाव

compulsory *a.* आवश्यक, अनिवार्य

compunction *n.* पश्चात्ताप, पछतावा

computation *n.* गणना*, हिसाब

compute *v.t.* गणना करना, लेखा करना

comrade *n.* मित्र, संगी, साथी

conceal *v.t.* छिपाना, परदा डालना

concede *v.t.* स्वीकार करना

conceit *n.* दंभ, कष्टकल्पना*

conceited *a.* दंभी, उद्धत, अभिमानी

conceivable *a.* बोधगम्य

conceive *v.t.* ध्यान में लाना, गर्भ से होना

concentrate *v.t. & i.* केंद्रित करना या होना; *n.* सारकृत द्रव्य

concentration *n.* एकाग्रता

concept *n.* धारणा*

conception *n.* सामान्य धारणा*, गर्भधारण

concern *v.t.* लगाव रखना, दिलचस्पी लेना; *n.* प्रसंग, चिंता*

concerning *prep.* ···के विषय में

concerned *a.* संबद्ध, चिंतित

concert *v.t.* एकत्र करना; *n.* मेल, सहगान, सहवादन

concession *n.* छूट*, सुविधा*

conch *n.* घोंघा, कौड़ी*, शंख, सीपी*

conciliate *v.t.* समझौता करना

conciliation *n.* समझौता

concise *a.* संक्षिप्त

conclave *n.* गुप्त सभा*

conclude *v.t. & i.* समाप्त करना या होना, निष्कर्ष निकालना

conclusion *n.* अंत, निष्कर्ष, परिणाम

conclusive *a.* निर्णयात्मक, अंतिम

concoct *v.t.* गढ़ना

concoction *n.* मनगढ़ंत बात

concomitance *n.* सहभाव

concord *n.* समझौता, मेल, तालमेल

concourse *n.* समागम, जमघट

concrete *a.* मूर्त्त, ठोस; *n.*

ठोस वस्तु*, कंकरीट; *v.t.* ठोस बनाना

concubine *n.* रखेल*

concurrence *n.* सहमति*, संगति*, अनुकूलता*

condemn *v.t.* दंड देना, अपराधी ठहराना, निन्दा करना

condemnation *n.* निन्दा*, दंडाज्ञा*

condense *v.t. & i.* घनीभूत या संक्षिप्त करना

condition *n.* दशा*, स्थिति*, शर्तें*

conditional *a.* सापेक्ष, शर्तबंद

condole *v.i.* शोक प्रकट करना, मातमपुर्सी करना

condolence *n.* शोक, मातम-पुर्सी*

condone *v.t.* दोष पर ध्यान न देना, क्षमा करना

conduce *v.i.* कारण या सहायक होना

conduct *v.t. & i.* मार्ग दिखाना, ताप या बिजली संवाहित करना; *n.* आचरण

conductor *n.* पथ-प्रदर्शक, बस आदि का परिचालक

confectioner *n.* हलवाई

confectionery *n.* मिठाइयां*, मिठाई-पाकशाला*, हलवाई की दुकान*

confederacy *n.* राज्यसंघ

confederate *v.t. & i.* संघ में शामिल करना या होना

confederation *n.* राज्यसंघ, महासंघ

confer *v.t. & i.* प्रदान करना, सलाह करना

conference *n.* सम्मेलन, मंत्रणा*

confess *v.t. & i.* दोष या पाप या अपराध स्वीकार करना

confession *n.* दोष या पाप या अपराध का स्वीकार, सकारी हुई बात*

confidant *n.* विश्वासपात्र

confide *v.t. & i.* विश्वास करना, भेद सौंपना

confidence *n.* विश्वास

confident *a.* आश्वस्त

confidential *a.* गोपनीय

confine *v.t. & i.* सीमाबद्ध या बंदी करना या रखना

confinement *n.* रोक*, कैद*

confines *n. & pl.* सीमाए*

confirm *v.t.* पुष्टि करना, प्रमाणित करना

confirmation *n.* पुष्टि, स्थायी-करण, प्रमाणीकरण

confiscate *v.t.* सर्वस्व हरण करना, जब्त करना

confiscation *n.* क़ानून द्वारा सर्वस्व-हरण, कुर्की*, जब्ती*

conflagration *n.* प्रचंड अग्नि*, अग्निदाह, अग्निकांड

conflict *v.i.* भिड़ना, मुठभेड़ होना; *n.* कलह, विग्रह, मुठ-भेड़*

confluence *n.* संगम

confluent *a.* साथ-साथ प्रवाहित

conform *v.t. & i.* अनुरूप या समान बनाना या होना, अनुमत होना

conformation *n.* अनुकूलन, समरूपता

conformity *n.* समरूपता, अनु-रूपता, संगति

confound *v.t.* व्यर्थ कर देना, भ्रमजाल में डाल देना

confront *v.t.* सामना करना

confrontation *n.* मुकाबला

confuse *v.t. & i.* गड़मड करना, घपला करना

confusion *n.* उलझन*, अस-मंजस, गड़बड़ी*

congenial *a.* सुखावह, सुहावना

congest *v.t.* घनीभूत करना

congestion *n.* भीड़भाड़*, लहू का जमाव

congratulate *v.t.* बधाई देना

congratulation *n.* बधाई*

congregation *n.* सभा*, जमाव

congress *n.* कांग्रेस, सम्मेलन

congruity *n.* साहृश्य, सामंजस्य

conjecture *n. & v.t.* अटकल* (लगाना), धारणा* भविष्य-वाणी*

conjugal *a.* वैवाहिक, दांपतिक

conjugation *n.* धातुरूप, मैथुन

conjunction *n.* संयोजक, समुच्चयवाचक पद

conjure *v.t.* शपथपूर्वक प्रार्थना करना, जादू करना या दिखाना

conjurer *n.* जादूगर

connect *v.t. & i.* जोड़ना, मिलाना, संबद्ध करना (होना)

connection *n.* संबंध, मेल

connivance *n.* उपेक्षा*, मूक आज्ञा*

connive *v.i.* अनदेखी करना

connote *v.t.* अर्थ सूचित करना, गुणार्थ देना, फल-रूप में सूचित करना, गुण-बोध करना

connubial *a.* वैवाहिक, दांपतिक

conquer *v.t.* जीतना, जीतकर अधीन करना

conquest *n.* विजय, जीता हुआ प्रदेश

conscience *n.* अंतःकरण, चैतन्य, भले-बुरे का विवेक

conscientious *a.* शुद्धमति, धर्मशील, विवेकात्मक

conscious *a.* सचेत, सबोध, चौकस

consciousness *n.* चेतना*, अनु-भव, व्यक्ति की भावसमष्टि*

conscript *n. & a.* जबरी रंगरूट

conscription *n.* जबरी या

अनिवार्य भर्ती*

consecrate v.t. संस्कार करना।

consecutive a. निरंतर, अनु-गामी

consent n. & v.t. स्वीकृति* या अनुमति* (देना), सम्मति*, आज्ञा*, (मानना)

consequence n. परिणाम, प्रभाव

consequent a. अनुवर्ती

conservative a. & n. अनुदार

conserve v.t. रक्षा करना, नष्ट होने से बचाना ; n. मुरब्बा, मिठाई*, पाग

consider v.t. & i. विचार करना, सोचना

considerable a. विचारणीय, काफी, मान्य

considerate a. विचारवान, सावधान

consideration n. विचार

consign v.t. भेजना, सौंपना

consignment n. भेजा हुआ माल

consist v.i. पता होना, निहित होना

consistence n. स्थिरता, अनु-कूलता*, संगति*

consistent a. अविचल, संगत

consolation n. धीरज, ढाढ़स

console v.t. दिलासा या ढाढ़स देना

consolidate v.t. & i. एकीकृत करना, ठोस करना या होना, एक पिण्ड बनाना

consolidation n. एकीकरण, चकबंदी*

consonant n. & a. व्यंजन, एक सुरवाला, सुरीला

conspicuous a. ध्यानाकर्षी, आकर्षक, सुस्पष्ट

conspiracy n. सांठगांठ*, षड्यंत्र

conspirator.n. षड्यंत्री, राज-द्रोही

conspire v.i. षड्यंत्र या राज-द्रोह करना

constable n. पुलिस का सिपाही

constant a. अचल, स्थिर, निरंतर

constipation n. कब्ज

constituency n. चुनाव-क्षेत्र

constituent n. भाग, अंश, अंग

constitute v.t. नियुक्त करना, अंग होना

constitution n. संविधान, शारी-रिक या मानसिक गठन*

constitutional a. संवैधानिक, गठन-संबंधी

constrain v.t. बाध्य करना, संयत करना

constraint n. संयम, नियंत्रण

construct v.t. निर्माण करना

construction n. निर्माण,

रचना*

construe v.t. & i. व्याख्या करना

consul n. वाणिज्यदूत

consult v.t. परामर्श करना

consultation n. विचार-विनिमय सलाह*

consume v.t. व्यय करना, खा-पी जाना, नष्ट करना

consummate v.t. पूर्ण करना, पक्का करना; a. पूर्ण, परम, पक्का

consummation n. समाप्ति*, सिद्धि*

consumption n. उपभोग, खपत*, क्षय, नाश, क्षयरोग

consumptive a. क्षयशील, क्षय-रोग-संबंधी; n. क्षयरोगी

contact n. & v.t. संपर्क या संसर्ग (में आना, करना); लगाव (रखना)

contagious a. संक्रामक

contain v.t. अपने में धारण करना

contaminate v.t. छूत फैलाना

contemplate v.i. & t. ध्यान लगाना, विचारना, मनन करना

contemplation n. ध्यान, विचार-मग्नता*

contemporary a. & n. सम-कालीन

contempt n. अपमान

contemptible a. घृणित, तुच्छ

contemptuous a. तिरस्कार-पूर्ण, धृष्ट

contend v.t. & i. तर्क या विवाद करना

content a. & v.t. संतुष्ट या तृप्त (करना); n. विचार-तत्त्व

contentment n. सन्तोष, तृप्ति*

contention n. विवाद-विषय

contest v.t. विवाद करना, झगड़ना; n. विवाद, कलह

context n. प्रकरण, प्रसंग

contiguity n. समीपता*, संलग्नता*, सम्पर्क

contiguous a. आसन्न, समीप

continent n. महाद्वीप

continental a. महाद्वीप संबंधी

contingency n. अनिश्चित संभावना*

continuation n. चालू क्रम

continue v.t. & i. जारी रखना या रहना, बना रहना, टिकना

continuity n. निरंतरता*

continuous a. निरंतर, लगा-तार, अबाध

contraband a. & n. अवैध, निषिद्ध, तस्करी

contract n., v.t. & i. ठेका (देना या लेना), पट्टा (लिखना या लिखाना)

contraction *n.* सिकुड़न*

contractor *n.* ठेकेदार

contradict *v.t.* खंडन करना

contradictory *a.* परस्पर-विरुद्ध

contrary *a.* विपरीत, पतिकूल

contrast *v.t. & i.* भेद दिख-लाना ; *n.* विरोध, अन्तर

contravene *v.t.* विरोध या उल्लंघन करना

contravention *n.* उल्लंघन, विरोध

contribute *v.t. & i.* चंदा देना

contribution *n.* चंदा

contributor *n.* चंदा देनेवाला, पत्रिका में लिखनेवाला

control *n. & v.t.* संयम या शासन (करना), नियंत्रण (करना)

controversial *a.* विवादग्रस्त

controversy *n.* विवाद

convalesce *v.i.* पुनः स्वस्थ होना

convalescent *a. & n.* क्रमशः रोगमुक्त होनेवाला या पुनः स्वास्थ्य पानेवाला (व्यक्ति)

convene *v.t.* आयोजित करना

convener *n.* संयोजक

convenience *n.* सुविधा*

convenient *a.* उपयुक्त, अनुकूल

convent *n.* ईसाई मठ

convention *n.* परंपरा*, सभा*, रीति*

conventional *a.* परंपरागत

converge *v.t. & i.* एक ही केंद्र की ओर बढ़ना, एक ही केंद्र पर मिलना, झुकाना, झुकना

conversant *a.* निपुण, सुपरिचित

conversation *n.* वार्तालाप

converse *v.t.* वार्तालाप करना, बोलना ; *n. & a.* उलटा, विपरीत प्रस्ताव

conversion *n.* धर्म-परिवर्तन

convert *v.t.* धर्म या मत बदलना ; *n.* स्वधर्म त्यागी

convertible *a.* बदलने या विनि-मय के योग्य

convey *v.t.* पहुंचाना, ढोना, संचारित या सूचित करना

conveyance *n.* संचार, वाहन, वहन

convict *v.t.* अपराधी ठहराना, दंड देना ; *n.* मुजरिम, कैदी

conviction *n.* दंड, दोष-निर्णय, दृढ़ विश्वास

convince *v.t.* प्रतीति कराना

convocation *n.* दीक्षांत समा-रोह

convolution *n.* ऐंठन*

convoy *v.t.* सुरक्षित ले जाना ; *n.* अनुरक्षक, रक्षक पोत

convulsion *n.* ऐंठन*, गड़बड़*, खलबली*

coo *n. & v.i.* कूजन (करना)

cook *v.t.* (भोजन) पकाना ; *n.* रसोइया

cooker *n.* कुकर, चूल्हा

cool *a.* ठंडा, उदासीन, मंद ; *v.t.* ठंडा करना

cooler *n.* ठंडा करने का साधन

co-operate *v.i.* मिलकर काम करना, सहयोग करना

co-operation *n.* सहयोग

co-operative *a.* सहकारी

co-opt *v.t.* (सदस्य) सहयोजित करना

co-ordinate *a.* सवर्गीय, समान पदवाला, तुल्य ; *v.t.* तालमेल करना

co-ordination *n.* समन्वय, समीकरण

co-partner *n.* साझीदार

cope *v.t. & i.* स्पर्धा करना

copious *a.* विपुल, भरपूर

copper *n.* तांबा

copy *n. & v.t.* कापी* या नकल* (करना), प्रति*, हस्तलिपि*

copyright *n.* कापीराइट

coral *n.* मूंगा

cord *n.* डोरी*

cordial *a.* हार्दिक, सच्चा ; *n.* पुष्टि-कर या उत्तेजक पेय

cordiality *n.* सौजन्य, मित्रभाव

corn *n.* अन्न, पैर का गोखरू

corner *n.* कोण, कोना, गुप्त स्थान ; *v.t.* कठिन अवस्था में रखना

corolla *n.* फूल का भीतरी भाग

coronation *n.* राज्रतिलक

coronet *n.* छोटा मुकुट

corporal ⚫*a.* शारीरिक ; *n.* कारपोरल

corporation *n.* निगम, महापालिका*

corporeal *a.* दैहिक, भौतिक, मूर्त

corps *n.* सेना की टुकड़ी*

corpse *n.* शव, लाश*

corpulence *n.* स्थूलता*, मोटापन

corpulent *a.* मांसल, मोटा*

corpuscle *n.* (रक्त-) कोशा*, कणिका*

correct *a.* ठीक, उचित, यथार्थ ; *v.t.* ठीक या शुद्ध करना, दंड देना

correction *n.* संशोधन, सुधार, दंड

correlate *v.t. & i.* सहसंबद्ध करना या कराना ; *n.* सहबद्ध

correlation *n.* सहसंबंध

correspond *v.i.* अनुरूप या जोड़ का होना, पत्रव्यवहार करना

correspondence *n.* संसर्ग, पत्रव्यवहार ; अनुरूपता*

correspondent *n.* संवाददाता

corridor *n.* गलियारा

corrigendum *n.* शुद्धिपत्र

corroborate *v.t.* प्रमाणित करना

corroboration *n.* संपुष्टि, प्रमाण

corrode *v.t. & i.* क्रमश: नष्ट करना या होना

corrosion *n.* क्रमिक क्षय

corrosive *a.* क्षयकारी

corrugate *v.t. & i.* लहरिया-दार या पनारीदार बनाना या बनना

corrupt *v.t. & i.* भ्रष्ट करना या होना, दूषित करना, घूस देना; *a.* भ्रष्ट, पतित

corruptible *a.* पतित या भ्रष्ट होने योग्य

corruption *n.* भ्रष्टाचार

cosmetic *a.* अंगराग, श्रृंगार-द्रव्य

cosmic *a.* विश्वीय, ब्रह्मांड-संबंधी

cosmology *n.* विश्व-शास्त्र

cosmopolitan *a.* सार्वभौमी; *n.* विश्व-मित्र

cosmos *n.* ब्रह्मांड

cost *v.t.* दाम लगना, लागत पड़ना, व्यय होना, हानि होना; *n.* लागत*, व्यय, दाम

costly *a.* बहुमूल्य, महंगा

costume *n.* पहनावा, वेश

cosy *a.* सुख-सुविधापूर्ण (स्थान)

cot *n.* खाट*, पालना, खटोला

cottage *n.* कुटी*, झोंपड़ी*

cotton *n.* रुई*, सूती कपड़ा, कपास

couch *n.* गद्देदार चौकी*, पलंग; *v.t. & i.* लिटाना, लेटना, (शब्दों में) लपेटना

cough *n.* खांसी*, बलग़म; *v.i.* खांसना

coulter *n.* हल का फल, फाल

council *n.* परिषद्*

councillor *n.* पारषद, सभासद

counsel *n.* सलाह, बैरिस्टर; *v.t.* सलाह देना

counsellor *n.* परामर्शदाता, बैरिस्टर

count *v.t. & i.* गिनना, विचारना; *n.* गणना*

countenance *n.* मुख की आकृति*; *v.t.* कृपा करना, बढ़ावा देना

counter *n.* लेनदेन की मेज़* या खिड़की*; *v.t. & i.* उलटा करना या होना, जवाबी चाल चलना, प्रतिघात करना, *a. & adv.* प्रतिकूल

counteract *v.t.* काट करना, हराना

counterbalance *v.t.* धड़ा बांधना; *n.* पासंग

counterfeit *n. & v.t.* कपट-मुद्रा* या खोटा सिक्का

(बनाना), जाल करना, छलना;
a. खोटा, जाली, नक़ली

counterfoil *n.* प्रतिपर्ण,
मुसन्ना (रसीद आदि की
नक़ल* या 'अधकट्टी'*)

counterpart *n.* प्रतिलिपि*,
प्रतिमूर्ति*

counterpoise *n.* समतोलन

countersign *n. & v.t.* प्रति-
हस्ताक्षर (करना)

countless *a.* असंख्य

country *n.* देश, प्रदेश, देहात

countryman *n.* ग्रामीण

county *n.* (इंगलैंड का) प्रान्त
या ज़िला

couple *n.* दंपति, जोड़ा; *v.t.
& i.* जोड़ना, मिलाना

couplet *n.* श्लोक, दोहा

coupon *n.* कूपन, पुरजी*,
रसीद*

courage *n.* साहस, वीरता*

courageous *a.* साहसी

courier *n.* दूत, हरकारा

course *n.* पाठ्यक्रम, गतिक्रम

court *n.* अदालत, आंगन, दर-
बार; *v.t.* रिझाना, प्रणय-
प्रार्थना करना

courteous *a.* शालीन, नम्र,
विनीत

courtesan *n.* गणिका*, वेश्या*

courtesy *n.* शालीनता*, विनय

courtier *n.* राजसभासद्, दर-

बारी

court-martial *n.* सैनिक
न्यायालय

courtship *n.* प्रेमचर्या*

courtyard *n.* आंगन

cousin *n.* चचेरा, ममेरा, मौसेरा
या फुफेरा भाई या बहन

cover *v.t.* ढकना, छिपाना,
रक्षा करना ; *n.* ढक्कन

coverlet *n.* बिछावन की चांदनी

covetous *a.* लालची

cow *n.* गाय; *v.t.* डराना

coward *a. & n.* कायर, डर-
पोक

cowardice *n.* कायरता*

coy *a.* विनीत, लज्जालु, संकोची

crab *n.* केकड़ा, कर्करराशि*, खट्टा
जंगली सेब, ऊंटड़ा (यंत्र)

crabbed *a.* खट्टा, चिड़चिड़ा

crack *v.t. & i.* तड़काना,
तड़कना ; *n.* तड़ाका, दरार*;
a. प्रत्युत्तम

cracker *n.* पटाखा

crackle *v.t.* तड़ककर टूटना

cradle *n.* पालना; *v.t.* पालने
में झुलाना

craft *n.* शिल्प, कौशल, व्यापार,
छल

craftsman *n.* शिल्पकार

crafty *a.* कपटी, धूर्त

cram *v.t. & i.* ठूंसना, कंठस्थ
करना

craving *n.* लालसा*

crawl *v.i.* रेंगना, सरकना; *n.* रेंगने की क्रिया या भाव (रिंगण रिंखण)

craze *v.t. & i.* सनक चढ़ना या चढ़ा लेना; *n.* भक*, सनक*

crazy *a.* सनकी, भक्की

creak *v.i.* चरमराना; *n.* कर्कश शब्द

cream *n.* मलाई*, सार

crease *n.* सिकुड़न*, चुन्नट*; *v.t.* सिकुड़न या चुन्नट डालना

create *v.t.* सृजन करना

creation *n.* सृष्टि*, रचना*

creator *n.* विधाता, सृष्टिकर्ता

creature *n.* जीव, प्राणी

credence *n.* प्रतीति*, विश्वास

credentials *n.* (*pl*) प्रमाणपत्र, परिचयपत्र, अधिकारपत्र

credible *a.* विश्वसनीय

credit *n. & v.t.* विश्वास (करना), रकममनामे लिखना, श्रेय (देना), साख*

creditable *a.* प्रशंसनीय, गौरव-कर

creditor *n.* लेनदार

credulity *n.* भोलापन

credulous *a.* भोला, सहज-विश्वासी

creed *n.* धार्मिक श्रद्धा*

creek *n.* खाड़ा, उप-नदी*, संकरा दर्रा

creep *v.i.* सरकना, रेंगना

creeper *n.* लता*

cremate *v.t.* दाह-संस्कार करना

cremation *n.* दाह-क्रिया*

creosote *n.* लोहबान

crescent *n.* बालचंद्र, मास के आरंभ या अंत का चांद

crest *n.* शिखा*, मुकुट, कलंगी*, ढाल पर बना राजचिह्न

crew *n.* मल्लाहों का जत्था, संघ

cricket *n.* क्रिकेट का खेल, झींगुर

crime *n.* अपराध, दुराचार

criminal *n. & a.* अपराधी, अपराध के समान

criminate *v.t.* अपराधी सिद्ध करना

crimson *a.* लाल

cringe *v.t.* चापलूसी करना

cripple *n. & v.t.* पंगु या अशक्त (बना देना)

crisis *n.* संकट

crisp *a.* कुरकुरा, कुंडकीला; *v.t.* लहरदार बनाना

criterion *n.* लक्षण

critic *n.* आलोचक

critical *a.* आलोचनात्मक, संकटमय

criticism *n.* आलोचना

criticize *v.t.* समालोचना करना

crochet *n.* कोशिये की कशीदा-

कारी*
crock *n.* घड़ा
crockery *n.* चीनी या मिट्टी के
बर्तन
crocodile *n.* घड़ियाल
crony *n.* परम मित्र
crop *n.* उपज*; *v.t. & i.*
उपजाना, उपजना
cross *n., v.t. & i.* सलीब (का
चिह्न '+' बनाना), काटना,
पार करना; *a.* दुरात्मा,
विपरीत
cross-breed *n.* संकरता, दोग़ला-
पन
crossing *n.* चौरस्ता, चौमुहानी*
crossword *n.* शब्दपहेली*
crouch *v.i.* विनीत भाव दिख-
लाना, झुकना
croup *n.* गलशोथ
crow *v.i.* कांव-कांव करना; *n.*
कौआ
crowd *n.* भीड़*; *v.t.* भीड़
लगाना
crown *n.* मुकुट, राजा, शिखर,
5 शिलिंग का सिक्का; *v.t.*
राजतिलक करना, पूर्ण करना
crucial *a.* निर्णायक, प्रामाणिक
crucifix *n.* सलीब पर ईसामूर्ति*
crucify *v.t.* शूली चढ़ाना
crude *a.* अपक्व, कच्चा, रूखा
crudity *n.* रूखापन कच्चापन
cruel *adj.* क्रूर, निर्दय, कठोर

cruelty *n.* क्रूरता*, निर्दयता*
cruiser *n.* युद्धपोत
crumb *n.* रोटी का छोटा टुकड़ा
या कोमल भाग
crumble *v.t.* चूरा करना या
होना
crumple *v.t.* तह बनाना
crunch *v.t.* चबाना, दबाना,
रौंदना
crusade *n.* ईसाइयों का धर्मयुद्ध
crush *v.t.* कुचलना; *n.* कुचलने
की क्रिया*, भीड़भाड़*
crust *n.* पपड़ी*, छिलका; *v.t.*
& *i.* पपड़ी जमाना या पड़ना
crutch *n.* टेक*, बैसाखी*
cry *v.i.* चिल्लाना, गरजना, रोना,
प्रार्थना करना; *n.* पुकार*,
चीख*, विलाप
crystal *n.* स्फटिक, बिल्लौर,
सीसा
crystallize *v.t. & i.* रवे
बनाना या बनना, स्थायी या
स्थिर रूप धारण करना
cub *n.* शेर या भालू या लोमड़ी
का बच्चा
cubbish *a.* अशिष्ट
cube *n.* घनफल, घन
cubic *a.* क्यूबिक, घनफल-
संबंधी, घनाकार
cubical *a.* घनाकार
cuckoo *n.* कोयल*
cucumber *n.* खीरा, ककड़ी*

cuddle *n., v.t. & i.* आलिंगन (करना) लाड़ करना, लिपट-कर सोना, गुड़मुड़ी होना

cudgel *n.* डंडा, सोटा ; *v.t.* डंडे से मारना

cue *n.* (नाटक में), संकेत-शब्द, खेल का डंडा

cuff *n. & v.t.* आस्तीन*, आस्तीन की कलाई-पट्टी*, मुक्का या घूंसा (मारना)

culminate *v.i.* परमकोटि को प्राप्त होना ; मध्याह्न-रेखा पर होना

culpability *n.* दंडनीयता*

culpable *a.* दंडनीय

culprit *n.* अपराधी

cult *n.* धर्मसंप्रदाय

cultivate *v.t.* खेती करना, बढ़ाना, पालना

cultivator *n.* किसान, पोषक

culture *n.* संस्कृति*, जुताई*

cumbersome, cumbrous *a.* कण्टकर, भारी, बेडौल

cumin *n.* जीरा

cumulative *a.* संचित, संचयी

cunning *a. & n.* चतुर (-ता*), धूर्त (-ता*), कुशल (-ता*)

cup *n.* प्याला, कटोरा

cupboard *n.* आलमारी*

Cupid *n.* कामदेव

cupidity *n.* अतिलोभ

curable *a.* इलाज के योग्य

curative *a. & n.* रोगनाशक (दवा*)

curator *n.* संग्रहालय का अध्यक्ष

curb *n. & v.t.* रोक (-ना)

curd *n.* दही

cure *n., v.t. & i.* इलाज (करना या होना), नीरोग करना या होना, नमक लगाना

curfew *n.* कर्फ्यू

curio *n.* कलावस्तु*, कौतूहल-जनक पदार्थ

curiosity *n.* उत्सुकता*, जिज्ञासा*

currency *n.* चलन, प्रचलित मुद्रा*

current *a.* वर्तमान, प्रचलित ; *n.* स्रोत, धारा*, प्रवृत्ति*

curriculum *n.* पाठ्यक्रम

currier *n.* चमड़ा कमानेवाला

curry *n.* कढ़ी, शोरबा ; *v.t.* चमड़ा कमाना, खरहरना

curse *n., v.t. & i.* धिक्कार या गाली* या शाप (देना) बला*, पाप, कोसना

cursory *a.* सरसरी

curt *a.* संक्षिप्त, रूखा, 'टका-सा'

curtail *v.t.* छोटा या संक्षेप या लोप करना

curtain *n.* परदा, चिक

curvature *n.* वक्रता*, घुमाव

curve *n.* वक्ररेखा*, चाप

cushion *n. & v.t.* गद्दा या

338

तकिया (लगाना), गुदगुदा
बनाना

custard *n.* ग्रंडे ग्रौर दूध की
फिरनी*

custard-apple *n.* शरीफ़ा

custodian *n.* निग्विपाल

custody *n.* रक्षा. पालन, निग-
रानी*, हिरासत*, हवालात*

custom *n.* रीति-रिवाज, ग्राचार,
ग्रभ्यास, चुंगी*

customary *a.* प्रथागन, चिर-
प्रचलित

customer *n.* ग्राहक

custom-house *n.* चुंगीघर

cut *v.t.* काटना, ग्रलग करना;
n. काट*, कटौती*

cutting *n.* कतरन*

cycle *n.* चक्र, कालचक्र, चक्कर,
साइकिल*

cyclic *a.* चक्रीय, चक्रवत्, काल-
चक्र-संबंधी

cyclist *n.* साइकिल सवार,
साइकिलबाज़

cyclone *n.* चक्करदार ग्रांधी*,
ववंडर, चक्रवात

cyclopaedia *n.* विश्वकोश,
ज्ञानकोश

cyclostyle *n.* कटाई-छापा,
स्टेंसिल की छपाई* (साइक्लो-
स्टाइल*)

cylinder *n.* बेलन के ग्राकार
का पोला ग्रथवा ठोस पदार्थ,
बेलन

cylindric (-al) *a.* बेलनाकार

cymbal *n.* भांभ*, मजीरा

cypress *n.* सरो

D

dabble *v.t.* छेड़ना, छिड़कना,
छींटें डालना, छपछपाना

dacoit *n.* डाकू

dacoity *n.* डकैती*

dad *n.* बापू, ग्रव्वा

daffodil *n.* पीला नरगिस

dagger *n.* कटारी*

daily *a.* दैनिक; *adv.* प्रतिदिन,
बहुधा; *n.* दैनिक समाचारपत्र

dainty *a.* रुचिर, स्वादिष्ट,

रम्य; *n.* स्वादिष्ट भोजन

dairy *n.* डेयरी, गोशाला*, दुग्ध-
शाला*

dais *n.* मंच, चबूतरा

daisy *n.* गुलबहार

dale *n.* घाटी*

dalliance *n.* रंगरेली*, टाल-
मटोल

dally *v.t. & i.* प्रेमक्रीड़ा करना,
इठलाना

dam.ᴐ *n.* सेतु, बांध, (पशु की)
मां*; *v.t.* बांध से धार रोकना

damage *n.* क्षति*, हरजाना ;
v.t. क्षति पहुंचाना

dame *n.* बेगम*ः गृहिणी*,
प्रौढ़ा*, महिला*

damn *n. & v.t.* निन्दा (करना),
धिक्कार (-ना), शाप देना

damp *a.* नम, सीला, गीला ;
n. नमी*, सील*, कुहरा ;
v.t. & i. तर करना, जी
तोड़न.

damsel *n.* कुंवारी युवती*

dance *v.t. & i.* नाचना, (बच्चे
को) उछालना ; *n.* नाच

dandle *v.t.* (बच्चे को) गोद
में या घुटने पर झुलाना

dandruff *n.* रूसी*

dandy *n.* छैला, बांका

danger *n.* खतरा, जोखिम*

dangerous *a.* खतरनाक, संकट-
मय

dangle *v.i. & t.* लटकना,
लटकाना, झूलना, झुलाना,
ललचाना, पीछे-पीछे फिरना

dank *a.* गीला, सीला

dare *v.i.* साहस या ढिठाई
करना, जानकर जोखिम उठाना

daredevil *n.* बेधड़क

daring *n.* साहस; *a.* साहसपूर्ण,
दिलेर

dark *a. & n.* काना (-रंग),
अंधेरा, घुंघ (-ला), सांझ*

darling *a. & n.* अतिप्रिय, प्रेम-
पात्र

dash *n., v.t. & i.* निक्षेपचिह्न
'डैश' : '—' (लगाना), जोश
का काम (करना)

dastard *n.* कायर

date *n. & v.t.* तिथि (डालना),
काल (निर्धारित करना)
घटनाकाल, खजूर

daub *n. & v.t.* लीप-पोत या
लीपापोती* (करना)

daughter *n.* बेटी*, पुत्री*

daughter-in-law *n.* पतोहू*

daunt *v.t.* उत्साह या धैर्य या
साहस तोड़ना

dauntless *a.* अ-भीत

dawn *n. & v.i.* अरुणोदय
(होना), प्रकट होना, फुरना

day *n.* दिन

daze *n. & v.t.* चौंध* (लगाना),
तिलमिला (-ना, हट*)

dazzle *n. & v.t.* चकाचौंध*
(में डालना), चकरा देना

dead *a.* मृत, जड़, सुन्न

deadlock *n.* गतिरोध

dead-shot *a. & n.* अचूक
निशानेवाला

deadly *a.* घातक, मृत्युवत्

deaf *a.* बहरा

deal *n., v.t. & i.* लेन-देन या
क्रय-विक्रय (करना), सौदा

(करना), सरोकार (रखना)

dealer *n.* वितरक, विक्रेता, व्यापारी

dealings *n.* (*pl.*) आचरण, व्यवहार, सरोकार, लेन-देन

dear *a.* प्यारा, महंगा

dearth *n.* दुर्लभता*; अकाल, महंगी*

death *n.* मृत्यु*, नाश

deathblow *n.* प्राणघातक चोट

deathless *a.* अमर

debar *v.t.* वंचित करना, रोकना, निषेध करना

debase *v.t.* भ्रष्ट करना, मूल्य घटाना

debate *v.t. & i.* विवाद करना, झगड़ना, सोचना ; *n.* विवाद, तर्क, चर्चा*

debauch *v.t.* दूषित करना, (सतीत्व) भ्रष्ट करना ; *n.* लंपट

debauchery *n.* लंपटता*, कामुकता*, व्यसन

debenture *n.* ऋणपत्र, प्रतिज्ञापत्र

debility *n.* दुर्बलता*, शक्तिहीनता*

debit *n.* नामे, लेनी*; *v.t.* रकम नामे लिखना

debris *n.* मलबा, अवशेष

debt *n.* ऋण, उधार, आभार

debtor *n.* ऋणी, देनदार

decade *n.* दशाब्द

decadent *a.* पतनोन्मुख

decamp *v.i.* भाग जाना, डेरा कूच करना

decay *v.i. & t.* क्षीण करना या होना, सड़ना, बिगड़ना ; *n.* क्षय, सड़न*

decease *v.i.* मरना ; *n.* मृत्यु*

deceit *n.* धोखा, छल

deceive *v.t.* ठगना, धोखा देना

December *n.* दिसंबर

decency *n.* विनय, शिष्टता*

decent *a.* प्रतिष्ठित, शिष्ट, उदार

decentralize *v.t.* विकेन्द्रित करना

deception *n.* छल, कपट, ढकोसला

decide *v.t. & i.* निर्णय करना या देना, निश्चित करना

decimal *n. & a.* दशमलव

decipher *n. & v.t.* गूढ़वाचन (करना), गूढ़लिपि पढ़ना

decision *n.* निर्णय, फैसला

decisive *a.* निर्णयकारी, निश्चित

deck *n.* जहाज़ की छत*; *v.t.* सजाना

declaim *v.t. & i.* रटा हुआ या जोशीला भाषण देना

declaration *n.* घोषणा*, घोषणापत्र

declare *v.t.* घोषणा करना

decline *v.t. & i.* अस्वीकार करना ; *n.* क्षय, पतन

decompose *v.t. & i.* सड़ना, सड़ाना

decorate *v.t.* सजाना, पदक आदि से विभूषित करना

decoration *n.* सजावट*, पदक आदि

decorum *n.* मर्यादा*, शिष्टाचार

decrease *v.t. & i.* घटाना, घटना ; *n.* कमी*

decree *n.* डिगरी, आज्ञा*, राजाज्ञा; *v.t.* हुक्म जारी करना

decry *v.t.* निन्दा करना

dedicate *v.t.* भेंट करना, समर्पण करना

dedication *n.* समर्पण

deduce *v.t.* तर्क से पता लगाना, अनुमान करना

deduct *v.t.* घटा लेना

deduction *n.* कटौती*

deed *n.* कार्य, कृति*, कारनामा

deep *a.* गहरा, गुप्त ; *n.* समुद्र

deer *n.* हिरन

defamation *n.* मानहानि*

defame *v.t.* मानहानि करना, बदनाम करना

default *n.* चूक*; *v.t. & i.* चूकना, पैरवी न करना

defeat *v.t.* हराना; *n.* पराजय*, हार*

defect *n.* कमी*, त्रुटि*

defence *n.* रक्षा*, प्रत्युत्तर

defend *v.t.* रक्षा करना

defendant *n.* प्रतिवादी, मुद्दालेह

defensive *a.* रक्षात्मक ; *n.* बचाव

deference *n.* आदर, वश्यता*

defiance *n.* विद्रोह, आज्ञाभंग

defiant *a.* निडर, विद्रोही, उपेक्षापूर्ण

deficit *n.* कमी*, टोटा

deficit budget *n.* घाटे का बजट

define *v.t.* परिभाषा देना, सीमा बांधना

definite *a.* निर्दिष्ट, सुनिश्चित

definition *n.* परिभाषा*

degenerate *v.i.* पतित होना ; *a.* पतित

degrade *v.t. & i.* पदच्युत करना या होना

degree *n.* उपाधि*, अंश (गणित)

deject *v.t.* दिल तोड़ना

dejection *n.* उदासी*

delegate *v.t.* प्रतिनिधित्व करना

delegation *n.* प्रतिनिधि

delete *v.t.* हटाना, मिटाना

deliberate *v.t. & i.* राय लेना, विचार करना ; *a.* सुचिन्तित

delicious *a.* स्वादिष्ट, रुचिकर

delight *v.t. & i.* सुखी होना ; *n.* हर्ष, खुशी*

deliver *v.t.* सौंपना, (डाक) बांटना

delivery *n.* डाक-वितरण, भाषण या उसका ढंग

delta *n.* डेल्टा, नदी का दहाना

deluge *n.* जल-प्रलय

delusion *n.* मोह, भ्रम, छल

demand *n. & v.t.* मांग* या दावा (करना), मांगना

demarcation *n.* सीमानिर्धारण

demeanour *n.* सलूक

demerit *n.* अवगुण, दोष

demise *n. & v.t.* मरण, 'हिब्बा' (करना)

democracy *n.* जनतंत्र

demolish *v.t.* ढाना, निगल जाना, नष्ट करना

demon *n.* दानव

demonstrate *v.t.* प्रयोग से समझाना, प्रदर्शित या प्रमाणित करना, प्रदर्शन करना

demoralize *v.t.* अनुशासन और उत्साह भंग करना, चरित्र भ्रष्ट करना

demur *n. & v.t.* आपत्ति* या आगा-पीछा (करना), शंका* (करना)

demure *a.* संकोची, धीर, विनीत

demy *n.* कागज़ का 18″ × 22″ आकार

den *n.* मांद*, गुप्त अड्डा

denotation *n.* संकेत (-न),

नाम, (तर्क में) व्याप्त्यर्थ

denote *v.i.* ···का नाम या वस्तुवाची होना, संकेतित या सूचित करना

denounce *v.t.* भर्त्सना करना

dense *a.* घना, गाढ़ा, मूर्ख

dentist *n.* दांत का डाक्टर

denude *v.t.* नग्न या वस्त्रहीन करना

deny *v.t.* अस्वीकार करना, ग़लत ठहराना, वंचित करना, निषेध करना

depart *v.t. & i.* चल देना, चला जाना, विदा होना, मरना

department *n.* विभाग, अंग

departure *n.* प्रस्थान

depend *v.i.* निर्भर या अवलंबित होना, अधीन या आश्रित होना, भरोसा करना

depict *v.t.* चित्रित करना, वर्णन करना

deplorable *a.* खेदजनक, शोचनीय

deplore *v.t.* विलाप करना, शोक करना, खेद या दुख प्रकट करना

deport *v.t.* निर्वासित करना

depose *v.t. & i.* पद या अधिकार या राजगद्दी से च्युत करना, गवाही या बयान देना, हटाना, साक्षी देना

deposit *v.t.* जमा करना, गिरवी या घरोहर रखना ; *n.* बैंक में

जमा धन, थाती*

depot *n.* गोदाम, मंडी*, डिपो

deprave *v.t.* चरित्र दूषित करना

depreciate *v.t. & i.* मान या मूल्य घटाना या घटना

depress *v.t.* खिन्न करना, नीचा करना, दबाना, झुकाना

depression *n.* मंदी*, उदासी*, गड्ढा

deprive *v.t.* वंचित करना, छीन लेना

depth *n.* गहराई*, गंभीरता*, मध्यभाग

deputation *n.* शिष्टमंडल

depute *v.t.* अधिकार या भार सौंपना, प्रतिनिधि नियुक्त करना

derail *v.t. & i.* पटरी से उतारना या उतरना

derange *v.t.* व्यतिक्रम करना, गड़बड़ करना

deranged *a.* अव्यवस्थित, पागल

deride *v.i.* हंसी उड़ाना, ताना देना

derision *n.* उपहास, ताना

derivation *n.* मूल, व्युत्पत्ति*

derive *v.t.* मूल या व्युत्पत्ति, खोजना, अनुमान करना

derogate *v.i.* अपमानित होना

descendant *n.* वंशज

describe *v.t.* वर्णन या चित्रण करना, लक्षण बताना

description *n.* वर्णन

desert *v.t. & i.* छोड़ना, छोड़ भागना, *n.* रेगिस्तान

deserve *v.t.* पात्र या योग्य होना

design *v.t.* रूपरेखा या खाका बनाना, मंसूबा या इरादा करना या होना; *n.* नमूना, रूपरेखा*, इरादा, ढांचा

designing *a.* छली, कुचक्री

desirable *a.* वांछनीय, इष्ट, श्रेय

desire *v.t.* चाहना, मनोरथ करना, मांगना; *n.* अभिलाषा*, इच्छा*

desist *v.t.* हाथ खींचना, बाज आना

desk *n.* डेस्क, ढलवां मेज*

despair *v.t.* निराश होना; *n.* निराशा*

desperate *a.* निराशांध

despicable *a.* तिरस्करणीय, घृणित

despise *v.t.* तिरस्कार या निंदा या घृणा करना

despite *n.* घृणा*, ईर्ष्या*; *prep.* के बावजूद

despondent *a.* हताश, विषण्ण, उदास

despot *n.* निरंकुश शासक, अत्ततायी

destination *n.* मंजिल*, गंतव्य, भाग्य

destiny *n.* दैव, भाग्य

destitute *a.* निराश्रय, विहीन

destroy *v.t.* ध्वस्त या नष्ट करना

destruction *n.* ध्वंस, नाश

desultory *a.* अस्थिर, अनियत, निरुद्देश्य

detach *v.t.* विच्छिन्न करना, अलगाना

detachment *n.* अलगाव, सेना की टुकड़ी* या जत्था

detail *n. & v.t.* ब्योरा (देना)

detain *v.t.* बिठाये रखना, हवालात में या नजरबंद रखना

detect *v.t.* पता लगाना, खोज निकालना, ताड़ना

detective *n.* जासूस, गुप्तचर

detention *n.* कैद*, नजरबंदी*

deteriorate *v.t. & i.* बिगाड़ना, बिगड़ना, क्षय करना या होना

determine *v.t. & i.* ठान लेना, निर्धारण करना, स्थिर करना, निपटाना

detest *v.t.* घृणा करना

dethrone *v.t.* राजगद्दी से उतारना

detract *v.t. & i.* साख या मान घटाना

detriment *n.* हानि*, अपकार

devastate *v.t.* बरबाद करना, उजाड़ना

develop *v.t. & i.* विकास करना या होना

development *n.* विकास, बढ़ती*

deviate *v.i.* भटकना

device *n.* साधन, उपाय

devious *a.* भ्रांत, कुटिल, चक्करदार

devil *n.* शैतान

devise *v.t.* उपाय निकालना

devoid *adj.* रहित

devote *v.t.* समर्पण या उत्सर्ग करना, लगाना, रत होना

devoted *a.* समर्पित, दृढ़ भक्त, अनुरक्त

devotee *n.* भक्त

devotion *n.* भक्ति*, प्रेम

devour *v.t.* निगलना, हड़प करना, भकोसना, नष्ट करना

dew *n.* ओस*

dexterity *n.* निपुणता*, चातुरी*

diabetes *n.* प्रमेह, मधुमेह

diabolic (-al) *a.* घोर, नारकीय, पैशाचिक

diagnose *v.t.* निदान करना

diagnosis *n.* निदान

dialect *n.* उपभाषा*

dialogue *n.* संवाद, कथोपकथन

diameter *n.* व्यास

diamond *n.* हीरा

diarrhoea *n.* अतिसार

diary *n* दैनन्दिनी*, रोजनामचा, डायरी*

dice *n. (pl.), v.t. & i.* पासा (खेलना)

dictate *v.t.* इमला लिखाना,

आज्ञा देना; n. आज्ञा*

dictation n. इमला

dictator n. तानाशाह

diction n. वाक्शैली*

dictionary n. शब्दकोश

dictum n. सिद्धांतवचन, नियम

didactic a. उपदेशात्मक

die n. सांचा, पट्टा, ठप्पा; v.i. मरना

diet n. आहार, भोजन, पथ्य

differ v.i. भिन्नमत होना

difference n. मतभेद, कलह, शेष

different a. भिन्न, विविध

difficult a. कठिन

difficulty n. कठिनाई*

dig v.t. & i. खोदना; n. खुदाई*

digest v.t. पचाना; n. सार-संग्रह

digestion n. पाचन, पाचनशक्ति*

digit n. अंगुल (नाप), उंगली*, (0 से 9 तक का कोई) अंक

dignify v.t. गौरव बढ़ाना

dignity n. गौरव, महिमा*, प्रतिष्ठा*

dilemma n. कशमकश

diligence n. अध्यवसाय

dilute a. & v.t. जलमिश्रित (करना)

dim a., v.t. & i. धुंधला (बनाना या होना)

dimension n. आयाम, (गणित में) 'घात'

diminish v.t. & i. कम करना या होना

diminutive a. & n. अतिलघु, ऊनवाचक (शब्द)

din n., v.t. & i. शोर (मचाना या मचना)

dine v.t. & i. मध्याह्न का भोजन करना या भोज देना

dingy a. काला, मैला, अंधेरा और गंदा

dinner n. दिन का प्रधान भोजन या ज्योनार

dip n., v.t. & i. डुबकी* (देना या लगाना)

diploma n. उपाधिपत्र, राजपत्र

diplomacy n. कूटनीति*, नीति-चातुरी*

diplomatic a. & n. राजनयिक, कूटनीतिक, कूटनीतिज्ञ

dire a. दारुण, भीषण

direct a. & adv. सीधा, खरा, प्रत्यक्ष; v.t. & i. निदेशन करना, राह बताना

direction n. पता, दिशा,* निदेशन

director n. संचालक, निदेशक, निर्देशक

directory n. डाइरेक्टरी, निदेश-संहिता*

dirt n. धूल*, कचरा

dirty a. मैला, गंदा

disability n. अपात्रता*,

अक्षमता*

disadvantage n. प्रतिकूल अवस्था* या प्रभाव, प्रसुविधा*

disagree v.i. असहमत होना

disagreeable a. अप्रिय, नागवार, दुर्विनीत

disappear v.i. लुप्त होना, खो जाना

disappoint v.t. विफल या निराश करना

disapprove v.t. & i. बुरा मानना, अस्वीकार या अस-मर्थन करना

disarm v.t. & i. निरस्त्र करना

disarmament n. निरस्त्रीकरण

disaster n. विपत्ति*

disastrous n. सर्वनाशी

discharge v.t. & i. कर्त्तव्य पूरा करना, मुक्त करना; n. छूट*, रिहाई*

disciple n. शिष्य

discipline n. अनुशासन; v.t. अनुशासित करना

disclose v.t. प्रकट करना, भेद खोलना

discomfort n. क्लेश, तकलीफ़*

disconnect v.t. संबंध तोड़ना

discontent n. असंतोष

discount n. बट्टा, सूद दर सूद

discourage v.t. हतोत्साह करना

discourse n. लेख, संलाप, बातचीत*

discourteous a. असभ्य, रूख

discover v.t. खोज करना

discovery n. खोज*, आविष्कार

discuss v.t. विवाद करना, तर्क करना

disease n. रोग, व्याधि*

disfranchise v.t. मताधिकार या नागरिकता से वंचित करना

disguise n. & v.t. भेस (बद-लना)

dish n. थाली*, तश्तरी*

dishonest a. बेईमान

dishonour n. & v.t. अपमान (करना)

dislike v.t. नापसन्द करना

disloyal a. राजद्रोही

dismiss v.t. बर्खास्त करना

disorder n. अशांति*

disparity n. विषमता*

dispensary n. दवाख़ाना

disperse v.t. & i. बिखेरना, तीन-तेरह करना या होना

displace v.t. स्थान से हटाना

display n. & v.t. प्रदर्शन (सजाना, करना)

displease v.t. रुष्ट करना

disposal n. निपटान*, व्यव-स्थापन

dispose v.t. निपटाना, बेचना

disposition n. प्रबन्ध, प्रकृति*, प्रवृत्ति*

disprove v.t. खंडन करना, झूठा

ठहराना

dispute *n., v.t. & i.* विचार या विवाद (करना), मतभेद (प्रकट करना)

disqualification *n.* अपात्रता*, अनर्हता*

disquiet *a. & v.t.* बेचैन (करना); *n.* बेचैनी*

disregard *n. & v.t.* उपेक्षा* या अनादर (करना)

disrepute *n.* अपयश, निन्दा*

disrespect *n.* अनादर, अशिष्टता*

disrupt *v.t.* तितर-बितर या नष्ट-भ्रष्ट करना

dissatisfaction *n.* असंतोष

dissect *v.t.* चीड़फाड़ करना, सूक्ष्म परीक्षण करना

dissipate *v.t.* छितराना, नष्ट करना

dissolve *v.t. & i.* गलाना, घुलाना, घुलना

dissuade *v.t.* विरत करना

distance *n.* दूरी*

distasteful *a.* अरुचिकर, स्वाद-हीन

distil *v.t. & i.* सत्त चुवाना या चूना

distillery *n.* शराब की भट्टी*

distinct *a.* स्पष्ट, अलग, विशिष्ट, नियत

distinction *n.* भेद, महत्ता*

distinguish *v.t. & i.* भेद करना या दिखाना, प्रसिद्ध होना

distort *v.t.* तोड़ना मरोड़ना

distraction *n.* विकर्षण, पागल-पन

distress *n.* यातना*, आपदा*, दरिद्रता*; *v.t.* सताना

distribute *v.t.* बांटना, अलग करना

district *n.* जिला, मंडल, जनपद

distrust *n. & v.t.* अविश्वास या सन्देह (करना)

disturb *v.t.* अशांत या आकुल करना, विघ्न डालना

ditch *n.* खाई*, गढ़ा, नाला, मोरी*

ditto *n. & a.* 'ऐजन' (वही, उसीकी प्रतिलिपि)

dive *n. & v.i.* डुबकी* (लगाना)

diver *n.* गोताखोर

diverse *a.* भिन्न, पृथक्, विविध

divert *v.t.* राह से परे मोड़ना या हटाना, मनोरंजन करना, वंचित करना

divide *v.t. & i.* बांटना, भाग देना

dividend *n.* भाज्य, लाभांश, सूद

divine *a.* दिव्य; *n.* पुरोहित; *v.t. & i.* भविष्य बताना

divinity *n.* देवता, देवत्व

division *n.* विभाजन, विभाग, (गणित में) भाग, खंड,

कमिश्नरी, सेना की टुकड़ी*,
श्रेणी* (-विभाग)

divorce *n. & v.t.* तलाक (देना)

divulge *v.t.* भेद खोलना

dizzy *a.* चकराहट या घुमरी से
ग्रस्त

do *v.t. & i., aux.* करना, पूरा
करना

docile *a.* सिखाने योग्य, सीधा

dock *n.* बंदरगाह, कठघरा

doctor *n.* डॉक्टर, चिकित्सक

doctorate *n.* डॉक्टर की उपाधि*,
आचार्य-पद

doctrine *n.* मत, वाद, सिद्धांत

document *n.* लिखित प्रमाण,
दस्तावेज़*

dodge *n. & v.t.* चकमा (देना)

doe *n.* हिरनी*

dog *n.* कुत्ता; *v.t.* खोज या पीछा
करना, पीछे लगा रहना

dogged *a.* हठी

doggerel *n.* तुच्छ

dogma *n.* हठधर्मिता*, रूढ़ि*

doings *n.* (*pl.*) कर्म, व्यवहार

dole *n.* क्षुद्र अंश; *v.t.* बांटना

doleful *a.* आर्त्त, भैरव, सुनसान

doll *n.* गुड़िया*, पुतली*

dollar *n.* डॉलर (मुद्रा*)

domain *n.* जागीर*, प्रदेश,
विचार-सीमा*

dome *n.* गुंबद

domestic *a.* घरेलू, पालतू;

n. गृहसेवक

domesticate *v.t.* पालतू या सभ्य
या वातावरण के अनुकूल
बनाना

domicile *n.* अधिवास; *v.t.*
& *i.* स्थायी अधिवासी होना

dominant *a.* प्रधान, प्रबल, हावी

dominate *v.t. & i.* प्रभुत्व
रखना

dominion *n.* अधिराज्य, प्रभुत्व,
राज्य

don *v.t.* पहनना

donate *v.t.* दान देना

donation *n.* दान, भेंट, चंदा

donkey *n.* गधा

donor *n.* दाता, दानी, देनेवाला

do-nothing *a. & n.* प्रमादी,
काहिल

doom *n.* नाश, भ्रांत, क़यामत*;
v.t. विनाश या दुर्भाग्य को
सौंप देना, दंडाज्ञा देना

doomsday *n.* क़यामत या प्रलय
का दिन

door *n.* द्वार

dormant *a.* सुप्त, निष्क्रिय, गूढ़

dose *n.* खूराक*

dot *n. & v.t.* बिंदी* (लगाना)

double *a., n., v.t. & i.* दूना
(करना), प्रतिमूर्ति*

double-dealing *n.* कपटाचार;
a. कपटाचारी

doubt *n., v.t. & i.* सन्देह

(करना), दुविधा (में होना)

dough *n.* लोई*, गुंधा आटा

dove *n.* कबूतर

dove-cot *n.* दरबा

down *adv. & prep.* नीचे

downcast *a.* खिन्न, अधोमुख

downfall *n.* पतन, नाश

downpour *n.* मूसलाधार वर्षा*

downright *adv.* पूर्णंत:,सर्वथा

downward *a. & adv.*, down-
    wards *adv.* नीचे, नीचे को

dowry *n.* दहेज

doze *n. & v.i.* झपकी* (लेना),
    ऊंघ* (-ना)

dozen *n.* दर्जन

drab *n., a. & v.t.* बादामी
    (रंग, कपड़ा), नीरस (-ता*)

draft *n. & v.t.* जबरिया भरती*
    (में लेना), हुडी* या 'ड्राफ्ट'
    (बुनाना), प्रारूप या ढांचा
    (तैयार करना)

draftsman *a.* मानचित्रकार,
    मसविदा-नवीस

drag *n., v.t. & i.* घसीट*(-ना),
    घिसटन*, घिसटना

dragon *n.* पौराणिक राक्षस

drain *n.* नाला, निकास ; *v.t.*
    & i. खींच या सोख लेना

drainage *n.* नालियों-मोरियों
    की व्यवस्था* या उनका गंदा
    पानी

dram *n.* 'ड्राम' ($=\frac{1}{16}$ औंस

ठोस या $\frac{1}{8}$ औंस तरल)

drama *n.* नाटक, अभिनय

draper *n.* बजाज़

drapery *n.* बजाज़ी*, परदे

drastic *a.* उग्र, कठोर

draught *n. & v.t.* प्रारूप या
    ढांचा या खाका (तैयार करना),
    हुंडी* भोंका

draughtsman *n.* मानचित्रकार,
    प्रारूपकार

draw *v.t. & i.* खींचना, खिंचना ;
    n. बराबरी पर छूटा खेल

drawback *n.* कमी*, खोट*,
    असुविधा*

drawers *n.* दराज*, जांघिया

drawing *n.* ड्राइंग, रेखांकन,
    रेखाचित्र

drawing-room *n.* ड्राइंगरूम,
    बैठक

dread *v.t. & i.* डरना, थर्राना ;
    a. & n. भयावह (वस्तु), डर

dream *n., v.t. & i.* सपना
    (देखना)

dreary *a.* मन्द, निरानन्द

drench *v.t.* सराबोर करना

dress *n., v.t. & i.* पहनावा
    (पहनना), सजाना, पहनाना

dressing *n.* मरहम-पट्टी

drill *n., v.t. & i.* बरमा (-ना),
    क़वायद (करना, कराना),ड्रिल

drink *n., v.t. & i.* पेय, पीना,
    मदपान (करना)

drip n. टपकन; v.t. & i. टप-
काना, टपकना, सराबोर होना

drive v.t. & i. हांकना, (गाड़ी)
चलाना; n. (गाड़ी या ग्रहाते
की) सड़क*, (गाड़ी पर) सैर*

driver n. चालक

drizzle n. & v.i. फुही*(पड़ना)

droll a. & n. हासकर, ठिठोलिया

drollery n. विनोद, विचित्र परि-
हास, हास्य-रचना*

drop n. बूंद*, पतन, मंदी*,
लोलक; v.t. गिराना, गिरना,
टपकाना, टपकना

drought n. ग्रनावृष्टि*, सूखा,
प्यास*

drown v.i. & t. डूबना, डुबाना

drowse n., v.i. & t. झपकी*
(लेना), ऊंघ (-ना), तंद्रिल
या निद्रालु बनाना

drudge v.i. खट मरना, जांगर
चलाना; n. मरखटट्टू, किराये
का टट्टू, गुलाम

drug n. ग्रौषध; v.t. & i.
(दवा में विष ग्रादि) मिलाना,
दवा पिलाना, कुछ खिला-
पिलाकर ग्रचेत करना

druggist n. ग्रत्तार, ग्रौषध-
विक्रेता

drum n., v.t. & i. ढोल या
नगाड़ा (बजाना), पीपा

drunkard n. पियक्कड़

dry a. मूखा, प्यासा, नीरस; v.i.
& t. सुखाना, सूखना

dualism n. द्वैत, द्वैतवाद, द्विवचन

dub v.t. उपाधि देना, उपनाम
रखना

dubious a. भ्रामक, संदिग्ध

duck n. बतख*, मादा बतख*;
v.t. & i. डुबकी लगाना

due n. & a. दाय, दावा, प्राप्य;
adv. ठीक, सीधे

duel n. & v.t. मल्लयुद्ध या द्वंद्व-
युद्ध (करना)

duke n. नवाब, 'ड्यूक'

dull a., v.t. & i. कुंठित (कर
देना या हो जाना), मूर्ख, जड़,
खिन्न

duly adv. यथोचित, यथासमय,
पर्याप्त रूप से

dumb a. & v.t. गूंगा या मूक
(बना डालना), हक्काबक्का
(कर देना)

dumbfound v.t. ग्रवाक् या
भौंचक्का कर देना

dum-dum a. & n. (बन्दूक की)
दमदम (गोली*)

dunce n. जड़मति

dune n. रेत का टीला

dung n. गोबर, खाद*

dungeon n. कालकोठरी*

duplicate a., n. & v.t. प्रति-
लिपि* या प्रतिरूप (बनाना),
दूना (करना), समानार्थ शब्द

duplicity n. द्वैधता*, दुरंगापन

durable *a.* टिकाऊ, स्थायी

duration *n.* अवधि*, मीयाद*, सत्र

during *prep.* तक, में, इतने में, दारान

dusk *n.* सांझ*

dust *n. & v.t.* धूल* (छिड़कना, पोंछना)

duster *n.* झाड़न*

dutiful कर्तव्यनिष्ठ

duty *n.* कर्त्तव्य, चुंगी*, पाबंदी*

dwarf *a., n. & v.t.* बौना (बनाना)

dwell *v.t.* बसना, रहना, ध्यान केन्द्रित करना

dwelling *n.* आवास, घर

dwindle *v.t.* कम या क्षीण या भ्रष्ट हो चलना, महत्त्व खोना

dye *n., v.t. & i.* रंग या रंगने का मसाला (बनाना), रंगना

dynamic *a.* गतिशील, ऊर्जस्वी

dynamics *n.* (*pl.*) गतिविज्ञान, 'गतिकी'*

dynamite *n.* 'डाइनेमाइट', बलस्फोट

dynamo *n.* बिजली उत्पन्न करने का यन्त्र, 'डाइनेमो'

dynasty *n.* राजकुल, वंश

dysentery *n.* ग्रामातिसार, ग्रांव, पेचिश*

dyspepsia *n.* अजीर्ण, मंदाग्नि*, बदहजमी*

E

each *a. & pron.* प्रति, प्रत्येक, परस्पर

eager *a.* उत्सुक, आतुर, उत्कट

eagle *n.* गरुड़

ear *n.* कान, ध्वनि-विवेक, अन्न की बाल*

early *a. & adv.* पूर्व, शीघ्र, सवेरे, अकालघटित

earn *v.t.* उपार्जन करना, प्राप्त करना, कमाना

earnest *a.* अकपट, तत्पर, उत्सुक *n.* बयाना, साई*, थाती*

earth *n.* पृथ्वी*, भूमंडल, संसार; *v.t. & i.* मिट्टी से ढंकना, मिट्टी में गाड़ना

earthen *a.* मिट्टी का (बना हुआ)

earthly *a.* पार्थिव, लौकिक

earthquake *n.* भूकम्प

earth-worm *n.* केंचुआ

ease *n., v.t. & i.* सुख या आराम (पहुंचाना)

easel *n.* चित्रफलक

east *n.* पूरब, पूरबी; *a.* प्राच्य; *adv.* पूर्व की ओर

Easter *n.* ईस्टर' (ईसा-पुन-
जीवन पर्व)

eastern *a.* पूरबी, पूर्वीय; *n.*
प्राच्यदेशवासी

easy *a.* सहज, सुलभ, मंदा ; *n.*
सुस्ताहट*; *adv.* सरलता से ;
v.i. धीमे चलो

eat *v.t. & i.* खाना

eatable *n.* (प्राय: *pl.*) खाद्य-
पदार्थ ; *a.* भोज्य, खाद्य

eavesdrop *v.i.* छिपकर बातें
सुनना

ebb *n. & v.i.* भाटा (ग्राना)

ebony *n.* ग्राबनूस

eccentric *a. & n.* केंद्रभ्रष्ट,
झक्की या विलक्षरा (व्यक्ति)

eccentricity *n.* सनक*

ecclesiastical *a.* गिरजा या
पादरी संबंधी, धार्मिक

echo *n., v.t. & i.* प्रतिध्वनि*
(-त करना या होना)

eclat *n.* शोभा*, भारी सफलता*

eclipse *n. & v.t.* ग्रहण (लगना),
ग्रस्त (करना)

ecliptic *n.* क्रांतिवृत्त (सूर्य का
मार्ग) ; *a.* ग्रहण-संबंधी

economic (-al) *a.* ग्रार्थिक,
ग्रर्थशास्त्रीय, लाभप्रद

economics *n.* (*pl.*) ग्रर्थशास्त्र,
ग्रर्थनीति*, ग्रार्थिक ग्रवस्था*

economize *v.t. & i.* खर्च कम
करना, कम खर्च करना

economy *n.* मितव्ययिता*,
ग्रर्थनीति*

ecstasy *n.* परमानंद

Eden *n.* भूस्वर्ग, सम्मोह,
परमानंद-दशा*

edge *n., v.t. & i.* धार*
(रखना), किनारा

edible *a. & n.* खाद्य (-पदार्थ),
खाने योग्य

edifice *n.* भवन, प्रासाद

edit *v.t.* संपादन करना

edition *n.* संस्करण, संपादन

editor *n.* सम्पादक

editorial *a. & n.* सम्पादक
संबंधी, सम्पादकीय ग्रग्रलेख

educate *v.t.* शिक्षा देना या
दिलाना

education *n.* शिक्षरण, नैतिक
या वौद्धिक विकास

educe *v.t.* निष्कर्ष या सार
निकालना, बिलगाना

efface *v.t.* मिटाना, पोंछ डालना,
नष्ट करना

effect *n.* परिराम, प्रभाव; *v.t.*
ग्रमल में लाना

effects *n.* (*pl.*) चल-संपत्ति*

effectual *a.* ग्रमोघ, वैध, समर्थ

effeminate *a.* स्त्रैरण, इंद्रिय-
परतंत्र

effete *a.* थका हुग्रा, दुर्बल,
ग्रशक्त

efficacy *n.* गुरण, गुरणकारिता*,

प्रभाव, सामर्थ्य

efficiency *n.* निपुणता*, कार्य-क्षमता*, योग्यता*

effigy *n.* प्रतिमा*, पुतला

efflorescent *a.* पुष्पित

effort *n.* प्रयास, उद्यम

effrontery *n.* धृष्टता*, गुस्ताखी*

effulgent *a.* दीप्तिमान

effusion *n.* बहाव, प्रसंयत वाक्य

egg *n.* अंडा; *v.t.* उकसाना

egg-plant *n.* भंटा का पौधा

ego *n.* अहं, आत्मा*

egotism *n.* अहंता*, अहंकार, आत्मचर्चा*

eight *n.* आठ

eighteen *n.* अठारह

eighty *n.* अस्सी

either *a. & pron.* दो में से एक या प्रत्येक, भी; *adv. & conj.* या तो

ejaculate *v.t.* बोल पड़ना, शरीर से निकाल फेंकना

eject *v.t.* बेदखल करना, फेंकना, निकालना

eke *v.t.* जैसे-तैसे निर्वाह करना

elaborate *v.t.* विस्तार से करना; *a.* विस्तृत, सुसम्पन्न

elapse *v.i.* बीत जाना

elastic *a. & n.* लचीला (फीता), प्रफुल्ल, नमनीय

elate *v.t.* उत्तेजित या उल्लसित या गर्वित करना

elbow *n., v.t. & i.* कोहनी (मारना), धक्कमधक्का करके घुसना या निकलना

elder *a. & n.* ज्येष्ठ या श्रेष्ठ (व्यक्ति)

elderly *a.* प्रौढ़, वयोवृद्ध

elect *v.t.* निर्वाचित करना

election *n.* चुनाव

electorate *n.* चुनावक्षेत्र, निर्वाचकवर्ग, निर्वाचकमंडल

electric *a.* बिजली का

electricity *n.* बिजली*

electrify *v.t.* बिजली लगाना

electropathy *n.* बिजली का (से) इलाज

electroplate *v.t.* बिजली से सोना-चांदी चढ़ाना

elegance *n.* चारुता,* शिष्टता*, रम्यता*

elegy *n.* शोकगीत

element *n.* तत्त्व, प्राथमिक शिक्षा*

elementary *a.* मौलिक, प्राथमिक, तात्त्विक

elephant *n.* हाथी

elephantiasis *n.* फ़ीलपांव

elevate *v.t.* ऊपर उठाना, पद या मान बढ़ाना

elevator *n.* उत्सेधक, 'लिफ्ट'

eleven *n.* ग्यारह

elf *n.* कल्पित बौना, बेताल या योगिनी*

elicit *v.t.* प्रकाश में लाना, निष्कर्ष या सार निकालना

eligible *a.* योग्य, वरणीय, पात्र

eliminate *v.t.* निकाल देना, दूर करना, लुप्त करना

elocution *n.* वाग्मिता*

elope *v.i.* साथ भाग जाना, गुप्त, रहना, फ़रार होना

eloquent *a.* सुवक्ता

else *adv.* अन्य, साथ ही, अन्यथा नहीं तो

elucidate *v.t.* विशद या स्पष्ट करना

elude *v.t. & i.* टाल जाना, टलना, बच निकलना

elusion *n.* छल, चकमा

elusive *a.* मायावी, हाथ न आनेवाला

emaciated *a.* दुर्बल, क्षीण

emanate *v.i.* उद्भूत या निर्गत होना

emancipation *n.* उद्धार, मुक्ति-दान

emasculate *v.t.* बधिया करना, शक्तिहीन या प्रभावहीन करना

embalm *v.t.* शवरक्षा-लेप करना

embank *v.t.* तटबंध या पुश्ता बांधना

embankment *n.* बांध, पुश्ता

embargo *n. & v.t.* घाटबंधी* या व्यापारावरोध (करना)

embark *v.t.* जहाज पर चढ़ना

embarrass *v.t.* असमंजस या झंझट या संकट में डालना, उलझाना

embassy *n.* राजदूतावास, राज-दूत का कार्य या पद

embattle *v.t.* व्यूह रचना, सन्नद्ध करना

embezzlement *n.* ग़बन

embitter *v.t.* कटुतर या दुखद-तर बना देना

emblem *n.* चिह्न, प्रतीक, राज्य-चिह्न

embodiment *n.* अवतार, मूर्त रूप*

embolden *v.t.* साहसी बनाना, उत्साह देना

embosom *v.t.* छाती से लगाना, मन या हृदय में गाड़ लेना, घेरना

emboss *v.t.* उभारदार नक्काशी करना

embrace *n. & v.t.* प्रेमालिंगन (करना)

embroidery *n.* कढ़ाई*, चिकन,* कारचोबी*

embryo *n.* भ्रूण, अविकसित गर्भशिशु; *a.* अपरिपक्व

embryology *n.* भ्रूणविज्ञान

emerald *n.* मरकत, पन्ना

emerge *v.i.* उभरना, प्रकट होना

emergency *n.* संकटकाल

emigrate v.i. & t. स्वदेश त्यागना, विदेशवास करना या कराना

eminent a. विशिष्ट, प्रख्यात, श्रेष्ठ

emissary n. दूत

emit v.t. निकालना, फेंकना

emolument n. आय,* वेतन, प्राप्ति*

emotion n. भावना,* भावावेश, जोश

emperor n. सम्राट्

emphasis n. जोर, प्रमुखता*

emphasize v.t. जोर देना, महत्त्व पर जोर देना

emphatic a. जोरदार, दृढ़, निश्चित

empire n. साम्राज्य

empiric a. & n. प्रयोगसिद्ध, अनुभवसिद्ध

employ n. & v.t. (अपनी) सेवा* या नौकरी* में (रखना), नियुक्त करना

employee n. नियुक्त, कर्मचारी, नौकर

employer n. मालिक

employment n. नौकरी*, रोजगार

emporium n. बिक्री-भंडार

empower v.t. अधिकार या सामर्थ्य देना

empress n. साम्राज्ञी*

empty n., v.t. & i. रीता या खाली या छूछा (करना या होना)

emulate v.t. प्रतियोगिता करना, सोत्साह अनुकरण करना

emulsion n. रासायनिक पायस, पायसन

enable v.t. योग्य या समर्थ या अधिकारी बनाना

enact v.t. कानून बनाना, अभिनीत करना

enamel n. & v.t. मीनाकारी* (करना), तामचीनी* (चढ़ाना)

enamour v.t. आसक्त या आकृष्ट या प्रेममत्त करना, आनंदित करना

encamp v.t. & i. पड़ाव डालना या पड़ना, पड़ाव में ठहरना

encase v.t. डिब्बा बंद करना, खोल चढ़ाना

encash v.t. भुनाना, नकद बनाना

enchant v.t. मंत्रमुग्ध करना, रिझाना

encircle v.t. घेरना, वृत्त बनाना, घेरा डालना

enclose v.t. बंद करना, घेरना, संलग्न करना

enclosure n. घेरा, अहाता, संलग्न पत्रादि

encomium n. अतिरंजित प्रशंसा,* चापलूसी*

encompass *v.t.* घेर लेना,
रखना, घरना

encounter *n. & v.i.* मुठभेड़*
या सामना (होना), आकस्मिक
मिलन या भेंट* (होना)

encourage *v.t.* बढ़ावा देना,
उकसाना

encroach *v.t. & i.* अनधिकार
प्रवेश या अतिक्रमण करना

encumber *v.t.* भारग्रस्त या
ऋणग्रस्त करना, रोड़े अटकाना,
उलझाना

encyclopaedia *n.* विश्वकोश

end *n., v.t. & i.* अंत (करना),
सीमा, अंतिम भाग, नाश, मृत्यु,
प्रयोजन, लक्ष्य

endanger *v.t.* जोखिम में डालना

endearment *n.* लाड़-प्यार,
प्यार की बात*

endeavour *n., v.t. & i.* प्रयास
या उद्यम (करना)

ending *n.* अन्त, समापन,
समाप्ति*

endorse *v.t.* अनुमोदन या पुष्टि
करना

endow *v.t.* धर्मस्व देना

endurable *a.* टिकाऊ, चिर-
स्थायी

endurance *n.* धैर्य, सहनशक्ति*

endure *v.t. & i.* सहना, भोगना

enemy *n.* शत्रु, शत्रु-सेना*

energy *n.* ऊर्जा,* स्फूर्ति*

enfeeble *v.t.* दुर्बल करना

enforce *v.t.* लागू करना, विवश
करना

enfranchise *v.t.* मताधिकार
देना

engage *v.t. & i.* नियुक्त करना,
सगाई में बंधना, व्यस्त रहना

engagement *n.* नियुक्ति*
सगाई*

engine *n.* इंजन

engineer *n.* इंजीनियर, अभि-
यन्ता

English *a. & n.* अंग्रेजी भाषा*
अंग्रेज, इंगलैंड संबंधी

engrave *v.t.* नक्काशी करना

engross *v.t.* ध्यानमग्न करना

engulf *v.t.* निमग्न करना
निगल जाना

enigma *n.* गूढ़ प्रश्न, पहेली*

enjoy *v.t.* आनन्द लेना, लाभ
उठाना

enlarge *v.t.* बड़ा करना या
बनाना

enlighten *v.t.* प्रबुद्ध करना

enlist *v.t.* भरती करना, सूची
बनाना

enliven *v.t.* अनुप्राणित करना

enmity *n.* शत्रुता*, वैर, विद्वेष

enormous *a.* बहुत बड़ा,
असाधारण

enough *a. & adv.* पर्याप्त
(मात्रा में); *n.* पर्याप्ति*

enrage *v.t.* कुपित करना

enrapture *v.t.* निहाल करना

enrich *v.t.* समृद्ध या उपजाऊ बनाना

enrol *v.t.* नाम लिखना, भरती करना

enshrine *v.t.* संदिर में रखना

enslave *v.t.* दास बनाना, वश में रखना

ensue *v.i. & t.* अनुघटित होना, खोज या पीछा करना

ensure *v.t.* पक्का या ठीक कर लेना, सुरक्षित रखना, निर्भय करना

entangle *v.t.* कठिनाइयों में डालना, जाल में फंसाना, उलभाना

enter *v.t. & i.* प्रवेश पाना या करना, दाखिल करना

enterprise *n.* उद्यम, दिलेरी*

entertain *v.t.* सत्कार करना, मनोरंजन करना, विचारना

entertainment *n.* मनोरंजन

enthrone *v.t.* राजसिंहासन पर बैठाना

enthusiasm *n.* उमंग*, जोश

entice *v.t.* लुभाना, ललचाना

entire *a.* सम्पूर्ण, समूचा

entitle *v.t.* उपाधि या अधिकार देना, नाम रखना

entity *n.* अस्तित्व, सत्त्व

entomb *v.t.* कब्र में रखना, दफ़न करना

entomology *n.* कृमिविज्ञान

entrails *n.* आंतड़ियां*

entrance *v.t.* मूर्च्छित या व्याकुल करना; *n.* प्रवेश, प्रवेश का अधिकार, द्वार, प्रवेशिका*

entrap *v.t.* फन्दे में फंसाना

entreat *v.t.* विनती करना, गिड़गिड़ाना

entrenchment *n.* खाई*

entrust *v.t.* सौंपना, जिम्म करना, विश्वास पर छोड़ना

entry *n.* प्रवेश, प्रवेशद्वार, इंदराज

enumerate *v.t.* गिनना, नाम ले-लेकर बताना

enunciate *v.t.* उच्चारित करना, प्रतिज्ञा करना

envelop *v.t.* ढंक लेना, घेरा बनाना या रचना

envelope *n.* लिफ़ाफ़ा, ग्लिाफ़

envious *a.* ईर्ष्यालु

environment *n.* परिवेश, वातावरण

envisage *v.t.* सामना या परिकल्पना करना, विशेष दृष्टि से सोचना

envoy *n.* दूत, राजदूत, प्रतिनिधि

envy *n. & v.t.* ईर्ष्या (करना), विद्वेष (रखना)

enwrap *v.t.* ढकना, आवरण चढ़ाना, लपेटना, तह करना

ephemeral *a.* क्षणभंगुर

epic *n. & a.* महाकाव्य (के उप-युक्त)

epidemic *n. & a.* महामारी*, संक्रामक (रोग)

epigram *n.* सूक्ति*, चुटकुला

epigraph *n.* पुरालेख, आदर्श वाक्य, सूक्ति*

epilepsy *n.* मिरगी*

epilogue *n.* उपसंहार, भरत-वाक्य

episode *n.* उपकथा*

epistle *n.* पत्र, पत्रकाव्य

epitaph *n.* समाधिलेख

epithet *n.* गुणसूचक नाम, विशेषण

epitome *n.* सार, सारग्रहण, प्रतीक

epoch *n.* युग, युगारंभ, काल, प्रवधि*

equal *a., v.t. & i.* बराबर या एक-सा (करना या होना); *n.* समकक्ष व्यक्ति, (*pl.*) समान वस्तुएं*

equanimity *n.* संतुलन, समभाव

equation *n.* समीकरण

equator *n.* भूमध्यरेखा*

equidistant *a.* समदूर, समानान्तर

equilateral *a.* समभुज, समभुजीय

equilibrium *n.* संतुलन

equip *v.t.* सन्नद्ध करना, संवारना, सजाना

equipment *n.* साज-सामान

equitable *a.* न्यायसंगत

equity *n.* न्यायसाम्य

equivalent *a. & n.* तुल्य (राशि, द्रव्य), समान (-मूल्य वस्तु), पर्याय

equivocal *a.* गोलमोल

equivocate *v.t.* गोलमोल बात कहना या जवाब देना

equivocation *n.* वाक्छल

era *n.* युग, अनुयुग

eradicate *v.t.* जड़ से उखाड़ना, पूर्ण रूप से नाश करना

erase *v.t.* खुरचना, मिटाना

ere *adv. & prep.* इससे पूर्व कि, पहले

erect *a. & v.t.* सीधा या खड़ा (करना)

erotic *a.* कामुक, कामोद्दीपक; *n.* प्रेमकाव्य

err *v.i.* ग़लती करना या होना

errand *n.* संदेश, दूतकर्म

errata *n. & (pl.)* अशुद्धिपत्र, शुद्धिपत्र

erroneous *a.* भ्रमपूर्ण, त्रुटिपूर्ण

error *n.* त्रुटि*, भूल*, ग़लती*

erudite *a.* पंडित, पांडित्यपूर्ण

erupt *v.i.* विस्फोट होना, फूटना, (ज्वालामुखी का) फटना

escape *n., v.i. & t.* पलायन

(करना), (गैस आदि का) निष्क्रम (होना)

eschew *v.t.* परिहार या त्याग करना, परहेज़ करना

escort *v.t.* रक्षार्थ साथ जाना या देना; *n.* अनुरक्षक (व्यक्ति या दल), अनुरक्षण, पहरा

especial *a.* अपवादभूत, विशिष्ट

Esperanto *n.* कृत्रिम विश्व-भाषा विशेष, 'एस्पेरांतो'

espionage *n.* जासूसी*

espouse *v.t.* मत अपनाना, पृष्ठपोषण करना

essay *v.t. & i.* प्रयास करना, परखना; *n.* निबन्ध

essence *n.* तत्त्व, सार, इत्र

essential *a.* सारभूत, आवश्यक

establish *v.t.* स्थापित करना, सिद्ध करना

establishment *n.* गृहस्थी*, संस्थान

estate *n.* जागीर*, रियासत*

esteem *n. & v.t.* मान (करना)

estimate *n. & v.t.* अनुमान (लगाना)

eternal *a.* शाश्वत

ether *n.* ईथर, तेजावह तत्त्व

ethics *n.*, (*pl.*) आचारशास्त्र, नीति*

etiquette *n.* शिष्टाचार

etymology *n.* शब्दविज्ञान, शब्द व्युत्पत्ति*

eunuch *n.* नपुंसक, हिजड़ा

evacuate *v.t.* खाली करना, छोड़कर अन्यत्र जाना

evacuee *n.* शरणार्थी

evade *v.t.* टाल जाना, बच निकलना

evasion *n.* छल, परिहार

even *a. & v.t.* चौरस (करना) सम (संख्या)

evening *n.* शाम*, संध्या*

event *n.* घटना*, वृत्तांत

eventual *a.* संभावित, अंतिम

ever *adv.* सदा, कभी, निरंतर

evergreen *a. & n.* सदाबहार (पेड़)

everlasting *a.* शाश्वत, टिकाऊ

every *a.* प्रति, प्रत्येक, हर एक

evict *v.t.* बेदखल करना

eviction *n.* बेदखली*

evidence *n.* गवाही*

evident *a.* प्रत्यक्ष

evil *a. & n.* अशुभ या अहित (वस्तु)

evince *v.t.* प्रकट करना, जताना

evoke *v.t.* आह्वान या आवाहन करना

evolution *n.* विकास

evolve *v.t. & i.* विकसित करना या होना

exact *a. & v.t.* यथार्थ, ठोस; बलपूर्वक वसूल या लागू करना

exaggerate *v.t.* अतिरंजित

करना

exaggeration *n.* अतिरंजना*, अतिशयोक्ति*

exalt *v.t.* ऊंचा पद देना, प्रशंसा करना

examination *n.* परीक्षा*, जांच-पड़ताल*

examine *v.t.* परीक्षा या जांच-पड़ताल या खोज या छानबीन करना

examinee *n.* परीक्षार्थी

examiner *n.* परीक्षक

example *n.* उदाहरण, नमूना

excavate *v.t.* खोदना

exceed *v.t. & i.* अधिक होना, बढ़ना

excel *v.t. & i.* विशिष्ट या श्रेष्ठ होना

excellence *n.* श्रेष्ठता*, महत्ता*

excellency *n.* महामान्य, परम-श्रेष्ठ

excellent *a.* अत्युत्तम

except *v.t. & i.* वर्जित करना, आपत्ति उठाना; *prep.* सिवाय

exception *n.* अपवाद, आपत्ति*

excess *n.* अति*, अतिरेक

exchange *n., v.t. & i.* विनि-मय (करना या होना)

exchequer *n.* राजकोष

excise *n.* आबकारी*, चुंगी*

excite *v.t.* उत्तेजित करना

exclamation *n.* विस्मयोद्गार

exclude *v.t.* बाहर रखना

exclusive *a.* विशेष, एकांतिक

excommunicate *v.t.* जाति या समाज या धर्म से बहिष्कृत करना

excursion *n.* सैर*, सैर-सपाटा

excuse *n.* क्षमायाचना*; *v.t.* क्षमा करना, बहाना बनाना

execute *v.t.* कार्यान्वित करना, फांसी देना

exempt *v.t.* बरी (करना), छूट देना; *n.* शर्तों से मुक्त व्यक्ति

exercise *n., v.t. & i.* व्यायाम (करना), अभ्यास (करना)

exhaust *v.t.* चुका डालना, निशक्त कर डालना

exhibit *n.* प्रदर्शनीय वस्तु, दस्तावेज़; *v.t.* प्रदर्शित करना

exhibition *n.* प्रदर्शनी*, नुमायश*

exile *n. & v.t.* निर्वासित (व्यक्ति, करना)

exist *v.i.* होना, जीना

existence *n.* अस्तित्व

exit *n.* बाहर जाने का मार्ग

expand *v.t. & i.* फैलाना, फैलना

expansion *n.* विस्तार

expansive *a.* विस्तृत

ex-parte *a. & adv.* एकतरफा

expect *v.t.* प्रत्याशा या अपेक्षा या प्रतीक्षा करना

expedient *a.* इष्ट, समयोचित;
n. युक्ति*, तदबीर*

expedite *v.t.* झटपट कर या
करा देना, शीघ्रता करना

expedition *n.* अभियान,
अभियानी-दल, मुस्तैदी*

expel *v.t.* खदेड़ देना, खारिज
करना

expend *v.t.* व्यय करना, खपाना,
उड़ा डालना

expenditure *n.* व्यय, लागत*

expense *n.* मूल्य, व्यय

expensive *a.* बहुमूल्य, महंगा

experience *n. & v.t.* अनुभव
(करना, से सीखना)

experiment *n. & v.i.* प्रयोग
(करना)

expert *a. & n.* कुशल या
विशेषज्ञ (व्यक्ति)

expire *v.t. & i.* बीत जाना,
मरना, अंत होना

expiry *n.* अंत

explain *v.t.* व्याख्या करना,
समझाना, सफ़ाई देना

explanation *n.* व्याख्या*
सफ़ाई*

explicit *a.* सुस्पष्ट, सुनिश्चित,
स्पष्टवादी

explode *v.t. & i.* विस्फोट
करना या होना

exploit *n.* पराक्रम, कारनामा;
v.t. काम लेना, शोषण करना

exploration *n.* अन्वेषण

explore *v.i. & t.* खोजना,
पता लगाना

explosion *n* विस्फोट, धमाका

explosive *a. & n.* विस्फोट
(द्रव्य)

exponent *a. & n.* व्याख्याता

export *n. & v.t.* निर्यात
(करना, माल)

expound *v.t.* व्याख्या करना

express *a., n. & adv.* द्रुत
(गति से), असंदिग्ध; *v.t.*
व्यक्त या प्रकट करना

expression *n.* अभिव्यक्ति*,
मुखमुद्रा*

expressive *a.* अर्थपूर्ण, भावपूर्ण

expulsion *n.* निर्वासन,
निष्कासन

expunge *v.t.* मिटाना

exquisite *a.* अतिसुंदर

extempore *adv.* बिना तैयारी
के; *a.* समय-स्फूर्त

extend *v.t.* विस्तृत करना या
होना

external *a.* बाह्य, वैदेशिक

extinct *a.* बुझा हुआ, मरा
हुआ, लुप्त

extinguish *v.t.* बुझाना, अन्त
करना

extol *v.t.* अति प्रशंसा करना

extra *a., adv. & n.* अतिरिक्त,
इतर, आदि

extract *n. & v.t.* रस या सत्त या निष्कर्ष (निकालना), उद्धरण (देना)

extraordinary *a.* अपूर्व, असाधारण

extravagance *n.* अपव्यय

extreme *a. & n.* चरम (सीमा*)

extremist *n.* अतिवादी

extricate *v.t.* निस्तार देना, उद्धार करना

exuberance *n.* प्रचुरता*,

ओजस्विता*, उर्वरता*, संपन्नता*

exude *v.i.* रसकर बहना, पसीजना, चूना

exult *v.i.* गर्व के अनुभव या हर्ष के मद या जय के उल्लास से फूला न समाना

eye *n.* आंख*; *v.t.* नज़र रखना

eyebrow *n.* भौं*

eyelash *n.* बरौनी*

eyelid *n.* पपोटा

F

fable *n.* आख्यायिका*, कपोल-कल्पना*

fabric *n.* बुनावट*, कपड़ा

fabricate *v.t.* निर्माण करना, जाल रचना

fabulous काल्पनिक, अविश्वस-नीय

facade *n.* अगवाड़ा, मोहरा

face *n.* मुख, चेहरा; *v.t. & i.* सामने आना या होना, सामना करना

facet *n.* पहल, पहलू, रुख, खंड

facetious *a.* हास्कर, ठिठोलिया

facial *a.* मुख-संबंधी, मुख का; *n.* चेहरे की मालिश*

facile *a.* सरलप्रकृति, सुगम,

सुलभ

facilitate *v.t.* सुगम या सुविधा-जनक बनाना

facility *n.* सुगमता* सहूलियत*

fac-simile *n. & v.t.* अनुचित्र (बनाना)

fact *n.* तथ्य, कार्य, यथार्थता*

faction *n.* गुट, गुटबंदी*

factitious *a.* कृत्रिम

factitive *a.* द्विकर्मक (क्रिया), पूरक

factor *n.* गुणनखंड, साधन, उपादान

factory *n.* कारख़ाना

faculty *n.* मनःशक्ति*, विश्व-विद्यालय का विभाग

fad n. धुन*, सनक*, प्रिय-
सिद्धांत

fade v.i. रंग उतरना, मुरझाना

faggot n. ईंधन का गट्ठा

fail v.i. विफल होना, अनुत्तीर्ण
होना

fain a. & adv. लाचारी से,
इच्छुक, प्रसन्नता से

faint n. मूर्च्छा*; v.i. मूर्च्छित
होना

fair n. मेला; a. निर्दोष, गोरा;
fair play उचित व्यवहार,
fair sex स्त्री जाति

fairly adv. बहुत कुछ

fairy n. परी*

faith n. श्रद्धा* भक्ति*, धर्म,
विश्वास

faithful a. भक्त, सच्चा, श्रद्धालु

falcon n. बाज

fall v.i. गिरना, टूट पड़ना ;n.
पतन, झरना, ढलान*

fallacy n. भ्रम, हेत्वाभास

fallow a. ऊसर, बंजर

false a. झूठा, बनावटी

falter v.i. हकलाना, डिगना

fame n. कीर्ति*, प्रसिद्धि*

famed a. प्रसिद्ध

familiar a. अंतरंग, सुपरिचित

family n. परिवार, वंश, जाति*

famine n. अकाल, कमी*

famous a. प्रसिद्ध

fan n. पंखा; v.t. पंखा झलना,
हवा देना

fanatic a. कट्टर, धर्मान्ध

fancy n. कल्पना*, पसंद*; v.t.
कल्पना करना

fantastic a. विलक्षण, ऊट-
पटांग

fantasy n. विलक्षण कल्पना*

far a. & adv. दूर, दूरवर्ती ; n.
दूरी*, अंतर

farce n. स्वांग, प्रहसन

fare n. भाड़ा; v.i. भोजन
करना, बसर होना

farewell n., interj. विदाई*
(का नमस्कार)

farm n. खेत, फ़ार्म; v.t. खेती
करना

farmer n. किसान, खेतिहर

farming n. खेती*, किसानी*

fashion n. फ़ैशन, शैली*; v.t.
आकार देना

fast n. & v.i. उपवास (करना);
a. द्रुतगामी ; adv. तेज,
स्थिरता से

fasten v.t. जकड़ देना

fat a. मोटा; n. चरबी

fatal a. घातक, भाग्यसंबंधी

fatalism n. भाग्यवाद

fate n. भाग्य, दैव

father n. पिता, प्रणेता

father-in-law n. ससुर

fathom v.t. गहराई नापना,
थाह लेना

fathomless *a.* अगाध

fatigue *n.* थकान; *v.t.* थकाना

fault *n.* दोष, क़सूर

fauna *n.* (*pl.*) (किसी प्रदेश या युग के) पशु, पशुवर्ग्ग्न

favour *n.* कृपा*, अनुग्रह; *v.t.* पक्ष लेना, कृपा करना

favourable *a.* अनुकूल, हितकर

favourite *a. & n.* प्रीतिपात्र या कृपापात्र (जन)

favouritism *n.* पक्षपात

fear *n.* भय, आशंका*, त्रास; *v.i. & t.* भयभीत या शंकित होना, डरना, डराना

feasible *a.* संगत, साध्य

feast *n., v.i. & t.* उत्सव या प्रीतिभोज (में भाग लेना)

feat *n.* करतब, कमाल; *a.* कुशल, चुस्त

feather *n.* पंख, पर

feature *n.* लक्षण, रूप, नाट्य-रूप्क, महत्त्वपूर्ण लेख; *v.t.* विशिष्ट होना

February *n.* फ़रवरी*

feckless *a.* विफल, निरर्थक, अबल, बेकार

feculent *a.* पंकिल, गंदला, मटमैला, बदबूदार

fecund *a.* उपजाऊ, फलप्रद

federal *a.* संघीय

federation *n.* संघराज्य, राज्य-संघ

fee *n. & v.t.* शुल्क या फ़ीस (देना), वेतन, परखना

feeble *a.* क्षीण, अस्पष्ट, मंद

feed *n., v.t. & i.* भोजन या निवाला (देना), रसद* (पहुंचाते रहना), खिलाना, पालना

feel *n., v.t. & i.* संवेदना* (प्राप्त करना, होना), सहानु-भूति में दुखी होना

feign *v.t & i.* गढ़ना, स्वांग या ढोंग या बहाना करना

felicitate *v.t.* अभिनंदित करना, बधाई देना

felicitous *a.* आनंदप्रद, धन्य

felicity *n.* आनंद, सौभाग्य, आशीर्वाद

fellow *n.* साथी, सहचर

felony *n.* घोर पाप, घोर अपराध

female *n. & a.* स्त्री*, मादा*, स्त्रीय

feminine *a.* स्त्रीवाची, स्त्री-जाति का

fence *n., v.i. & t.* बाड़ा (बनाकर घेरना), चहारदीवारी

fend *v.t. & i.* बचाव करना, मार भगाना, जुगाड करना

ferment *n., v.i. & t.* उबाल (-ना, खाना), विक्षोभ या उत्तेजना (भरना, लाना)

ferocious *a.* क्रूर, भयंकर, जंगली

ferry *n. & v.t.* नाव* (से पार

जाना या ले जाना), खेवा
(की व्यवस्था*)

fertile a. उपजाऊ

fertility n. उपजाऊपन

fertilizer n. उर्वरक, खाद*

fervent a. उत्कट

fervour n. उत्साह, चाव, जोश

festival n. उत्सव, त्योहार

festive a. उत्सव-संबंधी

festivity n. उत्सव

festoon n. & v t. तोरण
(बनाना, से सजाना)

fetch v.t. & i. जाकर लाना

fete n. & v.t. उत्सव (मनाना)

fetish n. जड़पूजा*

fetter n. & v.t. बेड़ी* (डालना),
रोक* (लगाना); (pl.) क़ैद

feud n. कलह, कुलवैर, अदावत*

feudal a. जागीरी, सामंती

feudalism n. जागीरदारी*,
सामंतवाद

fever n. ज्वर, ताप

few a. & n. कुछ, इने-गिने,
थोड़े

fiasco n. टांय-टांय फिस*

fibre n. तंतु, रेशा, ढांचा,
प्रकृति*

fickle a. चंचल, अस्थिर

fiction n. कथा* (-साहित्य),
गढ़ी बात*

fictitious a. कल्पित, मनगढ़ंत,
फ़र्जी

fiddle n., v.t. & i. बेला
(बजाना); interj. वाहियात

fidelity n. निष्ठा*, ईमानदारी*

fidget a., v.i. & t. बेचैन या
अधीर (डोलना या होना या
करना); n. स्नायविक
बेचैनी*, विकल मनोदशा*

fie interj. छि:-छि:

field n. क्षेत्र, मैदान, खेत; v.t.
& i. गेंद रोककर लौटाना

field-marshal n. सर्वोच्च सेना-
पति, फ़ील्डमार्शल

field-work n. क्षेत्रकार्य, अस्थायी
मोर्चाबंदी*

fiend n. क्रूर व्यक्ति, दीवाना,
दानव

fierce a. कोपाकुल, उग्र, रौद्र,
क्रूर, भयंकर

fiery a. उत्साही, कलहप्रिय,
प्रज्वलित

fifteen n. पन्द्रह

fifty n. पचास

fig n. अंजीर

fight n. लड़ाई; v.t. लड़ना

figment n. कल्पना, मनगढ़ंत

figuration n. रंगरूप, रूपरेखा*
अलंकरण

figurative a. आलंकारिक

figure n. आकृति*, मूर्ति*,
संख्या*; v.t. गिनती करना,
नक्काशी से सजाना; figure
of speech अलंकार

file *n.* फ़ाइल*, मिसिल*; *v.t. & i.* दाख़िल दफ़्तर करना, पंक्ति में चलना

fill *v.t. & i.* भरना, पूरा करना या होना

film *n.* फ़िलम*; *v.t. & i.* फ़िल्म बनना

filth *n.* गंदगी*, नीचता*

final *a.* अन्तिम, निर्णय किया हुआ

finance *n.* वित्त, (ब० व०) आर्थिक साधन; *v.t.* पूंजी लगाना

financial *a.* वित्तीय

financier *n.* वित्तदाता, राजस्व-विद, पूंजीपति

find *v.t* पाना, पता लगाना; *n.* खोज*

finger *n.* उंगली*

finis *n.* इति*

finish *n., v.t. & i.* अन्त या समापन करना या होना, निष्पन्न करना

finite *a.* परिमित, सांत

fir *n.* देवदार

fire *n., v.t. & i.* आग* (लगा देना, लगाकर भड़काना, लग जाना), गोली दागना, नौकरी से निकाल देना

fire-brand *n.* कलह भड़काने वाला व्यक्ति या वस्तु*

fire-brick *n.* आग में न गलने वाली ईंट*

fire-brigade *n.* आग बुझाने वालों का दल

fire-engine *n.* दमकल*

fire-fly *n.* जुगनू

fireproof *a.* अदाह्य, आगरोक

firework *n.* आतिशबाजी*

firm *a.* दृढ़, ठोस, स्थिर; *n.* कंपनी*, महाजनी या तिजारती कोठी*, साझे का व्यवसाय

first *a., n. & adv.* प्रथम (-त:) प्रमुख, पहले-पहल, प्रथम

first-aid *n.* प्राथमिक चिकित्सा*

fiscal *a.* राजकोषीय

fish *n., v.t. & i.* मछली* (मारना, पकड़ना), (जलतल से) निकालना, टोह में रहना

fisherman *n.* मछुआ

fishplate *n.* रेल की पटरिया जुड़ी रखने की 'पाटी'*

fissure *n.* दरार*

fist *n. & v.t.* मुक्का या घूंसा (मारना), मुट्ठी*

fistula *n.* नासूर

fit *a.* योग्य; *n.* मूर्च्छा*, दौरा; *v.t. & i.* योग्य बनना, फिट करना

fitful *a.* चपल

fitter *n.* मिस्त्री, फ़िटर

fittings *n.* (*pl.*) साज-सामान

five *n.* पांच

fix *v.t. & i.* निर्धारित या

पक्का करना, जमाना ;
n. असमंजस, जंजाल

flabby a. पिलपिला, शिथिल

flag n. & v.t. झंडा (लगाना),
झंडी* (से सूचित या सीमा-
बद्ध करना)

flagrant a. संगीन, घोर, खुला

flame n., v.t. & i. लौ* या
लपट* (उठना, बलना)

flannel n. फ़लालैन

flare n. & v.i. चौंधियाती
चंचल लौ* (से जगमगा
उठना)

flash n., v.t. & i. दीप्ति*,
दीप्त होना, कौंध (माना)

flask n. 'पलास्क', बोतल*

flat a. & v.t. समतल या चिकना
(करना)

flatter v.t. चापलूसी करना

flaunt n., v.t. & i. शान*
(दिखाना), अकड़* (-ना),
इठलाना

flavour n. विशिष्ट स्वाद या
गंध*

flaw n. त्रुटि*, खोट*, दोष

flee v.i. चंपत हो जाना

fleece n. & v.t. ऊन (कतरना)

fleet n. बेड़ा; a. चुस्त, छिछला;
adv. उथले में; v.i. चंपत
या गुम होना

flesh n. मांस, मोटापा, देह*

flexible a. लचीला, नम्र

flicker n. झिलमिलाहट*,
टिमटिमाहट*; v.t. झिल-
मिलाना, टिमटिमाना

flier, flyer n. हवाबाज़, उड़ाका

flight n. भगदड़*, (पक्षी-)वृंद,
झपट*

flimsy a. झीना, छिछला,
नि:सत्व

flint n. चकमक पत्थर

flip n. & v.t. टक्कर* (मारना)

flippancy n. वाणी की चपलता*
ओछापन

flirt n. चुलबुला या चोंचलेबाज़
विलासी व्यक्ति या स्त्री*;
v.t. & i. दिखावटी प्रेमलीला
करना

flitter v.i. फड़फड़ाना, फुदकना

float v.i. & t. तिरना, उतराना

flock n. यूथ, झुंड, समुदाय;
v.t. जुड़ना, दल बांधकर
जाना या चलना, भीड़ लगाना

flog v.t. कोड़े लगाना या
लगाकर हांकना

flood n. v.t. & i. बाढ़* (ला
देना), बहुतायत*

floor n., v.t. & i. फ़र्श
(जमाना), (मकान का) तल्ला

flora n. देशकाल-विशेष के
उद्भिज (-समुदाय की
तालिका* या सूची*;), पुष्प
देवी*

florescence n. पुष्पकाल

florid *a.* पुष्पसज्जित, प्रति-
अलंकृत

florist *n.* फूलों का खेतिहर या
व्यापारी या विणेपज्ञ

flotilla *n.* छोटे जहाजों का बेड़ा

flounder *n. & v.i.* गिरते-पड़ते
बढ़ने का प्रयास (करना),
गलतियां कर बैठना

flour *n.* आटा, महीन चूर्ण

flourish *n., v.t. & i.* विकास
(पाना)

flout *n. & v.t.* अवज्ञा* या
अनादर या उपहास या आक्षेप
(करना), ताना (मारना)

flow *n.* प्रवाह, बहाव; *v.i.*
बहना, हिलना

flower *n., v.t. & i.* फूल (देना),
विकसितावस्था* (में होना),
उत्तमांश, पुष्पित करना या
होना

flowery *a.* फूलों-भरा, अलंकृत,
लच्छेदार

fluctuate *v.i.* रूपांतरित होना,
लहराना, घटना-बढ़ना

fluent *a.* सहज, धाराप्रवाह

fluid *a. & n.* द्रव या तरल
(पदार्थ)

fluke *n.* संयोग से या अचानक
ठीक पड़ने वाली चोट*

flush *n., v.t. & i.* प्रबल जल-
वेग (से धोना) दमक (आ
जाना); *a.* भरपूर

fluster *n., v.t. & i.* हलचल*
या खलबली* (मचाना, में
पड़ना)

flute *n., v.i. & t.* बांसुरी
(बजाना), खांच* (डालना,
-दार बनाना)

flutter *n.* फड़फड़ाहट*, स्पंदन,
संत्रेग; *v.t. & i.* फड़फड़ाना,
लहराना, घड़कना ·

flux *n.* स्राव; *v.t. & i.* बहकर
निकलना, गलना, गलाना,
पिघलना

fly *n.* मक्खी*, घड़ी या यंत्र
की मक्खी*, उड़ान*; *v.i.*
& *t.* उड़ना, उड़ाना

foam *n. & v.i.* झाग (उठना)

focal *a.* नाभीय, किरणकेन्द्रीय

focus *n.* केन्द्र, किरणबिन्दु;
v.t. & i. केन्द्रित करना या
होना

fodder *n.* चारा

foe *n.* शत्रु

fog *n.* कुहरा

foil *v.t.* विफल या परास्त
करना

fold *n.* तह*, लपेट*; *v.t. &*
i. तह करना

foliage *n.* वनस्पति*

folk *n.* लोक, जनता*, लोग

folk-lore *n.* लोकगीत

follow *v.t. & i.* अनुगमन
करना, पीछा करना

follower *n.* शिष्य, अनुचर

folly *n.* मूर्खता*

foment *v.t.* गरम पानी से सेंकना, शह देकर उभाड़ना

fond *a.* प्रिय, अनुरक्त

fondle *v.t. & i.* प्यार करना, प्रणयक्रीड़ा करना

food *n.* आहार, भोजन, अन्न

fool *a. & n.* मूर्ख (व्यक्ति)

foolhardy *a.* अक्खड़, उजड्डु

foolish *a.* निर्बुद्धि, नासमझ

foolscap *n.* फूल्सकैप, (प्रायः) 17" × 13½" आकार का कागज़

football *n.* फुटबाल

footlights *n.* (*pl.*) फुटलाइट, रंगमंच की रोशनी*

footnote *n.* फुटनोट, पादटीका*

footprint *n.* पदचिह्न

for *prep., conj.* के लिए, के कारण, के प्रति, क्योंकि, की ओर

forbid *v.t.* मना करना, रोकना

force *n. & v.t.* बल, सैनिक बल (प्रयोग करना)

forcible *a.* प्रबल, बलात्कृत

forearm *n.* कलाची* (कुहनी से कलाई तक); *v.i.* तैयार होना या रहना

foreboding *n.* आपत्ति या अनिष्ट का पूर्वज्ञान

forecast *n. & v.t.* पूर्वानुमान या पूर्वकल्पना* या पूर्वकथन (करना)

forefather *n.* पूर्वपुरुष, पुरखा

forefinger *n.* तर्जनी*

forehead *n.* माथा, ललाट

foreign *a.* विदेशी, इतर, असंबद्ध, बाहरी

foreigner *n.* विदेशी या परदेशी आदमी

foreknowledge *n.* पूर्वज्ञान

foreleg *n.* चौपाये का अगला पैर

forelock *n.* माथे की लट*

foreman *n.* फोरमैन, चौधरी

foremost *a.* सर्वोत्तम, सर्वाधिक; *adv.* प्रथमतः

forerunner *n.* पूर्वज, अग्रदूत, हरकारा

foresee *v.t.* पहले से जान या भांप लेना

foresight *n.* दूरदर्शिता*

forest *n.* जंगल, वन

forestall *v.t.* पहले से कर लेना

forester *n.* वनवासी, जंगल का अफ़सर

forestry *n.* वनविद्या* वनप्रांत

foretell *v.t.* पहले से कह देना

forethought *n.* दूरदृष्टि*, अग्रचिंता*

forewarn *v.t.* आगाह कर देना

foreword *n.* प्रस्तावना*, भूमिका*

338

forfeit *a.*, *n.* & *v.t.* जब्त (वस्तु*, करा बैठना) (*pl.*) जब्तियों का खेल

forfeiture *n.* जब्ती

forgather *v.i.* समागम करना

forge *n.* लुहारखाना; *v.t.* & *i.* मन से गढ़ लेना

forgery *n.* जाली चीज़* जाल-साज़ी*

forget *v.t.* & *i.* भूलना, भुला देना

forgetful *a.* भुलक्कड़

forgive *v.t.* क्षमा करना (ऋण-) मुक्त कर देना

forgo, forego *v.t.* त्यागना

forlorn *a.* निराश, अनाथ, हत-भाग्य

form *n.*, *v.t.* & *i.* रूप (ग्रहण करना, देना), रीति*, शैली*, विद्या*, प्रपत्र (फ़ार्म), जाब्ता, (स्कूल की) कक्षा*

formal *a.* औपचारिक, ऊपरी, दिखाऊ

format *n.* पुस्तक का फ़र्मा

formation *n.* विन्यास, रचित वस्तु*, रचना*

former *a.*, *pron.* भूतपूर्व, प्राचीन काल का, अगला

formerly *adv.* प्राचीन समय में

formidable *a.* दुर्जेय, घोर, भयंकर

formula *n.* सूत्र, गुर, नुसखा

formulate *v.t.* सूत्रित या सुविन्यस्त करना

forsake *v.t.* त्यागना, मैत्री या संबंध तोड़ना

forswear *v.t.* भूठी सौगंध खाना, सौगंध तोड़ना, शपथ-पूर्वक त्यागना

fort *n.* दुर्ग, गढ़

forth *adv.*, *prep.* आगे (को), सामने, अब से

forthcoming *a.* आगामी, आसन्न

forthwith *adv.* तुरंत, झट से

fortification *n.* किलाबन्दी*

fortitude *n.* सहनशक्ति, पौरुष, धैर्य

fortnight *n.* पखवारा

fortunate *a.* भाग्यवान

fortune *n.* भाग्य, धन-दौलत*

forty *n.* चालीस

forum *n.* फ़ोरम, वादमंच, गोष्ठी*

forward *a.* अगला; *adv.* आगे; *v.t.* & *i.* आगे बढ़ना

fossil *n.* जीवाश्म; *a.* शीलीभूत

foster *v.t.* सस्नेह पालन करना, प्रोत्साहन देना; *n.* पोषक, धात्रेय

foul *a.* गंदा, कलुषित

found *v.t.* & *i.* नींव डालना, गलाना, ढालना

foundation *n.* स्थापना*,

आधार, नींव*

founder n. संस्थापक, प्रतिष्ठा-पक, प्रवर्त्तक; v.t. & i. थककर गिर पड़ना, पानी भरकर डुबो देना

foundry n. ढलाई-घर

fount n. झरना; सोता, फ़ौवारा, मूल, उद्गम, छापे के एक सांचे के अक्षर

fountain n. झरना, उद्गम, फ़ौवारा

four n. चार

fourteen n. चौदह

fowl n. मुर्गा या मुर्गी; v.t. वनपक्षी को फंसाना या मारना

fowler n. बहेलिया, चिड़ीमार

fowling-piece n. छोटी बंदूक*

fox n. लोमड़ी*, धूर्त्त व्यक्ति

foxy a. काइयां, फफूंदीदार, लाल-भूरा

fracas n. हुल्लड़

fraction n. भिन्न अंक, भाग, अंश

fractious a. कलहकारी

fracture n., v.t. & i. भंग या अस्थिभंग (करना), तड़काना, तड़कना

fragile a. भंगुर

fragment n. खंड, टुकड़ा, अपूर्ण, अंश

fragrance n. सौरभ, सुगंधि*

frail a दुर्बल, अनैतिक, व्यभि-चारिणी, भंगुर, नश्वर

frame n., v.t. & i. चौखटा (लगाना),ढांचा (खड़ा करना, बनाना), मनोदशा*

franchise n. मताधिकार

frangible a. भंगुर, नश्वर

frank a. निश्छल, खरा, खुला, स्पष्ट

frankincense n. लोहबान

frantic a. आपे से बाहर, (क्रोधादि से) पागल

fraternal a. भाईचारे का, बिरादराना, आपसी

fraternity n. भाईचारा, बन्धुता*, बिरादरी*

fraternize v.i. भाईचारा करना

fratricide n. भ्रातृघात, भ्रातृ-घातक

fraud n. छल, धोखा, चाल*

fraudulent a. छली, बेईमान

fraught a. भरपूर

fray n. कलह, दंगा; v.t. & i. उघेड़ना, घिस जाना

freak n. लीला*, उमंग* (का परिणाम)

free a. & v.t. स्वतंत्र, मुक्त (करना)

freebooter n. लुटेरा

freedom n. स्वतंत्रता*, स्वच्छंदता*

free-fight n. खुली लड़ाई*

freehand a. मुक्तहस्त (आलेखन)

freehold *n.* माफ़ी (निष्कर) ज़मीन

free-wheel *n.* (साइकिल का) 'फ़्रीह्वील'

freeze *v.i. & t.* बर्फ़ जमना, शीत से अकड़ जाना

freight *n.* माल का भाड़ा, भाड़े का कुल माल; *v.t.* (विशेष रूप से जहाज़ की) लड़ाई करना, भाड़े पर चलाना

French *a. & n.* फ़ांसीसी

frenzy *n. & v.t.* उन्माद का दौरा या उग्र आवेश (उत्पन्न कर देना)

frequency *n.* बारम्बार होना, पुनः-पुनः संघटन

frequent *a.* बार-बार या तीव्र गति से या अभ्यासवश होने वाला; *v.t.* बार-बार या प्रायः जाया करना

fresco *n. & v.t.* भित्तिचित्र (की विधि*) खचित करना

fresh *a.* ताज़ा, हाल का, स्वच्छ; *adv.* नवीनतापूर्वक, हाल में

fret *n.* झल्लाहट*, कुढ़न; *v.t. & i.* झल्लाना, चिड़चिड़ाना

friction *n.* रगड़, टकराव, मालिश

Friday *n.* शुक्रवार

friend *n.* मित्र, साथी, हितैषी, सहायक

frigate *n.* मार्गरक्षण और

पनडुब्बी-विरोधी कामों का युद्धपोत

fright *n.* भय, उद्वेग, त्रातंक

frighten *v.t.* डराना, त्रस्त करना

frigid *a.* ठंड से जमाया अकड़ा हुआ, कठोर भावनाशून्य

frill *n., v.t. & i.* झालर* (लगाना), झिल्ली सिकुड़ना

fringe *n. & v.t.* झब्बे या झालर या फुंदने की किनारी* (लगाना)

frippery *n.* उतरन*, सस्ती भड़कीली चीज़*

fritter *n.* फल आदि का पकौड़ा, *v.t.* व्यर्थ नष्ट करना

frivolous *a.* तुच्छ, ओछा, निरर्थक

frizzle *n. & v.t.* घूंघर (-दार बाल, डालना)

frock *n.* फ़ाराक, कुरती

frog *n.* मेढ़क

frolic *n. & v.i.* उल्लास, आनंद (मनाना); *a.* उल्लसित

from *prep.* से

front *n.* सामना, मोर्चा; *v.t. & i.* सम्मुख होना, सामना करना

frontier *n.* सीमाप्रदेश

frost *n. & v.t.* पाला, तुषार (पड़ना, मारना)

frown *n.* त्यौरी; *v.t.* घुड़की

जमाना

fructify *v.t.* *& i.* उपजाऊ बनाना, फलवान होना, गर्भा- धान करना

frugal *a.* मितव्ययी, कमखर्ची*

fruit *n.* फल, परिणाम, नतीजा

fruitful *a.* उपजाऊ, फलदायक, लाभदायक

fruitless *a.* फलहीन, निरर्थक, व्यर्थ, अकारथ, बेकार, विफल

frustrate *v.t.* हराना, निराश करना

frustration *n.* निराशा*, हार*

fry *v.t.*, *(p.t. fried)* आग में भूनना, तलना; *n.* भूना हुआ पदार्थ; *n.* अंडे से तुरत निकली हुई छोटी मछलियां*

fuel *n.* ईंधन, कोयला, लकड़ी*

fugitive *a.* भागनेवाला (आफत*, शत्रु, मालिक या न्याय से), *n.* फ़रारी* भागनेवाला, भग्गू

fulfil *v.t.*, *(p.t. fulfilled)* पूरा करना, सफल करना

fulfilment *n.* सिद्धि*

full *a.* परिपूर्ण, सफल, पर्याप्त, योग्य, अन्तिम; *n.* पूरा परिमाण; *adv.* पूरी तरह से

full-blown *a.* फूल के समान विकसित

fully *adv.* पूर्ण रूप से

full-stop *n.* पूर्णविराम चिह्न

fullness *n.* पूर्णता*

fumble *v.i. & t.* टटोलना, भद्दी तरह से पकड़ना, टोहना, घालमेल करना

fun *n.* क्रीड़ा*, खेल, तमाशा, दिल्लगी*

function *n.* समारोह, उत्सव; *v.t.* कर्त्तव्य पालन करना

functionary *n.* पदाधिकारी, अहलकार

fund *n.* सुरक्षित निधि*, कोष, पूंजी* फंड; *(pl.)* धन-निधि*, खजाना

fundamental *a.* आधारभूत, मौलिक, आवश्यक

funeral *n.* अन्त्येष्टि क्रिया*, शवयात्रा* जनाज़ा

fungus *n.* *(pl.* fungi, funguses)* फफूंदी* कुकुर- मुत्ता

funny *a.* विनोदी, खिलाड़ी, अजीब

fur *n.* महीन कोमल रोवें, पशम, (ब० व०) ऐसे रोवें के बने वस्त्र

furious *a.* अति क्रुद्ध, कोपातुर, प्रकुपित

furl *v.t.* लपेटना, मोड़ना, तह करना

furlong *n.* एक मील का आठबां भाग, 220 गज

furlough *n.* थोड़े दिन की छुट्टी

furnace *n.* धातु गलाने की

भट्टी*, ब्रंगीठी*

furnish v.t. तैयार करना, सजाना, जुहाना

furniture n. सामग्री*, ब्रसबाब

furrow n. हल-रेखा*, लीक*, नाली*; v.t. लीक बनाना, हल चलाना, जोतना

further adv. ब्रागे का, ब्रौर भी; a. दूर का, ब्रधिक; v.t. ब्रागे बढ़ाना

fury n. रोष, क्रोध, ब्रावेश, प्रकोप, (मौसम का) कोप

fuse v.t. & i. गलाना, जोड़ना,

एकरूप होना; n. फुस तार, फ़्यूज तार

fusible a. गलाने या जोड़ने योग्य, द्रवशील

fusion n. विलय, विलयन

fuss n. कोलाहल, गड़बड़, हंगामा; v.t. उपद्रव करना

fussy a. उपद्रवी, भमेलिया

futile a. व्यर्थ, निरर्थक, निस्सार

futility n. निरर्थकता*, निस्सारता*

future n. भविष्य, भावी*

G

gabarage n. पार्सल बनाने का मोटा कपड़ा

gabble v.i. वृथा बकबक करना, बड़बड़ाना

gabbler n. बड़बड़िया, बातूनी

gadfly n. (pl. gadflies) गोमक्खी*, डंस

gag v.t. (p.t. gagged) कपड़ा ठूंसकर मुंह बन्द करना, न बोलने देना, धोखा-घड़ी करना, भूठ बोलना

gage n. परा, ललकार, बीड़ा, ज़मानत*, जाकड़; v.t. गिरवी रखना, रेहन रखना

gaggle v.i. (बत्तख की तरह)

कलकल करना, करकराना, कूजना

gaiety n. ब्रानन्द, उत्सव

gaily adv. ब्रानन्द से, सुखपूर्वक

gain n. लाभ, सुविधा*; v.t. & i. प्राप्त करना, कमाना, जीतना, लाभ करना, पहुंचना

gainful a. लाभदायक

gainsay v.t. (p.t. gainsaid) ब्रस्वीकार करना, विरोध करना

gait n. गति*, चाल*, पग, चालढाल*

gala n. उत्सव, त्यौहार, पर्व

galactic a. ब्राकाशगंगा-संबंधी

galaxy n. (pl galaxies) आकाशगंगा*, प्रकाशयुक्त, तारक-पुंज, प्रसिद्ध मनुष्यों की मंडली*

gale n. आंधी*, भंभा, तूफ़ान

gallant a. वीर, श्रेष्ठ, भड़कीला, विनीत; n. लोकप्रिय मनुष्य

gallantry n. सज्जनता* वीरता*

gall-bladder n. पित्ताशय की थैली*

gallery n. गैलरी*, वीथी*, वीथिका*, दीर्घा*, दालान, चित्रशाला*

gallon n. तीन सेर दस छटांक की नाप*

gallop n. घोड़े की सरपट चाल*, पोइया; v.t. & i. सरपट दौड़ना या दौड़ाना, तेज पाठ करना

gallows n. pl. (used as sing.) फांसी देन की टिकठी*, फांसी का पट्टा, सूली* gallow-bird फांसी देने योग्य मनुष्य

galore n. अधिकता*, बहुतायत

galvanic a. बिजली उत्पन्न करनेवाली, विद्युत-शक्ति संबंधी

galvanism n. रासायनिक क्रिया से उत्पन्न होनेवाली विद्युत-शक्ति-विज्ञान

galvanize v.t. बिजली द्वारा धातु चढ़ाना, जस्ता चढ़ाना, कलई करना

galvanometer n. बिजली की शक्ति नापने का यन्त्र

gamble v.t. & i. दांव लगाकर जुआ खेलना, साहसपूर्ण कार्य करना, जान-बूझकर बड़े लाभ के लिए जोखिम उठाना

gambler n. जुआरी, जुएबाज़

game n. क्रीड़ा*, हँसी*, लड़ाई*, मैदान का खेल, आखेट; v.i. जुआ खेलना

gamecock n. लड़नेवाला मुर्गा

gamekeeper n. जंगली पशुओं की रक्षा करनेवाला

gamely adv. वीरता से

gamesome a. खिलाड़ी, चंचल, फुर्तीला

gamester n. जुआरी, खिलाड़ी

gander n. (fem. goose) राजहंस

gang n. मंडली, गरा, संघ, टोली*, गिरोह

gangrene n. मांस का सड़ाव, गैंग्रीन, कोथ

gangster n. दुष्ट मंडली का सदस्य, बदमाश

gangsaw n. दो या अधिक धार का आरा

gangway n. जहाज़ पर चलने का संकुचित मार्ग, गैंगवे, गलियारा

gaol n. कारागार, बंदीगृह, जेल

gap n. दरार*, फटन*, दून*,

घाटी*

gape v.t. मुंह बाना, जंभाई लेना, विस्मय से देखना, तड़पना, हक्काबक्का रह जाना; n. जंभाई, घूरने की क्रिया*, विच्छेद, भंग, दरार*

garage n. गैरेज, गेराज, मोटर-घर

garb n. वस्त्र, पहिनावा, आकृति; v.t. विशिष्ट कपड़े पहनना या ओढ़ना

garbage n. जूठन, मल, कूड़ा, गंदगी*

garden n. बगीचा*, फुलवारी*, बाड़ी*

gardener n. माली, बागबान

gardening n. बागबानी*

gargle n. गलगला, गलगला की द्रववस्तु*, कुल्ली*, गरारा; v.t. कुल्ला (गलगला) करना

garish a. सुहावना, दिखावटी, भड़कीला

garland n. फूलों की माला, गजरा; v.t. माला पहनाना, गजरा गले में डालना

garlic n. लहसुन

garment n. परिधान, वसन, पोशाक*

garret n. अटारी, छत का कमरा

garrison n. गढ़सेना*, दुर्गरक्षक; v.t. गढ़ में सेना* रखना, मोर्चाबन्दी करना, किले में रखना

garrot n. समुद्री बत्तख*

garter n. मोजा बांधने की पट्टी*, गेटिस*; v.t. मोजों के तसमे बांधना, गेटिस बांधना

gas n. (pl. gases.) गैस

gas-bag n. गैस का थैला

gas-engine n. गैस का इंजन

gasify v.t. (p.t. gasified) गैस बनाना, गैसीकरण करना

gasket n. पाल बांधने की रस्सी*

gas-meter n. गैस नापने का मीटर

gasometer n. बातिमान, गैस-पात्र, गैसभाण्डार, गैस आगार

gasp n. श्वास, कष्ट, हांफी, हांफा; v.t. & i. हांफना, दम लेना

gassy a. गैसपूर्ण, गैस-सा, (वात आदि) शब्दबहुल, शून्य

gastric a. जठर-संबंधी, पेट का

gastro a. उपसर्ग जिसका अर्थ 'पेट-सम्बन्धी' होता है

gate n. मार्ग, द्वार, फाटक, दर्रा, घाटी*

gate-keeper n. पहरेदार

gather v.t. इकट्ठा करना, बटोरना, संग्रह कराना, चुनना, प्राप्त करना, अनुमान करना, उन्नति* करना

gathering जनसमूह, सभा*, जलसा

gaudy *a.* भड़कीला, दिखौवा, शोख

gauge *n.* नाप, रेल की लाइन* का अन्तर, अनुमान; *v.t.* ठीक-ठीक नापना, एकसा करना

gauntlet *n.* हस्तत्राण, लोहे का दस्ताना; (*pick, take, up, the* ~) चुनौती स्वीकार करना, बीड़ा उठाना, मैदान में आना

gay *a.* (*comp.* gayer, *sup.* gayest) आनन्दित; प्रसन्न-प्रफुल्ल, दिखौवा, चमकीला

gaze *v.t.* टकटकी बांधकर देखना, घूरना; *n.* टकटकी* ताक*

gazette *n.* गज़ट, सरकारी समाचार-पत्र, राज-पत्र *v.t.* सरकारी समाचारपत्र में घोषित करना

gazetteer *n.* गजेटियर, भूगोल सम्बन्धी शब्दों का कोष, विवरणिका*

gear *n.* गियर, दांतेदार पहिया, कल-पुर्जे, औज़ार, माल-असबाब

gecko *n.* छिपकली*

geld *v.t.* बधिया करना

gelding *n.* बधियाकरण, बधिया घोड़ा, या अन्य पशु, खस्सी, आख्ता

gem *n.* रत्न, मणि*, बहुमूल्य पदार्थ; *v t.* (*p.t.* gemmed.) रत्नों से सजाना

gemini *n.* मिथुन राशि*, जोड़ा, युग्म

gemmy *a.* रत्नों से पूर्ण, रत्न-जटित

gender *n.* व्याकरण में जाति-विभाग, लिंग

general *a.* जातिवाचक, व्यापक, सामान्य, साधारण, प्रचलित; सेनापति, प्रधान अंश

generality *n.* सामान्यता*, व्यापकता*, अस्पष्टता* बहुमत, मुख्य रूप

generalize *v.t.* सामान्य सिद्धान्त बना लेना, विशेष से सामान्य अनुमान निकालना, अस्पष्ट बोलना या कहना

generally *adv.* सामान्य रूप से, सामान्यतः, आमतौर से, प्रायः, बहुधा

generate *v.t.* उत्पन्न करना, जनना, उपजाना

generation *n.* वंश, कुल, पीढ़ी*

generator *n.* जनक, उत्पादक, (वाष्प, विद्युत, गैस आदि*,) उत्पादक यंत्र, जेनरेटर

generosity *n.* उदारता*, त्यागशीलता*

generous *a.* उदार, दानी, त्यागी

genius *n.* (*pl.* geniuses.) स्वभाव, विशिष्ट स्वाभाविक योग्यता, अपूर्व बुद्धि का मनुष्य

gentle *a.* सज्जन, दयालु, सुशील, शांत

gentleman *n.* (*fem.* gentle woman) भद्र (शिष्ट) मनुष्य, सज्जन, भलामानुस

gentry *n.* कुलीन जन, सभ्य लोग

genuine *a.* प्रामाणिक, निर्मल, खरा, असली

geographer *n.* भूगोलशास्त्री

geographical *a.* भूगोल विषयक

geography *n.* भू-विवरण, भूगोल, भू-विज्ञान, भूपरिचय, भूवृत्तान्त, भूगोल का ग्रन्थ या विषय

geological *a.* भूगर्भशास्त्र-सम्बन्धी

geologist *n.* भूगर्भशास्त्री

geology *n.* भूगर्भशास्त्र

geometric(al) *a.* रेखागणित-सम्बन्धी

geometry *n.* रेखागणित, ज्यामिति*

germ *n.* अंकुर, बीज, मूल, जीवाणु

germicide *n.* अंकुर-नाशक दवा*

germinate *v t.* उगना, उत्पन्न होना

germination *n.* अंकुरन, अंकुरन काल, प्रस्फुटन, जनन, उद्भव

gerund *n.* अंग्रेज़ी क्रियापद में 'ing' प्रत्यय लगी हुई संज्ञा*

gesticulation *n.* हावभाव

gesture *n.* चेष्टा, भाव-संकेत, इंगिति*

get *v.t. & i.* (*p.t.* got, *p.p.* gotten, got) प्राप्त करना, पाना, कमाना, होना, get-up *n.* बनावट, ठाठ, वेष, भूषा

ghastliness *n.* विकटता*, भयंकरता*

ghastly *a.* विकट, भयंकर,

ghost *n.* प्रेत, भूत, प्रतिच्छाया*

ghostly *a.* भूत-सम्बन्धी, आध्यात्मिक

giant *n.* (*fem.* giantess) दीर्घकाय मनुष्य, राक्षस, दानव, असाधारण शक्ति*

gibbon *n.* लम्बे हाथ का लंगूर, गिबन

gibe *n.* ताना, ठट्टा, टिपोरी*, बोली-ठोली, *v.i. & t.* ताना मारना, चिढ़ाना

giddy *a.* (*comp.* giddier,

sup. giddiest.)घुमरीवाला, जिसका (बीमारी, सफलता आदि से) सर चकराता हो, चक्कर लानेवाला, चञ्चल, घबड़ानेवाला

gift *n.* उपहार, भेंट*, ईश्वरीय शक्ति*, दान, देन* हिब्बा, प्रतिभा*

gifted *a.* प्राकृतिक गुण-युक्त, मेधावी

gigantic *a.* विशाल, महाकाय

giggle *v.i.* मूर्ख मनुष्य की तरह हंसना, खिसियाना, खीसें पोरना, दांत निकालना

gild *v.t.* (*p.t. & p.p.* gilt) सोना चढ़ाना, मुलम्मा करना, चमकाना

gilt *a.* सोना चढ़ा हुआ, मुलम्मा किया हुआ

gin *n.* जौ की मदिरा*, फन्दा, जाल, रुई में से बिनौला निकालने का यन्त्र; *v.t.* रुई में से बिनौला निकालना

ginger *n.* अदरक, dry ginger सोंठ

gipsy *n.* (*pl.* gipsies)जिप्सी, कञ्जर या भ्रमणकारी (आवारा) जाति

giraffe *n.* जिराफ

gird *v.t.* (*p.t.* girded or girt.) लपेटना, घेरना, पेटी बांधना; सशक्त करना,

जकड़ना

girder *n.* घरन*, कड़ी*, छत या पुल की डाट*, गाटर

girdle *n. & v.t.* कटिसूत्र, कमरबन्द, लपेटना

girl (*mas.* boy) कुमारी*, कन्या*, बालिका*, बच्ची*, लड़की*, बाला*, प्रेयसी*

girlhood *n.* कुमारीत्व, बालिकावस्था*, कन्यापन

girlish *a.* कन्या के समान, शर्मीली*, भोली*

gist *n.* तात्पर्य, भाव, निष्कर्ष, सार, निचोड़

give *v.t.* (*p.t.* gave, *p.p.* given) देना, सौंपना, उत्पन्न करना, कहना

giving *n.* दान, अर्पण, समर्पण

glacier *n.* हिमनद, ग्लेसियर, हिमानी*, तुषार नदी*

glad *a.* (*com.* gladder, *sup.* gladdest)प्रसन्न, आनन्दित, तुष्ट, मगन

gladden *v.t.* प्रसन्न करना, तुष्ट करना

gladsome *a.* आनन्दमय, हर्षमय

glamour *n.* जादू, टोना, चकाचौंध*

glance *n.* दृष्टिपात, झलक*; *v.t.* दृष्टि डालना, चमकाना, उचटती नजर से देखना,

कनखी मारना

gland n. गिल्टी*, गाँठ*, ग्रन्थि*

glare n. चौंधाने वाला प्रकाश, चमक*, कड़ी दृष्टि*; v.t. तीव्र प्रकाश से चमकना

glass n. कांच, शीशा, कांच का गिलास, दर्पण ; glasses n. pl. उपनेत्र, चश्मा

glaucoma n. आँख का रोग, काँचबिन्दु, मोतियाबिन्दु

glaze v.t. शीशा लगाना, काँच की तरह चिकना और चमकाना

glazier n. खिड़कियों में शीशा जड़नेवाला

glee n. आनन्द, प्रसन्नता*

glide v.t. सरकना, धीरे से घसकना

glider n. बिना इंजन का वायुयान

glimpse n. क्षणिक दृष्टि*, झलक*, आभास

glitter v.i. चमकना; चमक*, दमक*

gloat v.t. बुरी या वासना की दृष्टि से देखना, घूरना

globe n. गोलार्द्ध, गोल पदार्थ, पृथ्वी*

gloom n. अन्धकार, धुंधलापन, विषाद

gloomy a. अन्धकारमय, खिन्न,

उदास

glorification n. महिमागान, स्तुति*, प्रशंसा*

glorify v.t. (p.t. glorified) पूजना, आसमान पर चढ़ाना, गुए गाना

glorious a. प्रसिद्ध, तेजस्वी, प्रतापी, महान

glory n. (pl. glories) बड़ी प्रतिष्ठा*, ख्याति*, प्रताप, शोभा*, प्रकाश, ईश्वर की महिमा*; v.t. आनन्द करना, गर्व करना

glossary n. अर्थ सहित शब्दसूची*, शब्दकोश

glossy a. चमकीला, चिकना

glove n. हाथ का मोजा, दस्ताना

glow v.i. लाल होना, तपना, चमकना

glow-worm n. खद्योत, जुगनू

glucose n. अंगूर से निकली हुई शक्कर*

glue n. सरेस

glum a. अप्रसन्न, मलिनमुख

glut v.t. भकोसना, अधिक भोजन करना

glutton n. भुक्खड़, पेटू

glycerine n. ग्लीसरीन

go v.t. (p.t. went, p.p. gone) जाना, चलना, प्रस्थान करना, आगे बढ़ना; the

story goes ऐसा कहा जाता है; to go ahead विश्वास-पूर्वक आगे बढ़ना; to go at आक्रमण करना; to go bad सड़ना; to go by आगे-पीछे जाना; to go through पूर्ण करना; to go with बराबर होना

goad *n.* बैल हांकने की छड़ी*; *v.t.* अंकुश लगाना, प्रेरित करना

goal *n.* दौड़ का अन्त, सीमा*, लक्ष्य, उद्देश्य

goat *n.* बकरा, व्यभिचारी, दुराचारी*

goatee *n.* बकरे की सी दाढ़ी*, कुच्ची दाढ़ी*

gobble *v.t.* जल्दी-जल्दी खाना

go-between *n.* मध्यस्थ, दलाल

goblet *n.* कटोरा, चषक, पान-पात्र

go-cart *n.* बच्चों को चलना सिखलाने की गाड़ी*

god *n.* (*fem.* goddess) परमेश्वर, देवता, स्रष्टा, नियन्ता, पूजायोग्य

godfather *n.* (*fem* god-mother) धर्म-पिता

godhead *n.* ईश्वर, ईश्वरत्व, देवत्व

godly *a.* धार्मिक, धर्मपरायण, धर्मात्मा

godsend *n.* ईश्वर-प्रेरित सौभाग्य

godspeed *n.* सफलता*, उन्नति*, यात्रा* या जोखिम के काम में किसी की मंगल-कामना*

goggles *n. pl.* धूप का चश्मा

goglet *n.* सुराही*, झझर

going *n.* गमन, प्रस्थान

gold *n.* सोना, धन, सम्पत्ति*

golden *a.* सोने का, प्रसन्न, बहुमूल्य

gold-field *n.* सोने की खान*, स्वर्ण-क्षेत्र

goldplate *n.* सोने के बने हुए पात्र

goldsmith *n.* सुनार, स्वर्णकार

goldthread *n.* कलाबत्तू

golf *n.* गॉल्फ़, गेंद और ग्रंटे का खेल

gong *n.* घंटा, घड़ियाल

good *a.* (*comp.* better, *sup.* best) शुभ, अच्छा, सच्चा, सन्तोषप्रद, उचित, पुष्ट, दयालु, योग्य; *n.* सुविधा*, लाभ, कल्याण; good-for-nothing व्यर्थ का, निष्प्रयोजन; good looking सुन्दर

good-breeding *n.* सभ्यता* शिष्टता*, भद्रता*

good-bye *interj.* विदाई* अलविदा*

goodly *a.* सुन्दर, सुडौल, प्रसन्न

goodness n. कृपा*, दया*, महत्त्व, गुण

goods n.pl. सामग्री* माल, घरेलू सामान

goodwill n. सद्भाव, हार्दिकता*, साख*

goose n. (pl. geese, mas. gander) कलहंस, दर्जी का इस्त्री करने का लोहा, मूर्ख

gooseberry n. (pl. gooseberries) करौंदा, झरबेर

gorgeous a. भव्य, भड़कीला

gorilla n. अफ्रीका का लंगूर, वनमानुस

gorse n. भटकटैया*

gospel n. सुसमाचार, इंजील

gossip n. प्रलाप, बकवाद* झूठी गप्प; v.i. बकबक करना

goth n. एक जर्मन कबीला जिसने 3-5वीं सदी में हमला करके इटली, फ्रांस और स्पेन में अपना राज्य बनाया था; अशिष्ट, असभ्य, जाहिल

gothic a. गॉथ कबीले से संबंधित, गॉथ मुद्राक्षर या टाइप, गॉथ स्थापत्य

gouge n. गोल रुखानी*; v.t. गोल रुखानी से काटना

gourd n. लौकी, कद्दू, तूंबी*, तुम्बा, तूमड़ी*

gout n. बातरोग, गठिया

gouty a. गठिया से ग्रस्त, वात-रोगी

govern v.t. & i. निर्देश देना, शासन करना, दमन करना, परिचालित करना

governess n. अध्यापिका* शासिका*, मास्टरनी*

government n. शासनक्रम, शासक लोग, राज्य, शासन, सत्ता*, सरकार*

governor n. शासक, राज्यपाल

governor-general n. (pl. governors general) बड़े लाट, महाराज्यपाल, महा-शासक

governorship n. राज्यपाल का पद

gown n. चोगा, लबादा, गाउन

grab v.t. (p.t. grabbed) झपटना, छीनना, हथियाना

grace n. सुन्दर ढंग, अनुग्रह, दया*, विनीत भाव, ईश्वर की कृपा*, ड्यूक इ० के प्रति विनय के शब्द; v.t. अनुग्रह करना, सजाना

gracious a. प्रसन्न, शिष्ट, नम्र अनुकूल

gradation n. क्रमिक स्थापन, परम्परा*, परिपाटी*

grade n. पद, श्रेणी*, पदवी*; v.t. क्रम में रखना

gradual a. by steps or degrees. क्रमिक

graduate *v.i. & t.* विश्व-
विद्यालय की उपाधि लेना,
विभाग करना; *n.* विश्व-
विद्यालय की उपाधि प्राप्त
मनुष्य, स्नातक

graft *v.t.* कलम बांधना,
अनुचित लाभ कमाने की
चेष्टा करना, एक तरह से
घूस लेना; *n.* कलम

grain *n.* दाना, बीज, कण, डेढ़
रत्ती के बराबर की अंगरेज़ी
तौल*; *v.t.* दाना बनाना

gram *n.* चना

grammar *n.* व्याकरण

grammarian *n.* व्याकरण
जानने वाला, वैयाकरण

gramme *n.* दशमलव प्रणाली
में तौल की इकाई (प्रायः
$15\frac{1}{2}$ ग्रेन)

gramophone *n.* ग्रामोफोन
बाजा

granary *n.* धान्यागार, खत्ती*,
कोठार

grand *a.* महान, उच्च पद का,
श्रेष्ठ, कुलीन, सुन्दर, शानदार,
गम्भीर

grandad *n.* दादा या नाना

grandam *n.* दादी* या नानी*,
आजी*

grandchild *n.* पोता, पोती*,
नाती, नतिनी*

grandee *n.* भद्र पुरुष, कुलीन,
रईस

grandeur *n.* महत्त्व, श्रेष्ठता*,
महिमा*, बड़ाई*, तेज

grandfather *n.* नाना, दादा

grandiloquent *a.* शब्दा-
डम्बरपूर्ण, अतिशयोक्ति का,
वागाडम्बर

grandiose *a.* प्रभावकारी,
दिखावटी, आडम्बरपूर्ण

grandmother *a.* नानी*
दादी*

grange *n.* खलिहान, खत्ती

granite *n.* एक प्रकार का कड़ा
स्फटिक पत्थर, कणाश्म

granitic *a.* कड़े, स्फटिक
पत्थर का

grant *v.t.* देना, मानना, स्वी-
कार करना; दान, जागीर*,
कानूनी स्वीकृति*

grantee *n.* जागीरदार*, अनु-
देयी, दानभोगी

grape *n.* अंगूर

grapery *n.* अंगूर का बगीचा

graph *n.* रेखाओं द्वारा गणित
अथवा रसायन शास्त्र इत्यादि
के सत्यों को दरसाने की
विधि, रेखाचित्र, लेखाचित्र

graphic (-al) *a.* रेखाचित्रीय,
स्पष्ट, भली भांति दरसाया
हुआ, (~s) ग्राफ से चित्र
बनाने की कला*

graphite *n.* काला सीसा

graphology n. हस्तलेख का
अध्ययन या विज्ञान

grapple v.t. & i. बांधना,
पकड़ना, संघर्ष करना; n.
एक प्रकार की हुक*

grasp v.t. पकड़ना, थामना,
समझाना; n. पकड़*, चंगुल*
समझ

grass n. तृण, घास*, दूव*,
शस्य, कुश

grasshopper n. तृणभोजी
पतिंगा या टिड्डा

grate n. अंगीठी की जाली*
भट्टी*

grateful a. स्वीकार के योग्य,
कृतज्ञ, सुखकर

gratification n. आनन्द,
तृप्ति,* पुरस्कार

gratis adv. बिना दाम का,
मुफ्त, निःशुल्क

gratitude n. कृतज्ञता*, आभार

gratuity n. ऐच्छिक दान,
सेवोपहार, अनुग्रह धन

grave v.t. खोदना, नक्काशी
करना; n. इमशान, समाधि*
कब्र*; a. गम्भीर, आवश्यक,
महान ; grave-yard समाधि-
स्थान, कब्रगाह

gravitate v.i. किसी वस्तु*
की ओर आकर्षित होना,
केन्द्र की ओर झुकना

gravitation n. आकर्षणशक्ति*,

गुरुत्वाकर्षण

gravity n. गम्भीरता,* भार,
महत्त्व,   आकर्षणशक्ति*;
centre of gravity. आक-
र्षण-केन्द्र; specific gravity
आपेक्षिक गुरुत्व या घनत्व

gray a. धूसर, खाकी

graze v.t. & i. चरना, घास
खाना, खुरचना

grease n. चर्बी* v.t. तेल या
चर्बी पोतना; to grease
the palm of घूस देना

greasy a. (comp. greasier,
sup. greasiest.) तेल-युक्त,
मैला, चिकना

great a. विशाल, बड़ा, प्रसिद्ध,
श्रेष्ठ, प्रधान, धनी, शक्ति-
शाली, महान

greed n. लोभ, लोलुपता*

greedy a. लोभी, लालची,
लोलुप, लुब्ध

Greek n. & a. यूनानी, यूनानी
भाषा*

green a. हरा, नया, अनुभव-
हीन, ताज़ा, कच्चा

greenery n. वनस्पति*, हरि-
याली* सब्ज़ा

green-room n. नेपथ्यशाला*

greet v.t. नमस्कार करना,
सत्कार करना, अभिनन्दन
करना

greeting n. नमस्कार, शुभ-

कामना,* अभिनन्दन, हर्ष-
ध्वनि,* जयजयकार*
grenade n. हथगोला
grey a. भूरा, चितकबरा,
प्राचीन, वयोवृद्ध
greyhound n. एक प्रकार का
कुत्ता
grief n. शोक, खेद, संताप,
व्यथा*
grievance n. कष्ट, विपत्ति*
दुख का कारण, शिकायत*
grieve v.t. & i. पीड़ा देना,
शोक करना, दुःखी होना
grievous a. पीड़ाकर, दुःखकर,
क्षतिकर
grim a. भयंकर, विकट, निर्दय,
कुरूप
grin v.i. (p.t. grinned)
मूर्खता से हंसना; n. हंसी*
grind v t. (p.t. & p.p.
ground) पीसना, कुचलना,
कष्ट देना, चोखा करना
grip v.t. (p.t. gripped)
कसकर पकड़ना, जकड़ना;
n. पकड़*, चंगुल, गिरफ़्त*
gripe v.t. पकड़ना; n. पकड़,*
तीव्र वेदना*
groan v.i. पीड़ा का शब्द
करना, कराहना; n. कराह*,
चीख,* तड़प
grocer n. बनिया, पंसारी
grocery n. (pl.-ies)किराना

groom n. साईस; v.t. घोड़े
की देखरेख करना; groom's
man विवाह के समय वर
के साथ रहनेवाला उसका
अविवाहित मित्र, सहबलिया
groove n. प्रणाली*, नाली*,
नाली*; v.t. नाली बनाना
grope v.i. अंधेरे में टटोलना
gross n. (pl. gross) बारह
दर्जन; a. मोटा, अशिष्ट, कुल,
निर्लज्ज; in the gross
सामान्य रूप से, थोक में
grotesque a. विलक्षण, भद्दा,
कुरूप
ground n. भूमि*, पृथ्वी*
नींव*, मूल, हेतु, पदार्थ,
पर्याप्त कारण; v.t. स्थापित
करना, स्थिर करना, भूमि
में लग जाना; to break
ground काम करने में अग्रुआ
होना; to gain ground
आगे बढ़ना; to give
ground पीछे हटना
ground-floor n. घर का
निचला खंड
groundless a. अकारण, निरा-
धार, निर्मूल, मिथ्या
ground-nut n. मूंगफली*
groundwork n. मूल सिद्धांत,
आधार, नींव*
group n. समुदाय झुण्ड;
गुटः(-ism) गुटबाजी; v.t.
338

क्रम में रखना

grove n. छोटा जङ्गल, कुञ्ज

grow v.i. & t. (p.t. grew, p. p. grown) बढ़ना, उगना विकसित होना, उपजाना; to grow out of निकलना; to grow up पूर्ण यौवन प्राप्त करना, पूरा जवान होना; to grow rich धनी होना

grower n. फल आदि उपजाने वाला

grudge v.i. & t. ईर्ष्या करना, कुढ़ना, अनिच्छा प्रकट करना; n. ईर्ष्या*; असन्तोष, घृणा का कारण

gruel n. मांड़

gruesome a. भयंकर, तिरस्कार-युक्त

grumble v.t. गुर्राना, असन्तोष दिखलाना

grumpy a. नीच, दुष्ट

guarantee n. गारंटी, बंधक, जमानत;* v.t. दूसरे की जमानत* करना या होना

guaranty n. बंधकत्व

guard v.t. रक्षा करना, बचाना, चौकसी करना; n. चौकसी, पहरेदार, रेलगाड़ी का रक्षक; to keep guard, to be on guard आक्रमण के लिए सचेत रहना

guardian n. पितृहीन शिशु का संरक्षक, अभिभावक, सरपरस्त

guardianship n. संरक्षक या अभिभावक का पद

guava n. अमरूद

guerilla n. छापेमार

guess v.i. & t. शीघ्र राय बनाना, अटकल करना, अनुमान करना; n. अनुमान

guest n. अतिथि, पाहुन, मेहमान

guidance n. मार्ग-प्रदर्शन

guide v.t. मार्ग दिखलाना, सिखलाना; n. गाइड

guild n. शिल्पी संघ, श्रमिक-निकाय

guile n. माया,* धोखा, छल

guilt n. अपराध, पातक, दुष्टता*, जुर्म

Guinea n. गिन्नी, 21 शिलिंग का सोने का अंग्रेजी सिक्का, गिन्नी प्रदेश (प॰ अफ्रीका) से संबंधित

guise n. रंगढंग, बाहरी आकृति* पहनावा, बहाना, छद्मवेष, स्वांग, बाना

guitar n. गिटार, सारङ्गी, छतारा

gulf n. खाड़ी,* गड्ढा

gull n. एक प्रकार की समुद्री चिड़िया*, मूर्ख मनुष्य; v.t. ठगना, धोखा देना

gulp v.t. जल्दी से निगलना;
n. कौर, ग्रास

gum n. गोंद, मसूड़ा; v.t.
(p.t. gummed) गोंद से
चिपकाना या गोंद लगाना

gummy a. चिपचिपा

gun n. तोप*, बन्दूक*

gunpowder n. अग्निचूर्ण,
बारूद

gust n. प्रचण्ड वायु*, उमंग,
झोंका

gutter a. जलमार्ग, परनाली*,
मार्ग, परनाला, गन्दा नाला;
v.i. बूंद-बूंद करके चूना, पोला

होना

guttural a. कण्ठस्थ, कण्ठ से
उच्चारण किया हुआ; n. कंठ
से उच्चारित स्वर जैसे हिन्दी
के क्, ख्, ग्, आदि

gymnasium n. (pl. -siums,
or -sia) व्यायामशाला*,
अखाड़ा, यूरोप में उच्च श्रेणी
की पाठशाला*

gymnast n. कुश्तीबाज, पहल-
वान

gymnastic a. व्यायाम-संबंधी

gymnastics n. व्यायाम, कसरत*

H

H रसायनशास्त्र में हाइड्रोजन
के लिए संकेत

habeas corpus n. व्यक्ति-
स्वातंत्र्य, बन्दी प्रत्यक्षीकरण,
अभियुक्त का उपस्थिति-पत्र

habit n. अभ्यास, व्यवहार, स्व-
भाव

habitable a. बसने योग्य

habitat n. किसी पक्षी या पशु
का प्राकृतिक निवास, आवास,
घाम, वास, घर, स्थान

habitation n. निवासस्थान

hack v.t. टुकड़ा करना, नोचना;
n. किराये का घोड़ा, घाव,

कटाव; hacksaw धातु
काटने की आरी*

hackle n. सन संवारने की
कंघी* कलंगी*, मछली* का
चारा; v.t. सन साफ करना,
चीरना फाड़ना, बोटी-बोटी
करना

hackney n. किराये का घोड़ा;
श्रमिक, टहलुआ; v.t. (p.t.
hackneyed) अधिक उपयोग
में लाना, सर्वसुलभ बनाना

hackney-carriage n. किराए
की गाड़ी*

hackneyed a. सामान्य, जीर्ण,

जर्जर, शिथिल, मन्द, सार्व-
जनिक, भाड़े का, घिसा-पिटा

hacksaw *n.* धातु काटने की
आरी*

haggard *a.* भयंकर आकृति का,
दुबला-पतला

haggle *v.t.* मोल-चाल करना,
झंझट करना

hail *n.* शिलावृष्टि,* ओला; *v.i.*
ओला पड़ना, वेग से गिरना;
v.t. नमस्कार करना, अभि-
वादन करना, दूर से पुकारना;
interj. जयजयकार का शब्द

hair *n.* बाल, रोवां; to a hair
भलीभांति, ठीक-ठीक

hair-breadth *n.* अति अल्प
अन्तर

hair-splitting *n.* बाल की खाल
खींचना

hale *a.* हट्टा-कट्टा, तन्दुरुस्त

half *n.* (*pl.* halves) आधा;
half as much again डेढ़-
गुना, ढेवढ़ा

half-blood *n.* सौतेला भाई-
बहिन*

half-bred *a.* अशिक्षित, असभ्य,
दोगला

half-hearted *a.* उदासीन,
उत्साहहीन, बेदिली, खिन्न
मन, अनमना, अन्यमनस्क

halftone *a.* फोटो द्वारा ब्लॉक
बनाने की एक विधि जिसमें

प्रकाश और छाया चिह्न छोटे-
छोटे बिन्दुओं द्वारा स्पष्ट किए
गए हों

half-way *adv.* बीच रास्ते में

hall *n.* हॉल, सभा के लिए
बड़ा कमरा, विशाल कक्ष;
hall of audience सभा-
मण्डप

hall-mark *n.* सोना या चांदी
को प्रमाणित करने का चिह्न,
प्रमाणांक

hallow *v.t.* पवित्र करना, पूजना

hallucinate *v.t.* चित्त पर
मिथ्या प्रभाव (मोह) डालना,
भ्रांत होना, करना, मायाजाल
में डालना

halt *v.t.* ठमकना, रुकना; *n.*
रुकावट*, पड़ाव, विराम,
डेरा, मंज़िल*, मुक़ाम

halve *v.t.* आधा करना

hamlet *n.* छोटा गांव, पुरवा,
पल्ली*

hammer *n.* बंदूक का घोड़ा,
हथौड़ा, मुगरी*, नीलाम करने
वाले की मुंगरी*; *v.t.* (*p.t.*
hammered) हथौड़ी* से
पीटना; to bring to the
hammer नीलाम करने के
लिए रखना

hand *n.* (*pl.*) हाथ, घड़ी* की
सूई*, लिखावट*, ताश का
दांव; (ब० व०) कर्मचारी;

v.t. अर्पण करना, देना; at
first hand बनाने वाले से
सीधे प्राप्त; at hand समीप
में; cap in hand विनीत
भाव से; from hand to
mouth किसी प्रकार गुज़र
होना; to lay hands on
पकड़ना; to live from
hand to mouth जो
कमाना सब खर्च कर डालना;
on hand अधिकार में; out
of hand अधिकार के बाहर;
with a heavy hand
कठोरता से

handbill *n.* विज्ञापन-पत्र,
पर्चा, इश्तहार

handbook *n.* छोटी पुस्तक

handcuff *n.* हथकड़ी*; *v.t.*
हथकड़ी डालना

handful *n.* मुट्ठीभर

handicap *v.t.* (*p.t.* handi-
capped) असुविधा या विघ्न
डालना *n.* एक प्रकार की घुड़-
दौड़ जिसमें प्रत्येक प्रतिस्पर्धी
को समान सुविधा दी जाती है

handicraft *n.* हस्तशिल्प*,
दस्तकारी*

handiwork *n.* हस्तकार्य, शिल्प

handkerchief *n.* (*pl.* hand-
kerchiefs) दस्ती* रूमाल

handle *n.* मूठ, मुठिया; *v.t.*
पकड़ना, प्रबंध करना, संभालना

handloom *n.* हाथकरघा

handsome *a.* सुंदर, उत्तम,
दयालु

handwriting *n.* हस्तलेख,
लिखावट*

handy *a.* (*comp.* handier,
sup. handiest) सुघर,
निपुण, सुविधा का, तैयार

hang *v.t.* (*p.t. & p.. p.*
hung) लटकाना, टांगना

hang *v.t* (*p.t. & p. p.*
hanged) फांसी लटकाना;
to hang about भटकना;
to hang together साथी
होना; to hang back
अनिच्छा प्रकट करना

hangman *n.* बधिक, फांसी देने
वाला

hanker *v.t.* उत्कण्ठा करना,
लालसा करना

happen *v.t.* आ पड़ना, बीतना,
घटित होना

happening *n.* अवसर, घटना,
संयोग

happily *a.* सुख से

happiness *n.* सुख, आनन्द

happy *a.* (*comp.* happier,
sup. happiest) भाग्यवान,
सुखी, धन्य

harass *v.t.* थकाना, व्यग्र करना,
घबड़ाना, दिक करना

harassment *n.* परेशानी*, दुःख

harbour *n.* बन्दरगाह; *v.t. &*
i. आश्रय देना, विचार करना

hard *a.* कड़ा, ठोस, कठिन, पुष्ट
क्रूर, न समझने योग्य; hard
by प्रति समीप; hard up
धन का अभाव; hard water
खारा पानी

harden *v.t.* कड़ा करना, सख्त
होना

hard-fisted *a.* लालची

hard-headed *a.* हठी

hard-hearted *a.* निर्दय

hardihood *n.* वीरता*, साहस

hardly *adv.* कठिनता* से,
मुश्किल से

hardship *n.* शारीरिक क्लेश

hardware *n.* धातु के सामान,
लोहे के सामान

hardy *adj.* (*comp*. hardier,
sup. hardiest) साहसी, वीर

hare *n.* शशक, खरहा, खरगोश

harm *n.* हानि*, अपकार,
अनिष्ट; *v.t.* कष्ट देना, चोट
पहुंचाना

harmonic (-al) *a.* सुरीला

harmonious *a.* सामंजस्यपूर्ण,
संगत, ऐक्यपूर्ण मधुर, सुरीला,
एकताल, समस्वर, संगीतमय

harmonium *n.* हारमोनियम
बाजा

harmonize *v.t. & i.* अनुरूप
करना, मिलाना, स्वर योजन

करना

harmony *n.* एकता*, स्वर का
मेल, शांति*, समन्वय

harness *n.* घोड़े का साज,
कवच, सामग्री*; *v.t. & i.*
साज चढ़ाना, जोतना, अधीन
करना; to die in harness
काम करते हुए मरना

harp *n.* बीन, वीणा*; *v.t.*
बीन बजाना; to harp on
one string एक ही बात को
बारम्बार दुहराना

harper, harpist *n.* बीन बजाने
वाला

harsh *a.* कर्कश, रूक्ष, कठोर,
निर्दय

harvest *n.* कृषि-फल, उत्पत्ति*
फ़सल*

harvester *n.* हारवेस्टर, फ़सल
काटने की मशीन*,

haste *n.* वेग, शीघ्रता*; *v.t.*
शीघ्रता करना, जल्दबाज़ी
करना

hat *n.* टोप, टोपी*; हैट;
v.i. टोप पहनना

hatch *v.t.* अंडा सेना, अंडे से
बच्चा निकालना, जाल
रचना; *n.* पक्षियों के बच्चे

hatchet *n.* छोटी कुल्हाड़ी*

hate *v.t.* घृणा करना, द्वेष
करना नफ़रत करना ; *n.*
घृणा*; नफ़रत*

haughty a. (comp. haugh-
tier; sup. haughtiest)
अभिमानी, घृष्ट, ढीठ

haunt v.t. बहुधा भेंट करना
गा आना-जाना; भूत आना,
बार-बार याद आना, छाना,
मंडराना; n. आश्रय, बसेरा

haunted a. प्रेतवाधित

have v.t. (p.t. & p. p. had)
रखना, वश में रखना, जानना,
लेना

havoc n. नाश; to cry havoc
सेना को लूटने की आज्ञा देना

hawk n. बाज पक्षी; v.t.
शिक्षित बाज पक्षी द्वारा
आखेट करना, वेग से खखा-
रना; v.t. फेरी करके माल
बेचना

hawker n. फेरीवाला,

hawthorn n. नागफनी

hazard n. संकट, विपत्ति*;
v.t. संकट में डालना;
at all hazards भला-बुरा
चाहे जो हो

hazardous a. संकटजनक

haze n. धुन्ध, कुहरा, मानसिक
व्यग्रता*

hazy a. धुंधला, अंधेरा, अस्पष्ट

he (pl. they) pron. 3rd.
pers. sing. वह (पुरुष-
वाचक)

head n. सर, मस्तक, शीर्ष,
मस्तिष्क, प्रधान शासक, मूल,
अन्तरीप, विवाद-विषय; v.t.
मार्ग दिखलाना, बढ़ाना
अगुवाई करना

headache n. सिर की पीड़ा*
सरदर्द

heading n. सिरनामा, शीर्षक,
सुर्खी*

head-dress n. मुरेठा, साफ़ा

headlong adv. शीघ्रता से

headmaster n. प्रधानाध्यापक

headmost a. सबसे आगे

headquarters n. pl. प्रधान
केन्द्र या कार्यालय

headstrong a. हठी, जिद्दी,
अड़ियल

headway n. उन्नति का क्रम

heal v.t. & i. स्वस्थ करना,
घाव भरना

healer n. आरोग्य करनेवाला

health n. आरोग्य, स्वास्थ्य

healthy a. (comp. healthier,
sup. healthiest) स्वस्थ,
रोगरहित, तन्दुरुस्त

heap n. समुदाय, ढेर; v.t.
ढेर लगाना

hear v.t. & i. कान लगाना,
सुनना, ध्यान देना, सूचित
होना

hearsay n. चर्चा, गप्प* अफ़-
वाह*

heart n. हृदय, मर्म, साहस,

सत्त्व, मध्य भाग; to learn
by heart कण्ठस्थ करना;
heart and soul पूर्ण शक्ति
से

heartache n. मानसिक व्यथा*,
दिल का दर्द

heart-broken a. मलिनचित्त,
उदास, टूटा हुआ दिल

heart-burning n. स्पर्धा, ईर्ष्या*

heart-felt a. आंतरिक, हार्दिक,
दिली

hearth n. अग्निकुण्ड, अग्नि का
पार्श्वस्थान, चूल्हा, भट्टी*

heartily adv. प्रसन्नता से, खुशी
मन से

heat n. दाह, क्रोध, वेग, ताप;
v.t. & i. गरम करना या
होना

heave v.t. & i. उठना, सांस
लेना, हांफना, आहें भरना;
n. गहरी सांस*, उभाड़,
उसांस*, आह*

heaven n. (usu. in pl.)
आकाश, स्वर्ग, अत्यन्त आनंद

heavenly a. दिव्य, स्वर्गीय

heavy a. (comp. heavier,
sup. heaviest) भारी,
गम्भीर, देर में पचने वाला,
मन्द, अत्याचारी; time
hangs heavy समय बहुत
धीरे बीतता है

Hebrew n. यहूदी, यहूदी भाषा*

hector n. गुण्डा, तंग करनेवाला
मनुष्य; v.t. कष्ट देना, तंग
करना

hedge n. झाड़ियों की टट्टी
रोक, बाड़ा, हाता; v.t. टट्टी
से घेरना, बाड़ा लगाना

heed n. ध्यान, सावधानी*;
v.t. ध्यान लगाना, मन
लगाना, चौकसी रखना

heel n. एड़ी*, पिछला भाग,
पशुओं का खुर; v.i. जहाज़
का एक ओर झुकना; v.t.
एड़ी लगाना; at one's
heels पीछे-पीछे, पास में;
out at heels दरिद्रता की
अवस्था में

hefty a. (comp. heftier, sup.
heftiest) पुष्ट

height n. ऊंचा स्थान, ऊंचाई*

heighten v.t. ऊंचा करना,
बढ़ाना

heinous a. अति दुष्ट, घृणित

heir n. (fem. heiress) उत्तरा-
धिकारी, अंशभागी, वारिस

heir-apparent n. युवराज

hell n. यमलोक, नरक, दोज़ख

helm n. पतवार; at the ~
of affairs किसी भी संगठन
या शासन का नेता होना;
take the ~ शासन-सूत्र
हाथ में लेना

helmet n. लोहे का टोप, शिर-

स्त्राएा

help *v.t.* सहायता* देना, अनुग्रह करना, बचाना; *n.* सहायता, आश्रय

helpful *a.* उपयोगी

helpless *a.* निराश्रय

helpmate *n.* सहायक

hemisphere *n.* गोलार्द्ध, अर्द्ध-गोल

hemp *n.* सुतली*, सनई*, सन, भांग*, गांजा

hen *n.* मुर्गी*

hence *adv.* यहां से, अब से, इसलिए; *interj.* हट

henceforth *adv.* अब से

henceforward *adv.* इस समय से आगे

henchman *n.* प्रधान सेवक, विश्वस्त अनुचर, राजनीति के क्षेत्र.में दलाल

henpecked *a.* स्त्रीवश

her *a.* उस स्त्री* का

herald *n.* अग्रदूत; *v.t.* घोषणा करना

herb *n.* औषधि*, जड़ी-बूटी*

herculean *a.* अत्यन्त बलवान, अति कठिन

herd *n.* पशु-समूह, झुण्ड; *v.i.* एकत्रित होना

herdsman *n.* चरवाहा, गडरिया

here *adv.* यहां, इस स्थान में

hereabouts *adv.* यहां, पास-पड़ौस में

hereafter *adv.* भविष्य में

hereby *adv.* इस रीति* से

hereditary *n.* पैतृक

heredity *n.* वंश-परम्परा*

heritable *a.* परम्परा* से प्राप्त होने योग्य

heritage *n.* बपौती, पैतृक सम्पत्ति*

hermit *n.* तपस्वी, संन्यासी

hermitage *n.* आश्रम, कुटी*

hernia *n.* हार्निया, आंत* उतरने का रोग

hero *n.* (*pl.* heroes) महावीर, शूरवीर, अर्द्ध-देवता, नाटक का नायक

heroic *a.* वीरता का

heroine *n.* वीरांगना*, नायिका*

heroism *n.* वीरता*

hero-worship *n.* वीरात्माओं का पूजन

herring *n.* एक प्रकार की समुद्री मछली*

hesitant *a.* दुविधा में पड़ा हुआ

hesitate *v.i.* हिचकिचाना, सन्देह करना

hesitation *n.* सन्देह, दुविधा*

heterogeneous *a.* पंचमेल, विविध, विरोधी, विजातीय, असदृश

heyday *n.* आनन्द या उमंग का समय

hiccup n. हिचकी*; v.i. (p.t. hiccuped) हिचकी* लेना

hide n. पशु की खाल*; v.t. (p.t. hid, p.p. hidden, hid) छिपाना, गुप्त रखना, छिपना; hide and seek आंखमुदौवल का खेल

hideous a. बड़ा भद्दा, डरावना

hierarchy n. देवदूतों का वर्ग, पुरोहितों का राज्य, महन्त-शाही

higgle v.i. मोल-भाव करना

high a. (com. higher, sup. highest) ऊंचा, महंगा, प्रसिद्ध, महान, क्रुद्ध, प्रचण्ड, गम्भीर; high-brow अति बुद्धिमान व्यक्ति; high-flown उन्नत; highhanded क्रूर, उद्धत; highminded महात्मा, उदार चित्त का; high road प्रधान मार्ग

high-born a. उच्च कुल में उत्पन्न

highbred a. कुलीन, शिष्ट

highlander n. पहाड़ी

highly adj. उच्चता से

highness n. महाराज, महा-रानी*; high-sounding आडम्बरपूर्ण; high-spirited साहसी, उद्दण्ड, क्रोधी; high-water दीर्घ ज्वार; highway-man डाकू, लुटेरा

highway n. बड़ी सड़क*

hilarious a. प्रफुल्ल, प्रसन्न

hilarity n. आनन्द

hill n. पहाड़, पहाड़ी*

hillock n. छोटी पहाड़ी*

hilly a. पर्वतमय, पहाड़ी

him pron. उस पुरुष को

hind n. दास, किसान, हिरनी*

hind a. (comp. hinder, sup. hindmost, hindermost) पिछला

hinder v.t. रोकना, अटकाना, विघ्न डालना

hindrance n. बाधा*, विघ्न

hint n. संकेत, सहायक प्रस्ताव या सूचना*; v.t. अर्थ लगाना, उल्लेख करना; to hint at संकेत करना

hip n. नितम्ब, कमर, कूल्हा

hip-hip-hurrah interj. आनन्द-सूचक शब्द

hire n. किराया, भाड़ा; v.t. भाड़े पर रखना

hireling n. ठेकेदार, मजूर

his pron. उस मनुष्य का

hiss v.i. सिसकारना; n. सिस-कार, सिसकारी*

historian n. इतिहास-लेखक

historical a. ऐतिहासिक

history n. इतिहास, प्राचीन कथा*

hit v.t. (p.t. hit) मारना,

पहुंचना, टकराना, निशाना
लगाना; n. प्रहार, चोट*,
सफलता*

hitch v.t. & i. झटके से हटाना,
पकड़ जाना; n. बंधन,
रुकावट*, एक प्रकार की गांठ*

hither a. & adv. यहां, इधर

hitherto adv. अब तक

hive n. मधुमक्खी का छत्ता v.i.
& t. मधुमक्खी* की तरह
जुटकर रहना, इकट्ठा करना

hoard n. ढेर, जखीरा; **hoarder**
जखीरेबाज़; v.t. संचय करना,
इकट्ठा करना

hoarse a. रूक्ष, कर्कश

hoax n. हंसी*, धोखेबाज़; v.t.
ठगना

hobby n. (pl. hobbies) हॉबी,
शौक, पुष्ट टट्टू

hobby-horse n. लिल्ली घोड़ी*,
बच्चों के खेलने का लकड़ी का
घोड़ा

hockey n. हॉकी

hoist v.t. उभाड़ना, उठाना,
ऊंचा करना; n. ऊपर उठाने
का यन्त्र

hold v.t. & i. (p.t. & p.p.
held) अधिकार में रखना,
धरना, अनुष्ठान करना, उत्सव
मनाना, लगा रहना, पकड़ना;
n. जहाज की पेंदी* में
सामग्री* रखने का स्थान,
पकड़, अधिकार

holdall n. होलडाल, बिस्तरबन्द;
to hold by स्वीकार करना;
to hold back ठमकना;
to hold forth सबके सामने
अपने विचार प्रकट करना;
to hold in रोक रखना;
to hold off देर करना;
to hold one's tongue
चुप रहना; to hold out
फैलाना; to hold over
स्थिर करना; to hold up
रोकना, सहारा देना; to
hold water सूक्ष्म परीक्षा*
करना

hole n. छेद, सूराख; v.t. छेद
करना; hole and corner
गुप्त बात*, रहस्य

holiday n. (pl. holidays)
छुट्टी का दिन, मनोरंजन,
त्योहार का दिन

hollow a. खोखला, छूछा, झूठा,
बेईमान; n. गड्ढा, घाटी;
v.t. गड्ढा करना; adv. पूर्ण
रूप से; hollow-hearted;
a. बेईमान; hollowness n.
खोखलापन; बेईमानी*

holocaust n. पूर्ण आहुति*,
प्रचण्ड अग्नि*

holy a. (comp. holier, sup.
holiest) धार्मिक, शुद्ध, पवित्र;
holy land पुण्यभूमि

homage *n.* श्रद्धांजलि*, आदर

home *n.* घर, वासःथान, जन्म-भूमि*, आश्रय; at home. घर पर, स्वदेश में, आनन्द से; home member गृह सचिव; homesick घर के बाहर रहने से खिन्न; homewards घर की ओर; to bring home to समझ में बैठा देना

homicidal *a.* मनुष्य-वध संबंधी

homicide *n.* नर-हत्या*, मनुष्य-घातक

homoeopath *n.* होमियोपैथ

homoeopathy *n.* होमियोपैथिक (सम) चिकित्सा

homoeopathic *a.* होमियोपैथिक चिकित्सा-सम्बन्धी

homogeneous *a.* सदृश, एकरूप

honest *a.* सच्चा, ईमानदार

honesty *n.* सच्चाई, ईमानदारी

honey *n.* मधु, शहद*

honeycomb *n.* मधुकोष का छत्ता

honeymoon *n.* विवाह के बाद दम्पति का उत्सव-काल

honorarium *n.* पारिश्रमिक

honorary *a.* बिना शुल्क का, अप्रवैतनिक

honour *n.* सम्मान, पूजा*,

सत्कार, आदर, कीर्ति*; *v.t.* प्रतिष्ठा करना

honourable *a.* प्रतिष्ठित, माननीय

hood *n.* हुड, ढकना, कन्टोप

hoodwink *v.t.* छलना, धोखा देना

hook *n.* कुलाबा, कांटा, मछली* फंसाने की बंसी* *v.t.* कंटिये से फंसाना, मोड़ना

hooligan *n.* गुण्डा

hoot *v.i.* तिरस्कार करना, उल्लू की तरह चिल्लाना; *n.* उल्लू की बोली*

hop *v.t.* (*p.t.* hooped) एक पैर के बल कूदना

hope *v.i.* आशा* करना; *n.* आशा*, विश्वास

hopeful *a.* आशाजनक

hopeless *a.* आशाहीन, निराश

horde *n.* कंजड़ों का जत्था, झुण्ड; *v.i.* खेमों में रहना

horizon *n.* क्षितिज

horn *n.* सींग*, भोंपा

hornet *n.* बर्र, हाड़ा, भिड़

horrible *a.* भयंकर, डरावना

horrify *v.t.* डराना

horror *n.* अत्यन्त भय या घृणा*

horse *n.* घोड़ा; *v.i.* घोड़े पर सवारी* करना

horse-power *n.* यंत्र की वह

शक्ति जिसके द्वारा 550 पाउण्ड का भार एक सैकण्ड में एक फुट उठ सके

horseshoe n. घोड़े की नाल*

horticulture n. बागबानी*, उद्यान-विद्या*

hose n. (pl. hose) पायजामा, मोजा, पानी छिड़कने की नली*

hosiery n. मोजे की तरह बुने हुए सामान, इस तरह के सामान की दूकान*

hospitable a. अतिथि-सत्कारी, मेहमाननवाज

hospital n. अस्पताल

hospitality n. अतिथि-सत्कार

host n. (fem. hostess) आतिथेय, मेज़बान, समुदाय, सेना

hostage n. शरीर बन्धक, ज़ामिन

hostel n. होस्टल, छात्रावास

hostile a. बैरी, विरुद्ध, लड़ाका

hostility n. शत्रुता*; hosti-lities n. pl. युद्ध के कार्य

hot a. गरम, तीता, उग्र, कामा-तुर, क्रोधी

hotbed n. खाद डालकर तैयार की हुई भूमि, बुरे तत्त्वों का अड्डा

hot-headed a. क्रोधी, उग्र स्वभाव का

hotchpotch n. गोलमाल

hound n. शिकारी कुत्ता; v.t. ऐसे कुत्ते से शिकार करना

hour n. घंटा, समय, अवसर; at the eleventh hour अन्तिम क्षण में; the man of the hour उस समय का प्रसिद्ध मनुष्य

house n. (pl. houses) घर, मकान, गृहस्थी, वंश; v.t. & i. घर में रखना या रहना

housebreaker n. सेंघ मारने वाला चोर, मकान ढहाने वाला; household n. & a. कुटुम्ब, कुटुम्ब का

housekeeper n. घर की देख-भाल करनेवाला

housemaid n. दासी*, नौक-रानी*

house-surgeon n. अस्पताल में रहने वाला डाक्टर

housewife n. गृहिणी*, घरवाली*

how adv. किस प्रकार से, कैसे

however adv. तो भी

howl v.t. गरजना, गुर्राना; n. भेड़िये का शब्द

howler n. गुर्रानेवाला, बहुत बड़ी गलती*

howling n. गर्जना*, चिल्ला-हट*

hub n. पहिए का धुरा

hubble-bubble *n.* हुक्का

hubbub *n.* कोलाहल, कलकल शब्द

huddle *v.t.* ढेर लगाना, भीड़ मचाना; *n.* भीड़भाड़*

huge *a.* बहुत बड़ा, विशाल

hum *v.t.* (*p.t.* hummed) भनभनाना, गुनगुनाना *n.* गुनगुनाहट*

human *a.* मनुष्य-जाति संबंधी

humane *a.* दयालु

humanitarian *a.* मानवीय

humanity *n.* मानवता*

humanize *v.t.* दयालु बनाना, मानवीयकरण करना

humble *a.* अधम, विनीत, नम्र; *v.t.* नम्र करना

humbly *adv.* नम्रता* से

humbug *n.* छल, कपट, पाखण्ड; *v.t.* धोखा देना

humdrum *a.* नीरस, फीका

humid *a.* गीला, तर, नम

humidity *n.* नमी*

humiliate *v.t.* विनीत करना, नीचा दिखलाना

humiliation *n.* घमंड चूर करना

humility *n.* दीनता*, विनय

humorist *n.* ठिठोलिया, हास्यरस का लेखक

humorous *a.* विनोदी, रसिक

humour *n.* हास्य, विनोद, मनोवृत्ति*, भाव, प्रवृत्ति, रसिकता*, शारीरिक रस; *v.t.* सन्तुष्ट करना; out of humour अप्रसन्न, क्रोध में

hunch *n.* कूबड़

hunch-backed *a.* कुबड़ा

hundred *n.* सौ

hundredth *a.* सौवां

hundredfold *n.* सौ गुना

hundredweight *n.* एक सौ बारह पाउण्ड की तौल*

hunger *n.* भूख*, तीव्र अभिलाषा*, *v.i.* तीव्र अभिलाषा करना

hungrily *adv.* भूखे ढंग से

hungry *a.* भूखा

hunt *v.t.* शिकार करना, पीछा करना, खोजना; *n.* आखेट खोज*

hunter *n.* (*fem.* huntress) शिकारी, बहेलिया

huntsman *n.* शिकारी, व्याध

hurdle *n.* टट्टी, टट्टर, रुकावट*; *v.t.* टट्टी में बन्द करना, रुकावट डालना

hurl *v.t.* वेग से फेंकना, उछालना, चक्कर देना

hurrah *interj.* आनन्द-सूचक अव्यय, वाहवाह

hurricane *n.* प्रचण्ड वायु* hurricane-lamp आंधी में न बुझने वाला लैम्प

hurriedly *adv.* शीघ्रता* से

hurry *n.* शीघ्रता, आकुलता; *v.t. & i. (p.t.* hurried) जल्दी करना, जल्दी* से जाना

hurt *v.i. & t.* कष्ट देना, घायल करना, पीड़ा* देना; *n.* कष्ट, घाव, पीड़ा*

hurtful *a.* पीड़ा-कारक

husband *n.* पति, शोहर; *v.t.* किफायत से, अच्छा प्रबन्ध करना

husband-man *n.* किसान, खेतिहर

husbandry *n.* कृषि*, खेती*, कम खर्ची*, किफायत*

hush *n.* चुपकी*; *interj.* चुप ! शान्त ! hushmoney किसी अपराध को छिपाने की घूस

husk *n.* छिलका, भूसी*; *n.* (व०व०) अवशेष; *v.t.* छिलका हटाना

huskiness *n.* छिलकापन

husky *a.* भूसी* भरा, कर्कश

hut *n.* कुटो*, झोंपड़ी*

hyaena *n.* लकड़बग्घा

hybrid *a.* वर्णसंकर

hydraulics *n.* उदिक, जलगति विज्ञान

hydro *pref.* 'जल' के अर्थ का उपसर्ग

hydrogen *n.* उदजन, जलजन

hydrometer *n.* तरल पदार्थों का घनत्व नापने का यंत्र

hydrophobia *n.* जलातंक

hydroplane *n.* एक प्रकार का वायुयान जो जल में दौड़कर हवा में उड़ता है

hygiene *n.* आरोग्यशास्त्र

hygienic *a.* आरोग्य संबंधी

hygrometer *n.* वायु में का जल नापने का यंत्र

hymn *n.* ईश्वर-स्तुति*, स्तोत्र

hyperbole *n.* अत्युक्ति*, किसी बात को बहुत बढ़ाकर या घटाकर कहने की रीति*

hyperbolical *a.* अत्युक्ति-पूर्ण

hypercritic (-al) *a.* दोष को ही विशेष रूप से देखने वाला, छिद्रान्वेषी

hypnotism *n.* सम्मोहन विज्ञान, कृत्रिम निद्रा लाने की कला*

hypnotize *v.t.* कृत्रिम निद्रा लाना

hypocrisy *n.* कपट, पाखंड

hypocrite *n.* छली, पाखंडी

hypocritical *a.* पाखण्डी

hypothesis *n.* (*pl*-ses) प्रतिज्ञा*, कल्पना*

hypothetical *a.* कल्पित माना हुआ

hysteria *n.* वातोन्माद, मूर्च्छा*, मिरगी*

hysterical मूर्च्छा रोग सम्बन्धी

I

I *pron.* (*pl.* we) मैं

ice *n.* बरफ*; *v.t.* बरफ से
ढांपना, to break the ice
काम शुरू करना

iceberg *n.* बहता हुआ बरफ का
पहाड़ या हिमशिला खण्ड

ice-cream *n.* आइसक्रीम, कुल्फी
बरफ*

icicle *n.* बरफ* की लटकती हुई
चट्टान*

icy *a.* बरफ* के समान ठण्डा

idea *n.* भाव, विश्वास, अभिप्राय,
विचार, कल्पना*

ideal *a.* & *n.* परम, निर्दोष,
आदर्श

idealist *n.* आदर्शवादी

idealistic *a.* आदर्श-संबंधी

idealize *v.t.* आदर्श बनाना

identical *a.* अभिन्न, समान,
एकसा

identically *adv.* अनुरूप रूप में,
अभिन्न रूप से

identification *n.* पहिचान*,
शिनाख्त

identify *v.t.* (*p.t.* identified)
पहिचानना, शिनाख्त करना

identity *n.* समानता*, सारूप्य

idiocy *n.* मूर्खता*, पागलपन

idiom *n.* मुहावरा, बोली

idiomatic (-al) *a.* मुहावरेदार

idiosyncrasy *n.* (*pl.* idio-
syncrasies) व्यक्तिगत
विशिष्टता*, स्वभाव, लत*

idiosyncratic विशेष स्वभाव
या प्रकृति* का

idiot *n.* जड़, उल्लू, मूर्ख

idiotic *a.* मूर्ख

idle *a.* आलसी, निरुपयोगी,
व्यर्थ, तुच्छ; *v.t.* समय वृथा
गंवाना

idleness *n.* सुस्ती*, बेकारी*,
आलस्य

idler *n.* आलस्य में अपना समय
बितानेवाला

idol *n.* प्रतिमा*, मूर्ति*, आराध्य
व्यक्ति

idolater *n.* (*fem.* idolatress)
मूर्तिपूजक

idolatrous *a.* मूर्ति-पूजन संबंधी

idolize *v.t.* मूर्ति* बनाना, देवता
मानना

if *conj.* यदि, जो; as if मानो

ignite *v.t.* & *i.* आग से जलाना,
आग लगना

ignoble *a.* अकुलीन, नीच,
अप्रतिष्ठित

ignominious *a.* लज्जाकर,
निद्य

ignominy *n.* बदनामी*, लज्जा*,
कलंक

ignorance n. अज्ञान, जहालत*

ignorant a. अशिक्षित, अबोध, विद्याहीन, जाहिल

ignore v.t. ध्यान न देना, उपेक्षा करना, हटाना

Iliad n. होमर कवि का प्रसिद्ध महाकाव्य

ill a. (comp. worse, sup. worst) बुरा, अस्वस्थ, रोगी; ill-advised मूर्ख; ill at ease व्यग्र; ill-blood शत्रुता*; ill-bred असभ्य, गंवार; ill-omened अभागा; ill-starred अभागा; ill-temper क्रोध; ill-treat बुरी तरह व्यवहार करना; ill-will शत्रुता*

illegal a. न्याय-विरुद्ध, गैर-क़ानूनी

illegality n. अवैधता*

illegibility n. अस्पष्टता*

illegible a. अस्पष्ट, गिचपिच

illegitimacy n. अवैधता*, अनुचित, हरामीपन, दोगलापन

illegitimate a. अनुचित, दोगला, विधि-विरुद्ध

illicit a. नियम या व्यवहार के विरुद्ध

illiteracy n. विद्याहीनता* निरक्षरता*

illiterate a. & n. अशिक्षित, विद्याहीन, निरक्षर

illness n. अस्वस्थता*, रोग, बीमारी*

illogical a. न्याय या तर्क-विरुद्ध

illude v.t. ठगना, धोखा देना

illuminate v.t. रोशनी करना, उजागर करना, चित्रों से सजाना

illumination n. प्रकाश, प्रभा*, दीपावली*

illusion n. छल, माया*, अयथार्थ

illustrate v.t. व्याख्या करना, दृष्टान्त देना, चित्र इत्यादि द्वारा समझाना, चित्रों से सजाना

illustration n. उदाहरण, दृष्टांत, चित्र

illustrative a. उदाहरण या दृष्टांतदर्शक

illustrious a. चमकीला, शानदार, महान, प्रसिद्ध

image n. प्रतिमा*, मूर्ति*, प्रतिबिम्ब, छाया*, v.t. दरसाना, चित्त में धारण करना

imagery n. कल्पना, विम्ब-विधान

imaginable a. कल्पनीय, संभाव्य

imaginary a. काल्पनिक, मन-गढ़न्त

imagination n. कल्पना*,
विचार

imaginative a. कल्पनामय,
भावनापूर्ण

imagine v.t. विचारना, अनुमान
करना, कल्पना करना

imitable a. अनुकरण करने
योग्य

imitate v.t. नक़ल करना,
अनुकरण करना; imitation
n. नक़ल*, अनुकरण, सादृश्य

imitative a. कृत्रिम, बनावटी,
नक़ली

imitator n. अनुकरण करने
वाला, नक़लची

immaculate a. शुद्ध, निर्मल,
निर्दोष

immaterial a. अभौतिक,
सारहीन, अनावश्यक

immature a. अधकचरा, अधूरा,
अपूर्ण

immaturity n. अधकचरापन,
अपरिपक्वता*

immeasurable a. अपरिमित,
अथाह, बहुत बड़ा

immediate a. तुरंत, शीघ्र,
समीप

immemorial a. अति प्राचीन,
पुरातन

immense a. बहुत बड़ा

immensely adv. अधिकता से

immensity n. विशालता*

immerge v.t. डूबना, डुबोना

immerse v.t. जलसमाधि देना,
डुबो देना, दफ़न करना

immersion n. गोता, अन्त्येष्टि*

immigrant n. परदेशवासी,
प्रवासी नागरिक

immigrate v.t. परदेश में बसना

immobile a. स्थिर, निश्चल

immobility n. स्थिरता*

immoderate a. अत्यंत,
अपरिमित

immodest a. निर्लज्ज, अशिष्ट

immodesty n. निर्लज्जता*,
अशिष्टता*

immoral a. अनैतिक, पापी

immorality n. अनैतिकता*,
अधर्म, पाप

immortal a. अमर, अविनाशी

immortality n. अमरत्व

immortalize v.t. अमर करना

immovability n. अचल स्थिति*

immovable a. अचल, स्थिर, दृढ़

immune a. (रोगादि से) मुक्त,
प्रतिरक्षित, बचा हुआ

immunity n. मुक्ति*, छुटकारा

immunize v.t. छुटकारा देना

impact n. मुठभेड़*, टक्कर*;
v.t. कसकर दबाना

impalpable a. अस्पृश्य, न
समझने योग्य

impanel v.t. सूची में रखना

impart v.t. भाग देना, ᴅᶠ

करना, समाचार पहुंचाना

impartial *a.* अपक्षपाती, सम-
दर्शी, न्यायी

impartiality *n.* अपक्षपात,
समदर्शिता*

impassable *a.* अगम्य, गहन

impasse *n.* बन्द गली*, कठिन
स्थिति*

impatience *n.* अधीरता*,
व्यग्रता*

impatient *a.* अधीर, व्यग्र,
उत्सुक

impeach *v.t.* अभियोग लगाना,
दोषी ठहराना

impeachment *n.* दोषारोपण

impede *v.t.* अवरोध करना,
रोकना

impediment *n.* अवरोध,
रुकावट*

impend *v.i.* लटकना, समीप
आ जाना

impendent *a.* निकटवर्ती

impending *a.* उपस्थित

impenetrability *n.* अभेद्यता*

impenetrable *a.* अभेद्य,
अप्रवेश्य

imperative *a.* आज्ञार्थक, अति
आवश्यक, कर्त्तव्य; impera-
tively *adv.* आदेशक रूप में

imperceptible *a.* अगोचर, न
जानने योग्य

imperfect *a.* अपूर्ण, अधूरा

imperfection *n.* दोष, त्रुटि*

imperial *a.* राज्य अथवा राजा-
धिराज संबंधी, शाही; *n.*
32×22 इंच नाप का कागज

imperialism *n.* साम्राज्यवाद

imperil *v.t.* (*p.t.* imperilled)
आपत्ति में डालना

imperishable *a.* अविनाशी,
अनश्वर

imperishably *adv.* अनश्वरता
से

impermanence *n.* अनस्थिरता*

impersonal *a.* व्यक्ति से संबंध
न रखने वाला

impersonate *v.t.* वेष बदलना,
जाली आदमी बनना

impersonation *n.* वेष बदलने
का कार्य

impersonator *n.* वेष बदलने
वाला मनुष्य

impertinence *n.* अशिष्टता*,
ढिठाई*

impertinent *a.* अशिष्ट, असंगत,
अविनीत

impetuous *a.* तीव्र, प्रबल,
साहसी

impetuosity *n.* साहस,
प्रचण्डता*

impetus *n.* शक्ति*, प्रेरणा*

implement *n.* हथियार, औजार;
v.t. कार्यान्वित करना

implicate *v.t.* चक्कर में डालना,

अपराध में फंसाना

implication n. फंसाव, लपेट*

implicit a. निहित, निर्विवाद

implicitly adv. निस्संदेह

implore v.t. प्रार्थना करना, याचना करना

imploringly adv. विनय-सहित

imply v.t. (p.t. implied) अर्थ निकालना, सूचित करना, संकेत करना

impolite a. असभ्य, अविनीत

import v.t. विदेश का माल देश में लाना, अर्थ होना, सूचित करना; n. आयात सामग्री*, तात्पर्य, अर्थ

importable a. देश में लाने योग्य (विदेशी माल)

importance n. महत्त्व, प्रभाव, महिमा*

important a. प्रभाव या महत्त्व का, आवश्यक

impose v.t. थोपना, प्रभाव डालना

imposing a. प्रभावशाली, रोबदार, धोखा देनेवाला

impossibility n. असंभावना*

impossible a. असंभव, दुष्कर

imposition n. कर, लगान, छल

impost n. महसूल, चुंगी*

impostor n. पाखण्डी, कपटी, छली

imposture n. छल, कपट

impotence n. शक्तिहीनता*, नामर्दी*

impotent a. नपुंसक, नामर्द, शक्तिहीन

impound v.t. बाड़े में बन्द करना, जब्त करना

impoverish v.t. दरिद्र बना देना, शक्तिहीन करना, साधन-हीन करना

impoverishment n. दरिद्रता*

impracticability n. असाध्यता

impracticable a. असाध्य, असंभव

impregnate v.t. गर्भवती करना, भरना

impress v.t. छापना, मुहर करना, चित्त पर प्रभाव डालना; n. छाप*, मुहर*

impression n. छाप*, विचार

impressive a. प्रभावशाली, गंभीर

imprint v.t. छापना, अंकित करना; n. छाप*

imprison v.t. बन्दी करना, बन्द करना

imprisonment n. कारावास, जेल*

improper a. अशुद्ध, अयोग्य, अनुचित

impropriety n. अनुचित बोली* या कार्य

improve v.t. & i अच्छा

करना या होना, सुधारना,
उन्नति करना

improvement n. उन्नति*,
सुधार

improvise v.t. तत्काल गीत
बनाना या व्याख्यान देना,
तत्काल तैयार करना

imprudence n. अविवेक

imprudent a. अविवेकी, ढीठ

impuissant a. लाचार, बेबस

impulse n. आवेगा, प्रवृत्ति*,
लालसा*

impulsive a. आवेग, संवेग-
शील

impunity n. दण्ड से मुक्ति*,
माफ़ी*

impure a. अशुद्ध, अपवित्र,
दूसरे पदार्थ से मिला हुआ

impurity n. अपवित्रता*

imputation n. दोषारोपरण

impute v.t. दोष लगाना,
कलंकित करना

in prep. में, बीच, भीतर, द्वारा,
कारण से; in as far as यहां
तक कि; in that क्योंकि;
ins and outs गुप्त तथा
प्रत्यक्ष बात

inability n. असमर्थता*

inaccurate a. अशुद्ध, बेठीक,
गलत

inaction n. निष्क्रियता*,
आलस्य

inactive a. निष्क्रिय, आलसी

inadmissible a. अग्राह्य,
अमान्य

inanimate a. निर्जीव, प्राराहीन,
मृत

inapplicable a. अनुचित,
अयोग्य

inasmuch adv. यद्यपि, इससे

inattentive a. अन्यमनस्क,
लापरवाह

inaudible a. न सुनाई पड़नेवाला

inaugural a. उद्घाटन-संबंधी,
अभिषेकात्मक

inauguration n. उद्घाटन

inauspicious a. अशुभ

inborn a. स्वाभाविक, सहज,
जन्म से प्राप्त

inbreathe v.t. भीतर को सांस
लेना

incalculable a. अनगिनत,
बेहिसाब

incantation n. मन्त्र, जादू

incapable a. अयोग्य

incapacitate v.t. अयोग्य करना

incapacity n. अयोग्यता*,
अक्षमता*

incarnate a. मूर्त, शरीरी; v.t.
शरीर धाररा करना, अवतार
लेना

incarnation n. अवतार

incautious a. असावधान

incense v.t. धूप देना, क्रोध से

उत्तेजित करना; *n.* धूप,
सुगंध*, प्रशंसा*

incentive *n.* प्रलोभन, उत्तेजना;
a. प्रवर्तक, उत्तेजक

inception *n.* आरंभ

inceptive *a.* आरंभ का

inch *n.* इंच

incident *a.* अनिवार्य रूप से
होनेवाला; *n.* घटना*, वृत्तांत

incidental *a.* आकस्मिक
अनावश्यक

incidentally *adv.* आकस्मिक
रूप में

incite *v.t.* प्रवृत्त करना, उत्तेजित
करना

incitement *n.* प्रोत्साहन,
उत्तेजना*

inclination *n.* झुकाव, प्रवृत्ति*

incline *v.t. & i.* झुकना, झुकाना,
इच्छा करना; to incline
one's ear ध्यान लगाकर
सुनना

inclined *a.* झुका हुआ, प्रवृत्त

include *v.t.* शामिल करना,
जोड़ना, समावेश करना, मिला
लेना

inclusion *n.* समावेश

inclusive *a.* संयुक्त किया हुआ,
सहित

incognito *a. & adv.* गुप्त, भेस
बदले हुए

incoherence *n.* बेतरतीबी*

incoherent *a.* असंगत, बेमेल

incohesive *a.* असंबद्ध

incombustible *a.* अदाह्य

income *n.* आय*, अर्थप्राप्ति*,
आमदनी*; income-tax
आयकर

incomer *n.* बिना आज्ञा प्रवेश
करनेवाला

incoming *a.* आनेवाला, (लाभ)
होनेवाला

incomparable *a.* अद्वितीय,
बेजोड़

incompetent *a.* अयोग्य

incomplete *a.* अपूर्ण, अधूरा

inconformity *n.* असमानता

incongruent *a.* अयोग्य, अपूर्ण,
अनमेल

incongruity *n.* अयोग्यता*,
अनुपपत्ति*

incongruous *a.* असंबद्ध, बेडौल

inconsiderate *a.* विचारशून्य

incontaminate *a.* अदूषित,
पवित्र

incontestable *a.* निर्विवाद

inconvenient *a.* असुविधाजनक

incorporate *v.t. & i.* मिलाना,
इकट्ठा करना; *a.* मिला हुआ,
संयुक्त

incorporation *n.* संसर्ग,
मण्डली*, सम्मेलन

incorrect *a.* असत्य, अशुद्ध
गलत

incorrigible *a.* असाध्य, लाइलाज

incorrupt *a.* पवित्र, ईमानदार, घूस न देने योग्य

incorruptible *a.* न सड़ने योग्य, शुद्ध, न भ्रष्ट होने योग्य

increase *v.t. & i.* बढ़ना, बढ़ाना, फैलाना; *n.* वृद्धि, उत्पत्ति*, उपज*

incredible *a.* विश्वास न करने योग्य

increment *n.* बढ़ती*, लाभ, वृद्धि*

incriminate *v.t.* दोषी* ठहराना

incriminatory *a.* अभियोगात्मक

incubate *v.i. & t.* अण्डा सेना

incubator *n.* अण्डा सेने की मशीन*

inculcate *v.t.* मस्तिष्क में बैठा देना, समझाना

inculcation *n.* अन्त:निवेशन, शिक्षा*, उपदेश

incumbent *a.* अवलंबी, आश्रित; *n.* वृत्तिभोगी

incur *v.t.* (*p.t.* incurred) अपने ऊपर लेना, ग्रस्त होना, सहना

incurable *a.* असाध्य, लाइलाज

incursion *n.* यकायक आक्रमण, चढ़ाई*

indecency *n.* घृष्टता*, अभद्रता*

indecent *a.* घृष्ट, अभद्र

indecision *n.* अनिश्चय, संदेह

indeed *adv.* वस्तुत:, यथार्थ में; *interj.* तिरस्कार-सूचक अव्यय, अरे !

indefensible *a.* अरक्षणीय, न बचाने योग्य

indefinite *a.* अनिश्चित, सीमा-रहित

indelicacy *n.* फूहड़पन, रूखापन

indemnity *n.* क्षतिपूर्ति*

indent *v.t & i.* दांतेदार बनाना, पंक्ति से हटाकर नया परिच्छेद आरंभ करना; माल का बीजक, (मोटर आदि में) खरोच

independence *n.* स्वतंत्रता*, आजादी*

independent *a.* स्वतंत्र, स्वेच्छाचारी, स्वाधीन

indescribable *a.* अवर्णनीय

index *n.* (*pl.* indexes) चिह्न, सूचीपत्र प्रदर्शक सिद्धांत; *v.i.* सूचीपत्र लगाना; *n.* (*pl.* indices) बीजगणित में प्रयुक्त विशेष चिह्न

India *pr. n.* भारतवर्ष

Indian *a.* भारतीय

Indian Penal Code भारतीय दंड संहिता*

indicate *v.t.* प्रकट करना, प्रकाशित करना, सूचित करना

indication n. चिह्न, सूचना*. लक्षण

indicative a. दर्शक, सूचक

indicator n. निर्देशक

indict v.t. न्यायालय के सामने दोषी ठहराना

indictment n. अभियोग, कलंक

indifference n. उदासीनता*, उपेक्षा*

indifferent a. तटस्थ, उदासीन, असावधान, अपक्षपाती, सामान्य

indigenous a. स्वदेशी, स्वदेश में उत्पन्न

indigestible a. न पचने योग्य

indigestion n. अजीर्ण, मन्दाग्नि*, बदहज़मी*

indigestive a. अजीर्ण करने वाला

indignant a. क्रोधित, घृणापूर्ण

indignation n. रोष, क्रोध

indigo n. नील का पौधा, इससे निकाला हुआ रंग

indirect a. अप्रत्यक्ष, परोक्ष

indiscreet a. अप्रौढ़

indiscretion n. मूर्खता*, धृष्टता*

indiscriminate a. अविवेकी, अव्यवस्थित

indispensable a. परम आव-श्यक

indisposed a. अनिच्छुक

अस्वस्थ

indisputable a. निर्विवाद, निश्चित

indissolubility n. अद्रवत्व

indissoluble a. जो घुल न सके, स्थायी

indistinct a. अस्पष्ट

indistinguishable a. पृथक् विचार न करने योग्य, अविवेच्य

individual n. एक व्यक्ति; a. अकेला, व्यक्तिगत, विशिष्ट

individualism n. व्यक्तिवाद

individuality n. व्यक्तित्व, विशेषता*

indivisible a. अभाज्य

indomitable a. दुर्जन, हठी, अदम्य

indoor a. घर के भीतर होने वाला

induce v.t. उभाड़ना, मनाना, अनुमान करना

inducement n. प्रलोभन, फुसलाहट*

induct v.t. प्रारंभ करना

induction n. अनुगम, उप-पादन (विद्युत का)

indulge v.t. & i. तुष्ट करना, प्रसन्न करना, आसक्त या लिप्त होना

indulgence n. तुष्टि*, क्षमा*, आज्ञा* अनुग्रह, आसक्ति*

indulgent *a.* अति दयालु, आसक्त

industrial *a.* औद्योगिक

industrial court *n.* औद्योगिक न्यायालय

industrious *a.* उद्योगी, परिश्रमी

industry *n.* उद्योग, परिश्रम, व्यवसाय

ineffective *a.* प्रभावहीन, बेअसर

inept *a.* अयोग्य, मूर्ख, अनाड़ी

ineptitude *n.* मूर्खता*, अयोग्यता*

inequitable *a.* अन्यायी, न्यायविरुद्ध

inequity *n.* अन्याय, पक्षपात

ineradicable *a.* जड़ से न उखाड़ने योग्य

inert *a.* गतिहीन, आलसी, जड़

inertia *n.* निश्चलता*, जड़ पदार्थ की एक विशिष्ट स्थिति*

inevitable *a.* अनिवार्य, आवश्यक

inevitably *adv.* अनिवार्य रीति से

inexorable *a.* अनाराध्य, निर्दय, कठोर

inexpensive *a.* सस्ता

inexperience *n.* अनुभव-शून्यता*

infallible *a.* अभ्रांत

infamous *a.* दुर्नाम, दुष्ट, निर्लज्ज

infamy *n.* अपकीर्ति*, कलंक

infancy *n.* बाल्यावस्था*, प्रथम अवस्था*

infant *n.* बालक, शिशु

infanticide *n.* शिशुहत्या*

infantile *a.* शिशु-सम्बन्धी, शिशु-तुल्य

infantry *n.* (*pl.* infantries) पैदल सेना

infatuate *v.t.* बुद्धि नाश करना, उत्तेजित करना

infatuation *n.* मूढ़ता*, मूर्खता*

infect *v.t.* छूत का रोग लगना, दूषित करना

infection *n.* सम्पर्क, स्पर्श रोग

infectious *a.* संक्रामक, रोग फैलाने वाला

infer *v.t.* (*p.t.* inferred) अनुमान करना, तर्क करना, परिणाम निकालना

inference *n.* अनुमान, परामर्श

inferior *a.* नीचा, न्यून, हीन

inferiority *n.* न्यूनता*, हीनता*

infernal *a.* नरक-सम्बन्धी, आसुरी, राक्षसी

inferno *n.* पाताल, नरक

infinite *a.* अपरिमित, अनन्त

infinity *n.* अनन्तता*

infirm *a.* दुर्बल, क्षीण, रोगी

inflame *v.t. & i.* उत्तेजित करना, भड़काना, फूल आना,

जलना

inflammable *a.* शीघ्र जलने वाला

inflammation *n.* सूजन*, दाह*

inflammatory *a.* दाहक, सूजन का

inflation *n.* मुद्रास्फीति*

inflexible *a.* अनम्य, हृढ़

inflict *v.t.* प्रयुक्त करना, दण्ड देना

influence *n.* शक्ति*, प्रतिष्ठा*; *v.t.* प्रभाव डालना, प्रवृत्त करना

influential *a.* प्रभावशाली

influenza *n.* इंफ्लुएंजा, एक तरह का बुखार

influx *n.* प्रवाह, प्रवेश

inform *v.t.* सूचित करना, बतलाना

informal *a.* अनौपचारिक

informant *n.* निवेदक, सूचना देनेवाला

information *n.* सूचना*, जान-कारी

information department सूचना विभाग

information minister सूचना-मंत्री

informative *a.* शिक्षाप्रद, जानकारी पैदा करने वाला

informatory *a.* शिक्षाप्रद, सूचना-पूर्ण

informer *n.* भेदिया

infringe *v.t.* उल्लंघन करना, तोड़ना

infringement *n.* उल्लंघन

infuriate *v.t.* कुपित करना, क्रुद्ध करना

infuse *v.t. & i.* उड़ेलना, मन में बैठाना, पानी में डालना, उत्तेजित करना

infusion *n.* जलसेक, आसव, प्रेरणा*, जान डालना, जान फूंकना

ingenuity *n.* कल्पनाशक्ति*, चतुराई*

ingenuous *a.* निष्कपट, शुद्ध, सरल

ingrain *v.t.* चित्त में बैठा देना

ingrained *a.* दीर्घस्थायी, दृढ़

ingrate *n.* कृतघ्न मनुष्य

ingratitude *n.* कृतघ्नता*

ingredient *n.* अंश, भाग

ingurgitate *v.t.* जल्दी-जल्दी खाना

inhabit *v.t.* निवास करना, बसना

inhabitable *a.* बसने योग्य

inhabitant *n.* निवासी

inhabitation *n.* घर, निवास, डेरा

inhale *v.t.* सांस खींचना, कश खींचना

inharmonic *a.* बेसुरा, अनमेल

inherent *a.* सहज, जन्मजात अंतर्निहित

inherit *v.t.* पैतृक सम्पत्ति पाना, प्रकृति से पाना

inheritable *a.* परंपरा द्वारा प्राप्य, दाय

inheritance *n.* उत्तराधिकार (*fem.* inheritress) उत्तराधिकारी

inhibit *v.t.* रोकना, मना करना

inhibition *n.* रुकावट*

inhibitory *a.* रोकनेवाला, निरोधात्मक

inhospitable *a.* असत्कारी

inhuman *a.* अमानुषी, निर्दयी

inhumation *n.* गाड़ने की क्रिया*

inimical *a.* शत्रुवत्, विरोधी

inimitable *a.* अननुकरणीय, अद्वितीय

inimitably *adv.* अननुकरणीय रूप से

iniquity *a.* अधर्म, अन्याय

initial *a.* आदि का, अपूर्ण; *n.* शब्द का आदि अक्षर; (*pl.*) किसी व्यक्ति के नाम के आदि अक्षर; *v.t.* (*p.t.* initialled) हस्ताक्षर करना

initiate *v.t.* आरम्भ करना, प्रथम संस्कार करना

initiation *n.* दीक्षा संस्कार

initiative *n.* पहल, आरम्भबल

initiator *n.* (*fem.* initiatrix) संस्कार करने वाला, चालक, सर्जक

inject *v.t.* सुई लगाना

injection *n.* इंजेक्शन, दवा की सुई

injudicious *a.* अविवेकी, विचारशून्य

injunction *n.* आज्ञा,* आदेश, निषेधाज्ञा, हिदायत*; sacred injunction शास्त्र की आज्ञा*

injure *v.t.* हानि पहुंचाना, पीड़ा देना, घायल करना

injured *a.* पीड़ा प्राप्त, व्यथित, घायल

injurious *a.* हानिकारक, पीड़ाकर

injury *n.* अपकार, हानि*, घाव

injustice *n.* अधर्म*, अनीति*, अन्याय

ink *n.* रोशनाई*, मसि*; *v.t.* रोशनाई लगाना

inkling *n.* संकेत, कानाफूसी*

inkstand *n.* मसिपात्र, दवात*

inky *a.* रोशनाई पोता हुआ

inland *a. & adv.* देश के भीतरी और, अन्तर्देशीय

inlander *n.* देश के भीतरी भाग में रहनेवाला

inlay *v.t.* (*p.t.* inlaid)

पच्चीकारी करना, जड़ना
inlet *n.* संकरी खाड़ी*
inmate *n.* निवासी, दूसरे के साथ रहनेवाला
inmost *a.* सबसे भीतरी
inn *n.* सराय*, धर्मशाला*; inns of courts इङ्गलैंड के वकीलों का समाज
innate *a.* सहज, स्वाभाविक
inner *a.* (*comp.* of in) अन्तरीय, भीतरी; inner-apartments अन्तःगृह; the inner man मनुष्य की अन्तरात्मा*
innermost *a.* सबसे भीतरी
innings *n. pl.* क्रिकेट में एक-एक पारी का खेल, अधिकार की अवधि*
innkeeper *n.* भटियारा
innocence *n.* सरलता*, निर्दोषता*
innocent *a.* निरपराध, सीधा, भोला
innocuity *n.* सज्जनता*, अनपकारिता
innocuous *a.* हानि न पहुंचाने वाला
innovate *v.t.* नई खोज करना, नई रीति चलाना
innovation *n.* नई रीति* या पद्धति* या खोज*
innovator *n.* प्रवर्तक, अन्वेषक

innumerable *a.* असंख्य, अगणित, अनगिनत
inoculate *v.t.* टीका लगाना
inoculation *n.* टीका
inoculator *n.* टीका लगाने वाला
inoffensive *a.* आपत्तिरहित, निरापद
inoperative *a.* बेकार, विफल
inopportune *a.* असामयिक, बेमौका
inquest *n.* अन्वीक्षण, जांच*
inquire *v.t. & i.* पूछना, जांचना
inquiry *n.* इन्क्वायरी, पूछ-ताछ*, तहक़ीकात*
inquisition *n.* जांच*, खोज*
inquisitive *a.* जिज्ञासु, कुतूहली
inquisitor *n.* जिज्ञासा दिखाने वाला
insane *a.* उन्मत्त, पागल
insanity *n.* उन्माद, पागलपन
inscribe *v.t.* लिखना, अंकित करना, एक आकृति के भीतर दूसरी आकृति बनाना
inscription *n.* शिलालेख
insect *n.* कृमि, कीड़ा-मकोड़ा, तुच्छ प्राणी
insecticide *n.* कीटनाशक
insecure *a.* अरक्षित
insensibility *n.* असंवेदन-शीलता, जड़ता*, मूर्च्छा*

insensible *a.* अरसंवेद्य, अचेत

insensibly *adv.* अलक्ष्य रूप में

inseparable *a.* न पृथक् करने योग्य

insert *v.t.* डालना, रखना, बैठाना

insertion *n.* बैठाना, जरदोजी का काम

inside *n., a. & adv.* भीतरी भाग, भीतर, अन्दर

insidious *a.* कपटी, छली, धूर्त

insignificance *n.* अगौरव, तुच्छता*

insignificant *a.* अनावश्यक, तुच्छ

insincere *a.* कपटी, भूठा

insinuate *v.t.* धीरे-धीरे भड़काना, संकेत करना

insinuation *n.* आक्षेप, फुसलाव

insinuator *n.* भड़काने वाला

insipid *a.* रसहीन, बेस्वाद, फीका, मंद

insipidity *n.* फीकापन

insist *v.t.* दृढ़ता से कहना, हठ करना

insistence *n.* हठ, जोर, जिद, आग्रह

insolate *v.t.* धूप में सुखाना

insolation *n.* शुद्ध करने के लिए सूर्य की किरणों के सामने रखना, आतपन

insolence *n.* घृष्टता*, गुस्ताखी*, बदतमीजी*

insolent *a.* घृष्ट, असभ्य, ढीठ

insoluble *n.* न घुलने योग्य, असाध्य, जटिल

insolvable *a.* व्याख्या न करने योग्य

insolvency *n.* दिवालियापन

insolvent *a.* दिवालिया

inspect *v.t.* निगरानी करना, मुआइना करना, जांचना

inspection *n.* निरीक्षण, मुआइना

inspector *n.* (*fem.* inspectress) इन्सपेक्टर, निरीक्षक

inspiration *n.* प्रेरणा*

inspirator *n.* हवा या भाप लेने का यन्त्र

inspire *v.t.* प्रेरित करना

instability *n.* अस्थिरता*, क्षणभंगुरता*

install *v.t.* अभिषेक करना, पदासीन करना, स्थापित करना, जमाना, गाड़ना, लगाना

installation *n.* अभिषेक, स्थापना

instalment *n.* किस्त*

instance *n.* उदाहरण, संकेत, घटना*, *v.t.* दृष्टान्त देना

instant *a.* आवश्यक, तुरंत; *n.* वर्तमान काल, क्षण

instantaneous *a.* क्षणिक

instantly *adv.* तत्काल, तुरंत

instigate *v.t.* उत्तेजित करना, बहकाना

instigation *n.* भड़काव, बहकाव

instigator *n.* बहकाने या भड़काने वाला व्यक्ति

instil *v.t.* (*p.t.* instilled) चित्त पर प्रभाव डालना

instinct *n.* सहज ज्ञान, स्वाभाविक बुद्धि*

instinctive *a.* स्वाभाविक, प्राकृतिक

institute *v.t.* खड़ा करना, स्थापित करना, आरम्भ करना; *n.* व्यवस्था*, नियम, संस्था*, संस्थान

institution *n.* सभा*, समाज, संस्था*

instruct *v.t.* शिक्षा देना, पढ़ाना, समझाना

instruction *n.* उपदेश (ब०व०) आज्ञा*

instructive *a.* उपदेशपूर्ण

instructor *n.* (*fem.* instructress) अध्यापक, शिक्षक

instrument *n.* यन्त्र, अस्त्र, साधन, लेख पत्र

instrumental *a.* साधक, सहायक, बाजा संबंधी; ∼ music वाद्य संगीत

instrumentalist *n.* वादक

insubordinate *a.* अवज्ञाकारी,

उद्धत

insubordination *n.* अविनय, आज्ञाभंग, अवज्ञा*

insufferable *a.* असह्य, दुःसह, दम्भी

insufficient *a.* अपर्याप्त, नाकाफ़ी

insular *a.* टापू संबंधी, संकुचित विचार का, जलवेष्टित

insularity *n.* जल से घिराव, संकीर्णता*

insulate *v.t.* बिजली की धारा जाने का मार्ग, अलगाना, अलग करना, संवाह रोकना

insulation *n.* पृथक्करण

insulator *n.* बिजली की धारा रोकने वाला

insult *n.* अपमान, अपकीर्ति*, तिरस्कार; *v.t.* निन्दा करना, अपमानित करना, गाली देना

insuperable *a.* अलंघ्य, अजेय

insupportable *a.* असह्य, असहाय

insurance *n.* बीमा, रक्षा*; life insurance जीवन-बीमा

insure *v.t.* बीमा करना

insurgent *a. & n.* राजद्रोही, बलवाई

insurmountable *a.* दुर्गम, अजेय

insurrection *n.* राजविद्रोह, बलवा

insurrectionary *a.* बलवाई, विद्रोही

intact *a.* अस्पृष्ट, अछूता, अक्षत, पूर्ण

intangible *a.* अग्राह्य, अस्पृश्य, न छूने योग्य

integral *a.* सम्पूर्ण, पूरा

integrate *v.t.* सम्पूर्ण करना, जोड़ना, एक करना

integration *n.* समाकलन, एकीकरण

integrity *n.* ईमानदारी*, पवित्रता*

intellect *n.* बुद्धि*, ज्ञान (समझ)

intellectual *a.* बुद्धि-संबंधी, अति बुद्धिमान

intelligence *n.* बुद्धि*, ज्ञान, समाचार, सूचना*

intelligent *a.* बुद्धिमान, सुबोध

intelligible *a.* सुबोध, स्पष्ट

intelligibly *adv.* बुद्धिमानी से

intense *a.* प्रचण्ड, तीव्र, अत्यन्त

intensify *v.t. & i.* (*p.t.* intensified) तीव्र करना या होना

intensity *n.* तीव्रता*, गहनता*

intensive *a.* प्रखर, प्रचण्ड, गहन, घन

intent *n.* अभिलाषा*, इच्छा*, उद्देश्य, इरादा; to all intents and purposes सर्वथा

intention *n.* अभिप्राय, आशय, इरादा

intentional *a.* इच्छानुरूप, जानबूझकर

interact *v.t.* परस्पर प्रभाव डालना

intercept *v.t.* अवरोध करना, रोकना

interchange *v.t.* लेन-देन करना, हेरा-फेरी करना; *n.* बदलाव, फेरा-फेरी*

intercourse *n.* अन्योन्य संसर्ग, समागम, मेलजोल, संभोग

interdepend *v.t.* एक दूसरे पर निर्भर करना

interdependence *n.* अन्योन्य या पारस्परिक आश्रय

interest *n.* लाभ, स्वार्थ, सूद, सुविधा*, कल्याण, हित, अनुराग, प्रेम; *v.t.* चित्त आकर्षित करना, अभिरुचि या दिलचस्पी पैदा करना

interested *a.* स्वार्थी, अनुरक्त, रुचि रखनेवाला

interesting *a.* चित्तरंजक, सुहावना, आनन्ददायक

interfere *v.t.* विघ्न डालना, निरोध करना, दखल देना, हस्तक्षेप करना

interference *n.* विघ्न, हस्तक्षेप

interim *adv.* बीच में; *n.* अन्तरिम

interior *a.* भीतरी; भीतरी भाग

interjacent *a.* मध्य का, त्रिचला

interject *v.t.* एकाएक बीच में बोल उठना

interjection *n.* विस्मयादि-बोधक शब्द

interlock *v.t. & i.* आलिंगन करना, गुथना

interlude *n.* नाटक के अंकों के बीच का छोटा अभिनय, विष्कम्भ, अन्तराल

intermeddle *v.t.* दूसरे के कार्य में हस्तक्षेप करना

intermediary *n.* मध्यस्थ, पंच

intermediate *n.* बीच का, मध्यवर्ती, इन्टर (कक्षा या परीक्षा)

intermingle *v.t. & i.* मिश्रण करना, मिलाना, मिलना

intern *v.t.* सीमा के बाहर जाने की अनुज्ञा न देना, नजरबन्द करना, कैद करना

internal *a.* आन्तरिक, भीतरी

international *a.* अन्तर्राष्ट्रीय

interplay *n.* परस्पर क्रिया*

interpret *v.t.* व्याख्या करना, भाषान्तर करना, अनुवाद करना

interpretation *n.* अर्थ, व्याख्या

interpreter *n.* व्याख्याकार, दुभाषिया

interrogate *v.t.* प्रश्न पूछना

interrogation *n.* प्रश्न; note of interrogation प्रश्न चिह्न; interrogative *a.* प्रश्नवाचक

interrupt *v.t.* रोकना, टोकना, विघ्न डालना

interruption *n.* विघ्न, रुकावट*

intersect *v.t.* एक दूसरे को काटना, दो टुकड़े करना

intersection *n.* कटाव

interval *n.* अन्तर, प्रधकाल, विराम, मध्यान्तर

intervene *v.i.* बीच में आना, विघ्न डालना

intervention *n.* व्यवधान, विघ्न, हस्तक्षेप

interview *n.* इन्टरव्यू, भेंट, साक्षात्कार

intestinal *a.* आंत-संबंधी

intestine *n.* (*usu. pl.*) आंतड़ी*, आंत*

intimacy *n.* प्रतिपरिचय, प्रतिसंसर्ग

intimate *a.* अन्तरंग, सुपरिचित; *v.t.* सूचना देना, सूचित करना

intimation *n.* सन्देश, सूचना*

intimidate *v.t.* डराना, धमकाना

intimidation *n.* धमकी*, डांट*

intimidator *n.* धमकाने वाला

into *prep.* भीतर, में

intolerable असह्य, न सहने योग्य

intoxicant *n. & a.* उन्माद लानेवाला, मादक, नशा

intoxicate *v.t.* मदिरा से उन्मत्त करना, मतवाला बनाना

intoxication *n.* उन्माद, नशा

intrench *v.t.* खाई बनाना

intrepid *a.* वीर, निडर, साहसी

intrigue *v.t.* साजिश करना; *n.* साजिश, षड्यन्त्र

intriguer *n.* साजिश करनेवाला, षड्यंत्रकारी

intrinsic *a.* स्वाभाविक, वास्तविक

introduce *v.t.* प्रवेश करना, लाना, परिचय कराना, आरम्भ करना, उत्पन्न करना

introduction *n.* परिचय, प्रस्तावना*

introductory *a.* परिचय संबंधी, आरम्भिक, प्रस्तावना का

introspect *v.i.* अन्तर्दृष्टि डालना, आत्मपरीक्षण करना, भीतर देखना

introspection *n.* आत्मपरीक्षण

intrude *v.t. & i.* घुस पड़ना, बिना अधिकार के प्रवेश करना

intrusion *n.* विना आज्ञा प्रवेश, अनुचित हस्तक्षेप

intrusive *a.* बिना अधिकार के प्रवेश करने वाला

intuition *n.* अन्तर्ज्ञान, सहज ज्ञान

intuitive *a.* अन्तर्ज्ञान से प्राप्त

invade *v.t.* चढ़ाई करना, लंघन करना

invalid *n.* अशक्त, अपाहिज

invalid *a.* दुर्बल, अशक्त, नियम-विरुद्ध

invalidate *v.t.* शक्ति कम करना, रद्द करना

invaluable *a.* बहुमूल्य, अनमोल

invasion *n.* आक्रमण, घावा

invective *n.* आक्षेप, गाली*, फटकार*

invent *v.t.* कल्पना करना, आविष्कार करना, मनगढ़न्त करना

invention *n.* ईजाद*, कल्पना*, आविष्कार

inventive *a.* कल्पनाचतुर, आविष्कार-कुशल

inventor *n.* (*fem.* inventress) आविष्कारक

invert *v.t.* उलटना क्रम बदलना

invest *v.t.* घेरना, लाभ के लिए धन लगाना, पद पर नियुक्त करना

investiture *n.* अधिकार देने

338

का संस्कार

investigate *v.t.* पता लगाना, जांच करना

investigation *n.* खोज*, जांच*

investment *n.* घिराव, घन लगाना, धन का विनियोग

invigilate *v.t.* परीक्षा में विद्यार्थियों की निगरानी करना

invigilation *n.* परीक्षा में निगरानी*

invigilator *n.* निरीक्षक

invincibility *n.* अजेयता*

invincible *a* न जीते जाने योग्य, अजेय

inviolable *a.* भ्रष्ट न करने योग्य, पवित्र

inviolably *adv.* पवित्रता से

invisible *a.* अदृश्य

invitation *n.* निमन्त्रण, बुलावा

invite *v.t.* मांगना, निमन्त्रण देना, आकर्षित करना

invoice *n.* बीजक, चलान

invoke *v.t.* अभिमन्त्रित करना, रक्षा के लिए ईश्वर से स्तुति करना

involve *v.t.* फंसाना, संयुक्त करना, मिलाना, लपेटना

inwards *adv.* भीतरी ओर

irate *a.* क्रुद्ध
क्रोध, रोष
a. आयरलैंड देश का, की भाषा

irksome *a.* क्लेश देनेवाला, दुःखदायी

iron *n.* लोहा, इस्त्री करने का लोहा, (ब० व०) हथकड़ी*, बेड़ी*; *a.* लोहे का, पुष्ट; *v.t.* लोहा देकर चिकनाना या इस्त्री करना, हथकड़ी लगाना; to have too many irons in the fire अनेक कार्यों में लीन होना; to rule with a rod of iron निर्दयता से राज्य करना; to strike while the iron is hot उचित समय पर काम करना

ironical *a.* ताने का, व्यंगात्मक

irony *n.* व्यंगोक्ति*, ताना, व्यंग्य

irradiate *v.i. & t.* चमकना

irrational *a.* विवेकरहित, तर्कहीन

irreconcilable *a.* असंगत, बेमेल, कट्टर दुश्मन, कट्टर विरोधी

irrefutable *a.* अखंडनीय

irregular *a.* नियम-विरुद्ध, बेडौल, टेढ़ा, मर्यादाहीन, अनियमित, अस्थायी (सेना)*

irregularity *n.* अव्यवस्था*, विषमता*, अनियम

irrelevant *a.* असंगत

irrespective *a.* बिना आक्षेप का, पृथक्

irresponsible *a.* अनुत्तरदायी

irrigate *v.t.* भूमि को जल से सींचना

irrigation *n.* सिंचाई*

irritable *a.* शीघ्र क्रुद्ध होने वाला, चिड़चिड़ा

irritant *a.* उत्तेजित करनेवाला

irritate *v.t.* क्रुद्ध करना, चिढ़ाना, कुढ़ाना, उत्तेजित करना

irritation *n.* संताप, आवेग

irruption *n.* विस्फोट, आक्रमण, चढ़ाई*

island *n.* द्वीप, टापू

isobar *n.* समदाब रेखा*, समपीड रेखा*

isolate *v.t.* अलग रखना

isolation *n.* अलग होने की स्थिति*, पृथक्करण

issue *v.i. & t.* बाहर आना, निकलना, आगे बढ़ना, बहना, प्रकाशित करना, अधिकार से देना; *n.* सन्तति*, निर्गम, वादविषय, प्रकाशन

Italian *a.* इटली देश का, इस देश की भाषा*

italics *n. pl.* छापे के अक्षर जो दाहिनी ओर झुके होते हैं, तिरछे अक्षर

item *n.* विषय, वस्तु*, मद*

itinerary *n.* यात्रा का विवरण

ivory *n.* हाथीदांत; *a.* हाथीदांत का बना हुआ

J

jab *v.t.* (*p.t.* jabbed) भोंकना, घुसाना

jabber *v.i.* बन्दर की तरह बड़-बड़ाना

jack *n.* 'जॉन' का प्रचलित रूप, दुष्ट, ताश में का गुलाम, भारी बोझ उठाने का यन्त्र, गधा, जहाज की झंडी*, कटहल

jack-boots *n. pl.* घुटने तक के जूते

jackal *n.* सियार

jacket *n.* जैकेट, मिरजई*, बंडी*, बाहरी ढपना

jade *n.* मरियल घोड़ा; *v.t.* थकाना

jail *n.* जेल*, बन्दीगृह, कैदखाना

jailer *n.* जेलर, बन्दीगृह का अध्यक्ष

jam *n.* मुरब्बा, मीठा अचार; *v.t.* (*p.t.* jammed) कसकर दबाना या निचोड़ना

January *n.* जनवरी

Japan *n.* जापान, जापान की बनी हुई एक प्रकार की कड़ी

वार्निश; *v.t.* ऐसी वार्निश
करना

jar *v.i.* (*p.t.* jarred) घड़घड़ाहट
का शब्द करना, झगड़ना;
n. कर्कश शब्द, मिट्टी या कांच
का घड़ा, जार

jargon *n.* निरर्थक बकवाद*,
बड़बड़ाहट*

jasmine (jessamine) *n.*
चमेली*, बेला*

jasper *n.* सूर्यकान्त मणि*

jaundice *n.* पाण्डु (कमला) रोग

javelin *n.* भाला, बरछी*

jaw *n.* जबड़ा; (ब० व०) मुख

jealous *a* ईर्षालु, डाह करने
वाला

jealously *adv.* ईर्ष्या से

jealousy *n.* डाह*, ईर्ष्या*

jean *n.* जीन नामक कपड़ा

jelly *n.* (*pl.* jellies) मुरब्बा,
मीठी चटनी; *v.t. & i.* जमाना,
जमना

jeopardize *v.t.* आपत्ति में
डालना

jerk *n.* धक्का, झटका

jerkin *n.* जरकिन, कुरती*,
मिरजई*

jerky *a.* धक्का देनेवाला

jersey *n.* जरसी, शरीर में
चिपकी हुई ऊनी बंडी*

jest *n* हंसी, ठट्टा; *v.t.* हंसी
करना

jet *n.* संगमूसा, जल या गैस की
धारा, फौवारा, टोंटी; jet
black चमकीले काले रंग का

Jew *n.* (*fem.* Jewess) यहूदी
जाति का मनुष्य; Jew's-
harp मुरचंग

jewel *n.* मणि*, रत्न; *v.t.*
रत्न-जटित करना

jeweller *n.* जौहरी

jewellery *n.* जवाहिरात

Jewish *a.* यहूदियों का

jilt *n.* दुष्ट स्त्री*; *v.t.* प्रेमी को
आश्वासन देकर तिरस्कार
करना

jingle *n.* टनटनाहट*; *v.i.* टन-
टन शब्द करना

job *n.* सामान्य या छोटा काम,
अवस्था; *v.i.* (*p.t.* jobbed)
छोटा काम करना

jobber *n.* छोटा काम करनेवाला

jobbery *n.* बेईमानी स्वार्थ-
साधन, घूसखोरी

job-work *n.* हलका काम,
ठेके का काम

jockey *n.* घुड़दौड़ का सवार;
v.t. ठगना, धोखा देना

jocular *a.* रसिक, ठिठोलिया

jog *v.t. & i.* (*p.t.* jogged)
हिलाना, ढकेलना, उत्तेजित
करना, धीरे से आगे बढ़ना

join *v.t. & i.* जोड़ना, बांधना,
मिलाना, साटना, साथ होना

joiner n. बढ़ई

joint n. जोड़; a. संयुक्त; joint-stock साझे की पूंजी*

jointly adv. एक साथ काम करते हुए

joke n. हंसी*, ठट्ठा; v.i. हंसी-ठट्ठा करना

joker n. ठिठोलिया, मसखरा

jolly a. विनोदी, रसिक

jolt n. झटका; v.t. झटका देना, हिलाना

jostle v.t. धक्का देना, ढकेलना; n. धक्का, झटका

jot n. कण, अति सूक्ष्म परिमाण या मात्रा; v.t. (p.t. jotted) यादगार के लिए संक्षेप में लिखना

journal n. दैनिक पत्र, बही-खाता, रोजनामचा

journalism n. पत्रकारिता*

journalist n. पत्रकार

journey n. (pl. journeys) देश-भ्रमण, यात्रा; v.i. (p.t. journeyed) यात्रा करना

jovial a. प्रसन्न

joviality n. आनन्द, प्रसन्नता*

joy n. आनन्द, हर्ष

joyful, joyous a. आनन्दपूर्ण, हर्षित

joyously adv. आनन्द से

jubilance n. परमानन्द

jubilant a. आनन्द करनेवाला

jubilate v.i. परम आनन्द दिखाना या मनाना

jubilation n. आनन्द-नाद

jubilee n. जयंती*; diamond-jubilee हीरक जयंती

judge v.t. & i. न्याय करना, राय बनाना निश्चय करना, अनुमान करना, आलोचना करना; n. जज, न्यायाधीश

judgment n. न्यायाधीश का निर्णय, दण्ड की आज्ञा, अनुमान, विचार; judgment-day प्रलय का दिन; judgment seat धर्मासन

judicature n. न्याय का अधिकार, न्यायालय

judicial a. न्याय-सम्बन्धी

judicious a. न्याययुक्त, उचित

jug n. जलपात्र, घड़ा, सुराही; v.t. (p.t. jugged) घड़े में उबालना

juggle v.i. बाजीगरी दिखाना

juggler n. बाजीगर

jugglery n. बाजीगरी*

juice n. रस, अर्क

July n. जुलाई

jumble v.t. बिना क्रम के मिलाना या रखना; n. गड़बड़, मेल, गड़बड़ी*

jump v.i कूदना, उछलना; n. कूदान, छलांग*, एकाएक दाम की वृद्धि; to jump out of

one's skin भय या आनन्द
से उछल पड़ना

junction *n.* जंकशन, संगम,
सन्धि*, रेलवे की लाइनों का
मेल

juncture *n.* उचित वेला या
समय

June *n.* जून

jungle *n.* जंगल, वन

junior *a.* आयु या पद में छोटा

juniority *n.* छोटापन

junk *n.* कूड़ा-कर्कट

Jupiter *n.* रोम के देवराज
बृहस्पति

jurisdiction *n.* अधिकारक्षेत्र

jurisprudence *n.* न्यायशास्त्र

jurist *n.* न्यायज्ञ

juror *n.* जूरियों में से एक व्यक्ति

jury *n.* जूरी, पंच

juryman *n.* पंचों में से एक

just *a.* सच्चा, धार्मिक, यथार्थ,
निष्पक्ष, नियमित, उचित;
just now अभी

justice *n.* न्याय, सत्यता*,
अपक्षपात, न्यायाधिपति; to
do justice to किसी को
अधिकार देना, सचाई का
व्यवहार करना, पूरी तरह से
आनन्द लेना

justifiable *a.* न्यायोचित

justification *n.* दोषमुक्ति*,
समर्थन

justify *v.t.* (*p.t.* justified)
न्याय्य ठहराना, निर्दोष
बतलाना, उचित कारण
बतलाना

justly *adv.* न्यायपूर्वक

jute *n.* जूट, पटुआ

juvenile *a.* यौवन-सम्बन्धी,
बालकपन का

juvenility *n.* नौजवानी*,
बालपन

K

Kaiser *n.* जर्मनी के राजा की
उपाधि*

kaleidoscope *n.* बहुरूपदर्शक

kaleidoscopic *a.* सर्वदा
बदलनेवाला

kangaroo *n.* कंगारू

keen *a.* चोखा, पुष्ट, कड़ुवा,
उत्कट, उत्सुक

keen *v.i.* मृतक के लिए विलाप
करना

keenness *n.* उत्सुकता*

keep *v.t. & i.* (*p.t. & p.p.*
kept) पकड़ना, सुरक्षित
रखना, यत्न करना, रक्षा

करना, रखना. उत्सव मनाना;
to keep an eye on नज़र
रखना; to keep company
with साथ देना; to keep
one's word प्रतिज्ञा पालन
करना; to keep under
अधीन रखना; to keep up
स्थापित रखना, गिरने से
रोकना

keeper *n.* रखनेवाला, रक्षा
करने वाला

kerchief *n.* रूमाल

kernel *n.* गुद्दा, गरी, तत्त्व,
सार

kerosene *n.* किरोसीन, मिट्टी
का तेल

kettle *n.* देगची*, पतीली*,
केतली*

key *n.* (*pl.* keys) ताली*,
कुंजी*, व्याख्या*, टीका*,
बाजे का पर्दा

key *n.* नीचा टापू

keyboard *n.* की-बोर्ड, बाजे या
टाइप-राइटर इ० में हाथ से
दबाने के पर्दे

key-note *n.* प्रधान राग

keystone *n.* कमान (मेहराब)
के बीच की ईंट या पत्थर,
प्रधान सिद्धांत

kick *v.t.* लात मारना, पर
झटकारना; *n.* लत्ती, पर
की फटकार

kid *n.* बकरी का बच्चा, इसकी
खाल का चमड़ा, बच्चा

kiddy *n.* छोटा बच्चा

kidnap *v.t.* (*p.t.* kidnap-
ped) चोरी से किसी मनुष्य
को भगा ले जाना

kidnapper *n.* चोरी से भगा ले
जानेवाला, उठाईगीर

kidney *n.* गुर्दा

kidney bean *n.* एक प्रकार की
सेम*, मूंग*

kill *v.t.* मार डालना, नष्ट
करना; to kill two birds
with one stone एक पंथ
दो काज

kiln *n.* भट्टी*, आवां

kilo *n.* मेट्रिक नाप में 'एक
हज़ार' के लिए उपसर्ग

kind *a.* दयालु, सदय, समवेदना-
पूर्ण; *n.* जाति*, रीति*,
प्रकृति*, प्रकार; payment
in kind रुपयों के बदले माल
द्वारा भुगतान

kindergarten *n.* किंडरगार्टेन,
बालकनजीबारी

kindle *v.t.* आग सुलगाना,
प्रज्वलित करना, उत्तेजित
करना

king *n.* (*fem.* queen) भूपति;
राजा; king of kings
ईश्वर; king of terror यम

kingdom *n.* राज्य

kinship *n.* रक्त-संबंध

kiss *v.t.* चूमना, लाड़ करना;
to kiss the book बाइबिल
चूमकर शपथ खाना; to kiss
the ground दण्डवत् करना;
to kiss the rod विनीत
भाव से दण्ड स्वीकार करना

kit *n.* सिपाही या मल्लाह की
सामग्री का झोला, चिकारा,
सारंगी*

kitchen *n.* रसोईघर, पाकगृह;
kitchen-garden फल या
तरकारी का बगीचा; kitchen
maid रसोईघर की दासी*

kite *n.* चील*, पतंग*, गुड्डी*,
कनकैया*; kite balloon
जमीन में बंधा हुआ गुब्बारा

kith *n.* जान-पहिचान संबंधी

kitten *n.* बिल्ली का बच्चा

kittle *a.* शान्त न करके योग्य,
दुराराध्य

kitty *n.* बिल्ली का बच्चा

knee *n.* घुटना; to bring one
to his knees अधीन करना;
knee-deep घुटने तक गहरा

kneel *v.i.* (*p.t. & p.p.*
knelt) घुटना टेकना

knife *n.* (*pl.* knives) छुरी*,
चाकू; *v.t.* छुरी भोंककर
मारना; to play a good
knife and fork पेट-भर
भोजन करना

knight *n.* योद्धा, शूरवीर,
अंग्रेजी सर की उपाधि, शतरंज
के खेल में 'वज़ीर'; *v.t.*
नाइट की पदवी देना

knight-errant (*pl.* knights-
errant) *n.* साहसिक कार्य
की खोज में घूमनेवाला वीर;
knight-errantry; *n.* इस
प्रकार की वीरता*

knighthood *n.* नाइट की
पदवी*

knightly *a.* नाइट् सम्बन्धी

knit *v.t.* (*p.t.* knitted,
knit) बुनना, जोड़ना,
मिलाना; knitting needle;
जाली बुनने की सलाई या
सूई; to knit one's brows
भौंह सिकोड़ना

knock *v.t. & i.* दस्तक देना,
धक्का देना, खटखटाना,
घूमना; *n.* धक्का, खट-
खटाहट*, दस्तक*; to knock
about रुखाई से व्यवहार
करना, बेकार घूमना; to
knock down मारकर गिरा
देना; to knock off काम
रोक देना, जल्दी से पूरा
करना; to knock out
पीटना; to knock together
जल्दी से मिला देना; to
knock under अधीन होना;
to knock up जगाना

knot *n.* गांठ*, गुच्छा, वृक्ष-संधि*, कठिनाई*, मण्डली*, 6080 फुट की नाप; *v.t.* (*p.t.* knotted) गांठ बांधना; to cut the knot कठिनता को जीतना

know *v.t. & i.* (*p.t.* knew, *p.p.* known) सूचित होना, जानना, समझना, पहिचानना, परिचित होना

knowledge *n.* ज्ञान, बोध, विद्या*, परिचय

kodak *n.* कोडक, फोटो उतारने का छोटा कैमरा

kudos *n.* कीर्ति*, यश

L

label *n.* लेबुल, नामपत्र; *v.t.* (*p.t.* labelled) नामपत्र या चिप्पी चिपकाना

labial *a.* ओष्ठ-सम्बन्धी; *n.* ओठ से उच्चारित अक्षर की ध्वनि*

laboratory *n.* (*pl.* laboratories) प्रयोगशाला*

laborious *a.* परिश्रमी, थकाने वाला

laboriously *adv.* श्रम से, उद्योग से

labour *v.i.* परिश्रम करना, कठोर श्रम करना, प्रयत्न करना; *n.* परिश्रम, उद्योग, व्यापार, प्रसव-वेदना; labour party श्रमिकों का दल, मजदूर दल, ब्रिटेन के मजदूर दल का नाम

labour welfare work *a.* श्रमिक-कल्याण-कार्य

laboured *a.* असरल, कृत्रिम

labourer *n.* श्रमिक, मजदूर

labourite *n.* लेबर पार्टी का सदस्य

labyrinth *n.* भूलभुलैया* भंवरजाल

lac *n.* लाह, लाख (संख्या*)

lace *n.* फीता, लेस, बिनी हुई डोरी*; *v.t.* फीते से बांधना, सजाना; lace pillow तकिया जिस पर आलपीन गाड़कर लैस बनाई जाती है

lack *n.* कमी*; *v.i. & t.* कमी होना, चाहना, छोड़ना

lackey *n.* (*pl.* lackeys) अनुचर, टहलुआ

lack-lustre *a.* मन्द, बिना चमक का

laconic *a.* अल्प, संक्षेप

lacuna *n.* (*pl.* lacunae) अन्तराल, शून्य स्थान

lad *n.* (*fem.* lass) बालक, छोकरा

ladder *n.* सीढ़ी

lade *v.t.* (*p.p.* laden) भार रखना, जहाज पर बोझ लादना

lady *n.* (*pl.* ladies) कुलस्त्री*, भद्र महिला*, घर की मालकिन*; lady-in-waiting रानी* की दासी*

lag *v.i.* (*p.t.* lagged) धीरे चलना, पिछड़ जाना

lake *n.* झील*, सरोवर; *n.* एक प्रकार का गुलाबी रंग; lake poets इंगलैंड के तीन प्रधान कवि कोलरिज, सदी तथा वर्ड्सवर्थ इस नाम से पुकारे जाते हैं

Lama *n.* लामा, तिब्बत के बौद्ध भिक्षु

lamasery *n.* तिब्बत के बौद्ध भिक्षुओं का मठ

lamb *n.* भेड़ का बच्चा, मेमना; like a lamb नम्रता से; a wolf in lamb's skin धूर्त मनुष्य

lame *a.* लंगड़ा, असन्तोषजनक, अपूर्ण; *v.t.* लंगड़ा करना

lament *v.i.* विलाप करना, रोना; *n.* विलाप

lamentable *a.* दुःखी, शोचनीय

lamentation *n.* विलाप, रुलाई*

lamp *n.* लम्प, दीपक; lampblack कालिख, काजल; lamplighter लम्प जलाने वाला; lamp-post बिजली का खम्भा; spirit lamp स्पिरिट से जलने का चूल्हा

lampoon *n.* निन्दालेख, आक्षेप; *v.t.* निन्दालेख लिखना

lance *n.* बरछा, बल्लम; *v.t.* भाला भोंकना, नश्तर लगाना

lancer *n.* बल्लमधारी सैनिक

land *n.* स्थल, भूमि*, पृथ्वी*, राष्ट्र, देश; *v.t. & i.* तीर पर रखना, भूमि पर उतरना; arable land जोतने की भूमि*; land of the living संसारी जीवन

landing *n.* भूमि पर उतार

landlord *n.* (*fem.* landlady) जमींदार, ताल्लुकेदार

landmark *n.* सीमाचिह्न

landscape *n.* नयन-गोचर प्रदेश, ऐसे स्थान का चित्र, प्राकृतिक दृश्य

lane *n.* संकरी गली*

language *n.* भाषा*, बोली*, बोलने का ढंग; dead language प्राचीन भाषा जो अब बोली नहीं जाती

languish *v.i.* शिथिल होना,

दुर्बल होना, मन्द होना

lanky *a.* (*comp.* lankier *sup.* lankiest) भद्दा, दुबला और लम्बा (मनुष्य)

lantern *a.* लालटेन, कण्डील; chinese lantern कागज़ की लालटेन, कण्डील; magic lantern एक प्रकार की लालटेन जिसमें रक्खे हुए कांच के छोटे चित्र का बड़ा प्रति-बिम्ब पर्दे पर पड़ता है, माया-दीप, चित्र-दीप

lap *n.* अंचल, गोद, पल्ला, किनारा; lap-dog एक प्रकार का छोटा कुत्ता

lapse *v.i.* सरकना, घसकना; *n.* पतन, गिराव, चूक*, lapse of time समय का बीतना

lapwing *n.* टिटिहरी*

large *a.* बड़ा, भारी, चौड़ा, विपुल, उदार; at large स्वतंत्र, मुक्त; gentleman at large बेकार मनुष्य; of large nature दयालु; people at large सामान्य लोग

largely *adv.* अधिक परिमाण में

lark *n.* भारद्वाज पक्षी, लवा

lascivious *a.* कामुक

lash *v.t. & i.* हिलाना, हिलना, ज़ोर से मारना; *n.* चाबुक की मार*

lass *n.* (*mas.* lad) कन्या*, कुमारी*

lassie *n.* कुमारी* के लिए प्रेम का शब्द

last *v.i. & t.* टिकना, सहना; *n.* जूता बनाने का फर्मा; *a. & adv* अन्तिम; last thing to do पक्का इरादा; to breathe one's last अन्तिम श्वास लेना, मरना; will last two weeks दो सप्ताह चल जाएगा

lasting *a.* स्थायी, देर तक ठहरनेवाला

lastly *adv.* अन्त में

latch *n.* अगड़ी*, सिटकिनी*; *v.t.* अगड़ी या सिटकिनी से बन्द करना

latchet *n.* जूता बांधने का तस्मा या फीता

late *a.* (*comp.* latter, later, *sup.* latest, last) विलम्ब से आया हुआ, पीछे का, बहुत दिन या रात चढ़े, गत, मृत; *adv.* अचिरकाल से, थोड़े दिन हुए

lately *adv.* थोड़े दिन हुए

latent *a.* अप्रत्यक्ष, गुप्त, छिपा हुआ

later *a.* उत्तरकाल का, बाद का

lathe *n.* खराद

lather *n.* साबुन का फेन या झाग; *v.i. & t.* फेन से भरना,

भागदार होना

Latin *a.* प्राचीन रोमवासी संबंधी, रोम की भाषा

Latinize *v.t.* शब्दों में रोम की भाषा का रूपान्तर करना

latitude *n.* चौड़ाई*, विस्तार, स्वतन्त्रता*, अक्षांश

latitudinal *a.* अक्षांश-संबंधी

latrine *n.* टट्टी*, संडास, शौचालय

latter *a.* पिछला

lattice *n.* जाली*, झंझरी*

laud *v.t.* प्रशंसा करना, गुण वर्णन करना; *n.* प्रशंसा*, स्तुति*

laudable *a.* सराहने योग्य

laugh *v.t. & i.* हंसना, हंसी उड़ाना; *n.* हंसी*, मुसकुराहट*; to laugh at हंसी उड़ाना; to laugh away किसी विषय को हंसकर उड़ा देना; to laugh down हंसकर चुप करा देना; to laugh in one's sleeve गुप्त रूप से प्रसन्न होना; to laugh off हंसकर समाप्त करना; to laugh over हंस-हंसकर शास्त्रार्थ करना

laughable *a.* हंसाने योग्य, हंसने योग्य, हास्यकर

laughing *n. & a.* हंसी, हंसने वाला

laughter *n.* हंसी*, खिलखिलाहट*

launch *v.t. & i.* पानी में सरकना या डालना, फेंकना, चालू करना; *n.* नए जहाज को पानी में उतारना, लड़ाई के जहाज की सबसे बड़ी नाव*

launder *v.t.* धोना और लोहा करना

launderer *n.* धोबी

laundress *n. fem.* धोबिन*

laundry *n.* लॉण्ड्री, कपड़ा धोने का स्थान

laurel *n.* चमकदार पत्तियों का एक पौधा, जयपत्र

lava *n.* लावा, भूराल, ज्वालामुखी पर्वत से निकलने वाला पिघला हुआ पदार्थ

lavatory *n.* शौचालय टट्टीघर

lavish *a.* अतिव्ययी, खर्चीला, शाहखर्च; *v.t.* व्यर्थ खर्च करना (उड़ाना)

law *n.* कानून, आचार, शासन, नियम, विधि*, सिद्धान्त; law-suit अभियोग, नालिश, मुकदमा; code of laws धर्मशास्त्र; versed in law विधि में प्रवीण; to go to law अभियोग करना; to take law into one's own hands शक्ति द्वारा बदला लेना

lawful *a*. शास्त्रोक्त, स्वत्व का; lawful age प्राप्त वय

lawgiver *n*. शास्त्रकार, विधि बनानेवाला

lawless *a*. नियम-विरुद्ध

lawn *n*. महीन मलमल, घास का मैदान, लॉन; lawn tennis लॉन टेनिस, घास पर खेलने का एक प्रकार का गेंद का खेल

lawyer *n*. वकील, मुख्तार

lax *a*. शिथिल, भ्रष्टचरित

laxative *a*. पेट को मृदु करने वाली या जुलाब की दवा

laxity *n*. शिथिलता*, ढीलापन

lay *v.t*. (*p.t*. laid, *p.p*. lain) रखना, लिटाना, दांव लगाना, अंडा देना, गाड़ना; to lay bare प्रगट करना, पता लगाना; to lay by संचित करना; to lay down भूमि पर रखना; to lay hands on पकड़ना, अधिकार में करना; to lay in wait घात में रहना; to lay out व्यय करना; to lay up सुरक्षित करना, अलग रखना, जमा करना; to lay waste नष्ट करना

lay *a*. अव्यावसायिक, जन-साधारण का

layer *n*. परत*, तह*

layman *n*. अप्रविज्ञ जन, साधारण आदमी

lazily *adv*. सुस्ती से

laziness *n*. आलस्य

lazy *a*. (*comp* lazier, *sup*. laziest) आलसी, अनुद्योगी काहिल, सुस्त

lead *n*. सीसा, पेंसिल में का भीतरी लिखनेवाला भाग; red lead सिन्दूर; white lead सफेदा

lead *v.t. & i*. (*p.t. & p.p*. led) मार्ग दिखलाना, नेतृत्व करना; *n*. नायकत्व, रहनु-माई*; to lead astray बहकाना; to lead on ललचाना

leaden *a*. भारी, सीसे का

leader *n*. लीडर, नेता, अग्रलेख; leader of the house सभाप्रणी; leader of opposition विरोधी दल का नेता

leading *a*. प्रधान, मुख्य

leaf *n*. (*pl*. leaves) पत्ता, पत्ती*, वर्क; to turn over a new leaf सुधरना

leafage *n*. पत्तियां*

leaflet *n*. छोटी पत्ती*, पर्चा

leafy *a*. पत्तियों से पूर्ण

league, *n*. संघटन, गुट्ट, तीन मील का नाप

leak *n.* छेद, दरार*; *v.i. & t.* छेद में से टपकना या चूना या टपकाना

leakage *n.* टपक, रसाव, रहस्योद्घाटन

lean *a.* कृश, दुर्बल; *v.t.* झुकाना, सहारा देना, टेकना

leap *v.i.* (*p.t.* leaped or leapt) उछलना, कूदना; *n.* छलांग*, कुदान*; leap-year वह साल जिसमें फरवरी महीने में 29 दिन होते हैं

learn *v.i.* (*p.t.* learned, learnt) विद्या, बुद्धि या अनुभव प्राप्त करना; to learn by heart कंठस्थ करना

learned *a.* विद्वान

learner *n.* शिक्षार्थी, नवसिखुआ

learning *n.* विद्या*, पाण्डित्य

lease *n.* पट्टा; *v.t.* पट्टा लेना या देना

lease-holder *n.* पट्टेदार

least *a.* (*sup.* of less) सबसे छोटा; at least कम से कम; in the least किंचितमात्र भी

leather *n.* पशु का कमाया हुआ चमड़ा

leave *v.t.* (*p.t. & p.p.* left) रहने देना, छोड़ना, चले जाना, छोड़कर मरना; *n.* अवकाश, छुट्टी*, प्रस्थान, विदाई*, आज्ञा*; to take leave of विदाई लेना; to leave off त्यागना, छोड़ना

lecture *n.* व्याख्यान, उपदेश, *v.t.* व्याख्यान देना, डांटना

lecturer *n.* व्याख्यान देनेवाला, कॉलेज का अध्यापक

ledger *n.* बहीखाता, प्रपंजी*

leech *n.* चिकित्सक, वैद्य, जोंक*, *v.t.* घाव में जोंक लगाना

leek *n.* प्याज के प्रकार की एक वनस्पति

left (*p.t. & p.p.* of leave, left) *a.* बायां, (राज.) वाम-पंथी; left-hander बयंहत्था, फूहर; ~handed compliment व्याजनिन्दा

leftward *a.* बाईं ओर

leg *n.* पैर, टेबुल का पाया; to shake a leg नाचना; to take to one's legs भाग जाना; to stand on one's own legs अपनी कमाई का भरोसा करना

legacy *n.* मृत्यु-पत्र, बपौती

legal *a.* वैध, कानूनी

legality *n.* वैधानिकता

legalize *v.t.* वैध बनाना, कानूनी रूप देना

legate *n.* दूत, उपराजदूत

legatee *n.* उत्तराधिकारी

legation *n.* दूतावास

legend *n.* पौराणिक कथा*, उपाख्यान, दिव्य-चरित्र

legendary *a.* पौराणिक कथा सम्बन्धी

legible *a.* स्पष्ट अक्षर का, पढ़ने योग्य

legibly *adv.*. स्पष्टता से

legion *n.* सेना*, लश्कर*

legislate *v.t.* विधान बनाना

legislation *n.* विधान

legislative *a.* विधान-संबंधी

legislator *n.* विधायक

legislature *n.* विधान सभा*

legitimacy *n.* वैधता*, सच्चाई*

legitimate *a.* न्याय्य, क़ानूनी

leisure *n.* अवकाश, छुट्टी; *a.* सावकाश. खाली

leisurely *a.* यथावकाश, धीरे-धीरे, आराम से

lemon *n.* नीबू

lemonade *n.* लेमनेड, नीबू का शर्बत

lend *v.t.* (*p.t. & p.p.* lent) उधार देना, किराए पर देना; to lend a hand सहायता देना

length *n.* लम्बान, फैलाव*, दूरी*; at length विस्तार-पूर्वक

lengthen *v.t.* बढ़ाना, लम्बा करना

lengthwise, (lengthways) *advs.* लम्बेबल

lengthy *a.* लम्बा

lenience, leniency *ns.* मृदुता*, कोमलता*, सदयता*, ढिलाई*

lenient *a.* मृदु, कोमल, दयालु

lens *n.* (*pl.* lenses) लेंस, शीशा, ताल

leopard *n.* चीता, तेंदुआ

leper *n.* कुष्ठ, रोगी, कोढ़ी

leperous, leprous *a.* कोढ़ रोग संबंधी

leprosy *n.* कुष्ठ, कोढ़*

less *a.* (*comp. of* little) अल्पतर, कमतर; *suf.* 'अभाव' अर्थ का प्रत्यय

lessee *n.* ठेकेदार, पट्टेदार

lessen *v.i. & t.* कम होना या करना

lesser *a.* दो पदार्थों में छोटा, कमतर, अल्पतर

lesson *n.* पाठ, शिक्षा*, उपदेश, उदाहरण, दण्ड; *v.t.* उपदेश देना

lest *conj.* नहीं तो, ऐसा न हो कि

let *v.t. & aux.* (*verb*) (*p.t. & p.p.* let) अनुमति देना, आज्ञा देना, छुट्टी देना, होने देना, किराए पर देना; to let किराए पर देना; to let alone मन पर छोड़

देना; to let down नीचा दिखाना, ढीलना; to let fall गिरने देना; to let go मुक्त करना; to let into प्रवेश करना; to let loose बंधन से मुक्त करना; to let out बाहर निकालना

let *suf.* अर्थार्थक प्रत्यय, यथा 'streamlet'

lethal *a.* घातक, जानलेवा

lethargic *a.* निद्रालु, सुस्त, भारी

lethargy *n.* आलस्य, तन्द्रा*

letter *n.* अक्षर, पत्र, चिट्ठी*; (ब॰व॰) साहित्य; *v.t.* पुस्तक पर नाम छापना या लिखना

level *n.* समतल; *a.* समतल, सपाट, चौरस; *v.t.* चौरस करना, चिकनाना, लक्ष्य करना

lever *n.* लीवर, उत्तोलनदण्ड, प्रभाव उत्पन्न करने का साधन

leverage *n.* लीवर के प्रयोग से प्राप्त शक्ति*

levy *v.t.* (*p.t.* levied) उठाना, कर लगाना; *n.* कर इकट्ठा करने की क्रिया उद्ग्रहण

lexicon *n.* शब्द-संग्रह, कोश

liabilities *n. pl.* ऋण

liability (*pl.* liabilities) दायित्व, देयता*

liable *a.* उत्तरदायी, जवाबदेह, अधीन

liar *n.* झूठा

liasion *n.* अवैध प्रेम, सम्पर्क, ~ officer सम्पर्क अधिकारी

libel *n.* निन्दालेख; *v.i.* (*p.t.* libelled) अपमान-सूचक शब्द व्यवहार करना

liberal *a.* उदार, स्वार्थहीन, शिष्ट, कुलीन

liberalism *n.* स्वतन्त्र विचार, उदारतावाद

liberality *n.* दानशीलता*, उदारता*, पक्षपातहीनता*

liberate *v.t.* मुक्त करना, स्वतन्त्र करना, छोड़ना, रिहा करना

liberation *n.* मुक्ति*, आज़ादी*

liberator *n.* मुक्ति दिलानेवाला

liberty *n. pl.* liberties) स्वाधीनता*, प्राकृतिक अधिकारों का स्वतन्त्र उपभोग, सुविधा*

librarian *n.* लाइब्रेरियन, पुस्तकालय का अध्यक्ष

library *n.* (*pl.* libraries) पुस्तकालय, पुस्तक-संग्रह; walking library बड़ा विद्वान मनुष्य

licence *n.* लेंसन्स, आज्ञा*, अधिकार, दुराचार, नियम का उल्लंघन

license *v.t.* आज्ञा देना, अधिकार देना

licensee *n.* लेंसन्सदार

licentiate *n.* विश्वविद्यालय से प्रमाण-पत्र पाया हुआ मनुष्य

lick *v.t.* जीभ से चाटना; *n.* चाटने की क्रिया; to lick one's shoes दासत्व दिखलाना; to lick the dust हार जाना

lid *n.* ढपना

lie *v.i.* (*p.t.* lay, *p.p.* lain) लेटना, विश्राम करना, पड़े रहना, अवस्थित होना; as far as in me lies यथा-शक्ति; to lie in ambush प्रतीक्षा करना

lie *n.* असत्य, झूठ; *v.i. & t.* (*p.t.* lied) झूठ बोलना

lieu *n.* स्थान, बदला; in lieu of बदले में

lieutenant *n.* लेफ्टिनेन्ट, प्रति-निधि; lieutenant-gover-nor उपराज्यपाल

life *n.* (*pl.* lives) जीवन, प्राणधारण, चेतना*, आयुष्य, उत्साह

life-belt *n.* जीवन-रक्षक पेटी

life-blood n. जीवन के लिए आवश्यक रक्त

life-boat *n.* जीवन-नौका*

life-guard *n.* शरीर-रक्षक

lifeless *a.* निर्जीव

life-like *a.* जीवित-तुल्य

lifelong *adv.* जीवन-पर्यन्त;

to bring to life मूर्च्छित को सचेत करना

lift *v t.* उठाना, उन्नति करना; *n.* लिफ्ट, उन्नति*, भार उठाने का यन्त्र; to lift up one's voice चिल्ला उठना

light *n.* प्रकाश, दीपक, ज्ञान, दृष्टि*; *v.t.* (*p.t.* lit or lighted)प्रकाश देना, जलाना; to come to light प्रकट होना the light of one's eyes पूजनीय व्यक्ति; to throw light upon समझाने में सहायता देना

light *a.* हल्का, अनावश्यक, मनोरम, सहज में पचन योग्य;

lighthanded *a.* सहज में काम करनेवाला; light-hearted प्रसन्नचित; light literature उपन्यास; light come light go जो सहज में प्राप्त होता है वह सहज में नष्ट होता है; light music सुगम संगीत

lighten *v.t. & i.* हल्का करना या होना

lightly *adv.* सहज में, बिना विचार के

lightning *n.* बिजली*

like *a.* (*comp.* more like, *sup.* most like) समान, सदृश, बराबर

like *v.i.* चाहना, इच्छा करना

likelihood, likeliness *ns.* सम्भावना*

likely *a. & adv.* (*comp. & sup.* with more & most) सम्भवत:, कदाचित्

liken *v.t.* सदृश करना, मिलाना

likeness *n.* समता*, चित्र

likewise *adv.* इसी रीति से

liking *n.* इच्छा*, रुचि*

lilac *n.* बकाइन का पेड़

lime *n.* चूना, लासा, जंभीरी नीबू; *v.t.* चूना फैलाना, लासे से पक्षी पकड़ना; lime-light गैस का तीव्र प्रकाश; lime-stone चूने का पत्थर

limit *n.* सीमा*, किनारा*, हद*; *v.t.* सीमा के भीतर बंद करना

limitable *a.* परिमित

limitation *n.* हद*, सीमा*

limited *a.* घिरा हुआ, संकुचित

limitless *a.* अमीम

line *n.* रस्सी*, तागा, रेखा*, पंक्ति*, रुक्का, तार, पैदल सेना*; *v.t.* रेखा से अंकित करना

linen *n.* लिनन का कपड़ा, छालटी

liner *n.* अनेक जहाजों की पंक्ति में का एक जहाज

linger *v.t.* विलम्ब करना, देर तक ठहरना

lingual *a.* जीभ संबंधी, भाषण या भाषा संबंधी

linguiform *a.* जीभ की शकल का

linguist *n.* अनेक भाषाओं में प्रवीण, बहुभाषी

linguistic *a.* भाषा या बहुभाषा संबंधी

lining *n.* कपड़े या बकस का अस्तर

link *n.* कड़ी*, संधि*, एक चैन का सौवां भाग (7·92 इंच), मशाल; *v.t.* मिलाना, जोड़ना

link-boy *n.* मशालची

lion *n.* (*fem.* lioness) सिंह, शेर; lion-hearted बड़ा वीर; lion's mouth भयंकर स्थिति; lion's share सर्वोत्तम भाग

lip *n.* ओंठ रद-पट, किनारा; *v.t.* (*p.t.* lipped) चूमना, बड़बड़ाना

liqueur *n.* मीठी सुगंधित मदिरा*

liquid *a.* तरल; *n.* द्रव, जल, रस

liquidate *v.t.* ऋणमुक्त करना, हिसाब बेबाक करना, (कम्पनी, फर्म आदि) बन्द करना

liquidity *n.* द्रवत्व

liquor *n.* तरल पदार्थ, मदिरा*

list n. सूची*; v.t. & i. इच्छा करना, सूची में नाम लिखना

listen v.i. ध्यान देकर सुनना, श्रवण करना

listener n. सुननेवाला, श्रोता

listful a. सावधान

listless a. असावधान

literacy n. पढ़ने-लिखने की योग्यता*, साक्षरता*

literal a. अक्षरशः; ठीक-ठीक, मूलार्थक

literary a. साहित्य-संबंधी

literate a. पढ़ा लिखा, पंडित, शिक्षित

literature n. साहित्य, शास्त्र-समूह

lithograph v.t. पत्थर के छापे से छापना; n. लिथोग्राफ

lithographer n. पत्थर के छापे से छापनेवाला

lithography n. लिथोग्राफी, पत्थर का छापा

litigant n. विवादी

litigate v.t. मुकदमा करना, अदालत लड़ना

litigation n. मुकदमेबाज़ी*

litre n. लिटर, प्रायः 1¾ पाइन्ट की तौल

litter n. भूसे का ढेर, कूड़ा-कर्कट, डोली*, टिखटी*, कुछ पशुओं के बच्चे; v.t. कूड़े से ढाँपना, बच्चा देना

little a. (comp. less, lesser, sup. least) अल्प, छोटा, थोड़ा, छोटे कद का; little man लड़का, छोकरा; a little बहुत थोड़ा, थोड़ा-सा; little by little; थोड़ा-थोड़ा करके; little known अप्रसिद्ध

live v.i. & t. जीना, रहना, वसना, बिताना, चलाना

live a. सजीव, जीवित, शक्ति-पूर्ण

livelihood n. जीविका*

livelong a. दीर्घकालिक

lively a. तीव्र, तीक्ष्ण, रोचक

live-stock n. पशु समुदाय

liver n. यकृत, जिगर

living n. & a. जीविका*, जीवित, समकालीन

lizard n. छिपकली*

load n. बोझ, माल, भार; v.i. लादना, बारूद, गोली इत्यादि भरना

loadstone n. चुम्बक

loaf n. (pl. loaves) पावरोटी*, कन्द (मिश्री) का पिण्ड; v.i. वृथा समय नष्ट करना

loafer n. उठाईगीर, आबारा, घुमक्कड़

loam n. चिकनी बलुई मिट्टी*

loan n. ऋण, उधार लिया हुआ धन; v.t. उधार देना

loath *a.* अनिच्छुक, विमुख

loathe *v.t.* नापसन्द करना, घृणा करना

loathing *n.* घृणा*

loathsome *a.* घृणित

lobby *n.* (*pl.* lobbies) लॉबी, सभाकक्ष, प्रकोष्ठ

local *n.* स्थानीय

locality *n.* स्थान, अवस्थिति*

localize *v.t.* किसी मुख्य स्थान में स्थिर करना

locate *v.t.* स्थापन करना, बैठाना, ठीक स्थान का पता लगाना

location *n.* स्थिति*, मौका

lock *n.* ताला, बन्दूक का घोड़ा, बांध, वालों की लट*; *v.t.* ताला लगाना, बन्द करना, आलिंगन करना

locker *n.* लॉकर, अलमारी*

locket *n.* लॉकेट, सोने या चांदी का कुंडा

lock-smith *n.* ताला बनाने या मरम्मत करनेवाला

lock-up *n.* बन्दीगृह, हिरासत*, हवालात*

locomotive *n.* लोकोमोटिव, चलित्र

locust *n.* टिड्डी*

lodestar *n.* ध्रुवतारा

lodge *n.* छोटा घर, समिति* (सभा*) स्थान; *v.t. & i.* बसना, स्थिर करना, टिकाना, सुरक्षित रखना, दायर करना

lodging *n.* निवासस्थान

loftiness *n.* ऊंचाई*, अभिमान

lofty *a.* (*comp.* loftier, *sup.* loftiest) ऊंचा, क्रोधी, घमंडी

log *n.* लकड़ी का कुन्दा, लट्ठा

logbook *n.* रोजनामचा, कार्य-पंजी*

loggerhead *n.* मूर्ख, लंठ; to be at loggerheads with कलह करना

logic *n.* तर्कशास्त्र, न्यायशास्त्र, तर्क

logical *a.* तर्कसंगत, तर्कशास्त्र संबंधी, न्यायसिद्ध

logician *n.* नैयायिक तार्किक

loin *n.* कूल्हा, कमर*; to gird up the loins कमर कसना; loin-cloth कौपीन, लंगोटी*

loiter *v.i.* धीरे चलना, देर करना, टालमटोल करना

lone, lonely *a.* निर्जन, अकेला

loneliness *n.* निर्जनता*, अकेलापन

lonesome *a.* अकेला, मन्द

long *a.* लंबा, फैला हुआ, कठिन, भारी; longcloth लट्ठा; in the long run अन्ततोगत्वा; longhand पूरे अक्षरों में (संकेतित से भिन्न) लिखावट; longheaded दूरदर्शी;

long-tongued बकवादी;
the long and short of a
matter किसी विषय का
सारांश

long v.t. अत्यन्त अभिलाषा
करना

longevity n. दीर्घायु

longing n. उत्कंठा*, लालसा*

longitude n. देशान्तर

look v.t. & i. देखना, आश्चर्य
दिखलाना, ध्यान लगाना,
मालूम होना, सामना करना;
n. रूप, आकृति*, आभा*;
to look about खोज में
रहना; to look after ध्यान
देना; to look ahead
भविष्य विचारना; look
before you leap बिना
विचारेकाम न करो; to look
black क्रुद्ध आकृति धारण
करना; to look down
upon तिरस्कार करना;
to look into पता
लगाना; look sharp जल्दी
करो

lookout n. (pl. lookouts)
चौकसी*

loom n. करघा; v.t. अस्पष्ट
देख पड़ना

loop n. फन्दा, गांठ*; v.t.
फन्दा लगाना

loop-hole n. छिद्र, भागने का

गुप्त मार्ग

loose a. ढीला, शिथिल.
अनिश्चित, अबद्ध, अशुद्ध,
दुराचारी; v.t. मुक्त करना,
जाने देना

loosen v.t. & i. ढीला करना
या होना

loot n. लूट का माल; v.t.
लूटना

lop v.t. (p.t. lopped) डाल
या शाखा काटना, कलम
करना; n. कटाव, कलम;
v.i. लटकना; lopsided एक
ओर से दूसरी ओर भारी,
एकअंगी, उलार

lord n. प्रभु, स्वामी, राजा,
शासक, सामन्त, नवाब

lordly a. तेजस्वी, गर्वित

lordship n. नवाब का पद या
महत्त्व

lorry n. (pl. lorries) लॉरी,
बड़ी खुली गाड़ी*

lose v.t. & i. (p.t. & p.p.
lost) त्यागना, छोड़ना, वंचित
होना, खोना, नष्ट होना,
असफल होना; to lose
ground पीछे को हटाया
जाना; to lose one's head
घबरा जाना; to lose heart
हतोत्साह होना; to lose
one's temper क्रुद्ध होना,
to lose one's way बहक

जाना, भटक जाना

loser *n.* हारनेवाला, खोनेवाला

loss *n.* हानि*, नाश, हार*, घाटा; to be at a loss घबड़ा जाना

lot *n.* भाग्य, अंश, भाग, चुनाव; a lot अधिक संख्या; to cast lots चिट्ठी गुट्टी डालना

lotion *n.* धोने की औषधि*, मलहम

lottery *n.* चिट्ठी डालकर बांटने की रीति*, लॉटरी

lotus *n.* कमल

loud *a.* बड़ी ध्वनि का, कोला-हल पूर्ण, दिखावा, भद्दा; loudspeaker लाउडस्पीकर, ध्वनि विस्तारक यंत्र

lounge *v.t. & i.* व्यर्थ समय नष्ट करना या घूमना; *n.* बैठक, एक प्रकार की आराम-कुर्सी*

lovable *a.* स्नेह के योग्य, चित्त आकर्षण करनेवाला

love *v.t.* प्रेम करना, बहुत चाहना; *n.* प्रेम, स्नेह, प्रेम-पात्र

lover *n.* प्रेमी, प्रेमिका*

lovely *a.* सुन्दर, प्यारा

loving *a.* प्यारा

low *a.* (*comp.* lower, *sup.* lowest) नीचा, धीमा, भूमि के समीप का, तल के पास,

विनीत; lowborn नीच कुल का; low sound धीमाशब्द; to have low opinion of तुच्छ जानना; lowbred अशिष्ट व्यवहार का

low *v.i.* बैल की तरह डकारना

lower *v.t. & i.* विनीत करना, असम्मान करना, उतारना, दाम कम करना, उतरना

lowering *a. & n.* नीचा करने वाला, घटानेवाला, नीचा करने या घटाने की क्रिया

lowland *n.* समतल नीची भूमि*

lowliness *n.* विनय, नम्रता*

lowly *a.* विनीत, नम्र

lowermost *a.* सबसे नीचा

loyal *a.* देशभक्त, विश्वासी, राजभक्त

loyalist *n.* राजभक्त

loyalty *n.* राजभक्ति*

lubricant *n.* चिकनाने का मसाला, 'स्नेह द्रव्य'

lubricate *v.t.* तेल देकर चिकनाना

lubricity *n.* स्निग्धता*, चिकना-पन

lucent *a.* प्रकाशमान

lucerne *n.* एक प्रकार की घास* जिसको पशु खाते हैं

lucid *a.* स्पष्ट अर्थ का, व्यक्त

lucidity *n.* स्पष्टता*

luck *n.* संयोग, भाग्य; good-

luck सौभाग्य; ill or bad luck दुर्भाग्य; to try one's luck साहस करना; as ill luck would have it दुर्भाग्य से

luckily *adv.* भाग्यवश

luckless *a.* अभागा, हतभाग्य

lucky *a.* (*comp.* luckier, *sup* luckiest) भाग्यवान, शुभ, मंगलकारी

lucrative *a.* लाभदायक, धन-दायक, फल देनेवाला

luggage *n.* यात्रा की गठरी*

lukewarm *a.* मन्दोष्ण, गुन-गुना, उदासीन

lull *v.t.* शान्त करना, गाकर सुनाना; *n.* शान्ति काल, मंदी*

lullaby *n.* (*pl.* lullabies) लोरी*

luminant *a.* & *n.* प्रकाश देनेवाला

luminary *n.* प्रकाशदायक पदार्थ, तारा, सूर्य, चन्द्रमा, अपूर्व बुद्धि का मनुष्य

luminous *a.* प्रकाशयुक्त, चम-कीला, स्पष्ट

lump *n.* पिण्ड, ढेर, सूजन*, *v.t.* ढेर करना

lunacy *n.* उन्माद, पागलपन

lunar *a.* चन्द्रमा-सम्बन्धी; lunar-month चान्द्रमास; lunar eclipse चन्द्रग्रहण

lunatic *n.* पागल मनुष्य; luna-tic asylum पागलखाना

lunch (-eon) *n.* लंच, मध्याह्न का थोड़ा भोजन; *v.t.* भोजन करना

lung *n.* फुफ्फुस, फेफड़ा

lure *v.t.* फुसलाना, लुभाना; *n.* लालच, फुसलाहट*

lurid *a.* घोररूप, भयंकर, अन्धकारनय

lurk *v.i.* घात में रहना, भटकना

lush *a.* रसदार; *n.* मदिरा; *v.t.* खूब शराब पीना या पिलाना

lust *n.* उत्कट इच्छा* या अभि-लाषा*, कामवासना*; *v.t.* तीव्र लालसा करना

lustful *a.* लम्पट, कामातुर

lustre *n.* चमक*, शोभा*, तेज

lustrous *a* तेजस्वी, चमकीला

luxurious *a.* सुखभोगी, आनन्द-पूर्ण, विलासी, सुखकर

luxury *n.* (*pl.* luxuries) सुख, विलास, विशिष्ट भोजन वस्त्र इ०, (ब० व०) सुखकर या विलास की सामग्री*

lying *a.* लेटा हुआ

lynch *v.t.* बिना बंध निर्णय के मार डालना, वध करना

lyric *a.* बीन सम्बन्धी, गीतात्मक सुरीला; *n.* लिरिक, गीत

M

macabre *a.* भयंकर

machine *n.* मशीन*, यन्त्र, इंजन, बिना समझे-बूझे काम करनेवाला व्यक्ति; machine-gun मशीनगन, चक्रतोप; machine-man मशीनमैन, यन्त्र पर काम करनेवाला मनुष्य

machinery *n.* मशीनरी*, यन्त्रों का समूह, साधन

mad *a.* पागल, उन्मत्त, मूर्ख, बौड़हा

madam *n.* (*mas.* sir) मादाम*, मैडम*, महाशया*, श्रीमती*

madcap *n.* झक्की मनुष्य

madden *v.t.* पागल करना, क्रुद्ध करना

mad-house *n.* पागलखाना

magazine *n.* शस्त्र, शस्त्रागार, पत्रिका; magazine-gun (rifle) बन्दूक या पिस्तौल जिसमें अनेक कारतूस भरे होते हैं जो पारी-पारी से छूट सकते हैं

magic *n.* मन्त्र, जादू, भूत-विद्या*; black magic हानिकारक जादू; white magic लाभकर जादू; magic lantern पर्दे पर बड़ा चित्र दिखलाने की लालटेन*, माया-दीप, चित्रदीप

magical *a.* ऐन्द्रजालिक, विलक्षण, जादू का

magician *n.* जादूगर

magisterial *a.* मजिस्ट्रेट-संबंधी, दण्डाधीश-संबंधी

magistracy *n.* दण्डाधिकार, मजिस्ट्रेट का पद, मजिस्ट्रेट लोग

magistrate *n.* मजिस्ट्रेट, जिला-धीश

magna charta *n.* इंगलैंड के राजा जॉन का 1215 ई० का प्रसिद्ध आज्ञापत्र, महाधिकार-पत्र

magnate *n.* उच्च पदाधिकारी, बड़ा रईस, बड़ा धनी

magnet *n.* चुम्बक

magnetic *a.* चुम्बक की शक्ति-वाला

magnetism *n.* आकर्षण शक्ति*

magnificent *a.* शोभायमान, तेजस्वी, प्रतापी

magnify *v.t.* (*p.t.* magnified) अधिक करना, बढ़ाना, अतिशय वर्णन करना

magnitude *n.* परिमाण, मात्रा*, आकार, महत्त्व

magpie *n.* नीलकण्ठ पक्षी

mahogany *n.* महोगनी या

महार्घ नामक वृक्ष

maid *n.* (*mas.* bachelor) कन्या*, कुमारी*, चेरी*; maid of honour रानी* (या राजकुमारी*) की अनुचरी* या दासी*; maid servant दासी*, नौकरानी*

maiden *n.* कुमारी*, बालिका*, नौकरानी*; *a.* प्रथम, पहिला, प्रयोग में न लाया हुआ; ~ speech प्रथम भाषण

mail *n.* शरीरत्राण, कवच, डाक का थैला, डाक विभाग; *v.t.* डाक द्वारा चिट्ठी इत्यादि भेजना

mail-coach *n.* डाक ले जाने की गाड़ी*, या गाड़ी का डब्बा; mail-train डाकगाड़ी

main *n.* शक्ति*, समुद्र, गैस या पानी की प्रधान नली* अथवा बिजली का तार; *a.* प्रधान, मुख्य

mainland *n.* महाद्वीप, प्रधान भूभाग, महादेश

mainly *adv.* प्रधान रूप से, विशेष करके

main spring *n.* घड़ी की बड़ी कमानी*

mainstay *n.* प्रधान आश्रय

maintain *v.t.* संभालना, पालन करना, समर्थन करना, रक्षा करना

maintenance *n.* जीविका*, रक्षा*, निर्वाह

maize *n.* मकई, भुट्टा, मक्का

majestic (-al) *a.* प्रभावशाली, ऐश्वर्ययुक्त

majesty *n.* महिमा*, गौरव, वैभव, राजत्व, महाराजा की उपाधि*

major *a.* बड़ा प्रधान, प्राप्तवयस्क; *n.* सेना का अध्यक्ष

majority *n.* बहुमत, प्राप्तवयस्कता

make *v.t.* (*p.t. & p.p.* made) निर्माण करना, विवश करना, बनाना, तैयार करना; *n.* आकार, रूप, बनावट*; to make a clean breast of बिना छिपाए सब कह डालना; to make a clean sweep of पूरी तरह से हटाना; to make after पीछा करना; to make away with नाश करना; to make believe बहाना करना; to make one's bread जीविका कमाना; to make faces मुंह बनाना, चिढ़ाना; to make good पूरा करना; to make off प्रस्थान करना; to make up टोटा पूरा करना; to make water

लघुशंका करना

maker *n.* बनानेवाला

makeshift *n.* क्षणिक उपयोग

making *n.* रचना*; बनावट*;

mal *pref.* 'बुरा, दुष्ट' के अर्थ
के उपसर्ग

maladjustment *n.* कुप्रबंध,
बुरी रीति*

maladministration *n.* कुशा-
सन

malady *n.* (*pl.* maladies)
रोग, व्याधि*; बीमारी*

malaria *n.* मलेरिया, शीतज्वर,
जूड़ी*;

malarial, malarious *a.* मले-
रिया ज्वर सम्बन्धी

malcontent *a.* अमन्तुष्ट

male *n.* पुरुष, नर

malicious *a.* द्रोही, दुष्टात्मा

malign *v.t.* कलंकित करना, *a.*
अयोग्य, कष्टकर

malignancy *n.* द्रोह, कपट

malignant *a.* द्रोही, कपटी

mall *n.* माल (रोड), ठण्डी
सड़क

mallard *n.* जंगली बत्तख

malnutrition *n.* कुपोषण,
अपर्याप्त पोषण

malpractice *n.* कदाचार

malt *n.* माल्ट, जौ या अन्य अन्न
जो मदिरा बनाने के लिए
तैयार किया जाता है

Maltese *n.* & *a.* माल्टा-
निवासी, माल्टा का या
सम्बन्धी

maltreatment *n.* बुरा व्यवहार,
अपकार

mamma *n.* मां*; अम्मा*;

mammal *n.* अपने बच्चों को
दूध पिलानेवाला प्राणी,
स्तनधारी प्राणी

mammoth *a.* बहुत बड़ा, महान

man *n.* (*pl.* men) मानव,
सयाना पुरुष, नर, नौकर,
पति; *v.t.* (*p.t.* manned)
सेना the innerman
आत्मा*; man-at-arms
सशस्त्र अश्वारोही सैनिक;
man-child बालक; man
in the street सामान्य
मनुष्य

manage *v.t.* & *i.* व्यवस्था
करना, प्रबन्ध करना, चलाना

manageability *n.* प्रबन्ध-
नीयता*

manageable *a.* प्रबन्ध करने
योग्य

management *n.* प्रबन्ध,
मालिक

manager (*fem.* manage-
ress) *n.* मैनेजर, प्रबन्धक,
व्यवस्थापक

mandarin *n.* छोटी चपटी
नारंगी*;

mandate *n.* श्राज्ञा-पत्र, फरमान

mandatory *a.* श्राज्ञा-संबंधी, श्रादेशात्मक

mane *n.* पशुश्रों की गर्दन पर के लम्बे वाल (श्रयाल)

manful *a.* पराक्रमी, दिलेर, साहसी

manfully *a.* वीरता तथा साहस सहित

manger *n.* घोड़े या चौपायों को खिलाने की नाद

mango *n.* (*pl.* mangoes.) श्राम

mangrove *n.* सुन्दर-वन के मुन्दरी का वृक्ष

manhood *n* पुरुषत्व

mania *n.* उन्माद, सनक*; भक* maniac *n.* पागल मनुष्य

manifest *a.* प्रकट, स्पष्ट, प्रत्यक्ष; *v.t.* स्पष्ट करना, प्रकट करना

manifestation *n.* श्राविर्भाव, प्रकाशन

manifesto *n.* (*pl.* manifestoes) राजकीय घोषणा, घोषणापत्र

manifold *a.* श्रनेक रूप तथा श्राकार का, पेचीला

manipulate *v.t.* दक्षता से चलाना, चातुरी से प्रबन्ध करना, छल-योजना करना

manipulation *n.* हस्त व्यापार, कारीगरी, छल-योजना

manipulator *n.* छल-योजक, पत्तेबाज़

mankind *n.* मनुष्यजाति*

manliness *n.* वीरता*, साहस

manly *a.* मनुष्यवत्, स्थिर, वीर, साहसी

manna *n.* (यहूदियों का) श्राध्यात्मिक श्राहार

manner *n.* रीति*, प्रथा*, नियम, (ब०व०) व्यवहार

mannerism *n.* व्यावहारिकता*

mannerly *a.* शिष्ट, विनीत

manoeuvre *n.* जुगत, कुशल-गति*, कपट प्रयोग, (ब०व०) सैनिक चातुरी*; *v.t.* चतुराई से प्रबंध करना

man-of-war *n.* लड़ाई का जहाज

mansion *n.* भवन, महल, हवेली*

mantel *n.* (mantelpiece or mantelshelf) श्रंगीठी के ऊपर की संकरी श्रलमारी

manual *a.* हाथ का, हाथ का किया हुश्रा; *n.* छोटी पुस्तक*, गुटका*, नियमावली

manufacture *n.* शिल्पकर्म; *v.t.* शिल्प द्वारा बनाना, पैदा करना, निर्माण करना

manufacturer *n.* निर्माता,

उत्पादक, शिल्पी, कारखाने-
दार

manure n. खाद*; v.t. खेत में
खाद डालना

manuscript n. (abbr. ms. ;
pl. mss.) पाण्डुलिपि*, हस्त-
लिपि*, हाथ से लिखी हुई
पुस्तक

many a. अनेक, बहुत; as
many उतने; the many
अनेक, बहुतेरे; manysided
विभिन्न; a good many
अधिक संख्या

map n. नकशा, मानचित्र; v.t.
(p.t. mapped) मानचित्र
बनाना; to map out प्रबन्ध,
करना

maple n. एक प्रकार का छाया-
दार वृक्ष

mar v.t. (p.t. marred) नष्ट
करना, बिगाड़ना

marble n. बिल्लौर, संगमरमर,
लड़कों के खेलने की गोली;
v.t. संगमरमर के समान
रंगना, अबरी बनाना

March n. मार्च, अंग्रेजी वर्ष
का तीसरा महीना

march n. सीमा प्रदेश, सेना
की क्रम में गति; v.t. क्रम में
चलना, प्रस्थान करना, कूच
करना मार्च करना

mare n. घोड़ी*

margin n. पार्श्व, उपान्त,
मात्रा*

marginal a. सीमांत

marigold n. गेंदे का फूल

marine a. समुद्री, जल सेना
सम्बन्धी

mariner n. नाविक, मल्लाह,
जहाजी

marital a. पति-सम्बन्धी,
विवाह-संबंधी

maritime a समुद्री, समुद्र-
संबंधी

mark n. चिह्न, लेख, लक्ष्य, अंक,
परीक्षा में दिया गया अंक;
v.t. चिह्न लगाना, सावधानी
से देखना; wide of the
mark लक्ष्य के बाहर; up to
the mark योग्य, उचित;
men of mark प्रसिद्ध लोग

marked a. अंकित, प्रसिद्ध,
सुस्पष्ट

markedly adv. सावधानी से

market n. हाट*, बाजार; v.t.
हाट में बिक्री-बट्टा करना

marketable a. बिक्री के योग्य

marking n. चिह्न, छाप*;
marking ink कपड़े पर
छापने की पक्की रोशनाई*

marksman n. निशानेबाज

maroon n. भूरा लाल रंग,
एक नीग्रो सम्प्रदाय; a. इस रंग
का; v.t. किसी मनुष्य को

निर्जन टापू पर छोड़ देना

marriage *n.* विवाह, शादी*

marriageable *a.* विवाह-योग्य

marry *v.t.* (*p.t.* married) विवाह करना

mars *n.* युद्ध-देवता, मंगल तारा

marsh *n.* कच्छभूमि, दलदल

marshal *n.* मार्शल, सेनापति; *v.i.* (*p.t.* marshalled) क्रम से रखना, सजाना

marshiness *n.* दलदली स्थिति*

marshy *a.* दलदली

mart *n.* मार्ट, हाट*, बाजार

martial *a.* सेना-संबंधी, सैनिक, लड़ाकू रणप्रिय; martial law मार्शल लॉ, सैनिक नियम

martyr *n.* शहीद, हुतात्मा

martyrdom *n.* शहादत, हुतात्मत्व

marvel *v.t.* (*p.t.* marvelled) आश्चर्य करना; *n.* कौतुक, चमत्कार

marvellous *a.* अद्भुत, आश्चर्य-जनक

masculine *a.* पुरुष जाति का, पुरुषोचित, मर्दाना

mash *n.* दलिया, महेला; *v.t.* कूंचकर मिलाना

mask *n.* घूंघट, स्वांग, रूप बदलने का चेहरा, बहाना; *v.t.* छिपाना, ढांकना

mason *n.* थवई, राज, फ्रीमेसन

mass *n.* पिण्ड, राशि* समूह, ढेर, संख्या*, प्रधान अंश, ईसाइयों का धर्मसमाज; *v t & i.* संघटित करना, इकट्ठा होना; mass meeting बड़ी सभा*

massacre *n.* मनुष्य संहार, खूनखराबी; *v.t.* निर्दयता से हत्या करना

massage *n.* मसाज, बदन में मालिश द्वारा चिकित्सा, शरीर-मर्दन

mast *n.* मस्तूल

master *n.* मास्टर, अधिकारी, शासक, प्रभु, प्रवीण, गृहपति. गुरु, विषय का ज्ञाता, नवयुवक बालक को पुकारने के लिए आदरसूचक शब्द; *v.t.* जीतना, पूर्ण ज्ञान प्राप्त करना; to be one's own master स्वतन्त्र होना

masterhand *n.* अति प्रवीण व्यक्ति

master-key *n.* मास्टरचाभी*, अनेक तालों को खोलनेवाली एक चाभी*

masterly *a.* उत्तम, प्रवीण

masterpiece *n.* प्रधान कृति* या रचना*

mastery *n.* जीत*, विजय*

mat *n.* चटाई*, आसन; *v.t.* (*p.t.* matted) गूंथना,

फंसाना; matting *n.* चटाई बनाने की सामग्री*

mat *a. & v.t.* बिना चमक का, मैला करना

match *n.* दियासलाई, तुल्य, बराबर, विवाह-सम्बन्ध, खेल, मैच, प्रतियोगिता*; *v.t. & i.* विवाह करना, बराबर करना या होना, अनुरूप होना

matchless *a.* अद्वितीय, बेजोड़

match-maker *n.* विवाह स्थिर करानेवाला

mate *n.* पति या पत्नी*, संगी, मित्र, जहाज पर का एक अधिकारी

material *a.* भौतिक, स्थूल, जड़, आवश्यक; *n.* पदार्थ, वस्तु*

materialize *v.t.* भौतिक बनाना, कार्यान्वित करना या होना

materially *adv.* आवश्यकरूप से

maternal *a.* माता-सम्बन्धी

maternity *n.* मातृत्व

mathematical *a.* गणित-सम्बन्धी

mathematician *n.* गणितज्ञ

mathematics *n. pl.* (used as *sing.*) गणित विद्या

matinee *n.* दिन का नाटक आदि

matricidal *a.* मातृहत्या-सम्बन्धी

matricide *n.* मातृहत्या*

matriculate *n.* मैट्रिक पास, मैट्रिक पास विद्यार्थी; *v.t.* मैट्रिक पास करना

matriculation *n.* मैट्रिक परीक्षा*

matrimonial *a.* विवाह-संबंधी, वैवाहिक

matrimony *n.* विवाह-संस्कार

matrix *n. (pls.* matrixes, matrices) सांचा, ठप्पा

matron *n.* मेट्रन, ब्याही स्त्री*, वृढ़ा*, किसी संस्था की मालकिन*, धात्री*

matter *n.* द्रव्य, पदार्थ, विषय, साधन, तत्व, पीव; *v.i.* आवश्यक होना; in the matter of विषय में; a matter of course सामान्य विषय; as a matter of fact वस्तुत:, सचमुच; no matter कोई चिन्ता नहीं; matter of fact वास्त- विकता*

matting *n.* चटाई बनाने की सामग्री*

mattress *n.* चटाई*, तोशक, गद्दा

mature *a.* परिपक्व, प्रौढ़, तैयार; *v.i. & t.* सिद्ध होना, प्रौढ़ करना

maturity *n.* परिपक्वता*, प्रौढ़ता*, सिद्धि*

maul *v.i.* कूंचना, पीसना, बुरी तरह से पकड़ना

mawkish *a.* घृणित नीरस, फीका, रूक्ष प्रकृति का

mawseed *n.* पोस्त का दाना

maxim *n.* कहावत*, सूत्र

maximize *v.t.* अत्यधिक बड़ा बनाना, सिद्धान्तों की सपरिश्रम व्याख्या करना

maximum *n.* (*pl.* maxima) सबसे अधिक संख्या या परिमाण

May *n.* मई

may *v. aux* (*p.t.* might) सम्भव होना, सकना; may be कदाचित्

Mayday *n.* मई दिवस

maypole *n* फूलों से सजा हुआ डंडा जिसके चारों ओर मई के उत्सव में लोग नाचते हैं

mayor *n.* (*fem.* mayoress) मेयर महापौर, नगर-प्रमुख

mayoral *a.* मैयर-संबंधी

mayoralty *n.* महापौर-पद, या कार्यकाल

me *pron.* मुझे, मुझको; ah me ! ओफ ओफ ! हाय !

meadow *n.* चरागाह*

meagre *a.* दुबंल, क्षीण, थोड़ा

meal *n.* आटा, भोजन

mealy *a.* आटे का सूखा; mealy-mouthed स्पष्ट रूप

में सच्ची बात न कहने वाला

mean *a.* नीच, अधम, गंवार, तुच्छ, दरिद्र

mean *v.t.* (*p.t.* meant) इच्छा करना, चाहना, मतलब रखना

mean *n. & a.* मध्य, मध्य-वर्ती, बीच का, औसत

meaning *n.* अभिप्राय, अर्थ

means *n. pl.* साधन, धन, उपाय, यंत्र; by no means अवश्य नहीं या निश्चय ही नहीं

mean-spirited *a.* नीच बुद्धि या प्रकृति का

meantime *n.* मध्यकाल; बीच का काल

meanwhile *adv.* इस बीच में

measles *n. pl.* एक प्रकार का शीतला रोग, खसरा, छोटी चेचक

measurable *a.* नापने योग्य

measure *n.* उपाय, परिमाण, प्रस्ताव, कार्यवाही; *v t.* कूतना, नापना; in a measure अंशतः; made to measure नाप से बना हुआ, out of measure अधिक परिमाण में; greatest common measure (G.C. M.) महत्तम समापवर्तक

measureless *a.* असीम, बिना नाप का

measurement n. परिमाण, नाप*

meat n. आहार का मांस; meat-safe मांस रखने की जालीदार अलमारी, मीटसेफ़

mechanic n. मेकेनिक यांत्रिक, मिस्त्री a. यंत्र-संबंधी

mechanical a. यंत्र-संबंधी, यंत्रवत्, बुद्धि-रहित

mechanics n. यन्त्र-विद्या*

mechanism n. यन्त्र-रचना*, यंत्रक्रिया-विधि*

mechanist n. यन्त्र-विद्या में कुशल

medal n. मेडल, मुद्रा, पदक, तमगा

medallist n. पदक बनानेवाला, पदक पाया हुआ मनुष्य, पदक या मुद्रा का चित्रकार

meddle v.t. विघ्न डालना, दखल देना

media n. साधन, हेतु, मार्ग

mediaeval (medieval) a. मध्ययुग (काल) सम्बन्धी

mediate v.i. बीच में पड़ना, पंच बनना

mediation n. बिचवई* मध्यस्थता*

mediator n. (fem. media-trix) मध्यस्थ, पंच

medical a. मेडिकल, भैषजिक

medicament n. दवादारु,

औषधि*, दवा

medicate v.t. दवा देना

medicinal a. भैषजीय

medicine n. भैषज, औषधि*

medico pref. 'डाक्टर' का अर्थ-सूचक उपसर्ग

mediocre a. सामान्य, साधारण

mediocrity n. सामान्यता*

meditate v.t. ध्यान करना, मनन करना, विचार करना, समाधि लगाना

meditation n. ध्यान, विचार, मनन, चिन्तन

mediterranean a. भूमध्य-स्थित; n. भूमध्यसागर

medium n. (pls. media, mediums) मध्य, साधन, कारण, मार्ग; a. सामान्य

meek a. विनीत, नम्र, कोमल

meet a. उचित, योग्य; v.i. & t. (p.p. met) इकट्ठा होना, संतुष्ट करना; to meet with भेंट करना

megaphone n. ध्वनिवर्द्धक यंत्र, लाउडस्पीकर

melancholia n. एक वात-व्याधि

melancholic a. वातव्याधि-सम्बन्धी

melancholy n. & a. खिन्नता*, उदासी*, चिन्ताकुल, उदासीन

mellow a. पका और कोमल,

पुष्ट, रुचिकर, मंजुल, सौम्य

melodious a. मधुर स्वर का,
सुरीला

melodrama n. मेलोड्रामा,
उत्तेजनापूर्ण सुखान्त नाटक

melodramatic a. मेलोड्रामा-
विषयक भावों को जागृत
करनेवाले नाटक का

melody n. (pl. melodies)
स्वर की मधुरता*, लय*,
राग, मूर्च्छना*

melon n. तरबूज; musk-
melon खरबूजा

melt v.t. & i. (p.p. melten)
गलाना, धुलाना, पिघलाना

member n. मेम्बर, अंग, अवयव,
सदस्य, सभासद; unruly
member जिह्वा*

membership n. मेम्बरी,
सदस्यता

memento n. (pls. mem-
entos, mementoes)
स्मारक, यादगार*, निशानी*

memo n. मेमो, ज्ञाप, ज्ञापन

memoir n. संस्मरण, वृत्तान्त

memorable a. स्मरणीय,
प्रसिद्ध

memorandum n. (pl.
memoranda, memoran-
dums) स्मृति पत्र, दस्तावेज

memorial a. & n. स्मारक,
यादगार

memory n. स्मरण-शक्ति*,
स्मृति*, याद*

menace v.t. डराना, धमकाना;
n धमकी*

mend v.t. ठीक करना, मरम्मत
करना, उन्नति करना; to
mend one's ways आचरण
सुधारना; to mend the fire
आग सुलगाना

menial n. चाकर, दास; a. नीच,
ओछा

menses n. स्त्री का आर्तव या
मासिक धर्म

mental a. मानसिक, बुद्धि-
संबंधी

mentality n. मनोवृत्ति*,
स्वभाव, मानसिक शक्ति*

mention v.t. निर्देश करना,
चर्चा करना; n. कथन, निर्देश,
उल्लेख, चर्चा

mentor n. विश्वासी मन्त्री,
अनुभवी सलाहकार

menu n. मेनू, भोज्य-सूची*

mercantile a. व्यापार-सम्बन्धी

mercenary a. धनलोलुप,
स्वार्थी, भाड़े का टट्टू

merchant n. व्यापारी, व्यव-
सायी

merciful a. दयालु, कृपालु

merciless a. निर्दय, क्रूर, बेरहम

mercury a. पारा, बुध तारा

merge v.t. & i मिलना,

338

मिलाना, विलयन करना,
समावेश करना, डूबना, डुबाना

merger n. विलय, विलयन

merit n. योग्यता*, पात्रता*,
दक्षता*

meritorious a. योग्य, दक्ष,
गुणी

mermaid (mas. merman)
n. मत्स्यांगना*

merriment n. आनन्द, विनोद

merry a. (comp. merrier,
sup. marriest) आनन्दित,
मगन, प्रसन्न; to make
merry उत्सव मनाना;
merry andrew मसखरा,
विदूषक

mess n. भोजनशाला*, घालमेल;
to make a mess of
कुप्रबन्ध करना; v.t. & i.
मलिन करना, मलिन होना,
गड़बड़ करना

message n. सन्देश, समाचार

messenger n. संदेशवाहक, दूत

messiah n. मसीहा, ईसा मसीह

metabolism n. शरीर में पोषक
पदार्थों का परिवर्तन, चया-
पचय

metal n. धातु*, पत्थर के टुकड़े;
(ब० व०) रेल की लाइन;
v.t. (p.t. metalled) पत्थर
के टुकड़ों से सड़क की मरम्मत
करना

metallic a. धातु-सम्बन्धी

metallurgy n. धातु-विज्ञान

metamorphosis n. (pl.
metamorphoses) रूपान्तर,
कायापलट, रूपभेद, रूपविकार
रूपविक्रिया

metaphor n. रूपक, लक्षण

metaphysical a. आध्यात्मिक,
आत्मविषयक

metaphysics n. अध्यात्म-
विज्ञान, आत्मतत्त्वज्ञान, तत्त्व-
विज्ञान, सिद्धान्तमात्र

meteorological a. ऋतुविज्ञान
संबंधी, अन्तरिक्ष विद्या-संबंधी;
meteorologist n. ऋतु-
विज्ञानी अन्तरिक्ष विद्याविद्

meteorology n. ऋतु-विज्ञान,
अन्तरिक्ष विद्या*, जलवायु
तथा आकाश-विषयक ज्ञान

meter n. मीटर, नाप, माप,
मापक यन्त्र

methinks v.t. मुझे जान पड़ता
है, मैं समझता हूं

method n. रीति*, नियम, ढंग,
विधि*, व्यवस्था*

methodical a. व्यवस्थित, यथा-
क्रम

methodist n. एक क्रिस्तानी पंथ

metric a. मीटर-संबंधी, दशांश

metropolis n. (pl. metro-
polises) मुख्य नगर, राज-
धानी*

metropolitan *a. & n.* राज-
धानी संबंधी, राजधानी का
निवासी, पादरी

mew *v.i* म्याऊं करना, बिल्ली
की तरह शब्द करना; *n.*
म्याऊं, बिल्ली का शब्द

mewl *v.i.* बिल्ली की तरह
धीमा शब्द करना

mica *n.* अबरक

mickle *a. & n.* अधिक, बहुत,
अधिक परिमाण

micro *pref.* एक अल्पार्थक उप-
सर्ग

microphone *n.* माइक्रोफोन

microscope *n.* माइक्रोस्कोप,
सूक्ष्मदर्शक यन्त्र

microscopic (-al) *a.* अणु-
वीक्षण यन्त्र-सम्बन्धी

mid *a.* मध्य का, बिचला

midday *n.* मध्याह्न

middle *a.* मध्य का, बिचला;
middle-aged अधेड़ अवस्था
का; middle ages मध्य युग
(प्रायः 1000 से 1400 ई०
सन् तक का समय); middle
class मध्य वर्ग

middleman *n.* मध्यस्थ, पंच

midst *adv.* बीच में

midsummer *n.* उत्तरायण
काल; midsummer day
21 जून का दिन

midwife (*pl.* midwives) *n.*

मिडवाइफ, प्रसव में सहायता
देनेवाली दाई*

might *n.* शक्ति*, सामर्थ्य,
पराक्रम, प्रभाव; with
might and main पूरी शक्ति
से

mighty *adv.* (*comp.* migh-
tier, *sup.* mightiest)
शक्तिमान, पुष्ट

migrate *v.t.* प्रवास करना,
स्थान बदलना, दूसरे स्थान
में बसना

migration *n.* देशान्तर निवास

mike *n.* माइक्रोफोन या
'माइक्रोस्कोप' का छोटा रूप;
v.t. काम से जी चुराना

milch *a.* दुधार, दूध देनेवाली

mild *a.* दयालु, कोमल, शान्त,
सौम्य

mileage *n.* मील-भत्ता, मीलों
की संख्या

milestone *n.* मील का पत्थर

militant *a.* लड़ाकू, जंगजोर

military *a.* युद्ध या सैनिक-
सम्बन्धी; *n.* सेना*, फौज*

militate *v.t.* लड़ना, विरोध
करना

militia *n.* देशरक्षिणी सेना*

milk *n.* दूध; *v.t.* दूध दुहना

milky *a.* दूध का, दूध के
सदृश; milky way आकाश-
गंगा*, अमंख्य तारों की

चमकती हुई पंक्ति*

mill *a.* चक्की*, जांता, कार-
खाना; *v.t.* (*p.t.* milled)
चक्की में पीसना, ठप्पा
करना, मुद्रा के किनारे पर
धारी बनाना

millenary *a.* एक हज़ार वर्ष
का; *n.* हज़ार वर्ष की जन्म-
गांठ, हज़ार वर्ष

millennial *a.* एक हज़ार का

millennium *n.* एक हज़ार वर्ष

milli *pref.* 'हज़ारवां' अर्थ का
उपसर्ग

milliner *n.* मेमों की टोपी
बनानेवाला

millinery *n.* मेमों की टोपी*
इत्यादि

million *n.* दस लाख

millionaire *n.* लखपती

mimic *a.* अनुकरण करने
वाला; *n.* बहुरूपिया, भांड;
v.t. बहुरूपिए के समान
अनुकरण करना

mimicry *n.* स्वांग, विडम्बना*

minaret *n.* मीनार, धौरहरा

mince *v.t.* छोटे-छोटे टुकड़े
करना, बनकर बोलना

mind *n.* मन, चित्त, विचार,
इच्छा*, अभिप्राय, निर्णय;
v.t. & i. ध्यान देना, याद
करना, सावधान होना; to
pass out of mind भूल

जाना; of one mind समान
मत का; to my mind मेरी
समझ में; to give one's
mind to ध्यान लगाना;
never mind कोई चिन्ता
नहीं; mind's eye कल्पना*

mindful *a.* सचेत, सावधान

mine *n.* खान*, सुरंग, बारूद
भरा हुआ पात्र: *v.t.* खान
खोदना, सुरंग बनाना

miner *n.* खान मज़दूर

mineral *n.* खनिज पदार्थ,
धातु*; *a* खनिज से प्राप्त;
mineral oil मिट्टी का तेल;
mineral water धातु का
अंश मिला हुआ जल

mineralogist *n.* खनिज विद्या
में निपुण

mineralogy *n.* खनिज विद्या*

mingle *v.t.* एकत्र करना,
मिलाना; to mingle tears
साथ मिलकर रोना

miniature *n.* छोटे आकार का
चित्र; *a.* अति सूक्ष्म; in
miniature छोटे रूप में

minimize *v.t.* अति सूक्ष्म
करना

minimum *n.* (*pl.* minima.)
अति सूक्ष्म परिमाण, न्यूनतम

minister *n.* मन्त्री, अधिकारी,
राजदूत, पुरोहित; *v.t. & i.*
सेवा करना, कर्त्तव्य करना

ministry *n. (pl.* ministries) मंत्रालय

minor *a.* छोटा, नाबालिग, अनावश्यक; *n.* नाबालिग व्यक्ति

minority *n.* नाबालिगी, अल्प-संख्यक

mint *n.* टकसाल; *v.t.* सिक्का ढालना

minus *prep.* कमी*, घटाव, ऋण (—) का चिह्न

minute *a.* बहुत छोटा, तुच्छ, सूक्ष्म, ब्योरेवार

minute *n.* मिनट, अंश, क्षण, अधिकृत पत्र, स्मरणार्थ लेख; minutehand घड़ी की बड़ी सुई; minutely *a.* मिनट में एक बार होने वाला

minutely *adv.* सूक्ष्म ढंग से

minutes *n. pl.* कार्यवाही*, कार्य-विवरण

miracle *n.* अद्भुत घटना*, चमत्कार

mirage *n.* मृगतृष्णा, मृग-मरीचिका*

mirror *n.* दर्पण; *v.t.* दर्पण से प्रतिबिम्बित करना

mirth *n.* आनन्द, प्रमोद

mis *pref.* 'बुरा, अशुद्ध' के अर्थ का उपसर्ग

misadventure *n.* अभाग्य, दुर्घटना*

misanthrope *n.* मनुष्य-द्रोही

misbehave *v.t.* दुर्व्यवहार करना

misbehaviour *n.* अशिष्ट व्यवहार

miscalculate *v.t.* अशुद्ध गणना करना

miscalculation *n.* अशुद्ध गणना*

miscarriage *n.* बुरा प्रबन्ध, विफलता*, गर्भपात

miscellaneous *a.* विविध, मिश्रित

miscellany *n.* मिश्रण, नाना विषयों का संग्रह

mischief *n.* शरारत*, हानि*

mischievous *a.* दुष्ट, शरारती

misconception *n.* भ्रान्ति*, मिथ्या धारणा*

misconduct *n.* बुरा व्यवहार; *v.t.* बुरा व्यवहार करना

misdeed *n.* कुकर्म, दुराचार

misdirection *n.* गलत दिशा*

miser *n.* कृपण, कंजूस

miserable *a.* तुच्छ, अधम, अभागा

miserably *adv.* अभाग्य से

miserly *a.* कंजूस की तरह का

misery *n. (pl.* miseries) दुर्गति*; अभाग्य

misfire *v.i.* बंदूक का न दगना, निशाना चूकना

misfit *n.* अनुपयुक्त वस्तु या वस्त्र या व्यक्ति; *v.t.* (*p.t.* misfitted) ठीक न बैठना

misfortune *n.* अभाग्य, दुर्गति*

misgiving *n.* अविश्वास

misguide *v.t.* बहकाना, भटकाना

mishap *n.* अभाग्य, आपत्ति*;

misjudge *v.t.* गलत फैसला करना

mislead *v.t.* बहकाना, धोखा देना

mismanagement *n.* कुप्रबन्ध

misnomer *n.* अशुद्ध नाम

misplace *v.t.* कुठौर रखना, बेठिकाने रखना

misprint *v.t.* अशुद्ध छापना; *n.* छापे की अशुद्धि*

miss *n.* युवती*; कुमारी*; कन्या*

miss *v.t. & i.* निशाना चूकना, न पाना, अभाव का अनुभव करना, विफल होना

missile *n.* क्षेप्यास्त्र

mission *n.* मिशन, शिष्टमंडल, कार्य, उद्देश्य, संदेश, दौत्य

missionary *n.* मिशनरी, धर्म-प्रचार के लिए नियुक्त मनुष्य, धर्म-प्रचारक

mistake *v.t.* (*p.t.* mistook, *p.p.* mistaken) भ्रम में पड़ना, सन्देह में होना; *n.* अशुद्धि*; भ्रम, गलती*

mistress *n.* (*mas.* mister) *abbr.* mrs.) श्रीमती*; महोदया*; गृहिणी*; स्वामिनी*; रखैल*

mistrust *n.* अविश्वास; *v.t.* सन्देह करना

misunderstand *v.i.* (misunderstood) मिथ्या जानना, गलत समझना,

misunderstanding *n.* गलत-फहमी*

misuse *n.* दुरुपयोग दुर्व्यवहार; *v.t.* बुरी तरह काम में लाना, अनुचित व्यवहार करना

mitigate *v.t.* शांत करना, घटाना

mix *v.i. & t.* मिलना, मिलाना, जोड़ना

mixture *n.* मिक्चर, मिश्रण, घोल

moan *v.i.* विलाप करना, कराहना; *n.* विलाप, कराह*

mob *n.* उपद्रवी मनुष्यों की भीड़*, *v i.* उपद्रव करना, भीड़ लगाना

mobile *a.* सचल, गतिशील

mobilize *v t.* जुटाना, संचालित करना, चलाना, सेना को युद्ध के काम में लगाना

mock *v.i. & t.* हंसी उड़ाना,

छलना, चिढ़ाना; *n.* अनु-
करण, तिरस्कार; *a.* बनावटी,
भूठा
mockery *n.* छल, विडम्बना*,
हंसी*
model *n.* प्रतिमा*, आदर्श,
नमूना; *v.t.* (*p.t.* modelled)
बनाना, ढालना
moderate *a.* परिमित, मध्यम-
श्रेणी का, संयमित, परिवर्तन-
विरोधी; *v.t. & i.* संयमित
करना, घटाना, शान्त करना,
मन्द या नरम होना
modern *a.* आधुनिक, नवीन
modernize *v.t.* नया बनाना
modest *a.* लज्जावान, शुद्ध,
सुशील, संकोची
modesty *n.* नम्रता*, विनय
modify *v.t.* (*p.t.* modified)
सुधारना, रूपभेद करना, कम
करना, कड़ाई कम करना
modulate *v.t.* स्वर ऊंचा नीचा
करना, न्यूनाधिक करना,
मिलाना, ठीक करना या होना
moist *a.* कुछ भीगा हुआ, तर
moisture *n.* गीलापन, तरी*,
नमी*
molasses *n.* राब, जूसी, शीरा,
गुड़
mole *n.* छछूंदर, तिल, मसा,
बांध
molest *v.t.* कष्ट देना, विघ्न

करना, छेड़ना
moment *n.* क्षण, आवश्य-
कता* at the present
moment अभी
momentary *a.* क्षणिक
momentous *a.* महत्त्व का
momentum *n.* (*pl.* mo-
menta) वेग, गति*, चाल*
monarch *n.* अधिप, राजा
monarchy *n.* राजतन्त्र
monastery *n.* मठ
Monday *n.* सोमवार
monetary *a.* धन या मुद्रा-
सम्बन्धी
money *n.* धन, मुद्रा*, बैंक के
या सरकारी नोट
monition *n.* भय सूचना*,
उपदेश
monitor *n.* (*fem.* moni-
tress) मॉनीटर, छात्रनायक
monk *n.* (*fem.* nun)
संन्यासी, उदासी
monkey *n.* बन्दर
mono *pref.* 'अकेला' के अर्थ
का उपसर्ग
monogamy *n.* एकपत्नी विवाह
monogram *n.* एक में गुथे हुए
अनेक अक्षर
monograph *n.* किसी एक
विषय पर लेख
monolith *n.* केवल पत्थर का
खम्भा

monologue *n.* स्वगत भाषण, एक-संभाषणीय नाटक, एक-पात्रीय रूपक

monopolist *n.* इजारेदार

monopolize *v.t.* इजारेदारी करना

monopoly *n.* (*p.l.* monopolies) इजारेदारी

monosyllable *n.* एकाक्षरी शब्द

monotonous एक तान, एक लय, नीरस, उबाने वाला, उकता देने वाला

monotony *n.* नीरसता, ऊब

monotype *n.* मोनोटाइप, एक मुद्र

monsoon *n.* मानसून, वर्षाऋतु

monster *n.* राक्षस, दैत्य, निर्दय मनुष्य, बड़े आकार का विलक्षण प्राणी

monstrosity *n.* भयंकरता*, दैत्यता*

monstrous *a.* राक्षसी, अद्भुत, विलक्षण, भयंकर

month *n.* मास, महीना

monthly *a.*, *adv.* & *n.* मासिक, प्रतिमास, मासिक पत्रिका*

monumental *a.* स्मारक-संबंधी वृहत् और चिरस्थायी

mood *n.* मूड, चित्तवृत्ति*, भाव, अवस्था*

moody *a.* मनमौजी, उदासीन, क्रोधी

moon *n.* चन्द्रमा; *v.i.* निरर्थक भटकना

moonshine *n.* चांदनी, स्वप्न-प्रलाप

mooring *n.* नौकाबंघ स्थल, घाट, नौकादि बांधने का रस्सा या जंजीर

mop *n.* कूंचा, झाड़ू; *v.t.* (*p t.* mopped.) झाड़ू से निर्मल या साफ करना

moral *a.* चरित्र-संबंधी, कर्तव्य-परायण, न्यायानुसारी; *n.* अभिप्राय

moralist *n.* नीतिज्ञ, सदाचार-मार्गी

morality *n.* नीति*, विद्या*, सदाचार

moralize *v.i.* नीतिसंगत करना, उपदेश करना

morbid *a.* अस्वस्थ, दूषित, रोगी

morbidity *n.* अस्वस्थता*

more *a.* अधिकतर; *adv.* अधिकता से; is no more मर गया है; more and more लगातार, बढ़कर; more or less न्यूनाधिक

moreover *adv.* इससे अधिक, सिवाय

morning *n.* & *a.* प्रातःकाल,

प्रातःकालीन; good morning to you आपका प्रातः-काल शुभ हो

morphia n. अफीम का सत्त्व

morrow n. आनेवाला दिन

mortal a. मरनेवाला, प्राण-घातक; n. मर्त्य

morality n. मरण, नाश

mortgage n. बन्धक, गिरवी*, v.t. बन्धक रखना

mortgagee n. रेहनदार, बन्धक-धारी

mortgagor n. बन्धक रखने वाला मनुष्य, गिरवी रखने वाला, राहित

mortify v.t. & i. (p.t. mortified) विनीत करना, क्लेश देना, मन मारना

mosaic n. मौजेक, पच्चीकारी*

mosque n. मसजिद*

mosquito n. (pl. mosquitoes) मच्छर

most a. & adv. अधिकतम, सबसे अधिक; for the most part विशेषकर, प्रायः; at the most अधिकतर; to make the most of सबसे अधिक सुविधा का होना

mother n. (mas. father) माता*, महतिन*, उद्गम-स्थान; v.t. पालन-पोषण करना; mother-country

मातृभूमि*; mother-of-pearl मोती का सीप; mother-tongue मातृभाषा*; mother-wit सामान्य बुद्धि*

motherhood n. मातृभाव, मातृत्व

mother-in-law (pl. mothers-in-law) n. सास

motherly a. माता सदृश

motif n. प्रधान विचार, (कला-कृति में) विशेष लक्षण

motion n. गति*, चिह्न, व्यापार, प्रस्ताव; v.i. संकेत करना; adjournment motion कामरोको प्रस्ताव, कार्यस्थगन प्रस्ताव

motionless a. स्थिर, अचल

motive n. प्रेरणा*, कारण

motley a. अनेक विभिन्न तत्त्वों का बना हुआ

motor n. & a. गति देनेवाला यन्त्र, गाड़ी-चालक यंत्र; v.i. मोटरगाड़ी द्वारा यात्रा करना

motorist n. मोटर गाड़ी चलाने वाला

motto n. (pl. mottoes) नीति-वाक्य, सिद्धान्त, आदर्श-वाक्य, कहावत

moujik n. रूसी किसान

mould n. रूप, नमूना, सांचा; v.t. सांचा बनाना, ढालना

mound n. छोटी पहाड़ी*

mount n. पहाड़ी*, तस्वीर का चौखटा या इसके चिपकाने की दवनी*, सवारी का घोड़ा; v.t. उठाना, चढ़ाना, सवार होना, बैठाना

mountain n. पर्वत, पहाड़; a. पहाड़ी, पर्वनीय

mountaineer n. पर्वतनिवासी, पर्वतारोही

mountainous a. पहाड़ी, पर्वत-मय

mourn v.t. विलाप करना, शोक करना

mourner n. विलाप करनेवाला

mournful a. शोकाकुल, उद्विग्न

mourning n. शोक, विलाप; mourning-dress अमंगल (शोक) सूचक काला वस्त्र

mouse n. (pl. mice) चूहा; mouse-trap चूहादानी*

moustache n. मूंछ*

mouth n. मुख, मुहाना; मार्ग; v.t. लालची की तरह खाना, रोब से बोलना

mouthful n. ग्रास, कौर

mouth-piece n. दूसरे के स्थान पर बोलने के लिए नियुक्त व्यक्ति, मुखपत्र

movables n. चल सम्पत्ति*

move v.t. & i. हटना, हटाना, चलना, उत्तेजित करना, चलाना, उकसाना, प्रस्ताव करना, प्रणाम करना; n. गति*, चाल*

movement n. गति*, चाल*, घड़ी का पुर्जा

mover n. प्रस्तावक

movies n. pl. चलचित्र

much a. & adv. बहुत, प्रत्यन्त

mud n. गीली मिट्टी*, कीचड़

muddle n. गड़बड़ी*; v.t. गड़बड़ करना

mudguard n. मडगार्ड, पंक-रक्षी

mug n. मग, लोटा, गड़ुआ

mulberry n. शहतूत

mule n. खच्चर, हठी मनुष्य, सूत कातने का यंत्र

muleteer n. खच्चर हांकनेवाला

multi, mult prefs. 'बहुत' 'अनेक के अर्थ के उपसर्ग

multifarious a. बहुविध, रंग-बिरंग

multimillionaire n. करोड़पति

multiple a. बहुभागी, विभिन्न; n. ऐसी संख्या जो बिना शेष के दूसरी संख्या को भाग दे सकती है; least common multiple लघुतम समापवर्त्य

multiplication n. गुणन-क्रिया*, गुणा*

multiplicity n. अनेक भेद

multiply v.t. (p.t. multi-plied) गुणा करना, बढ़ाना

multitude n. बड़ी संख्या*,
भीड़*, सामान्य लोग

mum a. मूक, चुप

mumble v.i. बुदबुदाना, अस्पष्ट
बोलना

mummy n. ममी, मसाला
लगाकर सुरक्षित शव

mundane a. संसारी, इस लोक
का

municipal a. नगरपालिका
संबंधी; ~ corporation
नगर-निगम

municipality n. नगरपालिका*

munitions n. युद्ध-सामग्री,
लड़ाई के सामान

mural a. भीत-संबंधी

murder v t. हत्या करना, नष्ट
करना; n. हत्या*, वध

murderer (fem. murderess)
n. हत्यारा

murderous a. निठुर, हत्यारा,
घातक

murmur n. बड़बड़ाहट*,
असन्तोष की ध्वनि*; v.t.
बड़बड़ाना, असन्तोष प्रकट
करना

muscle n. मांसपेशी*, पुट्ठा

muscular a. पेशी-संबंधी, मांसल

muse n. सरस्वती*, वाग्देवता,
काव्य प्रतिभा*; v.i. चिन्ता
में लीन होना, विचार करना

museum n. संग्रहालय, अजायब-
घर

mushroom n. कुकुरमुत्ता

music n. सङ्गीत, गानविद्या*,
सुर, सुरीला शब्द

musical a. सुरीला

musician n. संगीतज्ञ

musing n. ध्यान, चिन्तन

musk n. मृगमद, कस्तूरी;
    musk deer कस्तूरीमृग;
    musk melon तरबूज;
    musk-rat छछूंदर

musket n. छोटी बन्दूक*

musketeer n. बन्दूकधारी सैनिक

must v.i. & aux. अवश्य
चाहिए, अवश्य होना

mustard n. सरसों, राई

muster v.t. & i. इकट्ठा होना
या करना; n. समाज,
मण्डली*, जमाव; muster-
roll अधिकारियों और उनके
अनुचरों की सूची

mutation n. नाम परिवर्तन,
दाखिलखारिज

mutilate v.t. अंगभंग करना,
छांटना, खंडित करना

mutilation n. अंग का कटाव

mutinous a. विद्रोही

mutiny n. बलवा, विप्लव; v.t.
(p.t. mutinied) विप्लव या
बलवा करना

mutter v.t. & i. अस्पष्ट
बोलना, बरबराना; n. बड़-

वड़ाहट

mutton *n.* भेड़ का मांस

mutual *a.* पारस्परिक, अन्योन्य, आपस का

muzzle *n.* पशु के मुख का थूथन, बन्दूक का मुंह, पशु के मुख पर लगाने की जाली*; *v.t.* मुख पर जाली लगाना, काटने से रोकना

myopia, myopy *ns.* अल्प दृष्टित्व, जिसमें दूर का पदार्थ स्पष्ट नहीं दीख पड़ता

myopic *a.* अल्प दृष्टि सम्बन्धी

mysterious *a.* रहस्यपूर्ण, गुप्त, अस्पष्ट

mystery *n.* गुप्त बात, रहस्य

mystic, mystical *a.* रहस्य-वादी, सूफी

mysticism *n.* रहस्यवाद, सूफी-वाद

mystify *v.t.* (*p.t.* mystified) रहस्यमय करना, गूढ़ करना

myth *n.* पौराणिक कथा*, कल्पित कथा*, गप्प*

mythical *a.* पौराणिक कथा-सम्बन्धी

mythological *a.* पुराण शास्त्र संबंधी

mythology *n.* पौराणिक कथाएं*, पुराणशास्त्र

N

nail *n.* नख, पंजा, कील; *v.i.* कांटी से अड़ना; to hit the nail on the head सच्ची वार्ता कहना; on the nail बिना विलम्ब के

naive *a.* सीधा, प्राकृतिक

naked *a.* नंगा, वस्त्रहीन

name *n.* नाम, लक्षण, यश, जातीय, वंश; a good name प्रसिद्ध; persons of name प्रसिद्ध लोग ; *v.t.* नाम लेना, निर्धारित करना

namesake *n.* एक ही नाम का,

नामराशि*

napkin *n.* अंगौछी*, छोटी तौलिया*

narcosis *n.* मूर्च्छा*

narcotic *a. & n.* निद्रा लाने वाली, निद्राजनक औषधि

narrate *v.t.* विवरण-सहित वर्णन करना

narrator *n.* वर्णन करने वाला

narrow *a.* संकुचित, संकरा, छोटा; *v t. & i.* संकुचित करना या होना; narrow circumstances दरिद्रता*,

narrow-minded कृपण बुद्धिवाला, ओछा

nascent *a.* नवजात, वर्द्धमान

nasty *a* मलिन, कष्टकारक, अरोचक

nation *n.* जाति*, राष्ट्र

national *a.* राष्ट्रीय, जातीय; ~ anthem राष्ट्र गीत

nationalist *n.* राष्ट्रवादी

nationality *n.* राष्ट्रीयता*

nationalize *v.t.* राष्ट्रीयकरण

native *a.* सहज, स्वाभाविक, प्राकृतिक, सामान्य; *n.* देश-वासी, देशी जन

natural *a.* स्वाभाविक, प्राकृतिक, यथार्थ, सच्चा; natural history जीव-विज्ञान, पशु तथा वनस्पति जीवशास्त्र; natural philo-sophy भौतिक विज्ञान

naturalist *n.* प्रकृतिवादी

naturalize *v.t.* नागरिकता के अधिकार देना

naturally *adv.* स्वभावतः, प्रकृति से

nature *n.* प्रकृति*, भूमंडल, सत्व, स्वभाव, शक्ति*, धर्म, प्रकार; against nature अप्राकृतिक; contrary to nature विलक्षण; debt of nature मृत्यु*; nature study प्रकृति का अध्ययन;

to ease nature मल-मूत्र त्यागना

naughty *a.* दुष्ट, उपद्रवी

nausea *n.* जी को मिचलाहट*, मिचली*, ओकाई*

naval *a.* जहाजी, नावीय, समुद्री

navigability *n.* नाव ले जाने की योग्यता*, नौगम्यता*

navigable *a.* पोत या नाव ले जाने योग्य

navigate *v.t. & i.* समुद्र में यात्रा करना, पोत चलाना

navigation *n.* समुद्र-यात्रा*, नौ-गमन

navigator *n.* नाविक, मल्लाह

navy *n.* जहाजी बेड़ा, जलसेना, नौसेना; navy blue गाढ़ा नीला रंग

near *a. & prep. (comp.* nearer, *sup.* nearest) समीप, पास में; *v.t.* समीप, पहुंचना; far and near सर्वत्र

nearly *adv.* पास में, प्रायः nearly related घनिष्ठ रूप से सम्बन्धित

neat *n. (pl.* neat) चौपाया; *a.* शुद्ध, स्वच्छ, सुथरा

nebula *n. (pl.* nebulae) आंखों के आगे धुन्ध, तारा-मण्डल, नीहारिका*

necessary *n.* अति आवश्यक

पदार्थ; *a.* अपरिहार्य, आवश्यक, अनिवार्य; **necessarily** *adv.* अवश्य करके

necessitate *v.t.* आवश्यक करना, विवश करना

necessity *n.* आवश्यकता*, विवशता*

neck *n.* कण्ठ, गरदन*, भू-डमरूमध्य

necklace *n.* गले का हार

nectar *n.* अमृत, सुधा

need *n.* प्रयोजन, कष्ट, दरिद्रता*; *v.t.* चाहना, ज़रूरत होना; **needful** *a.* आवश्यक

needle *n.* सूई, कुतुबनुमा का कांटा

needlework *n.* ज़रदोज़ी का काम

needs *adv.* अवश्य, मजबूरन

needy *a.* (*comp.* needier, *sup.* neediest) अति दरिद्र, ज़रूरतमन्द

nefarious *a.* बड़ा दुष्ट

negate *v.t.* अस्वीकार करना

negation *n.* निषेध, अस्वीकार

negative *a.* निषेधार्थक, अभाव-सूचक; *n.* अभाव-सूचक शब्द, (बीजगणित में) ऋण परिमाण फोटो का निगेटिव; *v.i.* असिद्ध करना

neglect *v.t.* उपेक्षा करना, सुध न लेना, बिना पूरा किए

छोड़ना; *n.* उपेक्षा*, अशुद्धि*

negligence *n.* उपेक्षा*, भूल*

negligible *a.* उपेक्षा करने योग्य

negotiable *a.* विनिमेय, बिक्री करने योग्य

negotiate *v.t.* व्यापार करना, तय करना

negotiation *n.* व्यवहार, सौदा

negotiator *n.* व्यवहारी, मध्यस्थ, विचौलिया

Negro *n.* (*pl.* Negroes, *fem.* Negress) हबशी

neighbour *r.* पड़ोसी

neighbourhood *n.* पड़ोस

neither *a., conj. & pron.* दोनो में से कोई भी नहीं

neo *pref.* 'नवीन या आधुनिक' के अर्थ का उपमर्ग

nephew *n.* (*fem.* niece) भतीजा, भांजा

nepotism *n.* भाई भतीजावाद, कुनबापरस्ती

Neptune *n.* समुद्र देवता, वरुण, एक नक्षत्र

nerve *n.* शिरा*, ज्ञानतन्तु, दृढ़ता*, धैर्य; *v.t.* शक्ति देना; to lose one's nerve डर-पोक बन जाना

nerveless *a.* शक्तिहीन

nervous *a.* नाड़ीमंडल-संबंधी, ओजस्वी, डरपोक, मांसल,

पुष्ट nervous-system नाड़ी-मण्डल, नाड़ी-संस्थान

nest *n.* घोंसला, आनन्दगृह

nestle *v.i. & t.* घोंसले में रहना, शरण लेना, प्यार से सटना या दबाना, पालन-पोषण करना

net *n.* फन्दा, जाल, *v.t.* (*p.t.* netted) जाल में फंसाना; *a.* खर्चा, दस्तूरी आदि, छोड़ा हुआ, शुद्ध, मूल

network *n.* जाली का काम, जाली*

neuter *a.* नपुंसक, निरपेक्ष; neuter gender नपुंसक लिंग

neutral *a* तटस्थ, उदासीन

neutrality *n.* समदृष्टि*, तटस्थता*, उदासीनता*

neutralize *v.t.* निरर्थक या निष्क्रिय करना

never *adv.* कभी नहीं, अवश्य नहीं

nevertheless *conj.* तो भी, तिसपर भी

new *a.* नया, हाल का, ताज़ा; new comer नवागन्तुक; the new world अमेरिका महाद्वीप; new year's day जनवरी का पहला दिन

news *n.* वार्ता*, समाचार; news-agent समाचारपत्र का एजेण्ट; newsmonger समा-चार फैलानेवाला; news-paper समाचारपत्र; news-man पत्रकार

next *a.* (*sup.* of nigh) आगामी, निकट का; *adv.* अगले स्थान में, ठीक बाद में; *prep.* बगल में; next to nothing प्रायः कुछ नहीं

nice *a.* मनोहर, स्वाद, अच्छा, सूक्ष्मदर्शी

nickel *n.* निकल, गिलट; *v.t.* (*p.t.* nickelled) गिलट चढ़ाना

nickname *n.* उपनाम, चिढ़ाने का नाम

niece *n.* (*mas.* nephew) भतीजी*, भानजी*

night *n.* रात*, अन्धकार; night-bird उल्लू; night-blindness रतौंधी; night-fall *n.* सन्ध्या समय; night-long रात-भर; nightmare दुःस्वप्न; night-watch रात का पहरा

nightingale *n.* बुलबुल*

nightly *n. & adv.* रात का, प्रति रात्रि को

nil *n.* कोई संख्या नहीं

nine *a.* नौ; a nine day's wonder कुछ काल के लिए आश्चर्य उत्पन्न करनेवाला; **ninefold** *a.* नौगुना

nineteen *a.* उन्नीस

ninety *a.* नब्बे

nitro *pref.* उपसर्ग जो 'शोरे की उत्पत्ति' के अर्थ में प्रयुक्त होता है

nitrogen *n.* 'नाइट्रोजन' नामक वायुतत्त्व, नत्रजन

no *a.* कोई भी नहीं; *adv.* कुछ भी नहीं; *n.* नहीं' की सम्मति*; in no time जल्दी से; nobody कोई व्यक्ति नहीं; no doubt नि:सन्देह; no one कोई भी नहीं; noes *n. pl.* 'नहीं' की सम्मतियां; nowhere कहीं भी नहीं; nowise *adv.* किसी प्रकार से नहीं

nobility *n.* कुलीनता*, महत्त्व, सामाजिक उत्कर्ष, कुलीन लोग; noble-minded उदार चित्त का

noble *a.* कुलीन, सुप्रतिष्ठित, तेजस्वी, श्रेष्ठ, प्रभावशाली; *n.* कुलीन मनुष्य

nod *v.i. & t.* (*p.t.* nodded) सिर हिलाना, सिर झुकाकर अभिवादन करना; a nodding acquaintance सामान्य परिचय

noise *n.* कोलाहल, रव; *v.i.* कोलाहल करना

noiseless *a.* नीरव

nomad *n.* घूमनेवाला, बंजारा

nomenclature *n.* नाम, नाम-क्रम, पारिभाषिक शब्द

nominal *a.* नाम मात्र का, असत्य

nominate *v.t.* नाम लेना, नामजद करना, निर्दिष्ट करना, नियुक्त करना

nomination *n.* नामजदगी, नियुक्ति

nominee *n.* मनोनीत व्यक्ति

nonchalance *n.* उदासीनता*, शान्ति*

nonchalant *a.* उदासीन

nonconformist *n.* प्रचलित धर्म के मत का विरोधी, अननुवर्ती

non-co-operation *n.* असहयोग

none *pron., a. & adv.* कोई नहीं

nonentity *n.* अस्तित्वहीनता*, शून्यता*

none-the-less *adv.* तथापि, तो भी

nonsense *n.* बकवास*, असंगत वार्ता*

nonsensical *a.* असंगत, अनर्थक

norm *n.* नियम, आदर्श

normal *a.* यथाक्रम, सामान्य

normalize *v.t.* नियमित करना, सुव्यवस्थित करना, सामान्य स्थिति लाना

north *n.* उत्तर; north pole

उत्तरी ध्रुव

nose *n.* नाक*, किसी पदार्थ का नुकीला भाग; *v.t.* सूंघना, सूंघकर पता लगाना; to poke one's nose into हस्तक्षेप करना; to turn up one's nose at तिरस्कार करना; nose-band नकेल

nostril *n.* नाक का छेद, नथुना

not *adv.* नहीं, न, मत; not a few अधिक, बहुत; not at all कुछ भी नहीं; not but न केवल

notable *a.* स्मरणीय, प्रसिद्ध; *n.* प्रसिद्ध पुरुष

note *n.* टिप्पणी*, चिह्न, टीका*, व्याख्या*, पत्र, रसीद*, यादगार*; *v.t.* यादगार बना लेना, ध्यान देना

noteworthy *a.* विचार करने योग्य

nothing *n.* कुछ भी नहीं, तुच्छ वस्तु*; to dance on nothing फांसी पड़ना; for nothing निर्थक, व्यर्थ; to make nothing of निर्थक जानना, समझ में न आना; to come to nothing निर्थक होना; to have nothing to do with आशय न रखना; *adv.* किसी प्रकार से नहीं

notice *n.* नोटिस, सूचना*, निरूपण, विज्ञापन; *v.t.* ध्यान देना, निरूपण करना; to take no notice of ध्यान न देना

notification *n.* सूचना*, विज्ञापन

notify *v.t.* (*p.t.* notified) सूचना देना, जताना, प्रकाशित करना, विज्ञापित करना

notion *n.* कल्पना*, विचार, मत

notoriety *n.* कुख्याति*, प्रसिद्धि*

notorious *a.* प्रसिद्ध, दुर्नाम, कुख्यात

notwithstanding *conj.*, *adv.* & *prep.* यद्यपि, तो भी, होते हुए भी

nought *n.* कुछ नहीं, शून्य; to bring to nought नाश करना, व्यर्थ करना; to sit at nought तिरस्कार करना

noun *n.* संज्ञा*, नाम, विशेष्य

nourish *v.t.* पालन करना, पोषण करना

nourishment *n.* पौष्टिक आहार

novel *a.* अपूर्व, नवीन, अनोखा; *n.* उपन्यास

novelette *n.* लघु उपन्यास

novelist *n.* उपन्यासकार

novelty *n.* कौतुक, अद्भुत वस्तु*

November *n.* नवम्बर, अंग्रेजी वर्ष का ग्यारहवां महीना

novice *n.* नवसिखुवा, अनभ्यस्त, अनुभवहीन व्यक्ति

now *adv.* अभी; now-a-days इन दिनों, आजकल; now and then कभी-कभी

nuclear *a.* न्यप्टि न्येप्टिक, केन्द्रकीय, पारमाणविक

nude *a.* वस्त्रहीन, नंगा

nudity *n.* वस्त्रहीनता*, नंगापन

nuisance *n.* कण्टक, बाधा*, क्लेशकारक पदार्थ; commit no nuisance स्थान को गन्दा मत करो

null *a.* निष्फल, वृथा*, null and void निरर्थक

number *n.* संख्या*, गराना*, गिनती*, समूह, (ब०व०) कविता*; *v.t.* गिनती करना; science of numbers अंक-गणित

numerical *a.* संख्या-सूचक, संख्यायुक्त

numerous *a.* अनेक, बहुत

nun *n., fem.* (*mas.* monk) संन्यासिनी*, तपस्विनी, बैरागिन*

nurse *n.* नर्स*, परिचारिका*, धाय*; *v.t.* धाय की तरह काम करना, दूध पिलाकर बच्चे को पालना

nursery *n.* नर्सरी, पेड़-पौधों को रखने का कमरा, बच्चो का कमरा, पोषशाला*, शिशु-शाला*

nurture *n.* शिक्षा, पालन; *v.t* पालन करना, शिक्षा देना

nut *n.* गरीफल, कड़े छिलके का फल, काष्ठफल, लकड़ी की ढिबरी*; *v t.* कड़े फल इकट्ठा करना

nutrition *n.* पुष्टिकर भोजन

nutritious *a.* पोषक, पुष्टिवर्धक

nutritive *a.* पोषण-सम्बन्धी, पोषक, आहार के योग्य

nymph *n.* अप्सरा*, परी*, सुन्दर स्त्री*

nymphomania *n.* स्त्रियों में उत्कट कामुकता*

O

oak *n.* बलूत का पेड़ा; oak-apple माजूफल

oar *n.* पतवार, डांडा, मल्लाह; *v.t.* नाव खेना

oarsman *n.* मल्लाह

oasis *n.* (*pl.* oases) मरुद्वीप, नखलिस्तान

oat *n.* जई*

oatmeal n. जई का आटा

oath n. शपथ*, सौगन्ध*

obduracy n. हठ

obdurate a. हठी, कठोर हृदय

obedience n. आज्ञापालन, अनुसरण

obedient a. आज्ञाकारी, कर्तव्य-शील

obey v.t. & i. आज्ञा पालन करना, बात मनाना, अनुशासित होना

obituary a. मृत्यु-संबंधी; n. मृत्यु-समाचार, मृतक-परिचय

object n. इरादा, प्रयोजन, उद्देश्य, इन्द्रिय-विषय, द्रव्य, पदार्थ, (व्याकरण में) कर्म

object v.i. & t. विरोध करना, अस्वीकार करना

objection n. आपत्ति*, विरोध, आक्षेप

objectionable a. आपत्ति-जनक, अरुचिकर, विरोधी

objective n. परिश्रम का लक्ष्य, (व्या०) कर्म

objective a. वस्तुपरक; objective case (व्याकरण में) कर्म कारक

obligation n. बन्धन, प्रतिज्ञा*, बाध्यता*, कर्तव्य, धर्म, अनुग्रह, उपकार

obligatory a. बाध्यकारी, अवश्यकरणीय, आभार्य

oblige v.t. विवश करना, अनुग्रह करना, ऋणी करना

oblique a. झुका हुआ, तिरछा

obliterate v.t. मिटाना, नष्ट करना

obliteration n. लोप, नाश, उन्मूलन

oblivion n. विस्मृति*, उपेक्षा*

oblong a. दीर्घाकार, आयता-कार; n. आयत आकृति*

obnoxious a. घृणित, अनिष्ट-कारी, अप्रिय

obscene a. अश्लील, अपवित्र, फूहर

obscenity n. अश्लीलता*, फूहरपन

obscure a. अप्रसिद्ध, अस्पष्ट, गूढ़; v.t. छिपाना

obscurity n. अप्रसिद्धि*, गूढ़ता*

observance n. व्यवहार, रीति* आचरण

observant a. सावधान, चैतन्य, विवेकी

observation n. निरीक्षण, विचार

observatory n. वेधशाला*

observe v.t. & i. ध्यान देना, परीक्षा करना, अनुष्ठान करना

obsess v.t. प्रेत की तरह पीड़ा देना, कष्ट देना

obsession n. प्रेतबाधा*

obsolete *a.* अप्रचलित, पुराने ढंग का

obstinacy *n.* हठ

obstinate *a.* दुःसाध्य, हठी

obstruct *v.t.* अवरोध करना, रोकना

obstruction *n.* रुकावट*

obstructive *a.* प्रतिबन्ध करने वाला, रोकने वाला

obtain *v.t. & i.* प्राप्त करना, प्रवृत्त होना

obtainable *a.* प्राप्त करने योग्य, प्राप्य

obtuse *a.* मन्द, मूढ़, समकोण से बड़े कोण का, दीर्घकोणीय

obvious *a.* स्पष्ट, प्रत्यक्ष, सुबोध, सुगम

obviously *adv.* स्पष्ट रूप से

occasion *n.* अवसर, प्रसंग, प्रयोजन, हेतु, घटना*, कारण; *v.t.* उत्पन्न करना, घटित कराना या करना

occasional *a.* समयानुसार, प्रासंगिक

occasionally *adv.* कभी-कभी

occident *n.* पश्चिम दिशा*

occidental *a.* पश्चिमी, पाश्चात्य

occult *a.* जादू का, गुप्त, छिपा हुआ

occupant *n.* अधिकारी, मालिक

occupation *n.* अधिकार, व्यव-साय, पेशा

occupy *v.t. & i.* (*p.t.* occu-pied) अधिकार करना, व्याप्त करना पद धारण करना, धन्धे में लगना

occur *v.i. & t.* (*p.t.* occur-red) प्रकट होना, घटित होना, मन में आना

occurrence *n.* घटना*, वृत्तान्त

ocean *n.* महासागर; ocean-lane जहाज़ के चलने का समुद्र का मार्ग

octagon *n.* अष्टभुज

octagonal *a.* अठपहला

octangular *a.* आठ कोने का

octave *n.* सत्यक, अष्टक, आठ चरणों का पद, बाजे का पर्दा

October *n.* अक्तूबर

octroi *n.* चुंगी*

odd *a.* ताख (अयुग्म), बिल-क्षण, विचित्र; at odds विरोध में; odds and ends फुटकर पदार्थ; to take odds सुविधा स्वीकार करना; odd and even जस-ताख; odd number विषम संख्या*

oddity *n.* (*pl.* oddities) विचित्रता*, अपूर्वता*

odds *n. pl.* भिन्नता* अस-मानता*, सुविधा*

ode *n.* गीत, गीति-काव्य

odour *n.* गंध, सुगंध*

offence *n.* अन्यायाचरण, अप-
राध, आक्रमण, क्रोध का
कारण

offend *v.t.* क्रुद्ध करना, अप्रसन्न
करना, चित्त दुखाना, आज्ञा
भंग करना

offender *n.* दोषी, अपराधी

offensive *a.* आक्रामक, घृणा-
जनक, अप्रिय

offer *v.t. & i. (p.t.* offered)
निवेदन करना प्रस्ताव करना;
n. निवेदन, प्रार्थना*

offering *n.* बलिदान, उपहार,
भेंट*

office *n.* कर्त्तव्य, व्यापार,
कार्यालय, काम

officer *n.* पदाधिकारी, अफसर

official *n. & a.* अधिकार संबंधी,
कर्मचारी

officially *adv.* अधिकारपूर्वक

officiate *v.i.* किसी पदाधिकारी
के स्थान में काम करना, एवजी
करना

offing *n.* किनारे से दिखाई पड़ता
हुआ समुद्र का दूर का भाग,
दृश्य-क्षितिज

offset *n.* दीवार का सलामी
छज्जा, हरजाना, कलम लगाने
की टहनी, मुद्रण कला में रबर
की छपाई

offshoot *n.* शाखा*, अंकुर

offspring *n.* सन्तति*, परिणाम

oft *adv.* बहुधा

often *adv.* बहुधा, प्रायः

oil *n.* तेल; *v.t.* तेल पोतना या
लगाना; to pour oil in
the flame उत्तेजित करना;
to pour oil on the waters
झगड़ा तय करना; to burn
the midnight oil रात में
देर तक पढ़ना या काम करना;
to oil one's tongue चाप-
लूसी करना

oilcake *n.* खली*

oilcloth *n.* मोमजामा

oil-colour *n.* तेल में मिला हुआ
रंग

oil-painting *n.* तैलचित्र

ointment *n.* मलहम, उबटन

old *a. (comp.* older, elder,
sup. oldest, eldest) वृद्ध,
फटा-पुराना, जर्जर, प्राचीन;
old boy पाठशाला का प्राचीन
विद्यार्थी; old hand अनुभवी
मनुष्य; old - fashioned
पुराने ढंग का

oligarchy *n.* अभिजाततंत्र

olive *n.* जैतून का वृक्ष; olive-
branch शान्ति का चिह्न;
olive crown विजय-मुकुट

-ology *suf.* 'विज्ञान' के
अर्थ का प्रत्यय, यथा—
biology, theology etc.

olympian *a.* महत्त्व का, प्रभाव-
शाली

omega *n.* यूनानी वर्णमाला का
अन्तिम अक्षर

omen *n.* भविष्यवाणी*, शकुन,
लक्षण

ominous *a.* अपशकुन का

omission *n.* चूक*, भूल*

omit *v.t.* (*p.t.* omitted)
त्यागना, छोड़ देना

omnipotence *n.* अनन्त शक्ति*

omnipotent *a.* सर्वशक्तिमान

omnipresence *n.* विश्व-
व्यापकता*

omnipresent *a.* विश्वव्यापी

omniscience *n.* अनन्त ज्ञान

omniscient *a.* सर्वज्ञ, त्रिकाल-
दर्शी

on *prep.* पर, और, समीप, लिए,
ऊपर, लगा हुआ, कारण से;
on account of वास्ते, लिए;
on the wing उड़ता हुआ;
a. सहारे पर का, लगा हुआ;
on purpose जान-बूझकर;
to be on fire आग लग
जाना; on the move चालू;
from that day on उस दिन
से; on the instance तुरंत;
on the minute ठीक समय
पर, आगे को

once *adv.* एक बार, पहले;
at once तुरंत; once more

again दुबारा; once for
all सर्वदा के लिए

one *a. & pron.* एक व्यक्ति,
कोई, वही, संयुक्त; many a
one बहुतेरे एक साथ; one
and all एक साथ सब; one
by one एक-एक करके; one
another परस्पर; one-
sided पक्षपाती; with one
voice एक सुर में

onerous *a.* भारी, कष्टसाध्य

onion *n.* प्याज

on-looker *n.* दर्शक

only *a.* केवल, प्रधान; *adv.*
केवल; *conj.* सिवाय; not
only but न केवल

onset *n.* आक्रमण, धावा

onslaught *n.* भयंकर आक्रमण

onus *n.* (*no plural*) भार,
कर्त्तव्य, उत्तरदायित्व

onward *a.* आगे की ओर बढ़ा
हुआ

onwards *adv.* आगे की ओर

opal *n.* दूधिया पत्थर, पोलकी

open *a.* खुला हुआ, प्रकट; *v.t.*
आरम्भ करना, प्रकाशित
करना, खोलना, स्थापित
करना; open air घर के
बाहर की खुली वायु; open-
handed उदार, दानी; open-
minded पक्षपातरहित;
open-mouthed लालची,

स्पष्टवक्ता; open to dis-
pute विवादनीय ; open
weather स्वच्छ ऋतु; to
keep doors open
सबका आतिथ्य करना;
to receive with open
arms सहृदय स्वागत या
स्वीकार करना; with open
eyes स्पष्ट रूप से; to open
one's eyes आश्चर्य दिख-
लाना; to open up प्रका-
शित करना

opening *n.* आरम्भ, अवसर,
छिद्र

openly *adv.* स्पष्टता से, खुले-
आम

opera *n.* ऑपेरा, गीति-नाट्य;
opera-glass नाटक देखने
की दूरबीन

operate *v.t. & i.* कार्य करना,
यन्त्र चलाना, शल्य-क्रिया
करना; operating room
(theatre) डाक्टर के चीर-
फाड़ करने का कमरा

operation *n.* उद्यम, चीर-फाड़,
सेना की गति*

operative *a. & n.* काम करने
वाला, श्रमिक

operator *n.* काम करनेवाला

opinion *n.* राय*, विश्वास,
अभिप्राय, आशय, विचार;
I am of opinion मैं ऐसा

विचार करता हूं

opium *n.* अफीम*

opponent *n.* विरोधी, शत्रु

opportune *a.* सुगम, अनुकूल

opportunity *n.* अवकाश,
अवसर; to wait an oppor-
tunity *n.* अवसर की
प्रतीक्षा करना

oppose *v.t.* विरोध करना,
बाधा डालना, सामना करना

opposite *a.* सामने का, विपरीत,
प्रतिकूल; of an opposite
kind भिन्न प्रकार का; the
opposite sex स्त्री-जाति

opposition *n.* विरोध, वैर,
विरोधी पक्ष

oppositional *a.* द्वेष या विरोध
भाव का

oppress *v.t.* पीड़ा देना, सताना,
दबाना

oppression *n.* उपद्रव, निर्दयता

oppressive *a.* कठोर, निर्दय

oppressor *n.* अत्याचारी, क्रूर

optic (-al) *a.* नेत्रविज्ञान

optician *n.* चश्मा बेचनेवाला,
चक्षुविद्या में निपुण

optics *n.* प्रकाश-संबंधी विज्ञान

optimism *n.* आशावादिता*

optimist *n.* आशावादी

optimistic *a.* आशावादी

option *n.* विकल्प, रुचि*, पसन्द,
अभिलाषा*; left to your

option ग्रापके इच्छानुसार

optional *a.* इच्छानुसार,
वैकल्पिक

oracle *n.* ग्राकाशवाणी*,
भविष्यवाणी*, प्रसिद्ध विद्वान

oracular *a.* गुप्त, ग्रस्पष्ट

oral *a.* मौखिक, बोला हुग्रा

orally *adv.* मौखिक से

orange *n.* नारंगी* संतरा;
a. नारंगी के रंग का; orange-
colour नारंगी रंग

oration *n.* सार्वजनिक व्याख्यान

orator *n.* (*fem.* oratress)
सुवक्ता, वाग्मी

oratorial *a.* व्याख्यान-संबंधी

oratory *n.* भाषरा की शक्ति*
या कला*

orbit *n* ग्रहपथ, कक्षा, ग्रांख का
गड्ढा

orchard *n.* फल-वाटिका*;
orchard-house फल के वृक्षों
को उगाने का ग्राच्छादित गृह

orchestra *n.* ग्रार्केस्ट्रा, वादक-
दल, वाद्यस्थान

ordeal *n.* अग्नि-परीक्षा*,
कठिन परीक्षा*

order *n.* क्रम, शासन, ग्राज्ञा*,
सामाजिक पद, ग्राचार,
जाति*, ग्रादेश, दर्जा; *v.t.*
क्रम में रखना, ग्राज्ञा देना;
in order to वास्ते, लिए;
lower orders नीच जाति
के लोग; made to order
ग्राज्ञानुसार बनाई हुई वस्तु;
order-book ग्राहकों की
मांग की बही; order of
battle सैन्य रचना; order
of the day कार्य का व्यव-
स्थित क्रम; out of order
क्रमहीन

orderly *a. & n.* क्रमानुसार,
सेवक, ग्रदंली

ordinance *n.* नियम, विधि*,
व्यवहार

ordinarily *adv.* साधाररण रूप से

ordinary *a.* सामान्य, साधारण,
प्रचलित, नियम के ग्रनुसार

organ *n.* इन्द्रिय*, अंग, मुख-
पत्र भाग, बड़ा बाजा;
किसी कार्य का साधन;
mouth organ मुंह से
बजाने का बाजा

organic *a.* इन्द्रिय-संबंधी,
धार्मिक, क्रमिक

organism *n.* जीवधारी रचना'

organization *n.* संघटन,
निर्मारा, रचना*, संगठन;
संस्था*

organize *v.t.* क्रमबद्ध बनाना
संगठित करना

orient *n.* पूर्व दिशा*

oriental *a. & n.* पूर्वी, पूर्व
देश निवासी, पूर्व देश

origin *n.* मूल, ग्रारम्भ,

उत्पत्ति*, वंश या गोत्र

original *a. & n.* प्रथम, मौलिक (ग्रन्थ)

originality *n.* मौलिकता*, अपूर्व रचना-शक्ति*

originate *v.t. & i.* उत्पन्न करना या होना, निर्माण करना

originator *n.* उत्पन्न करने वाला

ornament *n.* अलंकार, आभूषण, श्रृंगार; *v.t.* सुशोभित करना, सजाना

ornamental *a.* सुशोभित करने वाला

ornamentation *n.* सजावट*

orphan *n.* अनाथ बालक

orphanage *n.* अनाथालय

orthodox *a.* सत्यधर्मानुसारी, नियमानुसारी, कट्टरपंथी

orthodoxy *n.* कट्टर धर्म-परायणता*

oscillate *v.i. & t.* झूलना, डोलना, हिलाना, कांगना

ostracize *v.t.* जाति के बाहर निकाल देना

ostrich *n.* शुतरमुर्ग; ostrich policy अपने को भ्रम में डालने वाली नीति*

other *a. & pron.* अन्य, दूसरा, भिन्न; every other day एक-एक दिन के अन्तर पर; some time or other किसी न किसी दिन; the other day कुछ दिन बीते; the other world भविष्य-जीवन

ottoman *a.* तुर्क संबंधी; *n.* तुर्क, एक प्रकार का गद्दा

ounce *n.* आधी छटांक के लगभग की अंग्रेज़ी तौल*, तेंदुआ

our *pron.* हम लोगों का

oust *v.t.* अधिकार छीन लेना, हटाना, बाहर करना

out *adv. a., & prep. (comp.* outer, *sup.* outmost, outermost) भीतर से प्रकट, प्रकाशित, समाप्त, घर के बाहर, भूला हुआ, बिना अधिकार का, बुझा हुआ; fire is out आग बुझ गई है; out with him उसको बाहर निकाल दो; out and away दूर तक; out and out पूर्ण रूप से; out of breath हांफता हुआ; out of में से; out of curiosity आश्चर्य से; out of doors खुले मैदान में; out of hand तुरन्त, out of order विधि विरुद्ध; out of the way असामान्य; out with मित्रभाव न रखता

हुआ; the book is out
पुस्तक प्रकाशित हो गई है;
the fire is out आग बुझ
गई; to be out प्रकाशित
होना

out *pref.* 'अधिक होना, बढ़ना
या बाहर' के अर्थ का उपसर्ग

outbalance *v.t.* भार में
बढ़ाना

outbid *v.t.* अधिक दाम लगाना

outbreak *n.* आकस्मिक
आरम्भ, उद्गार, हुल्लड़,
बलवा

outburst *n.* घड़ाका, विस्फोट

outcast *n.* निकलुआ;
a. गृहहीन, अधम, पतित

outcome *n.* परिणाम, फल

outdoor *a.* खुले स्थान में
किया हुआ, घर के बाहर का
(बाहरी)

outfit *n.* यात्रा-सामग्री, उप-
करण; *v.t.* (*p. t.* out-
fitted) तैयारी करना

outgrow *v.i.* वेग से बढ़ना
या उगना

outhouse *n.* घर के बाहर का
छोटा मकान

outing *n.* हवा खाने के लिए
बाहर गमन, प्रमोद-भ्रमण

outlandish *a.* अपरिचित,
बाहरी, अशिष्ट, गंवारू, प्रति
विलक्षण

outlaw *n.* न्यायविरुद्ध चलने
वाला मनुष्य; *v.t.* न्यायोचित
सुविधाओं से वंचित करना

outlet *n* निकास, द्वार

outline *n.* बाहरी सीमा*,
रूप-रेखा*, आकार मात्र,
ढांचा, सामान्य वर्णन; *v.t*
रेखांकित मानचित्र बनाना

outlive *v.i.* अधिक जीना या
रहना

outlook *n.* सामान्य दृश्य

outnumber *v.i.* संख्या में
बढ़ना

outpatient *n.* अस्पताल के
बाहर रहनेवाला रोगी

outpost *n.* सेना से दूर पर
की चौकी*

output *n.* उत्पादन, उत्पत्ति*,
उपज*

outrage *n* अत्याचार, उपद्रव;
v t. & i. उपद्रव करना,
अत्याचार करना

outright *adv.* पूर्ण रूप से,
सर्वथा

outshine *v.t.* अधिक चमकना

outside *n.* बाहरी भाग; *adv.*
बाहरी ओर

outsider *n.* परदेशी पुरुष

outsize *a.* सामान्य नाप से
बढ़कर

outskirt *n.* सीमाप्रान्त, सरहद*

outskirts *n. pl.* नगर के बाहर

का प्रदेश

outstanding *a.* बकाया; विशिष्ट

outward *a.* बाहरी

outwardly *adv.* बाहरी ओर

outweigh *v.t.* भार या महत्त्व में बढ़ना

outwit *v.t.* (*p.t.* outwitted) बुद्धि में बढ़ जाना, ठगना, धोखा देना

ovation *n.* स्वस्ति-वाचन, जय-जयकार

oven *n.* चूल्हा, तंदूर

over *prep. & adv.* अधिक, बिषय मे, ऊपर, आगे की ओर, अतिरिक्त, आरपार; all over India भारतवर्ष में सर्वत्र; over against सम्मुख; over and over again बारम्बार; over head and ears पूर्ण रूप से; over our heads हम लोगों के विचार के बाहर; the work is over कार्य समाप्त हो गया

overact *v.t.* सीमा के बाहर काम करना

overall *n.* ऊपरी लबादा

overawe *v t.* व्याकुल करना, डराना

overboard *adv.* जहाज की छत पर, नौका के बाहर

overburden *v.t.* अधिक बोझ लादना

overcast मेघाच्छन्न; *v.t.* अंधेरा करना

overcharge *v.t. & i.* अधिक दाम लगाना या लगना

overcoat *n.* ओवर कोट, बड़ा कोट

overcome *v.t.* (*p.t.* over-came, *p.p.* overcome) जीतना

overdo *v.t.* (*p.t.* overdid, *p.p.* overdone) बहुत ही दूर ले जाना, पीड़ा देना, थका देना

overdose *n.* औषधि की अधिक मात्रा*

overdraft *n.* बैंक में से जमा से अधिक रुपया निकालना, अधिकर्ष

overdraw *v.t.* (*p.t.* over-drew, *p.p.* overdrawn) जमा से अधिक रकम निकालना

overdue *a.* मिती बिताया हुआ, समय पर न चुकाया हुआ

overhaul *v.t.* मरम्मत करके नया बना देना, परीक्षा करना, जांचना

overhear *v.t.* छिपकर सुनना

overlap *v.t.* (*p.t.* over-lapped) एक के ऊपर दूसरे का किनारा रखना

overlook *v.t.* क्षमा करना,

उपेक्षा करना, जांचना

overpower *v.t.* पराजित करना, हराना

overrate *v.t.* अधिक मूल्य लगाना

overrule *v.t.* अधिशासित करना, रद्द करना

overrun *v.t. & i.* (*p.t.* over-ran) पददलित करना, लूटना

oversea *a.* समुद्र पार का

overseer *n.* अधीक्षक

overt *a.* स्पष्ट, प्रत्यक्ष, प्रकट

overtake *v.t.* (*p.t.* took *p.p.* taken) पीछा करके पकड़ लेना

overthrow *v.t.* (*p.t.* threw, *p.p.* thrown) वश में करना, जीतना, नाश करना; *n.* हार*

overtime *n.* निर्घारित से अधिक समय, ओवर टाइम, अतिरिक्त समय का काम

overture *n.* प्रस्ताव

overwhelm *v.t.* व्याकुल करना, कुचलना

overwork *v.t. & i.* (*p.t.* overwrought) अधिक काम कराकर थकाना, अधिक परिश्रम करना

owe *v.t. & i.* ऋणी होना

owl *n.* उल्लू पक्षी

own *a.* निजी; *v.t.* अपनाना, स्वामी होना, स्वीकार करना; of my own अपना निज का; of one's own accord अपनी स्वतन्त्र इच्छा से; to hold one's own अपना अधिकार या स्वत्व धारण करना; to make one's own अपनना

owner *n.* स्वामी

ox *n.* (*pl.* oxen) बैल, बरघ

oxide *n.* प्राणवायु का किसी तत्त्व से संयोग, आरेय

oxygen *n.* प्राणवायु, ओषजन, जारक

oyster *n.* सीप*, घोंघा

P

pace *n.* पग, चाल*, गति*; *v.i. & t.* चलना, गति ठीक करना; to keep pace with समान गति से चलना; to pace up and down इघर-उघर चलना

pacific *a.* शांत, स्थिर

pacify *v.t.* (*p.t.* pacified) शांत करना, शांति लाना

pack *n.* गठरी*, बोझ, गड्डी*,

शिकारी कुत्ते, भेड़िये इत्यादि का समुदाय; *v.t. & i.* माल से भरना, गठरी बांधना, भीड़ मचाना

package *n.* छोटी गठरी*

packet *n.* छोटा पार्सल या पुलिंदा

packing *n.* बांधने की सामग्री*; packing-needle गठरी सीने का सूत्रा; packing-sheet सामग्री बांधने का कपड़ा

pact *n.* बंधेज, इकरारनामा, ठेका, संधि*

pad *n.* गद्दी*, काठी*, सोख़्ता या कागज की गड्डी, पशुओं के पैर के नीचे का कोमल भाग; *v.t.* (*p.t.* padded) गद्देदार बनाना

padding *n.* गद्दी*

paddle *v.i. & t.* पानी में पैर मारना, नाव चलाना; *n.* छोटा डांड़ा, बाइसिकिल*, जहाज़ चलाने का साधन, क्षेपणी; paddle-wheel जहाज़ चलाने का पहिया, क्षेपड़ी चक्र; to paddle one's own canoe अपने सामर्थ्य पर निर्भर होना

paddy *n.* धान

page *n.* छोकरा, लड़का, पुस्तक के पत्र का एक ओर का भाग; *v.t.* पुस्तक आदि के पन्ने में

अंक डालना; page of honour रईस का सेवक लड़का

pageant *n.* आडम्बर, लीला*, तमाशा

pageantry *n.* आडम्बर, तड़क-भड़क, तमाशा

pagoda *n.* पगोडा, मेरु-मन्दिर

pain *n.* दुःख, पीड़ा*, क्लेश; प्रसव-वेदना*; *v.t.* पीड़ा देना, दुःख देना; bodily pain शारीरिक व्याधि; mental pain मनोव्यथा; sharp pain तीव्र वेदना, शूल; to take pains कष्ट सहना

painful *a.* दुःखदायी

painstaking *a.* परिश्रमी, उद्यमी

paint *n.* रंग, लेप; *v.t.* रंगना, चित्र बनाना

painter *n.* (*fem.* paintress) चित्रकार

painting *n.* रंगा हुआ चित्र

pair *n.* जोड़ा; *v.t.* जोड़ा लगाना या मिलाना; a married pair पति और पत्नी; to pair off दो-दो करके अलगाना; well-paired अच्छी तरह जोड़ा या मिलाया हुआ

palace *n.* राजभवन, महल

palanquin n. शिविका*, पालकी*

palatable a. स्वादिष्ट

palatal a. तालु-सम्बन्धी

palate n. तालु, स्वाद

palatial a. विशाल, बड़ा

pale n. बाड़ा, घेरा; a. पीला, धुंधला; v.t. & i. पीला करना, पीला होना

palette n. चित्रकार की रंग मिलाने की पटिया*; palette-knife रंग मिलाने की लोहे की पट्टी

palm n. हथेली*; v.t. हथेली में छिपाना; palm of victory जय-ध्वनि; to grease a person's palm घूस देना; to join the palms हाथ जोड़ना; to palm off धोखा देना. ठगना

palm n. ताड़ का पेड़, उत्तमता*, विजय-चिह्न; palm oil गरी का तेल

palmist n. हस्तरेखा-सामुद्रिक में निपुण

palmistry n. हस्तरेखा-सामुद्रिक विद्या*

palpable a. स्पष्टगोचर, स्पष्ट, प्रत्यक्ष

palpitate v.i. धड़कना, कांपना

palpitation n. धड़कन*

paltry a. तुच्छ, नीच

pamper v.t. & i. अधिक भोजन कराना, सन्तुष्ट करना

pampered a. हृष्टपुष्ट

pampering a. परिपोषक

pamphlet n. पैम्फलेट, पर्चा, छोटी पत्रिका*

pamphleteer n. पर्चा लिखने वाला, पत्रिकाकार

pandemonium n. पिशाच-सभा, अव्यवस्थित स्थान, बड़ा उपद्रव

pandora n. एक प्रकार की सारंगी*

pane n. कांच की पट्टी*

panegyric n. स्तुति*, प्रशंसा*

panel n. द्वारफलक, दिलहा, तैलचित्र बनाने की तख्ती* पंच, झालर; v.t. दिलहा या चौखटा लगाना

pang n. व्यथा*, संताप, वेदना

panic n. त्रास, आतंक, विप्लव, अकस्मात् भय; panic-monger आतंक फैलानेवाला; panic-struck आतंकित

panorama n. निरन्तर दृष्टिगत दृश्य, चित्रमाला*, इर्द-गिर्द का दृश्य

pant v.i. सांस लेना, हांफना, तीव्र इच्छा करना; n. धड़कन

pantheism n. विश्वदेवतावाद, सर्वेश्वरवाद, देवपूजा*

panther n. चीता, तेंदुआ

pantomime n. मूकाभिनय,

स्वांग

pantry *n.* (*pl.* pantries) भण्डारघर

papacy *n.* पोप (रोम के सबसे बड़े पादरी) का पद

papal *a.* पोप संबंधी

paper *n.* कागज, समाचारपत्र, लेख, प्रश्नपत्र, (ब० व०) चिट्ठी पत्री; *n.* कागज का बना हुआ; paper-hangings *n. pl.* कमरे की दीवारों पर चिपकाने के कागज; paper knife *n.* कागज काटने की छुरी*; paper-mill *n.* कागज बनाने का कारखाना; paper-money बैंक इत्यादि के नोट; paper-weight कागज दबाने का भार; to commit to paper कागज पर लिख लेना; to put pen to paper लिखना प्रारम्भ करना

papier-mache *n.* कागज की लुग्दी जिसके अनेक पदार्थ बनते हैं

par *n.* सममूल्य, समता*, वरा-बरी*; above par सामान्य मूल्य से अधिक; at par बराबर मूल्य का; below par घाटे पर, कमती भाव में

parable *n.* नीतिकथा*, कहावत*

parabolic (-al) *a.* नीतिकथा के रूप में वर्णित, अनुवृत्त

आकार का

parachute *n.* पैराशूट, हवाई छतरी

parachutist *n.* हवाई छतरी से उतरनेवाला सैनिक

parade *n.* परेड, कवायद, आडम्बर, सैन्य-व्यायाम, टहलने का मार्ग; *v.t.* सैन्य-व्यायाम करना, आडम्बर करना; parade ground कवायद करने का स्थान

paradise स्वर्ग, परम आनन्द का सुन्दर स्थान

paradox *n.* असत्याभास, परस्पर विरुद्ध मत

paradoxical *a.* असत्याभास रूप का

paraffin *n.* मोमबत्ती बनाने का एक प्रकार का पदार्थ, मृद्वसा; paraffin-oil स्वच्छ किया हुआ मिट्टी का तेल

paragon *n.* आदर्श या अत्युत्तम पदार्थ

paragraph *n.* अनुच्छेद, प्रकरण

parallel *a.* समानान्तर, सहृश, समान परिणाम का; *v.t.* समानान्तर करना, तुल्य करना; parallel lines समानान्तर रेखायें; parallels of latitude अक्षवृत्त, अक्षांश रेखाएं*

parallelism *n.* समानता*

parallelogram *n.* समानान्तर चतुर्भुज

paralyse *v.t.* लकवा मारना, शक्तिहीन करना

paralysis *n.* पक्षाघात, लहवा रोग

paralytic *n.* लकवा मारा हुआ

paramount *a.* सर्वश्रेष्ठ, सर्वोत्तम

paraphernalia *n. pl.* सज-धज, आडम्बर, सामग्री*

paraphrase *n.* टीका*, संक्षिप्त ब्याख्या*; *v.t.* संक्षिप्त ब्याख्या करना

parasite *n.* परोपजीवी जन्तु या पौधा

parcel *n.* पार्सल, खंड, पोटली*, गठरी*; *v.t.* खंड करना, बांटना; part and parcel अंगभूत; to parcel अलगाना

pardon *v.t.* क्षमा करना; *n.* क्षमा*

pardonable *a.* क्षमा के योग्य

parent *n.* माता*-पिता, उद्गम, प्रभव

parentage *n.* जाति*, कुल

parental *a.* पैतृक, प्रिय

parenthesis *n.* (*pl.* ses) निक्षेपवाक्य, प्रधान वचन, कोष्ठक का ( ) चिह्न

parish *n.* पादरी का प्रदेश

parity *n.* समानता*, बराबरी*

park *n.* पार्क, कीड़ावन, सर्व- सामान्य के घूमने का बगीचा; *v.t.* पार्क बनाना, मोटर आदि मोटर चौक में खड़ा करना

parlance *n.* संभाषण की शैली*

parley *n.* बातचीत*, संभाषण, सभा*; *v.t.* सभा करना

parliament *n.* पार्लमेन्ट, संसद*

parliamentarian *n.* संसत्पंडित, संसदवादी, संसदीय

parliamentary *a.* संसदीय

parlour *n.* बैठक*, दर्शन-गृह

parody *n.* पैरोडी*, हास्यानु- कृति*, अनुकरण-काव्य; *v.t.* (*p.t.* parodied) पैरोडी लिखना

parole *n.* पैरोल, साधि मुक्ति*, कारावकाश

parricide *n.* पिता की हत्या करनेवाला, पितृहत्या*

parrot *n.* सुग्गा, तोता; *v.t.* बिना अर्थ समझे शब्द दुहराना

parry *v.t.* (*p.t.* parried) रोकना, छेकना; *n.* छेकान

parson *n.* पादरी

part *n.* अंश, भाग, खंड, नाटक के पात्र का नियोग; *v.t.* बांटना, अलग करना; for my part जहां तक मेरा संबंध है; for the most part विशेषकर; I have done my part मैंने अपना निर्धारित कार्य कर लिया;

in parts थोड़े अंश में; part and parcel आवश्यक अंश; parts योग्यता; to have a part in संबंध रखना; to part the hair सिर के बालों को कंघी से संवारना; to part with सौंपना, विदाई लेना, त्यागना; to take part सहायता करना

partake *v.i.* (*p.t.*-took, *p.p.*-taken) भाग लेना, साझी होना

partial *a.* एक अंश का, अपूर्ण, पक्षपाती

partiality *n.* पक्षपात, स्नेह, असमदृष्टि*

participate *v.i.* हिस्सा लेना, साझी होना

participation *n.* हिस्सेदारी*, शिरकत*

particle *n.* कण, लेश, परमाणु

particular *a.* पृथक्, विशिष्ट, व्यक्तिगत, सावधान, निश्चित; विस्तृत वर्णन, ब्योरा; at a particular time किसी विशिष्ट समय पर; give the particulars उसका ब्योरा कहो

partisan *n.* पक्षधर, नेज़ा, भाला

partition *n.* बंटवारा, हिस्सा, अलगानेवाली भीत; *v.t.* बंटवारा करना, बांटना

partner *n.* मेली, सहकारी, साझीदार

partnership *n.* सहकारिता*, साझा

party *n.* (*pl.* parties) पार्टी*, दल, समुदाय, समाज, मुकदमा करनेवाला; of one's party अपने पक्ष का; of the opposite party विपक्ष का

pass *v.i.* & *t.* चले जाना, लुप्त होना, मर जाना, दूसरा समझा जाना, नियम होना, परीक्षा में उत्तीर्ण होना, बिताना, आज्ञा देना; to pass for स्वीकृत होना, मान जाना; to pass sentence upon दण्ड की आज्ञा देना; let it pass now अब ऐसा होने दो; read the paper and pass it on पत्र पढ़कर आगे को बढ़ाओ; this passes comprehension यह विचार से बाहर है; to come to pass घटित होना; to pass away मरना; to pass by तिरस्कार करना; to pass off लुप्त होना; to pass over त्यागना; to pass through प्रवेश करना, घुसना; to pass time समय बिताना; to pass water लघुशंका करना; *n.* घाटी*, परीक्षा में सफलता*,

338

प्रवेश का आज्ञापत्र, प्रवेश-पत्र

pass-book n. पासबुक, रुपये का लेन-देन लिखने की बैंक की किताब*

passenger n. यात्री, मुसाफिर

passion n. चित्त का आवेग, भावावेग

passionate a. तीव्र, तीक्ष्ण, क्रोधी, कामुक

passive a. निष्क्रिय, निश्चेष्ट, उदासीन; passive resistance सत्याग्रह; passive कर्मवाच्य

passport n. पासपोर्ट, पार-पत्र

past a. & n. बीता हुआ, पहले का, भूतपूर्व काल; prep. & adv. बाद, समयान्तर में; for some time past कुछ दिन हुए; half past four साढ़े चार बजे; ran past the garden बगीचे की ओर दौड़ा

paste n. आटे की लेई, साना हुआ आटा; v.t. लेई से चिपकाना

paste board n. दफ्ती*

pastel n. पेस्टल, रंगीन खड़िया

pastime n. क्रीड़ा*, खेल, मन-बहलाव

pastoral a. पादरी या गड़रिये से सम्बन्धित, ग्रामीण जीवन संबंधी

pasture n. चारा, घास*, चरागाह*; v.t. पशुओं को चराना

pat v.t. (p.t. patted) थप-थपाना, ठोकना; n. थपकी*; a. & adv. उचित, योग्य; pat on the back पीठ पर की थपथपाहट

patch v.t. मरम्मत करना; n. चिप्पड़, पेबन

patent a. स्पष्ट, प्रत्यक्ष; n. पेटेन्ट, एकस्व; v.t. आविष्कार की रजिस्ट्री कराना

paternal a. पैतृक

path n. मार्ग, पगडंडी*

pathetic a. हृदयस्पर्शी, कारुणिक

patience n. क्षमा*, सहन-शीलता*, धैर्य; out of patience with न सहने योग्य; to have no patience with उत्तेजित होना, क्रुद्ध होना

patient a. सहनशील, धैर्ययुक्त, जल्दी न करनेवाला; n. रोगी

patricide n. पितृहत्या*

patrimonial a. पैतृक, बपौती

patrimony n. पैतृक धन, विरासत

patriot n. देशभक्त

patriotic a. देशभक्तिपूर्ण

patriotism n. देशभक्ति*

patrol v.i. (p.t. patrolled)

पहरा देना, रक्षा करना; *n.*
रक्षा के निमित्त रात्रि में
चक्कर लगाना, पहरेदार

patron *n.* पोषक, संरक्षक

patronage *n.* सहायता*, अनुग्रह

patronize *v.t.* आश्रय देना,
सहायता देना

pattern *n.* आकार, सांचा

paucity *n.* लघुता*, कमी*

pauper *n.* अनाथ, दरिद्र, भिक्षुक

pause *n.* विराम, ठहराव; *v.i.*
विश्राम करना, ठहरना; to
pause upon चिन्तन करना

pave *v.t.* पत्थर या ईंट बैठाना,
मार्ग बनाना

pavement *n.* पत्थर या ईंट का
फर्श, सड़क की पटरी

pavilion *n.* पविलियन, तम्बू,
खेमा, मण्डप; *v.t.* पटमण्डप
लगाना, तम्बू लगाना

paw *n.* पंजा, चंगुल; *v.t.* पंजे से
खुरचना

pay *v.t.* (*p.t.* paid) ऋण
चुकाना, बदला देना, वेतन
देना; *n.* वेतन, मूल्य; to pay
attention to ध्यान लगाना;
to pay for बदले में देना;
to pay in अपने खाते में
देना; to pay in one's
own coin बदला चुकाना;
to pay off पूरा धन चुकाना;
to pay out दण्ड देना; to

pay up पूरा ऋण चुकाना;
paymaster वेतन बांटनेवाल

payable *a.* देय, शोधनीय

payee *n.* रुपया पानेवाला

payer *n.* रुपया देनेवाला

payment *n.* भुगतान, चुकौता

pea *n.* मटर; peascod मटर
की छीमी

peace *n.* शांति*, अविरोध,
मैत्री*; at peace शांति भाव
में; to hold one's peace
चुप रहना

peaceable *a.* शांतिप्रिय,
अव्याकुल

peaceful *a.* शांत

peacock *n.* (*fem.* peahen)
मोर

peak *n.* शिखर, पहाड़ की
चोटी*; peak and pine
क्षीण तथा दुर्बल

pearl *n.* मोती; mother of
pearl मोती का सीप; pearl
eye मोतियाबिंद; to cast
pearls before swine
अयोग्य व्यक्ति को अमूल्य
पदार्थ देना

peasant *n.* किसान, खेतिहर

peasantry *n.* किसान वर्ग

pebble *n.* पत्थर की गोली*,
कंकड़, स्फटिक

peck *n.* चोंच*, दो गैलन की
तौल*; *v.i.* चोंच मारना,

दाना चुगना; to peck out
छेद करना

peculiar *a.* असाधारण, विल-
क्षण

peculiarity *n.* विशेषता*,
विलक्षणता*

pecuniary *a.* धन-सम्बन्धी,
आर्थिक; pecuniary diffi-
culties आर्थिक कष्ट;
pecuniary loss आर्थिक
हानि*

pedagogue *n.* बाल-शिक्षक,
बाल-अध्यापक

pedagogy *n.* अध्यापकी विद्या*,
शिक्षण-शास्त्र

pedal *n.* पैडल, किसी यन्त्र का
पैर से चलाने का भाग
(साधन); *v.t.* पैडल चलाना

pedantic *a.* पाण्डित्य दिखलाने
वाला

pedestal *n.* पाद-पीठ*, चौकी*;
भवन का स्तम्भपाद, नींव*

pedestrian *n.* पाद-चारी या
पैदल चलनेवाला यात्री

pedigree *n.* वंशावली*

peel *v.t.* छिलका या छाल
उतारना; *n.* छिलका, छाल*

peep *v.i* चूं-चूं करना, चोरी से
देखना, भांकना, दिखाई देना;
peep of day अरुणोदय,
तड़का

peer (*fem.* peeress) *n.* शिष्ट-

जन, कुलीन पुरुष तुल्य, समान,
लार्ड

peerless *a.* अनुपम

peg *n.* कील*, खूंटी*, शराब
की छोटी प्याली; *v.t.* (*p.t.*
pegged) खूंटे से बांधना,
स्थिर करना; a peg to
hang अवसर, बहाना; to
peg away हठपूर्वक कार्य
करना; to peg down नियम-
बद्ध करना

pell-mell *a.* & *adv.* व्याकुलता
से

pellucid *a.* स्वच्छ और पार-
दर्शक, स्पष्ट

pen *n.* लेखनी*, *v.t.* लिखना

penal *a.* दण्डविषयक; penal
code दंड-विधान; penal
code दंड-संहिता*; penal-
law दण्ड के नियम; penal
servitude सपरिश्रम कारा-
वास

penalize *v.t.* दण्डनीय बनाना

penalty *n.* दण्ड, अर्थदण्ड

penance *n.* तपस्या*, प्राय-
श्चित्त; to practise penance तपस्या करना

pencil *n.* पेन्सिल; *v.t.* (*p.t.*
pencilled) पेन्सिल से
लिखना अथवा चित्र बनाना

pending *n.* अस्थिरता*,
विचाराधीन; *prep.* अनिश्चित

अवस्था में

pendulum n. पेण्डुलम, दोलक, लंगर; swing of pendulum राजनीतिक अवस्था में उलट-फेर

penetrate v.t. & i. चुभाना, अर्थ समझना, व्याप्त होना

penetration n. प्रवेशन, वेधन

penis n. शिश्न, लिङ्ग

penniless a. निर्धन, दरिद्र

penny n. (pl. pennies, pence) अंग्रेजी सिक्का जो प्रायः एक आने के बराबर होता है; penny a line सस्ता साहित्य

pension n. पेन्शन, पूर्व सेवा-वृत्ति*, v.t. पेन्शन देना

pensioner n. पेन्शन पानेवाला मनुष्य

pensive a. चिन्ताग्रस्त

pentagon n. पंचकोण, पंचभुज

peon n. चपरासी, चाकर

people n. जन, जनता (ब०व०) जाति; v.t. बसना, मनुष्यों से पूर्ण करना

pepper n. गोल मिर्च; v.t मिर्च मिलाना

peptic a. पाचक, अग्निवर्धक

per prep. में, द्वारा, प्रति; per annum प्रति वर्ष; per capita प्रति व्यक्ति पीछे; per diem प्रतिदिन; per

unit प्रति एकक

perambulator n. पेरम्बुलेटर बच्चा-गाड़ी*

perceive v.t. जानना, समझना, देखना

perceptibility n. अनुभव-गम्यता*, दृष्टिगोचरता*

perceptible a. देखने या समझने योग्य

perceptibly adv. प्रत्यक्ष रूप में

per cent adv. प्रति सैकड़ा

percentage n. फ़ीसदी, की सैकड़ा

perception n. बोध, अनुभव, ज्ञान

perceptive a. प्रत्यक्ष ज्ञानशील

perch n. मीठे जल की मछली, चिड़ियों के बैठने का अड्डा, 5½ गज की नाप; v.i. & t. अड्डे पर बैठना, ऊंचे पर रखना; to knock off the perch हराना, नष्ट करना; to hop the perch मर जाना

perennial a. वर्ष-भर रहने वाली, चिरस्थायी; n. बारहमासी पौधा

perfect a. सम्पूर्ण, निर्दोष, उत्तम, प्रवीण, अखण्ड; v.t. पूरा करना, निर्दोष बनाना

perfection n. परिपूर्णता*, निर्दोषता*, उत्तमता*

perfidy *n.* विश्वासघात, छल, कपट, घोखा

perforate *v.t.* छेद करना

perforce *adv.* बलपूर्वक, हठ से

perform *v.t. & i.* करना, पूर्ण करना, नाटक करना, बाजा बजाना

performance *n.* पूर्ति*, अभिनय, कार्य, क्रिया*

performer *n.* कार्य करनेवाला, नाटक करनेवाला

perfume *n.* सुगन्ध*, इत्र, धूप*; *v.t.* सुगन्धित करना

perfunctory अन्यमनस्क, बेमन

perhaps *adv.* कदाचित्, संयोगवश

peril *n.* विपत्ति*, आशंका*, खतरा; *v.t.* (*p.t.* perilled) विपत्ति में डालना

perilous *a.* संकटमय

period *n.* समय, काल अवधि*, युग, परिमाण, पूर्ण विराम; last period अन्त की अवस्था; period of life जीवन-काल

periodical *n.* पत्रिका*, नियत कालिक पत्रिका, सावधिक पत्र

periodically *adv.* नियत समय पर

peripheral *a.* परिधि-सम्बन्धी

periphery *n.* बाहरी सीमा* परिधि*

perish *v.i.* मरना, सड़ना, नाश होना

perishable *a.* नाश होने योग्य; perishables *n. pl.* नाश होने वाले पदार्थ

perjure *v.i.* झूठी गवाही देना, प्रतिज्ञा भंग करना

perjury *n.* झूठी गवाही*

permanence (-cy) *ns.* स्थिरता*, नित्यता*

permanent *a* स्थिर, स्थायी, नित्य, टिकाऊ

permeable *a.* रसने या प्रवेश करने योग्य

permissible *a.* आज्ञा पाने योग्य

permission *n.* आज्ञा*, अनुमति*

permissive *a.* क्षमा देने वाला

permit *v.t.* (*p.t.* permitted) आज्ञा देना; *n.* परमिट, अनुमतिपत्र

permittance *n.* प्रवेश की आज्ञा*

permutation *n.* परिवर्तन, उलट-पलट

permute *v.t.* क्रम बदलना या उलटना

pernicious *a.* अपकारक, नाशक

perpendicular *a.* लम्बरूप, खड़े बल का; *n.* समकोणिक रेखा*

perpetrate *v.t.* अपराध या मूर्खता का कार्य करना

perpetual *a.* निश्य, सतत, लगातार

perpetuate *v.t.* जारी रखना

perplex *v.t.* व्याकुल करना, घबड़ाना

perplexity *n.* व्यग्रता*, भंझट*

persecute *v.t.* पीड़ा देना, कष्ट देना, सताना, चोट पहुंचाना

persecution *n.* उत्पीड़न, उपद्रव

persecutor *n.* दुःख या पीड़ा देनेवाला, सतानेवाला

perseverance *n.* अध्यवसाय, दृढ़ता*, हठ, धुन*

persevere *v.i.* अध्यवसाय में लगा रहना, निरन्तर प्रयत्न करना

persist *v.t.* दृढ़ रहना, हठ करना

persistence (-cy) *n.* अध्यव- साय, प्रयत्न, विलम्बन, अनु- लम्बन, दृढ़ता*

persistent *a.* दृढ़, हठी, आग्रही

person *n.* मनुष्य, व्यक्ति, मानव- शरीर; first person उत्तम पुरुष; second person मध्यम पुरुष; third person अन्य पुरुष

personage *n.* श्रेष्ठ पुरुष, सम्भ्रान्त जन

personal *a.* व्यक्तिगत, निजी, अपना

personality *n.* व्यक्तित्व, विशे- षता*

personification *n.* मानवी- करण, चेतनद्वारोपण, मूर्ति- करण

personify *v.t.* (*p.t.* per- sonified) मानवीकरण या मूर्तिकरण करना, आत्मीभूत होना, मूर्तिमान होना

personnel *n.* कार्यकर्त्ता वर्ग, कर्मचारी दल

perspective *n.* दृश्य-भूमिका*, दृश्य, दृष्टि*, दृष्टिसीमा*

perspiration *n.* पसीना

perspire *v.i.* पसीना निकलना

persuade *v.t.* फुसलाना, बह- काना, मनाना उकसाना, प्रबोधना

persuasion *n.* प्रतीतीकरण प्रोत्साहन

pertain *v.i.* उपांग होना, संदर्भ रखना, स्वामित्व होना, संबंध होना

pertinent *a.* योग्य, ठीक, उचित

perturb *v.t.* व्याकुल करना, घबड़ाना

perusal *n.* अध्ययन, वाचन, पठन

peruse *v.t.* चित्त लगाकर पढ़ना

pervade *v.t.* व्याप्त करना,

फैलाना

perverse *a.* पतित, प्रतिकूल, विकृत, भ्रान्त, दुःशील

perversion *n.* विकृति*, भ्राचार-भ्रष्टता*, दोष

perversity *n.* दुःशीलता*, प्रतिकूलता*, हठ

pervert *v.t.* सन्मार्ग से हटाना, दूषित करना

pervious *a.* प्रवेश्य, सछिद्र

pessimism *n.* निराशावाद

pessimist *n.* निराशावादी

pessimistic *a.* निराश, निराशा-वादी

pest *n.* महामारी*, नाशकारक वस्तु*; pest of the people लोक कंटक

pestilence *n.* प्लेग, महामारी*

pet *n.* प्यारा, पालतू जानवर, क्रोध; pet name प्यार का पुकारने का नाम; *v.i. (p.t.* petted) प्यार करना पोसना

petal *n.* फूल की पंखड़ी, दलपत्र

petition *n* याचिका, अर्जी; प्रार्थना*; *v.t.* प्रार्थना पत्र भेजना

petitioner *n.* निवेदक, अभ्यर्थी

petrol *n.* पेट्रोल

petty *a.* (*comp.* pettier, *sup* pettiest) छोटा, अल्प, तुच्छ, क्षुद्र

petulance *n.* दुःशीलता*

petulant *a.* कर्कश, बिड़चिड़ा, भ्रधीर, ढीठ

phallus *n.* लिंग, लिंग-पूजन

phantom *n.* प्रेत की छाया*, प्रेत; *a.* भ्रसत्य, छाया मात्र

Pharaoh *n.* मिस्र देश के प्राचीन राजाभ्रों की उपाधि, फ़ैरोह

pharmaceutical *a.* भ्रौषधि-निर्माण-विद्या सम्बन्धी

pharmacy *n.* भ्रौषधि बनाने की विद्या*, भ्रौषधालय, दवा-खाना

phase *n.* भ्राकृति*, स्थिति*, परिवर्तन की स्थिति*

phenomenal *a* प्रकृतिविषयक, भ्रद्भुत

phenomenon *n.* (*pl.* phenomena) प्राकृतिक घटना*, भ्रद्भुत पदार्थ

phial *n.* शीशी*, छोटी बोतल*

philanthrope *n* मनुष्य मात्र से स्नेह करनेवाला, मानव-प्रेमी, जनहितैषी, समाजसेवी

philanthropic (-al) *a.* सर्व-जन-उपकारी, लोकानुरागी, विश्वमित्र, उदार

philanthropist *n.* मनुष्यमात्र से प्रेम करनेवाला व्यक्ति, जन-हितैषी, समाजसेवी

philanthropy *n.* लोक-कल्याण की भावना*, विश्वप्रेम, लोकोपकार, मानव-सौहार्द

philistine *n.* बाहरी मनुष्य, अशिक्षित मनुष्य; *a.* अशिक्षित, असंस्कृत

philologer, philologian, philologist *ns.* भाषा-विज्ञान-विद्, भाषा-शास्त्री

philology *n.* भाषा-विज्ञान

philosopher *n.* तत्त्वज्ञानी, दार्शनिक

philosophical *a.* दार्शनिक, तत्त्वज्ञान-सम्बन्धी

philosophize *v.t.* दार्शनिक रूप से तत्त्व अन्वेषण करना, तत्त्व निरूपण करना

philosophy *n.* दर्शनशास्त्र, तत्त्वज्ञान-विज्ञान

phone *n.* फोन, 'टेलीफोन' शब्द का छोटा रूप

phonetic *a.* ध्वनि-संबंधी

phonetics *n.* ध्वनि-विज्ञान, स्वर-शास्त्र

phono *pref.* 'ध्वनि' के अर्थ का उपसर्ग

phonogram *n.* फोनोग्राम, ध्वनि-संकेत, ध्वनि-प्रतीक ध्वनिलेख, ध्वनिग्राम

phosphate *n.* फॉस्फोरस तत्त्व से बना हुआ लवण, भास्वीय लवण

phosphorus *n.* फास्फोरस, एक जलनेवाला तत्त्व जो अंधेरे में चमकता है, भास्वर

photo *n.* (*pl.* photos) फोटो, अक्स से उतारा हुआ चित्र, भा. चित्र

photograph *v.t.* फोटो उतारना

photographer *n.* फोटोग्राफर, फोटो उतारनेवाला

photographic *a.* फोटो-सम्बन्धी

photography *n.* फोटो खींचने की कला*

photometer *n.* भामिति*, प्रकाश का घनत्व नापने का यंत्र

phototype *n.* फोटोटाइप, धातु-पट पर फोटोग्राफकी सहायता से चित्र खोदने की विधि*

phrase *n.* वाक्य, खण्ड, वचन, उक्ति* वाक्यशैली*; *v.t.* शब्दों में व्यक्त करना, बोलना

phraseology *n.* वाक्यरचना*, कथनशैली*

physic *n.* औषधि-शास्त्र, औषधि*; *v.t.* इलाज करना, दवा देना

physical *a.* पदार्थ-विज्ञान संबंधी, शारीरिक, पार्थिव, जड़; physical exercise शारीरिक परिश्रम; physical science पदार्थ-विज्ञान, भौतिक विज्ञान

physician *n.* डाक्टर, वैद्य, चिकित्सक

physicist *n.* भौतिकशास्त्री,

पदार्थ विज्ञानविद्

physics *n.* भौतिक विज्ञान, पदार्थ-विज्ञान

physiognomy *n.* प्राकृति देख- कर चरित्र बतलाने की विद्या* मुख की प्राकृति*

physiography *n.* प्राकृतिक भूगोल

physiology *n.* शरीरशास्त्र, शरीर-विज्ञान, देह-व्यापार, जीवक्रिया-विज्ञान

physique *n.* शरीर-रचना, डीलडौल

pianist *n.* पियानिस्ट, पियानो- वादक

piano *n.* (*pl.* pianos) पियानो

pick *v.t.* तोड़ना, इकट्ठा करना, चुनना, चोंच मारना, खोलना; *n.* फावड़ा, चुनाव, सबसे उत्तम पदार्थ; ear pick कनखोदनी; pick a-back गट्ठर की तरह पीठ पर लादे हुए; pick-me- up उत्तेजक पेय; toothpick दंतखोदनी; to pick holes in दोष निकालना; to pick off एक-एक करके गोली से मारना; to pick out चुन लेना

picket *n.* नोंकदार छड़, सैन्य- दल, धरना देना; *v.i.* (*p.t.* picketed) इस प्रकार धरना देना

picketing *n.* पिकेटिंग, धरना

pickle *n.* अचार, मुरब्बा, सिरका; *v.t.* अचार या मुरब्बा बनाना

picnic *n.* पिकनिक, वनभोजन, घर के बाहर का प्रामोद; *v.t.* (*p.t.* picnicked) पिकनिक में भाग लेना

pictorial *a.* सचित्र, चित्रमय

picture *n.* चित्र, दृश्य, अति सुन्दर पदार्थ; *v.t.* चित्र खींचना, स्पष्ट वर्णन करना; pic ure book बच्चों के पढ़ने की चित्रपूर्ण पुस्तक; picture-gallery चित्रशाला*; picture-house (-palace) सिनेमा या नाटकघर

picturesque *a.* चित्र के समान सुन्दर, स्पष्ट

piece *n.* भाग, खण्ड मुद्रा*, बन्दूक* रचना*, एक अकेली वस्तु*, *v.t.* चिप्पड़ लगाना, टुकड़ा करना; to break to pieces टुकड़े-टुकड़े करना; piece of work कोई कार्य; piece of water जलाशय; of a piece एक ही प्रकार का; piece goods नये कपड़ों के थान

pierce *v.t. & i.* छेदना, घुसाना, प्रवेश करना

piety *n.* ईश्वरभक्ति*, धर्म-

परायणता*, भक्ति*

pig n. सुग्रर, सुग्रर का बच्चा,
ढाली हुई धातु*; pig-iron
बिना ग्राेचा हुग्रा लोहा, pig-
headed हठी; pig-style
सुग्ररबाड़ा

pigeon n. कबूतर; pigeon-
hole ग्रलमारी में कागज
रखने के छोटे खाने; pigeon-
hearted डरपोक

pigmy (pygmy) ns. बौना

pile n. लट्टा, ढेर. ग्ररथी*; v.t.
ढेर लगाना, इकट्ठा करना;
to pile on ढेर लगाना

piles n. pl. बवासीर

pilfer v.t. (p.t. pilfered)
थोड़ा-थोड़ा करके चुराना

pilferer n. चोर, ठग

pilgrim n. तीर्थयात्री

pilgrimage n. तीर्थयात्रा*

pill n. गुटिका*, गोली*

pillar n. स्तम्भ, खम्भा, ग्राधार;
v.t. स्म्भा लगाना; driven
from pillar to post एक
ग्राश्रय से दूसरे ग्राश्रय को
फेंका हुग्रा; pillar of faith
श्रद्धा का स्तम्भ

pillow n. तकिया*; v.t. तकिया
लगाना; pillow-case तकिए
का गिलाफ; to take coun-
sel of one's pillow विचार
करने के लिए रात का ग्रवसर

लेना

pilot n. पाइलट, विमान चालक;
v.t. मार्ग दिखलाना, विभाग
चलाना

pilot-engine n. पाइलट इंजन
मार्गदर्शी इंजन

pin n. ग्रालपीन*, खूंटी*, ग्रल्प
मूल्य की वस्तु*; v.t. (p.t.
pinned) ग्रालपीन से नत्थी
करना

pinhole n. बहुत महीन छेद

pinch v.t. & i. चिकोटी काटना,
बलपूर्वक धन लेना, दुःख देना,
प्रेरणा करना; n. चिकोटी*,
कोंचन, चुभन*, चुटकी-भर

pine n. चीड़ का वृक्ष, देवदार;
v.t. विलाप करना, सूख जाना,
लालायित होना

pine apple n. ग्रनन्नास या
उसका पेड़

pink n. एक सुगंधित फूल,
ग्रापद, प्याजी रंग; a. हलके
गुलाबी रंग का

pinkish a. हलका गुलाबी

pinky a. गुलाबी रंग का

pinnacle r. ग्रटारी*, कलश,
चरमसीमा*

pioneer n. मार्ग-दर्शक, प्रथम
ग्रन्वेषक, ग्रग्रसर, नेता; v.t.
मार्ग दिखलाना, मार्ग बतलाना

pious a. पवित्र, धार्मिक, भक्ति-
मान

pipe n. पाइप, बांसुरी, नली*, पक्षी का गायन; v t. बांसुरी या सीटी बजाना; pipeclay चिलम बनाने की मिट्टी; tobacco-pipe चिलम

piquant a. तीखा, सरस, रुचि-कर, स्वादिष्ट, उत्तेजक

piracy n. समुद्री डकैती*

pirate n. समुद्री डाकू; v.t. जहाज पर डाका डालना

pistol n. पिस्तौल

piston n. पिस्टन, पिचकारी का डट्टा, मुशली*

pit n. गड्ढा, शरीर पर छोटे गर्त, पशुओं को फंसाने का जाल, समाधि*; v t. छोटे गड्ढे बनाना; pit of the stomach नाभि*

pitch n. राल, तारकोल, धूना, ऊंचाई*, स्वरमान, ढाल*, चढ़ाव; v.t. राल पोतना; mineral pitch शिलाजीत; pitch-black गहरा काला रंग

pitch v.t. & i. फेंकना, भूमि पर गाड़ना, स्थिर करना, निश्चय करना; n ऊंचाई*, सीमा*, ढाल*, फेंकान; pitched battle स्थायी रूप का युद्ध, जमी हुई लड़ाई; pitch-fork सूखी घास हटाने का लम्बा पांचा

pitcher n. घड़ा, मटका

piteous a. दयापूर्ण, दीन

pitfall n. फंसाने का जाल, गुप्त प्राप्ति*

pitiable a दया का पात्र, दीन

pitiful a. दयापूर्ण, करुणामय

pitiless a निर्दय, कठोर

pitman n. खान में काम करने-वाला श्रमिक

pittance n. क्षुद्र वेतन, अल्प पारिश्रमिक

pity n. दया*, करुणा*; v.t. (p t. pitied) दया करना, तरस खाना

pivot n. चूल या कील जिस पर कोई यन्त्र घूमता है, कील, प्रधान आधार; v.t. चूल लगाना, चूल पर घुमाना

placable a. आराध्य, शान्त, क्षमाशील, सरल

placard n. प्लेकार्ड, विज्ञापन पत्र

place n. स्थल, भूमि*, स्थिति*, श्रेणी*, उद्यम, कार्य, स्थान, पद; v.t. नियुक्त करना, स्थिर करना, लगाना; in the first place पहली बार; out of place अनुचित, अयोग्य; to take place घटना होना

placid a. शांत, नम्र, गम्भीर

plague n. प्लेग, महामारी*, उत्पात, उपद्रव; v.t. पीड़ा देना, कष्ट देना

plain *a.* चौरस, सपाट, सामान्य, स्पष्ट, प्रत्यक्ष, सीधा; *n.* मैदान; plain dealing सरल, निष्कपट व्यवहार; plain - speaking स्पष्ट-वादिता* या कथन

plaint *n.* अभियोग, नालिश

plaintiff *n.* अभियोगी, वादी, मुद्दई

plan *n.* योजना*, मानचित्र, ढांचा, कल्पना*, उपाय; *v.t.* (*p.t.* planned) योजना बनाना, ढांचा बनाना, उपाय रचना; planning आयोजन, नियोजन

plane *n.* चौरस भूमि*, जीवन-स्थिति*, बढ़ई का रन्दा, *v.t.* चौरस करना; *a.* चौरस; *n.* वायुयान का पंखा, वायुयान; jack-plane बढ़ई का बड़ा रन्दा; trying-plane बढ़ई का छोटा रन्दा

planet *n.* नक्षत्र, ग्रह

planetary *a.* ग्रह-संबंधी

plant *n.* वनस्पति*, पौधा, यंत्र, यंत्रसमुच्चय, कारखाना; *v.t.* जमाना, स्थिर करना, नियुक्त करना

plantain *n.* केले का वृक्ष, केले का फल

plantation *n.* रोपाई*, वृक्ष-रोपण, खेती* खेत, उद्यान, नवउपनिवेश, बस्ती*, कृत्रिम वन, झुरमुट

plaster *n.* भीत पर लगाने का पलस्तर, औषधि का लेप; *v.t.* पलस्तर लगाना, लेप लगाना

plate *n.* प्लेट, पत्तर, चद्दर, थाली, गृहस्थों के पात्र; *v.t.* चद्दर बैठाना, मुलम्मा करना; name plate नाम लिखी हुई पट्टी*, नामपट; plate powder *n.* धातु को चमकाने की बुकनी; plate-rack *n.* थाली इत्यादि सुखाने की अलमारी*

plateau *n.* (*pls.* plateaux, plateaus) पठार, भूमि*

platform *n.* मंच, चबूतरा, मचान; the platform व्याख्यान, वक्तृता*

platinum *n.* प्लेटिनम नामक एक बहुमूल्य श्वेत धातु*, कलधौत

platitude *n.* सामान्य वार्ता*, तुच्छ बात*, तुच्छता*, ओछा-पन, खोखलापन, निरर्थकता*

platonic *a.* तत्त्वज्ञानी प्लेटो-संबंधी

platoon *n.* पलटन*, पैदल सेना*

plausible *a.* सत्याभासी, स्वीकार्य, स्पष्ट-कथित, युक्ति-संगत, न्यायसंगत, घोषेबाज

play *n.* गति*, क्रिया-शीलता*, हंसी*, विनोद, खेल, क्रीड़ा*,

नाटक, अभिनय, जुम्रा; v.t.
& i. खेलना, नाटक करना,
जुम्रा खेलना, कूद-फांद मचाना,
बाजा बजाना; playhouse
n. नाटकगृह; playingcard
खेलने का ताश; fairplay
पक्षपातहीनता; foul play
कपट व्यवहार; out of play
खेल के नियमों के विरुद्ध; to
play fast and loose
बेईमानी करना

plea n. तर्क, हेतु, कारण,
बहाना, प्रार्थना*

plead v.i. वकालत करना, पक्ष
समर्थन करना

pleader n. अभिवक्ता, वकील

pleasant a. मनोहर, सुहावना

pleasantry n. आनन्द, हंसी*

please v.t. & i. प्रसन्न करना,
आनन्दित करना, सन्तुष्ट
करना, रुचिकर या अच्छा
लगना

pleasure n. आनन्द, सुख, रुचि*,
अभिलाषा*

plebiscite n. जनमत संग्रह

pledge n. प्रतिज्ञा*, बन्धक,
प्रण; v.t. बन्धक रखना,
वचन देना, प्रतिज्ञा करना

plenary a. समग्र, पूर्ण, विस्तृत,
निर्बाध

plenipotentiary a. & n.
परमशक्तिमान, निरंकुश, पूर्ण

सामर्थ्य-सम्पन्न राजदूत

plenty n. पूरी सामग्री*,
बहुतायत* ; in plenty
बहुतायत से

plenum n. पूर्ण समाज, सर्वां-
गीण सभा

plight n. दुर्दशा*, दशा*, वृत्ति*,
भाव

plot n. भूमि*, देश, क्षेत्र, गुप्त-
योजना*, कूटप्रबन्ध, उपन्यास
या नाटक का कथानक; v.t.
(p.t. plotted) रूपरेखा या
खाका बनाना, कपट प्रबन्ध
करना; to plot against
षड्यन्त्र रचना

plough n. हल; v.t. हल में
भूमि जोतना

ploughman n. हलवाहा

pluck v.t. तोड़ना, छीनना,
इकट्ठा करना, ऐंठना; n.
साहस, परीक्षा में असफलता*;
to pluck off नोंच लेना

plug n. डट्टा, ठेंपी*, गुल्ली*,
v.t. (p.t. plugged) डट्टा
लगाकर बन्द करना

plum n. आलूबुखारा, आलूचा,
बेर

plumber n. पानी का नल
बैठानेवाला, नलकार

plump a. स्थूल, पुष्ट, गोल-
मटोल, भरा हुआ; v.t. & i.
धड़ाके से गिरना या गिराना

plunder *v.t.* लूटना; *n.* लूट का माल.

plunge *v.t. & i.* डुबाना, डूबना, गोता लगाना; *n.* डुबकी*, प्रवेश

plural *a.* अनेक, बहुवचन

plurality *n.* अनेकता*, अधिकता*

plus *adv.* अधिक; *n.* जोड़ने का (धन +) चिह्न

ply *v.i. & t.* (*p.t.* plied) निरंतर कार्य करना, परिश्रम से करना बल लगाकर प्रयोग करना, प्रार्थना करना; *n.* तह दिशा*, रुझान

ply-wood *n.* अनेक तहों का तख्ता, पर्तदार लकड़ी*

pneumonia *n.* न्यूमोनिया, फेफड़ों की सूजन

pocket *n.* पाकिट, जेब*, खलीता; *v.t.* जेब में रखना, अपने काम में लाना; to pocket an insult चुपचाप अपमान सह लेना; empty pocket निर्धन मनुष्य

pocket-book *n.* जेबी पुस्तक*

pocket-money *n.* जेब खर्च

poem *n.* पद्यकाव्य, कविता*

poesy *n.* काव्य-रचना*, काव्य-कला*

poet *n.* (*fem.* poetess) कवि; a ready poet आशुकवि

poetaster *n.* क्षुद्र कवि, तुक्कड़

poetess *n. fem.* कवयित्री*

poetic *a.* कविता-संबंधी

poetics *n. pl.* काव्यशास्त्र

poetry *n.* कविता*, काव्य-रचना, पद्य

poignancy *n.* तीखापन, तीक्ष्णता*

poignant *a.* तीखा, मर्मवेधी, उत्कट

point *n.* बिन्दु, यन्त्र की नोक, नोकदार शस्त्र, अन्तरीप, अवसर, क्षण, काल परिमाण, विरामचिह्न; *v.t.* चोखा करना, ध्यान आकृष्ट करना, लक्ष्य करना, सीमेन्ट से भरना; at all points सब अंश में; make a point ध्यान आकर्षित करना; on the point of death मृत्यु के समीप; point at issue विवाद विषय; on the point of उद्यत; to carry one's point लक्ष्य स्थिर करना; to gain a point अभीष्ट सिद्ध करना; to mark a point स्थिर करना; point of view दृष्टिकोण

poise *v.t. & i.* तौलना, पसंघा करना, संभलना; *n.* पसंघा, सन्तुलन

poison *n.* विष, गरल, हानि-

कारक प्रभाव; *v.t.* जहर देना,
मारना, नष्ट करना

poisonous *a.* विषैला, जहरीला

polar *a.* ध्रुवीय, ध्रुव के समीप
का

pole *n.* लम्बा डंडा, लम्बा,
5½ गज की नाप; ध्रुव चुम्बक
के दोनों छोर

polemic *a. & n* विवादास्पद,
शास्त्रार्थ करनेवाला, टण्टा,
बखेड़ा, हुज्जती

polemics *n. pl.* वादानुवाद

pole-star *n.* ध्रुवतारा

police *n.* पुलिस, आरक्षी;
police-station थाना चौकी,
आरक्षालय

policeman *n.* पुलिस का सिपाही

policy *n.* नीति*, राजनीति*,
युक्ति, राज्य-शासन-पद्धति*;
prudential policy समीक्षा*;
bad (crooked) policy
कुनीति*, छल प्रयोग

polish *v.t. & i.* चमकाना या
चमकना, स्वच्छ करना; *n.*
पॉलिश, चमक*, शोभा*,
शिष्टता*, रोगन

polished *a.* शिष्ट, विनीत,
परिमार्जित

polite *a.* शिष्ट, विनीत

politeness *n.* शिष्टता*, विनय

politic *a.* नीति-चतुर, बुद्धिमान

political *a.* राजनीतिक; poli-

tical economy राजनैतिक
अर्थशास्त्र; political geography राजनैतिक भूगोल;
political science राजनीति
विज्ञान

politician *n.* राजनीतिज्ञ

politics *n. pl.* (used as
sing.) राजनीति-शास्त्र

polity *n.* नीति*, राज्यशासन-
पद्धति*, राज्यतंत्र

poll *n.* मस्तक, निर्वाचकों की
नामावली, मतदान; *v.t. &
i.* (*p.t.* polled) बाल
काटना, सूचीपत्र में लिखना,
मतदान करना, वोट पाना;
poll-tax प्रत्येक मनुष्य पर
लगनेवाला कर

pollute *v.t.* दूषित करना, भ्रष्ट
करना

polo *n.* पोलो, चौगान

poly *pref.* 'अनेक' के अर्थ का
उपसर्ग

polygamic *a.* बहुपतित्व या
बहुपत्नीत्व-संबंधी

polygamous *a.* एक से अधिक
पत्नीवाला

polygamy *n.* बहुविवाह

polyglot *n.* बहुभाषी, बहुभाषा-
विद्

polytechnic *a.* पॉलीटेकनीक,
विविधकला-विषयक, विविध-
कला विद्यालय

polytheism n. बहुदेववाद

polytheist n. बहुदेवपूजक

polytheistic a. बहुदेववादी

pomp n. आडम्बर, विभव, ठाटबाट

pomposity n. आडम्बर

pompous a. आडम्बरी, विभव-युक्त

pond n. छोटा तालाब, हौज

ponder v.t. मन में तौलना विचार करना

ponderable a. विचारणीय.

pontiff n. रोम का प्रधान पादरी, पोप

pony n. (pl. ponies) टट्टू, छोटा घोड़ा

poor a. दीन, तुच्छ, दरिद्र, अधम, अभागा, विनीत, अन-उपजाऊ

pop v.t. & i. (p.t. popped) धड़ाके का शब्द करना या होना, बन्दूक छोड़ना; n. धड़ाके का शब्द; adv. एक-एक, तुरत; pop-gun बच्चों के खेलने की बन्दूक; to pop the question विवाह का प्रस्ताव करना; pop art एक तरह की आधुनिक चित्रकला; pop music एक तरह का आधुनिक संगीत

pope n. पोप, रोम का बड़ा पादरी; pope's head लम्बे डंडे की झाड़ू

poplar n. चिनार

poplin n. पॉपलीन कपड़ा

populace n. साधारण लोग, जन-समूह

popular a. लौकिक, सर्वप्रिय, प्रचलित, सर्वमान्य मनुष्यों के समझने योग्य; popular language प्रचलित भाषा*; popular scandal लोकाप-वाद

popularity n. लोकप्रियता*, प्रसिद्धि*

popularize v.t. लोकप्रिय या प्रसिद्ध बनाना, प्रचलित करना, जनप्रिय करना, लोक-गम्य बनाना

populate v.t. जनपूर्ण करना, बसाना

population n. जनसंख्या*, आबादी*

populous a. जनपूर्ण, घना आबाद

porcelain n. चीनी मिट्टी*, उसके बर्तन

porch n. ड्योढ़ी, ओसारा

pork n. सूअर का मांस

porridge n. लपसी*, हलुआ; keep your breath to cool your porridge अपनी सलाह अपने पास रक्खो

port n. बन्दरगाह; v.t. बन्दर-

338

गाह की ओर जहाज़ का घुमाना

portable *a.* ले जाने योग्य, वहनीय

portage *n* ढुलाई* ले जाने का भाड़ा

portal *n* सदर दरवाज़ा

portend *v t.* शकुन बतलाना, पहिले से सूचना देना, आगाह करना, चेतावनी देना

porter *n.* (*fem.* portress) द्वारपाल, दरबान

portfolio *n.* (*pl.* -s) पोर्ट-फोलियो, खुले पत्र, मानचित्र आदि रखने का बस्ता, मन्त्रि-पद

portico *n.* (*pl.* -es) पोर्टिको, द्वार-मण्डप, बरसाती*

portion *n* अंश, भाग, वांट, दहेज, भाग्य; *v.t.* बांटना, दहेज देना

portrait *n.* छविचित्र, व्यक्ति-चित्र, चित्र, फोटो

portraiture *n.* चित्रण, आले-खन, चित्रकारी*, चित्र, चित्रात्मक वर्णन

portray *v t.* चित्र बनाना, वर्णन करना

portrayal *n.* चित्रलेखन, वर्णन

pose *v.t. & i.* मुद्रा बनाना, विशेष स्थिति में बैठना, स्तम्भित करना, चक्कर में डालना; *n.* मुद्रा*, स्थिति*,

छवि*, ढव, ढोंग

position *n.* स्थान, स्थिति*, पदवी*, मनोभाव, अंगस्थिति*, out of position अनावश्यक, अयोग्य

positive *a.* वास्तविक, निश्चित, पक्का, आवश्यक, घनराशि का; positive laws स्थिर नियम

possess *v.t.* अधिकार रखना, धारण करना, दखल करना, अधिक प्रभाव डालना

possession *n.* अधिकार, अधीन, पदार्थ, भोग

possibility *n.* सम्भावना*

possible *a.* होने योग्य, सम्भव

post *pref.* 'बाद' का अर्थ-सूचक उपसर्ग

post *n.* खम्भा, थूनी; *v t.* खम्भे पर लगाना, सार्वजनिक विज्ञापन लगाना

post *n.* पद, अधिकार, डाक-विभाग; *v.t.* नियुक्त करना, चिट्ठी छोड़ना, वेग से यात्रा करना; *adv* शीघ्रता से; post-paid *a.* डाक महसूल पहिले से दिया हुआ

postage *n.* डाक महसूल

postal *a.* डाक-सम्बन्धी

post-card *n.* पोस्टकार्ड

post-date *v.t.* लिखने के बाद की तिथि डालना

poster *n.* पोस्टर, विज्ञापन, विज्ञापन चिपकानेवाला

posterity *n.* सन्तति*, वंश, भावी पीढ़ी*

posthumous *a.* मरणोत्तर, पिता के मरण के उपरान्त उत्पन्न, लेखक के मरण के उपरान्त प्रकाशित

postman *n.* डाकिया, पत्रवाहक

postmark *n.* डाकघर की मोहर*

postmaster *n* पत्रपाल, डाक-पति; postmaster general महापत्रपाल

post-mortem *a.* मृत्यु के पश्चात्; *n.* शव-परीक्षा*

post-office *n.* डाकघर

postpone *v.i & t.* स्थगित करना, टालना

postponement *n.* स्थगन, विलम्बन

postscript *n.* (*abbr.* P.S.) अनुलेख, पत्र समाप्त करने पर लिखा हुआ अंश, पुनश्च

postulate *n.* स्वीकृत पक्ष, स्वयंसिद्ध; *v.t.* & *i.* स्वयंसिद्ध मान लेना

posture *n.* मनःस्थिति*, मुद्रा*, आसन, अंग-विन्यास हाव-भाव, चाल-ढाल*, दशा*

pot *n.* पात्र, भाण्ड, गमला; *v.t.* पात्र में रखना, गमले में

पेड़ लगाना; pot-boiler जीविकार्थ साहित्य, साहित्य-जीवी

potash *n.* पोटाश, सज्जी, खार

potassium *n.* पोटैशियम, पोटाश का आधारभूत तत्त्व, दहातु

potato *n.* (*pl.* potatoes) आलू; quite the potato योग्य वस्तु

potency *n.* शक्ति*, अधिकार, प्रभावशीलता*, पुंसकता*

potent *a.* प्रबल, बलवान

potential *a.* प्रबल, गुणकारक, शक्य

potentiality *n.* सम्भावना*, शक्यता*

pottery *n.* मिट्टी के पात्र, कुम्हार का व्यापार

poultry *n.* घरेलू मुर्गी*, बत्तख इत्यादि; poultry farming मुर्गीपालन

pounce *v.t.* झपटना, आक्रमण करना

pound *n.* पौंड, आध सेर तौल. सोने की प्रायः 15 रुपये की मुद्रा; penny wise and pound foolish छोटे व्यय में मितव्ययता और बड़ी रकम उड़ाना, मोहरों की लूट में कोयलों पर छाप

pound *v.t.* कूटना, पीसना,

टुकड़े करना

pour *v.t.* धार गिराना, बोलना, उंडेलना, अधिक संख्या में निकालना; it never rains but pours आपत्तियां एक साथ आती हैं; to pour cold water on हताश करना; to pour forth arrows तीरों की वर्षा करना; to pour oil upon troubled waters उपद्रव शान्त करना

poverty *n.* दरिद्रता*, कमी*, प्रभाव, आवश्यकता*, reduced to poverty दरिद्रताग्रस्त

powder *n.* पाउडर, बुकनी*, अग्निचूर्ण, बारूद; *v.t.* बुकनी करना, छिड़कना; to reduce to powder बुकनी करना

powder-magazine *n.* बारूद-घर

power *n.* शक्ति*, ऊर्जा*, बल, अधिकार, प्रभाव. राज्य, शासन; according to one's power यथाशक्ति; in one's power अपने अधीन; to exercise power शासन करना; power politics अधिकारार्थ कूटनीति*, बड़े राष्ट्रों की कूटनीति*

practicability *n.* करणीयता*, साध्यता*, सम्भावना*

practicable *a.* करने योग्य, सम्भव

practical *a.* व्यावहारिक, अभ्यास-सम्बन्धी, प्रायोगिक; practical knowledge व्यावहारिक ज्ञान; practical scheme व्यवहार के योग्य उपाय

practice *n.* अभ्यास, व्यवसाय

practise *v.t. & i.* अभ्यास करना, साधना, जीविका करना

practitioner *n.* व्यवसायी

pragmatic (-al) *a.* व्यवहार-मूलक, राज-कार्य या इतिहास विषयक, हस्तक्षेपी ढीठ

pragmatism *n.* पांडित्य का अभिमान, व्यवहारवाद, फलवाद, उपयोगवाद

praise *n.* प्रशंसा*, स्तुति*; *v.t.* प्रशंसा करना, स्तुति करना

praiseworthy *a.* सराहने योग्य

pram *n.* प्राम, बच्चागाड़ी*

prance *v.i. & t.* पैरों उछलना, उछलनेवाले घोड़े पर चढ़ना; *n.* उछल-कूद*

prank *v.t. & i.* सजाना, तड़क-भड़क दिखाना; *n.* क्रीड़ा*, खेल; mischievous prank दुष्टता*

pray *v.t. & i.* प्रार्थना करना, स्तुति करना, विनती करना

prayer n. प्रार्थना* स्तुति*, भजन

preach v.i. धर्म का उपदेश करना; to preach down उपदेश देकर नीचा दिखलाना

preacher n. धर्मोपदेशक

preamble n. भूमिका*, प्रस्तावना*; v.i. प्रस्तावना लिखना

precarious a. अनिश्चित, अररक्षित, संकटपूर्ण

precaution n. चौकसी*, सावधानी*

precautionary a. सतर्कता विषयक

precautious a. पहिले से सचेत

precede v.i. आगे होना, पूर्वकालीन होना

precedence (-cy) n. पूर्व आगमन, प्राथमिकता*, श्रेष्ठता*; प्रथम अधिकार

precedent n. पहिले का निर्णय, प्रमाण, दृष्टान्त, पूर्वोदाहरण, नज़ीर, पूर्वघटना

precept n. नियम, उपदेश, मर्यादा*, अधिपत्र

preceptor (fem. preceptress) n. उपदेशक, गुरु

precious a. मूल्यवान, महंगा, बहुमूल्य; precious metals सोना चांदी; precious stone मणि, रत्न

precipice n. करारा, कगार, खड़ी* ढाल*

precipitate v.t. .& i. फेंकना, प्रेरणा करना, शीघ्रता करना, पेंदी में बैठना या बठाना; a. बड़ी जल्दी करनेवाला; n. तलछट, पेंदी में बैठनेवाला पदार्थ

precis n. संक्षेप, सार

precise a. निश्चित, यथार्थ

precision n. यथार्थता*, शुद्धता*, सूक्ष्मता*

preclude v.t. बन्द करना, रोकना, पृथक् रखना

preclusion n. रुकावट*, अवरोध, बहिष्कार

preclusive a. प्रतिरोधक, रोकनेवाला

precocious a. समय से पहिले पकनेवाला, घृष्ट, बाल-प्रौढ़, अकाल-प्रौढ़

preconceive v.t. पहले से निश्चय कर लेना, पूर्व धारणा बनाना, पहले से सोच रखना

predecessor n. पूर्व अधिकारी, पूर्ववर्ती, पूर्वगामी, पूर्वज

predestination n. भाग्य, प्रारब्ध

predetermine v.t. पहिले से निर्णय कर लेना

predicament n. कठिन परिस्थिति*, विषमावस्था*, पदार्थ, अरस्तू के दस पदार्थ

predicate n. (व्याकरण में) विधेय

predict v.t. भविष्यवाणी करना

prediction n. भविष्यवाणी*

predominance n. अधिकता*, प्रबलता*, प्रभुत्व, सत्ता*, प्राधान्य

predominant v. प्रबल, प्रधान, हावी

predominate v.i. प्रबल होना, अधिकार रखना, विशिष्ट होना, हावी होना

pre-eminence n. श्रेष्ठता*, उत्तमता*

pre-eminent a. सर्वोत्तम

preface n. प्रस्तावना*, भूमिका*, v i. प्रस्तावना करना, भूमिका लिखना

prefect n. प्रीफेक्ट, अधिनायक, कक्षा का प्रमुख विद्यार्थी

prefer v.t. (p.t. preferred) अधिक चाहना, पहले चुनना, विचारार्थ उपस्थित करना

preferable a. उत्तम, श्रेष्ठ

preference n. प्राथमिकता* वरीयता*

preferential a. पक्षपाती, अधिक आदर का

prefix n. उपसर्ग; v.t. उपसर्ग लगाना, पुस्तक में भूमिका लगाना

preform v.t. पहिले से बना लेना

pregnancy n. गर्भावस्था*

pregnant a. गर्भवती*, फलदाता

prehistoric a. लिखित इतिहास के पहिले का, पूर्व-ऐतिहासिक

prejudice n. पूर्वाग्रह, दुराग्रह. पक्षपात, हानि*

prejudicial a. पक्षपातपूर्ण, हानिकारक, पक्षपाती

preliminary a. प्रारम्भिक; n. (pl. -ries) आरम्भ का कार्य, उपक्रम, तैयारी*

prelude n. आरम्भ, प्रस्तावना; v.t. प्रस्तावना करना

premature a. अकाल-प्रौढ़, कालपूर्व, असमय, कच्चा

premeditate v.t. पूर्व-चिन्ता करना या योजना बनाना, पूर्व-संकल्प करना, पूर्व-मनन करना

premeditation n. पूर्व-विचार, पूर्व चिन्तन

premier a. प्रधान, मुख्य; n. प्रधान मन्त्री

premise (premiss) n. पूर्वाधारित तथ्य (ब० व०) गृहोपान्त, गृहसीमा*, अहाता

premise v.t. प्रस्तावना के रूप में कहना

premium n. पारितोषिक, लाभ, बढ़ोत्तरी*, अधिक मूल्य, जीवन बीमा की किस्त

premonish *v.t.* पहिले से सचेत
करना

premonition *n.* पूर्व-सूचना*

preoccupation *n.* पूर्व-
अधिकार, पूर्वाग्रह, पक्षपात,
पूर्व-निर्णय, सर्वोपरि
व्यापार, तल्लीनता*

preoccupy *v.t.* (*p t.* pre-
occupied) पूर्वाधिकार
करना, पूर्वक्रम करना, निमग्न
करना

preparation *n.* पूर्व-व्यवस्था*,
तैयारी*, निर्मित पदार्थ

prepare *v.t.* तैयार करना

preponderance *n.* प्रबलता*,
प्राधान्य, अतिरेक, प्राचुर्य,
बाहुल्य

preponderant *a.* अतिरिक्त,
प्रचुर

preponderate *v.i.* अधिक
होना, अतिरिक्त होना, भारी
होना, प्रभाव रखना

preposition *n.* कारक-चिह्न
पूर्व-विभक्ति चिह्न

preposterous *a.* अनर्थक,
अयुक्त

prerequisite *adv.* पूर्वाकांक्षित

prerogative *n.* विशेष अधि-
कार

presbyterian *a.* गिरजाघर के
प्रधान पादरी के शासन से
संबंधित

prescribe *v.t.* आज्ञा देना;
नुसखा लिखना

prescript *n.* नियम, उपदेश

prescription *n.* निर्देशन,
शासन, उपचार - विधि*,
नुसखा, सनातन रीति*

presence *n.* उपस्थिति*, समी-
पता* चाल-ढाल; in the
presence of सम्मुख, प्रत्यक्ष;
presence of mind प्रतिभा-
शक्ति*, तत्काल बुद्धि*

present *a.* उपस्थित, इस समय
का; *n.* वर्तमान काल उप
हार; *v.t. & i.* उपहार देना,
उपस्थित करना, प्रस्तावना
करना; at present इस
समय, अभी; by these pre-
sents इस लेख द्वारा; in
the present case वर्तमान
अवस्था में

presently *adv.* अतिशीघ्र

preservation *n.* रक्षा*, पालन

preserve *v.t.* रक्षा करना,
बचाना, सड़ने से सुरक्षित
रखना; *n.* मुरब्बा, रक्षास्थान

preside *v.i* निरीक्षण करना,
अध्यक्ष होना, किसी सभा का
सभापति बनना; presiding
officer अधिष्ठाता

presidency *n.* अध्यक्ष का पद,
देश-विभाग, महाप्रान्त प्रदेश

president *n.* सभापति, राष्ट्र-

पति; president - elect
मनोनीत सभापति

press v.t. & i. निचोड़ना,
दबाना, ढकेलना, शीघ्र चलना
या जाना, भीड़ मचाना,
आग्रह करना; n. दबाव,
भीड़*, दबाने का यन्त्र,
छापने का यन्त्र, शीघ्रता*;
the press प्रकाशक लोग,
वर्तमान पत्र; to press
against टकराना; to press
upon प्रेरित करना; to
press upon mind चित्त
पर अत्यन्त प्रभाव डालना;
press information bureau
(P I.B.) पत्रसूचना विभाग;
press note प्रेस-विज्ञप्ति*

pressman n. (pl. pressmen)
छापनेवाला, पत्रकार

pressure n. बल, आवश्यकता*,
बाघकता*; financial pres-
sure घन-संकट; pressure
of business कार्य-भार

prestige n. गौरव, प्रतिष्ठा*

presume v.t. अनुमान करना,
तर्क करना, साहस करना,
मान लेना, घृष्टता करना

presumptuous a. साहसी,
ढीठ, अभिमानी

presuppose v.t. पूर्व भावना
बनाना, पूर्वानुमान करना,
पूर्वधारणा करना, लक्षित

करना

pretence n. बहाना, छद्म, छल

pretend v.t. छल करना, बहाना
करना

pretender n. कपटी, भूठा
दावेदार

pretension n. छल, वृथा-
भिमान

pretentious a. छली, कपटी

pretext n. कपट, बहाना; v.t.
बहाना बनाना

pretty a. (comp. prettier;
sup. prettiest) सुन्दर,
शोभायुक्त, आकर्षक; pretty
clear प्राय: शुद्ध; pretty
warm गुनगुना; adv. सामान्य
रूप में

prevail v.i. प्रबल होना, जीतना,
बहकाना, प्रचलित होना; to
prevail upon प्रवृत्त करना,
राजी करना

prevalent a. प्रबल, प्रचलित

prevent v.t रोकना

prevention n. प्रतिबन्ध, रुका-
वट*

preventive a. रोकनेवाला,
निषेधात्मक; preventive
detention रोघात्मक कारा-
वास, नज़रबन्दी; preventive
detention act नज़रबन्दी
कानून

previous a. अगला, पहिले का

prey n. प्रहेर, प्राबेट, शिकार, लूट का माल; v.i. लूटना, प्राबेट करके खाना; to prey upon प्राक्रमण करना

price n. मूल्य, दाम, क्षतिपूर्ति; at any price प्रत्येक प्रवस्था में, किसी भी मूल्य पर; price current पदार्थ के प्रचलित मूल्य की सूची; without price प्रमूल्य

priceless a. प्रनमोल

prick n. नुकीला शस्त्र, छिद्र, कष्टकारक विचार; v.t. छेदना. पीड़ा देना; to prick up one's ears सचेत होना

pride n. प्रभिमान, प्रहंकार, गर्व; v.t. गर्व करना; pride of one's birth प्रपने कुल का प्रभिमान; to pride oneself प्रात्मगौरव करना

priest n. (fem. priestess) पुरोहित. पादरी

priesthood n. पुरोहित का पद

prima facie n. पहिली दृष्टि में, देखते ही

primarily adv प्रधान रूप से

primary a. मुख्य; primary education प्रारम्भिक शिक्षा

prime a. प्रधान, प्रति उत्तम; n. प्रारम्भ, प्रौढ़ता; prime of life युवावस्था*; prime cost लागत; prime minis-

ter प्रधान मन्त्री

primer n. प्रवेशिका*, पहली बाल पाटी*

primeval a. पहिला, प्रादि प्रवस्था का

primitive a. प्राचीन, पुरानी रीत का, गंवार

prince n (fem. princess) राजा, राजकुमार, राजपुत्र;. prince - consort राज्य करनेवाली रानो का पति; Prince of Wales इंगलैंड के सबसे बड़े राजकुमार की पदवी

principal a. प्रधान, मुख्य, श्रेष्ठ, प्रमुख; n. प्रधानाचार्य

principality n. राज्य. प्रदेश

principe n. मूल सिद्धान्त, नियम, कारण. जीवन-विधि*; on principle सिद्धान्त के प्रनुसार

print v.t. मोहर लगाना, टाइप से छापना; n. चिह्न, छाप*; finger-print प्रंगूठे की छाप; footprint पैर का चिह्न; out of print छपी पुस्तक के मिलने का प्रभाव, प्रप्राप्य

printer n. मुद्रक

printing n. छपाई*

prison n कारागार, बंदीगृह; v.t. बन्धन में डालना, बन्दी करना; prison-bird कारागार का बन्दा

prisoner n. बन्दी; state prisoner राजनीतिक बंदी

prisonment n. कैदखाने में बंद करने का कार्य

privacy n. गुप्तता*, निर्जनता*, अन्तरग

private n. अनधिकारी, गुप्त, अप्रकट; in private गुप्त रूप से; private apartment अन्तःपुर private profit निजी लाभ; private road निजी सड़क

privation n. अभाव, हानि*, लोग

privilege n. विशेष अधिकार या सुविधा*; privilege committee विशेषाधिकार समिति*. विशेष अधिकार देना

privileged a विशेष अधिकार-युक्त

prize n. पारितोषिक, बहुमूल्य वस्तु; v t. अधिक मूल्य का समझना

pro pref. 'पहिले' 'वास्ते' के अर्थ का उपसर्ग; pro bono publico सर्वजनहिताय; pro forma adv. नियमानुसार किया हुआ; pros and cons विधि तथा निषेध दोनों पक्ष का

probability n. सम्भावना*; in all probability प्रायः; pro-bably adv. संयोगवश; pro-

-bable a. संभव, प्रायः होनेवाला

probation n. परीक्षण काल

probationer n. काम सीखने के लिए नियुक्त पुरुष, परीक्ष्य-माण व्यक्ति

probational a. परीक्षाधीन

probe v.i. अन्वीक्षण करना, खोज करना, परीक्षा करना; n. घाव की परीक्षा करने की सलाई* अनुसंधान, खोज*, जांच*

problem n. विवाद-विषय, समस्या*, कठिन प्रश्न, रेखा-गणित में उपपाद्य विषय

problematic(al) अनिश्चित, शंकायुक्त

procedure n. कार्य करने की रीति*, विधि*, व्यवहार, कार्यनीति*, विधान, क्रिया-विधि*

proceed v i. बढ़ना, आगे जाना, प्रवृत्त होना, अभियोग करना; the play will now proceed अब खेल आरम्भ होगा

proceeding n. कार्य, ब्यापार, न्याय-सम्बन्धी कार्यवाही*; to institute legal pro-ceedings न्यायालय में अभि-योग चलाना

proceeds n. pl. प्राप्त धन, लाभ

process n. प्रगति-क्रम, विधि
व्यवहार; in process of
time कालक्रम से

procession n. सवारी*, जुलूस,
शोभा-यात्रा*

proclaim v.t. घोषणा करना,
प्रकाशित करना

proclamation n. घोषणा*,
ढिंढोरा

proctor n. प्रॉक्टर, कार्याध्यक्ष

procure v t. उपार्जन करना

procurement n. प्राप्ति*,
वसूली*

prodigal a. अपव्ययी, फिजूल-
खर्च; prodigal son लौटा
हुआ घुमक्कड़

prodigious a. अद्भुत, विल-
क्षण

prodigy n. विलक्षण पदार्थ या
मनुष्य, शकुन

produce v.t. बढ़ाना, उत्पन्न
करना; n. उत्पत्ति*, लाभ,
उपज*

producer n. उत्पादक

product n. फल, परिणाम,
गुणनफल

production n. उत्पादन,
रचना* उपज*

productive a. बहुत उत्पन्न
करनेवाला, उगाऊ

profane a. अपवित्र, अशुद्ध;
v.t. & i. अपवित्र करना,

दूषित करना

profess v.t. & i. स्वीकार
करना प्रतिज्ञा करना, मानना

profession n. प्रतिज्ञा*,
व्यापार, व्यवसाय

professional a. किसी व्यवसाय
का

professor n. प्रोफेसर,
स्वीकार करनेवाला, विश्व-
विद्यालय का अध्यापक

proficiency n. प्रवीणता*

proficient a. प्रवीण, कुशल

profile n. प्रोफाइल, ढांचा,
बगली चित्र; v.t. प्रोफाइल
बनाना

profit n. लाभ, सुविधा*,
प्राप्ति*; v.t. & i. (p.t.
profited) लाभ उठाना

profiteer n. अनुचित लाभ
उठानेवाला, मुनाफाखोर; v.i.
अधिक लाभ उठाना

profiteering n. मुनाफाखोरी*

profound a. गम्भीर, अति
विद्वान, विलक्षण; profound
sleep गाढ़ी निद्रा; pro-
found sigh गाढ़ा उच्छ्वास

profuse a. मुक्तहस्त, लुटाऊ,
अत्यधिक

profusely adv. फिजूलखर्ची के
साथ, मुक्तहस्त ढंग से,
विपुल मात्रा में

profusion n. समृद्धि* अधि-

कता*

progeny n. संतान, वंश

programme n. कार्यक्रम, क्रमावली

progress n. वृद्धि*, उन्नति*, उपज*, यात्रा* v.t.बढ़ाना, उन्नति करना progress in learning विद्या की उन्नति

progressive a. क्रम से बढ़ने-वाला, प्रगतिशील, प्रगतिवादी

prohibit v.t. (p.t. prohibited) निषेध करना, मना करना

prohibition n. निषेध, मनाही*

prohibitive a. निषेध करने-वाला

prohibitory a. निषेध करनेवाला

project n. योजना*, उपाय, कल्पना*, विचार; v.t. & i. आगे को फेंकना, योजना बनाना, खाका खींचना, विचार करना; to project oneself दूसरे के प्रभाव में जा पड़ना

projectile n. वायु में फेंका हुआ पदार्थ

projector n. प्रोजेक्टर, चल-चित्र दर्शित्र, प्रक्षेपक यंत्र

proletarian n. सर्वहारा

prolific a. फलवान, उपजाऊ

prologue n. प्रस्तावना*, नाटक का आरंभ

prolong v.t. बढ़ाना, विस्तार करना

prominence (-cy) ns. ऊंचाई*, उन्नति*, श्रेष्ठता*

prominent a. मुख्य, प्रधान

promise n. प्रतिज्ञा*, आभास, आशा*; v.t. प्रतिज्ञा करना, आशा दिलाना; a hollow promise झूठी प्रतिज्ञा; to break a promise. प्रतिज्ञा भंग करना; to fulfil a promise. प्रतिज्ञा पालन करना

promising a. होनहार

promissory a. प्रतिज्ञायुक्त; promissory note प्रतिज्ञा-पत्र

promote v.t. बढ़ाना, ऊंचे पद पर पहुंचाना, उत्साह देना, संस्था स्थापित करना

promotion n उन्नति*, उच्च पद की प्राप्ति*

prompt a. उद्धत, द्रुत, समय का पक्का; v.t. प्रवृत्त करना, उकसाना

prompter n. नाटक में पात्र को स्थान-स्थान पर स्मरण करानेवाला

promulgate v.t. प्रकाशित करना प्रसिद्ध करना, घोषित करना, जारी करना

promulgation n. प्रवर्तन,

विषोषण
pronoun *n.* सर्वनाम शब्द
pronounce *v.t. & i.* उच्चारण करना, निर्णय सुनाना
pronunciation *n.* उच्चारण या इसकी रीति*
proof *n* प्रमाण, परीक्षा*, शक्ति का प्रमाण, प्रूफ पहिली छाप*, शोध्यपत्र; *a.* परीक्षित शक्ति का; burden of proof साघन धर्म; proof reader छपे कागज (प्रूफ) को शुद्ध करनेवाला, शोधन- कर्ता: to put to the proof परीक्षा करना; writ- tten proof लिखित प्रमाण
propaganda *n.* प्रचार
propagate *v.t.* उत्पन्न करना, बढ़ाना, फैलाना, विस्तृत करना
propagation *n.* वृद्धि*, फैलाव
propeller *n.* जहाज या वायु- यान को आगे बढ़ानेवाला पंखा, चालक-यंत्र
proper *a.* आत्मीय, निजी, योग्य, वास्तविक ठीक, यथार्थ, उचित; proper fraction भिन्न जो इकाई से कम हो; proper noun व्यक्तिवाचक संज्ञा*
property *n.* निजी संपत्ति* या अधिकार, घन, लक्षण, गुण,

सम्पत्ति*, जायदाद*; lan- ded property स्थावर सम्पत्ति*; public property सार्वजनिक सम्पत्ति*
prophecy *n.* भविष्यकथन या सूचना*
prophesy *v.t. & i.* (*p.t.* prophesied) भविष्य बतलाना
prophet *n.* (*fem.* pro- phetess) भविष्यवक्ता, पैगम्बर
prophetic (-al) *a.* भविष्य- कथन सम्बन्धी
proportion *n.* तुलनात्मक अंश, सापेक्ष सम्बन्ध, समाना- नुपात, साहश्य, अनुरूपता*, भाग, हिस्सा; *v.t.* समानु- पातिक बनाना; in propor- ion to अनुरूप, सहश
proportionate *a.* आनुपातिक, यथोचित, बराबर; *v.t.* बरा- बर करना
proposal *n.* प्रस्ताव, विवाह का वचन
propose *v.t. & i.* विवाह का प्रस्ताव रखना, प्रस्ताव करना, प्रस्तुत करना, अनुमान करना
proposition *n.* प्रस्ताव, प्रमेय
proprietary *a.* स्वामी संबंधी; proprietary medicines ऐसी औषधियां जिनके बनाने

और बेचने के अधिकार
सुरक्षित हों; proprietary
rights स्वामित्व अधिकार

proprietor n. (fem. -tress)
स्वामी, मालिक

propriety n. योग्यता*, शुद्धता*,
सच्चरित्रता*; (ब०व०) शुद्ध
चरित्र

prorogation n. स्थगन, सत्राव-
सान

prorogue v.t. सभा को कुछ
काल के लिए स्थगित करना

prosaic a. गद्य की तरह, नीरस

proscribe v.t. जब्त करना,
रोकना, त्यागना

proscription n. निवारण का
कार्य, बहिष्कार, जब्ती*

prose n गद्य, गद्यकाव्य; a.
गद्यरूप; v.i. गद्य में बात
करना; prose poem गद्य-
काव्य

prosecute v.t. & i. अनुसरण
करना, कार्य में लगना, अभि-
योग करना; to prosecute
studies अध्ययन करना

prosecution n. अभियोग

prosecutor n. अभियोग चलाने-
वाला

prosody n. छन्द:शास्त्र

prospect n. विस्तृत दृश्य,
दर्शन, मनोभाव, आशा; v.i.
खोज करना

prospectus n. (pl. -es) प्रास-
पेक्टस, पुस्तक*, व्यवसाय
इत्यादि या नियमावली की
विवरण पत्रिका*

prosper v.i. सफल होना,
धनवान होना, उन्नति करना

prosperity n. सम्पत्ति*,
सौभाग्य

prosperous a. सफल धनी,
सम्पन्न

prostitute n. वेश्या*, तवायफ

prostrate a. लम्बा पड़ा हुआ,
दण्डवत् किए हुए; v.t. दण्ड-
वत् करना

protagonist n. नायक, मुख्य
अभिनेता, प्रवक्ता, हिमायती,
तरफदार

protect v.t. आपत्ति से बचाना,
रक्षा करना, सहायता देना

protection n. रक्षा*, घरण

protector n. (fem. -ress)
रक्षक

protege n. (fem. protegee)
आश्रित, पालित, पोष्य, उप-
जीवी, संरक्षणाधीन व्यक्ति

protein n. एक रासायनिक
सत्त्व, प्रोभूजिन

protest n. दृढ़ उक्ति*, प्रति-
वाद, विरोध; v.t. & i. दृढ़ता
के शब्द कहना, निषेधपूर्वक
कहना

protestant n. प्रोटेस्टेंट,

ईसाइयों के उस धर्म का अनुयायी जो पोप के अधिकार को स्वीकार नहीं करता

protestantism प्रोटेस्टेंट मत का सिद्धान्त

proto *pref.* 'प्रथम, आदि' के अर्थ का उपसर्ग

protocol *n.* प्रोटोकोल, विदेश-मंत्रालय का शिष्टाचार विभाग नयाचार. मूल संधि-पत्र, मूलपत्र

protoplasm *n.* परस, जीवद्रव्य

prototype *n.* मूलरूप, मूलादर्श

protract *v.t.* बढ़ाना, फैलाना

protrude *v.t.* ढकेलना, आगे को बढ़ाना

proud *a.* अभिमानी, गर्वी, घमंडी, उद्धत, विशाल, शान-दार, दिखौवा

prove *v.t. & i.* परीक्षा करना, सिद्ध करना, अनुभव करना, प्रकाशित करना

proverb *n.* जनोक्ति*, कहावत*

provide *v.i. & t.* तैयार होना, तैयारी करना, सामग्री जुटाना, नियुक्त करना; to provide against पहिले से प्रबन्ध कर लेना

providence *n.* पूर्वविचार, सावधानी, परमेश्वर

province *n.* देश का विभाग, प्रान्त, व्यापार, कर्त्तव्य, कार्य-गति*

provision *n.* तैयारी*, पूर्व-कल्पना, विधान; (ब० व०) भोजन

provisional *a.* क्षणिक, सामयिक

provocation *n.* उनेजना*, प्रेरणा*, तैश, आवेश, उक-साव

provocative *a.* उत्तेजक, प्रेरक, उकसानेवाला, तैश में आ जाने-वाला

provoke *v.t.* उकसाना, कुद्ध करना

prowess *n.* शूरता*, साहस

proximity *n.* समीपता; proximity of blood समीप का संबंध

prudent *a.* बुद्धिमान, दूरदर्शी, सावधान

prudence *n.* दूरदर्शिता*, चातुरी*

prudish *a.* मिथ्याविनयी, अति-सुशील

pry *v.t.* (*p.t.* pried) निहारना, सूक्ष्म निरीक्षण करना

pseudo *pref.* 'मिथ्या, दिखा-वटी' के अर्थ का उपसर्ग

pseudonym *n.* छद्मनाम

psyche *n.* आत्मा*, मन, मानस, चित्त

psychic *a.* मानस, मानसिक;

n. संवेदनशील व्यक्ति, साधन; (ब० व०) मनोविज्ञान

psycho *pref.* 'आत्मा या मन' के अर्थ का उपसर्ग

psychological *a.* मनोवैज्ञानिक

psychologist *n.* मनोविज्ञान-वेत्ता

psychology *n.* मनोविज्ञान*

puberty *n.* यौवन, युवावस्था

public *a.* लोक-सम्बन्धी सार्वजनिक, सामान्य प्रचलित; *n.* जन-साधारण; in public प्रत्यक्ष रूप में; public-good लोकहित; public - house मद्यगृह; public-road सार्वजनिक मार्ग, public-spirit जनकल्याण भावना*; public spirited जनकल्याण की भावनावाला; public-works सार्वजनिक हित के निर्माण-कार्य

publication *n.* प्रकाशन, प्रकाशित पुस्तक*

publicist *n.* वृत्तकार, पत्रकार

publicity *n.* लोक-प्रसिद्धि*, प्रचार

publish *v.t.* प्रकाशित करना

publisher *n.* प्रकाशक

pudding *n.* पुडिंग, एक प्रकार का मांस और अन्न का बना हुआ पक्वान्न; more praise than pudding वास्तविक

उपहार; pudding-hearted डरपोक मनुष्य

puerile *a.* बालक के समान, बच्चों-जैसा

puff *n.* वायु का झोंका, भाप की भभक*, धुएं की फूंक* पाउडर लगाने का साधन (रोएंदार गद्दी); *v.i. & t.* फूंकना, वृथा प्रशंसा करना; to puff and blow हांफना; to puff up फुलाना; to puff out हांफकर बोलना

pull *v.t.* खींचना, तोड़ना; *n.* खिंचाव, नौका - संचालन; pull-back असुविधा*; pulled *a.* अस्वस्थ; to pull about इधर-उधर हिलाना; to pull a thing to pieces किसी वस्तु को टुकड़े-टुकड़े करना; to pull back रोकना; to pull caps झगड़ा करना; to pull down ढाहना; to pull off one's hat टोपी उतारकर अभिवादन करना; to pull through आपत्ति से सुरक्षित निकल जाना

pulp *n.* गुद्दा; *v.t.* गुद्दा बनाना

pulpy *a.* गुद्देदार

pulpit *a.* व्याख्यान-मंच, आसन, पीठ*, व्यासपीठ*

pulsate *v.i.* धड़कना

pulse *n.* कलाई पर की नाड़ी*;
v.t. नाड़ी चलना; to feel
the pulse नाड़ी-परीक्षा
करना; (*pl.*)*n.* दाल

pump *n.* पम्प, उदंच; *v.i.*
& *t.* पम्प चलाना, पिचकारी
से हवा भरना या निकालना

pun *n.* श्लेप, शब्दक्रीड़ा*,
अनेकार्थ शब्द; *v.t.* ऐसे श्लेप
का प्रयोग करना

punch *n.* छेद करने का यंत्र,
हंसानेवाली मूर्ति, एक प्रकार
की मदिरा; *v.t.* छेद करना

punctual *a.* समयनिष्ठ, यथा-
समय

punctuate *v.t.* विराम-चिह्न
लगाना, चिह्नांकित करना,
व्यवधान डालना, टोकना

punctuation *n.* चिह्नांकन,
विराम-चिह्न

puncture *n.* पंक्चर, छोटा
छिद्र वेध; *v.t.* छोटा छिद्र
करना

pungent *a.* कड़वा, तीखा, उग्र

punish *v.t.* दण्ड देना, ताड़ना
देना

punishment *n.* दण्ड; capital
punishment प्राणदण्ड

punitive *a.* दण्डात्मक

pupil *n.* शिष्य, विद्यार्थी, आंख
की पुतली*; pupil-teacher
शिक्षक-विद्यार्थी, छात्र-शिक्षक

puppet *n.* गुड़िया*, कठपुतली*,
मनुष्य जो दूसरे के अधीन हो;
puppet-play कठपुतली का
खेल

puppy *n.* पिल्ला, घमण्डी मनुष्य

purchase *n.* क्रय, खरीद, मोल
लिया हुआ पदार्थ; *v.t.* क्रय
करना, मोल लेना, खरीदना;
purchasing power क्रय-
शक्ति*

pure *a.* शुद्ध, स्वच्छ, बिना
मेल का, निर्मल, केवल

purgatory *n.* पापमोचन, पाप-
मोचनस्थान, सुधारगृह, तपो-
भूमि*

purge *v.t.* शुद्ध करना, पाप
हटाना, पेट साफ करना

purify *v.t.* (*p t.* purified)
शुद्ध करना निर्मल करना

purist *n.* भाषा की शुद्धता पर
अधिक ध्यान रखनेवाला,
शुद्धतावादी

puritan *n.* एक ईसाई मत का
अनुयायी, निष्ठावान

puritanic (·al) *a.* प्रोटेस्टेंट
मतानुयायी, विशुद्धिवादी,
कट्टरतावादी

purity *n.* पवित्रता*, शुद्धता*

purl *n.* कलाबत्तू का किनारा,
लहर का मन्द शब्द; *v.i.*
मन्द शब्द करना

purple *n.* & *a.* बैंगनी बैंगनी

रंग का; purple robe राज-
कीय वस्त्र

purport n. आशय, अभिप्राय;
v i तात्पर्य बतलाना

purpose n. हेतु. अभिप्राय,
तात्पर्य; v.i. अभिप्राय रखना

purposely adv जान-बूझकर;
fixed purpose दृढ़ संकल्प;
on purpose उद्देश्य से; to
no purpose व्यर्थ, निरर्थक;
for the purpose of वास्ते,
लिए

purse n. पर्स, रुपया रखने की
थैली*, धन की भेंट*; v.t.
थैले में रखना; light purse
निर्धनता*; public purse
सार्वजनिक सम्पत्ति* to hold
the purse व्यय पर अधिकार
रखना

pursue v.t. पीछा करना, लक्ष्य
करना

pursuit n. अनुसरण, उद्यम,
व्यवसाय

purview n. विस्तार, फैलाव;
पर्यवलोकन

push v.t. & i. ढकेलना, बढ़ाना,
हटाना; n. धक्का, शक्ति*,
उद्योग; to push afar दूर
हटाना; to push forward
आगे को ढकेलना; to push
off नाव ढकेलकर धारा में
करना; to push on जल्दी

करना, to push aside
हटाना

pushing a. उत्साही, उद्यमी

put v.i. & t. (p.t. & p.p
put) रखना, स्थापित करना,
प्रश्न पूछना, प्रस्ताव करना;
put to it बाध्य करना; to
put a bullet through
गोली मारना; to put aside
अलग करना; to put back
रोकना; to put blame on
कलंकित करना; to put by
धन बचाना; to put down
दबाना; to put forth
प्रस्ताव करना; प्रकाशित
करना; to put in भरना,
लिखना; to put into one's
hands सौंपना; to put in
order क्रम में रखना; to put
off टालना; to put on
वस्त्र धारण करना, पहिनना;
to put out उलटना,
घबड़ाना; to put to a
stand रोकना; to put to
death हत्या करना; to put
to it बाध्य करना; to put
to the hammer नीलाम
करना; to put up इमारत
बनाना, बसेरा लेना; to put
up with सहन करना; well
put अच्छी तरह वर्णन किया
हुआ

putrid *a.* सड़ा हुआ, दुर्गन्धित

puzzle *n.* कूट प्रश्न, कठिन प्रश्न, पहेली*; *v.t.* घबड़ाना, व्याकुल करना

puzzling *a.* भ्रमकारी, घबड़ाने-वाला

pygmy (pigmy) *ns.* (*pl.* pygmies) नाटा मनुष्य, बौना

pyorrhoea *n.* पायरिया, मसूड़े में से पीव निकलने का रोग, शीताद

pyramid *n.* पिरामिड, स्तूप, मीनार

pyramidal *a.* स्तूपाकार, सूच्या-कार

pyre *n.* चिता*

Q

quack *v.t.* बतख की तरह टर्राना, गर्व करना; *n.* बतख का शब्द, ठगविद्या करनेवाला, नीमहकीम

quackery *n.* मिथ्याभिमान, नीमहकीमी*

quadrangle *n.* चौकोर आंगन, चतुर्भुज

quadrangular *a.* चतुष्कोणीय, चतुर्भुजीय

quadrate *a.* वर्गाकार; *n.* चौकोर टुकड़ा या चद्दर

quadri *pref.* 'चार' के अर्थ का उपसर्ग

quadrilateral *a. & n.* चार भुजा का, चतुर्भुज आकृति*

quadruped *n.* चौपाया, चतुष्पद

quadruple *n.* चौगुनी संख्या*; *v.t.* चौगुना करना

quadruplet *n.* एक साथ जन्म लेनेवाले चार बच्चे

quadruplicate *v.t.* चौगुना करना

quadruply *adv.* चतुर्गुण रूप में

quaint *a.* विचित्र, विलक्षण, पुराने ढंग का

quake *v.i.* कांपना, थर्राना; *n.* कंपकंपी*, थर्राहट*

quaker *n.* (*fem.* quakeress) क्वेकर, एक परोपकारी मण्डली का सभासद

qualification *n.* योग्यता*, मर्यादा*, विशिष्टता*

qualify *v.t. & i.* (*p.t.* quali-fied) योग्य बनाना या बनना, परीक्षा या प्रतियोगिता में उत्तीर्ण होना

qualitative *a.* जाति-स्वभाव या गुण-संबंधी

quality *n.* (*pl.* qualities)

गुण, जाति*, पद, स्वभाव,
धर्म, लक्षण; man of qua-
lity कुलीन पुरुष

quandary n. दुविधा*, व्या-
कुलता*, घबराहट*

quantitative adv. परिमाण
संबंधी

quantity n. परिमाण, विस्तार,
मात्रा*, अंश

quantum n. आवश्यक परिमाण
या मात्रा*

quarantine n. गमनागमन-
निषेध, संसर्गरोध, रोग-
प्रतिबन्ध, संसर्गरोध काल

quarrel n. कलह, झगड़ा,
विवाद; v.i. (p.t. quarrel-
led) झगड़ना

quarrelsome a. झगड़ालू,
लड़ाका; to pick up a
quarrel झगड़ा आरम्भ
करना; to quarrel with
one's bread and butter
अपना व्यवसाय त्यागना

quarry n. खदान*, खान*,
आखेट, लक्ष्य; v.i. (p.t.
quarried) खान से पत्थर
निकालना

quarter n. चतुर्थ भाग, चौदह
सेर का भार, स्थान, दिशा,
(ब॰व॰) सैनिकों के ठहरने
का स्थान; v.t. चार भाग
करना, ठहराना; in every

quarter सब दिशा में;
quarter of a century
पच्चीस वर्ष; quarter of an
hour पन्द्रह मिनट का समय;
quarter past four सवा-
चार बजे; to come to
close quarters मुठभेड़
करना

quarterly adv. & n. तीसरे
महीने, त्रैमासिक, त्रैमासिक
पत्रिका*

quartermaster n. सेना का
प्रधान अध्यक्ष

quasi pref. & conj. अर्ध

queen n. (mas. king) राज-
पत्नी*, महारानी*, रानी*,
अपूर्व वस्तु*, (शतरंज में)
वजीर, (ताश में) बेगम*

queen-mother n. fem राज-
माता*

queer a. अनूठा, विलक्षण,
अद्भुत, अनोखा

quell v.t. वश में करना
दबाना, शान्त करना

quench v.t. आग या प्यास
बुझाना, दबाना, शांत करना
चुप कर देना

quenchless a. न बुझाने योग्य,
अदम्य, अतृप्य

query n. (pl. querises) प्रश्न,
पूछताछ*; v t. (p.t. queri-
ed) प्रश्न करना, सन्देह करना

quest *n.* अन्वेषण, खोज*, अनुसंधान; *v.i. & t.* खोज करना

question *n.* प्रश्न, जांच*, विवाद या विचार का विषय; *v.t.* प्रश्न पूछना, जांचना, सन्देह करना

questionable *a.* सन्देहयुक्त, अनिश्चित; to beg the question सिद्ध करने के विषय को मान लेना; out of the question न विचारने योग्य; the topic in question प्रस्तुत विषय; to put a question प्रश्न पूछना, प्रश्न करना; to call in question सन्देह उत्पन्न करना

queue *n.* क्यू, कतार*, वेणी*

quibble *n.* वाक्छल, वक्रोक्ति* शब्द श्लेष; *v.t.* वाक्छल करना टेढ़ा बोलना, शब्द-श्लेष का प्रयोग करना

quick *a.* फुर्तीला, प्रस्तुत, तीव्र, सजीव; *n.* शरीर का जीवित (मर्म) भाग; be quick जल्दी करो; piercing to the quick मर्मभेदी

quicksand *n.* नदी या समुद्र का घसकनेवाला बालू का किनारा

quicksilver *n.* पारद, पारा

quiet *a.* निश्चल, शांत, सौम्य, चुपचाप, *n.* शांति*, स्थिरता*; *v.i.* स्थिर करना, शान्त करना

quilt *n.* रजाई*, तोषक, गद्दा, तोषक की खोली*; *v.t.* तोषक सीना, गद्दा बनाना

quinine *n.* कुनैन

quit *v.t.* (*p.t.* quitted छोड़ना, चुकाना, त्यागना

quite *adv.* सर्वथा, पूरी तरह से, बिलकुल; quite another सर्वथा, भिन्न; not quite proper अनुचित; quite so बहुत ठीक, मैं स्वीकार करता हूं

quits *n.* चुकती*, बदला; to cry quits झगड़ा तय करना, मेल करना

quiver *n.* तरकस; *v.i. & t.* कांपना, थर्राना, कंगाना

quixotic *a.* विलक्षण, अद्भुत, व्यर्थ

quorum *n.* (*pl.* quorums) कोरम, किसी सभा के कार्य के लिए सभासदों की निर्दिष्ट संख्या*

quota *n. pl.* (*sing.* quotum) कोटा, अंश, स्थिर भाग

quotation *n.* उद्धरण, प्रचलित मूल्य; quotation-marks निर्धारित वाक्य के

आगे-पीछे लगे हुए (" ") चिह्न

quote *v.t.* किसी के शब्द का उद्धरण करना, अधिकार के वचन कहना, मूल्य बतलाना

R

Rabbi *n.* रबी, यहूदी धर्मा-धिकारी

rabbit *n.* खरगोश

rabid *a.* उन्मत्त, विक्षिप्त, बावला

race *n.* वंश कुल, सन्तति*, जाति*, दौड़*, तीव्र जल-धारा*; *v.i.* वेग से दौड़ना; race-course दौड़ का मैदान; race-horse घुड़दौड़ का घोड़ा

racial *a.* कुल-संबंधी, जातीय, जातिमूलक

racialism *n.* जातिवाद, जाती-यता*

rack *n.* सचल घन, उड़ते हुए बादल, प्रलय; चारा रखने का कठौता, बोतल इ० रखने की टांड़, हत्या करने का साधन; *v t.* कसकर फैलाना, कष्ट देना, हत्या करना; rack rent अधिक से अधिक किराया

racket (racquet) *n.* टेनिस खेलने का बैट, बरफ पर चलने का जूता, कोलाहल; racket-ball एक प्रकार का कठोर छोटा गेंद; racket-press टेनिस के बैट को दबाने का साधन

radiance *n.* प्रभा*, चमक*, प्रकाश

radiant *a.* दीप्तिमान, उज्ज्वल, प्रसन्नमुख

radiate *v.i.* & *t.* किरण फेंकना, फैलाना

radiator *n.* रेडियेटर, विकि-रक, तापविकिरक कर्म, ताप-नाशक यंत्र

radical *a.* पूर्ण, समस्त, मौलिक; *n.* मूल सिद्धान्त

radio *n.* रेडियो, आकाशवाणी*; *v.t.* रेडियो समाचार भेजना, आकाशवाणी द्वारा प्रसारित करना; *pref.* 'रेडियम-संबंधी' अर्थ का उपसर्ग

radiograph *n.* रेडियोग्राफ, एक्सरे द्वारा उतारा हुआ चित्र

radiogram *n.* रेडियोग्राम, रेडियो-समाचार

radiophone *n.* रेडियो-टेली-फोन

radium *n.* रेडियम, एक बहु-मूल्य धातु जिसमें से बिजली की किरणें निकला करती हैं

radius *n.* (*pl.* radii) अर्घ-व्यास

rag *n.* चीर, चिथड़ा, लत्ता, टुकड़ा; *v t.* गाली देना, कष्ट देना

rage *n.* क्रोध, रोष, तीव्रता*; *v.t.* क्रुद्ध होना

raid *n.* धावा, चढ़ाई*; *v.t.* चढ़ाई करना, आक्रमण करना

raider *n.* आक्रमणकारी

rail *n.* रेल, रेल की लाइन*; *v.t.* पटरी लगाना या जड़ना; by rail रेल द्वारा; off the rails क्रमहीन

rail *v.t & i.* (*p t* railed) बाड़ लगाना, रेल लगाना

railing *n.* कटघरा, छड़ की बनी हुई आड़*

railway *n.* रेलवे, रेलमार्ग

rain *n.* वर्षा*, वृष्टि*; *v.i.* वर्षा होना; to rain in torrents, to rain cats and dogs मूसलधार वृष्टि होना

rainbow *n.* इन्द्रधनुष

rainfall *n.* वर्षा*, वृष्टि*

raise *v.t.* उभाड़ना, उठाना, बढ़ाना, जागृत करना, बनाना, धन बटोरना, उन्नति करना, शब्द करना; to raise a cry कोलाहल मचाना; to raise a dust उपद्रव खड़ा करना; to raise a laugh दूसरों को हंसाना; to raise a siege घेरनेवाली सेना को हटाना; to raise bread रोटी बनाने के लिए खमीर उठाना; to raise the wind किसी कार्य के लिए धन इकट्ठा करना

rally *v t. & i* (*p t.* rallied) समेटना, बटोरना, फिर से जुटाना; *v t.* ताना मारना

ramble *v.t.* भ्रमण करना, विचरना, असंबद्ध लिखना या बात करना; *n.* परिभ्रमण

rampant *a.* उग्र, प्रचण्ड, अनियंत्रित

rampart *n.* दुर्ग प्राचीर, शहर पनाह

rancour *n.* शत्रुता*, घृणा*, द्वेष

random *a.* क्रम-रहित, बिना सोचे-समझे; at random असंगत अटकलपच्चू

range *v.t.* पंक्ति में रखना, क्रम से करना; *n.* श्रेणी*, पंक्ति*, लक्ष्य लगाने का स्थान; **range-finder** लक्ष्य लगाने

की दूरी नापने का यंत्र

ranger *n.* रेंजर, वनपालक या वन या उद्यान का रखवाला, (ब० व०) घुड़सवार लोग

rank *a.* तीखा, उग्र गन्ध का; *n.* पंक्ति*, श्रेणी*, विभाग-क्रम प्रतिष्ठा, गौरव, पंक्ति-बद्ध सैनिक; *v.t.* पंक्ति या क्रम में रखना; a man of rank कुलीन मनुष्य

ransom *n.* बंदी को छोड़ने के लिए दिया हुआ धन; *v.t.* धन देकर बन्दी को मुक्त करना

rapacious *a.* लालची, अति लोलुप

rape *n.* बलात्कार

rapport *n.* संबंध, सारूप्य

rapt *a.* निमग्न, लीन

raptured *a.* हर्ष से उन्मत्त

rare *a.* विरल, अपूर्व, अनूठा

rascal *n.* दुष्ट, नीच, पापी

rash *a.* उतावला, हठी, अविवेकी; *n.* चकत्ता, दिदोरा

rat *n.* चूहा, मूसा, साथ छोड़ने-वाला व्यक्ति; to smell a rat संदेहयुक्त होना; rat-trap चूहादानी*

rate *n.* प्रमाण, महसूल, दर*, मूल्य, गति*, वेग, कर, अनु-पात, अनुमान; *v.t.* प्रमाण स्थिर करना, विचारना, नियत करना, गाली देना

rather *a.* वस्तुत:, कुछ अपेक्षा, अथवा

ratification *n.* अनुसमर्थन, विशोधन, दृढ़ीकरण

rating *n.* कर स्थिर करना; at any rate किसी न किसी प्रकार से; market rate बाजार दर; rate of interest व्याज की दर

ratify *v.t* (*p.t.* ratified) स्थिर करना, प्रमाणित करना, विशोधन करना, दृढ़ करना

ratio *n.* (*pl.* ratios) अनुपात

ration *n.* राशन, रसद

rational *a* तर्क संबंधी, तर्क-युक्त, विवेकी

rationale *n.* उपपत्ति*, मूल कारण

rationality *n.* तर्क* गति*, युक्तता*, चेतना*

rationalize *v.t. & i.* तर्कान्वित करना, सिद्ध करना; rationalisation of indus-try उद्योग समीकरण

rattle *v.i.* खड़खड़ करना; *n.* खड़खड़ का शब्द, एक प्रकार का शब्द करनेवाला खिलौना; to rattle along खड़खड़ करते हुए चलना; to rattle the sword युद्ध करने के लिए डराना

ravage *v.t.* नाश करना, लूटना;

n. नाश, लूट*

rave *v.i.* पागल की तरह बकबक करना, पागल होना

ravine *n.* कन्दरा*, खोह*, गहरी पतली घाटी*

raving *n. & a.* क्रोधपूर्ण वार्ता*, पागल

raw *a.* कच्चा, अधूरा, प्राकृतिक, अप्रौढ़, अशिक्षित; raw cloth बिना माड़ी लगा वस्त्र, raw head *n.* बच्चों को डराने का भूत; to touch one on the raw मर्मस्पर्श करना

ray *n.* किरण, प्रभाव, थोड़ी आशा*; *v.i* चमकना

raze *v.t.* भूमिसात करना, ढहाना, मटिया मेट करना, नष्ट करना

razor *n.* हजामत बनाने का उस्तरा; razor-strop उस्तरा पैना करने का चमोटा

re *prep.* विषय में; *pref.* 'फिर से, दूर, किनारे' के अर्थ का उपसर्ग

reach *v.t. & i.* पहुंचना प्राप्त करना; *n.* पहुंच*, विस्तार; beyond his reach उसकी शक्ति के बाहर; within the reach of प्राप्य, लभ्य

react *v.i.* प्रतिकार करना, परस्पर प्रतिक्रिया करना

reaction *n.* प्रतिक्रिया*, उत्तेजना के बाद की मलिनता*

reactionary *a. & n.* प्रतिक्रियावादी, उन्नति-रोधक

read *v.t.* (*p.t. & p.p* read) पढ़ना, व्याख्या करना, समझना, अध्ययन करना, to read a person's hand हस्तरेखा देखकर फल बताना; to read through आदि से अन्त तक पढ़ना; well-read विद्वान

readable *a.* पढ़ने योग्य, पठनीय

reader *n.* रीडर, विश्वविद्यालय का अध्यापक, प्रेस की छपी पुस्तक शुद्ध करनेवाला, पाठ्यपुस्तक*, पाठक

readily *adv.* सहज में, इच्छापूर्वक

readiness *n.* उत्साह, शीघ्रता*

ready *a. & adv.* उद्यत, इच्छुक, तैयार, सहज में प्राप्त; ready to go जाने को तैयार; ready at hand उपस्थित; ready-made तैयारी माल; ready money नगद रुपया

reagent *n.* एक रासायनिक पदार्थ को दूसरे तत्त्वों के अन्वेषण में सहायता देता है; प्रतिकर्त्ता

real *a.* सत्य, वास्तविक, यथार्थ

realistic *a.* यथार्थवादी, वास्तव-

वादी

reality n (pl. realities) यथार्थ, सत्यता*; in reality वास्तव में, सचमुच

realize v.t. & i. प्रत्यक्ष करना, जानना, स्पष्ट सुनना या देखना, मूल्य पाना

really adv. सचमुच, वस्तुत:

realm n. राज्य, देश, विषय

realty n. (pl. realties) अचल सम्पत्ति*

ream n. रीम, बीस जिस्ता कागज; v.t. टेकुवे से धातु में छिद्र बढ़ाना

reap v.t. & i. फसल आदि काटना, फल भोगना; as you sow so you reap जैसी करनी तैसी भरनी; to reap the fruits of one's deeds अपने किए का फल भोगना

reaper n. काटनेवाला, लवन करनेवाला

reason n. विवेक-बुद्धि*, तर्क, युक्ति*, कारण, प्रयोजन; v.i. & t. तर्क करना, विचार करना

reasonable a. उचित, यथार्थ, सर्वमान्य

reasonably a. युक्तिपूर्वक, यथोचित

reasoning n. विवेकबुद्धि*,

विचार

reassemble v.t. & i. फिर से इकट्ठा करना या होना

reassess v t. फिर से कर आदि स्थिर करना, पुनराकलन करना, दुबारा जांचना या कूतना

reassure v.t. विश्वास दिलाना

rebate v i. शक्ति कम करना, घटाना; n. रिबेट, बट्टा, छूट

rebel v.i. (p t. rebelled) राजद्रोह या विप्लव करना; n. राजद्रोही, विप्लवकारी

rebellion n. राजद्रोह, विप्लव

rebellious a. बलवाई, राज-द्रोही

rebound v.i. प्रतिक्षिप्त होना, उलट आना

rebuff n. प्रतिघात, रोक, झिड़की*; v.t. हटाना; रोकना, झिड़कना

rebuild v.t. (p.t. rebuilt) दुबारा बनाना, फिर से बनाना

rebuke v.t. निन्दा करना, गाली देना; n. गाली*, झिड़की*

recall v.t. स्मरण करना याद करना

recapitulate v.t. संक्षेप में वर्णन करना, पुनरावृति करना

recapitulation n. संक्षिप्त, पुनर्कथन, आवृत्ति*, भूगों

की पुनरुत्पत्ति*

receipt n भरपाई*, स्वीकार-पत्र, रसीद*

receive v t. प्राप्त करना, लेना, ग्रहण करना, स्वागत करना

receiver n. रिसीवर, लेनेवाला, तार, टेलीफोन आदि के समाचार ग्रहण करने के यंत्र का प्रधान भाग, प्रादाता

recent a. नया, प्राधुनिक

reception n. स्वागत, ग्रहण, प्रतिग्रह, अगवानी*; reception room स्वागत-कक्ष

receptive a. प्राशुग्राही मेधावी

recess n पीछे हटना, कोना, विश्रान्ति*, प्रवकाश

recession n. पीछे हटना, निकासी*, व्यापारिक मंदी*

recipe n. (pl. recipes) विधि*, नुसखा, प्रयोग, तालिका*, साधन

recipient n. ग्रहण करनेवाला, प्राधार

reciprocal a. परस्पर का, ग्रापस का, ग्रापस के संबंध का

reciprocate v.t. & i. परस्पर लेन-देन करना, विनिमय करना, प्रतिदान करना, प्रतिफल चुकाना

recital n. प्रपठन, प्राख्यान, वाचन, गायन, वादन

recitation n. सस्वर पाठ, प्रवचन

recite v.t. वर्णन करना, व्याख्या करना, चर्चा करना

reckless a. प्रसावधान, धृष्ट

reckon v.t. गणना करना, प्रनुमान करना, विश्वास करना

reckoning n. गणना*, हिसाब-किताब

reclaim v.t. & i. प्राप्त करना, सुधारना, पालना, कृषि योग्य बनाना, विरोध खड़ा करना

reclination n. झुकाव

recline v.t. & i. झुकाना, झुकना, सहारा लेना, विश्राम करना

recluse a. एकान्तवासी; n. संन्यासी, वैरागी

reclusion n. वैराग्य

recognition n. प्रभिज्ञान, पहचान*, स्वीकरण, मान्यता*

recognize v.t. पहचानना, स्वीकार करना, प्रमाणित करना

recoil v.i. पीछे हटना, कूदना, ठमकना; n. परावर्तन, प्रतिक्षेप

recollect v.t. फिर से इकट्ठा करना, स्मरण करना

recollection n. प्रनुस्मरण, स्मरण-शक्ति*

recommend v t. संस्तुति करना, प्रनुशंसा करना, प्रनुग्रह करना, सलाह देना,

सिफारिश करना

recommendation *n.* संस्तुति*, अनुशंसा*, गुण-कीर्तन, सिफारिश*

recompense *v.t.* बदला चुकाना, पारितोषिक देना, मुद्रा विज़ा देना

reconcile *v.t.* झगड़ा मिटाना, संधि कराना

reconciliation *n.* विरोध की शान्ति*, संधि*, पुनर्मिलन, संतोष, संराधन

reconnaissance *n.* किसी स्थान की सैनिक परीक्षा*, जासूसी देखभाल*, गश्त*, पैमाइश*

reconsider *v.t.* पुनर्विचार करना

record *v.t.* लिपिबद्ध करना, टांकना, रजिस्टर में लिखना *n.* रेकर्ड, अभिलेख, ग्रामोफोन बाजे का तवा, सरकारी कागज, गति*, धैर्य इत्यादि का आदर्श

recoup *v.t. & i* कमी करना, क्षति-पूर्ति करना

recourse *n.* आश्रय, शरण, सहारा, उपाय, साधन

recover *v.t. & i.* पुनः प्राप्त करना, बचाना, स्वस्थ होना, पुनः सम्पत्तिलाभ करना

recovery *n.* आरोग्य प्राप्ति*, पुनः प्राप्ति*

recreation *n.* विश्राम, मनोरंजन

recrimination *n.* परस्पर दोषारोपण

recruit *v.t. & i.* सामग्री पहुंचाना. नया बल प्राप्त करना, सैनिक की भरती करना; *n* रंगरूट, नया सैनिक

rectangle *n.* समकोण, चतुर्भुज, आयत

rectangular *a.* समकोण, आयताकार

rectification *n.* समाधान, शुद्धि*

rectify *v.t. (p.t.* rectified शुद्ध करना, संशोधित करना, ठीक करना, आसव बनाना

rector *n. (fem.* rectoress रेक्टर, अधिशिक्षक, मुख्याधिष्ठाता

rectum *n.* मलनाली, मलाशय

recur *v.i. (p.t.* recurred) फिर से याद पड़ना, दुबारा होना

recurrence *n.* पुनरागमन, पुनरावृत्ति*

recurrent *a.* बारम्बार होने वाला

red *a.* लाल रंग का; *n.* लाल रंग; red cap सैनिक; red flag भयसूचक चिह्न; red rag क्रोध उत्पन्न करनेवाला

पदार्थ; red-hot जलता हुआ, आगबबूला; red-handed अपराध करता हुआ; red-letter उत्सव का दिन; red tape लाल फीता।

redeem v.t. पुनः मोल लेना, धन देकर बचाना, बदला देना, मुक्त करना, दरहम-बरहम करना, वचन निभाना

redemption n. ऋणमुक्ति*, विमोचन

redirect v.t. फिर से निर्देशन करना

redolence (-cy) ns. सुगन्ध

redress v.t. प्रतिकार करना, सुधारना; n. प्रतिकार, समाधान, कष्टनिवारण

reduce v.t. क्रम में लाना, छोटा करना, अधीन करना, दुर्बल करना; to reduce to ashes भस्म करना; reduced circumstances दरिद्र अवस्था*; reduced in body क्षीण शरीर, दुर्बल; to reduce to a system व्यवस्था करना; to reduce to a skeleton अस्थि - पंजर (ठठरी) हो जाना

reduction n. कमी*, छूट*, छंटनी*

redundant a. व्यर्थ, अनावश्यक

reenactment n. पुनर-विनियमन

reel n. चरखी*, गड़ारी, एक प्रकार का नाच; v.i. लड़खड़ाना, चक्कर मारना; n. चक्कर; off the reel बिना रुकावट के, शीघ्रता से

refer v.t. & i. (p.t. referred) निर्देश करना, लक्ष्य करना, सूचित करना, उद्देश्य करना

referee n. रेफ्री, पंच, खेल पंच

reference n. अधिकार-सीमा*, संदर्भ, हवाला, निर्देश, संकेत, आश्रय; cross reference एक ही पुस्तक के अनेक स्थलों का निर्देश; with reference to संबंध में, विषय में

referendum n. मतसंग्रह

refill v.i. फिर से भरना; n. पुनः भरने या बैठाने की वस्तु*

refine v.t. & i. निर्मल करना, सिद्ध करना, संस्कार करना, सुधारना, चमकाना

refinement n. संशोधन, शिष्टता*, विनय

refinery n. रिफायनरी, किसी पदार्थ को शुद्ध करने का स्थान, शोधशाला*

reflect v.t. & i. प्रतिबिम्ब डालना, बिचारना, निन्दा या स्तुति करना, दोष निकालना

reflection n. प्रतिबिम्ब,

भावना*, विचार

reflective a. विचार-संबंधी

reflector n. प्रतिबिम्ब फेंकने-
वाला पदार्थ दर्पण

reflex a. पलटा हुआ, चित्त में
विचार किया हुआ; n. प्रति-
बिम्ब, छाया*

reflexive a. परावर्ती, कर्ता-
संबंधी

reform v.t. & i. सुधारना,
फिर से बनाना; n. सुधार,
दोषनिवृत्ति*

reformation n. सुधार

reformative a. संस्कारक

reformatory n. बाल-सुधार
विद्यालय

reformer n. refrain v.i. & t.
सुधारक

refrain v.i. & t. अड़ना,
रुकना; n. गीत के अन्त के
शब्द, टेक

refresh v.t. नया करना,
आनन्दित करना, ताजादम
करना या होना, जलपान
करना

refreshment n. अल्प आहार,
जलपान

refrigerate v.t. ठण्डा करना,
जमाना

refrigerator n. रेफरीजरेटर,
प्रशीतक

refuge n. आश्रय, शरण, आश्रय

देनेवाला; house of refuge
अनाथालय

refugee n. शरणार्थी

refund v.t. लौटाना, वापस
करना

refusal n. अस्वीकृति*

refuse v.t. & i. न मानना,
अस्वीकार करना

refuse n. अवशिष्ट, जूठन,
कचरा

refutable a. खंडन करने योग्य

refutation n. खण्डन

refute v.t. झूठा ठहराना, खण्डन
करना

regal a. राजकीय, महत्त्वपूर्ण

regard v.t. & i. आदर करना,
विचार करना, मानना, संबंध
रखना

regency n. राजप्रतिनिधि का
पद, उसका राज्य-काल

regenerate v.t. & i. नई शक्ति
और जीवन देना, अवस्था
सुधारना

regeneration n. पुनर्जीवन

regent n. राज्यसंरक्षक

regime n. शासन, शासनपद्धति*
शासनकाल

regiment n. सैन्य दल, पलटन*,
अनुशासन; v.t. नियंत्रण में
रखना

regimental a. पलटन संबंधी

region n. प्रदेश, क्षेत्र; lower

regions पाताल; upper regions स्वर्ग

regional *a.* क्षेत्रीय, प्रादेशिक

register *n.* रजिस्टर, पंजी*, हिसाब-बही*, गणनापत्र; *v.t.* रजिस्टर में लिखना, पंजीयित करना

registered *a.* गणनापत्र में लिखा हुआ, पंजीकृत

registrar *n.* रजिस्ट्रार, पंजिका-धिकारी, (विश्वविद्यालय में) कुलसचिव

registry *n.* रजिस्ट्री, पंजीयन लेखशाला*

regress *n.* वापसी*, निकासी*; *v.i.* लौटना, वापस आना; *v.t.* पीछे की ओर हटाना या घुमाना

regret *v.i.* (*p.t.* regretted) पछतावा करना, दुःखी होना

regular *a.* नियम के अनुसार, यथार्थ, व्यवस्थित, प्रचलित, एक समान, सामान्य; *n.* स्थायी सेना का सैनिक

regularity *n.* एकसमानता*, व्यवस्था*, नियम, विधि*

regulate *v.t.* विनियमन करना, क्रम में रखना

regulation *n.* अधिनियम

regulator *n.* रेगुलेटर, विनि-यमक, क्रम स्थापित करने-वाला

rehabilitate *v.t.* पुनरावास देना, अधिकार प्रदान करना, पुन: प्रतिष्ठित करना

rehabilitation *n.* पुनर्वासन, पुनस्थापन

rehearsal *n.* रिहर्सल, प्राभ्यास

rehearse *v.t.* रिहर्सल करना

reign *v.t.* शासन करना, राज्य करना; *n.* शासन राज्य

reimburse *v.t.* वापस करना, फेरना: reimbursement भरपायी, अदायगी

rein *n.* बागडोर*, लगाम*; *p.t.* संयम करना, अधीन करना

reinforce *v.t.* शक्ति बढ़ाना, पुन: लागू करना; rein-forced concrete लोहे की छड़, गिट्टी इत्यादि डालकर पुष्ट किया हुआ मसाला

reinforcement *n.* अतिरिक्त सैन्य, संवृहण, पोषण, बलवृद्धि*

reinstate *v.t.* पुन: नियुक्त करना, बहाल करना

reinstatement *n.* बहाली*, पुन: स्थापन

reiterate *v.t.* बारम्बार दुहराना

reject *v.t.* अस्वीकार करना, त्यागना

rejection *n.* अस्वीकरण

rejoice *v.i.* प्रसन्न होना,

आनन्द मनाना

rejoin *v.t. & i.* फिर मिलना या जोड़ना, उत्तर देना

rejoinder *n.* प्रत्युत्तर

rejuvenate *v.t.* फिर से युवा करना

rejuvenation पुनर्युवाकरण काया-कल्प

rekindle *v.t.* फिर से जलाना

relapse *v.i.* पहली अशुद्धि में दुबारा पड़ना, आरोग्य होकर फिर रोगी होना; *n.* पुन: स्वास्थ्य पतन या रोगाक्रमण

relate *v.t. & i.* कहना, सूचना देना, मिलाना, वर्णन करना

relation *n.* सूचना*, वर्णन, संबंध, संबंधी

relative *a.* सगोत्र संबंधी; *n.* संबंधी, नातेदार

relax *v.t.* शिथिल करना, कोमल करना

relaxation *n.* शिथिलता*, विश्राम

relay *n.* घोड़े, मनुष्य, सामग्री इत्यादि की नयी भरती, पुनर्योजन, पुन: प्रचालन

release *v.t.* मुक्त करना, छुटकारा देना, त्यागना; *n.* निस्तार, मुक्ति* छुटकारा

relent *v.i.* मृदु या कोमल होना, मान जाना

relentless *a.* निर्दय, दयाहीन

relevance (-cy)*ns.* सम्बन्वता*, सगति*, योग्यता*

relevant *a.* अनुरूप, योग्य, उचित

reliable *a.* विश्वास के योग्य

reliance *n.* भरोसा, विश्वास

relic *n.* मृत व्यक्ति का स्मारक, चिह्न, मृत शरीर

relief *n.* सहायता* सुख, दु:खी की सहायता, उभड़ी हुई नक्काशी*, relief fund सहायता के लिए एकत्रित धन; relief works व्यवसाय-हीन मनुष्यों को कार्य देने के लिए निर्माण-कार्य

relieve *v.t.* सहायता देना, पीड़ा हटाना, कार्य से हटाना

religion *n.* धर्म

religious *a.* धार्मिक, भक्तिमान

relinquish *v.t.* छोड़ना, त्यागना, अलग करना

relish *v.t. & i.* स्वाद लेना, आनन्द लेना, प्रसन्न होना; *n.* रस, स्वाद, रुचि*, आनन्द reluctance (-cy) अरुचि*, अनिच्छा*

reluctant *a.* अनिच्छुक, असन्तुष्ट

rely *v.i.* (*p.t.* relied) विश्वास करना, भरोसा करना

remain *v.i.* रहना, पीछे ठहरना, भरोसा करना; **let**

it remain as it is. जैसा
है वैसा छोड़ दो

remainder n. शेष भाग,
अवशिष्ट

remains n. pl. अवशेष, मृतक
शरीर

remand v.t. वापस भेजना,
बंधन में रखना; n. वापस
भेजने की आज्ञा*

remanent a. & n. अवशिष्ट,
अवशेष, बचा हुआ भाग

remark v.t. & i. ध्यान देना,
विचारना, बोलना; n.
भाषण, चर्चा, टीका-टिप्पणी*

remarkable a. ध्यान में रखने
योग्य

remedy n चिकित्सा, औषधि,
कष्ट-निवारण का उपाय;
v.t. (p.t. remedied)
चिकित्सा करना, उपचार
करना, प्रतिकार करना

remember v.t. स्मरण रखना,
याद करना

remembrance n. स्मरण,
यादगार*, स्मारक वस्तु; to
put in remembrance
स्मरण कराना

remembrancer n. राजकोष का
अध्यक्ष

remind v.t. स्मरण कराना,
स्मरण करना

reminiscence n. स्मृति*,

संस्मरण

reminiscent a. अतीत का
स्मरण दिलाने वाला

remission n. ऋण की
चुकती*, क्षमा*

remit v.t. (p.t. remitted)
छोड़ना, रुपया भेजना, ढीला
करना, छूट देना

remittance n. भेजा हुआ धन

remodel v.t. (p.t. remo-
delled) फिर से तैयार
करना या बनाना

remorse n. पश्चाताप, पछतावा

remote a. दूरवर्ती, असमीप,
एकान्त, निर्जन

removable a. हटाने योग्य

remove v.t. & i. स्थान
बदलना या हटाना, अलग
करना; to remove moun-
tains विलक्षण कार्य करना

remunerate v.t. पुरस्कार
देना, पारिश्रमिक देना

remuneration n. पारितोषिक,
पारिश्रमिक

remunerative a. लाभकारी,
पारिश्रमिक-संबंधी

renaissance n. रिनायसां,
पुनर्जागरण, नवयुग,
नवजागरण, पुनरुद्धार

render v.t. देना, प्रतिपादन
करना, अनुवाद करना

rendering n. प्रतिपादन, अनुवाद
३३१

rendezvous n. (pl. -ooz)
समागम या सभा का स्थान,
विनोदस्थल

renegade n. स्वधर्मत्यागी,
पाखण्डी, विश्वासघाती

renew v.t. & i. नया करना
या होना, पूर्व अवस्था में
लाना, दुहराना

renounce v.t. & i. त्यागना,
दूर करना, छोड़ना; to
renounce the world
संन्यास ग्रहण करना

renovate v.t. नया करना,
सुधारना ·

renown n. यश, कीर्ति*

renowned a. प्रसिद्ध

rent n. दरार*, भूमिकर,
किराया; v.t. & i. किराये
पर या पट्टे पर देना;
rent-free निःशुल्क, बिना
कर का

renunciation n. आत्मत्याग,
संन्यास, प्रस्वीकार

repair v.t. & i. सुधारना, मर-
म्मत करना, जाना, शरण
प्राप्त करना, आरोग्य होना

repartee n. हाज़िर-जवाबी*,
व्यंग्य-उक्ति*: v.i. व्यंग्य
बोलना

repatriate v.i. अपने देश को
लौट आना

repatriation n. स्वदेश में

repay v.t. & i. (p.t. re-
paid) चुकाना, प्रतिफल देना,
बदला देना

repayment n. दुबारा भुगतान

repeal v.t. खण्डन करना,
तोड़ना; n. प्रचार, भंग, लोप

repealable a. खंडन करने योग्य

repeat v.t. & i फिर से कहना
या करना, आवृत्ति करना

repel v.t. (p.t. repelled)
हटाना, टालना

repent v.t. & i. पश्चाताप
करना, पछताना

repentance n. पछतावा

repentant a. पछतावा करनेवाला

repercussion n. प्रतिघात,
प्रतिप्रभाव, अप्रत्यक्ष प्रभाव,
प्रतिक्रिया*

repetition n. पुनरुक्ति*,
आवृत्ति*, दुहराव

replace v t. पुनःस्थापित करना,
हानि की पूर्ति करना

replenish v.t फिर से भरना

replete a. भरपूर, भरा हुआ

replica n. प्रतिरूप, प्रतिकृति*,
प्रतिचित्र, नकल*

reply n., v i. & t. (p.t.
replied) उत्तर, उत्तर देना;
reply-paid telegram तार
जिसके उत्तर के लिए भेजने-
वाले ने रुपया जमा कर दिया

हो

report *v.t. & i.* रिपोर्ट देना, वृत्तान्त कहना, सूचना देना, वर्णन करना, घोषणा करना; *n.* रिपोर्ट*, वर्णन, चर्चा*, तीव्र शब्द; bad report झूठी चर्चा*; the report goes ऐसा सुना जाता है

reporter *n.* सूचना देनेवाला, संवाददाता

repose *v.t. & i.* विश्राम करना, सोना, विश्वास रखना

repository *n.* कोष, भण्डारघर

reposure *n.* शान्ति*

reprehension *n.* निन्दा*, कलंक

represent *v.t.* वर्णन करना, दरसाना, चित्त में लाना, प्रतिनिधि होना; to represent in writing लेख रूप में रखना

representation *n.* प्रतिनिधि- त्व, वर्णन, प्रतिरूप, मूर्ति*

representative *a. & n.* प्रति- निधि

repress *v.t.* रोकना, दबाना, अधिकार में लाना

repression *n.* रोक*, निरोध, दमन

reprieve *v.t.* दण्डविराम करना, अवकाश देना, फांसी स्थगित करना; *n.* दण्डविराम

reprimand *v.t.* डांटना; झिड़- कना; *n.* झिड़की*, घुड़की*

reprint *v.t.* दुबारा छापना या प्रकाशित करना; *n.* पुस्तक का नया प्रकाशन या संस्करण

reproach *v.t.* गाली देना, निन्दा करना, धिक्कारना; *n.* निन्दा*, तिरस्कार

reptile *n.* सांप, रेंगनेवाला जन्तु

republic *n.* गणराज्य, गणतंत्र

republican *a. & n.* रिपब्लि- कन, गणतंत्रवादी, प्रजातंत्र राज्य का समर्थक

repudiate *v.t.* प्रत्याख्यान करना, परित्याग करना, अलग करना, अधिकार से हटा देना

repugnance *n.* विरोध, घृणा*, अरुचि*

repugnant *a.* विरुद्ध, प्रतिकूल, घृणास्पद

repulse *v.t.* हटाना, अस्वीकार करना

repulsion *n.* प्रपकर्षण, घृणा*, अरुचि*

repulsive *a.* प्रतिघाती, घृणित, अप्रिय

reputation *n.* कीर्ति* यश, मान

repute *v.t.* विचार करना; *n.* यश, कीर्ति*, प्रसिद्धि*

request *v.t.* प्रार्थना करना,

विनय सहित मांगना; *n.* प्रार्थना*, मांग*

require *v.t.* मांगना, चाहना, आकांक्षा करना

requirement *n.* आकांक्षा*, मांग, जरूरत*

requisite *a.* आवश्यक, प्रयोजनीय

requisition *n. & v.t.* प्रार्थना*, मांग*, प्रार्थना करना

rescue *v.t.* बचाना, मुक्त करना, छुटकारा देना; *n.* त्राण, छुटकारा, मुक्ति*

research *n.* अन्वेषण, खोज*

resemblance *n.* सादृश्य, तुल्यता*

resemble *v.t.* सदृश होना, तुल्य होना

resent *v.t.* क्रोध करना, बुरा मानना

resentment *n.* क्रोध, ईर्ष्या*, द्वेष

reservation *n.* आरक्षिति*, रोक*, निग्रह

reserve *v t.* अलग रखना, रोकना, बचा रखना; *n.* रोक, संशय, सावधानी*, निग्रह, आत्मसंयम, मानसिक गम्भीरता*; reserve fund सुरक्षित कोष; without reserve पूर्ण रूप से

reservoir *n.* जलाशय, कुंड

reshape *v.t.* नयी आकृति प्रदान करना

reside *v.i.* बसना

residence *n.* रहने का स्थान, निवास

residency *n.* राजकीय अधिकारी के रहने का स्थान

resident *n.* निवासी, राजकीय अधिकारी

residual *n. & a.* शेष, बचत*

residuary *a.* बचत का

residue *n* परिशिष्ट, बाकी*, छाछ

resign *v.t.* पद का त्याग करना; to resign one's claims अधिकार त्यागना; to resign to fate भाग्य के अधीन होना

resignation *n.* पद का परित्याग

resist *v.t.* अवरोध करना, बाधा डालना

resistance *n.* विरोध, रुकाव

resistant *a.* अवरोध करनेवाला, अवरोधक

resolute *a.* स्थिर, दृढ़, साहसी

resolution *n.* निश्चय, स्थिरता*, चित्त की दृढ़ता* प्रस्ताव

resolve *v.t. & i.* अलगाना, भाग करना, ठानना, निश्चय करना

resonance *n.* प्रतिध्वनि*

resonant *a.* प्रतिध्वनित, गूंजनेवाला

resort *v i.* कहीं जाना, प्रयोग करना; *n.* आश्रय, अड्डा

resound *v.t. & i.* गूंजना, यश फैलाना

resource *n.* साधन. सहारा; (ब० व०) द्रव्य प्राप्ति का साधन

respect *v.t.* प्रतिष्ठा करना, सत्कार करना; *n.* प्रतिष्ठा*, सम्मान, विषय; in all respects सर्वथा; in respect of विषय में; self-respect आत्मगौरव; to pay one's respects प्रणाम करना

respective *a.* अलग-अलग, निज का, संबंधी

resplendent *a.* बड़ा चमकीला

respond *v.i.* उत्तर देना, अनुकूल होना

respondent *n.* प्रतिवादी

response *n.* उत्तर, प्रतिवचन

responsibility *n.* उत्तरदायित्व

responsible *a.* उत्तरदायी, विश्वस्त

rest *n.* स्थिरता*, शान्ति*, विश्राम, शेष भाग; *v t. & i.* विश्राम करना, स्थापित करना, बैठाना, ठहरना, भरोसा करना

restaurant *n.* रेस्तरां, भोजनालय, जलपान-गृह

restive *a.* अड़ियल, हठी, अशांत

restoration *n.* उद्धार, आरोग्य

restore *v.t.* वापस देना, सुधारना, आरोग्य करना

restrain *v.t.* रोकना, दबाना, अधीन करना

restrict *v.t.* सीमित करना, रोकना

result *v.i.* परिणाम होना, निकलना; *n.* अन्त, परिणाम, नतीजा

resume *v.t.* दुबारा आरम्भ करना, फिर शुरू से करना; *n.* सार, संक्षिप्त विवरण

resumption *n.* पुनर्ग्रहण

resurrect *v.t.* पुनर्जीवित करना

resurrection *n.* मसीह के कब्र से उठने की स्मृति में मनाया जानेवाला एक ईसाई पर्व, प्रलय के दिन मृतोत्थान, पुनरुज्जीवन, पुनः उभड़ना, पुनर्जीवन

resuscitate *v.i. & t.* पुनर्जीवित होना या करना

resuscitation *n.* पुनर्जीवन

retail *v.t. & i.* फुटकर बिक्री करना दुबारा समाचार कहना; *n.* फुटकर बिक्री*

retailer *n.* खुदरा बेचनेवाला

retain *v.t.* रोकना, धारण करना, चित्त में रखना

retainer *n.* प्रनुचर, सेवक, प्राश्रित

retaliate *v.i* बदला लेना

retaliation *n.* प्रतिशोध, बदला

retard *v.t.* कम करना, रोकना

retardation *n.* विरोध, रुकावट*

retention *n.* धारण करना या धारण करने की शक्ति*

retentive *a.* धारण करने की शक्ति वाला

retina *n.* (*pl.* retinae) प्रांख के पिछले भाग का चित्रपट, मूर्ति-पटल

retinue *n.* परिचारक या प्रनुचर वर्ग

retire *v.i* & *t.* प्रवकाश ग्रहण करना, पीछे को हटना, निद्रा लेना, शरण लेना; to retire from the world संसारी कार्यों से प्रलग होना

retirement *n.* प्रवकाश-ग्रहण, एकान्त स्थान

retort *v.i.* & *t.* प्रत्युत्तर देना, बदला लेना *n.* प्रत्युत्तर, प्रर्क उतारने का भबका

retrace *v.t.* खोजना, याद करना

retreat *v.i.* & *t.* पीछे हटना, स्थान छोड़ना; *n.* शरण, प्राश्रय, निर्जन स्थान

retrench *v t.* छंटनी करना

retrenchment *n.* छंटनी*

retrieve *v.t.* & *i.* पुन: प्राप्त करना, चंगा करना, बचाना, क्षतिपूर्ति करना, भूल सुधारना

retrim *v.t.* (*p.t.* retrimmed) काट-छांट कर फिर से सुधारना

retrograde *v.t.* पीछे हटना, पतित होना

retrospect *n.* सिंहावलोकन, प्रतीत-पर्यालोचन, पूर्व हृष्टांत गत प्रभाव

return *v i.* & *t.* फिर जाना या प्राना, वापस करना, उत्तर देना, सदस्य चुनना; *n.* पुनरागमन, वापसी*, हिसाब का लेखा; return-ticket वापसी टिकट

returning-officer *n.* निर्वाचन-प्रधिकारी

reunion *n.* पुनर्मिलन, सम्मिलन, मण्डली*

reveal *v.t.* प्रत्यक्ष करना, प्रकाशित करना, प्रकट करना

revel *v i.* (*p.t.* revelled) कोलाहल सहित खाना-पीना, प्रति प्रानन्द लेना

revelation *n.* प्राकाशवाणी, दैवी प्रकाश

reveller *n.* मद्यपान करके उपद्रव मचानेवाला

revelry *n.* मद्यपान का उत्सव

revenge *v.t.* वैर करना, बदला लेना; *n.* प्रतिकार, बदला

revenue *n.* राजस्व, राज्य की आय*

reverberate *v.i.* प्रतिध्वनि करना, गूंजना

revere *v t.* आदर करना, पवित्र मानना

reverence *n.* आदर, सत्कार, भक्ति*, act of reverence नमस्कार; his reverence महामान्यवर, प्रभु

reverend *a. & n.* माननीय, पादरी की उपाधि*

reverie *n.* ध्यान, भावना*, मन की लहर*

reversal *n.* उलट*, परिवर्तन

reverse *n.* विपरीत अवस्था*, हार*, पिछला भाग; *a.* विपरीत, उलटा; *v.t.* उलटना, औंधा करना

revert *v.t. & i.* पलटना लौटाना

review *v.t.* स लोचना करना, दोहराना; *n.* गुए दोष-निरू-पए, सैनिकों की जांच*, समीक्षा*

revise *v.t.* दोहराना, दुबारा विचार करना, दुबारा जांचना, दोष संशोधन करना

revision *n.* दुबारा परीक्षा* या संशोधन

revival *n.* चेतना-प्राप्ति*, पुनरुत्थान

revive *v.t. & i.* फिर से जीवित करना, पूर्वरूप में लाना; प्रसन्न करना

revocable *a.* खण्डन करने योग्य

revoke *v.t.* खण्डन करना, रद्द करना

revolt *v.i. & t.* राजद्रोह करना, विप्लव करना, घृणा उत्पन्न होना, धक्का देना

revolution *n.* क्रान्ति*, राज्य क्रान्ति*, चक्कर, भ्रमण

revolutionary *a.* राज्य-परि-वर्तन संबंधी, क्रान्तिकारी

revolve *v.i. & t.* चक्कर खाना, घूमना, विचार करना

revolver *n.* रिवाल्वर, एक बार भर कर अनेक बार चलाने की पिस्तौल*

reward *n.* प्रतिफल पारि-तोषिक; *v.t.* पारितोषिक देना

rhapsody *n.* असंबद्ध काव्य

rhetoric *n.* अलंकार-शास्त्र, रीति-शास्त्र

rhinoceros *n.* (*pl* -es) गैंडा

rhyme (rime) *n.* अनुप्रास, पदक, कविता* *v.i.* कविता लिखना, पद्य बनाना

rhymer, rhymester *ns.* पद्य-कार, तुच्छ कवि

rhythm *n.* ताल*, लय, ठेका

rhythmic (-al) *a.* तालबद्ध,

ताल-सुर संबंधी

rib n. पसुली*, पत्ती की नस*

ribald n. अशिष्ट नीच मनुष्य;
a. नीच, अशिष्ट

ribbon n. रिबन, पतला फीता;
(ब॰व॰) घोड़ा हांकने की
रास*

rice n. चावल

rich a. घनी, बहुमूल्य, उपजाऊ,
अनोखा, मसालेदार, चम-
कीला; riches n. pl. धन,
संपत्ति*

richly adv. बड़े प्रताप से,
सम्पन्न रूप में

richness n. अतिशोभा*,
उपजाऊपन, अधिकता*

rickshaw n. रिक्शा

rid v.t. (p.t. rid or rid-
ded) मुक्त करना, छोड़ना,
हटाना

riddle n. कूट प्रश्न, पहेली*,
बड़ी चलनी*; v.t. चलनी
से चालना

ride v.t. (p.t. rode p p.
ridden) घुड़सवारी करना,
गाड़ी इ॰ पर सवार होना,
जल पर तैरना; n. सवारी*;
to ride on कष्ट देना;
to ride one down घोड़ा
दौड़ाकर पकड़ लेना

ridge n. पर्वत-पृष्ठ, उभाड़,
टीला; v.t. टीला बनाना

ridicule v.t. हंसी उड़ाना,
ताना मारना, ठिठोली करना

ridiculous a. हास्यास्पद, भद्दा

rifle v t. & i. लूटना, बन्दूक
की नली में चक्करदार छेद
बनाना; n. राइफल

rifler n. लुटेरा

rift n. दरार*, छेद, फूट*; v.t.
फाड़ना

right a. & n. शुद्ध, सीधा,
नियमानुसार, उचित, दाहिना;
rights n. pl. अधिकार;
v.t. & i. ठीक स्थान
पर रखना, ठीक करना,
न्याय करना; bill of rights
अधिकार पत्र; right down
पूर्ण रूष से; right to the
bottom ठीक पेंदी तक;
right and left प्रत्येक दिशा
में; right angle समकोण;
to put to right क्रम में
रखना

righteous a. धार्मिक, पवित्र,
सच्चा

rigid a. कड़ा, कठोर, दृढ़

rigmarole n निरर्थक वार्ता-
लाप

rigorous n. कठिन, दृढ़

rigour n. दृढ़ता, *कठोरता*,
निठुरता*

rimple n. झुर्री*, सिकुड़न*

ring n. वृत्त, अंगूठी*, चक्राकार

पदार्थ, भंवर*, बाड़ा, घंटी
का शब्द, मनुष्यों का जत्था;
v.t. (p.t. ringed) मुंदरी
चढ़ाना, घेरना

ring v.t. & i. (p.t. rang,
p.p. rung) घंटी के समान
बजना; the coin rings
true (or untrue) सिक्के
की ठनकार ठीक (या बेठीक)
है; to ring the bell घण्टी
बजाकर सेवक को बुलाना;
to ring off टेलीफोन से
बातचीत समाप्त करना; to
ring up टेलीफोन पर घण्टी
बजाना

ring-master n. सर्कस का प्रबन्ध
करनेवाला

ringlet n. बालों की लट*

ringleader n. नायक, सरदार

ringworm n. दद्रु, दाद

riot n. दंगा, कोलाहल, उपद्रव,
विप्लव; to run riot उपद्रव
मचाना; v.t. विप्लव करना,
कोलाहल करना

riotous a. उपद्रवी

rip v.t. (p.t. ripped) फाड़ना,
चीरना; n. चीर, फटन

ripe a. प्रौढ़, तैयार, पका हुआ,
योग्य, सिद्ध, पूर्ण सम्पन्न;
ripe occasion उचित अवसर

ripple v.t. लहराना, लहर के
समान शब्द करना; n. लहरी,

कोमल शब्द

rise v.i. (p.t. rose, p.p.
risen) उठना, मींघा होना,
चढ़ना, उद्गम होना विप्लव
करना, फूलना, त्यागना; n.
उदय, चढ़ाव, ऊंचाई*, वृद्धि*,
अधिकता*; rising gene-
ration नयी पीढ़ी*; spirits
rise प्रति प्रसन्न है; the
pillar rises fifteen feet
खंभा पंद्रह फीट लम्बा है; to
rise against विद्रोह करना;
to rise betimes प्रातःकाल
उठना; to give rise to
उत्पन्न करना

risk n. विपत्ति*, आशंका*,
संकट; v.t. संकट या आपत्ति
में डालना; to run the risk
आपत्ति का सामना करना

risky a. आपत्तिपूर्ण, संकटमय

rite n. आचार, संस्कार; rite
of hospitality आतिथ्य-
सत्कार

ritual a संस्कार-संबंधी; n.
धार्मिक क्रिया*, पद्धति*
शास्त्रविधि*

rival n. प्रतिस्पर्धी; a. स्पर्धा
करनेवाला; v.t. (p.t. rival-
led) स्पर्धा करना

rivalry n. विरोध, स्पर्धा*

river n नदी*; river-bed
नदी का तल

rivulet *n.* छोटी नदी*, नाला

road *n.* सड़क*, राजपथ

roadstead *n.* जहाज का लंगर
डालकर ठहराने का स्थान;
high road राजपथ, बड़ी
सड़क; on the road यात्रा
करते हुए; royal road
राजगथ, बड़ी सड़क*, सीधा
मार्ग

roam *v.t.* घूमना, टहलना; to
roam about इधर-उधर
भटकना

roar *n.* जंगली पशु की गरज*,
चिल्लाहट*, चीख*; *v.t.*
गरजना, चिल्लाकर बोलना

roast *v.t.* भूनना, आंच पर या
धूप में सुखाना; *n.* भुना हुआ
मांस

rob *v.t.* (*p t.* robbed) बल-
पूर्वक छीनना, लूटना

robber *n.* डाकू, लुटेरा

robbery *n.* डाका, लूट*

robe *n.* जामा, लबादा घाघरा;
v.i & t. लबादा पहिनना,
पहिनाना; gentleman of
the robe वकील या बैरिस्टर

robot *n.* मनुष्य के आकार का
यन्त्र जो आज्ञानुसार अनेक
कार्य करता है

robust *a.* पुष्ट, हट्टा-कट्टा

rock *v.i. & t.* धीरे-धीरे
डोलना, हिलना, हिलाना

rock *n.* चट्टान*; rock-bottom
सबसे नीचे का भाग

rocket *n.* राकेट, अग्निबाण;
v.t. राकेटों से बमबारी करना

rod *n.* छड़, लग्गी*, डंडा,
छड़ी*; to kiss the rod
शान्तिपूर्वक दण्ड स्वीकार
करना

rogue *n.* धूर्त्त, शठ, कपटी
मनुष्य, *v.t. & i.* शठ की
तरह व्यवहार करना, ठगना

role *n.* भूमिका*, महान कार्य,
कृत्य

roll *v.i. & t.* पहिए की तरह
चलना, चक्कर में मुड़ना,
लपेटना, गरड़ना; *n.* सूची*,
तालिका*, नियमावली*;
roll-call हाजिरी लेना, roll
of honour युद्ध में मरे हुए
व्यक्तियों की सूची

rollick *v.i.* आनन्द मचाना,
मौज उड़ाना

Roman *n.* रोम देशवासी, *a.*
रोम देश का; Roman
Catholic ईसाइयों के धर्म का
एक सदस्य

romance *n.* प्रणय, कल्पित
कथा, झूठी कहानी*, उपन्यास;
v.t. झूठ कहना, गप्प हांकना

romantic *a.* कल्पित, विलक्षण,
रूमानी

romp *v.i.* कोलाहल करते हुए

खेलना ; *n.* इस प्रकार खेलने-
वाली लड़की*

rood *n.* ईसामसीह के शूली पर
चढ़ने की प्रतिमा*, एक एकड़
का चौथाई भाग

roof *n.* छत*, पाटन, शरण,
ऊपरी भाग; *v.t.* छत लगाकर
ढांपना;   roof of the
mouth तालु; under the
same roof एक ही घर में

room *n.* स्थान, कमरा, अधि-
कृत भूमि*, अवसर

roomy *a.* विशाल, फैला हुआ

roost *n.* पक्षी का अड्डा, वसेरा;
v.t. अड्डे पर बसेरा लेना;
to go to roost रात में
विश्राम करना

root *n.* जड़*, मूल*, नीचे का
भाग, कारण, हेतु, यौगिक
शब्द. *v.t.* जड़ पकड़ना,
स्थिर होना; root and
branch पूर्ण रूप से; to
root out जड़ से उखाड़ना

rope *n.* रस्सा, डोरी*; *v.t.*
रस्से से बांधना; on the
high ropes पारितोषिक के
लिए लड़नेवाले; rope of
sand माया*; rope-dancer
नट

rosarian *n.* गुलाब के फूल का
प्रेमी

rosary *n.* माला*, सुमिरनी*,

भजन*, गुलाब का बगीचा

rose *n.* गुलाब का फूल, गुलाबी
रंग, फीते का गुच्छा; life's
roses जीबन के आनन्द;
otto of roses गुलाब का
अतर; rose without a
thorn अलभ्य आनन्द

roseate *a.* गुलाबी रंग का

rosemary *n.* मेंहदी*, दौना

rosewater *n.* गुलाब-जल

rosewood *n.* एक प्रकार की
सुगन्धित लकड़ी*

rostrum *n.* (*pls.* rostrums,
rostra) व्याख्यान मंच या
चबूतरा

rosy *a.* गुलाबी, प्रसन्न, आन-
न्दित

rot *n.* दुर्गन्ध*, सड़ांध*;   *v.i.*
& *t.* सड़ना, सड़ाना

rotary *a.* घूमने या चक्कर
मारनेवाला; Rotary Club
रोटरी क्लब

rotate *v.i.* & *t.* चक्कर खाना

rotation *n.* परिभ्रमण, चक्कर

rotator *n.* अंग को घुमानेवाली
पेशी*

rote *n.* आवृत्ति; to learn by
rote कण्ठस्थ करना

rouble *n.* रूबल, रूसी सिक्का

rough *a.* विषम, रूक्ष, बिना
चमक का, असभ्य, बेढंगा,
अपूर्ण; rough-hewn भद्दा,

बनाया हुआ; rough-rider बिना फिरे हुए घोड़े पर सवारी करनेवाला; rough-shod घोड़े की नाल में के उभड़े हुए कांटे

round a. मण्डलाकार, गोलाकार, पूरा, निश्चित, पुष्ट, मोटा, फूला हुआ; v.t. & i. गोल होना या बनाना, पूरा करना; n. गोल पदार्थ, कार्यक्रम, परिधि*, सीढ़ी का डंडा, मोड़*, चाल*, चक्र स्थिति*; adv. चक्रवत, चारों ओर; all the year round वर्ष-भर; all round चारों ओर; merry - go - round फिरहरी*; rounds of ladder सीढ़ी के डंडे; the daily round प्रतिदिन का सामान्य कार्य

rouse v.i. उत्तेजित करना, जगाना, चौंकाना

rout v.t. भगाना, हराना; n. कोलाहल, उपद्रव विप्लवकारियों की मंडली*

route n मार्ग, क्रम; enroute मार्ग में

routine n. दिनचर्या* बंधा-बंधाया काम

rove v.i. भ्रमण करना, घूमना

rover n. घुमक्कड़, समुद्री लुटेरा

row ‍n. पंक्ति*, पद, पांति*, विप्लव, उपद्रव, नाव को सैर*; v.t. डांडे से नाव खेना; to kick up a row कोलाहल मचाना

rowdy a. कोलाहली, उपद्रवी; n. उपद्रवी पुरुष

royal a राजकीय, शिष्ट, महत्त्वपूर्ण; n. 20 × 25 इंच नाप का कागज

rub v.t. (p.t. rubbed) घिसना, रगड़ना, मलना, स्वच्छ करना, पालिश करना; n. रगड़*, रुकावट*; to rub in बुकनी करना; to rub up रगड़कर चमकाना, स्मरणशक्ति ताजा करना

rubber n. रबर

rubbish n. तुच्छ पदार्थ, कूड़ा-कर्कट

rubble n. पत्थर या ईंट के टुकड़े

ruby n. लाल रत्न; a. गहरे लाल रंग का

rude a. (comp. ruder, sup. rudest) रूखा, अशिष्ट, मूर्ख असभ्य, उद्धत

rudiment n. आरम्भ, (ब०व०) प्रथम (मूल) तत्त्व

rudimentary a. मौलिक, प्रथम

rue v.t. शोक करना, पछताना

rueful a. शोकार्त, उदास

ruffian n. गुण्डा, बदमाश,

ग्राततायी मनुष्य

ruffle *v.t. & i.* व्याकुल करना, झालर बनाना; *n.* झालरदार गुलूबन्द

rugged *a.* रूखा, बिना चमक का, ग्रसभ्य, झुर्रीदार

ruin *n.* नाश, पतन, (ब० व०) टूटा-फूटा भाग; *v.t. & i.* नाश करना, ग्रपमानित करना, नाश होना

rule *n.* शासन, राज्य, निर्देश, नियम, ग्रधिकार, सिद्धान्त, व्यवस्था*, ग्रविमान, शासक; *v.t.* निर्देश करना, शासन करना, राज्य करना, लकीर खींचना; according to rule यथाविधि; general rules सामान्य विधि; golden rule सुन्दर नियम; moral rules मर्यादा, नैतिक नियम; rule of action क्रिया विधान; rule of thumb ग्रनुभवसिद्ध रीति

ruler *n.* शासक, लकीर खींचने की पटरी*

ruling *a.* राज्य करता हुग्रा, उपदेश करनेवाला, प्रचलित; *n.* न्याय, न्यायाधीश का निर्णय

rum *n.* रम*, ऊख की मदिरा*; *a.* विलक्षण

rumble *v.i.* गड़गड़ शब्द करना; *n.* गड़गड़ाहट का शब्द

rumbler *n.* गड़गड़ शब्द करनेवाला

rumour *n.* लोकवार्ता*, गप्प*, ग्रफवाह*, चर्चा*; *v.t.* गप्प या ग्रफवाह उड़ाना, बात फैलाना

run *v.i. & t.* (*p.t.* ran, *p.p.* run) दौड़ना, वेग से चलना, कूदना, बढ़ना, फैलना, फैलाना, बहना; *n.* दौड़ान*, चाल*, यात्रा*, क्रम; to run riot मर्यादा भंग करना; a run on किसी वस्तु की बड़ी मांग; at a run दौड़ता हुग्रा; common run of men सामान्य मनुष्य; his blood ran cold वह बहुत डर गया; his tongue runs वह वकवास करता है; in the run ग्रन्त में; news ran समाचार फैल गया; on the run भागता हुग्रा; to run about भटकना; to run across टकराना; to run after पीछा करना; to run at ग्राक्रमण करना; run-away ग्रापत्ति से भागनेवाला, भगेड़ू

runner *n.* दौड़नेवाला, हरकारा

rupee *n.* रुपया

rupture *n.* टूटन*, बिगाड़,

प्रलगाव; *v.t. & i.* तोड़ना,
टूटना

rural *a.* देहाती, गंवारू

rush *n.* सरहरी*, झपट*,
आक्रमण; *v.t.* झपटना, बिना
समझे-बूझे काम करना, जल्दी
करना; to rush a bill
through जल्दी में नियम
स्थिर करना; to rush at
आक्रमण करना; to rush
into print जल्दी से छाप

देना

rust *n.* मुर्चा, प्रस्वस्थ दशा*;
v.i. मुर्चा लगना

rustic *a.* ग्रामीण, देहाती,
प्रसभ्य

rusticate *v t.* निस्सारित करना

rustication *n.* निस्सारण

rut *n.* पहिया चलने की लकीर*

ruth *n.* दया*

ruthless *a.* निर्दय, क्रूर

ryot *n.* रैयत

S

sabaoth *n. pl.* सेनाएं*

sabbath *n.* धार्मिक विश्राम का
दिन, सप्ताह का पहला दिन

sabotage *n.* तोड़-फोड़

sabre *n.* कृपाण, तलवार*;
v.t. कृपाण से हत्या करना

sack *n.* बोरा; लूटपाट; *v.t.*
बोरे में भरना; *v.t.* नगर को
जीतकर लूटना

sacrament *n.* धर्मविधि*,
संस्कार

sacred *a.* पुनीत, पवित्र, दैबी;
sacred grove तपोवन;
sacred knowledge वेदों
का ज्ञान

sacrifice *n.* बलिदान, यज्ञ, होम,
समर्पण, हानि*; *v.t. & i.*

बलिदान करना, अर्पण करना,
त्याग करता

sacrificial *a.* यज्ञ-संबंधी, बलि-
दान संबंधी

sacrilege *n.* पवित्र वस्तु को
दूषित करने या लूटने का कार्य

sacrilegious *a.* अपवित्र, भ्रष्ट,
पवित्र वस्तु को चुरानेवाला,
धर्म का उल्लंघन करनेवाला

sacrosanct *a.* पवित्र

sad *a.* (*comp.* sadder, *sup.*
saddest) उदास, दु:खी, खिन्न

sadden *v.t.* खिन्न या दु:खी
करना

saddle *n.* जीन, बैठकी*,
खोगीर; *v.t.* घोड़े की पीठ
पर जीन कसना, भार रखना

sadism *n.* क्रूरतापूर्ण विकृत
सम्भोग या मैथुन, दूसरे को
दुखी करके आनन्दित होने
की प्रवृत्ति*

safe *a.* सुरक्षित, स्वस्थ,
विश्वस्त, निश्चित; *n.* सेफ,
लोहे की संदूक*, तिजोरी*,
भोजन - सामग्री रखने की
जालीदार अलमारी*; safe
and sound कुशलपूर्वक

safeguard *n.* रक्षा*, साव-
धानी*; *v.t.* रक्षा करना

safety *n.* रक्षा*; safety lamp
खान में ले जाने का लम्प;
safety match केवल विशेष
प्रकार के मसाले पर रगड़ने
से ही जलनेवाली दियासलाई;
safety pin कोना न चुभने-
वाली आलपीन; safety-razor
ऐसा उस्तरा जिससे हजामत
बनाने में दाढ़ी न कटे; safety-
valve भाप का दबाव अधिक
बढ़ जाने पर स्वयं खुल जाने-
वाला इंजन का झट्टा

saffron *n.* केशर, कुंकुम; *a.*
केशरिया

sagacious *a.* मेधावी, बुद्धिमान,
चतुर, तीक्ष्ण बुद्धि का

sagaciously *adv.* चतुराई से

sagacity *n.* सूक्ष्म बुद्धि*, चतु-
राई*

sage *a.* पंडित, ज्ञानी; *n.* ऋषि,
मुनि

sail *n.* पाल, जहाज, जलयात्रा*,
वायु से चलनेवाली चक्की का
पंखा; *v.t. & i.* जल में
चलना या चलाना, वायु में
चलाना, नाव चलाना, जल-
यात्रा करना

sailer *n.* पाल पर चलनेवाला
जहाज

sailor *n.* नाविक

saint *n.* ऋषि, मुनि, सिद्धजन

saintly *a.* पवित्र, पुण्यात्मा

saintliness *n.* पुण्यात्मापन

salad *n.* कच्चे साग का अचार,
रायता; salad days युवा-
वस्था*, अनुभवहीन अवस्था*

salary *n.* वेतन; *v.t.* नियम से
वेतन देना

sale *n.* बिक्री*, नीलाम, कम
मूल्य की बिक्री*

salesman *n.* विक्रेता

salient *a.* उभड़ा हुआ, प्रधान,
मुख्य

sallow *a.* पीला, रोगी

sally *n.* झपट्टा, आक्रमण,
विप्लव, बुद्धिविलास; *v.t.*
(*p.t.* sallied) आक्रमण
करना।

saloon *n.* संलून, सजा हुआ
बड़ा कमरा, जहाज का बड़ा
कमरा, रेलगाड़ी का बिना
विभाग का बड़ा डब्बा

salt n. नमक, तीखापन, बुद्धि*;
a. नमकीन; v t. नमक
छिड़कना, नमक पोतना; not
worth his salt न रखने
योग्य; the salt of the
earth संसार की श्रेष्ठ जाति;
to eat a master's salt
स्वामी का काम ईमानदारी
से करना; to eat one's
salt प्रतिथि होना; salt-
cellar नमक रखने का छोटा
पात्र

salty a. नमकीन

salute n. सत्कार, नमस्कार,
चुम्बन, तोप को सलामी; v.t.
नमस्कार करना, स्वागत
करना

salvage n. अंशोद्धार, अग्नि
इत्यादि से सम्पत्ति को
बचाना, जहाज की सामग्री
को डूबने से बचाना

salvation n. पाप से मुक्ति*,
मोक्ष, उद्धार; salvation
army मुक्तिसेना*

salve n. शांतिप्रद औषधि*,
मलहम; v.t. नाश से बचाना

same a. & adv. अभिन्न,
समान, यही, एक ही, पहले
कहा हुआ; all the same
तिसपर भी; at the same
time उसी समय; just the
same ठीक ऐसा ही; of the

same age एक ही वय का

sample n. प्रतिरूप, आदर्श;
v.t. परीक्षा करना

samson n. अति बलवान मनुष्य

sanatorium (pl. sanatoria)
n. स्वास्थ्यसदन

sanctification n. पवित्र करने
का कार्य, पवित्रकरण

sanctify v.t. (p t sanctified)
पवित्र करना, पाप से मुक्त
करना

sanctimonious a. कपटधर्मी,
पाखण्डी

sanctimony n. बनावटी पुण्य,
पवित्रता* का बहाना

sanction n. आज्ञा*, अनुमोदन,
प्रोत्साहन; v.t. आज्ञा देना,
अधिकृत करना

sanctity n. (pl. -ties)
पवित्रता*, निर्मलता*, शुद्धता*

sanctuary n. (pl. -ries)
शरणस्थान

sand n. बालू मरुस्थल; v.t.
बालू मिलाना; sand bank
बलुआ किनारा; sand bath
औषधि इत्यादि पकाने का
बालू का यंत्र; sand-blast
कांच, धातु आदि के चमकीले
भाग को खुरखुरा करने का
यंत्र; sand-blind चौंधर,
कुछ अंधा; sand-box बालू-
दानी; sand-paper स्वच्छ

(पालिश) करने का बालू का कागज; sand-piper टिटिहरा; sand shoes बालू पर चलने का जूता; sandstone बलुआ पत्थर

sandal *n.* चप्पल*, चट्टी*

sandlewood *n.* चन्दन, सन्दल

sandwich *n.* मेवा, मांस इत्यादि भरी हुई कचौड़ी*; *v.t.* दो पदार्थों के बीच में कुछ रखना

sane *a.* स्वस्थ चित्त का, बुद्धिमान

sanguine *a.* रक्तवर्ण का, आशायुक्त, प्रसन्न, चमकीला; *n.* लोहू का रंग

sanitary *a.* स्वास्थ्य-संबंधी

sanity *n.* चित्त की स्थिरता*, मानसिक स्वास्थ्य

sapling *n.* छोटा पौधा

sarcasm *n.* आक्षेप, उपहास, व्यंग्य, ताना

sarcastic (-al) *a.* ताने का, व्यंग्यात्मक

sardonic *a.* उपहास या ताने का

Satan *n.* पिशाच, दैत्य

satellite *n.* उपग्रह, किसी मनुष्य का सर्वदा पीछा करनेवाला

satiate *v.t.* सन्तुष्ट करना, नाक तक भरना; *a.* अत्यन्त भरा हुआ

satire *n.* आक्षेप का लेख. उपहास, ताना

satirist *n.* व्यंग्यकार

satirize *v.t.* व्यंग्य करना

satisfaction *n.* इच्छा-पूर्ति*, सन्तोष, ऋण का चुकौता, निस्तार

satisfactory *a.* सन्तोषजनक, तृप्तिकर

satisfy *v.t.* (*p.t. & p.p.* satisfied) सन्तुष्ट करना, ऋण इत्यादि चुकाना, पूर्ण करना, विश्वास दिलाना

saturate *v.t.* पूर्ण रूप से सोखना, चूसना, पूरा भरना, मिलाना

saturation *n.* भराव, पूर्णता*

Saturday *n.* शनिवार, घनीचर

Saturn *n.* शनिग्रह

sauce *n.* मसाला, चटनी*, घृष्टता*; *v.t. & i.* मसालेदार बनाना, घृष्टता का व्यवहार करना

saucer *n.* तश्तरी*, रकाबी*

saunter *v.i.* टहलना, निरर्थक घूमना, अपना समय नष्ट करना, मस्ती से घूमना, मटरगश्ती करना

savage *a.* असभ्य, निर्दय, अशिष्ट, क्रोधी; *n.* निर्दय या क्रूर मनुष्य, असभ्य मनुष्य

savagery *n.* जंगलीपन, कूरता*

savant *n.* विद्वान, पंडित, ज्ञानी

save *v.t.* रक्षा करना, बचाना, रोकना, अल्प व्यय करना; *prep.* अतिरिक्त, छोड़कर

savings *n.* बचत*, संग्रह, संचित धन; savings bank बचत का धन, जमा करने का बैंक, संचय, अधिकोष

saviour *n.* उद्धारक, रक्षक, मुक्तिदाता

savour *n.* स्वाद, रस, रुचि*; *v.i. & t.* स्वाद लेना, तारीफ करना आभास देना

saw *n.* आरा आरी*; *v.t.* आरी से काटना

saw-dust *n.* आरे से निकला हुआ लकड़ी का बुरादा

say *v.t. & i.* (*p.t. & p.p.* said) बोलना, कहना, बताना, वर्णन करना; *n.* बात*, उक्ति*, कथन, मत, कहावत*; I say मैं दृढ़तापूर्वक कहता हूं; say no more बोलना बंद करो; that is to say अर्थात्; to say out स्पष्ट रूप से प्रकट करना

scaffold *n.* फांसी का तख्ता; *v.t.* मचान बांधना

scale *n.* मछली के चमड़े पर की परत*, चोइयां*, पतली तह*; *v.i.* परत उखड़ना; on a large scale स्थूल परिमाण में; to hold the scale पक्षपात न करना; to sink in the scale नीच अवस्था को प्राप्त करना; to turn the scale अवस्था बदल देना

scale *n.* तराजू का पलड़ा, तुला*, सीढ़ियों का क्रम, क्रमिक प्रबन्ध, नापने का चिह्न, सरगम का क्रम, कार्य-क्रम; *v.t.* ऊपर को चढ़ना

scalp *n.* खोपड़ी, मस्तक पर की त्वचा और बाल; *v.t.* मस्तक की खाल उखाड़ना

scan *v.t.* जांचना, सूक्ष्म परीक्षा करना, छन्द की मात्राओं की गणना करना

scandal *n.* आक्षेप, निन्दा*, कलंक, लोकापवाद; *v.t.* (*p.t.* scandaled) कलंक लगाना, निन्दा करना

scandalous *a.* कलंक लगाने वाला, अपवादक

scandalize *v.t.* निन्दा करना, कलंक लगाना

scant *a.* कम, थोड़ा; *adv.* कम मात्रा में

scape *v.t.* भाग जाना; scape-gallows फांसी पड़ने से बाल-बाल बचा हुआ; scape-goat बलि का बकरा, दूसरों के अपराध का फल भोगनेवाला:

scape-grace निर्लज्ज मनुष्य

scar *n.* घाव का चिह्न; *v.i.* (*p.t.* scarred) घाव का चिह्न पड़ना

scarce *a.* कम, थोड़ा, दुर्लभ; *adv.* प्रायः नहीं

scarcity *n.* न्यूनता*, कमी*

scare *n.* अकारण भय; *v.t.* डराना, चौंकाना

scarecrow *n.* विभीषिका*, चिड़ियों को डराने का पुतला, कागभगौड़ा

scathing *a.* अति कठोर, विनाश

scatter *v.t.* & *i.* छितराना, बिखेरना, फैलाना, प्रसारित करना

scatter-brain विचारहीन पुरुष

scavenger *n.* मेहतर, भंगी

scene *n* घटनास्थल, दृश्य, नाटक का अंश, रंगभूमि*, नाटक का पर्दा

scenery *n.* दृश्यावली*, सीनरी*

scenic (-al) *a.* सुरम्य, नाटक-संबंधी

scent *n.* सुगन्ध*, वास*; *v.t.* सूंघना, सुगन्धित करना; on the scent खोज में; to put off the scent धोखा देना

sceptic *n.* सन्देहवादी, संशयात्मा, नास्तिक वहमी, शक्की

sceptical *a.* सन्देह-युक्त

scepticism *n.* संदेहवाद,

अविश्वास

sceptre *n.* राजदण्ड, राज्यचिह्न

schedule *n.* सूची*, नामावली*, कार्यक्रम; *v.t.* सूची में लिखना, सूचीपत्र बनाना; scheduled time निर्धारित समय

scheme *n.* स्कीम, योजना* प्रारूप, उपाय, प्रबन्ध, व्यवस्था*; *v.t.* प्रबन्ध करना, उपाय करना, योजना बनाना

schism *n.* मतभेद, फूट*, लड़ाई*

scholar *n.* विद्यार्थी, छात्र, विद्वान

scholarship *n* पाण्डित्य, विद्वत्ता*, छात्रवृत्ति*

scholastic *a.* विद्वान या विश्वविद्यालय संबंधी, पंडिताऊ

school *n.* स्कूल विद्यालय, पाठशाला*, शाखा* सम्प्रदाय; *v.t.* अध्ययन करना, सिखलाना

schooling *n.* शिक्षा, उपदेश

school-master *n.* (*fem.* mistress) स्कूल का अध्यापक; school of fish मछलियों का झुण्ड

science *n.* विज्ञान, विद्याशास्त्र

scientific *a.* वैज्ञानिक, शास्त्रानुरोधी, शास्त्रीय

scientist *n.* वैज्ञानिक

scissors *n. pl.* कतरनी*, कैंची*; lamp-scissors लैम्प की बत्ती काटने की कैंची; nail scissors नाखून काटने की कैंची*

scoff *n.* प्राक्षेप, तिरस्कार; *v.t.* घृणा करना, ताना मारना

scold *v.t.* झिड़की देना, गाली देना; *n.* झिड़की*, गाली*

scoop *n.* फरसा, बड़ा चम्मच कल्छुल, विशेष खबर; *v.t.* उठाना, खोदना, विशेष खबर का पता लगाना

scope *n.* हेतु, रुचि*, विस्तार, प्रवसर, सीमा*

scorch *v.t. & i.* जलाना, झुलसाना, सूख जाना

score *n.* दरार*, फटन*, कोड़ी*, लम्बी लकीर*, कूंड़, खेलों में बनाए गए प्रंक; *v.t. & i.* खेल में प्रंक बनाना, गोल करना, रन बनाना, सफल होना, लाभ उठाना, हाज़िर जवाबी से काम लेना; on the score उस विषय में; scorebook गणना करने की पुस्तक; scores of people मनुष्यों की अधिक संख्या; to pay one's score गिनती ठीक करना, to score under रेखांकित करना

scorn *n.* तिरस्कार, निन्दा*;

v.t. तिरस्कार करना, प्रपमान करना

Scot *n.* स्कॉटलैंड देश का निवासी; scot *n.* कर

scot-free *a* बिना चोट लगे, बिना कर दिए

Scotch *a. & n.* स्कॉटलैंड देश का, इस देश का निवासी, इनकी भाषा, स्कांच ह्विस्की

scotch *v.t.* क्षत-विक्षत करना, जख्मी करना; *n.* छोटा घाव, खरोंच

scoundrel *n.* नीच, दुष्ट, लुच्चा

scout *n.* स्काउट, बालचर, भेदिया, जासूस, द्रुतगामी छोटा वायुयान; *v.t. & i.* स्काउट की तरह काम करना, भेद जानना; boy scout बालचर

scowl *v.t.* भौंह चढ़ाना, मुंह सिकोड़ना; *n.* भ्रूभंग, क्रोध-पूर्ण प्राकृति*

scramble *v.i. & t.* छीना-झपटी करना, पेट के बल चढ़ना; *n.* छीना-झपटी*, झगड़ा, कलह

scrap *n.* रद्दी माल, खण्ड, टुकड़ा, टूटा भाग; *v.t.* (*p.t.* scrapped) व्यर्थ जानकर टुकड़े करना, रद्दी की ढेर में डालना

scrape *v.t.* रगड़कर या खुरच

कर चिकना करना; n. खुरचन;
to scrape one's boots
जूते के तल्ले की मिट्टी हटाना;
to scrape one's plate
सब खा जाना, थाली में कुछ
न छोड़ना

scratch v.t. खुरचना, खोदना,
अलगाना; n. छोटा घाव,
खरोंच

scrawl v.i. घसीट लिखना; n.
घसीट लिखावट या चित्र

scream v.i. चीखना, ठहाका
मारकर हंसना; n. चीख*,
चिल्लाहट*, हंसी*

screen n. रक्षा करने या छिपाने
का पदार्थ, ओट, पर्दा, बड़ी
चलनी*; v.t. शरण देना,
रक्षा करना, तलाशी लेना,
सिनेमा दिखाना

screw n. पेंच, कंजूस मनुष्य;
v.t. & i. ऐंठना, रूक्षता का
व्यवहार करना, पेंच से
कसना; to have a screw
loose मनुष्य जिसका मस्तिष्क
ठीक काम नहीं करता; to
put the screw on पूरा
प्रयत्न करना

screw-bolt n. ढिबरीदार पेंच
screw-driver n. पेंचकस
script n. लिपि*, हस्तलिपि*,
वर्णमाला*, लिखावट*, मूल
लेख, चलचित्र-नाट्य, या

फिल्मी नाटक की टंकित
लिपि*, रेडियो-भाषण या
वार्ता* का पाठ, लेख, निबन्ध

scripture n. धर्म-पुस्तक,
बाइबिल*, बाइबिल का अंश

scroll n. कुंडली*, लपेटे
हुए कागज़ का मुट्ठा, सूची-
पत्र, घुमौवा फीता; v.t.
बेलबूटे काढ़ना, बेलबूटों से
सजाना

scrutinize v.t. छानबीन
करना, जांचना

scrutiny n. सूक्ष्म परीक्षा*;
छानबीन

scuffle n. झगड़ा, हाथापाई*
v t. झगड़ना, खींचातानी
करना

sculptor n. मूर्तिकार, संग-
तराश, नक्काश

sculptural a. मूर्तिकला-
विषयक

sculpture n. मूर्तिकला*, शिल्प
कला*, संगतराशी*, मूर्ति*,
v.t. मूर्ति बनाना

scum n. फेन, झाग, मैल*
v.t. & i. (p.t. scummed)
मैल हटाना

scurf n. चोइयां* रूसी*

scurvy a. नीच, तिरस्कृत; n.
एक प्रकार का रक्त-रोग,
लवणरक्त, दन्तरोग

scuttle n. कोयला रखने का

पात्र, छोटी डलिया*; *v.i.*
खिसकना, जल्दी करना,
दुम दबाकर भागना
sea *n.* समुद्र, बड़ी झील*,
समुद्र की बड़ी लहर*,
seaboard समुद्र तट; **sea-
coal** जहाज़ से लाया हुआ
कोयला; **sea-cow** समुद्री
घोड़ा; **seafarer** मल्लाह,
समुद्र-यात्रा करने वाला;
seaman मल्लाह, मांझी;
seamanship नाविक
विद्या*; **sea-rover** समुद्री
डाकू; **seascape** समुद्र का
चित्र; **seaworthy** समुद्र
यात्रा करने के योग्य; a
rough sea प्रचण्ड लहर;
mistress of the seas
प्रधान समुद्री शक्ति; sea of
blood हत्याकाण्ड; to go
to sea मल्लाह बनना; to
put to sea समुद्र पार जाना
seal *n.* एक प्रकार की समुद्री
मछली,* सुईस*
seal *n.* मुद्रा,* मुहर की छाप,*
विशिष्ट चिह्न; *v.i.* मुहर
लगाना, बन्द रखना, दृढ़
करना
search *v.t. & i.* खोजना, जांच
करना, परीक्षा करना; *n.*
जांच,* खोज,* परीक्षा*
to search into परीक्षा

करना; to search out जांच-
पड़ताल करना
searching *a.* कठोर अनुसंधान
या परीक्षा या जांच करने
वाला
searchlight *n.* सर्चलाइट,
बिजली की तेज़ रोशनी वाला
यंत्र
season *n.* ऋतु,* समय, काल,
उचित अवसर; *v.t.* स्वादिष्ट
करना, अभ्यास करना, सुखा-
कर पुष्ट करना; **auspi-
cious season** अच्छा
अवसर; in season, out
of season सब काल में;
out of season अकाल में;
season ticket रेलवे इत्यादि
का कुछ समय के लिए रिया-
यती टिकट
seasonable *a.* मौसमी, प्रसंगो-
चित, समय की आवश्यकताओं
को पूरा करने वाला
seasonably *adv.* उचित अवसर
का
seat *n.* आसन, बैठने का अधि-
कार, स्थान, ग्रामीण वास-
स्थान *v.i.* स्थापित करना,
नियुक्त करना
secede *v.t.* पृथक् होना, भिन्न
मत ग्रहण करना, अलग होना
secession *n.* पार्थक्य, अलगाव,
फूट*

seclude v.t. समाज से अल-
गाना, एकान्त में रखना, दूर
रखना, निकालना

secluded a. एकान्त स्थित,
निर्जंन, एकान्त

seclusion n. अकेलापन,
निर्जंनता

second a. दूसरा; n. सेकण्ड,
मिनट का साठवां भाग, रद्दी
माल; v t. अनुमोदन करना,
साहस देना; second to
none अद्वितीय, अपूर्व;
second-floor दूसरी मंज़िल;
second-hand दूसरे का
व्यवहार किया हुआ, जीर्ण;
second-rate सामान्य

secondary a. अमुख्य,
अप्रधान, दूसरे क्रम का,
सहायक; secondary edu-
cation माध्यमिक शिक्षा

seconder n. प्रस्ताव का
समर्थक

secrecy n. गुप्तता*, एकान्तता*

secret a. गुप्त, गूढ़, छिपा
हुआ; n. भेद, रहस्य; in
secret एकांत में; open
secret आम बात*; secret
counsel गुप्त मन्त्रणा;
secret information गुप्त
मन्त्र; secret ballot गुप्त
मतदान

secretarial a. सचिव-संबंधी

secretariat (e) n. सचिवालय

secretary n. सेक्रेटरी, सचिव,
मंत्री; secretary of state
राज्यमंत्री (ब्रिटेन), परराष्ट्र
मंत्री (अमरीका); under-
secretary अवर सचिव;
joint secretary संयुक्त
सचिव

secretaryship n. सचिवत्व,
मंत्रित्व

secretive a. रहस्यपूर्ण, छिपाऊ,
चुप्पा

sect n. सम्प्रदाय, पंथ

sectarian a. संकीर्ण, कट्टर

sectarianism n. संकीर्णतावाद

section n. कटाव, खण्ड, जाति,
वर्ग, भाग, प्रकरण; section-
mark प्रकरण का चिह्न

sectional a. खंड संबंधी

sector n. वृत्तखण्ड, रेखागणित
का एक यन्त्र

secular a. धर्मनिरपेक्ष, पार्थिव,
संसारी; n. धार्मिक सत्य

secure a. चिन्ता-रहित,
सुरक्षित, निर्भय, दृढ़,
विश्वासी; v t. निश्चित
करना, प्राप्त करना, पुष्ट
या सुरक्षित करना

security (pl. securities)
n. रक्षा*. बचाव, प्रतिभू

sedate a. गम्भीर. शान्त,
सौम्य, धीर, सयत

sediment *n.* तलछट, अवसाद

sedition *n.* राजद्रोह, विद्रोह, संक्षोभ

seditious *a.* राजद्रोही, विद्रोही

seduce *v.t.* सतीत्व नष्ट करने के लिए फुसलाना, चरित्र भ्रष्ट करने के लिए बहकाना, सत्पथ से डिगाना, सतीत्व नष्ट करना, पाप या अपराध की ओर लुभाना

seduction *n.* सतीत्वहरण, चरित्रदूषण

see *v.t. & i.* (*p.t.* saw, *p.p.* seen) देखना, विचारना, समझना, प्रबन्ध करना; परीक्षा करना; भेंट करना; I see मैं समझता हूं; to see after संभालना; to see good भला विचारना; to see into विचार करना; to see life अनुभव प्राप्त करना; to see the light उत्पन्न होना; to see off हटाना; to see one's way प्रबन्ध करना; to see the back त्याग देना; to see with one's eyes प्रत्यक्ष साक्षी होना; to see to परीक्षा करना

seek *v.t. & i.* (*p.t. & p.p.* sought) खोजना, जांचना, प्रत्यक्ष करना; to seek out अलगाना; to seek through खोज निकालना

seem *v.i.* जान पड़ना, देख पड़ना

seer *n.* (*fem.* seeress) भविष्यदर्शी, सिद्ध पुरुष, ऋषि, पैगम्बर, नबी

segment *n.* भाग, खण्ड, छिन्न अंश

segregate *v.t. & i.* पृथक् करना, अलगाना

segregation *n.* पृथक्त्व, अलगाव

seize *v.t.* पकड़ना, धरना, आक्रमण करना, विचारना

seizure *n.* आक्रमण, धावा, कानूनी अभिग्रहण

seldom *adv.* कदाचित, विरले ही

select *v.t.* बराना, चुनना; *a.* उत्तम, चुना हुआ

selection *n.* चुनाव

selective *a.* चुनने योग्य

self *n.* (*pl.* selves) स्व, आपा, स्वयं, निज, आत्म, अहं, आत्महित, स्वार्थ; self-acting स्वयं कर्म करने वाला; self-assumed बिना अधिकार के स्वीकृत; self-collected शान्त; self-evidence स्वतः सिद्ध; self-interest निजी स्वार्थ;

self-made अपने परिश्रम से महत्त्व प्राप्त किया हुआ; self-will हठ

selfish *a.* स्वार्थपर, स्वार्थी

sell *v.t.* • (*p.t.* & *p.p.* sold) बिक्री करना, धोखा देना; to sell off सब सामग्री बेच डालना

seller *n.* बेचने वाला, विक्रेता

sematic *a.* सार्थ, भय-सूचक

semblance *n.* रूप, आकार, समानता*

semen *n.* शुक्र, वीर्य

semi *pref.* (*as bemi demi*) 'आधा' के व्यर्थ का उपसर्ग

seminal *a.* शुक्र-संबंधी, प्रजनन-विषयक

seminary *n.* सेमिनरी, पाठशाला*

senate *n.* सेनेट, मन्त्रिसभा*, विश्वविद्यालय की प्रबन्ध-कारिणी सभा*

senatorial *a.* सेनेट-संबंधी, राजसभा या समिति-संबंधी

send *v.t.* & *i.* (*p.t.* & *p.p.* sent.) भेजना, प्रस्थान कराना; send off बिदाई; to send away प्रस्थान करना, भेजना; to send bullet गोली चलाना; to send for बुलाना; to send forth भेजना

senile *a.* वृद्धावस्था-संबंधी, जरा-सूचक

senior *a.* सीनियर, बड़ी अवस्था या पद का, वयोवृद्ध ज्येष्ठ, वरीय, प्रधान व्यक्ति

seniority *n.* वरीयता*; ज्येष्ठता*, जेठापन*

sensation *n.* संवेदना*, मनोवेग, उद्वेग, तीव्र अनुभूति*, अनुभव, उत्तेजना, सनसनी*

sensational *a.* संवेदनात्मक, उत्तेजनात्मक, सनसनीखेज, चेतना-विषयक, इन्द्रियबोध-संबंधी

sense *n.* इन्द्रिय-ज्ञान, बुद्धि*, चेतना*, बोध, विचार, तात्पर्य, होश; a man of sense बुद्धिमान पुरुष; common sense विवेक, बुद्धि*, साधारण ज्ञान; literal sense शब्दार्थ; out of sense बुद्धि-भ्रष्ट, पागल; pleasures of senses विषय-सुख, इन्द्रिय-सुख; sense of action कर्मेन्द्रिय; sense of obligation कृतज्ञता; sense of perception ज्ञानेन्द्रिय; sense of pleasure सुख का अनुभव

senseless *a.* ज्ञानहीन, दुर्बुद्धि, बेहोश

sensibility n. इन्द्रियग्राह्यता*, अनुभवशीलता*, ग्रहणशक्ति*, चेतना*, एहसास

sensible a. संवेदनशील, इन्द्रियगम्य, श्लाघनीय, संचेतन, उचित

sensibly adv. सद्बुद्धि से

sensitive a कोमलहृदय, सूक्ष्म-ग्राही; sensitive market जल्दी-जल्दी भाव बदलने की हाट; sensitive paper प्रकाश का प्रभाव पड़नेवाला फोटो का कागज

sensual a. इन्द्रियसुख-संबंधी, वासनात्मक, विलासप्रिय, शारीरिक, संसारी

sensualist n. विलासी, विषयी, सुखभोगवादी

sensuality n. कामासक्ति*, विषयरति*

sensuous a. इन्द्रियजनित, ऐन्द्रिक

sentence n. वाक्य, दण्ड की आज्ञा*, सूत्र; v.t. दण्ड की आज्ञा देना ।

sentiment n. मनोभाव, भावना*, भाव

sentimental a. भावुक, भावुकतापूर्ण

sentry n. सन्तरी, चौकीदार

separable a. अलगाने योग्य

separate v.t. & i. विभाग करना, अलगाना, पृथक् होना या करना; a. विभक्त, पृथक्, अकेला

separation n. वियोग, विरह, विभेद, आंशिक तलाक

September n. सितम्बर

septic a. & n. रक्त-दूषक, रक्त-दूषक पदार्थ, सेप्टिक

sequel n. अन्त, परिणाम

sequence n. अनुक्रम, परम्परा*, श्रेणी*

serene a. शान्त, स्वच्छ, निर्मल

serenity n. निर्मलता*, शान्ति*, स्थिरता*

serf n. दास, किसान, कपड़ा धोने का पाउडर

serfdom n. दासवृत्ति*, अर्ध-दासता*

serge n. एक प्रकार का ऊनी वस्त्र, सरज

sergeant n. सेना का अध्यक्ष, पुलिस का अफसर; lance-sergeant पुलिस का घुड़सवार सिपाही; sergeant-major सेनाध्यक्ष का सहायक

serial a. धारावाहिक, क्रमशः; n. क्रमिक प्रकाशन

series n. (sing. & pl.) सीरीज, श्रेणी*, ग्रंथमाला*, लेखमाला*

serious a. गम्भीर, सच्चा, उत्सुक

sermon n. धर्मोपदेश, प्रवचन,

उपदेश

serpent *n.* सर्प, सांप;
pharaoh's serpent एक
प्रकार की बत्ती जो जलाने
पर सर्प के आकार की हो
जाती है

servant *n.* सेवक, दास, मज़दूर,
नौकर

serve *v.t. & i.* सेवा करना,
सहायता देना व्यवहार करना,
परोसना, कार्य करना; it will
serve यह पर्याप्त होगा; to
serve a sentence पूरी
अवधि तक दंड भोगना; to
serve out बांटना, to serve
the devil निर्दय बनना; to
serve the purpose of
उपयोग का होना

service *n.* सेवा*, नौकरी*,
उपयोगिता*, दया*, आरा-
धना*, उपासना*; at his
service उसके अधीन; to
take service with नौकरी
करना, नौकरी में लगना

serviceable *a.* उपयोगी, लाभ-
दायक

servile *a.* दासवत्, गुलाम वृत्ति
का

session *n.* सेशन, न्यायालय या
सदन या सभा की बैठक,
कार्यकाल, पाठशाला का सत्र

sesspool *n.* चहबच्चा

set *v.t. & i.* (*p.t. & p.p.*
set) रखना, नियुक्त करना,
बैठाना, ठीक करना, बोना या
लगाना, स्थिर करना या
जमाना, फैलाना, फलना,
चुनना, स्थापित करना,
क्षितिज में डूबना; *a.* स्थिर,
नियुक्त; *n.* प्रेरणा*, समुदाय,
मण्डली*, संघ; set speech
पहले से प्रस्तुत व्याख्यान; to
set about आरम्भ करना;
to set a trap फन्दा लगाना;
to set apart अलगाना;
to set a defiance
ललकारना; to set at
liberty स्वतन्त्र करना; to
set at naught तिरस्कार
करना; to set by बचा
रखना; to set fire to आग
लगाना; to set forward
उत्पत्ति में सहायता देना; to
set free मुक्त करना; to set
in आरम्भ करना; to set
one's hand कार्य आरम्भ
करना; to set table भोजन
के लिए टेबुल बिछाना; to set
the watch घड़ी मिलाना;
set-back अवरोध, रोक; set-
off मुजरा, छूट

settle *v.t. & i.* स्थापित करना,
शांत करना, निर्णय करना,
राज़ी होना, नियुक्त करना,

स्वच्छ होना

settlement n. निर्णय, व्यव-
स्था*, उपनिवेश, निपटारा,
चुकौती*

settler n. उपनिवेशी, नया
बसनेवाला

seven n. सात; seventeen
सत्रह; seventeenth a.
सत्रहवां; seventy सत्तर;
seventieth a. सत्तरवां

sever v.t. & i. अलग करना,
अलग होना, तोड़ना

severance n. अलगाव, विच्छेद

several a. अनेक, अलग, पृथक्

severe a. तीक्ष्ण, कठोर,
अत्यन्त कष्टदायक

sew v.t. (p.t. sewed, p.p.
sewn) सीना, टांका लगाना

sew v.t. & i. पानी बहाना या
बहना, पानी का धीरे-धीरे
निकलना

sewage n. कीच, मल,
परनालियां*

sewer n. नाली*, मोरी*

sewerage n. परनाला

sex n. जाति*, लिंग, योनि*;
the fair sex स्त्रीजाति*,
the male sex पुरुष जाति*

sexual a. स्त्री या पुरुष जाति
संबंधी; लैंगिक, कामवासना-
संबंधी, योनि-संबंधी

sexualist n. लिंग-सिद्धान्तवादी,

लिंग या जातित्व विभाजन
का पंडित

shabby a. जर्जर, कुत्सित,
दरिद्र, मलिन, मैला

shackle n. श्रृंखला*, बंधन;
v.t. बांधना, रोकना

shade n. छाया*, अन्धकार,
पर्दा, रंग का उतार-चढ़ाव,
चित्र का गहरे रंग का भाग,
प्रेत, थोड़ा अन्तर; v.t. छाया
करना, अंधेरा करना, ढांकना;
to throw into the shade
निन्दा करना

shadow n. छाया*, परछाईं*,
आभा, रक्षा*, अनुचर, प्रेत;
v.t. छाया करना, अन्धकार
करना, ढांकना

shaft n. डंडी*, मुठिया*, पतला
डंडा, तीर, यन्त्र का लम्बा
घुरा

shake v.t. & i. (p.t. shook,
p.p shaken) हिलना,
कांपना, लड़खड़ाना, ब्याकुल
करना, थर्राना, निर्बल करना;
n. धक्का, थर्राहट*, हाथ-
मिलौवल; to shake about
हिला देना; to shake down
हिलाकर भेजना या लाना; to
shake in one's shoes भय
से कांपना; to shake off
छुटकारा पाना; to shake
off the dust from one's

feet सब संबंध त्याग देना

shaky *a.* अनिश्चित, डावांडोल

shall *v. aux.* (*p.t.* should) भविष्यकाल-सूचक क्रिया गा, गी

shallow *a.* (*comp.* shallower, *sup.* shallowest) छिछला, हलका, तुच्छ, ओछा

shallowness *n.* छिछलापन, ओछापन

shame *n.* लज्जा*, शर्म*, अपमान, कलंक; *v.t.* लज्जित करना

shameful *a.* लज्जापूर्ण, लज्जास्पद

shameless *a.* निर्लज्ज, बेशर्म

shampoo *v.t.* साबुन रगड़कर सिर धोना; *n.* शैम्पू, बाल धोने का पाउडर या लेप

shanty *n.* (*pl.* shanties) झोंपड़ी*

shape *v.t.* (*p.t.* shaped, *p.p.* shaped *or* shapen) आकार धारण करना, बनाना, ढालना, रचना, मूर्ति बनाना; *n.* आकृति*, आकार, रूप, सांचा

shapeless *a.* निराकार, भद्दा

shapely *a* सुरूप, सुन्दर, सुडौल

share *n.* अंश, भाग, हिस्सा, हल का फार; *v.t.* भाग करना, अंश लेना; share holder हिस्सेदार

sharer *n.* अंशभागी, हिस्सेदार

shark *n.* एक भयंकर समुद्री मछली, धूर्त पुरुष

sharp *a.* तीखा, नोकदार, तीव्रबुद्धि, सावधान, रसिक, कर्कश, छली, उग्र, पीड़ाकर; *n.* ठग; *adv.* ठीक समय पर, अभी; sharp-cut स्पष्ट रूप से निरूपित; sharp-set भूखा; sharp-shooter सही या ठीक लक्ष्य लगानेवाला मनुष्य

sharpen *v.t. & i.* तीखा करना या होना, अधिक बुद्धिमान बनाना

sharpener *n.* सान धरनेवाला

sharper *n.* ठग

sharply *adv.* रूखेपन से, पैने ढंग से

shatter *v.t. & i.* टुकड़े-टुकड़े करना, छितराना, क्रम बिगाड़ना

shave *v.t. & i.* (*p.t.* shaved, *p.p* shaved or shaven) हजामत बनाना या बनवाना, महीन काटना

shaver *n.* नापित, बाल मूंड़नेवाला, छोकड़ा, लौंडा, महंगा बेचनेवाला व्यापारी

shaving *n.* हजामत*, मुण्डन

shawl *n.* शाल, दुशाला

she *pron.* (*obj.* her, *poss.* hers, her, *pl.* they) वह

(स्त्री), यह (स्त्री)

shed *v.t.* (*p.t. & p.p.* shed)
फेंक ॥, गिराना; *n.* शेड,
भोंपड़ी*, प्रोसारा

sheep *n.* (*pl.*sheep), (*male*
ram, *female* ewe, *young
one* lamb) भेड़ी; sheep
without a shepherd बिना
नेता की मण्डली; to cast
sheep's eyes प्रेम-दृष्टि
डालना; to follow like
sheep सर्वदा अनुकरण
करना

sheepish *a.* डरपोक, लज्जालु

sheer *a.* केवल, मात्र, निपट,
खड़े बल का; *v.i.* अलग होना,
धिसकना

sheet *n.* चादर, चौड़ा वस्त्र,
विस्तार, पाल

shelf *n.* (*pl.* shelves) अल-
मारी*, टांड, उभड़ी हुई
चट्टान*

shell *n.* छिलका, खोली, नम
का गोला, ढांचा; *v.t. & i.*
छिलका उतारना, बम गोले
से उड़ाना; shell-buttons
कपड़ा चढ़े हुए घातु के बटन;
shell-proof गोली के लक्ष्य
से बचने योग्य

shelter *n.* आश्रय, शरण, रक्षा
करनेवाला; *v.t.* रक्षा करना

shepherd *n.* (*fem.* shepher-

dess) गड़रिया, चरवाहा;
v.t. रखवाली करना

sheriff *n.* शेरिफ, नगराधिप

sherry *n.* स्पेन देश की श्वेत
मदिरा*, शेरी

shield *n.* ढाल, रक्षा करनेवाला
मनुष्य या पदार्थ, पदक; *v.t.*
रक्षा करना, बचाना; the
other side of the shield
प्रस्तुत विषय का अनावश्यक
अंश

shift *v.t. & i.* हटाना, हटना,
अवस्था या स्थान बदलना,
स्थानापन्न करना, विचार
पलटना, प्रयत्न करना,
टालना; *n.* पाली*, बदला,
छल, साधन; to shift about
एक स्थान से दूसरे स्थान
को जाना; to shift one's
ground नई स्थिति धारण
करना

shin *n.* पिंडली*

shine *v.i.* (*p.t.* shone)
चमकना, जगमगाना; *n.*
प्रकाश, चमक

ship *n.* जहाज, पोत; *v.t.* (*p.t.*
shipped) जहाज पर लादना
या रखना

shipment *n.* जहाज पर लादी
गई सामग्री*

shipping *n.* जहाज, नौबहन

shipwright *n.* जहाज बनाने-

वाला

shipyard *n.* जहाज का कार-
खाना

shirt *n.* कमीज*

shit *v.i.* मल त्यागना; *n.* अप-
शब्द, गाली*

shiver *v.i. & t.* कांपना,
टूटना, टुकड़े करना; *n.* कंपन

shock *n.* आघात, धक्का,
टक्कर*, चोट*; *v.t. & i.*
धक्का देना, धक्का लगना,
दुःखी करना

shoe *n.* जूता, नाल; *v.t.* (*p.t.*
shod) जूता पहनाना, नाल
बांधना; shoe-black जूते पर
पालिश करनेवाला; shoe-
horn जूता पहनने का साधन;
shoer *n.* नालबन्द; to die
in one's shoes फांसी
पड़कर मरना

shoot *v.t. & i.* (*p.t.* shot)
मारना, फेंकना, छूटना एका-
एक उठ आना, अंकुरित होना;
n. फेंकान, लक्ष्यभेदी या
निशानेबाज़ों का दल, नई
डाल*; shooting star उल्का,
टूटनेवाला तारा

shop *n.* दुकान*; *v.i.* (*p.t.*
shopped) सामग्री मोल
लेने के लिए दूकान पर जाना

shopping *n.* खरीद*

shore *n.* समुद्रतट

short *a.* छोटा, नाटा, थोड़ा,
कम, संक्षेप, शीघ्र; *adv.*
यकायक, तुरन्त; in short
संक्षेप में, a short cut सरल
मार्ग; to cut short शीघ्र
समाप्त करना; shorthand
संक्षिप्त या संकेत लिपि;
shorthanded कम सहायकों
वाला; to come to short
निराश करना; to fall
short कम होना; to take
short views केवल वर्तमान
का विचार करना

shortage *n.* न्यूनता*, कमी*

shortcoming *n.* दोष, न्यूनता*

shortly *adv.* शीघ्र, भट से

shortness *n.* अल्पता*, लघुता*

shorts *n. pl:* घुटने तक का
पाजामा, जांघिया*

short-wind *a.* जल्द थक जाने-
वाला

short-witted *a.* कम बुद्धिवाला

shot *n.* गोली मारने की
क्रिया*, गोली*, बन्दूक या
तोप का गोला, गोली चलाने-
वाला

shoulder *n.* कन्धा, आधार,
सहारा; *v.t. & i.* कन्धे से
धक्का देना, कन्धा लगाना,
दायित्व लेना; of broad
shoulders बलवान; old
head on young shoul-

ders ग्रहण वय का बुद्धिमान पुरुष

shout n. डांट*, चिल्लाहट*, कोलाहल; v.i. चिल्लाना, कोलाहल करना; to shout at चिल्लाकर बोलना

shove v.t. & i. ढकेलना, किनारे पर से गिराना; n. धक्का

shovel n. फावड़ा; v.t. (p.t. shovelled) फावड़े से हटाना

show (shew) v.t. & i. (p.t. showed, p p. shown) प्रकट करना, प्रदर्शित करना, निर्देश देना, सिद्ध करना, मार्ग दिखलाना, देख पड़ना; n. दर्शन, प्रदर्शन या प्रदर्शनी*, दिखाव, कौतुक

shower n. वृष्टि*, बौछार, झड़ी*, फुहार*; v.i. बरसना, झड़ी लगाना

shrewd a. चतुर, धूर्त, तीक्ष्ण

shriek n. चीख*, कर्कश शब्द, चिल्लाहट*; v.i. चीखना, ठहाका मारकर हंसना

shrill a. तीव्र, कर्कश, उग्र, कर्णकटु

shrine n. पुण्यस्थान, तीर्थस्थान, मन्दिर, मठ

shrink v.t. & i. (p.t. shrank p.p. shrunken,

shrunk) सिकुड़ना, सिकोड़ना, सकुचाना

shrinkable a. सिकुड़ने योग्य

shrinkage; n. सिकुड़न*

shrunken a. सिकुड़ा हुआ

shroud n. शव-वस्त्र, कफन, ढकना; v.t. ढांकना, छिपाना, आश्रय देना

shrug v.t. & i. (p.t. shrugged) असन्तोष, सन्देह इत्यादि सूचित करने के लिए कन्धा सिकोड़ना

shudder v.i. कांपना, थर्राना

shuffle v.i. & t. स्थान बदलना, उलट-पुलट करना, गड़बड़ करना, पैर घसीट कर चलना. ताश फेंटना; n. गड़बड़ी, धूर्तता; to shuffle the cards नई विधि ग्रहण करना या अपनाना

shun v.t. (p.t. shuned) त्यागना, अलगाना, पहलू बचाना, किनारा कसना

shunt v.t. गाड़ी का मार्ग बदलना, बिजली की धारा का क्रम पलटना; n. बगल की लाइन*

shut v.t. & i. (p.t. & p. p. shut) बन्द करना, रोकना, बन्द होना, अलगाना; to shut down दृढ़तापूर्वक बन्द

करना; to shut off प्रवाह रोकना; to shut one's eyes न देखने का बहाना करना; to shut the door upon विचार न करना, प्रसम्भव करना

shutter *n.* शटर, बन्द करने का साधन, झांप; to put up the shutters दिन-भर के लिए व्यवसाय बन्द करना

shuttle *n.* ढरकी*, सूत्र यंत्र

shuttlecock *n.* पर लगा हुआ काग जो बैडमिन्टन के खेल में प्रयुक्त होता है

shy *a.* (*comp.* shyer or shier, *sup.* shyest or shiest) लज्जालू, समाज,से दूर रहने वाला डरपोक; *v.i.* भड़कना, लजाना

shyly *adv.* लज्जा से

Siamese *a.* स्याम देश का निवासी, इस देश की भाषा

Siberian *a.* साइबेरिया देश के निवासी का

sick *a.* पीड़ित, दुखी, रोगार्त, वमनेच्छु

sicken *v.t. & i.* रोगी होना या करना, जी मचलाना, घृणा होना; sick leave रोगों के कारण छुट्टी, रोगा-वकाश

sickle *n.* हसिया* हंसुवा

sickliness *n.* अस्वस्थता*

sickly *a.* अस्वस्थ, रोगी, वृणित

side *n.* किनारा,. छोर, बगल, तरफ*, दल, वश; *v.i. & t.* पक्ष लेना, भाग लेना; on all sides चारों श्रोर; on both sides दोनों श्रोर; on the other side उस पार; opposite side विपक्ष; on this side of the grave संसार में, जीवन में; outer side बाहरी भाग; side by side पास-पास; side-issue चित्त हटाने वाला विषय; side-line अप्रधान व्यवसाय

siege *n.* सेना से किले का घिराव; to lay siege to घेरा डालना

siesta *n.* दोपहर की झपकी*

sigh *n.* गहरी सांस*, उच्छ-वास*; *v.i. & t.* आह भरना, दुःख प्रकट करना

sight *n.* दृष्टि*, दर्शन, दृश्य, दिखाव, चमत्कार, निरीक्षण; *v.t.* देखना, लक्ष्य लगाना; at first sight देखते ही; in sight of दृष्टिगोचर; out of sight दृष्टि से परे; out of sight, out of mind अनुपस्थित को भूल जाना; payment at sight

दर्शनी हुंडी; to know by sight देखते ही पहचान लेना; to put out of sight छिपा देना; within sight दृष्टिगोचर

sightly *a.* सुन्दर, मनोहर

sign *n.* प्रतीक, प्रारूप, लक्षण, संकेत, भाव, इशारा, विशेष चिह्न; *v.t.* चिह्न करना, हस्ताक्षर करना; sign-board नामपट्ट; sign-post मार्ग-दर्शक पटरा

signal *n.* सिगनल, संकेत; *a.* प्रपूर्व, प्रसाधारण; *v.t.* (*p.t.* signalled) संकेत द्वारा सूचित करना

signaller *n.* रेलगाड़ी के प्राने का संकेत करने वाला

signatory *a.* हस्ताक्षर-संबंधी; *n.* हस्ताक्षरकर्त्ता

signature *n.* हस्ताक्षर, दस्त-खत

significance *n.* अभिप्राय, अर्थ, महत्त्व

significant *a.* अभिप्रायपूर्ण, प्रसिद्ध, विख्यात

signify *v.t. & i.* (*p.t.* signi-fied) अर्थ प्रकट करना, बतलाना

silence *n.* मौन, शान्ति*, गुप्त भाव; *interj.* चुप हो ! *v.t.* चुप करना, मुंह बन्द करना

silencer *n.* मशीन की प्राबाज कम करने का साधन

silent *a.* निःशब्द, चुप

silently *adv.* मौन होकर, चुप-चाप

silhouette *n.* केवल बाहरी रेखा दिखलानेवाला चित्र, तिमिर-चित्र, छाया-चित्र

silk *n.* सिल्क, रेशम, रेशमी कपड़ा

silk-cotton *n.* सेमल

silken *a.* रेशमी, रेशम के समान

silkworm *n.* रेशम का कीड़ा

silky *a.* रेशम के समान कोमल

silly *a.* (*comp.* sillier, *sup.* silliest) मतिहीन, प्रनाड़ी, मूर्ख

silver *n.* चांदी, चांदी की चद्दर, मुद्रा* इत्यादि; *v.t.* चांदी चढ़ाना; silver plate चांदी के चढ़े पात्र; silver-smith चांदी का काम बनानेवाला, सुनार

similar *a.* समान, तुल्य

similarity *n.* सादृश्य, समानता*

simile *n.* (*pl.* similes) उपमा*, समानता*

simmer *v.i. & t.* धीरे धीरे उबलना या उबालना; *n.* मन्द, उबाल

simple *a.* अमिश्र, सरल, एक ही प्रकार का, सहज, निष्कपट,

साधारण, ईमानदार, सीधा-
सादा; simple diet सामान्य
भोजन; simple-hearted
सरल हृदय का

simpleton n. मूर्ख, अनाड़ी

simplicity n. भोलापन, सरलता*

simplify v.t. (p.t. simplified) सरल करना, आसान
बनाना, सुगम करना

simultaneous a. एक ही समय
में होनेवाला, समकालीन,
एक साथ

simultaneously adv. एक ही
समय में, एक साथ

sin n. पाप, अनैतिकता*, दुष्ट-
आचरण; v.i. (p.t. sinned)
पाप करना, अपराध करना

since adv., prep. & conj.
से, जबसे, बाद में, क्योंकि,
आरम्भ करके; ever since
तब से; not long since
थोड़े दिन हुए

sincere a. निष्कपट, सच्चा,
यथार्थ

sincerity n. ईमानदारी*,
सच्चाई*, खरापन

sinful a. पाप-पूर्ण, दुष्ट

sing v i. & t. (p.t. sang,
p.p. sung) गाना, कविता
रचना; to sing out चिल्ला-
कर पुकारना; to sing to
sleep गाकर सुलाना

singer n. गायक, गवैया, गान-
वाला

single a. एक, अकेला, अवि-
वाहित, असहाय; v.t. चुन
लेना; single-eyed एक
आंख का काना

singular a. अकेला, अपूर्व,
विचित्र, असाधारण

singularity n. अपूर्वता*,
विलक्षणता*

singularly adv. विशेष प्रकार
से

sinister a. कुटिल, बुरा, दुष्ट

sink v.t. & i. (p.p. sunk)
डूबना, कुआं खोदना, दबना
या दबाना, कम करना, लुप्त
होना; n. मोरी*, परनाला

sinless a. पाप-रहित, शुद्ध

sinner n. पापी

sip v.t. थोड़ा-थोड़ा करके पीना,
चुस्की लेना; n. चुस्की*

sir n. (fem madam) महाशय,
महोदय, आर्य, श्रीमान, जनाब

siren n. अप्सरा*, मोहिनी*,
स्त्री*, तीव्र शब्द उत्पन्न करने
का भोंपा

sister n. (mas. brother)
बहिन*, धार्मिक सम्प्रदाय की
सदस्या*, भगिनी*

sisterhood n. भगिनीत्व; sister-in-law ननद*, साली*,
भौजाई*

sisterly *a.* बहिन के समान

sit *v.t. & i. (p.t.* sat) बैठना, स्थिर होना, विश्राम करना, बैठाना, भण्डा सेना, भण्डे पर बैठना; to sit at home कार्यहीन रहना; to sit out किसी विषय में भाग लेना; to sit up उठ बैठना

situate-(d) *a.* स्थित, स्थापित

situation *n.* स्थिति*, भ्रवस्था*, कार्य

six *a. & n.* छः ; sixfold छः गुना ; sixth *a.* छठा, sixteen सोलह ; sixteenth *a.* सोलहवां ; sixty *n.* साठ ; sixtieth *a.* साठवां ; at sixes and sevens ब्याकुलता से, घबड़ाहट में

size *n.* परिमाण, भ्राकृति*, रूप, भ्राकार, सरेस, लासा ; *v.t.* भ्राकार के भ्रनुसार क्रम में रखना, सरेस लगाना

skate *n.* स्केट बरफ पर सरकनेवाला जूता ; *v.i.* ऐसा जूता पहनकर सरकना ; roller-skate बरफ घर सरकनेवाला पहिया लगा जूता ; skating-ring इस प्रकार के जूते पहनकर दौड़ने का स्थान

sketch *n.* रेखाकृति*, स्थूल वर्णन, ढांचा ; *v.t.* खाका बनाना, ढांचा बनाना, मान-चित्र खींचना ; sketch-book खाका बनाने की पुस्तक

skilful *a.* प्रवीण, कुशल, चतुर, निपुण

skill *n.* कुशलता*, युक्ति*, चातुरी*

skilled *a.* चतुर, भ्रभ्यस्त

skin *n.* छाल, चमड़ा, झिलका ; *v.t. (p.t.* skinned) खाल उतारना ; only skin and bone कंकाल मात्र ; to change one's skin भ्रसंभव परिवर्तन होना ; to save one's skin सुरक्षित रहना

skirmish *n.* बिना क्रम का युद्ध, हलकी लड़ाई* ; *v.i.* भिड़न्त करना, हलकी लड़ाई लड़ना

skirt *n.* स्कर्ट, वस्त्र का लटकता भाग, स्त्रियों का घावरा, किनारा ; *v.t.* किनारा लगाना

skit *n.* हंसी का भ्रभिनय, भंड़ई*

sky *n. (pl.* skies) भ्राकाश, ऋतु* ; *v.t. (p.t.* skied) गेंद इत्यादि को भ्राकाश में फेंकना ; sky-lark चकोर, चकवा ; skylight छत में खिड़की* ; skyline क्षितिज ; sky-scraper गगन-चुम्बी प्रासाद

slab *n.* पत्थर की चौरस पटिया* ; *v.t.* पटिया या परत भ्रलग'ना

slack *a.* शिथिल, मन्द, कार्य-हीन, ढीला; *v.t. & i.* ढीला करना या होना; to slack off शक्ति कम करना; to slack up गति कम करना

slander *n.* अपवाद, दुर्नाम; *v t.* कलंक लगाना, दुर्नाम करना

slanderous *a.* कलंकी

slang *n.* अशिष्ट भाषा, गंवारू बोलचाल के शब्द

slap *n.* तमाचा; *v.t.* थप्पड़ मारना

slash *v.t.* दीवार या आड़ बनाने के लिए पेड़ों को गिराना, लंबी फांक करना; *n.* लम्बी फांक* लंबी चीर*

slate *n.* स्लेट पत्थर, स्लेट पट्टी*; *v.t.* स्लेट पत्थर बैठाना

slate *v.t.* कड़ी आलोचना करना, धज्जियां उड़ाना, डांटना, फटकारना, गाली देना

slaughter *n.* हत्या, संहार, वध; *v.t.* हत्या करना, वध करना; slaughter-house वधस्थान, कसाईखाना

slave *n.* दास, चाकर; *v.i.* दास की तरह काम करना; slave-bangle कुहनी पर पहनने की बरेखी; slave-born जन्म से दास; slave-hunter दास खोजनेवाला; **slave-trade** दास बेचने और मोल लेने का व्यापार

slavery *n.* दासत्व, गुलामी

slavish *a.* दास तुल्य, तुच्छ, नीच

slay *v.t.* (*p.t.* slew, p p. slain) वध करना, नाश करना

sleek *a.* मुलायम, चिकना, चमकीला

sleekness *n.* चिकनाहट*

sleep *v i.* (*p t. & p.p.* slept) सोना, मरना; *n.* निद्रा*, विश्राम

sleeper *n.* सोनेवाला; आलसी मनुष्य, लकड़ी की धरन जिस पर रेल की लाइन जड़ी होती है

sleeve *n.* बहोली*, आस्तीन*; to laugh in one's s'eeve छिपकर हंसना; to roll up one's sleeve झगड़ा करने के लिए तैयार होना; sleeve-link आस्तीन में लगाने का बटन

slender *a.* दुबला-पतला, छोटा, क्षीण, दुर्बल

slice *v.t.* चौड़े पतले टुकड़े करना; *n.* टुकड़ा, फांक

slick *a.* सामान्य, चतुर, भड़-कीला

slide *v.i. & t.* (*p.t.* slid) बसकना, फिसलना, सरकना;

n. सरकनेवाला भाग, सरकन, स्लाइड

slight *a.* छोटा, तुच्छ, अनावश्यक; *n.* अनादर, तिरस्कार; *v.t.* तिरस्कार करना

slim *a.* दुबला-पतला, धूर्त

sling *v.t. & i.* (*p.t.* slang) फेंकना, लटकना; *n.* ढेलवांस, गांठ उठाने का रस्सा, बरही*

slip *v.t. & i.* (*p.t.* slipped) सरकना, फिसलना, झूठा पैर पड़ना, भूल करना, भागना, ध्यान न देना, चुपके से ले जाना; *n.* दोष, भूल* ढीला बस्त्र, तकिये की खोली*, लकड़ी की पट्टी*

slipper *n.* घर में पहनने का ढीला जूता, चप्पल*, चट्टी*

slippery *a.* सरकनेवाला, अस्थिर

sliver *n.* काठ का टुकड़ा, फरी

slogan *n.* नारा

slope *n.* ढालुआं भूमि*, ढलवान, पर्वत का किनारा; *v.t. & i.* तिरछा या ढालुआं करना या होना; *a.* ढालुआं

slow *a.* मन्द, आलसी, विलम्ब करनेवाला, असावधान; *v.t.* गतिक्रम करना

slowly *adv.* धीरे से, मन्दता से

slowness *n.* मन्दता*, आलस्य

slow-witted *a.* मन्द बुद्धि का

slug *n.* एक प्रकार का घोंघा, आलसी पुरुष, बंदूक की अंडाकार गोली; **slug abed** देर तक चारपाई पर पड़ा रहनेवाला पुरुष

sluggard *n.* निद्रालु, आलसी मनुष्य

sluggish *a.* आलसी, ढीला

sluggishly *adv.* मंद गति से

slum *n.* गन्दी बस्ती*

slumber *v.i.* झपकी लेना, ऊंघना; *n.* झपकी*; to **slumber away** झपकी लेते हुए समय नष्ट करना

slumberous *a.* निद्रालु

slump *n.* किसी पदार्थ के मूल्य में एकाएक ह्रास या गिरावट*, मंदी*

slur *v.t. & i.* (*p.t.* slurred) अस्पष्ट बोलना, शीघ्रता करना, अपमान करना; *n.* निन्दा*, कलंक

slut *n.* (*mas.* solven) मैली-कुचैली स्त्री*

sly *a.* (*comp.* slyer, *sup.* slyest) धूर्त, दुष्ट

smack *n.* स्वाद, अल्प परिमाण, अल्प ज्ञान, मछली मारने की नाव*, ओंठ का शब्द; *v.t. & i.* स्वाद लेना, पटाखा छोड़ना

small *a.* अल्प, थोड़ा, छोटा,

तुच्छ, विनीत; *n.* कोमल
भाग; *adv.* विनीत; भाव से;
small arms बारूद से चलने-
वाले छोटे शस्त्र; smallpox
शीतला रोग, चेचक; small
cause court अदालत
खफीफा, लघुवाद न्यायालय

smart *n.* तीव्र वेदना*; *v.t.*
पीड़ा का अनुभव करना; *a.*
तीव्र, तीक्ष्ण, कठिन, कुशल,
चतुर, तीक्ष्णबुद्धि

smartly *adv.* तीव्रता से,
शीघ्रता से

smash *v t. & i.* टुकड़े करना,
नष्ट होना

smear *v.t.* धब्बा लगाना, मलिन
करना; *n.* धब्बा, मलिनता*

smell *v.t.* (*p.t.*, smelled or
smelt) सूंघना, शंका करना;
n गन्ध ग्रहण करने की
शक्ति*, गन्ध*

smelt *v.t.* गलाकर धातु अल-
गाना

smile *v.t. & i.*, मुस्कराना,
कृपा करना; *n.* मुस्कराहट*
अनुग्रह

smiling *a.* मुस्कराता हुआ,
प्रसन्न

smith *n.* धातु का काम करने-
वाला

smoke *n.* धुआं; *v.t. & i.* धुआं
फेंकना, तमाखू पीना

smoking *n.* धूम्रपान

smoky *a.* धुएं से भरा हुआ,
धुएं के रंग का

smooth *a.* चौरस, चिकना,
मृदु, प्रसन्न, विनीत; *v.t.*
चिकना करना, शांत करना;
smoothing-iron इस्त्री
करने का लोहा; smooth-
tongued चापलूस

smoothen *v.t.* चिकना करना

smoothing *a.* चिकनानेवाला

smoothly *adv.* निर्विघ्नता से

smother *v t.* गला घोंटना,
दबाना, छिपाना; *n.* धूल का
बादल

smoulder *v.i.* बिना ज्वाला के
धुआं देना, भीतर ही भीतर
जलना

smug *n.* बना-ठना हुआ, अपने
ही में प्रसन्न

smuggle *v t.* कर लगनेवाली
सामग्री को चोरी से मंगाना
या बाहर भेजना

smuggler *n.* इस प्रकार (कर न
देने की) चोरी करनेवाला,
चुंगीचोर

smuggling *n.* कर लगनेवाले
माल को चोरी से मंगाना या
भेजना, चुंगीचोरी*

snack *n.* अल्प भोजन, भाग

snag *n.* ठूंठ, उभड़ा हुआ कोना,
आकस्मिक व्यवधान, झड़-

चन*, वाघा*, रुकावट*

snail *n.* घोंघा, आलसी मनुष्य

snake *n.* सांप, धूर्त मनुष्य;
snake-charmer मदारी;
snake-gourd चिचिंडा

snaky *a.* सांप के आकार का

snap *v.t. & i.* (*p.t.*
snapped) भपटना, दांत
काटना, तोड़ना, क्रोध से
बोलना. चलते-फिरते पदार्थ
का छायाचित्र (फोटो) लेना;
n. कड़कड़ाहट*, खटका;
to snap at काटने का
प्रयत्न करना; to snap
out क्रोध से बोलना; to
snap teeth together दांत
कड़कड़ाना; snapshot
चलते-फिरते पदार्थ की फोटो

snarl *n.* गुर्राहट*; *v.i.* गुर्राना

snatch *v.t.* भटके से पकड़ना,
छीन ले जाना; *n.* भपट्टा,
छोटा भाग; by snatches
टुकड़े-टुकड़े करके; to
snatch at पकड़ने के लिए
प्रवृत्त होना; to snatch
off चुरा लेना

sneak *v.t. & i.* चुपके से
देखना, चुराना, चोर की तरह
भागना, नीचता का व्यवहार
करना

sneaking *a.* रहस्यमय, गुप्त,
अधम, नीच

sneeze *v.i.* छींकना; *n.* छींक*

sniff *v.i.* शब्द करते हुए नाक
से हवा खींचना, घृणा प्रकट
करना

snob *n.* गंवार, मोची का
सेवक; भद्रमानी, वर्गदम्भी,
नकचढ़ा अमीर

snobbery *n.* कपटभद्रता*,
मिथ्या वैभव-प्रेम, सभ्यम्म-
न्यता*, अमीरी की अकड़

snobbish *a.* मिथ्या वैभव-प्रेमी,
बना अमीर

snore *v.i.* नींद में खर्राटा लेना

snoring *n.* खर्राटा, घुरकन*

snort *v.i.* नाक से घर्रघर्र का
शब्द करना

snout *n.* पशु का थूथुन

snow *n.* बरफ* तुषार, पाला;
v.i. बरफ की तरह गिरना;
snow-drift वायु से हटाया
हुआ हिम; snow-line जिस
ऊंचाई के ऊपर पर्वत सर्वदा
बरफ से ढका रहता है;
snow-plough बरफ हटाने
का साधन

snowless *a.* बिना बरफ का

snowy *a.* बर्फीला, हिमपूर्ण

snub *n.* भर्त्सना*, गाली*,
ताना; *v.t.* (*p.t.* snubbed)
विनीत करना, भिड़कना;
snub-nose चपटी छोटी
नाक*

snubbing *n.* भिड़की*,
फटकार*

snuff *v.t.* सूंघना; *n.* सूंघनी*,
मोमबत्ती का गुल

so *adv. conj. & pron* इस
प्रकार से, ऐसा, तो भी इस-
लिए; quite so बिलकुल
ठीक या ऐसा ही; so and
so प्रमुक व्यक्ति; so be it
ऐसा ही हो; so far अब तक;
so long तब तक; so to
say मानो, कहने के लिए

soak *v.t. & i.* भिगोना, तर
करना, खूब मदिरा पीना;
n. भीगन

soap *n.* साबुन; *v.t.* साबुन से
धोना

soapy *a.* साबुन के समान,
खुशामदी; soap-nut रीठी

soar *v.i.* ऊपर की ओर उड़ना,
बहुत ऊंचे पर चढ़ना;
n. उड्डयन, उड़ान*

soaring *n.* ऊपर की ओर
उड़ान

sob *v.i.* (*p.t* sobbed)
सिसकना; *n.* सिसकी*

sobbing *n.* सिसकी*, सुबकी*

sober *a.* संयमी, विचारवान,
सचेत, गंभीर शांत, अप्रमत्त;
v.t. & i. संयतमन होना,
अनुत्तेजित होना, शांत
करना, होश में लाना या

होना

sobriety *n.* संयम, स्थिरता*,
गम्भीरता*

sociability *n.* मिलनसारी*
मेल-मिलाप

sociable *a.* मिलनसार, मैत्री-
पूर्ण, मेलमिलापी

sociably *adv.* मिलनसारी से

social *a.* सामाजिक, संघप्रिय
समाज-सम्बन्धी, सांसर्गिक,
मिलनसार, संबंधप्रिय

socialism *n.* समाजवाद,
समाजतंत्र

socialize *v.t.* समाजीकरण
करना, सामाजिक करना,
समाजवादी सिद्धान्तों पर
व्यवस्थित करना

society *n.* समाज, सभा*,
सामाजिक जीवन

sociology *n.* मनुष्य-समाज के
नियम तथा उन्नति का
शास्त्र, समाजशास्त्र, मानव-
समाज तत्व, समाज विज्ञान

sock *n.* (*pl.* sox) छोटा मोजा

socket *n.* सॉकेट, खाना, कोटर,
छेद जिसमें कोई वस्तु बैठाई
जाती हो

soda *n.* सोडा, खार

sodium *n.* सफेद धातु जो सोडा
में पाई जाती है, क्षीरधातु*

sofa *n.* सोफा, पलंग*, सेज*

soft *a.* कोमल, लचीला,

चिकना, सामान्य मृदु, सुकुमार, मधुर; *interj.* चुप; soft colours हलके रंग; soft goods कपड़े; soft-water ऐसा जल जिसमें क्षारीय पदार्थ तथा नमक का अंश बहुत कम हो, कोमल या मृदु जल

soften *v.t. & i.* कोमल करना या होना

softly *adv.* कोमलता से

soil *n.* भूमि*, धरती*, प्रदेश; *v.t. & i.* मैला करना या होना, अपवित्र करना

sojourn *v.i.* प्रवासी होना, प्रवास करना, अस्थायी रूप से वास करना; *n.* अल्पवास, प्रवास, बसेरा

solace *v.t.* धीरज देना, ढांढ़स देना; *n.* ढाढ़स, सान्त्वना*, दिलासा*

solar *a.* सौर, सूर्य-संबंधी; solar eclipse सूर्य-ग्रहण, solar system सौर-मण्डल, सौर-जगत

solarium *n.* रोग निवृत्ति के लिए सूर्य की किरणों के सेवन करने का घर, सौर-चिकित्सालय

soldier *n.* सैनिक, फौजी

soldierly *a.* सैनिक की तरह

sole *n.* तलवा, जूते का तल्ला;

a. अकेला, केवल, अनन्य, एकमात्र, सिर्फ, एक ही

solemn *a.* गम्भीर, धार्मिक, प्रभावशाली, पवित्र

solemnity *n.* गम्भीरता*, शांतचित्तता*

solemnize *v.t.* उत्सव मनाना, संस्कार करना, यथाशास्त्र अनुष्ठान करना

solicit *v t. & i.* (*p.t.* solicited) अनुनय करना, याचना करना, प्रार्थना करना

solicitation *n.* प्रार्थना*, विनती*, मिन्नत*

solicitor *n.* सालीसिटर, उपवकील, निवेदक; S∼ General सॉलिसिटर जनरल, महावादेक्षक

solicitous *a.* उत्सुक, उत्कंठित

solicitude *n.* चिन्ता*, व्यग्रता*, बेचैनी*

solid *a.* संपूर्ण, घन, ठोस, तत्त्वपूर्ण, अविभक्त

solidarity *n.* एकता*, पारस्परिक दायित्व

soliloquy *n.* (*pl.* -quies) स्वगत भाषण, अपने आप बकना

solitary *a.* निर्जन, अकेला, एकान्त

solitude *n.* निर्जन स्थान, अकेलापन

solo n. (pl. solos) सोलो, अकेले का गीत, अकेले बाजे का राग ; solo flight वायुयान पर अकेले उड़ना

soluble a. घुलनशील, हल करने योग्य

solution n. हल, घुलाव, पिघ- लाव, घोल. व्याख्या*, साधन या उत्पत्ति* chemical solution रासायनिक घोल

solve v.t. स्पष्ट करना, व्याख्या करना, प्रश्न का उत्तर निकालना; to slove a doubt सन्देह निवृत्त करना; to slove a question प्रश्न का उत्तर निकालना

solvency n. ऋण चुकाने की योग्यता*

solvent a. &. n. गलाने या घोलनेवाला, घोलक, ऋण चुकाने में समर्थ

some a. pron. & adv. कुछ मात्रा, कुछ संख्या, कोई, करीब-करीब, थोड़ा; some- body n. कोई एक व्यक्ति; somehow किसी प्रकार से ; sometimes कभी-कभी ; somewhat कुछ, थोड़ा-सा ; somewhere किसी अज्ञात स्थान में, कहीं भी

some suf a. उत्पन्न करने वाला' के अर्थ में प्रयुक्त होने- वाला प्रत्यय

somersault n. कलाबाज़ी, गुलांट

son n. (fem. daughter) पुत्र; son-in-law दामाद

song n. गायन, गीत, राग, अनुप्रासयुक्त कविता*

sonnet n सॉनेट, चौदह पंक्ति का गीत

sonometer n. सोनोमीटर, ध्वनिमान, बहरे आदमी की श्रवण-शक्ति जांचने का यंत्र

sonorous a. घोषपूर्ण, मधुर, मंजुल, सुरीला, ओजस्वी, गूंजायमान

soon adv. (comp. sooner, sup. soonest) थोड़े समय में, शीघ्र, झटपट, तुरन्त; no sooner than ज्योंही; soon as त्योंही, तुरन्त; sooner or later देर-सबेर; too soon अति शीघ्र

soot n. कजली, कालिख; v.t. कालिख लगाना

soothing a. शांत करनेवाला, तापहर

sophism n. मिथ्यावाद, सत्या भास, वाक्छल

sorcerer n. (fem. ·ess) जादूगर, ऐन्द्रजालिक

sordid a. नीच, अधम, घटिया, क्षुद्र

sore *a*. पीड़ायुक्त, दुःखदायी, क्षतयुक्त; *n*. घाव, जलन, फोड़ा-फुंसी कसक; *adv*. दुःख से, कष्ट से

sorrow *n*. शोक, खेद, संताप ब्यथा*; *v.i.* शोक करना, दुःख करना

sorrowful *a*. उदास, दुःखी

sorry *a*. दुःखी, खिन्न, उदास, नीच; in a sorry plight शोचनीय अवस्था में

sort *n*. प्रकार, जाति*, ढंग, रीति*; out of sorts अस्वस्थ, रोगी; *v.t. & i.* मेल लगाना, चुनना

soul *n*. शरीरात्मा*, जीव, तेज, तत्त्व, आदर्श

sound *a*. स्वस्थ, भला-चंगा, पूरॆ, ठीक, समूचा, शुद्ध

sound *v.t.* पानी की गहराई नापना, किसी के विचार का पता लगाना

sound *n*. शब्द, कोलाहल; *v.t. & i.* जोर से बोलना, परीक्षा करना

soundly *adv*. स्वस्थ रूप में, दृढ़ता से

soup *n*. सूप, भोल, जूस, शोरबा

sour *a*. खट्टा, तीखा, चिड़चिड़ा; *v.t. & i.* खट्टा करना या होना

source *n*. स्रोत, मूल, आदि-कारण

south *n*. दक्षिण दिशा*; south-east आग्नेय या दक्षिण-पूर्व दिशा*; south-west नैॠत्य या दक्षिण-पश्चिम दिशा*

southern *a*. दक्षिनी

souvenir *n*. स्मारक, पदार्थ, यादगार

sovereign *a*. प्रभुसत्ताधारी, प्रधान, श्रेष्ठ, मुख्य; *n*. राजा, इंग्लैंड का 20 शिलिंग का सोने का सिक्का

sovereignty *n*. प्रभुसत्ता*, प्रभुत्व

Soviet *n*. सोवियत, रूसी श्रमिकों तथा सैनिकों द्वारा निर्वाचित जिला - परिषद, पंचायत, अखिल रूस की प्रतिनिधि कांग्रेस

sow *n*. (*mas*. boar) सुअरी; *v.t.* (*p.t.* sowed, *p p.* sown) बीज बोना, फैलाना

space *n*. अन्तरिक्ष, स्थान, अन्तर, प्रदेश; *v.t.* स्थान छोड़ते हुए क्रम में रखना; pervading all space सब दिशाओं में व्यापक, सर्व-व्यापी; to space out अधिक स्थान फैलाना

spacious *a*. विस्तीर्ण, लम्बा-चौड़ा

spaciousness *n.* विस्तार, फैलाव

spade *n.* कुदाली*, फावड़ा; *v.t.* कुदाली से खोदना

spade-work *n.* आरम्भिक तथा कठिन परिश्रम

span *n.* बित्ता, मेहराव की चौड़ाई, विस्तार, फैलाव; *v.t.* (*p t.* spanned) फैलाना, मेहराब लगाना, बित्ते से नापना

Spaniard *n.* स्पेन देश का निवासी

Spanish *a.* स्पेन देश संबंधी; *n.* स्पेन देश की भाषा

spare *v.t & i.* बचाना, अल्प व्यय करना, रक्षा करना, क्षमा करना; *a.* अल्पव्ययी, थोड़ा, परिमित, कम

spark *n.* चिनगारी*, प्रतिभांश, ज्योति*

sparkle *v.i.* चिनगारी फेंकना, चमकना; *n.* छोटी चिनगारी*

sparrow *n.* चटक, गौरंया पक्षी

Spartan *a.* स्पर्टा नगर संबंधी, वीर और साहसी

spatial *a.* स्थान-संबंधी

speak *v.i. & t.* (*p.t.* spoke, spake, *p p.* spoken) भाषण देना, बोलना, व्याख्या करना; speaking trumpet दूर तक शब्द पहुंचाने- वाली तुरही; speaking-tube बोलने की नली; to speak up चिल्लाकर बोलना; to speak fair शिष्ट भाषा का प्रयोग करना; to speak for किसी के लिए बोलना; to speak ill of निन्दा करना; to speak one's mind अपना विचार प्रकट करना; to speak out प्रकाशित करना

speaker *n.* व्याख्यान देनेवाला, लोकसभा या विधानसभा का अध्यक्ष, वक्ता

specialist *n.* विशेषज्ञ

speciality *n.* विशिष्टता*

specialize *v.t. & i.* विशेषज्ञ होना, अलगाना, विशिष्ट करना, सीमा बांधना

specific *a. & n.* निश्चित, विशिष्ट, स्पष्ट, रोग हटाने की निश्चित औषधि; specific gravity विशिष्ट भार; spec fic medicine किसी रोग को हटाने की विशिष्ट औषधि

specification *n.* विशेष निर्देश, विस्तृत ब्योरा, इमारत का नक्शा और लागत का हिसाब

specify *v.t.* (*p.t.* specified) विशेष रूप से कहना, निश्चित रूप से उल्लेख करना

specified *a.* निर्दिष्ट*, विशिष्ट

specimen *n.* नमूना, बानगी*

spectacle *n.* चमत्कार, कौतुक, तमाशा, (ब०व०) उपनेत्र, चश्मा

spectacled *a.* चश्मा पहने हुए

spectacular *a.* चमत्कारपूर्ण, भव्य, प्रतिदर्शनीय

spectator *n.* (*fem.* spectatress) दर्शक, देखनेवाला, तमाशबीन

spectre *n.* भूत, पिशाच, प्रेतच्छाया*

spectrum *n.* (*pl.* spectra) रूपच्छटा*, वर्ण-क्रम, वर्ण-पट

speculate *v.i.* विचार करना, कल्पना करना, ख्याली घोड़े दौड़ाना, सट्टा करना

speculation *n.* सट्टेबाजी*, चिन्तन, दूरकल्पना*, अटकल-बाजी*

speech *n.* वाणी*, भाषा* व्याख्यान; eloquence of speech पदलालित्य; figure of speech अलंकार; maiden speech व्याख्यान-दाता का पहला भाषण; parts of speech शब्दभेद

speechless *a.* मूक, गूंगा

speed *v.t. & i.* (*p.t.* sped) शीघ्रता करना, सफल होना, सहायता देना; *n.* शीघ्रता*, सफलता*, गति*, रफ्तार*

speedily *adv.* झट, तुरन्त

speediness *n.* शीघ्रता*, जल्दी

speedy *a.* तीव्र, शीघ्र

spell *n.* जादू, टोना, मोहन-मन्त्र; spell-bound जादू से मोहित

spell *v.t.* (*p.t.* spelled *or* spelt) हिज्जे करना; to spell back-wards अर्थ बदलना; to spell out अक्षरों के क्रम से उच्चारण करना

spelling *n.* अक्षर-विन्यास, हिज्जे

spend *v.t.* (*p.t. & p.p.* spent) व्यय करना, लुटाना, खर्च करना

spendthrift *n.* अपव्ययी, खर्चीला, फिजूलखर्च, धन उड़ानेवाला मनुष्य

sphere *n.* गोलक, नक्षत्र, व्यवसाय, क्षेत्र

spheric (-al) गोलाकार, दिव्य

spice *n.* सुगन्धित द्रव्य, मसाला; *v.t.* मसालेदार बनाना

spicy *a.* सुगन्धित, दिखौवा, मसालेदार, तीखा

spider *n.* मकड़ा

spill *v.t.* (*p.t.* spilled *or* spilt) गिराना, बहाना; *n.*

बहाव, गिराव; to spill
blood हत्या करना

spin v.t. (p.t. span p p.
spun) सूत कातना, घुमाना
या चक्कर देना; n. चक्कर,
घुमाव

spinal a. रीढ़ की हड्डी का;
spinal column पीठ की
रीढ़, मेरुदण्ड; spinal cord
इस रीढ़ के भीतर की नाड़ी*,
सुषुम्ना*

spindle n. धुरा, टेकुआ,
तकुआ, तकली*

spine n. पीठ की रीढ़*, कांटे-
दार उभाड़

spinner n. कातनेवाला

spiral a. चक्राकार, पेचदार,
नोकदार; n. चक्कर, चक्कर-
दार कमानी

spirit n. प्राण, आत्मा*, प्रेत,
चित्तवृत्ति, वीरता, साहस,
प्रसन्नता*, चेष्टा*, प्रभाव,
सत्त्व सारांश, स्पिरट, (ब॰व॰)
मदिरा*; v.t. प्रसन्न करना,
उत्तेजित करना; departed
spirit प्रेतात्मा; gentle
spirit स्वभाव की सुजनता;
the spirit of the age
युग-भावना*; in good
spirits प्रसन्नतापूर्ण; in
high spirits उत्साह सहित;
spirit level समतल नापने

का यन्त्र

spirited a. साहसी, तेजस्वी

spiritless a. तेजहीन, उत्साह-
हीन

spiritual a. आध्यात्मिक,
धार्मिक, पवित्र

spiritualism n. अध्यात्मवाद

spiritualist n. अध्यात्मवादी,
ब्रह्मवादी

spirituality n. आध्यात्मिकता*,
पवित्रता*, धार्मिकता*

spit n. सींकचा थूक*; v.t.
(p.t. spitted) सींक भोंकना;
v.i. (p.t. spat) थूकना,
फूही पड़ना, खखारना

spitfire n. अति क्रोधी मनुष्य

spittoon n. पीकदान, उगालदान

splash v.t. पानी का छींटा
देना, कीचड़ उड़ाना; n.
छींटा, बौछार, छपाके का
शब्द

spleen n. प्लीहा, बरबट, रोष,
क्रोध

splendent a. चमकीला,
उज्ज्वल, देदीप्यमान, धातु के
समान चमकता हुआ

splendid a. श्रेष्ठ, प्रतापवान,
भव्य, महान

splendour n. शोभा*, प्रताप,
विभव

splinter n. चीरी हुई पट्टी; v.t.
पतली पट्टी चीरना

split v.t. & i. (p.t. split)
फाड़ना, धज्जी करना, फूटना,
अलग होना; n. दल में
विघटन*, फूट*, विभेद,
दरार*, फटन*

splitter n. तोड़क, अलगाने-
वाला

spoil v.t. & i. (p.t. spoiled,
spoilt) नष्ट करना, भ्रष्ट
करना या होना, लूटना;
n. लूट

spoke n. पहिए की तीली*,
सीढ़ी का डण्डा

spokesman n. प्रतिनिधि,
प्रवक्ता

sponge n. एक समुद्री प्राणी,
स्पन्ज, जलसोख; v.t. स्पन्ज
से धोना सुखाना

sponsor n. ज़ामिन, प्रतिभू,
धर्मपिता

spontaneity n. स्वयंस्फूर्ति*,
सहजता*

spontaneous a. आत्मस्फूर्त,
अपने आप, स्वयंजात, नैसर्गिक,
स्वाभाविक

spoon n. चम्मच, मूर्ख मनुष्य;
v t. चम्मच से लेना; born
with a silver spoon in
one's mouth जन्म से
भाग्यवान; desert-spoon
दो ड्राम का चम्मच

sporadic a. छिटपुट, कहीं-

कहीं, जहां-तहां

sport n. खेल, क्रीड़ा*, हंसी*,
लीला*; v.t. & i. खेलना,
हंसी करना, प्रसन्न करना;
to make sport of उपहास
करना, हंसी उड़ाना

sportive a. विनोदी, खिलाड़ी,
चंचल

sportsman n. मृगयासेवी,
खिलाड़ी

sportsmanlike a. खिलाड़ी की
तरह का

spot n. स्थान, कलंक, लांछन;
v t. (p.t. spotted) धब्बा
डालना, चिह्नित करना

spotless a. पवित्र कलंकहीन

sprain v.t. पेशी को मरोड़ना,
ऐंठना; n. मरोड़*, मुरक*,
मोच*

spray n. पतली शाखा*,
टहनी*, फूलों का गुच्छा,
बौछार; v.t. (p.t. sprayed)
छिड़कना, फुहार डालना

spread v.t. (p.t. & p p.
spread) फैलाना, तानना,
छितराना ढांपना; n. फैलाव,
विस्तार

spree n. आनन्द का उत्सव,
नाच-रंग

spring v.i. &t. (p.t. sprang,
p p. sprung) निकलना,
उगना, कूदना, चौंकना, प्रकट

होना, प्रस्ताव करना, फूटना, फाड़ना; *n.* कुदान*, लचीला- पन, कमानी का बल, शक्ति*, स्फूर्ति* उद्गम, भरना, वसन्त ऋतु*; spring-tide ज्वार; sprung from a noble family उच्च कुल में उत्पन्न; sprung from a royal family राजकुल में उत्पन्न

sprinkle *v.t.* छिड़कना; *n.* छिड़काव

sprout *v.i.* अंखुवा निकलना, जमना; *n.* पौधे का अंखुआ, कोंपल

spurious *a.* मिथ्या, बनावटी, जाली

sputum *n.* (*pl.* sputa) लार, थूक

spy *v.i.* (*p.t.* spied) दूर से देखना, जांच करना, भेद लगाना; *n.* जासूस, भेदिया

squad *n.* दस्ता, जत्था, झुंड

squadron *n.* सैनिक सवारों का जत्था, जहाज़ी बेड़े का भाग, विमान दल

squalor *n.* गंदगी*, दरिद्रता*, मलिनता*

squander *v.t.* वृथा व्यय करना, धन लुटाना

square *a.* समचतुर्भुज के आकार का, ठीक बराबर, चौरस,

निष्कपट; *n.* समकोण चतु- र्भुज, चौकोर मैदान जिसके चारों ओर घर बने हों, गोनिया, वर्ग, द्विघात; *v.t.* चौकोर करना, ठीक करना, हिसाब तय करना; on the square सचाई से; square root वर्गमूल; square deal- ing निष्कपट व्यवहार; to square the circle असंभव कार्य करना; to square up घूस देना

squarely *adv.* पूर्ण रूप से

squash *v.t.* कुचलना, दबाना, विनती करना; *n.* रस, कुचला, मुलायम वस्तु के गिरने की आवाज

squeak *v.i* चीखना, चिल्लाना; *n.* चीत्कार; a narrow squeak बाल-बाल बचना

squeeze *v.t.* दबाना, निचोड़ना, दबाव डालकर धन लेना

squint *v i.* कनखी से देखना; *n.* कनखी, ऐंची आंख

squire *n.* स्क्वायर, एक अंग्रेजी पदवी*, देहात का ठाकुर, जमींदार, नवाब का सेवक

squirrel *n.* गिलहरी*, चिखुरी*

stab *v.t.* (*p.t.* stabbed) नुकीले अस्त्र से प्रहार करना; *n.* छुरे का घाव, खोंच, भोंक; to stab in the back निन्दा

338

करना; to stab in the secret परोक्ष में मर्मभेद करना

stability *n.* स्थिरता*

stable *a.* स्थिर, निश्चल, ठिकाऊ

stable *n.* घुड़साल *v t.* घुड़साल में रखना

stadium *n.* स्टेडियम, क्रीड़ागन, मञ्च

staff *n.* (*pls.* staves, staffs) डण्डा, आबार, मूठ, स्टाफ, अधिकारियों का समूह

stag *n.* (*fem.* hind) हिरन, बारहसिंगा

stage *n.* मचान, चबूतरा, रंग-भूमि*, नाट्यशाला*, दृश्य, विश्रामस्थान, कार्यक्रम; *v.t.* & *i.* नाटक खेलना; stage-coach यात्रियों को ले जाने-वाली गाड़ी*;'डाक*; stage-craft नाटक खेलने की कला; stage-manager सूत्रधार

stagnant *a.* गतिहीन, स्थिर, मन्द

stagnate *v.i.* प्रवाह का रुकना, स्थिर होना, थम जाना

stagnation *n.* स्थिरता*, निश्चलता*

stainless *a.* निर्मल, कलंकरहित

stair *n.* सीढ़ी*; down-stairs घर का नीचे का खंड, flight

of stairs सीढ़ियों की पंक्ति; spiral staircase घुमौवा सीढ़ी; staircase सीढ़ियों की पंक्ति

stake *n.* खूंटा, शंकु, दांव, परण; *v.t.* दांव लगाना, खूंटे म बांधना; at stake सन्देह में, कठिनाई में

stale *a.* पुराना, बासी, बेस्वाद, नीरस; *v.t.* बेस्वाद करना, पुराना करना, बासी बनाना

stall *n* घुड़साल, छोटी दूकान*; *v.t.* घुड़साल में बांधना, बिक्री के लिए सजाना

stalwart *a.* वीर, साहसी, राजनीतिक दल का पक्का समर्थक, जीवट का, दिलेर

stamina *n.* बल, सहनशक्ति*, जीवट

stammer *v.t.* हकलाना, रुक-रुककर बोलना

stamp *v t* & *i.* पैर पटकना, ठप्पा लगाना, कुचलना, टिकट लगाना, दबाना; *n.* ठप्पा, मुहर* टिकट, मुहर करने का यंत्र, चरित्र; of the common stamp सामान्य प्रकृति का; of high stamp महानुभाव; of the same stamp तुल्य स्वभाव का; to stamp out ग्रत करना, समाप्त करना

stampede *n.* भगदड़*, खल-
बली*

stanch *v.t. & i.* घाव से खून
का बहाव रोकना, बहाव बन्द
करना, सूख जाना; *a.* स्थिर

stand *v.i. & t.* (*p.t. & p.p.*
stood) खड़ा होना या रखना,
रुकना, ठहरना, स्थिर रहना,
सहना, चुनाव के लिए खड़ा
होना, किसी सिद्धान्त पर दृढ़
रहना; hair stands on
end रोमांचित होना, रोंगटे
खड़ा होना; it stands to
reason यह न्यायसंगत है;
stand ly *n.* सहारा, आश्रय;
the matter stands thus
विषय ऐसा है; to stand
against बाधा डालना; to
stand at bay ठमककर
लड़ना; to stand by सहायता
देना, समर्थन करना, अड़ जाना;
to stand off हट जाना;
to stand on हठ करना;
to stand out आक्षेप करना;
to stand over टालना; to
stand still निश्चल खड़े
होना; to stand the test
परीक्षा की कसौटी पर चढ़ना
stand *n.* स्थिर दिशा*, रुका-
वट*, स्थान, व्याकुलता*,
आश्रय, चबूतरा, गाड़ियों के
ठहरने का अड्डा

standard *n.* मापदण्ड, पताका*,
झण्डा, नियम, रीति*, आदर्श,
मान, प्रमाण; *a.* अति उत्तम;
standard author प्रामा-
णिक ग्रन्थकार

standardize *v.t.* प्रमाण के
अनुसार करना

standing *a. & n.* खड़ा, स्थायी,
स्थिर पद, प्रसिद्धि*

standpoint *n.* सिद्धान्त

stanza *n.* पद्यांश, श्लोक, छन्द

staple *a.* मुख्य, प्रधान; *n.*
कुलाबा, कुण्डा; सौदा.
सामग्री*, प्रधान अंश, रेशम
या सूत का रेशा

star *n.* तारा, प्रसिद्ध पुरुष, छापे
में तारे का चिह्न; *v.t.* (*p.t.*
starred) तारों से सजाना

stare *v.t.* घूरना, ताकना; *n.*
टकटकी*

starry *a.* तारों से पूर्ण

start *v.i. & t.* चौंक पड़ना,
चिहुँक उठना, चल देना.
आरम्भ करना. कूदना, चालू
करना; by fits and starts
आकस्मिक प्रयत्न से; to get
a start of सुविधा पाना;
to start aside स्थान से
विचलित होना; to start in
आरम्भ करना; to start up
चौंक उठना; to start with
आरम्भ में; *n.* चिहुँक*, यका-

यक गति*, प्रारम्भ

starting n. प्रस्थान; starting-post जिस खंभे से घुड़दौड़ इत्यादि का आरंभ होता है

startle v.t. चौंकाना, घबड़ाना

startling a. चौंकानेवाला

starvation n. उपवास, अनशन

starve v.t. & i. क्षुधा से पीड़ित होना, भूखों मरना, ठंड से कष्ट उठाना, उपवास करना, अकालग्रस्त होना, अभावग्रस्त होना

starving a. क्षुधा से पीड़ित, निराहार

state n. अवस्था*, दशा*, पद, धूमधाम, जीवनवृत्ति*, राज्य; v.t. वर्णन करना, प्रकट करना, स्थिर करना; a. सर्वसामान्य, राजकीय; state affairs राजकीय; in state वैभव में; chair of state राजसिंहासन; statecraft राजकार्य-पद्धति, राजनीति

stateliness n. महत्त्व, गौरव

stately a. महत्त्व का, वैभवयुक्त

statement n. वक्तव्य, बयान, वर्णन

statesman n. नीतिमान, राजनीतिज्ञ, राज्यमर्मज्ञ, राजनायक

statesmanlike a. राजनीतिज्ञ के सदृश

statesmanship n. राज-

नीतिज्ञता*

station n. स्थान, पद, स्थिति*, रेल के ठहरने का स्थान, थाना, शस्त्र रखने का स्थान, ठिकाना; v.t. बैठाना

stationary a. अचल, निश्चल, स्थिर

stationer n. स्टेशनर, लेखन-सामग्री बेचनेवाला

stationery n. स्टेशनरी, लेखन-सामग्री*

statistician n. सांख्यिक, आंकिक

statistical a. आंकड़ा-संबंधी

statistics n. pl. सांख्यिकी*, आंकिकी*, आंकड़े

statue n. मूर्ति*, प्रतिमा*, बुत*

stature n. डील-डौल, आकार; of dwarfish stature बौने के आकारवाला; of low stature नाटा; of short stature नाटे कद का

status n. पद, सामाजिक स्थिति*

statute n. विधि*, व्यवस्था*, स्थिर नियम

statutory a. वैधिक, संविहित, कानूनी; statutory rationing संविहित राशन व्यवस्था*

staunch, stanch a. दृढ़, पक्का विश्वसनीय, कट्टर, मजबूत

stave n. डंडा, पीपा बनाने की

पटरी*; *v.t.* (*p.t. & p p.* staved *or* stove) छेद करना, टालना; to stave in कुचलकर टेढ़ा-मेढ़ा करना; to stave off हटा देना

stay *v.t. & i.* (*p.t.* stayed) ठहराना. रोकना, ठिकाना, सहारा देना; *n.* ठहराव, रुकाव; stay order निर्णय का कुछ काल के लिए स्थगन; to stay one's progress गति या उन्नति रोकना

steadfast *a.* स्थिर, अटल

steady *a.* (*comp.* steadier, *sup.* steadiest) दृढ़, प्रचल, स्थिर, विश्वासी; *v.t. & i.* (*p.t.* steadied) स्थिर होना या करना

steal *v.t. & i.* (*p.t.* stole, *p.p.* stolen) चोरी करना, खिसक जाना, चुपके से भाग जाना

stealthily *adv.* चोरी से, चुपके से

steam *n.* भाप*, शक्ति*, उत्साह; *v.t. & i.* भाप निकालना, भाप बनकर उड़ना

steamer *n.* स्टीमर, भाप से चलनेवाला जहाज

steel *n.* इस्पात, पक्का लोहा, वज्रलोह के बने शस्त्र,

स्थिरता*; steel-hearted कठोर-हृदय, निर्दय; *a.* इस्पात का बना हुआ या इसके समान; *v.t.* कड़ा करना, पक्का करना

steep *v.t.* भिगोना, गीला करना; *n.* गीला करने की विधि*

steer *v.t. & i.* जहाज, नाव, मोटर, वायुयान, बाइसिकिल इ० चलाना, मार्ग दिखलाना; steersman जहाज चलाने-वाला, कर्णधार, मांझी

stencil *n.* स्टेंसिल, पतले धातु इत्यादि के पत्तर पर कटा हुआ चित्र इ० जिसकी छाप दूसरे पदार्थ पर रंग की कूंची से उतारी जाती है; *v.t.* (*p.t.* stencilled) स्टेंसिल से छापना

stenographer (-ist) *n.* स्टेनो-ग्राफर, शीघ्रलिपिक, शार्टहैंड राइटर

step *n.* पग, थोड़ी दूरी*, गति*, कार्य, क्रम, पद, सीढ़ी का डण्डा; *v.t.* (*p.t.* stepped) चलना, डग बढ़ाना; to step back पीछे को हटना; to step in घुसना; stepping-stone कीचड़, पानी इत्यादि से पार जाने के लिए रक्खी हुई शिला, उन्नति का मार्ग;

step-brother, step-child, step-mother &c. सौतेला भाई, बालक, बालिका, माता इत्यादि

steppe *n.* स्टेपी, वृक्षहीन विस्तृत भूभाग या तृण-क्षेत्र, घास का मैदान

stereoscope *n.* एक प्रकार की दूरबीन जिसके द्वारा चित्र ठोस दीख पड़ते हैं, सैरबीन

stereotype *n.* छापने का ठोस सीसे का पटरा; *v.t.* ऐसे पटरे पर से छापना

stereotyped *a.* दृढ़, घिसा-पिटा

sterile *a.* बांझ, ऊसर

sterility *n* निष्फलता*, ऊसर-पन, वन्ध्यात्व

sterilization *n.* जीवाणुहनन, वन्ध्यकरण, निष्कीटन, बांझ बनाने का कार्य

sterilize *v.t.* जीवाणुशून्य करना, वन्ध्य या बांझ करना विनिवृत्त करना

sterling *a.* खरा, सच्चा; *n.* शुद्ध, प्रामाणिक, खरा (सोने का) सिक्का, पौण्ड ; ∼ balance पौण्ड पावना

stethoscope *n.* स्टेथेस्कोप, हृदय या फेफड़े की गति सुनने का यंत्र, हृद्ध्वक्षण-यंत्र

stevedore *n.* जहाज़ी कुली

stew *v.t.* धीमी आंच देकर पकाना; *n.* मन्द अग्नि पर पका हुआ मांस या तरकारी;

stewpan *n.* छिछली कड़ाही; to stew in one's own juice अपना ही स्वार्थ देखते रहना

steward *n.* (*fem.* stewardess) जागीर का प्रबंधक, गृह प्रबन्धक, कार्याध्यक्ष, जहाज़ी यात्रियों का सेवक

stick *v.t. & i.* (*p t.* stuck) भोंकना, कोंचना, ऐंठना, चिपकाना; stuck in the mud उन्नति न करनेवाला; to stick in चिपकाना; to stick in the throat गले में फंसना, निगलने में कष्ट होना; to stick out फैलाना; to stick to a point अपने सिद्धान्त पर दृढ़ रहना; to stick up खड़ा होना

stick *n.* डण्डा, लकड़ी*, छड़ी*

sticky *a.* चिपचिगा, चिपकने-वाला

stiff *a.* कड़ा, मोटा, हठी. कठिन; stiff-necked हठी; stiff-price ऊंचा दाम

stifle *v t* गला घोंटना; मन्द करना, दबाना

stifling *a.* गलाघोंटू

stigma *n.* (*pls.* stigmas, stigmata) अपमान, लांछन,

कलंक का धब्बा

still *a.* शान्त, निश्चल, स्थिर, चुप; *v.t* शान्त करना; *adv.* तो भी, अब भी, सर्वदा, कभी-कभी; *n.* अर्क खींचने का डेग, बंकयंत्र, भबका; **still-birth** मरा बच्चा पैदा होना; **still lake** बिना लहर की झील; **still life** स्टिल-लाइफ चित्र

stillness *n.* शान्ति*, मौन*

stimulant *a* & *n.* उत्तेजक, शक्तिवर्धक, शक्ति वढ़ानेवाली औषधि*

stimulate *v i.* प्रेरित करना, उत्तेजित करना, उसकाना

stimulation *n.* उत्तेजना*, प्रोत्साहन

stimulative *a* प्रवृत्त करनेवाला, उत्तेजक

stimulus *n.* (*pl.* stimuli) प्रोत्साहन, उसकाव

sting *v t.* & *i.* (*p.t.* & *p p.* stung) डंक मारना, अत्यन्त पीड़ा देना; *n.* डंक, विष का दांत, घाव, मर्म

stink *v i.* & *t.* (*p.t.* stank, *p.p* stunk) दुर्गन्ध निकलना या निकालना; *n* दुर्गन्ध*

stipend *n.* छात्रवृत्ति*, वेतन, वृत्ति*

stipulate *v.t.* & *i.* प्रतिज्ञा करना, बन्धेज करना, अनुबन्ध करना, समझौते की आवश्यक शर्तें पर बल देना

stipulation *n.* नियम, प्रतिज्ञा*, अनुबन्ध, करार

stir *v.t.* & *i.* (*p.t.* stirred) हिलाना, चलना, उत्तेजित करना, चालू करना; **to stir abroad** घर के बाहर जाना; **to stir the fire** आग को तेज करना; **to stir up** उत्तेजित करना

stitch *v.t.* सीना, टांका लगाना; *n.* सियन, टांका; **a stitch in time saves nine** समय पर किया हुआ थोड़ा-सा यत्न भी बड़े लाभ का होता है; **to drop a stitch** सियन की रचना काटकर रोक देना; **to put a stitch** घाव में टांका लगाना

stock *n.* तना, मूठ, आधार, वंश, कुटुम्ब, सामग्री*, मूल सामग्री*, मूलधन, पशु; *v.t.* इकट्ठा करना, ढेर लगाना, बिक्री के लिए रखना; *a.* अचल, सामान्य; **stocks and stones** निर्जीव पदार्थ, उत्साहहीन मनुष्य; **laughing stock** तिरस्कार का पात्र; **to have in stock** भंडार में होना; **stock-**

exchange सरकारी हुण्डी खरीदने या बेचने का स्थान

stocking n. पैर का मोजा

stoic n. सुख-दुःख को समान समझनेवाला, उदासी, वैरागी

stomach n पेट ग्रामाशय, रुचि*; v.t. धैर्य से सहना

stone n. शिला*, पत्थर, रत्न, स्मरणार्थ शिला*, कड़ा बीज, पथरी जो मूत्राशय में पड़ जाती है सात.सेर की तौल; v.t. पत्थर से मारना, पत्थर बैठाना; a heart of stone कठोर हृदय; stone blind पूरा ग्रन्धा; stonecutter संगतराश; stone-mill जांता; stones will cry out ऐसी निदयता जो प्राणहीन को भी प्रभावित कर देती है; to give a stone for bread दिखावटी सहायता करना; to leave no stone unturned कोई उपाय बाकी न छोड़ना; to stone to death ढेलों से मार डालना

stony a पत्थर के समान, कड़ा, दयाहीन

stool n. तिपाई*, चौकी*, मल, ठूंठ

stoop v.i. & t. शरीर का झुकना, झुकाना, अधीन होना; n. शरीर का झुकाव

stop v.t. & i. (p t. stopped) ठमकना, रुकना, रोकना, ग्रन्त करना; to stop a bullet गोली खाना; to stop down फोटो के कैमरे के ताल का छिद्र कम करना; to stop one's ears बातें न सुनना; to stop short एका-एक रुक जाना; n. रुकावट*, विश्राम, ग्रन्त, विराम का चिह्न; full stop पूर्ण विराम का चिह्न

stoppage n. अवरोध, रुकावट*

store n. संचय, सामग्री*, अधिकता* कार्यालय, (ब०व०) भण्डार; in store तैयार; store-house भण्डारघर; v.t. इकट्ठा करना, भण्डार में रखना

storey, story n. (pls. storeys, stories) मकान का खण्ड

stork n. सारस

storm n. ग्रांधी*, संक्षोभ, विप्लव, झगड़ा, किले पर आक्रमण; v.t. & i. क्रोध करना. आक्रमण करना; storm-bound ग्रांधी के कारण किनारे पर रुका हुआ (जहाज); storm in a tea-cup थोड़ी-सी बात के लिए भयंकर उपद्रव

stormy *a.* तूफानी

story *n.* (*pl* stories) कहानी*, वृत्तान्त. कथा*; quite another story दूसरा ही वृत्तान्त; the story goes ऐसा कहा जाता हैं

stout *a.* बलवान मोटा, साहसी, स्थूल शरीर का; stout-hearted *a.* वीरहृदय

stove *n.* चूल्हा, भट्टी*

straight *a.* सीधा, सच्चा, ईमानदार

straighten *v.t.* सीधा करना

straightforward *a* स्पष्टवक्ता, सत्यवादी, ईमानदार

straightway *adv.* तुरन्त

strain *v.t. & i.* तानना कसकर पकड़ना, थकाना, छानना; *n* श्रम, तनाव, कविता*, गीत; in another strain दूसरे लय में

strand *n.* तीर, तट, रस्से का बल, भांज; *v t.* किनारे पर लगना, असहाय हो जाना

strange *a.* अद्भुत, परदेशी, अपरिचित

stranger *n.* परदेशी

strangely *adv.* विलक्षण प्रकार से

strangle *v.t.* गला घोंटकर मारना, दबाना

strap *n.* तस्मा, चमोटा; *v.t.*

(*p.t.* strapped) तस्मे से बांधना, चमोटे पर उस्तरा तेज करना

strategic (-al) *a.* रणनीति-* सबंधी

strategy *n.* रणनीति*, व्यूह रचना*

stratum *n.* (*pl* strata) तह*, परत*, स्तर

straw *n.* पुआल, भूसा, तुच्छ पदार्थ; man of straw निःसत्त्व पुरुष; to catch at a straw शक्तिहीन वस्तु का सहारा लेना; to make a straw of तृण समान जानना

strawberry *n.* फरबेर

stray *v.t.* (*p t.* strayed) विचरना, भटकना; *a.* बिखरा हुआ, कभी-कभी भेंट करनेवाला

stream *n.* स्रोत, धारा*, प्रवाह; *v.i.* धारा में बहना, फैलना

streamer *n.* लम्बा संकरा झण्डा, आलोकप्रवाह

streamlet *n.* छोटी धारा*

streamy *a.* धारायुक्त, धारा में बहनेवाला

street *n.* गली*; on the street वेश्यावृत्तिवाली स्त्री; royal street राजमार्ग; the man in the street

सामान्य मनुष्य

strength n. शक्ति*, बल, पुष्टता*, प्रभाव, दल ; on the strength of प्रोत्साहन से, अवलंबन करके; strength of mind बुद्धि का बल

strengthen v.t. & i. पुष्ट करना या होना, उत्साह देना

strenuous a. उत्साही, उद्योगी, हठी

stress n. दबाव, बल, शक्ति*, प्रयत्न, किसी शब्द या अक्षर का विशिष्ट उच्चारण; v.t. विशिष्ट उच्चारण करना

stretch v.t. बढ़ाना, लम्बा करना, खींचना, तानना; n. विस्तार, फैलाव; to stretch one on the ground मार-कर भूमि पर लिटा देना; to stretch out फैलाना; to stretch the truth अत्युक्ति करना

stretcher n. स्ट्रेचर, डोली*, टिखठी*

strict a. नियत, दृढ़, प्रलंघनीय, सख्त

strictly adv. वस्तुत:

stricture तीव्रालोचना*, निन्दा-त्मक प्रभुक्ति*

stride v.i. (p.t. strode, p.p. stridden) लम्बे-लम्बे डगों से चलना; n. लम्बा डग

strife n. कलह, झगड़ा, शत्रुता*

strike v.t. (p.p. stricken) हड़ताल करना, मारना, धक्का देना दबाना, घुसाना, घण्टा बजाना हिसाब तय करना, खेमा उखाड़ना; n. हड़ताल*; struck with wonder चकित; to strike accounts हिसाब करना; to strike at the root of जड़ समेत नष्ट करना; to strike back जवाबी हमला करना; to strike fear in the mind चित्त में भय उत्पन्न करना; to strike one's flag गढ़ को शत्रु के हाथों समर्पण करना; to strike up acquaintance शीघ्र परिचय करना; to strike while the iron is hot उत्साह के समय काम करना

striking a. प्रभावशाली

string n. डोरी*, रस्सी*, तांत*, बन्धन; string of pearls मोतियों की माला*; v.t. तार चढ़ाना, तांत लगाना; to harp on the same string एक ही विषय में लीन होना; to have two strings to one bow दुहरा लाभ उठाना; to pull the strings किसी

कार्य का सूत्रधार होना; to touch the strings सारंगी बजाना आरम्भ करना

stringency *n.* कठोरता*, दृढ़ता*; अर्थ संकट, तंगी*

strip *v t.* (*p.t.* stripped) नंगा करना, छिलका उतारना, छांटना; *n.* धज्जी*, पट्टी*, टुकड़ा; to strip a cow गाय का सब दूध दुह लेना; to strip off सब कपड़े उतारना

stripe *n.* पट्टी*, धारी*, लकीर*, कोड़े का चिह्न; *v.t.* लकीर डालना

strive *v.i.* (*p.t.* strove, *p.p.* striven) प्रयत्न करना, उद्यम करना, झगड़ना

stroke *n.* आघात, धक्का, चोट*, रोग का एकाएक आक्रमण, लेखनी या कूंची से बनाई हुई लकीर*; *v.t.* आघात पहुंचाना, धक्का मारना; on the stroke ठीक समय पर; stroke of business लाभ का व्यापार

stroke *v t.* सुहराना, थपथपाना; *n.* थपकी*, to stroke one down शांत करना, ठण्डा करना; to stroke one's hair the wrong way उत्तेजित करना, क्रुद्ध करना

stroll *v.i.* विचरना, इधर-उधर भटकना; *n.* परिभ्रमण

strong *a.* पुष्ट, बलवान, प्रबल, तीव्र पराक्रमी दृढ़, समर्थ, सुरक्षित; of strong smell उग्र गन्ध का; of strong mind तीक्ष्ण बुद्धिवाला; strong market भाव बढ़ने का बाजार; strong support पूर्ण रूप से सहायता; strong verbs जिस क्रिया का भूतकाल का रूप शब्द के भीतरी स्वर के बदलने से बनता है

stronghold *n.* किला, दुर्ग, आन्दोलन का केन्द्र

structural *a.* रचना-संबंधी

structure *n.* रचना*, बनावट*, आकार ढंग

struggle *v.t.* प्रयत्न करना, संघर्ष करना, छटपटाना

strut *n.* अकड़ की चाल*; *v.i.* अकड़कर चलना

stubborn *a.* हठी, अड़ियल

stud *n.* फूलदार माथे का कांटा, कमीज का दोहरे सिरे का बटन; *v.t.* फूलदार कांटा जड़ना; collar-stud कालर में लगाने का बटन; studded with stars तारे जड़े हुए; studfarm घोड़ा पालने का स्थान

student *n.* छात्र, अध्येता,

विद्यार्थी

studio *n.* (*pl.* studios) स्ट्डिग्रो, चित्रशाला*, रंग-शाला*

studious *a.* विचारवान, परि-श्रमी, विद्याभ्यासी

study *n.* (*pl.* studies) विचार, अध्ययन, विद्या*, लेख, ध्यान, पढ़ने-लिखने का कमरा; *v.t. & i.* (*p.t.* studied) विचारना, परिश्रम से विद्याभ्यास करना; in brown study विचार से लीन; to study for the bar विधि (कानून) पढ़ना; to make a study of भली-भांति अन्वेषण करना; to study out ध्यान देकर अन्वेषण करना; to study up परीक्षा के लिए तैयारी करना

stuff *n.* सामग्री*, पदार्थ, तुच्छ पदार्थ, वृथा-वकवाद; *v.t.* भरना, बन्द करना

stuffy *a.* भरा हुआ, गला घोंटनेवाला।

stumble *v.i. & t.* ठोकर खाना, गिर पड़ना, भूल करना, अनायास मिलना; stumbling-block अवरोध, कठोर रुकावट*

stun *v.t.* (*p.t.* stunned) स्तम्भित करना, मूर्च्छित करना, घबड़ाना

stunt *v.t.* इश्तहारबाज़ी करना, बौना करना, नाटा करना

stupefy *v.t.* (*p.t.* stupefied) मूर्च्छित करना, मतिमन्द करना

stupendous *a.* विलक्षण, अपूर्व

stupid *a.* मन्द, मूर्ख, निर्बुद्धि, बुद्धिहीन

stupidity *n.* मूर्खता*, अज्ञानता*

sturdy *a.* पुष्ट, दृढ़, प्रबल

style *n.* नुकीली लेखनी*, रीति* वाग्व्यवहार, गढ़ना*, रीति*, पदवी*; *v.t.* (*p.t.* styled) नाम लेना, पदवी देना

suave *a.* शांतकर, नम्र, विनीत

sub *pref.* 'अधीन, सहायक' अर्थ का उपसर्ग

sub-committee *n.* उपसमिति*, छोटी कमेटी*

subdivide *v.t.* विभाग करना, हिस्सों का भाग करना

subdivision *n.* उपविभाग, उपविषय

subdue *v.t.* जीतना, वश में करना, अधीन करना, दमन करना, मृदु करना

sub-editor *n.* सह-सम्पादक

subject *a.* आश्रित, अधीन,

विवश; *n.* प्रजा*, प्रकरण, विषय, कार्य-साधन, कर्त्ता, कर्तृ पद, उद्देश्य, विषेय; subject to अधीन; subject in hand प्रस्तुत विषय; *v.t.* वश में करना, परवश करना

subjection   *n.* अधीनता*, दासता*, दमन

subjective *a.* आत्ममुख, आत्मगत; *n.* आत्मपरक, व्यक्तिपरक, आत्मनिष्ठ

subjectivism   *n.* आत्मवाद, ज्ञानसापेक्षतावाद, विषयविज्ञानवाद

subjudice *a.* विचाराधीन

subjugate *v.t.* वशीभूत करना, अधीन करना

subjugation   *n.* अधीनता*, दबाव

sublet *v.t.* उपपट्टे पर उठाना, शिकमी देना, पट्टे पर ली हुई वस्तु को दूसरे को पट्टे पर देना

sublimate *v.t.* उन्नत करना, शोधना, निर्मल करना, आदर्श रूप देना, आदर्श बनाना

sublime *a.* भव्य, प्रतिउदात्त, लोकोत्तर; *n.* भव्यता*, महानता*

sublimity *n.* प्रतिष्ठा*, गौरव

submarine *a.* जलवर्ती, समुद्रीय, अन्तःसागरीय; *n.* पनडुब्बी*, पानी के भीतर चलनेवाला युद्धपोत

submerge *v.t. & i.* पानी. में डुबाना या डूबना

submission *n.* निवेदन, शरणागति*, आत्मसमर्पण, आज्ञापालन, सहिष्णुता*

submissive *a.* नम्र, आज्ञाकारी

submit *v.t & i.* (*p.t.* submitted) स्वीकार करना, अधीन होना, वश में करना, अनुरोध करना

subordinate *a.* अधीन, नीचे पद का, अप्रधान; *n.* अधीनस्थ, अवर, मातहत; *v.t.* अधीन करना; subordinate officer अधीन (मातहत) अधिकारी; subordinate court अधीन न्यायालय

subordination *n.* अधीनता*, मातहती*

subscribe *v.t. & i.* नीचे हस्ताक्षर करना, स्वीकार करना, अंशदान देना, चन्दा देना

subscriber *n.* चन्दा देनेवाला, गाहक

subscription *n.* चंदा, हस्ताक्षर, अंशदान

subsequent *a.* उत्तरकालीन, परवर्ती

subsequently *adv.* तदनन्तर, बाद में

subserve *v.t.* उपयोगी होना, सहायता देना, नीचे पद पर काम करना

subservience *n.* अधीनता*, अनुसेवा*

subservient *a.* अधीन, मातहत, उपयोगी

subside *v.i.* डूबना, शान्त होना

subsidiary *a.* सहायक, अधीन, पूरक, गौण

subsidy *n.* आर्थिक सहायता*, इमदादी रकम*

subsist *v.i.* प्राणरक्षा करना, जीना

subsistence *n.* जीविका*, वृत्ति*

substance *n.* सार, तत्त्व, द्रव्य, गुण, सारांश; man of substance धनी मनुष्य; sum and substance निष्कर्ष, सार

substantial *a.* वास्तविक, अधिक, ठोस, धनी

substantially *adv.* वास्तव में

substantiate *v.t.* सत्यता प्रमाणित करना, सिद्ध करना, सबूत देना, पक्का करना

substantive *a.* सत्ता-सूचक, अस्तित्वसूचक, स्वाधीन, मूल-भूत; *n.* विशेष्य, संज्ञा*

substantively *adv.* विशेष्य रूप में

substitute *v.t.* दूसरे के स्थान में रखना; *n.* प्रतिनिधि, स्थानापन्न, एवजी

subterfuge *n.* छल, कपट, धोखा

subterranean *a.* भूमि के भीतर का

subtle *a.* चतुर, सूक्ष्म, कोमल, निपुण

subtlety *n.* सूक्ष्मता* सूक्ष्म-दर्शिता*, मक्कारी*

subtract *v.t.* घटाना, मुजरा करना

subtraction *n.* शेष, घटाव

suburb *n.* नगरपरिसर, उप-नगर, नगरांचल

suburban *a.* अन्तर्नगरीय, उप-नगर संबंधी

subversion *n.* तोड़-फोड़, ध्वंस, नाश

subversive *a.* विध्वंसात्मक

subvert *v.t.* उलटना, फेंकना, नाश करना

succeed *v.t. & i.* बाद में होना, स्थान ग्रहण करना, सफल होना, अपना इष्ट साधना

success *n.* सफलता*, काम-याबी*

successful *a.* सफल, कृतार्थ

succession *n.* परम्परा*,

पंक्ति*, माला*, वंशक्रम; in succession यथाक्रम क्रम से; law of succession उत्तराधिकार का नियम

successive *a.* क्रमानुसार, उत्तरोत्तर

successor *n.* उत्तराधिकारी

succumb *v.i.* वशीभूत होना, मान जाना, मरना

such *a.* उसी प्रकार का, समान, वैसा; such and such अमुक, इस नाम का

suck *v.t.* चूसना, दूध पीना; *n.* स्तनपान; a child that sucks the breast स्तनपान करनेवाला बच्चा; to suck out चूसकर खाली करना; to suck up चूमना, सोखना

suckle *v.t.* स्तन से दूध पिलाना

sudden *a.* आकस्मिक, यकायक, अलक्षित, तीव्र

suddenly *adv* यकायक

sue *v.t. & i.* अभियोग चलाना, विवाह के लिए प्रार्थना करना

suffer *v.t. & i.* आज्ञा देना, प्राप्त करना, सहना, अनुमोदन करना

sufferance *n* अनुज्ञा*, सहन-शीलता*, क्षमा*

sufferer *n.* कष्ट सहनेवाला, दुःखी, कष्टभोगी

suffering *n.* क्लेश, पीड़ा*,

दुःख, विपात्त

suffice *v.t. & i.* पर्याप्त होना, सन्तुष्ट करना

sufficiency *n.* पर्याप्ति*

sufficient *a.* पर्याप्त, उचित, काफी

suffix *n.* प्रत्यय; *v.t.* शब्द के अन्त में प्रत्यय जोड़ना, अन्त में जोड़ना या बढ़ाना

suffocate *v.t.* गला घोंटना, सांस रोकना

suffocation *n.* श्वासावरोध, दमघुटी*

suffrage *n.* मताधिकार, अनु-मोदन, मतदान

sugar *n.* शुगर, शक्कर*, चीनी*; *v.t.* मीठा करना, चीनी मिलाना; sugar-candy मिश्री*, कन्द; sugar-cane ऊख*

suggest *v.t.* सुझाव देना, प्रस्ताव करना

suggestion *n.* सुझाव, अनु-मति*, प्रस्ताव

suggestive *a.* सूचक, सांकेतिक, बतलाने वाला

suicidal *a.* आत्महत्या-संबंधी

suicide *n.* आत्महत्या*; to commit suicide आत्म-हत्या करना

suit *n.* प्रार्थना*, विवाह के लिए प्रस्ताव, अभियोग,

कपड़ों का एक जोड़ा, *v.t.*
& i. योग्य होना या करना,
सन्तुष्ट करना

suitability *n.* योग्यता*,
औचित्य

suitable *a.* योग्य, उचित

suitably *adv.* यथायोग्य,
अनुसार

suite *n.* नौकर चाकर, सेट,
संयोग

suitor *n.* विवाहार्थी, प्रेमी,
अभियोक्ता, मुद्दई

sullen *a.* उदास, चिड़चिड़ा

sulphur *n.* गन्धक

sulphuric *a.* गन्धकजात,
गन्धकीय

sultry *a.* अति उष्ण तथा
कष्टकर

sum *n.* जोड़, गणित का प्रश्न,
राशि*, तात्पर्य; *v.t.* जोड़ना,
मिलाना, संचय करना;
sum total पूरा जोड़

summarily *adv.* संक्षिप्त
रूप से, शीघ्रता से

summarize *v.t.* संक्षेप करना,
सारांश निकालना

summary *n.* संक्षेप, सारांश;
a. संक्षिप्त, अल्प

summer *n.* ग्रीष्म ऋतु*;
summer-house गर्मी में
रहने का बंगला, ग्रीष्मावास;
summer-tree खम्भा,

रोक*, थून

summit *n.* शिखर, चोटी*,
ऊंचाई*

summon *v.t.* आने की आज्ञा
करना, बुलाना, जागृत करना

summons *n.* (*pl.*
summonses) निमन्त्रण,
सम्मन

sumptuous *a.* अत्युत्तम,
बहुमूल्य

sumptuously *adv.* अति-
उत्तम ढंग से

sun *n.* सूर्य, धूप*; *v.t. & i.*
(*p t.* sunned) धूप दिखाना;
sun-bath धूप खाना, सूर्य-
स्नान; sun blind धूप रोकने
की खिड़की का पर्दा; sun-
dial धूपघड़ी*; sun-flo-
wer सूरजमुखी फूल; sun-
like सूर्य की तरह का; sun-
proof सूर्य की किरणों
के लिए अप्रवेश्य; sunshade
स्त्रियों का छोटा छाता;
sunless *a.* छायादार; sunstroke लू, आतप या लू
लगना; the sun is set
ऐश्वर्य के दिनों का अन्त हो
गया; to rise with the
sun सूर्योदय पर उठना;
to see the sun जीवित
रहना; to take the sun
धूप खाना; under the sun

संसार में

Sunday *n.* रविवार, इतवार

sunder *v.t. & i.* अलग करना या होना

sundry *a.* अनेक

sunny *a.* चमकीला, धूप से गरम प्रसन्न

super *pref.* 'ऊपर, आगे, बढ़कर' के अर्थ का उपसर्ग

superable *a.* जीतने योग्य, वश्य, निवार्य

superabundant *a.* अत्यधिक

superb *a.* महत्त्व का, गर्वपूर्ण, शानदार

supereminent *a.* अति उत्तम

superficial *a.* बाहरी, छिछला, दिखाऊ

superficiality *n* अल्पज्ञता*, सतहीपन

superfine *a.* अति उत्तम

superfluity *n.* अधिकता*, बाहुल्य, फालतू धन

superfluous *a.* अनावश्यक, फालतू

superhuman *a.* अलौकिक, दैवी

superintend *v.t.* देखभाल करना, अधीक्षण करना, प्रबन्ध करना, निगरानी करना

superintendence(-y) *ns.* प्रबन्ध, जांच*, निगरानी*, अधीक्षण, सुपरिंटेंडेंट का पद

superintendent *n.* अधीक्षक, सुपरिंटेंडेंट

superior *a.* प्रवर, वरिष्ठ, श्रेष्ठ

superiority *n.* श्रेष्ठता*, वरिष्ठता*

superlative *a.* सर्वोत्तम, अत्युत्तम

superlativeness *n.* अत्युत्तमता*

supernatural *a.* प्रकृति से परे, अलौकिक, अद्भुत, आधिदैविक, लोकातीत, अतिमानवीय

supersede *v.t.* उल्लंघन करना, पीछे छोड़ देना, अधिक्रमण करना, स्थानच्युत करना

supersensitive *a.* अति सूक्ष्मग्राही, अति संवेदनशील, अति विकारशील

superstition *n.* अन्धविश्वास, मिथ्या धर्म, वहम

superstitious *a.* अन्धविश्वासी, वहमी

supertax *n* अतिरिक्त कर

supervise *v.t.* निरीक्षण करना, देखरेख करना, सुपरवाइज़ करना

supervision *n.* प्रबन्ध, देखभाल*

supervisor *n.* सुपरवाइज़र, निरीक्षक

supplant *v t.* हटाना, अधिकार में लेना

supple *a.* नमनशील, लचीला, 338

अधीन
supplement *n.* परिशिष्ट,
पूरक, अतिरिक्त अंश; *v.t.*
जोड़ना, बढ़ाना, अनुपूरित
करना
supplementary *a.* पूरक
supply *v.t.* (*p.t.* supplied)
सप्लाई करना, पूर्ति करना,
कमी पूरी करना, भरना; *n.*
सप्लाई, पूर्तिकरण
support *v.t.* समर्थन करना,
संभालना, सहायता देना,
पोषण करना, सहना; *n.*
समर्थन, आश्रय, सहारा; to
support a motion प्रस्ताव
का अनुमोदन करना; to
support oneself गुजर
करना
supported *a.* समर्थित, पोषित
supporter *n.* समर्थक, पोषक,
संभालनेवाला
suppose *v.t. & i.* अनुमान
करना, सोचना, मान लेना,
कल्पना करना
supposition *n.* अनुमान,
कल्पना*
suppress *v.t.* शमन करना,
रोकना, छिपाना, दबाना,
रोक देना, नियंत्रित करना
suppression *n.* अवरोध, दमन
supra *pref.* 'ऊपर या अधिक'
के अर्थ का उपसर्ग

supremacy *n.* श्रेष्ठता*, प्रभुत्व
supreme *a.* परम, अति, श्रेष्ठ
अधिक; supreme being
परमेश्वर
sur *pref.* अधिक' के अर्थ का
उपसर्ग
surcharge *n.* अतिरिक्त बोझ,
अतिरिक्त किराया या कर;
v.t. अतिरिक्त कर लगाना
sure *a.* स्थिर, रक्षित, दृढ़,
अवश्य; to be sure
निःसन्देह; to make sure
निश्चय करना
surely *adv.* अवश्य, निःसन्देह
surf *n.* लहर*, तरंग*
surface *n.* सतह*, ऊपरी तल
surge *n.* बड़ी लहर*; भावुकता*,
उभार; *v.i.* लहर उठना,
उभड़ना
surgeon *n.* सर्जन, शल्यवैद्य;
surgeon dentist दांतों का
शल्यवैद्य
surgery *n.* शल्यविद्या*
surmise *n.* अनुमान; *v.t.* सन्देह
करना, वितर्क करना
surmount *v.t.* जीतना, ऊपर
चढ़ना
surmountable जीतने योग्य
surname *n.* उपनाम, कुलनाम;
v.t. कुलनाम रखना
surpass *v.t.* बढ़ना, प्रतिक्रमण
करना

surpassable a. अतिक्रमणीय

surplus n. अतिरिक्त भाग, बढ़ोतरी*

surprise v.t. चकित करना, घबड़ा देना; n. अचरज, आकुलता*

surprising a. विचित्र, अद्भुत

surrender v.t. & i. आत्म-समर्पण करना, वश में होना, सौंपना, त्यागना; n. आत्म-समर्पण, त्याग

surround v.t. चारों ओर से घेरना

surroundings n. परिस्थिति*

surtax n. अतिरिक्त कर

surveillance n. रखवाली*, चौकसी*

survey v.t. (p t. surveyed) परीक्षा करना, अधीक्षण करना, नापना; n. सर्वेक्षण, परीक्षा*, नाप

surveyor n. परिमापक

survival n. अति जीवन, अनु-जीवन

survive v.t. अस्तित्व बनाए रखना, बचा रहना, टिका रहना, जीवित रहना

susceptibility n. भाव-प्रवणता*, ग्रहणक्षमता*, ग्रहणशीलता*, योग्यता*

susceptible a. ग्रहणशील, कोमल हृदय का, अनुभवक्षम,

संवेदनशील, ग्रहणशील, सुप्रभाव्य

suspect v.t. शंका करना, सन्देह करना, अविश्वास करना, अनुमान करना

suspend v.t. मुअत्तल करना, लटकाना, देर करना, रोकना, अस्थिर दशा में रखना, विघ्न डालना, भुगतान रोकना

suspense n. दुविधा*, अनिश्चय, चिन्ता* ; ~account निलम्बित लेखा

suspension n. मुअत्तली*, निलम्बन

suspension bridge n. झूले का पुल

suspicion n. अविश्वास, शंका*, संदेह

suspicious a. शंकायुक्त, अविश्वासी

sustain v.t. संभालना, सहना, सिद्ध करना, जीवित रखना, उत्साह देना

sustenance n. आश्रय, आहार

suzerain n. राजाधिराज

suzerainty n. आधिपत्य

swagger v.i. अहंकार से बोलना, अकड़कर चलना; n. शेखी*; a. तेजस्वी, फुर्तीला, रोबदार

swallow n. अबाबील; v.t. निगलना, पी लेना; n. स्वाद;

one swallow does not make a summer एक उदाहरण से कोई सिद्धान्त निकालना उचित नहीं होता

swan n. राजहंस

swarm n. समूह, समुदाय, मधुमक्खियों का झुण्ड; v.t. इकट्ठा होना, भीड़ मचाना

swarthy a. धुंधला, काले चमड़े का

sway v.t. & i. (p.t. & p.p. swayed) झुकना या झुकाना, हिलाना, प्रभाव डालना, शासन करना; n. शासन, झुकान

swear v.t. & i. (p.t. swore, p.p. sworn) शपथ लेना, दृढ़ता से कहना

swearing n. शपथ*

sweat n. पसीना, परिश्रम; v.i. पसीना निकलना, परिश्रम करना; by the sweat of one's brow बड़े परिश्रम से

sweater n. स्वेटर, ऊनी बनियान

sweep v.t. & i. (p.t. & p.p. swept) झाड़ना, घसीटना, वेग से चलना; n. झाड़ू देने की क्रिया, धुम्रांकश, स्वच्छ करनेवाला, क्रम, मोड़, घुमाव

sweeper n. झाड़ू देनेवाला, भंगी

sweet a. मधुर स्वाद का, मीठा,

सुगंधित, सुन्दर, ललित, प्रिय; n. मिठाई*, मधुर पदार्थ; according to one's sweet will स्वेच्छानुसार; sweet-heart प्रेमीजन

sweeten v.t. मधुर या मीठा करना

sweetmeat n. मिठाई*, मुरब्बा

swell v.t. & i. (p.t. swelled, p.p. swelled or swollen) फैलाना, फुलाना, बढ़ाना, हवा से भरना; n. बढ़ती*, लहरों का उठना

swift a. शीघ्रगामी, वेगवान; swift-footed वेग से चलने- वाला ; swift - handed शीघ्रता से काम करनेवाला

swim v.t. & i. (p.t. swam, p.p. swum) तैरना, तैरकर पार करना

swimmer a. तैराक

swimming n. तैराकी*

swindle v.t. ठगना, धोखा देना; n. ठगी*, धोखा

swindler n. ठग, चोर

swine n. (pl. swine) सुअर

swing v.t. (p.t. swung) इधर- उधर हिलना या झूलना, वेग से चलना, फांसी पड़ना; n. झूला पालना, उन्नति

Swiss n. स्विट्जरलैंड देशवासी

switch n. स्विच, बिजली का

बटन, कमची*, छड़ी*; *v.t.*
कोड़े से मारना या लाइन
बदलना ; switch · board
बिजली की अनेक धाराओं
का संबंध बदलने का साधन,
स्विच बोर्ड

sword *n.* तलवार; to sheathe
the sword युद्ध समाप्त
करना ; to put to the
sword जान से मार डालना

sycophant *n.* पराश्रयी, चाटु-
कार

syllabic *a.* पूर्णाक्षर-सूचक,
शब्दांश का

syllable *n.* पदांश, शब्दांश

syllabus *n.* (*pls.* sylla-
buses, syllabi) पाठ्यक्रम,
संक्षेप, सारांश

symbol *n.* चिह्न, लक्षण, प्रतीक

symbolic (-al) *a.* प्रतीकात्मक,
सांकेतिक, लिपिचिह्न द्वारा
निर्दिष्ट, लाक्षणिक

symbolism *n.* प्रतीकवाद

symbolize *v.t.* प्रतीक द्वारा
दरसाना

symmetry *n.* सुडौलपन

symmetric(-al) *a.* सुडौल

sympathetic *a.* समदुःखी,
सहानुभूति का

sympathize *v.i.* सहानुभूति
प्रकट करना

sympathy *n.* सहानुभूति*,
दया*

symphony *n.* स्वर की समता*,
स्वर का मिलान, पूर्ण वाद्यवृन्द
के साथ बजाया गया गीत,
सिम्फनी

symptom *n.* लक्षण, चिह्न

symptomatic *a.* लक्षण-संबंधी

syndicate *n.* सिण्डीकेट,
व्यवसायी संघ

synonym *n.* पर्याय अथवा
तुल्यार्थ शब्द

synonymous *a.* पर्यायवाची

synopsis *n.* (*pl.* -ses) संक्षेप,
रूपरेखा*

syntax *n.* वाक्यरचना*, कारक-
प्रक्रिया*

synthesis *n.* (*pl.* -ses)
समन्वय, संयोग, संकलन,
संश्लेषण, शब्द संयोग, समास

syringe *n.* पिचकारी*; *v.t.*
पिचकारी देना

syrup *n.* सिरप, चाशनी*,
शर्बत

system *n.* व्यवस्था*, संहति*,
तंत्र-पद्धति*, रीति*, क्रम,
प्रयोग, प्रबन्ध, विश्व, अंग,
रचना

systematic *a.* यथाक्रम

systematize *v.t.* व्यवस्था
करना, क्रमबद्ध करना

table   326   talk

T

table n. टेबुल, मेज़*, चिकनी
समतल भूमि*, चौकी*,
लेखनाधार, सूची*, सूचीपत्र;
v.t. सूचीपत्र बनाना; at
table भोजन करते हुए; to
lay on the table टालना; to
turn the table स्थिति
बदलना; table-land ऊंची
समतल भूमि; table-money
अधिकारियों का भत्ता;
table-spoon आध आउंस
तरल पदार्थ रखने का चम्मच;
table talk सामान्य वार्ता-
लाप

tablet n. छोटा टेबुल, पटिया*,
औषधि की टिकिया*

tabloid n. औषधि की छोटी
टिकिया*

taboo n. रोक, निषेध, बहि-
ष्कार; v.t. निषेध करना

tabulate v.t. सूचीपत्र
बनाना; सारणीबद्ध करना

tacit a. मौन, अनकहा; tacit
consent चुपचाप या मौन
स्वीकृति

tackle n. उपकरण, हथियार,
कीलकांटा; v.t. गुंथ जाना,
सामना करना, काबू करना

tact n. व्यवहार-कुशलता*,
निपुणता*, युक्ति*

tactful a. व्यवहार-कुशल,
निपुण

tactician n. युद्ध-विद्या में
निपुण

tactics n. (sing. & pl.) व्यूह
रचना*, युद्ध-विद्या*, युक्ति*

tag n. फीते या डोरी के किनारे
पर लगी हुई धातु की नोक,
पुछिल्ला, तुच्छ पदार्थ; v.t.
जोड़ना, पुछिल्ला लगाना

tail n. पूंछ*, पिछला भाग

tailor n. (fem. tailoress)
दर्जी; tailor-bird n. बया
पक्षी

take v.t. (p.t. took, p.p.
taken) ग्रहण करना,
थामना, हाथ में लेना,
पकड़ना; to take away
वंचित करना; to take
down गिराना, लिखना;
to take fire आग लगना;
to take off हटाना; to
take up उठाना

tale n. कथा*, कहानी*,
गणना*

talent n. प्रतिभा*, क्षमता*,
योग्यता*

talented a. प्रतिभावान, योग्य,
काबिल

talk v.t. & i. बातचीत करना,

बोलना; *n.* वार्ता*, बात-
चीत*, खाली बातें*

talkative *a.* बातूनी, बक्की,
वकवादी

talkativeness *n.* बकवाद,
बक्कीपन

talkies *n. pl.* सवाक चलचित्र,
बोलता सिनेमा

tall *a.* ऊंचा, लम्बा, बड़ा

tally *n.* (*pl.* tall es) गणना-
पट, हिसाब-पट्टी*, हिसाब-
किताब का मिलान; *v.t. &*
i. (*p.t.* tallied) मिलान
करना या मिलाना

tamarind *n.* इमली का पेड़

tamarisk *n.* भाऊ का वृक्ष

tame *a.* पालतू, पलुप्रा, सौम्य,
निस्तेज, मन्द; *v.t.* पालना,
वश में करना

tamper *v.t. & i.* विघ्न डालना,
लिखित पत्र में चोरी से अदल-
बदल करना, गुप्त व्यवहार
करना

tan *v.i.* (*p.t.* tanned) चमड़ा
कमाना, भूरा करना; *a.*
पीले भूरे रंग का

tanner *n.* चमड़ा कमानेवाला,
चर्मकार

tannery *n.* चमड़ा कमाने का
कारखाना

tangent *n.* स्पर्श रेखा*, स्पर्श

tangible *a.* स्पर्शनीय, व्यक्त,

वास्तविक, शारीरिक

tangle *n.* फांस*, फंदा, उल-
झन*; *v.t.* फंसाना, उलझाना

tank *n.* टैंक, हौज, जलाशय,
बावली, सब सामग्री-युक्त
सैनिक मोटर गाड़ी

tantalize *v.t.* कष्ट देना झूठी
आशा दिलाकर व्याकुल
करना

tantamount *a.* समान,
तुल्यार्थक

tantrum *n.* आवेश, क्रोध

tap *n.* दस्तक*, टोंटी*, थप-
थपाहट*; *v.t. & i.* दस्तक
देना, टोंटी से पानी निका-
लना, धीरे से थपथपाना;
tap-room मद्यगृह, कल-
वरिया

tape *n.* फीता, पट्टी*; *v.t.*
फीते से बांधना; tape-
measure नापने का फीता;
to breast the tape
दौड़ में जीतना

tapestry *n.* टेपेस्ट्री, चित्र कढ़ा
पर्दा, चित्रमय पर्दा

tapis *n.* चित्रमय पर्दा, मेजपोश

target *n.* लक्ष्य, निशाना, गोला

tariff *n.* तटकर, चुंगी, निखे-
नामा *v.t.* चुंगी ठहराना,
तटकर निर्धारित करना,

tarnish *v.t.* मलिन करना
धब्बा लगाना

task *n.* सौंपा हुआ कार्य, काम,
कर्तव्य; *v.t.* काम लेना;
to take to task भिड़की
देना, गाली देना

taste *v.t.* स्वाद लेना, आनन्द
लेना; *n.* स्वाद, रस, अच्छी
प्रवृत्ति*; a man of taste
सुरुचिवान पुरुष

tatter *n.* चिथड़ा, फटन

tattoo *n.* गोदना; *v.i.* गोदना
लगाना

taunt *n.* ताना. निन्दा*,
तिरस्कार; *v.t.* निन्दा करना,
ताना मारना

tavern *n.* मदिरागृह, कल-
वरिया, सराय

tawdry *a.* भड़कीला, सस्ता
और भ्रष्ट

tax *n.* कर; corporation tax
निगम कर entertainment
tax मनोरंजन कर; tax-
free करमुक्त; income
tax आयकर; tax payer
करदाता; sales tax बिक्री-
कर; terminal tax सीमा-
कर; trade tax व्यापार
कर; taxable कर योग्य;
v.t. कर लगाना, पीड़ा देना

taxation *n.* कर निर्धारण

taxi *n.* टैक्सी

tea *n.* चाय*; tea-spoon एक
ड्राम तरल पदार्थ रखने का

छोटा चम्मच

teach *v.t.* (*p.t. & p. p.*
taught) शिक्षा देना, पढ़ाना,
उपदेश देना

teacher *n.* अध्यापक, शिक्षक

teaching *n.* शिक्षा*, उपदेश

teak *n* सागौन का वृक्ष

team *n.* एक साथ जुते हुए पशु,
खिलाड़ियों का एक दल,
टीम* *v.t.* एक साथ जोतना

teamster *n.* जोड़ी हांकने
वाला

teapoy *n.* तिपाई*, चौकी*

tear *n.* आंसू

tear *v.t.* (*p.t.* tore, *p.p.*
torn) चीरना, फाड़ना;
n. चीर*, फटन tear gas
आंसू गैस; to tear off झटके
से खींचना; to tear from
छीनना; to tear out जड़
से उखाड़ना

tearful *a.* रोता हुआ, अश्रुपूर्ण

tease *v t.* पीड़ा देना, चिढ़ाना,
ऊन संवारना

technical *a.* टेक्नीकल, पारि-
भाषिक तकनीकी

technicality *n.* कलाविज्ञता*
बारीकी*

technically *adv.* तकनीकी
रीति के अनुसार

technique *n.* प्रविधि*,
तकनीक

technological *a.* प्रौद्यो-
गिक, प्रावेधिक, शिल्प-विज्ञान
विषयक

technologist *n.* प्रौद्योगविज्ञ,
शिल्पज्ञ

technology *n.* प्रौद्योगिकी*
शिल्प-विज्ञान

tedious *a.* थकानेवाला, परि-
श्रम का

teem *v.t. & i.* बहुतायत से
उत्पन्न करना, फलयुक्त होना,
परिपूर्ण होना

teeming *a.* उत्पादी, बहुप्रज,
बहुप्रसवी

teens *n. pl.* तेरह वर्ष से
उन्नीस वर्ष तक की अवस्था

teethe *v.i.* दांत निकलना

teetotal *a.* सब मादक पदार्थों
का बहिष्कार करनेवाला

teetoalism *n.* मद्य परिवर्जन

teetotaller *n.* कभी मदिरा न
पीनेवाला मनुष्य

teil *n.* नीबू का वृक्ष

telegram *n.* टेलिग्राम, तार;
v.t. तार द्वारा समाचार भेजना

telegraphic *a.* तार-संबंधी

telegraphist *n.* तारबाबू

telegraphy *n.* तार-प्रणाली*

telephone *n.* टेलीफोन

telescope *n.* दूरदर्शक यंत्र

telescopic *a.* दूरदर्शक यंत्र के
सदृश

tell *v.t.* (*p.t. & p.p.* told)
वर्णन करना, कहना, बत-
लाना, गिनना

telling *a.* अधिक प्रभाववाला

telltale *n.* चुगलखोर

temper *n.* शील, स्वभाव,
प्रकृति*, गुणों का मेल, घातु
पर की कड़ाहट या पानी;
to loose temper क्रुद्ध
होना; out of temper
क्रुद्ध *v.t.* पानी रखना,
मिलाना, कम करना

temperament *n.* प्रकृति*,
स्वभाव

temperance *n.* संयम, बराव

temperate *a.* संयमी, शांत,
शीतोष्ण

temperately *adv.* संयम से

temperature *n.* तापमान

tempest *n.* आंधी, बवंडर,
हलचल*

tempestuous *a.* तूफानी,
प्रचण्ड

temple *n.* मन्दिर, देवालय,
कनपटी*

temporal *a.* सामयिक,
सांसारिक

temporary *a.* अस्थायी,
क्षणिक

temporize *v.i.* देर करना,
आगा-पीछा करना, समयो-
चित व्यवहार करना, ढील

देना

tempt *v.t.* प्रयत्न करना, ललचाना, बुराई करने के लिए तैयार करना, बहकाना

temptation *n* प्रलोभन, लालच

tempter *n.* (*fem.* temptress) लुभानेवाला, परखनेवाला, कुवृत्ति उत्तेजक

ten *n.* दस; tenth *a.* दसवां

tenable *a.* रक्षणीय, टिकाऊ

tenacious *a.* हृढ, हठी, कड़ा, हृढसंलग्न

tenacity *n.* हठ, हृढता*

tenancy *n.* काश्तकारी*, लगान-दारी*

tenant *n.* काश्तकार, असामी, किरायेदार

tend *v.t. & i.* प्रवृत्त होना, रक्षा करना, लक्ष्य करना किसी दिशा में चलना

tendency *n.* प्रवृत्ति*, स्वभाव अभिप्राय

tender *n.* टेण्डर, ठेका, भेंट प्रदत्त पदार्थ; legal tender मान्य सिक्का; *v.t.* भेंट करना, स्वीकार करने के लिए प्रस्तुत करना

tender *n.* जहाज के साथ की छोटी नाव*, इंजन के साथ की कोयला-पानी गाड़ी*

tender *a.* सुकुमार, दयालु;

tender age बाल्यावस्था*

tenderling *n.* लाड़ला, बच्चा

tenderly *adv.* कोमलता से

tenderness *n.* मृदुता*, कोम-लता*

tending *n* पालन, रक्षा*; tending to fall पतनशील

tenet *n.* मत, अभिप्राय, सिद्धान्त, नीति*

tennis *n.* टेनिस, गेंद का एक खेल

tenor *n.* क्रम, प्रवृत्ति*, भाव, पुरुष का उच्चतम स्वर

tense *a.* खींचा हुआ, ताना हुआ, उद्विग्न, क्षुब्ध

tension *n.* खिंचाव, कसाव, तनाव

tent *n.* पटमण्डप, तम्बू, छोल-दारी*

tentative *a.* परीक्षात्मक, प्रयोगात्मक

tenure *n.* पट्टा, पट्टे का काल, पदावधि*

term *n.* अवधि*, स्थिर काल, अन्त, नाम, दो छुटिटयों के बीच का काल; *v.t.* पुका-रना, नाम लेना या रखना; on friendly terms मित्र भाव से; to come to terms स्वीकार कर लेना

terminable *a.* अन्त करने योग्य

terminate v.t. & i. समाप्त
करना

termination n. अन्त समाप्ति*

terminology n. पारिभाषिक
शब्दावली*

terminus n. (pl. termini)
सीमा चिह्न, रेलवे लाइन के
अन्त का स्टेशन

terrace n चबूतरा, छत, घरों
की पंक्ति*

terracotta n. टेराकोटा मूर्ति
बनाने की एक प्रकार की कड़ी
मिट्टी*

terrible a. भयंकर, डरावना

terrific a. भयानक, भय उत्पन्न
करनेवाला

terrify v.t. (p.t. terrified)
डराना, भय दिखलाना

terrifying a. डरानेवाला

territorial a. प्रादेशिक, राज्य-
क्षेत्रीय

territory n. भूमि*, प्रदेश,
राज्य, क्षेत्र

terror n. आतंक, त्रास, भय,
डर; terror-struck भयग्रस्त

terrorist n. आतंकवादी

terrorize v.t. भयभीत करना,
डराना

terse a. लघु, सुथरा, संक्षिप्त,
सुगठित

test v t. प्रयोग करना, सिद्ध
करना, परीक्षा करना; n.
परीक्षा, कसौटी, जांच,
प्रमाण, मानदण्ड

testament n. मृत्युलेख,
वसीयत*

testify v.i. & t. (p.t. testi-
fied) सिद्ध करना, गवाही
देना, प्रमाणित करना

testimonial n. प्रमाणपत्र,
प्रशंसापत्र

testimony n. साक्षी, प्रमाण,
सबूत, गवाही*, शपथपूर्ण
घोषणा*; (बाइबिल में)
ईश्वर की दस आज्ञाएं*

text n. मूल, मूलपाठ, सूत्र, उद्-
धृत अवतरण; text book
n. पाठ्य-पुस्तक*

textile a. बुना हुआ, बुनाई-
संबंधी, बुनने योग्य; textile
industry सूती वस्त्रोद्योग;
n. बुना हुआ वस्त्र

textual a. मौलिक, पाठगत

texture n. रचना*, विन्यास,
बुनावट*

thank v.t. धन्यवाद देना

thankful a. कृतज्ञ

thankless a. कृतघ्न

thanks n. आपको धन्यवाद

thanks-giving n. धन्यवाद
प्रदान या प्रकाशन

thatch n. छप्पर, फूस*; v.t.
छप्पर से छाना

thaw v.t. & i. गलाना, पिघ-

लाना, ढीला पड़ना; *n.* द्रवए, पिघलान

theatre *n.* थियेटर, नाट्य-शाला*, व्याख्यान-मन्दिर; operation theatre शल्य-कक्ष

theatrical *a.* नाटक, नाटकीय प्रदर्शन, नाट्यक्रीड़ा, नाटक का खेल, नाटक-संबंधी

theft *n.* चोरी* तस्करता*

theism *n.* ईश्वरवाद, आस्ति-कता*

theist *n.* आस्तिक

theme *n.* निर्धारित विषय, प्रकरण

theologian *n.* ब्रह्मज्ञानी, वेदान्ती

theology *n.* ब्रह्मज्ञान, वेदान्त

theorem *n.* प्रमेय, उपपत्ति*, सूत्र

theoretical *a.* सिद्धान्त-संबंधी

theorist *n.* सिद्धान्ती

theorize *v.i.* सिद्धान्त स्थिर करना

theory *n.* सिद्धान्त, कल्पना*, उपपत्ति

therapeutic *a.* चिकित्सा-संबंधी

there *adv.* उस स्थान में, उस विषय में; thereabouts उस स्थान के पास, वहीं पर; thereafter उसके उपरान्त;

thereat उस कारण से; thereby उसके द्वारा; therefore उस कारण से; therefrom उस स्थान से; thereof उसका; thereon उसपर; thereto उस तक; thereupon उसपर, तुरन्त; therewith उससे; therewithal सर्वोपरि

thermo *pref.* 'गरम (उष्ण)' के अर्थ का उपसर्ग

thermometer *n.* थर्मामीटर, तापमापक यंत्र

thermos, thermos flask *ns.* थर्मस, स्थिरतापकूपी*

thesis *n.* (*pl.* theses) थीसिस, शास्त्रार्थ का विषय, निबन्ध

thick *a.* मोटा, गाढ़ा, स्थूल; *adv.* निरन्तर, अविरल; *n.* किसी पदार्थ का घना भाग; through thick and thin सब स्थितियों में; thick-headed मन्द, मूर्ख

thicket *n.* झाड़ी*, छोटा जंगल

thief *n.* (*pl.* thieves) चोर

thieve *v.t. & i.* चुराना, चोरी करना

thievery *n.* चोरी*

thigh *n.* जंघा*, जांघ*

thin *a.* (*comp.* thinner, *sup.* thinnest) कोमल, पतला, छिछला; *v.t. & i.* पतला

करना या होना

thing *n.* वस्तु*, बात*, द्रव्य, पदार्थ, काम, जन्तु

think *v.t. & i. (p.t. & p.p.* thought) विचारना, कल्पना करना, निर्णय करना

thinkable *a.* विचार करने योग्य

third *a.* तीसरा

thirdly *adv.* तीसरे स्थान में

thirst *v i.* प्यास लगना, उत्कंठित होना; *n.* प्यास*, तृष्णा*

thirsty *a.* प्यासा

thirteen *n.* तेरह

thirteenth *a.* तेरहवां

thirtieth *a.* तीसवां

thirty *n.* तीस

thorn *n.* कांटेदार वृक्ष, कांटा

thorough *a.* संपूर्ण, पर्याप्त, पूरा

thoroughfare *n.* राजमार्ग, सड़क

thoroughly *adv.* पूर्ण रूप से

thought *n.* विचार, कल्पना*, बुद्धि, ध्यान; thought-reading दूसरे के मन के विचार को जान लेना

thoughtful *a* विचारवान, सावधान

thoughtfully *adv.* विचार-पूर्वक

thoughtless *a.* भ्रमावधान,

मूर्ख

thousand *n.* हजार

thrash *v t.* पीटकर अन्न अलगाना, चाबुक से मारना, पराजित करना, रास्ता काटना

thread *n.* तागा, डोरा; *v.t.* सूई में तागा पिरोना; gold-thread कलाबत्तू

threat *n.* घुड़की*, घमकी*

threaten *v.t.* डांटना, घमकाना

three *a. & n.* तीन; three-fold तिगुना

threshold *n.* देहली*, द्वार, फाटक

thrice *adv.* तीन बार

thrift *n.* मितव्यय, कमखर्ची*

thrifty *a.* अल्पव्ययी

thrill *n.* स्पन्दन, पुलक; thriller रोमांचकारी कहानी*

thrilling *a.* उत्तेजक, सनसनी-खेज

thrive *v i. (p.t.* throve, *p.p.* thriven) बढ़ना, उन्नति करना, सफल होना

throat *n.* कण्ठ, गला, नरेटी*; sore throat गले की सूजन

throb *v.i. (p t.* throbbed) कांपना, घड़कना; *n.* स्फुरण, घड़कन

throne *n.* राजसिंहासन, राज-पद; *v.t.* राजसिंहासन पर बैठाना

throng n. समुदाय, भीड़*; v.t. & i. भीड़ करना, इकट्ठा होना

throttle n. गला, टेंटुआ; v.t. गला घोंटना

through prep. आरपार, एक ओर से दूसरी ओर तक; to carry through पूरा करना

throughout adv. & prep. सर्वत्र, सब ओर

throw v.t. & i. (p.t. threw, p.p. thrown) उछालना, फेंकना, ऐंठना; n. उछाल*, फेंक*, क्षेपण

thud n. धमाका; v.i. धमाके का शब्द करना

thumb n. अंगूठा; rule of thumb व्यवहार; under one's thumb वश में, अधीन

thump n. घड़ाका; v t. & i. भड़भराना, पीटना, ठोंकना; a. thumping बहुत बड़ा; thumping majority बहुत बड़ा बहुमत

thunder n. मेघ की गरज*; v.i. गरजना

thunderbolt n. वज्र, बिजली*

thunderstruck a. चकित, हक्का बक्का

Thursday n. गुरुवार, बृहस्पति-वार

thwart v.t. विरोध करना, हराना

ticket n. निर्देशपत्र, टिकट

tide n. ज्वारभाटा, समय, क्रम, पलट*

tidings n. pl. सन्देश, समाचार

tidiness n. स्वच्छता*

tidy a. स्वच्छ, सुथरा

tie v.t. (p.t. tied) संयुक्त करना, बांधना; n. बन्धन, ग्रन्थि*, गुलूबन्द, संबंध, टाई*

tiffin n. दूसरे पहर का जलपान, कलेवा

tiger n. (fem. tigress) चीता, बाघ

tight a. दृढ़, कसा हुआ; tight-fisted a. कृपण, कंजूस

tigress n. fem. बाघिन*

tile n. खपड़ा, पटिया*; v.t. खपड़ा छाना

till n. रुपया रखने का मेज का दराज; v.t. भूमि जोतना; tiller किसान

timber n. घर बनाने की लकड़ी, जहाज की सिरेवाली एक लकड़ी

time n. अवधि*, समय, जीवन, युग, ताल, लय*; v.t. समयानुकूल करना; for a long time बहुत दिनों तक; at all times सर्वदा; in the meantime इस बीच में; against time बड़ी शीघ्रता

से; at times बहुधा; time-
honoured बहुत समय से
पूजित; time-table समय-
सूची*; timepiece मेज-घड़ी

timely *a. & adv.* समय पर,
शीघ्र

timid *a.* डरपोक, कायर

timidity *n.* कायरता*

tin *n.* रांगा, टीन का डब्बा,
धन; *v.t.* (*p.t.* tinned)
रांगा चढ़ाना

tincture *n.* टिंचर, आभा*,
हलका रंग, औषधियों का
सत्त्व; *v t.* रंगना, स्वादिष्ट
बनाना

tinge *n.* हलका रंग, स्वाद; *v.t.*
हलका रंग देना

tiny *a.* (*comp.* tinier, *sup.*
tiniest) बहुत छोटा, नन्हा

tip *v.t.* (*p.t.* tipped) थप-
थपाना, भेद बतलाना, सेवक
को अल्प धन या इनाम देना;
n. थपकी*, सूचना*, अल्प
उपहार

tipsy *a.* मदिरा पिए हुए, मत-
वाला

irade *n.* निन्दापूर्ण भाषण

tire *v.i & t.* थकना. थकाना

tissue *n* जाल, रचना, तन्तु;
tissue paper पतला कागज

titan *a. & n.* दानवी, बड़ा
भारी दैत्य

title *n.* पुस्तक का नाम, पदवी*,
अधिकार; title-deed आगम-
पत्र

titular *a.* नाम मात्र का, नाम-
धारी

toast *n.* अंगार पर सेंकी हुई
रोटी*, जिसके आरोग्य के
निमित्त मदिरा पी जाए; *v.t.*
भूनना, सेंकना, किसी के
स्वास्थ्य या प्रतिष्ठा के लिए
मदिरा पीना

tobacco *n.* (*pl.* tobaccos)
तमाखू की पत्ती*

today *n. & adv.* आज, आज के
दिन

toddy *n.* ताड़ी*

toe *n.* पैर की अंगुली, खुर का
अगला भाग

toffee *n.* टाफी, एक प्रकार की
मिठाई*

toil *n.* कठोर परिश्रम, कष्ट,
फंदा, जाल; *v.i.* परिश्रम
करना

toilet *n.* श्रृंगार करने की
रीति*, परिधान, पोशाक*
हाथ-मुंह धोने का कमरा

tolerable *a.* सहने योग्य,
कामचलाऊ

tolerance *n.* सहनशक्ति*, धैर्य

tolerant *a.* सहनशील

tolerate *v.t. & i.* सहन करना,
होने देना, कष्ट उठाना

toleration *n.* सहन, क्षमा*,
घार्मिक स्वतन्त्रता*

toll *n.* मार्ग का कर, हाट में
बेचने की भरी; *v.t. & i.*
कर देना या लेना; toll-bar
चुंगी का फाटक; tollhouse
चुंगीघर

toll *n.* घण्टे का शब्द; *v.t.*
घण्टी बजाना

tomato *n.* (*pl.* tomatoes)
विलायती बैंगन, टमाटर

tomb *n.* कब्र, समाधि-स्थान

tombstone *n.* समाधि-शिला*

tome *n.* बड़ा ग्रन्थ

tomorrow *n. & adv.* कल,
श्रागामी दिन

ton *n.* 28 मन की तौल

tone *n.* स्वर ध्वनि* शब्द,
प्रकृति*, रीति*, फोटो में
प्रकाश तथा अन्धकार का
दिखाव; to tone down रंग
हलका करना

tongue *n.* जीभ*, भाषा*'
जीभी*; mother-tongue
मातृभाषा*; hold your
tongue चुप रहो; tongue-
tied खुलकर न बोल सकना

tonic *a.* स्वर-सम्बन्धी, बल-
वर्धक; *n.* बलवर्धक औषधि*

to-night *adv. & n.* श्राज की
रात में

tonsil *n.* गले में की एक गिलटी

tool *n.* श्रोजार, साधन, शस्त्र

toothache *n.* दांत का दर्द

top *n.* शिखर, सिरा, चोटी*,
लड़कों के खेलने का लट्टू;
v.t. & i. ढकना लगाना,
शिखर पर पहुंचना; *a. sup.*
(topmost) मुख्य, सर्वश्रेष्ठ

topic *n.* बात का विषय

topical *a.* प्रकरण-संबंधी,
सामयिक

topography *n.* मानचित्र पर
का विस्तृत वर्णन

topographic (-al) *a.* मान-
चित्र के विस्तृत वर्णन-संबंधी

topple *v.t.* लुढ़ककर गिर
पड़ना

topsyturvy *adv. & a.* उलटे
हुए, पूर्ण अव्यवस्थित, बिलकुल
गड़बड़

torch *n.* मशाल, पलीता;
torch-bearer मशालची

torment *n.* सन्ताप, पीड़ा*,
यातना*; *v t.* कष्ट देना,
सताना

torpedo *n.* (*p.* torpedoes)
एक प्रकार की मछली*,
जहाज़ की पेंदी तोड़ने का
गोला; torpedo-boat ऐसा
गोला फेंकने के लिए वेग से
जानेवाला पोत

torrent *n.* जल-प्रवाह, स्रोत

torrential *a.* जलप्रवाह संबंधी

tortoise *n.* कछुवा; tortoise-shell कछुवे की पीठ की हड्डी

torture *n.* दारुण वेदना*, यातना*, बड़ा दुख; *v.t.* अत्यन्त पीड़ा या कष्ट देना

tory *n.* ब्रिटेन के अनुदार दल का सदस्य

toss *v.t. & i.* फेंकना, उछालना, उछलना, झगड़ा तय करना; *n.* ऊपर को उछाल

total *a.* पूरा, सब; *n.* कुल परिमाण, कुल जोड़

totality *n.* पूर्णता*, पूर्ण संख्या*: totalize *v.t.* जोड़ना

touch *n.* स्पर्श, संसर्ग, जांच; *v.t. & i.* स्पर्श करना, पहुंचना, जांचना

touching *a.* करुणात्मक, हृदयस्पर्शी

touchstone *n.* कसौटी*

tough *a.* चिमड़ा, हठी, कठिन

tour *n.* दौरा, पर्यटन

tourist *n.* भ्रमणार्थी, पर्यटक

tournament, tourney *ns.* क्रीड़ा-युद्ध, दंगल, जंगी खेल

tower *n.* अटारी*, बुर्जी*, किला; *v.i.* ऊंचाई पर पहुंचना

towering *a.* बहुत ऊंचा, अति तीव्र

town *n.* छोटा शहर; town-clerk नगर का लेखा रखने वाला; town hall नगर का सार्वजनिक भवन; towns-folk नगरवासी

toy *n.* क्रीड़ा की वस्तु*, तुच्छ पदार्थ, खिलौना; *v.i* आनन्द मचाना, क्रीड़ा करना

trace *n.* चिह्न, मार्ग, पैर का चिह्न, अल्प मात्रा*; *v.t.* पीछा करके खोजना, चिह्न करना, आभा की सहायता से रेखा खींचना

track *n.* मार्ग, पगडंडी*, पैर का चिह्न; *v.t.* पदचिह्न द्वारा पता लगाना

trade *n.* व्यापार, व्यवसाय, लेनदेन; *v.i. & t.* लेन-देन का काम करना, व्यापार करना; trade-mark व्यावसायिक नाम या संकेत; tradesman व्यापारी, दुकानदार trade winds *n. pl.* अटलांटिक तथा प्रशांत महासागर में नियम से बहने वाली वायु, व्यापारिक पवन

tradition *n.* परम्परा*, परंपरागत कथा*, पुराण-कथा*, प्राचीन रीति*

traditional *a.* परम्परागत

traffic *n.* ट्राफिक, व्यापार,
338

व्यवसाय, एक स्थान से दूसरे स्थान को जाना या माल भेजना; *v t.* व्यवसाय करना

tragedy *n.* दुःखान्त नाटक, दुर्घटना

tragic (-al) *a.* दुःखात्मक, शोकजनक, भयंकर

trail *n.* पैर का चिह्न *v.t.* भूमि पर खींचना, पीछे घसीटना

trailer *n.* एक गाड़ी से खींची जानेवाली दूसरी गाड़ी लता

train *n.* ट्रेन*, रेलगाड़ी*, पीछे से ढकेला हुआ पदार्थ, वस्त्र का लहराना हुआ छोर

train *v.t. & i.* प्रशिक्षण देना, पढ़ाना, अभ्यास करना

training *n.* प्रशिक्षण

trait *n.* लक्षण, रेखा*, स्पर्श, विशेष चिह्न

traitor *n.* (*fem.* traitress) विश्वासघाती, छली, गद्दार

traitorous *a.* कपटी, विश्वासघाती

tram, tram-car *ns.* ट्राम गाड़ी*, खान में कोयला ढोने की गाड़ी*; **tramway** *n.* ट्राम गाड़ी की सड़क*

trammel *v.t.* (*p.t.* trammelled) फंसाना, रोकना

trample *v.t.* पैर से कुचलना; *n.* रौंदन

trance *n.* प्रचेत अवस्था*, मूर्छा*

tranquil *a.* शांत, गम्भीर, निश्चित

tranquillity *n.* शांति*, स्थिरता*

tranquillize *v.t.* शांत करना, धीरज देना

trans *pref* 'पार, दूसरी और अथवा परे' के अर्थ का उपसर्ग

transact *v.t. & i.* साधन करना, कार्य करना

transaction *n.* प्रबन्ध, कार्य, व्यवहार

transcend *v.t. & i.* ऊंचा होना, पार करना

transcendent *a.* प्रतिश्रेष्ठ

transcribe *v.t.* प्रतिलिपि करना, लिपि बदल कर लिखना

transcription *n.* प्रतिलिपि*, अनुकृति*

transfer *v.t.* (*p.t.* transferred) अपना अधिकार दूसरे को देना, हटाना, स्थानान्तरण करना; *n.* हटाव, स्थानान्तरण, बदली*, बदला हुआ पदार्थ

transferable *a.* स्थान बदलने योग्य, विनिमेय

transfigure *v.t.* रूप या आकार

बदलना

transform *v.t.* रूप या आकार बदलना

transformation *n.* रूपान्तर

transit *n.* गति*, क्रान्ति*, संक्रमण, मार्ग

transition *n.* परिवर्तन, संक्रमण

transitive *a.* सकर्मक क्रिया-संबंधी

transitory *a.* क्षणिक, अनित्य

translate *v.t.* भाषान्तर करना, अनुवाद करना

translation *n.* भाषान्तर, अनुवाद, उल्था

translator *n.* (*fem.* translatress) अनुवादक

transmigrate *v.i.* एक देश से दूसरे देश में जाना, काया पलट करना, पुनर्जन्म प्राप्त करना

transmigration *n.* पुनर्जन्म

transmit *v.t.* (*p.t.* transmitted) भेजना, पहुंचना, स्थान्तरित करना

transmitter *n.* ट्रान्समिटर, दूरविक्षेपक, पार भेजनेवाला

transparent *a.* पारदर्शक, स्वच्छ, निर्मल

transplant *v.t.* प्रतिरोपण करना, रोपना, पौधा लगाना, दूसरे स्थान में जमाना

transport *v.t.* परिवहन करना, ले जाना, देश-निकाला देना, आनन्द मनाना; *n.* परि-वहन, यातायात, आनन्द

transportation *n.* परिवहन, निर्वासन, काले पानी की सज़ा

trap *n.* फन्दा, पिंजड़ा, छल, कपट; *v.t.* (*p.t.* trapped) फन्दे में फंसाना; trap-door छत में लगी हुई खिड़की

trash *n.* निरर्थक पदार्थ, कूड़ -कर्कट

travel *v.t..* (*p.t.* travelled) यात्रा करना, घूमना; travels *n.* यात्रा का वर्णन

traveller *n.* यात्री

tray *n.* ट्रे, धातु या लकड़ी की थाली*

treacherous *a.* विश्वासघाती

treachery *n.* विश्वासघात

tread *v.t. & i.* (*p.t.* trod, *p.p.* trodden, trod) पग रखना, पर कुचलना; *n.* चलने का ढंग, टाप

treason *n.* राजद्रोह, राज-विरोध high treason राजा को गद्दी से उतारने या उसकी हत्या करने का कार्य

treasonable *a.* राजहत्या-संबंधी

treasure *n.* कोष, धन, बहुमूल्य पदार्थ; *v.t.* बटोरना, बहुमूल्य

मानना; treasure - trove
पृथ्वी में का गड़ा हुआ धन

treasurer   *n.*   कोषाध्यक्ष,
खजान्ची

treasury *n.* कोष-गृह, खजाना

treat *v.t. & i.* व्यवहार करना,
प्रबन्ध करना, न्योता देना,
सौदा करना; *n.* न्योता,
भोज

treatise   *n.*   निबन्ध, लेख,
पुस्तक*. कृति*

treatment *n.* व्यवहार, रोग
की चिकित्सा

treaty *n.* संधिपत्र, मेल

tree *n.* वृक्ष, पेड़

trek *v.i.* (*p.t.* trekked) बैल-
गाड़ी पर यात्रा करना, धीरे-
धीरे वढ़ना

tremble *v.i.* कांपना, थर्राना

trembling *n.* कंपन

tremendous *a.* भयंकर, बहुत
बड़ा

tremor *n.* कंपकंपी*, थरथराहट*

trend *v.i.* किसी दशा में झुकना;
n. झुकाव, प्रवृत्ति*

trespass *v.t.* अतिक्रमण करना,
विघ्न डालना, बिना अधिकार
प्रवेश करना; *n.* अतिक्रम,
बिना आज्ञा प्रवेश

trial *n.* परीक्षा*, जांच*, अभि-
योग; on trial परीक्षा के
निमित्त

triangle *n.* त्रिकोण, त्रिभुज

triangular *a.* त्रिभुजाकार

tribal *a.* जाति-संबंधी, कबायली

tribe *n.* जाति*, वंश, कबीला

tribulation *n.* क्लेश, कष्ट

tribunal *n.* न्यायालय

tribune *n.* जनरक्षक, प्रजा-
नायक, धर्माध्यक्ष-सिंहासन
बिशप की कुर्सी, मंच

tributary *a.* कर देनेवाला,
आश्रित; *n.* सहायक नदी*

tribute *n.* राजकर, प्रशंसा

trick *n.* कपट, छल, चाल*,
v.t. छलना, ठगना

trickle *v.i.* टपकना, रसना; *n.*
बहनेवाली धारा*

tricoloured *a.* तीन रंग का,
तिरंगा

tricycle *n.* ट्राइसिकिल

trifle *n.* तुच्छ या अल्प मूल्य
का पदार्थ, एक प्रकार की
मिठाई*; *v.t.* समय नष्ट
करना; to trifle with
तिरस्कार करना, चुटकियों में
उड़ाना

trigger *n.* बन्दूक इत्यादि का
घोड़ा

trigonometry   *n.*   त्रिकोण-
मिति*

trinity *n.* त्रिमूर्ति*

trip *v.i.* (*p.t.* tripped) हलके
पैरों से चलना, लुढ़कना; *n.*

छोटी यात्रा*, पर्यटन

tripartite a. त्रिदलीय, त्रिखंड

triplicate a. & n. तीन प्रतियां*, तीसरी प्रति*; v.t. तिगुना करना, तीन प्रतिलिपि बनाना

trisect v.t. तीन बराबर टुकड़े करना

triumph n. विजय*, प्रसन्नता*; v.t. विजय प्राप्त करना

triumphal a. विजय-संबंधी

triumphant a. विजयी

Trojan n. & a. ट्राय देश संबंधी, योद्धा

troop n. दल, यूथ, सेना*; v.i. दल बांधकर चलना

trooper n. अश्वारोही, घुड़सवार

trophy n. (pl. trophies) जय-स्मारक, विजय-चिह्न, बहुमूल्य उपहार

tropic n. अयनवृत्त, क्रान्ति-मण्डल

tropical a. अयनवृत्त-संबंधी

trouble n. दुःख, पीड़ा*, क्लेश, खेद, आपत्ति*, व्यग्रता*; v.t. व्याकुल करना, कष्ट देना

troublesome a. दुःखदायी

troupe n. खिलाड़ी लोग, नाटक करनेवालों की मण्डली

trousers n. pl. पाजामा, पतलून

truant n. स्कूल से भागनेवाला

छात्र, आलसी मनुष्य

truce n. क्षणिक सन्धि*

truck n. छकड़ा, सग्गड़, बिना छत की रेलगाड़ी या मोटर. v.t. लेन-देन करना, अदल-बदल करना

true a. सत्य, यथार्थ, निष्कपट, सच्चा

truism n. यथार्थता*, सचाई*

truly adv. वस्तुन:, सचमुच

trumpet n. तुरही*; v.t. घोषणा करना, प्रकाशित करना

trunk n. वृक्ष का तना, पशु का शरीर, वस्त्र रखने का बक्स, हाथी की सूंड़*

trust n. ट्रस्ट, विश्वास, प्रतीति*, भरोसा, खास, अनेक व्यव-सायियों का संघ; trust money घरोहर; v.t. विश्वास करना

trustee n. ट्रस्टी, घरोहर रखने-वाला, किसी की सम्पत्ति का प्रबन्ध करनेवाला

trustful a. विश्वस्त

trustworthy a. विश्वास के योग्य

truth n. सत्यता*, सचाई*, ईमानदारी*

truthful a. सत्यवादी, सच्चा

try v.t. (p.t. tried) शक्ति लगाना, परखना, परीक्षा

करना, विधि के अनुसार
परीक्षा करना

trying *a.* कष्टकारी, पीड़ाकर

tube *n.* ट्यूब, नली, रेल की
सुरंग*

tuberculosis *n.* क्षय रोग

tug *v.t. & i.* (*p.t.* tugged)
कसकर खींचना, घसीटना;
tug of war रस्साकशी

tuition *n.* ट्यूशन, शिक्षण

tulip *n.* कन्द पुष्प, नलिनी*,
लाबा

tumble *v.i.* एकाएक गिरना,
उलटना

tumbler *n.* लुढ़कने वाला, नट,
काच-पात्र, गिलास ।

tumour *n.* व्रण, गिल्टी*

tumult *n.* उपद्रव, हलचल*,
कोलाहल

tune *n.* सुर, ताल, उचित
प्रकृति*, योग्य स्वभाव; *v.t.*
ताल-स्वर में रखना

tunnel *n.* सुरंग*; *v.t.* (*p.t.*
tunnelled) सुरंग बनाना

turban *n.* पगड़ी*, मुरेठा

turbine *n.* जलचक्की*

turbulence (-y) *ns.* विप्लव,
उपद्रव

turbulent *a.* विक्षुब्ध, उपद्रवी

turmoil *n.* कष्ट, विप्लव,
उपद्रव

turn *v.t. & i.* घूमना, चक्कर

देना, बदलना, पलटना
खरादना; to turn over
उलटना; to turn to ashes
भस्म कर देना; *n.* चक्कर,
आकृति*, स्वरूप, कार्य,
पारी*; turncoat स्वपक्ष-
त्यागी; turntable इंजन
का मुंह घुमाने का चबूतरा

turner *n.* खरादनेवाला

turpentine *n.* फीरोजा ताड़पीन

turpitude *n.* नीचता*,
दुष्टता*

turquoise *n.* फीरोजा, हरित-
नील-मणि

tutle *n.* जंगली कबूतर, समुद्री
कछुआ

tussle *n.* झगड़ा मुठभेड़

tutelage *n.* संरक्षण, रक्षा*

tutelar, tutelary *a.* संरक्षक

tutor *n.* (*fem.* tutoress)
ट्यूटर, निजी शिक्षक गुरु

tutorial *a.* शिक्षा-संबंधी

twelfth *a.* बारहवां

twelve *n. & a.* बारह

twentieth *a.* बीसवां

twenty *n. & a.* बीस

twi *pref.* 'दो' के अर्थ का उप-
सर्ग

twice *adv.* दुबारा, दो बार

twilight *n.* सन्निप्रकाश, गो-
धूलि-वेला*

twin *n.* यमज या जुड़वां बच्चे

twinkle   *v i.*   जगमगाना, चमकना

twist *v.t. & i.* ऐंठना, मोड़ना; *n.* ऐंठन, मोड़, एक प्रकार का पाश्चात्य नृत्य

twitter *n.* पक्षियों के कूकने का शब्द; *v.i* चूं-चूं करना

two *n. & a.* दो

twofold *a.* दूना, दुहरा

type *n.* बिंब, आदर्श, प्रति-मूर्ति*, आकृति*, छापने के अक्षर इत्यादि

typewriter *n.* टाइपराइटर

typhoid *n. & a.* टाइफायड, आंत्र-ज्वर

typhoon *n.* बड़ी आंधी*, बवंडर

typhus *n.* भयंकर सन्निपात ज्वर

typical *a.* विशिष्ट, आदर्शभूत

typify *v.t.* (*p.t.* typified) प्रतिरूप में प्रकट करना

typist *n.* टाइपिस्ट

tyranny *n.* क्रूरता*, निरंकुशता*

tyrant *n.* निरंकुश शासक, अत्याचारी व्यक्ति, निर्दयी मनुष्य, उपद्रवी व्यक्ति

tyre (tire) *n.* टायर

Tzar *n.* (*fem.* Tzarina) जार, पुराने रूसी राजा की उपाधि*

U

ugliness *n.* कुरूपता*, भद्दापन

ugly *a.* कुरूप, भद्दा, घृणित

ulcer *n.* नासूर, व्रण, फोड़ा

ulcerous *a.* व्रणयुक्त, नासूरदार

-ule *suf.* 'छोटा' के अर्थ में प्रयुक्त होनेवाला प्रत्यय यथा, globule

ulterior *a.* परोक्ष, दूर का, आगे का

ultimate *a.* अति दूर का, पिछला, अन्तिम

ultimatum *n.* (*pls.* ulti-mata, ultimatums) अन्तिम प्रतिज्ञा* या मांग या चेता-वनी*

ultra *pref.* 'दूसरी ओर, आगे, पार' के अर्थ का उपसर्ग

umbrella *n.* (*pl.* umbrellas) छाता, छतरी*

umpire *n.* अम्पायर, विपंच, खेल-पंच

-un *pref.* रहित या हीन' के अर्थ का उपसर्ग जो संज्ञा, विशेषण तथा सर्वनाम के पहिले जोड़ा जाता है

unable *a.* अप्रयोग्य, अशक्त

unanimity *n*. एकमत

unanimous *a*. सर्वसम्मत

unaware *a*. अनभिज्ञ, अनजान, असावधान

unawares *adv*. एकाएक, अकस्मात्

unburden *v.t*. भार हटाना, स्वीकारोक्ति करके चित्त शान्त करना

uncanny *a*. प्रारब्धिक, अस्वाभाविक, अद्भुत, विलक्षण, डरावना, मनहूस

uncle *n*. (*fem*. aunt) चाचा या मामा

uncouth *a*. कुत्सित, भद्दा. अनोखा, विलक्षण

uncrown *v.t*. राज्यपद से हटाना

under *prep*. नीचे, तले, अधीन, कम, हस्ताक्षर सहित; *adv*. नीची अवस्था में, अधीन; *a*. नीचे का

undercurrent *n*. अन्तर्धारा; *a*. अदृश्य, गुप्त, प्रच्छन्न, अदेखा

undergo *v.t*. (*p.t*. underwent, *p.p*. undergone) सहना, भोगना

undergraduate *n*. विश्वविद्यालय का विद्यार्थी जिसने उपाधि परीक्षा पास नहीं की है, अवर या उपस्नातक

underhand *a*. गुप्त, छलपूर्ण

underline *v.t*. रेखांकित करना

undermine *v.t*. गुप्त रीति से क्षति पहुचाना, भूमि में खोदना, सुरंग लगाना, नष्ट करना

understand *v.t. & i*. (*p.t. & p p*. understood) अर्थ समझना, सूचित करना, भलीभांति जानना, सूचित किया जाना

undertake *v.t. & i*. (*p.t*. undertook, *p.p*. undertaken) आरम्भ करना, प्रयत्न करना, साहस करना

undertone *n*. धीमा स्वर

underwear *n*. जांघिया, गंजी*

undo *v t*. (*p.t*. undid, *p p*. undone) किए हुए कार्य को भ्रष्ट करना, नाश करना, खोलना

unearth *v t*. धरती में से निकालना, पता लगाना

unfair *a*. अनुचित, छली, अन्यायी

unfold *v.t*. उघारना, फैलाना, प्रकाशित करना

unfortunate *a*. अभागा, बदकिस्मत

ungainly *a*. कुरूप, भद्दा

unhorse *v.t*. घोड़े पर से गिरा देना

unhouse *v.t*. घर से निकालना

uniform *a*. एकरूप; *n*. यूनिफार्म, वर्दी*

unify *v.t.* (*p.t.* unified) एकरूप बनाना, समान करना, एकता कायम करना

union *n.* यूनियन, मिलाप, संघ

unionist *n.* मेल का प्रचार करनेवाला; Union Jack इंगलैंड की राष्ट्रीय पताका*

unique *a.* अनोखा, अनूठा

unison *n.* एकता*, एक तान या सुर

unit *n.* एक व्यक्ति, इकाई*, एकांग, पृथक् भाग, तौल या नाप का स्थिर परिमाण

unite *v.t. & i.* मिलाना, मिलना, एक करना, जोड़ना

unity *n.* (*pl.* unities) योग, मेल, एकता*, संघबढ़ता*, संगति*, समानता*

universal *a.* विश्वव्यापी, सार्व-लौकिक

universality *n.* विश्वव्यापकता*

universe *n.* सृष्टि*, सम्पूर्ण जगत, विश्व

university *n.* (*pl.* univer-sities) विश्वविद्यालय

univocal *a.* एकार्थ, एकतानिक, एकस्वरीय

unjust *a.* अन्यायी, अनुचित, न्यायविरुद्ध

unless *conj.* जब तक न, सिवाय, यदि नहीं, न कि, मगर

unmanned *a.* मनुष्यों की सहायता न प्राप्त किए हुए

unmannered *a.* अशिष्ट, असभ्य

unprincipled *a.* सिद्धान्तहीन, अनैतिक

unreliable *a.* विश्वास न करने योग्य

unrest *n.* अशान्ति*, व्याकुलता*

unruly *a.* अधीन न करने योग्य, बुरे व्यवहार का, अविनीत

unsafe *a.* अरक्षित, खतरनाक

unsettle *v.t. & i.* अस्थिर करना, व्यग्र होना

unsheathe *v.t.* म्यान से बाहर निकालना

unsmooth *a.* खुरखुरा, रूखा

unspent *a.* अक्षय, न खर्च किया हुआ

until *prep. & conj.* जब तक, तक

untoward *a.* हठी, कष्टकारी, भद्दा, अभागा

unwell *a.* रोगी, अस्वस्थ

unwittingly *adv.* अनजाने, अज्ञानता से

up *adv.* ऊपर, ऊपर की ओर, तक; ups and downs भाग्य का चढ़ाव-उतार; up to तक

uphill *a.* दु:साध्य, कठिन; *adv.* ऊपर की ओर

uphold *v.t.* (*p.t. & p.p.* up-held) उठाना, समर्थन करना,

बचाना

upkeep n. पालन, समारक्षण, मरम्मत*

uplift v.t. उठाना, उभाड़ना

upright a. खड़ा, सीधा, न्यायी, ईमानदार

uprising n. विद्रोह, बगावत*, बलवा

uproar n. उपद्रव, हुल्लड़, ऊधम

uproarious a. उपद्रवी

uproot v.t. जड़ से उखाड़ना

upset v.t. (p t. & p.p. up-set) घबरा देना, उलटना, औंधाना

urban a. नगरीय, नगर का, शहरो

urbane a. शीलवान, शिष्ट, भद्र

urbanity n. शिष्टता*, सुज-नता*, भद्रता.*

urchin n. बच्चा, छोकरा

urge v t. प्रवृत्त करना, उत्तेजित करना

urgency n. आवश्यकता*, आग्रह, जरूरत*

urgent a. अति आवश्यक

urinal n. मूत्रस्थान, मूत्रालय

urinate v.i. मूत्र त्याग करना

urine n. मूत्र, पेशाब

usage n. व्यवहार आचरण, रीति*, प्रथा*, दस्तूर

use n. व्यवहार, उपयोग, रीति*, चलन*; v.t. & i. प्रयोग

करना, व्यवहार करना, अभ्यास होना, अपने काम में लाना

useful a. प्रयोग करने योग्य, उपयोगी

useless a. निष्फल, व्यर्थ, बेकार

usher n. प्रवेशक, भेंट कराने-वाला, उपशिक्षक; v.t. प्रवेश करना, भेंट कराना

usual a. सामान्य, व्यावहारिक, प्रसिद्ध

usually adv. सामान्य या साधारण रीति से

usurp v t. बिना अधिकार के किसी की सम्पत्ति को छीन लेना, हड़पना

usurpation n. बलापहार, अप-हरण

usury n. सूदखोरी*

utensil n. बर्तन, बासन

utility n. उपयोगिता*, उपयोग, लाभ

utilize v.t. उपयोग करना, काम में लाना

utopia n. आदर्शलोक, काल्प-निक आदर्श, आदर्श सुख-शान्ति का स्थान या स्थिति*

utopian a. काल्पनिक, अव्यव-हार्य मात्रविचारक, स्वप्नदर्शी सुधारक

utterly adv. सम्पूर्णतः, सर्वथा, निपट, सरासर, निरा, बिलकुल

V

vacancy n. रिक्तता, शून्य पद

vacant a. शून्य, रिक्त, छूछा, विचारशून्य; vacant-minded खोखले दिमागवाला

vacate v.t. खाली करना, रिक्त करना छोड़ना

vacation n. छुट्टी*, अवकाश, विश्राम-काल

vaccinate v.t. टीका लगाना

vaccination n. टीका

vaccinator n. टीका लगानेवाला

vaccine n. वैक्सीन, टीका लगाने में प्रयुक्त दवा, रस, लासा

vacuum n. (pl. vacuums, vacua) शून्य, शून्य स्थान, आकाश; vacuum flask ऐसी बोतल जिसमें रखा हुआ तरल पदार्थ अपनी शीतोष्ण अवस्था देर तक बनाए रखता है

vagabond n. स्वेच्छाचारी या घुमक्कड़ व्यक्ति, आवासहीन व्यक्ति; a. स्वेच्छाचारी, घुमन्तू

vagary n. (pl. vagaries) विचित्र कल्पना*, विभ्रम, तरंग*, खब्त*, वहम

vague a. अनिश्चित, अस्थिर, सन्दिग्ध, अस्पष्ट

vaguely adv. अनिश्चित ढंग से

vagueness n. अस्थिरता*, अस्पष्टता*

vain a. शून्य, गर्वी, असार, व्यर्थ, दिखौवा; in vain वृथा, व्यर्थ

vainglory n. वृथा अभिमान

vainly adv. गर्व से, मूर्खता से

valiant a. पराक्रमी, वीर, साहसी

valid a. पुष्ट, सप्रमाण, मान्य, वैध

validity n. मान्यता*, वैधता*

validate v.t. वैध करना, मान्य करना, प्रमाणित करना, सही करना

valley n. (pl. valleys) दर्रा, घाटी*

valour n. शूरता*, वीरता*, पराक्रम

valuable a. बहुमूल्य, मूल्यवान

valuables n. pl. बहुमूल्य द्रव्य, जवाहरात

value n. उपयोगिता*, मूल्य, अच्छाई*, महत्त्व; v.t. दाम आंकना, आदर करना

valve n. एक ओर खुलनेवाला कपाट, रेडियो के यंत्र का कुम्बा, वाल्व

van n. सेना का अगला भाग, रेलगाड़ी का माल रखने का

डब्बा, वैन ; vanguard n. सेना-मुख, सेना का अगुझा, हिरावल दस्ता

vanish v.t. लुप्त होना, नष्ट होना

vanishing a. अदृश्य होता हुआ

vanity n. वृथा अभिमान, अहंकार

vanquish v.t. जीतना

vaporize v.t. भाप बनना

vaporous a. वाष्पपूर्ण, वाष्पीय, अस्पार

vapour n. वाष्प, भाप

varied a. विविध, नानारूप, विभिन्न

variety n. भेद, विविधता*, विभिन्न प्रकार; variety entertainment or show वैराइटी मनोरंजन, वैराइटी शो

various a. भिन्न, विविध, अनेक

varnish n. वार्निश, रोगन, कलफ; v.t. वार्निश या रोगन लगाना, चमकाना

vary v.t. & i. (p.t. varied) बदलना, भिन्न रूप धारण करना, रूपान्तर होना

vaseline n. वैसलिन, मृतैलवसा

vassal n. कृषक, असामी, दास

vast a. विशाल, बहुत बड़ा

vastly adv. बहुतायत से

vault n. गुम्बज, गुफा*, कंदरा*, अन्त:कक्ष, तहखाना, कुदान; v t. & i. मेहराब बनाना, छलांग मारना; the vault of heaven आकाश

vaultage n. मेहराबदार तह-खाना

vegetable n. शाक, वनस्पति*, तरकारी*

vegetarian n. शाकाहारी

vegetate v.i. वनस्पति की तरह उगना

vegetation n. वनस्पति-जीवन, तृणजाति*, हरियाली. सब्जा

vegetative a. वनस्पति के समान उगनेवाला, वानस्प-तिक, वर्द्धनशील, उत्पादनक्षम

vehement a. प्रचण्ड, उत्सुक, बलवान

vehemently adv. बड़े वेग या बल से

vehicle n. गाड़ी*, सवारी*, वाहक, माध्यम, साधन, उप-करण, द्वार; अनुपान

veil n. घूंघट, पर्दा, छद्य वेश; v.t. घूंघट लगाना, छिपाना; to throw the veil off प्रकट होना

vein n. शिरा*, पत्ती की नस*

velocity n. वेग, गति*, चाल*

velvet n. मखमल

velvety n. मखमल के समान

चिकना

velveteen *n.* बनावटी सूती मखमल

vender, vendor *n.* बेचनेवाला

venerable *a.* आदरणीय, पूज्य

venerate *v.t.* प्रतिष्ठा करना, सम्मान करना

vengeance *n* प्रतिशोध, बदला

venom *n.* विष, हानिकारक पदार्थ, द्वेष; *v.t.* विष प्रयोग करना

venomous *a.* विषैला, द्वेषी

ventilate *v.t.* संचारित करना, समालोचना करना, प्रचार करना

ventilation *n.* संवातन, प्रका- शन, बहस*

ventilator *n.* वातायन

venture *n.* साहस, संशय, संकट, जोखिम का काम; *v.t. & i.* जोखिम उठाने का साहस करना

veracious *a.* सच्चा, निष्कपट

veracity *n.* सचाई*, यथा- तथ्यता*

verandah *n.* अलिन्द, बरामदा

verb *n.* क्रियापद

verbal *a.* कहा हुआ, वाचिक, मौखिक, क्रियापद से बना हुआ

verbally *adv.* यथाशब्द, मुख से, जबानी

verbatim *adv.* शब्दशः

verbose *a.* शब्दाडम्बरपूर्ण

verbosity *n.* शब्दाडम्बर, वाक्- प्रपंच

verdict *n.* पंचनिर्णय, निश्चित मत

verge *n.* छड़ी*, डंडा, किनारा, सीमाप्रान्त, स्थान; *v.i.* झुकना, पहुंचना

verification *n.* प्रमाणीकरण

vermillion *n.* सिन्दूर

vernacular *a.* देशी, अपने देश का. *n.* मातृभाषा*; verna- cular language प्राकृत भाषा*

versatile *a.* बहुविद्य, बहुश्रुत, बहुमुखी, परिवर्तनशील, चंचल, अस्थिर

versatility *n* सर्वतोमुखी प्रतिभा, बहुशस्त्रज्ञता; परि- वर्तनशीलता, चंचलता, अस्थिरता

verse *n.* पाद, कविता*, पद्य; blank-verse अतुकान्त पद्य

versed *a.* प्रवीण, निपुण, दक्ष, कुशल

versification *n.* कविता-लेखन

versify *v.i. & t.* (*p.t.* versi- fied) कविता बनाना

version *n.* अनुवाद, पाठान्तर, विवरण

versus *prep.* विपरीत, प्रति

vertical *a.* लम्बरूप, खड़े बल का

vertically *adv.* लम्बरूप में

vertigo *n.* चक्कर, घुमरी*

verve *n.* उत्साह, ओज, बल

very *a.* सत्य, ठीक, सच्चा; *adv.* प्रति, बहुत

vessel *n.* पात्र, पोत या जहाज, रक्तवाहिनी*

vestige *n.* पदचिह्न, अवशिष्ट भाग

veteran *a.* वृद्ध तथा अनुभवी; *n.* दक्ष व्यक्ति, कुशल व्यक्ति

veterinary *a.* पशु-चिकित्सा संबंधी

veto *n.* (*pl.* vetoes) विटो, निषेधाधिकार, प्रतिषेध; *v.t.* निषेध करना, विटो का प्रयोग करना

vex *v.t.* खिजलाना, पीड़ा देना, कष्ट देना

vexation *n.* कष्ट, दुःख

via *n.* मार्ग; *adv.* मार्ग से

vibrate *v. i. & t.* थर्राना, हिलना, कांपना, झूलना, झुलाना, स्पन्दित होना

vibration *n.* कंपकंपी, थरथरी*

vibratory *a.* थर्राता हुआ

vicar *n.* ग्राम-पादरी

vicarious *a.* प्रतिनिधिरूप, स्थानापन्न, प्रतिरूपी, परार्थ कार्य करनेवाला

vice *n.* दोष, पाप, प्रघर्म, बांक, शिकंजा

vice *pref.* 'प्रतिनिधि, बदले में' अर्थ का उपसर्ग

viceregal *a.* वाइसराय के प्रतिनिधि से संबंधी

viceroy *n.* (*fem.* vice-reine) वायसराय, बड़ा लाट

vicinity *n.* समीपता*, पड़ोस

vicious *a.* दूषित, दुराचारी, पापी

viciously *adv.* दुष्टता से

victim *n.* शिकार, बलि, पीड़ित व्यक्ति

victimize *v.t.* बलि देना, ठगना, पीड़ित करना

victor *n.* विजयी, युद्ध में जीतनेवाला

victorious *a.* विजयी

victory *n* विजय*, जीत*

view *n.* आलोकन, दृष्टि*, दृष्टिपथ, उद्देश्य, इच्छा*, *v.t.* देखना, पर्यवेक्षण करना; point of view पक्ष; in view of विचार से

viewer *n.* पर्यवेक्षक, समीक्षक

viewless *a.* अदृश्य, अगोचर, अलक्ष्य

vigil *n.* सजगता*, जागृति*, चौकसी* रात्रि में जागरण, रतजगा

vigilance *n.* सावधानी*, चौकसी*

vigilant *a* सावधान

vigour *n.* शक्ति*, बल, प्रभाव

vigorous *a.* बलवान, प्रबल

vigorously *adv.* उत्साह से

vilify *v.t.* निन्दा करना, कलंक लगाना

villa *n.* विला, गांव का बंगला

village *n.* गांव, देहात

villager *n.* ग्रामनिवासी, देहाती

villain *n.* दुष्ट मनुष्य, खल-नायक

vincibility, vincibleness *ns* जीतने की योग्यता*

vincible *a.* जीतने योग्य

vindicate *v.t.* प्रतिपादन करना, निर्दोष सिद्ध करना, बचाना, समर्थन करना, प्रमा-णित करना

vindication *n.* प्रतिपादन, पुष्टीकरण, दोष-मुक्ति*, परिशोधन

vinegar *n.* सिरका, खट्टा पदार्थ

vineyard *n.* अंगूर का उद्यान

vintage *n.* द्राक्षा, अंगूर, द्राक्षा-चयन ऋतु*, अंगूर आने का मौसम

violate *v.t.* उल्लंघन करना, भंग करना, तोड़ना

violation (नियम का) उल्लंघन

violence *n.* हिंसा*, बल, उत्पात, अपराध; to do violence to आक्रमण करना

violent *a.* प्रबल, तीखा

violet *n.* बनफशा, वायलेट, पीले, बैंगनी तथा कई प्रकार के रंगों वाला पौधा; *a.* पाटल, नील लोहित, जामनी रंग का, बैंगनी

violin *n.* वायलिन, चिकारा, बेला*

violinist *n.* वायलिन बजाने-वाला

virgin *n.* कुमारी*, कन्या*; *a.* कन्यानुरूप, निर्मल, पवित्र

virginity *n.* कुमारीत्व, अक्षतावस्था*, सतीत्व, पवित्रता*

Virginia *n.* एक प्रकार की अमेरिका देश की तम्बाकू

virile *a.* पौरुषेय, वीर्यवान, पुष्ट

virose *a.* विषाणु, वाइरस

virtual *a.* यथार्थ, आभासी

virtually *adv.* यथार्थतः, वस्तुतः

virtue *n.* धर्म, सदाचार, नीति*, गुण; in virtue of प्रभाव से

virtuous *a.* सच्चरित्र, धार्मिक

virulence *n.* प्रचण्डता*

virulent *a.* प्रचण्ड, तीव्र

visibility *n.* दृश्यता*, प्रत्य-क्षता*

visible *a.* दृष्टिगोचर, प्रत्यक्ष

vision *n.* दृष्टि*, कल्पना*, छाया*, स्वप्न

visionary *a. & n.* मानसिक, काल्पनिक, स्वप्न देखने (काल्पनिक विचार करने) वाला

visit *n.* दर्शन, भेंट; *v.t. & i.* भेंट करना, मिलना

vista *n.* वृक्षों के बीच का सुन्दर पथ, वीथिका*, मानसिक सिंहावलोकन या आभास

visual *a.* दृष्टिगत, चाक्षुष

visualize *v.t.* कल्पना में देखना, मानसिक दर्शन करना

vital *a.* जीव-संबंधी, आवश्यक

vitality *n.* चेतना*, प्राण, जीवनशक्ति*

vitalize *v.t.* जीवन प्रदान करना, जिलाना

vitals *n. pl.* शरीर के मर्म-स्थान

vitamin *n.* विटामिन

vitiate *v.t.* दूषित करना, बिगाड़ना

vivacious *a.* प्रफुल्न, उत्साह-युक्त

vivacity *n.* उत्साह, प्रफुल्लता*

vivavoce *adv.* मौखिक, संभाषण द्वारा

vivid *a.* सजीव, स्पष्ट, तीव्र

vividly *adv.* स्पष्ट रूप में या से

vividness *n.* स्पष्टता*, सजीवता*, तीव्रता*

vivisect *v.t.* चीर-फाड़ करना

vocabulary *n.* शब्द-भण्डार, शब्दकोश

vocalist *n.* गायक, गानेवाला

vocalize *v.t.* शब्दयुक्त करना

vocation *n.* व्यवसाय, व्यापार, काम

vociferous *a.* कोलाहलपूर्ण, चीखनेवाला

vogue *n.* व्यवहार, ढंग, रीति*; in vogue प्रचलित

voice *n.* स्वर, वचन, वाणी*, सम्मति*, अभिप्राय, मत; *v.t.* शब्द करना, शब्दों में कहना; with one voice एकमत होकर; active voice कर्तृवाच्य; passive voice कर्मवाच्य

void *a.* शून्य, रिक्त, निरर्थक; to make void निरर्थक करना; *n.* शून्य स्थान; *v.t.* छोड़ना, त्यागना

voidness *n.* शून्यता*

volcanic *a.* ज्वालामुखी पर्वत संबंधी

volcano n. (pl. volcanoes) ज्वालामुखी पहाड़

volition n. इच्छाशक्ति*, संकल्प

volley n. (pl. volleys) शस्त्रों (गोलियों) की वर्षा*; v.t. गोलियों की वर्षा करना

volt n. बिजली की शक्ति की नाप की इकाई*, वोल्ट

voltage n. वोल्टों की नाप*

volume n. पुस्तक, ग्रंथ, विस्तार, परिमाण, घनफल

voluminous a. अनेक ग्रंथों का, लम्बा, विस्तीर्ण

voluntarily adv. स्वेच्छापूर्वक

voluntary a. इच्छापूर्वक, आप ही आप, ऐच्छिक

volunteer n. स्वयं-सेवक ; v.t. स्वयंसेवक बनना

voluptuous a. विषयी, विलासी

vomit v.t. & i. (p.t. vomited) कै या वमन करना ; n. वमन किया हुआ पदार्थ

vomiting n. वमन, कै

votary n. (fem. votaress) पूजक, भक्त, उपासक, कट्टर अनुयायी

vote n. वोट, मत, सम्मति*, अनुमोदन, राय; v.t. & i. वोट देना, मत देना, सम्मति देना

voucher n. प्रमाणपत्र, रसीद, खर्च का पुर्जा, बीजक, वाउचर

vouchsafe v.t. & i. साक्ष्य देना, कृपा करके देना, स्वीकार करने की कृपा करना

vow n. व्रत, प्रतिज्ञा; v.t. & i. प्रतिज्ञा करना, वचन देना

vowel n. स्वर (अक्षर); a. स्वरपूर्ण

voyage n. समुद्र-यात्रा*

voyager n. समुद्र-यात्रा करनेवाला

vulcanization n. गन्धकपूर्ण रबड़ बनाने की विधि, वलकनीकरण

vulcanize v.t. & i. गन्धक मिलाकर रबड़ का गुण बदलना, वलकन करना

vulgar a. भद्दा, देहाती, अशिष्ट, नीच

vulgarism n. गंवारपन, भद्दापन

vulgarize v.t. असभ्य बनाना, अति साधारण बन कर नष्ट करना

vulgarity n. गंवारपन, भद्दापन

vulnerable a. छेद्य, भेद्य, वेध्य, आलोच्य, आक्रमणीय

vulture n. गिद्ध, लोभी व्यक्ति

W

wade *v.i.* पानी में हल कर चलना, कठिनता से चलना

wafer *n* पतली रोटी*, मुहर करने की टिकिया*, 'वेफ़र, पतला बिस्कुट

waft *v i.* जल या वायु में तैरना

wage *v.t.* दांव लगाना, साहस. करना

wager *n.* दांव, *v.i.* दांव लगाना

wages *n. pl.* वेतन, मज़दूरी*

waggle *v.i. & t.* हिलना, घुमाना

wagon *n.* वैगन, रेल का डब्बा

wail *v.i.* विलाप करना, रोना; *n.* विलाप, रुलाई*

waist *n.* कमर*, कटिभाग, जहाज का सबसे चौड़ा भाग

wait *v.i. & t.* प्रतीक्षा करना, भेंट करना; to wait for घात में रहना; to wait upon नौकरी करना; waiting-maid दासी*

waiter *n.* वेटर, सेवक

waive *v.t.* त्यागना, छोड़ना, हटाना

wake *v.i. & t.* (*p.t.* woke or waked) जागना, जगाना; *n.* जागरण

waken *v.t. & i.* जगाना, जगना

walk *v.i.* पैदल चलना, टहलना, प्रस्थान करना; *n.* मार्ग, चाल*, कार्य का विस्तार, टहलने का स्थान; to walk away भाग जाना

wall *n.* दीवार*, (ब०व०) किलाबन्दी*; *v.t.* दीवार से घेरना; to go to the wall हटा दिया जाना

wallet *n.* बटुआ, भोला, थैली*

wander *v.i.* घूमना, विचरना, भटकना

wanderer *n.* विचरनेवाला

wandering *a. & n.* भ्रमण, अस्थिरता*

wane *v i.* कम होना, घटना, घटाव, क्षय

want *n.* अभाव, दरिद्रता*; *v.t. & i.* इच्छा करना, चाहना, कम होना, आवश्यकता होना

wanton *a.* खिलाड़ी, मर्यादा-हीन, लम्पट

war *n.* युद्ध, संग्राम, लड़ाई*, शत्रुता*; *v i.* (*p.t.* warred) युद्ध करना

warfare *n.* युद्ध, संग्राम

warlike *a.* रणप्रिय, संग्राम के योग्य

ward *n.* रक्षक, रक्षित व्यक्ति, ताले की भर, ग्रस्पताल का भाग; *v.t.* ग्राक्रमण से बचाना, रक्षा करना

warden *n.* वार्डेन, रक्षक, रक्षापुरुष

warder *n.* वारडर, द्वारपाल, पहरेदार

wardrobe *n.* वस्त्र रखने का कमरा या ग्रलमारी*

ware *n.* भाजन, पात्र, द्रव्य

wares *n. pl.* सौदा, माल-ग्रसबाब; warehouse माल रखने का गोदाम; *v.t.* गोदाम में रखना

warm *a.* गरम, तीव्र, उत्सुक, तीक्ष्ण, सहानुभूति-युक्त, क्रुद्ध; warm-colours पीले या लाल ग्राधार का रंग; warm-welcome उत्साह-सहित स्वागत; warm-hearted ग्रति स्नेह दिख-लानेवाला; *v.t. & i.* गरम करना या होना

warmth *n.* साधारण गरमी, उत्साह

warn *v.t.* सावधान करना, चेतावनी देना

warning *n.* चेतावनी*

warrant *n.* ग्रधिकार, प्रमाण, पकड़ने का हुकमनामा, वारंट; *v.t.* प्रमाणित करना, स्थिर करना

warrior *n.* वीर, योद्धा

warship *n.* युद्ध का जहाज

wash *v.t. & i.* धोना, गोला करना, बहाना, स्नान करना, शुद्ध करना; *n.* धोने का कार्य, तरल पदार्थ, पतला रंग

washable *a.* धोने योग्य

washer *n.* धोनेवाला, धोबी, वाशर

washerman *n.* (*fem.* washerwoman) धोबी

waste *a.* परती, जंगली, निरर्थक; *n.* जंगल, क्षय, नाश, कूड़ा-कर्कट; *v.t. & i.* उड़ाना, नाश करना, क्षय होना

wasteful *a.* ग्रपव्ययी, उड़ाऊ, हानिकारक

watch *v.t. & i.* चौकसी करना, सावधानी से देखना; *n.* रक्षा*, चौकसी*, रक्षक, जेब घड़ी*; to be on the watch राह देखना; to keep watch रखवाली करना; to watch over सचेत होना

watchful *a.* सावधान, चौकन्ना

watchword *n.* प्रत्यय वचन, प्रहरी-संकेत, दल-सिद्धान्त

water *n.* जल, नदी*, भील*, रत्नों की चमक*; *v.t. & i.*

जल से सींचना, पानी
पिलाना, पीना; water-
colour पानी मिलाकर
पोतने का रंग, ऐसा रंगा
हुआ चित्र; water-course
जलमार्ग, प्रबाह; watering-
place जल प्राप्त करने का
स्थान

waterfall n. झरना

water-melon n. तरबूज़

water-mill n. पनचक्की*

waterproof a. & n. वाटर-
प्रूफ, जल प्रवेश न करने
योग्य, ऐसा वस्त्र

watershed n. दो नदियों के
बीच की भूमि*

water-way n. नहर*

waterworks n. जलकल

watt n. बिजली की नाप*

wave n. लहर*, तरंग*; v i.
& t. लहराना, लहरिया
बनाना, संकेत करना

wax n. मोम, कान का खूंट,
मुहर लगाने की लाह*;
v.i. & t. मोम रगड़ना,
बढ़ना, बढ़ाना

way n. सड़क, मार्ग, दिशा*,
विधि*, प्रकार, दूरी*;
a little way थोड़ी दूरी;
by the way प्रसंगवश;
to give way पीछे हटना;
a long way off बहुत दूर;

in every way सर्वथा

waylay v.t. (p.t. waylaid,
p p. waylain) घात में
रहना

wayward a. स्वेच्छाचारी,
हठधर्मी

weak a. दुर्बल, अशक्त, अस्थिर,
कोमल, मूर्ख

weaken v.t. & i. दुर्बल करना
या होना

weak-headed a. कमज़ोर
बुद्धि का

weak-hearted a. साहसहीन,
डरपोक

weakling n. दुर्बल प्राणी

weakly a. दुर्बल

weakness n. दुर्बलता*

wealth n. धन, वैभव, सम्पत्ति*

wealthily adv. वैभव से

wealthy a. धनी

weapon n. शस्त्र, आयुध

wear v.t. & i. (p t. wore
p. p. worn) पहिनाना,
नष्ट होना, सहना; n. कपड़ा,
वस्त्र, कमी*; to wear
away घिसकर कम होना;
to wear out विस जाना

weary a. थका हुआ, रोगी,
खिन्न; v.t. & i. (p.t.
wearied) थकना, थकाना

weather n. मौसम, वायु की
अवस्था* समय; v.t. वायु के

सम्मुख करना, सहन करना,
जहाज को वायु की ओर ले
जाना;   weather-beaten
a. सब प्रकार की जलवायु
के सम्मुख किया हुआ;
weathercock वायु की
दिशा बतलाने की पंखी*

weave   *v t.* (*p.t.* wove,
p. p. woven) कपड़ा बुनना,
बैठाना

weaver *n.* जुलाहा

web *n.* जाला, मकड़े का जाला,
जल-पक्षियों के पंजे की
झिल्ली*;   web-footed
झिल्लीदार पंजेवाला

wed *v.t.* (*p.t.* wedded)
विवाह करना, मिलाना

wedded *a.* विवाहित

wedding *n.* विवाह, विवाह-
संबंधी

wedlock *n.* विवाह

wedge *n.* पच्चड़, फन्नी;
v.t. पच्चड़ ठोंकना, फाड़ना

Wednesday *n.* बुधवार

week *n.* सप्ताह, हफ्ता; week-
day रविवार के अतिरिक्त
सप्ताह का कोई दिन; week-
end सप्ताहान्त, शनिवार
की रात्रि से सोमवार के
प्रातःकाल तक

weekly *a.*, *adv.* & *n.*
साप्ताहिक, साप्ताहिक पत्र

weep *v.i.* (*p.t.* & *p. p.*
wept) आंसू बहाना, रोना,
विलाप करना

weeping *n.* विलाप

weigh *v.t.* & *i.* तौलना,
विचार करना, लंगर उठाना,
मनन करना, दबाना; to
weigh down उदास करना;
to weigh down upon
पीड़ा देना

weight *n.* भारीपन, तौल,
बटखरा, प्रभाव, बोझ;
v.t. बोझ लादना

welcome *a.* अभिनन्दित, मनो-
रंजक, रमणीय, शुभ; *n.*
स्वागत; *v.t.* स्वागत करना;
अभिनंदन करना

weld *v.t.* पीटकर धातु को
जोड़ना, मिलाना; *n.* इस
प्रकार का जोड़

well *a.* (*comp.* better. *sup.*
best) स्वस्थ, कुशल, नीरोग,
सुखी, योग्य; *adv.* अच्छी
तरह से, भली भांति, उचित
रीति से; as well as साथ,
भी;   well-nigh प्रायः;
well-to-do धनवान; *interj.*
बहुत ठीक ! अच्छा ! very
well बहुत ठीक; well then
तब तो

well *n.* कुआं, झरना

welt *n.* किनारा, गोट, मगजी*;

v.t. मगज़ी लगाना

West *n.* पश्चिम दिशा*; *a.* पश्चिमी; westerly, western *a.* पश्चिमी

westward *adv.* पश्चिम की ओर

wet *a.* भीगा, बरसाती; *n.* गीलापन; *v.t.* पानी से तर करना

wet-nurse *n.* दूध पिलाने-वाली धाय*

whale *n.* हेल, बड़ी समुद्री मछली*

what *interj. & pron.* क्या, कौन, जो कुछ, कितना; whatever *pron.* जो कुछ; whatnot *n.* बिना दरवाज़े की अलमारी*, टांड; whatsoever जो कुछ

wheat *n.* गेहूं

wheel *n.* चक्र, पहिया*, चाक, चक्र के आकार का यंत्र; *v.t. & i.* चक्कर देना, चक्कर खाना; wheel-barrow एक पहिये की ठेलागाड़ी*

when *adv.* जब, जिस समय, जबकि

whence *adv.* किस कारण से, कैसे

whenever *adv.* जब कभी

whensoever *adv.* जिस किसी समय

where *adv.* जहां, जिस स्थान में; whereabout किस स्थान के पास; whereabouts जहां कोई पाया जाता हो; where-by जिससे; wherefore जिस हेतु से; whereof जिसके; whereon जिसपर; wheresoever जिस किसी स्थान पर; whereupon जिसपर

which *pron.* जो, कौन-सा; whichever जौन-सा, चाहे यह या वह; whichsoever जो कोई भी

while *n.* क्षण, उचित समय; *conj. & adv.* जिस समय, जब तक; *v.t. & i.* वृथा समय बिताना, आनन्द से समय काटना

whilst *adv.* जब तक

whim *n.* मन की लहर*, चित्त की तरंग*

whimsical *a.* तरंगी, मनमौजी

whimsy *n.* झक*, लहर*

whip *v.t.* (*p t.* whipped) कोड़ा मारना, चाबुक से मारना; *n* चाबुक, कोचवान, सचेतक, whip-hand प्रभाव, सुविधा*

whipping *n.* बेंत की मार*

whirl *v.t. & i.* वेग से चक्कर खाना, शीघ्रता से ले जाना;

n. चक्कर, घुमान

whirlpool *n.* जल का भंवर

whirlwind *n.* चक्रवात, बवण्डर

whisky *n.* व्हिस्की*, जौ से बनी हुई मदिरा*

whisper *n.* कानाफूसी*, फुस-फुसाहट; *v.t.* कानाफूसी करना, धीरे से बोलना

whistle *v.i. & t.* सीटी बजाना, सीटी बजाकर पुकारना; *n.* सीटी*, सीटी का शब्द

white *a.* सफेद, शुभ्र, बिना घबने का; *n.* कोई सफेद पदार्थ; *v.t.* सफेद करना

whitewash *n. & v.t.* सफेदी*, सफेदी करना, चूने से पुताई करना

whither *adv.* जिधर, जहां तक

whithersoever *adv.* जिस किसी स्थान में

who *relative or interrogative pron.* कौन, किसने; whoever जो कोई; whosoever कोई भी व्यक्ति

whole *a.* पूर्ण, स्वस्थ; *n.* पूरी वस्तु*, सम्पूर्ण भाग; on the whole साधारणतः सब बातों का विचार करके; whole-hearted हार्दिक

wholesale *n.* थोक बिक्री; *a.* समग्र रूप का, थोक

wholesome *a.* स्वास्थ्यकर,

आनन्दकर

wholly *adv.* पूर्ण रूप से, सर्वथा

whom *pron. objective case of* 'who' जिसको; whomsoever जिस किसी मनुष्य को

whore *n.* वेश्या*, कसबिन*

whose *pron. possessive case of* 'who' *or* 'which' जिसका, किसका

why *adv.* क्यों? किस कारण से? किस लिए?

wicked *a.* पापी, दुष्ट, दुश्चरित्र

wicket *n.* खिड़की*, छोटा किवाड़, विकेट या क्रिकेट के खेल का गड़ा हुआ डंडा जिस पर गेंद मारा जाता है

wide *a.* चौड़ा, विस्तीर्ण, लक्ष्य से दूर

wideawake *a.* सचेत, चैतन्य

widen *v.t. & i.* चौड़ा करना या होना

widespread *a.* दूर तक फैला हुआ

width *n.* चौड़ाई*

widow *n.* (*mas.* widower) विधवा, रांड; *v.t.* विधवा करना

widower *n.* विधुर, रंडुआ

wife *n.* (*pl.* wives) पत्नी*, भार्या*, जोरू*

wild *a.* बनैला, बिना जोता-बोया, जंगली, क्रोधी, तीव्र, उन्मत्त, अस्थिर, बुद्धिहीन, व्याकुल

wilderness *n.* उजाड़ स्थान, जंगल

will *n.* इच्छा-शक्ति*, इच्छा*, आज्ञा*, संकल्प, दृढ़ता*, मृत्युपत्र, वसीयत*; *v.t.* इच्छा करना, संकल्प करना, आज्ञा देना, वसीयतनामा लिखना

willing *a.* इच्छुक, उद्यत

willingness *n.* सम्मति*, रजा-मंदी*

win *v t. & i.* (*p.t. & p.p.* won) जीतना, प्राप्त करना, विजयी होना

wind *n.* वायु*, हवा*. सांस*, बातरोग, वृथा वार्ता*; *v.i. & t.* (*p.t.* wound) बहना, फूंकना, तेज हांकना; how the wind blows कैसी स्थिति या अवस्था है

wind *v.t. & i.* (*p.t. & p p.* wound) लपेटना, मोड़ना, घुमाव में होना; wind up समेटना, समाप्त करना

windmill *n.* हवा-चक्की*

window *n.* खिड़की*, झरोखा

wind-up *n.* अन्त, परिणाम

windward *n.* पवन की दिशा*; *a. & adv.* जिस दिशा से वायु बहती है, वायु की ओर

windy *a.* हवादार, बक्की

wine *n.* अंगूर की मदिरा*

wing *n.* पर, डैना, रंगमंच का पार्श्व भाग; *v.t. & i.* उड़ना, पर लगाना; on the wing उड़ता हुआ

winter *n.* जाड़े की ऋतु*, शिशिरकाल; *v.t.* जाड़ा बिताना

wipe *v.t.* पोंछना, मिटाना, रगड़कर स्वच्छ करना

wire *n.* धातुसूत्र, तार, तार का समाचार; *v.t.* तार से बांधना, तार द्वारा समाचार भेजना

wireless *a* बिना तार का; *n.* बिना तार द्वारा समाचार भेजने या मंगाने का यंत्र, वायरलेस

wirepuller *n.* षड्यंत्र रचने-वाला

wisdom *n* चतुराई*, पाण्डित्य, बुद्धि*, विवेक

wise *a.* विद्वान, पंडित, चतुर; *n.* प्रकार, रीति*, ढंग

wiseacre *n.* अपने को बुद्धिमान समझनेवाला मनुष्य, लाल-बुझक्कड़, ज्ञानाभिमानी

wish *n.* इच्छा*, अभिलाषा*, आकांक्षा*; *v.t. & i.* अभि-

लाषा करना, इच्छा करना

wishful *a.* उत्सुक, अभिलाषी, इच्छुक

wit *n.* बुद्धि*, बुद्धिचातुर्य, रसिकोक्ति*, ममखरापन, हाज़िरजवाबी

witless *a.* मूर्ख

witch *n. fem.* (*mas.* wizard) जादूगरनी*, डाइन*; *v.t.* जादू-टोना करना

witchcraft *n.* इन्द्रजाल, जादू

witchery *n.* जादू, टोना

with *prep.* साथ, से

withal *adv.* साथ, और भी

withdraw *v.i. & t.* (*p.t.* withdrew, *p.p.* withdrawn) लौटना, लौटाना, वापस हट जाना

withdrawal *n.* वापसी*, धन की निकासी*

withhold *v.t.* (*p.t. & p.p.* withheld) रोक रखना, थामना

within *prep.* भीतरी भाग में

without *prep., adv & conj.* बिना, सिवाय, रहित छोड़-कर; without delay शीघ्र, अबिलम्ब; without doubt नि:सन्देह, अवश्य

withstand *v.t.* (*p t. & p p.* withstood) विरोध करना, रोकना

witness *n.* साक्षी, गवाह, प्रमाण; *v.t. & i.* प्रमाणित करना, साक्षी देना

witness-box *n.* अदालत में गवाह के खड़े होने का कटघरा

witty *a.* ठिठोलिया. प्रत्युत्पन्न-मति

wizard *n.* (*fem.* witch) जादूगर, ओझा

wolf *n.* (*pl.* wolves) भेड़िया

woman *n.* (*mas.* man, *pl.* women) नारी*, स्त्री*, औरत*, दासी*

womanhood *n.* स्त्रीत्व, नारी-त्व, स्त्री-समाज

womb *n.* गर्भ, कन्दरा*

wonder *n* आश्चर्य, विस्मय, अद्भुत पदार्थ या मनुष्य; *v i.* चकित होना, सन्देह करना

wonderful *a.* विलक्षण, अद्भुत

wonderfully *adv.* आश्चर्य से, बहुत ही

wont *a.* अभ्यस्त; *n.* रीति*, स्वभाव

woo *v.t* प्रणय-निवेदन करना, फुसलाना, राज़ी करना

wood *n.* जंगल की लकड़ी*, काठ; *a.* लकड़ी का; wood-apple *n.* कैथ; woodbine *n.* एक प्रकार का सुगन्धित फूल; woodcock *n.* जंगली मुर्ग

woodcut *n.* काष्ठ-चित्र, काष्ठ-फलक-चित्र

wool *n.* भेड़ का कोमल रोवां, ऊन: wool-gathering वृथा कार्य

woollen *a.* ऊन का बना हुआ, ऊनी

word *n.* पद, शब्द, आरूया*, बात*, सन्देश, वचन; *v.t.* शब्दों में कहना

work *n.* कार्य, व्यापार, परिश्रम, उद्यम, व्यवसाय, ग्रन्य, (ब० व०) कार्यालय, यंत्र-समुदाय, कारखाना

work *v.t. & i.* (*p.t.* worked *or* wrought) परिश्रम करना, काम में लगना या लगाना, प्रबन्ध चलाना, करना, ढलना, कसीदा काढ़ना, जहाज चलाना; workaday *a.* परिश्रमी; work-box *n.* सूई*, पेचक इत्यादि रखने की पेटी*; workhouse *n.* दरिद्रों के काम करने का घर; workmanlike *a.* कुशलता से किया हुआ: workman-ship *n.* कारीगरी*, कर्म-कौशल

world *n.* संसार, जगत, मनुष्य-जाति*, जन-रीति*, जन-व्यवहार, जीवन, संसारी, पृथ्वी*

worldly *a.* लौकिक, संसारी; world-wide संसार-भर में व्याप्त; the next world परलोक; all the world सर्वस्व

worm *n.* कृमि*, कीड़ा*, पेंच की चूड़ी*, टेढ़ी नली*, प्रभागा प्राणी; *v.i. & t.* उत्तेजित करना, भेद लेना, गेंठना; wormcast कीड़ों से फंकी हुई मिट्टी; worm-eaten कीड़ों से खाया हुआ; wormwood एक प्रकार का कड़वा पौधा, चिरायता

worry *n.* चिन्ता*, व्याकुलता*; *v t.* (*p.t.* worried) क्लेश देना, पीड़ा देना

worship *n.* पूजा*, आराधना*, भक्ति*, अत्यधिक प्रशंसा*, सम्मानसूचक पदवी*; *v.t.* (*p.t.* worshipped) पूजा करना, आदर करना

worshipful *a.* पूजनीय, आदरणीय

worshipper *n.* उपासक, पूजक

worth *n.* मूल्य, गुण, योग्यता*; worthwhile योग्य, उचित

worthless *a.* बेकार, गुणहीन, प्रसार

wound *n.* चोट*; हानि*; *v.t.* चोट पहुंचाना

wrangle *v.i.* भगड़ा करना,

शास्त्रार्थ करना
wrath n. रोष, क्रोध
wrathful a. प्रति क्रुद्ध
wreck n. जहाज का टूट जाना, नाश, जिसका स्वास्थ्य बिगड़ गया हो, v.t. & i. टकराना, नाश करना, नष्ट होना
wreckage n. टूटे जहाज़ का शेष भाग
wrestle v.t. & i. मल्लयुद्ध करना, कुश्ती लड़ना
wrestler n. पहलवान, कुश्ती-बाज़
wrestling n. मल्लयुद्ध, कुश्ती*
wriggle v.t. & i. तड़फड़ाना, कठिनाई से बच निकलना
wrinkle n. झुर्री*, सिकुड़न;

v.t. & i. झुर्री डालना, झुर्री पड़ना
wrist n. कलाई*
writ n. लेख्य, समादेश-पत्र, हुकमनामा, परवाना; Holy Writ बाइबिल
write v.t. & i. (p.t. wrote, p.p. written or writ) लिखना, पत्र लिखना, ग्रन्थ बनाना, रचना करना
writer n. लेखक, ग्रन्थकार
wrong a. अशुद्ध, अयोग्य, अनुचित, उलटा; v.t. अभ्यास करना, अपराध करना; n. अपराध; अन्याय, भ्रम
wrongful a. अवैध, अनुचित, बेजा, दोषपूर्ण, अन्यायपूर्ण

X

xanthoma n. पीतचर्म रोग, खाल पर पीली चित्ती वाला रोग
xanthopsy n. पीतदृष्टि*, कमला रोग
xenial a. प्रतिथि-संबंधी, सत्कार का
xenium n. प्रतिथि को दिया हुआ उपहार
xenomorphic a. विचित्र आकृति का

xerantic a. सूखनेवाला
x-rays n. (pl.) एक्स-रे, क्ष-रश्मि, क्ष-किरण
xylophagous a. लकड़ी खाने-वाला
xylophilous a. लकड़ी खाकर निर्वाह करने वाला (कीड़ा)
xylophone n. एक प्रकार का जलतरंग बाजा
xyster n. हड्डी खुरचने का जर्राही यंत्र

Y

yacht *n.* विहार करने की या दौड़ लगाने की नाव; *v i.* ऐसी नाव में यात्रा करना

yachting *n.* नौका-विहार

yak *n.* सुरागाय*, याक

Yankee *n.* अमेरिका निवासी

yard *n.* गज (=३ फुट), पाल लटकाने के लिए मस्तूल के ऊपर लगा हुआ वर्तुलाकार डण्डा

yardstick *n.* तीन फुट की छड़ी प्रामाणिक नाप*, तुलना का स्तर

yawn *v.i.* जंभाई लेना, उबासी लेना; *n.* जंभाई*, उबासी*

year *n.* वर्ष (३०व०) वृद्धावस्था; current year वर्तमान वर्ष; last year गत वर्ष; leap-year अंग्रेजी वर्ष जिसमें फरवरी मास में २६ दिन होते हैं; year-book वर्षबोध, ग्रन्थकोश

yearly *a. & adv.* वर्ष में एक बार

yearn *v.t.* इच्छा करना, उत्सुक होना

yellow *a.* पीला, सुनहला; *n.* पीला रंग; *v.i. & t.* पीला होना या करना

yellow fever *n.* पाण्डुज्वर

yellow boy *n.* मुहर, गिन्नी*, अशरफी*

yellowish *a.* कुछ पीलापन लिए हुए

yelp *n.* कुत्ते का पीड़ा में भूंकना; *v.i.* तेज़ी से भूंकना

yesterday *n.* गत दिवस, गत कल; yestern गत दिवस संबंधी; yesternight गत रात्रि*

yet *adv.* तो भी, अब भी, तथापि

yield *v.t.* आत्मसमर्पण करना, उत्पन्न करना, देना, स्वीकार करना; *n.* उत्पत्ति*, स्वीकृति*, आत्मसमर्पण

yoke *n.* जुग्रा, अधीनता*, बैल की जोड़ी*; *v.t.* पशु के कंधे पर जुग्रा रखना; under the yoke of परवश

yolk *n.* अण्डे का पीला भाग

young *a.* युवा, तरुण, जवान

youngster *n.* लड़का, छोकरा

youth *n.* यौवन, जवानी*, युवा मनुष्य

youthful *a.* युवा, पुष्ट

yule *n.* ईसाइयों का बड़े दिन का त्यौहार

yule-tide *n.* बड़े दिन के त्यौहार का समय

Z

zabrus n. एक प्रकार का बड़ा गुबरैला या भींगुर

zany n. ठिठोलिया; v.t. हंसी उड़ाना

zeal n. उत्साह, व्यग्रता*

zealot n. अति उत्साही, झक्की मनुष्य

zealous a. उत्साही, लवलीन

zealously adv. उत्साह से

zebra n. जेबरा, गोरखर

Zend n. पारसियों की धर्म-पुस्तकों की ज़ेन्द भाषा

zenith n. उच्च कोटि*, पराकाष्ठा*, शिरोबिंदु

zero n. (pl. zeroes) शून्य, बिन्दु

zest n. स्वाद, अभिरुचि*; v.t. स्वादिष्ट बनाना

ziganka n. रूस देश का एक प्रकार का नाच

zigzag n. तिर्छी या टेढ़ी-मेढ़ी लकीर*; a. मोड़दार, टेढ़ा-मेढ़ा; v.i. (p.t. zigzagged) शीघ्रता से आगे पीछे करना

zinc n. जस्ता

zip n. बन्दूक की गोली की सरसराहट का शब्द

zone n. क्षेत्र, मण्डल, मेखला, भू-कटिबन्ध, परिधि*, घेरा

zoo n. चिड़ियाघर, पशुवाटिका

zoology n. प्राणिविद्या*, जन्तुविज्ञान

zoological a. जन्तुविज्ञान-संबंध; zoological garden जंगली पशु पक्षी इ० रखने का बगीचा

zoologist n. जन्तुविज्ञानी, जीवशास्त्री

zoonomy n. जन्तुजीवन के नियम

zoopathology n. पशुओं के रोगों की विद्या*

zoophilist n. पशुओं का प्रेमी

zootechny n. पशुओं को पालने की विधि

Zoroastrianism n. पारसियों का धर्म, जरस्तुत मत

zoster n. एक प्रकार का चर्म-रोग

zumbooruk n. ऊंट की पीठ पर लदी हुई तोप*

zuna n. एक प्रकार की भेड़*

zymurgy n. आसब बनाने का रसायन

zythepsary n. मद्य बनाने का स्थान

zythum n. एक प्रकार की मदिरा*

❖❖❖

परिशिष्ट १

APPENDIX 1

प्रशासकीय शब्द

ADMINISTRATIVE TERMS

Accountant General : महा-लेखाकार

Accounts Clerk : लेखा-लिपिक/क्लर्क

Accounts Department : लेखा विभाग

Accounts Officer : लेखा-अधिकारी/अफसर

Additional Accountant General : अपर महा लेखाकार

Administration Division : प्रशासन प्रभाग

Administration and External Affairs Division : प्रशासन और परराष्ट्र प्रभाग

Administrator General : महा प्रशासक

Advisory Board : सलाहकार बोर्ड/मंडल

Advisory Committee : सला-हकार समिति

Advisory Council : सलाहकार परिषद्

Advocate General : महा-अधिवक्ता, एडवोकेट जनरल

Agriculture Ministry : कृषि-मंत्रालय

Circonditioning Division : वातानुकूलन प्रभाग

Air Headquarters : वायुसेना मुख्यालय/हैडक्वार्टर

All India Handicrafts Board : अखिल भारतीय दस्तकारी बोर्ड

All India Radio : आकाश-वाणी

Anti-corruption Branch : भ्रष्टाचार-विरोधी शाखा

Archaeological Department : पुरातत्त्व विभाग

Armed Forces Informa-

tion Office : सशस्त्र सेना सूचना कार्यालय/दफ्तर

Army Headquarters : सेना मुख्यालय/हेडक्वार्टर

Attache : अटैशे, सहचारी

Attorney General : महा-न्यायवादी

Backward Classes Commission पिछड़े वर्ग कमीशन

Bibliographer : ग्रन्थ-सूचीकार

Board of Censors : सेंसर बोर्ड

Board of Directors : निदे-शक-बोर्ड/मंडल

Board of Revenue : राजस्व बोर्ड/मंडल

Board of Scientific Terminology : वैज्ञानिक शब्दा-वली बोर्ड/मंडल

Board of Studies : पाठ्य-पर्षद

Botanical Survey of India : भारतीय वनस्पति सर्वेक्षण संस्था

Cabinet Secretariat : मंत्रि-मंडल/केबिनेट सचिवालय

Central Institute of Education : केन्द्रीय शिक्षण संस्थान

Central Intelligence Bureau : केन्द्रीय खुफिया ब्यूरो

Central Public Works Department : केन्द्रीय निर्माण विभाग

Central Recovery Office : केन्द्रीय वसूली कार्यालय/दफ्तर

Central Road Research Institute : केन्द्रीय सड़क अनुसंधानशाला

Central Social Welfare Board : केन्द्रीय समाज कल्याण बोर्ड/मंडल

Central Water and Power Commission : केन्द्रीय जल और बिजली कमीशन

Chamber of Commerce : वाणिज्य-मंडल

Chartered Accountant : चार्टर प्राप्त लेखाकार, चार्टर्ड अकाउण्टेण्ट

Chief Commissioner : मुख्य आयुक्त/कमिश्नर

Chief Engineer : मुख्य इंजीनियर

Chief Executive Officer : मुख्य कार्यकारी अधिकारी/अफसर

Chief Justice : मुख्य न्याया-धिपति

Chief Labour Commissioner : मुख्य श्रम आयुक्त/कमिश्नर

Chief Minister : मुख्य मंत्री

Chief Secretary : मुख्य सचिव

Child Welfare Centre : बाल कल्याण केन्द्र

Circle Inspector : परिमण्डल निरीक्षक, हलका इन्सपेक्टर

Circuit Court : दौरा-न्यायालय

Civil Aviation Department : सिविल/नगर विमानन विभाग

Civil Court : दीवानी न्यायालय/अदालत

Civil Dispensary : सरकारी औषधालय/दवाखाना

Civil Supplies and Rationing Department : सिविल रसद और राशन विभाग

Commissioned Officer : राजादिष्ट अधिकारी/अफसर

Communication Directorate : संचार मंत्रालय

Comptroller and Auditor General नियंत्रक और महालेखा परीक्षक

Conservator of Forests : वनसंरक्षक

Controller : नियन्त्रक

Co-operative Societies Department : सहकारी समिति विभाग

Co-opted Member : सहयोजित सदस्य

Co-ordination and complaint Section : समन्वय और शिकायत अनुभाग

Copyist : नकलनवीस

Cottage Industries Section : कुटीर उद्योग अनुभाग

Council of States : राज्य-सभा

Counsel : परामर्शदाता

Criminal Investigation Department : खुफिया पुलिस-विभाग

Custodian of Evacuee Property : निष्क्रान्त सम्पत्ति-परिरक्षक

Customs Department : सीमा-शुल्क-विभाग

Deputy Collector : डिप्टी कलक्टर/उपसमाहर्ता

Deputy Director : उप-निदेशक

Deputy Minister : उपमन्त्री

Deputy Secretary : उप-सचिव

Deputy Speaker : उपाध्यक्ष

Despatch Clerk : प्रेषण क्लर्क/लिपिक

Despatcher : प्रेषक

Development Minister : विकास मंत्री

Diarist : दैनिकी-लेखक/डायरी-लेखक

Director of Public Health :
लोक स्वास्थ्य-निदेशक

Director of Public Instructions : लोक शिक्षा-निदेशक

Directorate of Economics
and Statistics : अर्थ और
संख्यान निदेशालय

Directorate of Employ-
ment Exchange : रोज़गार
निदेशालय

Directorate of Training :
प्रशिक्षण निदेशालय

Directorate General : महा-
निदेशालय

Disease   Investigation
Officer : रोग-जांच अधि-
कारी/अफसर

Distillery Inspector : शराब-
ख़ारखाना-निरीक्षक

Distribution Section : वित-
रण-अनुभाग

District Council : जिला-
परिषद्

District Judge : जिला-जज/
न्यायाधीश

District Magistrate : जिला-
धीश, ज़िला मजिस्ट्रेट/दंड-
नायक

Economic Adviser : अर्थ-
सलाहकार

Editor, Chief : मुख्य-सम्पादक

Editor, Managing : प्रबंध-
सम्पादक

Editor, News : समाचार-
सम्पादक

Editor, Sub : उप-सम्पादक

Editorial Section : सम्पाद-
कीय अनुभाग

Education Directorate :
शिक्षा-निदेशालय

Education Minister : शिक्षा
मन्त्री

Election Commission :
चुनाव आयोग/कमीशन

Employment Exchange :
रोज़गार कार्यालय/दफ्तर

Enquiry Office : पूछताछ
कार्यालय/दफ्तर

Entertainment Tax Com-
mission : मनोरंजन-कर-
कमीशन/आयोग

Estate Office : राज सम्पत्ति
कार्यालय/दफ्तर

Excise Commissioner :
उत्पाद-शुल्क आयुक्त/कमिश्नर

Executive Officer : कार्यकारी
अधिकारी/अफसर

Ex-officio : पदेन

Exports Division : निर्यात
प्रभाग

External Publicity Divi-
sion : परराष्ट्र-प्रचार-प्रभाग

Federal Court : संघ न्याया-
लय

Finance Minister : वित्त मंत्री

Financial Adviser : वित्त सलाहकार

Fire Service : अग्नि-शमन व्यवस्था

Food Minister : खाद्य-मन्त्री

Foreign Minister : विदेश-मन्त्री

Forest Department : वन विभाग

Forest Research Institute : वन अनुसंधानशाला

Gazetted Officer : राजपत्रित अधिकारी/अफसर

Gazetted Post राजपत्रित पद

General Manager : महा-प्रबंधक

Geological Survey of India : भारतीय भूगर्भ सर्वेक्षण संस्था

Government House : राज-भवन

Government pleader : सर-कारी वकील

Governor General : महा-राज्यपाल

Head Clerk : प्रधान लिपिक/क्लर्क

Head Cons'able : प्रधान सिपाही/कांस्टेबल

Head Office : प्रधान कार्यालय /दफ़्तर

Health officer : स्वास्थ्य अधि-कारी/अफसर

Her Excellency : परम श्रेष्ठ

His Excellency : परम श्रष्ठ

Home Minister : गृह मन्त्री

Horticulture Department : उद्यान-विभाग

House of People : लोक-सभा

Improvement Trust : नगर-सुधार-विभाग

Incharge : कार्यभारी

Income Tax Officer आयकर अधिकारी/अफसर

Indian Administrative Service : भारतीय प्रशासन सेवा

Indian Air Force : भारतीय हवाई सेना

Indian Air Lines Corporation : भारतीय हवाई कम्पनी निगम

Indian Bureau of Mines : भारतीय खनिज-विभाग

Indian Civil Service : भार-तीय सिविल सेवा

Indian Council of Cultural Relations : भारतीय सांस्कृतिक संपर्क परिषद्

Indian Council of Medical Research : भारतीय चिकित्सा अनुसंधान परिषद्

Indian Council of World

Affairs : भारतीय विश्व-बिचार परिषद्

Indian Police Service : भारतीय पुलिस-सेवा

Indian Standards Institution भारतीय मानक-संस्था

Industries and Labour Directorate : उद्योग और श्रम निदेशालय

Information Department : सूचना विभाग

International Labour Office : अन्तर्राष्ट्रीय श्रम कार्यालय/दफ्तर

Irrigation Department : सिंचाई-विभाग

Issue Department : निकासी विभाग

Joint Secretary : संयुक्त सचिव

Judicial Department : न्याय विभाग

Labour Department : श्रम विभाग

Land and Development Office : भूमि और विकास कार्यालय/दफ्तर

Leader of the House : सदन-नेता

Legal Adviser : विधि-सलाह-कार

Legislative Assembly : विधान-सभा

Legislative Council : विधान-परिषद्

Lessor : पट्टदाता

Lexicographer कोशकार

Licenser लाइसेंसदाता

Lieutenant Governor : उप-राज्यपाल

Lighthouse Department : प्रकाश-स्तम्भ-विभाग

Local Government : स्थानीय सरकार

Local Self Government : स्थानीय स्वायत्त शासन

Locust Department : टिड्डी विभाग

Lower Chamber : प्रवर सदन

Lower Division Clerk : प्रवर श्रेणी लिपिक/क्लर्क

Lower House : प्रवर सदन

Managing Director : प्रबन्ध-निदेशक

Marine Officer : समुद्री अधिकारी/अफसर

Marketing Officer : पण्यन अधिकारी/अफसर

Mechanical and Workshop Division : मशीन और कारखाना प्रभाग

Medical Practitioner : चिकित्सा-व्यवसायी

Member of Parliament :

संसद सदस्य

Member Secretary : सदस्य सचिव

Meteorological Office मौसम कार्यालय/दफ्तर

Meter Reader : मीटर पढ़ने वाला

Military Officer : सेना अधिकारी/अफसर

Mining Board : खनि-बोर्ड

Minister of State : राज्य-मंत्री

Ministry of Commerce and Industry : वाणिज्य और उद्योग मन्त्रालय

Ministry of Communications : संचार मंत्रालय

Ministry of Defence : रक्षा-मंत्रालय

Ministry of Education : शिक्षा-मंत्रालय

Ministry of External Affairs : परराष्ट्र मंत्रालय

Ministry of Finance : वित्त-मंत्रालय

Ministry of Food and Agriculture : खाद्य और कृषि मंत्रालय

Ministry of Health : स्वास्थ्य-मंत्रालय

Ministry of Home Affairs : गृह-मंत्रालय

Ministry of Information and Broadcasting : सूचना और प्रसार मंत्रालय

Ministry of Internal Affairs : स्वराष्ट्र-मंत्रालय

Ministry of Irrigation and Power : सिंचाई और बिजली मंत्रालय

Ministry of Labour : श्रम-मंत्रालय

Ministry of Natural Resources and Scientific Research : प्राकृतिक साधन और वैज्ञानिक अनुसंधान-मंत्रालय

Ministry of Production : उत्पादन-मंत्रालय

Ministry of Railways : रेलवे मंत्रालय

Ministry of Rehabilitation : पुनर्वास-मंत्रालय

Ministry of Transport : परिवहन मंत्रालय

Ministry of Works, Housing and Supply : निर्माण, आवास और संभरण मंत्रालय

Municipal Board : नगर-पालिका

Municipal Commissioner : नगरपाल

National Archives of India : भारत का राष्ट्रीय अभिलेखा-

गार

National Art Gallery : राष्ट्रीय कला वीथी

National Physical Laboratory : राष्ट्रीय भौतिक प्रयोग-शाला

News Agent : समाचारपत्र/अखबार एजेंट

Nominator ; नामनकर्ता नामज़द करने वाला

Oath Commissioner : शपथ अधिकारी

Office Superintendent : कार्यालय/दफ्तर अधीक्षक

Officer-in-charge : कार्यभारी अधिकारी/अफसर

Officer on Special duty : विशेष कार्य अधिकारी/अफसर

Officiating : स्थानापन्न

Operator : प्रचालक

Overseas Communications Service : समुद्रपार संचार व्यवस्था

Parliamentary Secretary : संसद सचिव

Pay & Accounts Officer : वेतन व लेखा अधिकारी/अफसर

Paymaster : वेतनदाता

Personal Assistant : व्यक्तिक सहायक

Planning Officer : आयोजना

अधिकारी

Plant Protection Adviser : वनस्पति-रक्षा-सलाहकार

Polling Officer : मतांकन अधिकारी/अफसर

Port Officer : पत्तन अधिकारी/अफसर

Post & Telegraph Department : डाक-तार-विभाग

Postmaster General : पोस्टमास्टर जनरल, महाडाकपाल

Presiding Officer : अधिष्ठाता

Press Information Bureau : प्रेस-सूचना-ब्यूरो

Press Representative : पत्र प्रतिनिधि

Principal Officer : प्रमुख अधिकारी/अफसर

Principal Private Secretary : प्रमुख निजी सचिव

Private Secretary : निजी सचिव

Production Commissioner : उत्पादन आयुक्त/कमिश्नर

Propaganda Office : प्रचार कार्यालय/दफ्तर

Proposer : प्रस्तावक

Public Health Department : लोक-स्वास्थ्य विभाग

Public Service Commission : लोक-सेवा आयोग/कमीशन

Public Works Department : लोक निर्माण-विभाग

Publications Division : प्रकाशन प्रभाग

Publicity Office : प्रकाशन-कार्यालय/दफ्तर

Purchase Directorate : क्रय-निदेशालय

Railway Board : रेलवे बोर्ड/मंडल

Railway Conference Association : रेलवे सम्मेलन-निकाय

Receiving Centre : प्रादान केन्द्र

Reception & Enquiry Office : स्वागत और पूछ-ताछ कार्यालय/दफ्तर

Receptionist : स्वागती

Record Keeper : अभिलेख-पाल

Record Office : अभिलेख-कार्यालय/दफ्तर

Regional Languages Section : प्रादेशिक भाषा-अनुभाग

Regional Meteorological Centre : प्रादेशिक मौसम सूचना केन्द्र

Regional Tourist Office : प्रादेशिक पर्यटन कार्यालय/दफ्तर

Regional Transport Officer : प्रादेशिक परिवहन अधिकारी/अफसर

Registration Officer : रजिस्ट्री अधिकारी/अफसर

Rehabilitation Division : पुनर्वास-प्रभाग

Rehabilitation Minister : पुनर्वास-मंत्री

Remitter : प्रेषक/भेजने वाला

Rent Controller : भाड़ा नियंत्रक

Research Assistant : अनु-संधान सहायक

Resettlement & Employment Directorate : पुनःस्थापन और रोजगार निदेशालय

Resident Representative : स्थानिक प्रतिनिधि

Revenue Commissioner : राजस्व/माल आयुक्त/कमिश्नर

Revenue Minister : राजस्व/माल मंत्री

Road Transport Authority : सड़क परिवहन प्राधिकरण

Rural Development Department : ग्राम-बिकास विभाग

Scholarships & Informa-

tion Division : छात्रवृत्ति और सूचना-प्रभाग

School of Foreign Languages : विदेशी-भाषा विद्यालय

Sanitary Inspector : सफाई-निरीक्षक

Scientific Research Committee : वैज्ञानिक अनुसन्धान-समिति

Secretariat Security Organisation : सचिवालय सुरक्षा संगठन

Secretariat Training School : सचिवालय ट्रेनिंग-स्कूल/प्रशिक्षणशाला

Section Officer : अनुभाग अधिकारी/अफसर

Select Committee : प्रवर-समिति

Small Scale Industries Directorate : लघु उद्योग-निदेशालय

Stationery Section : लेखन-सामग्री/स्टेशनरी अनुभाग

Statistical Branch : संख्यान-शाखा

Storage & Inspection Directorate : संचय और निरीक्षण निदेशालय

Superintendent of Excise & Salt : उत्पाद शुल्क और नमक अधीक्षक

Supply & Disposals Directorate : संभरण व निपटान निदेशालय

Surveyor General of India : भारत का महासर्वेक्षक

Taxation Enquiry Committee : कर जांच-समिति

Tax Collector : कर-समाहर्ता

Technical Assistant : तकनीकी सहायक

Technical Directorate : तकनीकी निदेशालय

Telegraph Complaint Officer : तार-शिकायत अधिकारी/अफसर

Telephone Supervisor : टेलीफोन-पर्यवेक्षक

Teleprinters Section : दूर मुद्रक-अनुभाग

Textile Enquiry Committee : कपड़ा-जांच-समिति

Timekeeper : समयपाल

Tools Development Directorate : औज़ार विकास निदेशालय

Trade Commissioner : व्यापार आयुक्त/कमिश्नर

Traffic Inspector : यातायात निरीक्षक

Traffic Manager : यातायात-प्रबन्धक

Traffic Superintendent :

यातायात प्रवीक्षक

Translation Department : अनुवाद विभाग

Transmitting Station : प्रेषण-केन्द्र

Transport Service : परिवहन व्यवस्था

Treasury Officer : कोषा-धिकारी, खजाना अफसर

Under Secretary : अवर सचिव

Upper Division Clerk : उच्च श्रेणी लिपिक/क्लर्क

United Nations Organisation : संयुक्त राष्ट्र-संघ

University Grants Commission : विश्वविद्यालय अनुदान आयोग कमीशन

Vacation Department : अवकाश-विभाग

Valuation Officer : मूल्यांकन अधिकारी/अफसर

Village Defence Society : ग्राम-रक्षा-समिति

Warrant Officer : वारंट अधिकारी/अफसर

Welfare Officer : कल्याण अधिकारी/अफसर

Whip : सचेतक, ह्विप

Wireless & Cipher Office : बेतार और बीज-लेख कार्या-लय/दफ्तर

Wireless Operator : बेतार प्रचालक

Works Manager : निर्माण प्रबन्धक

Zoological Survey of India : भारतीय प्राणि-सर्वे-क्षण विभाग

परिशिष्ट २

APPENDIX 2

अंग्रेज़ी तथा हिन्दी की कहावतें

ENGLISH PROVERBS AND THEIR
HINDI EQUIVALENTS

A bad man is better than a bad name—बद अच्छा बदनाम बुरा ।

A bad workman quarrels with his tools—नाच न जाने आंगन टेढ़ा ।

A bird in hand is worth two in the bush—नौ नगद न तेरह उधार ।

A bitter jest is the poison of friendship—लड़ाई की जड़ हांसी ।

A blind man is no judge—बंदर क्या जाने अदरख का स्वाद ।

A boaster and a liar are cousins—चोर का भाई गंठकटा

A burnt child dreads the fire—दूध का जला छाय को फूंककर पीता है ।

A drop in the ocean —ऊंट के मुंह में जीरा ।

Advice has no effect on those used to rod—लातों के भूत बातों से नहीं मानते ।

A figure among cyphers—अंधों में काना राजा ।

A fog cannot be dispelled by a fan—झोस चाटे प्यास नहीं बुझती

A gift will make its way—भगवान जब देता है तो छप्पर

फाड़कर देता है ।

A good name is better than bags of gold—साख जाय पर साख न जाय ।

A good servant should have good wages—खरी मजूरी चोखा काम ।

A good tongue is a good weapon—जबान सीरी मुलकगीरी ।

A guilty conscience self accuses—चोर की दाढ़ी में तिनका ।

A honey tongue, a heart of gall—मुख में राम बगल में छुरी ।

A little knowledge is a dangerous thing—नीम हकीम खतरे जान ।

All's well that ends well—अन्त भला सो भला

All that glitters is not gold—जो गरजते हैं वे बरसते नहीं ।

A man of no principle—गंगा गए गंगाराम जमना गए जमनाराम ।

An empty door will tempt the saint—मुफ्त की शराब काजी को भी हलाल ।

An empty vessel sounds much—थोथा चना बाजे घना ।

A nine days' wonder—चार दिन की चांदनी फिर अंधेरी रात ।

A robber in the garb of a saint—राम नाम जपना पराया माल अपना ।

A rotten sheep infects the whole flock—एक मछली सारे तालाब को गन्दा कर देती है ।

As gods so are the worshippers—जैसी रूह वैसे फरिश्ते ।

A single sinner sinks the boat—एक पापी नाव को ले डूबता है ।

As the king so are the subjects—यथा राजा तथा प्रजा ।

As you sow, so you reap—जैसी करनी वैसी भरनी ।

Avarice is the root of all evils—लालच बुरी बला है ।

A wolf in lamb's clothing—इंसान की शकल में शैतान ।

Barking dogs seldom bite—जो गरजते हैं सो बरसते नहीं ।

Bear and forbear is a good philosophy—संतोष का फल

सदा मीठा ।

Beauty has wings—चार दिन की चांदनी फिर अंधेरी रात ।

Beggars and borrowers could not be choosers—दान की बछिया का दांत नहीं देखा जाता ।

Beneath the rose lies the serpent—विष-रस भरा कनक घट जैसे ।

Better wear your shoes than your bed clothes—बैठे से बेगार भली ।

Between the devil and deep sea —इधर कुआं उधर खाई ।

Between two stools we come to the ground—दुविधा में दोनों गए, माया मिली न राम ।

Birds of a feather flock together—चोर-चोर मौसेरे भाई ।

Black will take no other hue—सूरदास की काली कमरिया चढ़े न दूजो रंग ।

Blood is thicker than water—अपना-अपना पराया-पराया ।

By the throat expressed by the world possessed—कही बात पराई हो जाती है ।

Cast in the same mould—एक ही थैली के चट्टे-बट्टे ।

Cattle do not die from crow's cursing—बिल्ली के सरापे छीका नहीं टूटता ।

Coming events cast their shadows before—होनहार बिरवान के होत चीकने पात ।

Contentment is happiness—संतोषी सदा सुखी ।

Crows are never the whiter for washing—भीम न मीठी होय सींचो गुड़ घी से ।

Crying in wilderness—भैंस के आगे बीन बजाना ।

Cut your coat according to your cloth—उतने पांव पसारिए जितनी लम्बी सौड़ ।

Danger past, God is forgotten—दुख गुजरा राम बिसारा ।

Death defies the doctor—टूटी की बूटी नहीं ।

Death keeps no calendar—मौत और गाहक का कुछ भरोसा नहीं कब आ जाए ।

Death makes no distinction of person—मौत न जाने बूढ़ा या जवान ।

Death's day is Doom's day—ग्राप मरे जग परलय ।

Deep rivers move with silent majesty, shallow brooks are noisy—प्रघजल गगरी छलकत जाय, भरी गगरिया चुप्पे जाय ।

Diamonds cut diamonds—लोहे को लोहा काटता है ।

Difficulties give way to diligence—मेहनत से मुसीबत भागती है ।

Distant drums sound well—दूर के ढोल सुहावने ।

Do at Rome as the Romans do—जैसा देश वैसा भेष ।

Do evil and look for like—कर बुरा तो हो बुरा ।

Do good and cast it into the river—नेकी कर दरिया में डाल ।

Drowning man catches at straw—डूबते को तिनके का सहारा ।

Dry bread at home is better than roast meat—बाहर की चिकनी-चुपड़ी से घर की रूखी अच्छी है ।

East or west home is the best—पूरब या पश्चिम घर सब से उत्तम ।

Empty vessels make much noise—थोथा चना बाजे घना ।

Empty words buy no barley—खाली बातों से काम नहीं चलता ।

Errors and omissions accepted—भूल-चूक लेनी-देनी ।

Escaped with life, millions found—जान बची और लाखों पाए ।

Errors like straws upon the surface flow.
One who is in search of truth must dive below.
जिन खोजा तिन पाइयां गहरे पानी पैठ ।
मैं बपुरी ढूंढन गई रही किनारे बैठ ।।

Even death cannot be had for the asking—मांगे मौत भी नहीं मिलती ।

Every body's business is no body's business—साझे की हांडी चौराहे पर फूटे ।

Every dog has his way—बारह वर्ष में कूड़ी के दिन भी

फिरते हैं ।

Every man's house is his castle—अपना मकान कोट समान ।

Every potter praises his pot—अपना पूत सब ही को प्यारा, अपने दही को सभी मीठा कहते हैं ।

Everything looks yellow to a jaundiced eye—सावन के अन्धे को हरा ही हरा दीखता है ।

Evil beginnings have bad endings—आदि बुरा अन्त बुरा ।

Evil got, evil spent—चोरी का माल मोरी में ।

Example teaches better than precept—औरों को नसीहत खुद को फजीहत ।

Face is the index of mind—चेहरा मन का आइना है ।

Face to face the truth comes out—मुंह के सामने झूठ नहीं बोला जाता ।

Feed the mouth, shame the eyes—मुंह खाए आंख लजाए ।

Fool to others, to himself a sage—अपने मुंह मियां मिट्ठू ।

Forced labour is better than idleness—बेकार से बेगार भली ।

Fortune favours the brave—पुरुषसिंह जे उद्यमी लक्ष्मी ताकी चेरि ।

Friends are plenty when the purse is full—बनी के सब यार ।

From a bad paymaster get what you can—भागते चोर की लंगोटी ही सही ।

Gather thistles and expect pickles—बोए पेड़ बबूल के तो आम कहां से होय ।

Give him an inch and he will take an ell—उंगली पकड़ते-पकड़ते पहुंचा पकड़ना ।

Gods' will be done—ईश्वरेच्छा बलीयसी ।

Good health is above wealth—तन्दुरुस्ती हज़ार नियामत ।

Good marksman may miss—घोड़े का सवार भी गिरता है, बड़े-बड़े भी चूक जाते हैं ।

Good mind, good find—आप भला तो जग भला ।

Good swimmers are very often drowned—तैराक ही डूबते हैं ।

Gone the goose that did lay golden eggs—वो दिन गए जब पसीना गुलाब था ।

Great cry little wool—ऊंची दूकान फीका पकवान ।

Guilty conscience is always suspicious—पापी का मन सदा शंकित रहता है ।

Half a loaf is better than no bread—कुछ नहीं से थोड़ा भला, नाहीं मामा से काना मामा अच्छा ।

Hard nut to crack—लोहे के चने चबाना ।

Haste is waste   उतावला सो बावला ।

He breaks his wife's head and then buys a plaster for it—चूहा मारकर गोबर सुंघाना ।

He cooks his own broth—अपनी खिचड़ी अलग पका रहा है ।

He giveth thrice that giveth in trice—तुरत दान महा-कल्याण ।

He jests at scars who never felt a wound—जाके पैर न फटी बिवाई, सो क्या जाने पीर पराई ।

He stumbled at the threshold—सर मुंडाते ही ओले पड़े ।

He, that is warm, thinks all are so—आप सुखी तो जग सुखी ।

He who would catch fish must not mind getting wet—नाचने उठे तो घूंघट कैसा ।

He who would sow well, must reap well—अच्छा करो अच्छा पाओ । कर भला तो हो भला ।

High winds blow on high hills—बड़ों की बड़ी बात ।

His bread is buttered on both the sides—चुपड़ी और दो दो ।

His wits are gone a wool-gathering—उसकी अकल चरने गई है ।

Hold your soul in patience—तेल देख तेल की धार देख ।

Honey is not for asses' mouth—यह मुंह और मसूर

की दाल ।

Hopeless fellow, driving from pillar to post—धोबी का
कुत्ता न घर का न घाट का ।

Hunger is the best sauce—भूख में किवाड़ भी पापड़ ।

Hurry spoils curry—आगे दौड़ पीछे चौड़ ।

If you want a thing well done, do it yourself—बिना
अपने मरे स्वर्ग नहीं दीखता ।

Ill got, ill spent—सूम का धन शैतान खाए ।

Ill gotten goods seldom prosper—चोरी का धन मोरी में ।

In calm sea every one is pilot—लड़ाई के बाद सभी बहादुर ।

Innocent have nothing to fear—सांच को आंच नहीं ।

I stout thou stout, who will carry the dirt out—मैं भी
रानी तू भी रानी कौन भरेगा घर का पानी ।

I talk of chaff and you hear of a cheese—पूछे खेत की
कहे खलियान की ।

It is easier to say than to do—कहना आसान है करना
मुश्किल है ।

It never rains, but it pours—मुसीबत अकेली नहीं आती ।

It is foolish sheep that makes the wolf his confessor—
बिल्ली और दूध की रखवाली ।

It is good sometimes to hold candle to the devil—
जरूरत पड़ने पर गधे को भी बाप बनाया जाता है ।

It is hard to live in Rome and to fight with the Pope—
जल में रहकर मगरमच्छ से बैर ।

It is no use crying over spilt milk—बीती ताहि बिसारि दे,
आगे की सुधि लेय ।

It is too late to lock the stable-door when the steed
is stolen—अब पछताय होत क्या जब चिड़ियां चुग गईं खेत ।

It is work that makes a workman—काम काम को
सिखाता है ।

It takes two to make a quarrel—एक हाथ से ताली
नहीं बजती ।

Killing two birds with one stone—एक पंथ दो काज ।
एक तीर से दो शिकार ।

Let bygones be bygones—बीती सो बीती । बीती ताहि
बिसार दे, ग्रागे की सुधि लेय ।

Let sleeping dogs lie—भिड़ों के छत्ते को मत छेड़ो ।

Let the past bury the dead—गड़े मुर्दे न उखाड़ो ।

Let us see which way the wind blows—देखें ऊंट किस
करवट बैठता है ।

Like cures like—विषस्य विषमौषधम् ।

Like draws like—चोर चोर मौसेरे भाई ।

Like father, like son—जस बाप तस बेटा ।

Little drops make the ocean—बूंद-बूंद से तालाब भर
जाता है ।

Living from hand to mouth—रोज़ कुग्रां खोदना, रोज़
पानी पीना ।

Long absent is soon forgotten—ग्रांख ग्रोफल पहाड़ ग्रोफल ।

Make hay while the sun shines—बहती गंगा में हाथ धोना ।

Man is one, destinies varies—परमेश्वर की माया कहीं
धूप कहीं छाया ।

Man proposes, God disposes—मेरे मन कुछ और है, कर्त्ता
के मन और ।

Many a slip between the cup and the lip—कानी के
ब्याह को सौ जोखों ।

Many men, many minds—जितने नर उतनी बुद्धि । नाना
मुनि नाना मति ।

Measure for measure—हत्या के बदले फांसी, जैसे को तैसा ।

Might is right—जिसकी लाठी उसकी भैंस ।

Misfortune finds out its victim—दुर्भाग्य जब ग्रावे ऊंट चढ़े
कुत्ता काटे ।

Misfortunes never come singly—मुफलिसी में ग्राटा गीला ।
मुसीबत ग्रकेले नहीं ग्राती है ।

Money begets money—पैसा पैसे को खींचता है ।

Money for money and interest besides—ब्याम के ब्याम और गुठलियों के दाम ।

Money makes the mare go—घी बनाए खीचड़ी नाम बहू का होय ।

Much cry and little wool—ऊंची दुकान फीका पकवान ।

No one knows the weight of another's burden—जाके पांव न फटी बिवाई, सो का जाने पीर पराई ।

No pains no gains—सेवा बिना मेवा नहीं ।

One flower makes no garland—एक फूल से माला नहीं बनती ।

One good turn deserves another—इस हाथ दे उस हाथ ले ।

One nail drives out another—कांटे से कांटा निकलता है ।

One post and hundred candidates—एक अनार सौ बीमार ।

One slays another pays—करे कोई भरे कोई ।

One swallow does not make a summer—अकेला चना भाड़ नहीं फोड़ सकता ।

One to-day is better than two to-morrow—नौ नगद न तेरह उधार ।

Only the wearer knows where the shoe pinches—जिसके पैर न फटी बिवाई वह क्या जाने पीर पराई ।

Out of the frying-pan into the fire—ब्याम से टपका, बबूल में अटका ।

Over shoes over boots—ओखली में सिर दिया तो मूसलों से क्या डर ।

Penny wise pound foolish—मोहरें लुटी जाएं कोयलों पर छाप ।

Poverty breeds strife—गरीबी झगड़े की जड़ है ।

Practice makes a man perfect—काम को काम सिखाता है ।

Prettiness dies quickly—चार दिन की चांदनी फिर अंधेरी रात ।

Pride goeth before a fall—घमंड का सिर नीचा ।

Public voice is God's voice—जबाने खल्क को नक्कारे खुदा

समझो ।

Puff not against the wind—आसमान का थूका मुंह पर ही आता है ।

Pure gold does not fear the flame—सांच को आंच नहीं ।

Quit not certainty for hope—आधी छोड़ सारी को धावे, आधी रहै न सारी पावे ।

Respect yourself and you will be respected—अपनी मर्यादा अपने हाथ ।

Riches have wings—लक्ष्मी चंचला होती है ।

Rod tames everyone—डंडे के आगे भूत नाचता है ।

Rome was not built in a day—हथेली पर दही नहीं जमता ।

See what airs he is giving himself—मेंढकी को भी जुकाम होने लगा ।

Self praise is no recommendation—अपने मुंह मियां मिट्ठू बनने से काम नहीं चलता ।

Society moulds men—खरबूजे को देखकर खरबूजा रंग बदलता है ।

Solid worth is not sullied by slander—धूल डाले चांद नहीं छिपता ।

Something is better than nothing—भागते चोर की लंगोटी ही सही ।

Something is wrong at the bottom—कुछ दाल में काला है ।

Soon ripe is soon rotten—जल्दी पका सो जल्दी सड़ा ।

Steal a goose and give giblets in alms—निहाई की चोरी और सुई का दान ।

Strike the iron while it is hot—अवसर को कभी न गंवाओ ।

Sweep before your own door—तुझको पराई क्या पड़ी अपनी निबेड़ तू ।

Temperance is the best physique—परहेज़ सब से अच्छा नुस्खा है ।

The belly teaches all arts—पेट सब कुछ कराता है ।

The cheap buyer takes bad meat—महंगा रोए एक बार

सस्ता रोए बार-बार ।

The deeper the well the cooler the water—जितना गुड़ डालो उतना मीठा ।

The innocent have nothing to fear—सांच को आंच नहीं ।

The priest sees no further than the church—मुल्ला की दौड़ मस्जिद तक ।

The thief threatens the constable—उलटा चोर कोतवाल को डांटे ।

There are man and man, every stone is not gem— आदमी-आदमी अन्तर कोई हीरा कोई कंकर ।

There is a world of difference between a king and a beggar—कहां राजा भोज कहां गंगू तेली ।

Think twice before you speak—पहले तोलो फिर मुंह से बोलो ।

Tit for tat— जैसे को तैसा । शठे शाठ्यम् ।

To cast pearls before swine—बन्दर क्या जाने अदरख का स्वाद ।

To count one's chickens before they are hatched—घर घोड़ा नकास मोल ।

To dig one's own grave—अपने पैरों पर आप कुल्हाड़ी मारना ।

To end in a fiasco—टांय-टांय फिस ।

To hunt with the hound and run with the fox—चोर से कहे चोरी कर शाह से कहे जागता रह ।

To invite one and feast another—एक को साई दूसरे को बधाई ।

To kill two birds with one stone—एक पंथ दो काज ।

To lock the stable-door when the steed is stolen—का वर्षा जब कृषी सुखानी ।

To make a mountain of a mole hill—राई का पहाड़ बनाना । तिल से ताड़ बनाना ।

To make castles in the air—हवाई किले बनाना ।

Tomorrow will take care of itself—अब की अब के साथ जब

की जड़ के साथ ।

To much courtesy, to much craft—मधुरी बानी दगाबाज की निशानी ।

To rob Peter to pay Paul—गाय मार कर जूता दान ।

Union is strength—एकता ही बल है ।

Vows made in storm are forgotten in calm — दुःख में सुमरिन सब करें, सुख में करे न कोय ।

Where there is a will there is a way—जहां चाह तहां राह ।

Whistling maid and crowning hen are neither fit for gods nor men—धोबी का कुत्ता न घर का न घाट का ।

Wisdom is more powerful than strength—अक्ल बड़ी कि भैंस ।

परिशिष्ट ३

APPENDIX 3

महत्त्वपूर्ण पद और मुहावरे
IMPORTANT PHRASES AND IDIOMS

NOUN PHRASES

An apple of discord—झगड़े की जड़

An apple of one's eye— बहुत प्यारा

A bed of roses—आराम देने वाली वस्तु

A bird of passage —एक स्थान पर जम कर न ठहरने वाला

Break of day—नड़का, प्रातःकाल

A child's play—बच्चों का खेल, बहुत सरल कार्य

Dead of night—आधी रात

A dead letter—बिना प्रभाव की बात

A fool's errand—मूर्खता का कार्य

A foul play—बेईमानी का खेल

A free port—बगैर कर का वन्दरगाह
The golden age—स्वर्ण युग
A golden opportunity—सुनहला अवसर
Hide and seek—आंख मिचौनी का खेल
The lion's share—सब से बड़ा भाग
A make-believe—बहाना
A make-weight—पासंग
A man of mark— विशेषता रखने वाला आदमी
A man of parts—अच्छे गुणों वाला आदमी
A man of letter—विद्वान
A man of war—लड़ाई का जहाज
A matter of fact—सच्चाई
At the nick of time—ऐन मौके पर
A pass-port— दूसरे देश जाने की आज्ञा
Petticoat government— जनाना राज्य
A pitched battle—डट कर लड़ी हुई लड़ाई
Ready money—नकद रुपया
Ring leader—सरदार
Sun-set—सूर्य अस्त होने का समय
A thankless task—बिना लाभ का कार्य

ADJECTIVAL PHRASES

Stark naked—बिल्कुल नंगा
Stone blind—निपट अंधा
Quick-witted—तुरत बुद्धि
Milk white—दूध जैसा सफेद
Ink-black—रोशनाई जैसा काला
Jet-black—काजल जैसा काला
Blood-red—रक्त जैसा लाल
Sky-blue—आकाश जैसा नीला
Gold-yellow—सोने जैसा पीला

Ashen grey—राख जैसा खाकी
Half-dead—अधमरा
Half-hearted—बिना मन के
Ice-cold—बर्फ़ जैसा ठण्डा
Honey-sweet—शहद जैसा मीठा
Butter-soft—मक्खन जैसा नरम
Heart rending—हृदय-विदारक
Lion-hearted—शेर दिल
Well-to-do—मालदार
Ease-loving—आराम-पसन्द
Pretty to look at—देखने में सुन्दर
Hard of hearing—कम सुनने वाला
Endowed with uncommon intelligence—असाधारण
    बुद्धिमान
Destitute of wealth—धनहीन
Hard pressed with need—ज़रूरत का मारा हुआ
Next to impossible—लगभग असम्भव
Last but one—एक छोड़ अन्तिम

ADVERBIAL PHRASES

All the day long—सारा दिन
All the year round—-साल-भर
All the week through—सप्ताह-भर
The other day—किसी दिन
All the world over—संसार-भर में
As far as—जहां तक
As long as—जब तक
As soon as—ज्योंही
At every step—प्रत्येक पद पर
At any cost—हर कीमत पर
At any rate—किसी न किसी तरह

At random—बिना किसी उद्देश्य के
At the eleventh hour—अंतिम समय
By the bye—अवसर आने पर
By and by—जल्दी ही
By chance—संयोग से
By no means—हर तरह से
By mistake—गलती से
By over sight—दृष्टि न पड़ने की वजह से
By way of—बतौर
By virtue of—कारण से
En route —जाते हुए
Ere long—जल्दी ही
Ever and anon—कभी-कभी
Every now and then—बहुधा
For good—सदैव के लिए
For nothing—प्रकारण
Heart and soul—जी जान से
In black and white—लिखकर
In cold blood—निर्दयता से
In no time—फौरन, तुरन्त
In the long run—अन्त में
In the nick of time—ऐन समय पर
In the prime of youth—भरी जवानी में
In a round about way—हेर-फेर से
In season and out of season—मौका-वे-मौका
In the twinkling of an eye—पलक मारते ही
Of late—हाल ही में
Of one's own accord—खुद-ब-खुद
Of course—वास्तव में
Off and on—लगातार नहीं
On and on—लगातार
On the eve of—मौके पर

On the spur of the moment—ठीक उचित समय पर
Over and above—अतिरिक्त
Through and through—पूर्ण रूप से

VERB PHRASES

To blow away—उड़ा देना
To blow down—नीचे गिरा देना
To blow out—फूंक मार कर बुझाना
To blow up—बारूद से उड़ा देना
To blow over—गुज़र जाना या थम जाना
To bear down—दबा देना
To bear upon—सम्बन्ध रखना
To break down—गिर जाना, बीच में रुकना
To break in—सधाना
To break into—चुपके से प्रवेश करना, नकब लगाना
To break open—ज़ोर लगा कर तोड़ना
To break off—रुक जाना
To break up—सभा आदि का समाप्त होना
To bring about—फल निकालना
To bring to light—प्रकट करना
To bring to a stand-still पूर्णतया रोक देना
To bring to bay—ऐसा घेर लेना कि बचाव न हो सके
To bring up—पालन करना
To call in question—सन्देह करना
To call names—गाली देना
To call to account—जवाब तलब करना
To carry weight—प्रभाव डालना
To cast a slur upon—धब्बा डालना
To change hands—कई हाथों में पहुंचना
To come of age—बालिग होना
To come off—होना या पड़ना

To come to blows—हाथापाई हो जाना
To come to grief—आपत्ति में पड़ना
To come to light—सब को मालूम होना
To count on, upon—भरोसा करना
To do away with—अलग कर देना
To fall in—एक पंक्ति में खड़े होना
To fall out—झगड़ा कर देना
To fall on, or upon—आक्रमण करना
To fall short—कमी हो जाना
To find fault with—दोष निकालना
To flock together—इकट्ठा हो बैठना
To gather strength—जोर पकड़ जाना
To get in—अन्दर आना
To get out—बाहर चले जाना
To get up—उठ बैठना
To give ear—ध्यान देना
To give in—हार मान लेना
To give up—त्याग देना
To give place—जगह छोड़ना
To give way—मान जाना, टूट जाना
To go about—किसी कार्य में लग जाना
To go astray—भटक जाना
To go hard with—हक में बुरा होना
To go off—बन्दूक आदि का एकदम छूट जाना
To go on—तरक्की करते जाना
To go through—समाप्त करना, सहन करना
To go to pieces—टुकड़े-टुकड़े होकर नष्ट होना
To go under the name of—कहलाना, विख्यात होना
To go without saying—स्वयं सिद्ध होना
To hold off—दूर रहना
To hold in play—रोके रखना
To hold one's own—मुकाबले पर डटे रहना

To hold one's tongue—ज़बान बन्द रखना
To hold good—ठीक सिद्ध होना
To hold on—डटे रहता
To hold together—मिले रहना
To hold with—सहमत होना, तरफदारी करना
To hold down—अधीन रखना
To keep back—पीछे हटना
To keep to—लगा रहना, डटा रहना
To keep on—आगे बढ़ते रहना, जारी रखना
To keep to one's self—छिपाकर रखना
To lay anchor—लंगर डाल देना
To lay by—भविष्य के लिए बचाकर रखना
To be laid up—बीमार पड़ जाना
To lay down—सुपुर्द करना
To lay open—भेद खोल देना
To lay waste—बरबाद कर देना
To be in wait—ताक में रहना
To look about one's self—चौकन्ना रहना
To look after—देख-भाल करना
To look blank—भौचक्की सूरत बनाना
To look down upon—घृणा की दृष्टि से देखना
To look for—तलाश में होना
To look in the face—किसी के सामने न झेंपना
To look into—जांच-पड़ताल करना
To look on—तमाशा देखते रहना
To lose ground—हारते जाना
To lose heart—हताश होना
To lose the day—पराजित होना
To lose sight of—न दिखाई देना
To make after—पीछा करना
To make a living—जीविका पैदा करना
To make amends—हरजाना देना

To make away with—चुरा ले जाना

To make bold—साहस करना

To make good—पूर्ति करना

To make light of—तुच्छ समझना

To make merry—आनन्द लूटना

To make of—समझ सकना

To make out—साफ-साफ समझ लेना

To make over—सौंपना

To make up one's mind—दृढ़ संकल्प करना

To make up for—कमी पूरी करना

To pass away—चल बसना

To pass by—समीप से होकर जाना

To pass for—समझा जाना

To put in mind—याद दिलाना

To put in practice—प्रयोग में लाना

To put off—रख छोड़ना, टालना

To put on—पहनना

To put out—बुझाना

To put to flight—मार भगाना

To put to sea—जहाज़ पर चला जाना

To put to the sword—तलवार के घाट उतारना

To put up—ठहरना

To put up with—सहन करना

To run after—पीछा करना

To run away—भाग जाना

To run high—भड़क उठना, उफान लेना

To run into debt—ऋणी हो जाना

To run riot—बेकाबू हो जाना

To run short—कम पड़ जाना, समाप्त होना

To set about—प्रारम्भ कर देना

To set afloat—बहा देना, प्रारम्भ करना

To set against—विरुद्ध खड़ा कर देना

To set agoing——चालू कर देना

To set apart——अलग रख छोड़ना

To set aside——हटा देना

To set at defiance——बिल्कुल बेपरवाही कर देना

To set free——स्वतन्त्र कर देना

To set in——आरम्भ होना

To set on foot——आरम्भ कर देना

To set out——चल पड़ना

To set right——ठीक कर देना

To set sail——समुद्र यात्रा पर चलना

To stand aloof——अलग रहना

To stand by——समीप खड़े रहना, साथ देना

To stand for——प्रतिनिधिरूप से खड़े होना

To stand off——दूर खड़े होना

To take aim——निशाना लगाना

To take air——बात फूट पड़ना

To take effect——कार्य रूप में लाना

To take down——लिख लेना

To take for——समझना

To take to heart——दिल में घर कर जाना

To take ill——बुरा मान जाना

To take hold of——अधिकार में कर लेना

To take in hand——किसी काम को हाथ में लेना

To take leave of——विदा लेना

To take notice of——ध्यान देना

To take to a thing——कोई काम करने लग जाना

To take place——होना

To take prisoner——कैद कर लेना

To take root——जड़ पकड़ जाना

To take to one's heels——भाग जाना

To take to the road——डाकू बन जाना

To throw about——बिखेरना

To throw away—फेंक देना, खो देना
To throw back—अस्वीकार कर देना
To throw dust in the eye of—धोखा देना
To turn aside—एक तरफ हट जाना
To turn out—बाहर निकाल देना, सिद्ध होना
To turn over a new leaf—जीवन में नवीन परिवर्तन होना
To turn one's back—पीठ दिखाकर भागना
To turn tail—दुम दबा कर भागना
To turn up—हो जाना, आना
To turn the tables—तख्ता पलट देना

MISCELLANEOUS IDIOMS

A bolt from the blue—अचानक चोट
A white elephant—बहुत खर्च वाला
Add fuel to the fire—जलती पर तेल डालना
A grey head on young shoulders—बुद्धि अधिक आयु कम
A white lie—सफेद झूठ
At a stone's throw—समीप
A turn coat—स्वपक्ष त्यागी
A beast of burden—लादू जानवर
A bird's eye view—एक दृष्टि
A snake in the grass—छुपा हुआ शत्रु
Herculean task—कठिन काम
A wild goose chase—व्यर्थ प्रयत्न
At daggers drawn—पक्के शत्रु
A fish out of water—दुविधा में
At sixes and sevens—बिखरे हुए होना
A blue stocking—पढ़ा-लिखा होने का बहाना करना
To show the white feather—डर कर भागना
A nine days' wonder—चार दिन की चांदनी
A hard nut to crack—कठिन समस्या
To all intents and purposes—वास्तव में

To blow one's trumpet—अपनी प्रशंसा करना

To breathe one's last—मर जाना

To burn the candle at both ends—फज़ूलखर्ची करना

Bury the hatchet—दुश्मनी दूर करना

To burn the mid night oil—बहुत परिश्रम करना

To be born with a silver spoon in one's mouth—
अमीर घराने में पैदा होना

A cock and bull story—बनावटी कहानी

Crocodile tears—बनावटी आंसू

To cut the Gordian knot—कठिन काम को शीघ्र करना

Part and parcel—अभिन्न अंग

By hook or by crook—जैसे भी हो

From hand to mouth—कठिनता से निर्वाह

To win laurels—प्रसिद्धि प्राप्त करना

To leave in lurch—मंझधार में छोड़ना

Under lock and key—सुरक्षित रखना

Sum and substance—किसी बात का निचोड़

To end in smoke—मिट्टी में मिलना

Tall talk व्यर्थ बात

Yeoman's service—महान सेवा

Jack of all trades—जो सब काम जानता हो, हर फन मौला

To take French leave—बिना आज्ञा के छुट्टी

To move heaven and earth—बहुत प्रयत्न करना

To let the grass grow under one's feet—अवसर खोना

To throw the gauntlet—चुनौती देना

To take the bull by the horn—वीरता से सामना करना

To pocket an insult—अपमान सहन करना

To leave no stone unturned—कोई कसर न छोड़ना

To be on the horns of a dilemma—दुविधा में

A close fisted man—कंजूस

In a nut-shell—संक्षेप में

More Dictionaries from Hippocrene Books:

ENGLISH-ALBANIAN DICTIONARY
0081   ISBN 0-87052-480-1 $12.50 cloth

ENGLISH-ARABIC CONVERSATIONAL DICTIONARY
Richard Jaschke
0093   ISBN 0-87052-494-1 $8.95 paper

CAMBODIAN-ENGLISH/ENGLISH-CAMBODIAN STANDARD DICTIONARY
0143   ISBN 0-87052-818-1 $14.95 paper

CZECH-ENGLISH/ENGLISH-CZECH CONCISE DICTIONARY
Nina Trnka
0276   ISBN 0-87052-586-7 $6.95 paper

DANISH-ENGLISH/ENGLISH-DANISH PRACTICAL DICTIONARY
0198   ISBN 0-87052-823-8 $9.95 paper

DUTCH-ENGLISH/ENGLISH-DUTCH CONCISE DICTIONARY:
With a Brief Introduction to Dutch Grammar
0606   ISBN 0-87052-910-2 $7.95 paper

FINNISH-ENGLISH/ENGLISH-FINNISH CONCISE DICTIONARY
0142   ISBN 0-87052-813-0 $8.95 paper

FRENCH-ENGLISH/ENGLISH-FRENCH PRACTICAL DICTIONARY
Rosalind Williams

| 0199 | ISBN 0-88254-815-8 | $6.95 paper |
| 2065 | ISBN 0-88254-928-6 | $12.95 cloth |

GERMAN-ENGLISH/ENGLISH-GERMAN PRACTICAL DICTIONARY
Stephen Jones

| 0200 | ISBN 0-88254-813-1 | $6.95 paper |
| 2063 | ISBN 0-88254-902-2 | $12.95 cloth |

CONCISE, PHONETIC ENGLISH-HEBREW/HEBREW-ENGLISH CONVERSATIONAL DICTIONARY (Romanized)
David C. Gross

| 0257 | ISBN 0-87052-625-1 | $7.95 paper |

HINDI-ENGLISH PRACTICAL DICTIONARY
R.C. Tiwari, R.S. Sharma and Krishna Vikal

| 0186 | ISBN 0-87052-824-6 | $11.95 paper |

HUNGARIAN-ENGLISH/ENGLISH-HUNGARIAN DICTIONARY
Magay Tamas, et al.

| 2039 | ISBN 0-88254-986-3 | $7.95 cloth |

HUNGARIAN-ENGLISH/ENGLISH-HUNGARIAN CONCISE DICTIONARY: With Complete Phonetics

| 0254 | ISBN 0-87052-891-2 | $6.95 paper |

ICELANDIC-ENGLISH/ENGLISH-ICELANDIC CONCISE DICTIONARY
Arnold Taylor
0147   ISBN 0-87052-801-7 $7.95 paper

INDONESIAN-ENGLISH/ENGLISH-INDONESIAN PRACTICAL DICTIONARY
Helen and Rossall Johnson
0127   ISBN 0-87052-810-6 $8.95 paper

ITALIAN-ENGLISH/ENGLISH-ITALIAN PRACTICAL DICTIONARY
Peter Ross
0201   ISBN 0-88254-816-6 $6.95 paper
2066   ISBN 0-88254-929-4 $12.95 cloth

NORWEGIAN-ENGLISH/ENGLISH-NORWEGIAN DICTIONARY
E.D. Gabrielsen
0202   ISBN 0-88254-584-1 $7.95 paper

PILIPINO-ENGLISH/ENGLISH-PILIPINO CONCISE DICTIONARY
Sam and Angela Bickford
2040   ISBN 0-87052-491-7 $6.95 paper

POLISH-ENGLISH/ENGLISH-POLISH STANDARD DICTIONARY (Revised)
Iwo Cyprian Pogonowski
0207   ISBN 0-87052-882-3 $12.95 paper
0665   ISBN 0-87052-908-0 $22.50 cloth

**POLISH-ENGLISH/ENGLISH-POLISH
PRACTICAL DICTIONARY**
Iwo Cyprian Pogonowski
2041   ISBN 0-87052-064-4 $8.95 paper

**PORTUGUESE-ENGLISH/ENGLISH-
PORTUGUESE PRACTICAL DICTIONARY**
Antonio Houaiss and I. Cardin
0477   ISBN 0-87052-374-0 $9.95 paper

**RUSSIAN-ENGLISH/ENGLISH-RUSSIAN
PRACTICAL DICTIONARY:
With Complete Phonetics**
O.P. Benyuch and G.V. Chernov
0164   ISBN 0-87052-336-8 $10.95 paper

**RUSSIAN-ENGLISH/ENGLISH-RUSSIAN
DICTIONARY**
W. Harrison and Svetlana Le Fleming
2344   ISBN 0-87052-751-7 $9.95 paper

**SERBO-CROATIAN-ENGLISH/ENGLISH-
SERBO-CROATIAN POCKET DICTIONARY**
0136   ISBN 0-87052-806-8 $11.95 cloth

**SPANISH-ENGLISH/ENGLISH-SPANISH
PRACTICAL DICTIONARY**
Arthur Butterfield
0211   ISBN 0-88254-814-X $6.95 paper
2064   ISBN 0-88254-905-7 $12.95 cloth

**SWEDISH-ENGLISH/ENGLISH-SWEDISH
STANDARD DICTIONARY**
Vincent and Kerstin Petti
0755   ISBN 0-87052-870-X $11.95 paper
0761   ISBN 0-87052-871-8 $19.95 cloth

**TURKISH-ENGLISH/ENGLISH-TURKISH
CONCISE DICTIONARY**
0569   ISBN 0-87052-241-8 $5.95 paper

**TURKISH-ENGLISH/ENGLISH-TURKISH
POCKET DICTIONARY**
0148   ISBN 0-87052-812-2 $14.95 paper